Crime, Poverty and Survival in the Middle East and North Africa

Crime, Poverty and Survival in the Middle East and North Africa

The 'Dangerous Classes' since 1800

Edited by Stephanie Cronin

I.B.TAURIS

LONDON • NEW YORK • OXFORD • NEW DELHI • SYDNEY

I.B. TAURIS
Bloomsbury Publishing Plc
50 Bedford Square, London, WC1B 3DP, UK
1385 Broadway, New York, NY 10018, USA
29 Earlsfort Terrace, Dublin 2, Ireland

BLOOMSBURY, I.B. TAURIS and the I.B. Tauris logo are trademarks
of Bloomsbury Publishing Plc

First published in Great Britain 2020
Paperback edition published 2021

Cover design: Adriana Brioso
Cover image © Shanty town, Tehran, Iran, 1980. (© Kaveh Kazemi/Getty Images)

ISBN HB: 978-1-7883-1371-1
       PB: 978-0-7556-4501-5
   eISBN: 978-1-8386-0398-4
    ePDF: 978-1-8386-0397-7

Typeset by Integra Software Services Pvt. Ltd.

To find out more about our authors and books visit www.bloomsbury.com
and sign up for our newsletters.

Publication supported by Elahé Omidyar Mir-Djalali, Founder and Chair,
Roshan Cultural Heritage Institute

Roshan ✳ Cultural Heritage Institute

Contents

Notes on contributors

Francesca Biancani is Assistant Professor of Middle Eastern History and International Relations in the Department of Political and Social Sciences of Bologna University. Her research focuses on Egyptian modern and contemporary history, especially on issues of gender, biopolitics, sexuality, labour and migration. Among her publications, 'International Migration and Sex Work in Early Twentieth Century Cairo', in L. Kozma, A. Witznisher and C. Shayegh (eds.), *Globalization and the Making of the Modern Middle East* (2014); 'Globalization, Migration, and Female Labour in Cosmopolitan Egypt, 1860–1937', in Mirjam Hladnik (ed.), *From Slovenia to Egypt: Aleksandrinke's Trans-Mediterranean Domestic Workers' Migration and National Imagination* (2015); 'Prostitution in Cairo', co-authored with Hanan Hammad, in M. Rodríguez García, L. Heerma van Voss and E. van Nederveen Meerkerk (eds.), *Selling Sex in the City: a Global History of Prostitution, 1600s-2000s* (2017). She is author of the book *Sex Work in Colonial Egypt. Women, Modernity and the Global Economy* (2018).

Mattin Biglari is a PhD student studying at SOAS, University of London. His thesis is on a social history of the oil industry in Iran, focusing on experiences of work, training and knowledge production in the Abadan refinery during the 1940s and 1950s. His wider research interests include the social and cultural history of modern Iran, global labour history and energy humanities. He has previously written on the US government's perceptions of Shi'ism during the Iranian revolution in the journal *Diplomatic History*.

Stephanie Cronin is Elahé Omidyar Mir-Djalali Research Fellow at St Antony's College and is a member of the Faculty of Oriental Studies, University of Oxford. She is the author of *Armies and State-building in the Modern Middle East: Politics, Nationalism and Military Reform* (2014); *Shahs, Soldiers and Subalterns in Iran: Opposition, Protest and Revolt, 1921–1941* (2010); *Tribal Politics in Iran: Rural Conflict and the New State, 1921–1941* (2006); and *The Army and the Creation of the Pahlavi State in Iran, 1910–1926* (1997). She is the editor of *Anti-Veiling Campaigns in the Muslim World: Gender, Modernism and the Politics of Dress* (2014); *Iranian-Russian Encounters: Empires and Revolutions since 1800* (2013); *Subalterns and Social Protest: History from Below in the Middle East and North Africa* (2007); *Reformers and Revolutionaries in Modern Iran: New Perspectives on the Iranian Left* (2004); and *The Making of Modern Iran; State and Society under Riza Shah, 1921–1941* (2003). She is the co-editor, with Edmund Herzig, of 'Russian Orientalism to Soviet Iranology: The Persian-speaking world and its history through Russian eyes', *Iranian Studies*, volume 48, no. 5, 2015. She is currently working on a social history of modern Iran 'from below'.

Olmo Gölz is a postdoctoral researcher in Islamic and Iranian Studies at the University of Freiburg, Germany. As a member of the interdisciplinary collaborative research centre 'Heroes – Heroizations – Heroisms' he is currently working on dynamics of the heroic in the Iran–Iraq War. In March 2017 he finished his PhD at the University of Freiburg. In his thesis 'Racketeers in Pahlavi-Iran – Violent Entrepreneurs and the Gendered Meaning of Protection' he discusses topics of urban violence and configurations of masculinities in twentieth-century Iran from a sociological perspective. From 2012 to 2016 he worked as a research fellow in Islamic and Iranian Studies in Freiburg and as a teaching fellow for Middle Eastern Studies at the University of Basel, Switzerland. He obtained a master's degree in Islamic and Iranian Studies at the University of Freiburg in 2012.

Jairan Gahan is Assistant Professor of History and Religious Studies at the University of Alberta, Canada. Her research broadly investigates microhistories of precarious populations in the modern Middle East, spanning the twentieth century, with a focus on Iran. She is currently working on her book manuscript 'Red-Light Tehran: Prostitution, Islamism, and the Rule of the Sovereign', which investigates non-Western genealogies of modern Islamic state formations in Iran, through an exploration of the role of Islamic ideas and ideals in the governance of the red-light district of Tehran from its inception in 1921 to its erasure in the aftermath of the Islamic Revolution (1979) in 1981.

Maziyar Ghiabi is Lecturer in Modern Iranian History at the University of Oxford and Titular Lecturer at Wadham College. Prior to this position, he was a postdoctoral fellow at the Paris School of Advanced Studies in Social Sciences (EHESS), where he was a member of the research lab IRIS. Maziyar obtained his DPhil in Politics at the University of Oxford (St Antony's College) where he was a Wellcome Trust Scholar in Society and Ethics (2013–2017). He is the editor of *Power and Illicit Drugs in the Global South* (2018) and the author of *Drugs Politics: Managing Disorder in the Islamic Republic of Iran* (2019). Besides his interest in global drug history, Ghiabi works on history and politics from below, urban and rural ethnography and visual research methods.

Till Grallert is Social Historian and Research Associate at the Orient-Institut Beirut of the Max Weber Foundation. He completed his PhD with a thesis titled 'To Whom Belong the Streets? Property, Propriety, and Appropriation: The Production of Public Space in Late Ottoman Damascus, 1875–1914' in 2014 at the Berlin Graduate School Muslim Cultures and Societies. His current research project aims at establishing a genealogy of urban food riots in the Eastern Mediterranean between the eighteenth and the twentieth centuries. In addition to the social and spatial history of late Ottoman cities, he has developed a strong interest in digital humanities and the socio-linguistics of early Arabic newspapers. He is a co-organizer of the 'Digital Humanities Institute – Beirut' (since 2015), the lead developer for and a contributor to the online chronology of nineteenth-century Arabic periodicals (Project Jarā'id) and a contributor to the recent collection of essays titled *Digital Humanities and Islamic & Middle East Studies* (edited by Elias Muhanna, 2016). He works on open, collaborative and scholarly digital editions of early Arabic periodicals such as Muhammad Kurd ʿAli's journal *ʿal-Muqtabas'* and ʿAbd al-*Qadir al-Iskandarani*'s *ʿal-Haqa ʾiq'* in the framework of his research project 'Open Arabic Periodical Editions' (OpenArabicPE). He occasionally blogs at tillgrallert.github.io.

Hanan Hammad is Associate Professor of History and the Director of Middle East Studies at Texas Christian University. Her book *Industrial Sexuality: Gender, Urbanization, and Social Transformation in Egypt* (2016) received book awards from the National Women's Studies Association (NWSA), The Political Economy Project (PEP) and the Association for Middle East Women's Studies (AMEWS) as well as honourable mentions from the Roger Owen Book Award (MESA) and from the Arab American Book Award. She has also published more than a dozen articles and book chapters on gender, sexuality, working-class history and comparative cultural history of Egypt and Iran.

Murat Metinsoy is Associate Professor in the Department of Political Science and International Relations, Faculty of Economics, Istanbul University. He received his PhD degree from Bogazici University in 2010 with a dissertation titled 'Everyday Politics of Ordinary People: Public Opinion, Dissent, and Resistance in Early Republican Turkey.' Based on police and gendarme reports, court records, politicians' reports, local newspapers and petitions, his dissertation revealed the daily and informal patterns of interactions between the state and society. Metinsoy studies the history and politics of modern Turkey, poor people's movements and popular resistance under authoritarian regimes. His MA thesis, 'Wars outside the War: The Social Impact of the Second World War on Turkey' was published in Turkish (*İkinci Dünya Savaşı'nda Türkiye: Gündelik Yaşamda Devlet ve Toplum*) in 2007 (two revised editions, 2016 and 2017). The book was awarded 'the Best Young Social Scientist Award' by the Turkish Social Science Association and 'the Best Book Award' by the Ottoman Bank Archives and Research Center. His papers were published in *IJMES, Int. J. of Turcologia, Int. J. of Turkish Studies, Toplum ve Bilim, Tarih ve Toplum, Toplumsal Tarih* and several international and national edited collections. His research has been supported by Boğaziçi University, ODTÜ, Istanbul University Scientific Research Council, the Scientific and Technological Research Council of Turkey, Turkish Academy of Sciences and American Research Institute in Turkey. He is currently revising his dissertation for publication and gives lectures on world history, history of civilizations, social history of modern Turkey and theory of social history.

Müge Özbek received her PhD at Boğaziçi University, Turkey, in 2017 with a dissertation titled 'Single, Poor Women in Istanbul, 1850–1915: Prostitution, Sexuality, and Female Labor.' She is currently a Post-Doctoral Fellow at the Research Center for Anatolian Civilizations, Koç University, Istanbul–Turkey. Her research focuses on female migration, sexuality and labour in the late Ottoman period.

Antonin Plarier has received his PhD in contemporary history at Panthéon Sorbonne University. His thesis was focused on rural banditry in Algeria during the colonial period (1871–1920s). His research work is centered on links existing between banditry and different types of dispossessions. He is also a temporary teacher and researcher (ATER) at the Institute of Political Studies in Grenoble

Acknowledgements

I would like to thank Elahé Omidyar Mir-Djalali, Founder and Chair, Roshan Cultural Heritage Institute, for her generous support of the intellectual activities which have made this collection possible, in particular, her funding of the Elahé Omidyar Mir-Djalali Research Fellowship at St Antony's College, University of Oxford. I would also like to thank the Gerda Henkel Foundation for their support for the conference which formed the basis of this book. The Middle East Centre at St Antony's graciously offered its facilities for the conference and the John Fell Fund provided additional funding. Lubica Pollakova did sterling work on editing and indexing the text and Thomas Stottor and Sophie Rudland at I.B. Tauris offered indispensable encouragement. I am grateful to them all.

Three of the chapters in the collection have been published before in scholarly journals. 'Noble Robbers, avengers and entrepreneurs: Eric Hobsbawm and banditry in Iran, the Middle East and North Africa' by Stephanie Cronin was originally published in *Middle Eastern Studies*, vol. 52, no. 5, 2015, pp. 845–870; 'Disreputable by Definition: Respectability and Theft by Poor Women in Urban Interwar Egypt' by Hanan Hammad first appeared in the *Journal of Middle East Women's Studies*, vol. 13, no. 3, 2017, pp. 376–394. An earlier version of Maziyar Ghiabi's chapter, 'The "Virtual Poor" in Iran: The Dangerous Classes and Homeless Life in Capitalist Times', was published (Open Access) in *Ethnography* (Sage Publications). See Maziyar Ghiabi, 'Under the Bridge in Tehran: Addiction, Poverty and Capital', *Ethnography*,https://doi.org/10.1177/1466138118787534. Published online August 2, 2018. The chapter in this book is a revised, extended and adapted version of the original article. The chapter entitled 'Disciplining Sex Work in Colonial Cairo' by Francesca Biancani is a version of chapters two and three of *Sex Work in Colonial Egypt* (I.B. Tauris, 2018). All are reproduced here with permission and I am grateful to the editors and publishers of the journals and the publisher of the book.

Note on transliteration

There has been no attempt to impose a uniform system of transliteration for the Arabic, Turkish and Persian names and terms employed in the chapters contained in this collection. Decisions about transliteration have been left to individual authors.

The use of diacritical marks has also been left to the discretion of individual authors.

The Dangerous Classes in the Middle East and North Africa

Stephanie Cronin

The contributions collected here grapple with the concept, well known to European social history, of 'the dangerous classes', seeking to apply it to the Middle East and North Africa, to understand and elucidate its role in subaltern experience and its contribution to the formulation of elite discourses and to state-building more generally. The book's geographical scope is the entire region, from Algeria in the west to Iran in the east and, although it does not deal specifically with every country of the region, the broad conceptual approaches and conclusions of each chapter are framed to have a wider and more generally applicable regional relevance. Most of the chapters focus on the late nineteenth to early twentieth centuries, the account of petty female crime looks at interwar Egypt, while the final two pieces bring the story to more recent and contemporary periods. The reasons for this chronological preference are similar to those which have made these decades so central to European and British social history. The years covering the late nineteenth century to the Great War constitute a watershed moment of global social transformation, the sometimes sudden arrival of modernity permitting the sharpest delineation of both the dangerous classes themselves and of elite attitudes towards them. The focus on the late nineteenth to early twentieth centuries, furthermore, has been made startlingly relevant by contemporary developments across the region. Mass population movements from and via North Africa across the Mediterranean have meant that the European respectable classes have turned on 'swarming', 'swamping' migrants a gaze similar to that of elites witnessing the subaltern upheavals of the late nineteenth century. More broadly, recent years have seen the emergence and political and social salience of a precariat, especially visible during the early days of the Arab Spring, and the growth of a lumpenproletariat of marginal youth available for recruitment to jihadi movements, both these phenomena predicated on the failure and defeat of older political organizations and ideologies. This has resulted in the contemporary Middle East and North Africa often bearing a greater resemblance to the nineteenth century than to the epoch of high nationalist modernism which lasted roughly from the 1920s until the triumph of neo-liberalism in the 1970s to 1980s.

The collection openly acknowledges, indeed celebrates, its debt to the pioneers of modern social history 'from below'. Certain figures loom particularly large. Part Two, which deals with banditry and crime is obviously profoundly influenced by the work of Eric Hobsbawm, and each of the chapters in this part frames its analysis in relation to Hobsbawm's much criticized but hugely influential foundational text and the elaborations and refinements of his thesis which were made over the decades subsequent to its first appearance.[1] Other pioneers of social history, without whose work Till Grallert's chapter in Part Three on bread riots would scarcely have been possible, are Charles Tilly, George Rudé and, especially, E. P. Thompson. The latter, whose seminal article of 1971 introduced the concept of the moral economy deployed here, has shaped all subsequent work on subaltern discursive worlds and modes of action.[2]

The book has more specific debts, namely to those social historians who have directed their attention to the lives of members of the European dangerous classes. First among these is Louis Chevalier, whose *Labouring and Dangerous Classes* discussed at length the social conditions of the Parisian working poor and drew the contours of their almost indistinguishable linkages to the dangerous classes proper.[3] Among the more general influences on the chapters in this collection, two may be mentioned: Marx and Foucault. Marx's influence on the British social historians is well known, but he is also of more direct interest to this collection in terms of his formulation of the concept of the lumpenproletariat, a concept which is overtly deployed by the chapters in Part Three. In his *Eighteenth Brumaire of Louis Napoleon*, Marx provided a colourful description of the lumpenproletariat, a description which is of key importance in explaining what he considers, in contrast to often romanticized views, to be their typically reactionary political role.[4] The other major figure of relevance here is, of course, Michel Foucault, whose wirk on punishment, madness and sexuality has been central to the recent flourishing of scholarly interest in marginality in general and in the role of the marginal in the construction of modern regimes of surveillance and discipline.

The chapters in this collection have at their centre the lives and experiences of various categories of the 'dangerous classes'. In order to understand such lives and experiences, however, equal attention must be paid to the changing character of the political, economic, social, cultural and ideological contexts within which those experiences are formed, and the practices and discourses of the authorities whom the 'dangerous' seek to avoid, evade, cheat or resist. By integrating the marginal and the apparently peripheral into larger historical narratives, indeed placing them at the centre of such narratives, the collection hopes to contribute to a greater understanding not only of the marginalized themselves, but also of elites and reformers, of power and authority, of nationalism, modernism and state-building, of economic, political and social transformations, and of their parallel discursive accompaniments, indeed to reconfigure the very essence of the dominant narratives of Middle Eastern and North African history.

The collection assumes profound similarities between Middle Eastern and European subaltern experience. The question then arises as to whether there are any particular features of Middle Eastern and North African lived experience which make these parallels inappropriate. It may be noted here how muted the role of Islam appears in these narratives. In a period when the region is seen primarily, and often even exclusively, through a religious lens, religion in general is remarkably absent from the chapters contained here. When they are visible, Islamic precepts appear rather as cultural tropes or as underpinnings of legitimacy, rather than as an active force in their own right. The chapters on prostitution, for example, mention the *Shari'a* mainly in terms of its avoidance by state legal systems and political authorities. A perhaps rather surprising apparent pre-modern toleration of 'deviance' of various kinds seems in fact to have had very little to do with prescriptive religious texts, and everything to do with the smallness and weakness of pre-modern states and the strengths and cohesion of pre-modern societies.

What then is the origin of the notion of the 'dangerous classes'? It was born in early nineteenth-century France, spreading rapidly across a western Europe then in the throes of unprecedented and sometimes traumatic political, economic, social and cultural transformation, reaching the USA with the publication in 1872 of a book with the same title by the American social reformer Charles Loring Brace.[5] The 'dangerous classes', sometimes the 'criminal classes', sometimes the lumpenproletariat, became common ways of describing all those who had fallen out of the respectable working class into the lower depths of the new urban and industrial environments, and survived there by their wits and by various amoral, disreputable or criminal strategies. It included beggars and vagrants, paupers, gypsies, pickpockets, burglars and fences, prostitutes and pimps, army deserters, ex-prisoners, tricksters, drug-dealers, the unemployed and unemployable, indeed every type of the criminal and marginal, and who were drawn from among women as well as men, and children as well as adults. Such representatives of the dangerous classes were extraordinarily well represented in literature, notable by Émile Zola, Victor Hugo and Charles Dickens in the nineteenth century and by Maxim Gorky and Bertolt Brecht in the twentieth, and in popular culture of all kinds.

The 'dangerous classes', sometimes barely distinguishable from the newly assembling proletariat from among whom they invariably originated, were a constant preoccupation, indeed obsession, of the emerging European bourgeoisie, an apparent threat both to its property, through crime, and to its political power, through revolution, or at least of social and moral chaos. The resulting fear permeated both the discourse and the policies of the period, including, and perhaps especially among, elite reformers, and was central to the construction of new mechanisms of control, modern regimes of surveillance and discipline, including policing, legal and penal, and even medical and psychiatric, systems. Although the term fell into disuse in the twentieth century, it is often argued that the concept remains embedded in elite formulations of the connections between propertylessness, poverty, immorality, criminality and the 'underclass'.

The construction of the concept of the 'dangerous classes' was not the exclusive preserve of right-wing or conservative political observers. As Olmo Gölz points out below in his discussion of the role of Iranian *lutis* in the overthrow of Muhammad Musaddiq, from a classical Marxist point of view the terms lumpenproletariat and dangerous classes are synonyms.[6] As mentioned above, Marx provided a ferocious description of the lumpenproletariat. He wrote: 'alongside ruined and adventurous scions of the bourgeoisie, there were vagabonds, discharged soldiers, discharged criminals, escaped galley slaves, swindlers, confidence tricksters, *lazzaroni* [gangmembers], pickpockets, sleight-of-hand experts, gamblers, *maquereaux* [pimps], brothel-keepers, porters, pen-pushers, organ-grinders, rag-and-bone merchants, knife-grinders, tinkers, and beggars'. Concluding his list, Marx, assessing their social existence, predicts their political inclinations: an 'indeterminate, fragmented mass, tossed backwards and forwards'.[7] Potentially available to any political tendency, such elements were most likely to be mobilized in opposition to the organized working class and, for Marx, it was in this that they constituted a serious danger.

Such figures were certainly not themselves a modern phenomenon, either in Europe or beyond. Indeed, a subaltern subculture had thrived among the urban lower classes across the Middle East and North Africa for centuries. Premodern Middle Eastern cities, like their European counterparts, seem to have had no lack of the lumpen, the marginal and the semi-criminal. Indeed, classical literature, medieval poetry and shadow-plays are replete with descriptions of these 'tricksters of all kinds'.[8] The medieval manuscript, *Kashf al-Asrar* by Abdurrahman al-Jawbari, provides vivid details of their elaborate deceptions.[9] His list of such characters is remarkably similar to Marx's lumpenproletariat and includes all kinds of swindlers, imposters, snake charmers, jugglers, slave-traders, fraudulent jewellers, drug sellers and money-changers, quacks and alchemists.[10] A particularly tricky subgroup were those posing as sufis and dervishes in order to exploit the piety of the faithful to obtain money from them.[11] Certainly elite literature was harsh in its condemnation of this subculture. Beggars, for example, the most numerous category in this subculture, were depicted exclusively as professional confidence tricksters running lucrative rackets, with no regard for the realities of poverty and pauperism and their genuine victims, often widows, children, the sick and disabled. Such attitudes survived under the surface of twentieth-century elite discourses of reform and modernity and continued to colour policy. Those closer to the risk of themselves falling into destitution, however, often took a rather more nuanced and even sympathetic view.[12]

During the nineteenth century, such groups and figures ceased providing picturesque vignettes for European travelogues but were transformed into the 'dangerous classes'. Their transition from being merely a nuisance, a threat confined to unwary individuals, to a collective menace is inextricably tied up with the arrival of modernity. What, then, was it exactly which made this subculture dangerous, not merely a perhaps regrettable but unavoidable feature of urban life? Certainly the poor had been an historically perennial presence in cities and towns, both in Europe and the Middle East, as were the more colourful and marginal figures and groups which emerged from among them. However, again in both Europe and the Middle East, the poor, the disreputable and even the criminal were not, before the nineteenth century, conceptualized as an existential threat to the moral, social and political order. Perceptions changed, however, in tandem with the accelerating transformations of urbanization and industrialization. As the populations of the cities exploded, the large majority, poor and even semi-destitute, concentrated in slums inaccessible to the authorities, and threatened with starvation by the smallest rise in the price of bread. In these environments, not only were the modern poor different to the poor of the past, and not only were there more of them in absolute terms and in terms of their proportion of the population, but elite attitudes towards them also changed. Crime, for example, was no longer an incidental and exceptional occurrence with no wider significance beyond the damage to the victim but, now commonplace, anonymous and pervasive, began to be perceived as a threat to society, along with the poor who perpetrated it, part of the fabric of the city, a veritable product of the new environment itself.[13] Indeed the city itself increasingly seemed to represent a site of essential danger, this new sensibility to a specific urban pathology expressed in novels such as Sayyid Murtaza Mushfeq-i Kazimi's *Tehran-i Makhuf* (Terrible Tehran).[14]

Across the region, modernists themselves began to fear the consequences of modernity, especially for women and especially as symbolized by the city, which became synonymous with anonymity, danger, and sexual crime.[15] As in Europe, the combination of a new fascination with female sexuality and prostitution, the frightening consequences of uncontrolled lower class migration and the growth of urban slums, the development of a modern police force equipped with forensic science, and the stimulation of an appetite and a market for crime fiction and lurid press reports, created the phenomenon of the sensational murder, even the serial killer, usually involving sexual motives.[16] One early but typical episode, which created a sensation in Istanbul in 1896, concerned the murders of an Ottoman Greek woman, whose moral transgressions were hinted at, her mother and their servant.[17] In 1920 an even more spectacular episode hit the newspaper headlines, the first reported full-blown case of serial murder in the Middle East. A police search in Cairo for four missing women led to the discovery of seventeen female bodies buried under the floors of houses in a district with a reputation for crime and deviance.[18] Two women, Raya and Sakina, both prostitutes, were arrested, and after interrogation confessed to murder. In Tehran in 1934 another exemplary serial murder case burst upon the public. Ali Asghar Burujirdi, quickly acquiring the soubriquet Asghar Qatil (Asghar the murderer), was arrested and confessed to the killing of eight boys, most of them homeless vagrants. He further confessed to having previously, while living in Baghdad, sexually abused adolescent boys and to having killed twenty-five of them.[19] Asghar Qatil and Raya and Sakina were tried and executed, entering urban mythology in Cairo and Tehran much as Jack the Ripper had done in the Victorian London of thirty years earlier, and for much the same reasons.

The extraordinary explosion of the urban populations, especially of the poor, in the late nineteenth- to early twentieth-centuries Middle East is sometimes overlooked. Hanan Hammad points out below that the 1907 Egyptian census recorded that one-third of Cairo residents were immigrants to the city while in the interwar years the urban population increased by over 50 per cent.[20] A similar story comes from Iran. Estimates suggest that Tehran, with a population of 85,000 in 1867, possessed 200,000 by 1900 and grew to 350,000 by 1913. Tabriz, between the same dates, doubled and then trebled, reaching 300,000.[21] Relative as well as absolute poverty increased, as did the struggle for employment and housing. Crime also increased, the perception of crime increasing even faster. The presence of such numbers in such conditions, the result of uncontrolled and uncontrollable population movements and demographic changes, led to both specific legislation and to more ambitious plans for the general remodelling of urban space along modernist lines. The 1909 Ottoman Committee of Union and Progress 'Law on vagrants and suspected persons' was an exemplary tool for disciplining the urban poor in general, particularly that most dangerous element, young, single men.[22] Liat Kozma has also pointed to the slightly earlier efforts made in Egypt, especially through the 1880 Police Act, to discipline the perceived chaos on the streets, especially, according to article 5 of the Act, those 'who wander about as they pleased without work, home or source of income'.[23] Such individual measures, however, did not satisfy the enthusiasms of modernism for the creation of entirely new urban environments. Plans were drawn up and energetic efforts made to remodel the capital cities of the Middle East according to new principles of space, order, health, policing, political control, culture and, eventually, consumerism.[24] Older notions of organic urban space were cast aside, networked residential quarters dissolved, their relationship to bazaar/suq and mosque destroyed, to be replaced by wide boulevards á la Hausmann constructed on a grid, or left to the poorest of the population to die slowly of neglect, from now on always synonymous with disease, disorder and backwardness.[25] Such 'town planning' led to one observer commenting in the 1930s that parts of Tehran looked at if they had been bombed from the air.[26]

Before the twentieth century, Middle Eastern societies had possessed an organic integrity. There were certainly sharp divisions into social classes, immense wealth down to abject poverty, and into estates, landowners, ulama, men of the sword and of the pen, artisans and paupers. But although possessing vastly unequal access to material resources and power, these classes and strata recognized each other as parts of the same society, broadly shared a common culture and inhabited the same mental universe. Quality and expense aside, they wore similar styles of clothing, appreciated the same kinds of entertainment, understood gender roles and family structure according to similar expectations. The twentieth century, however, brought with it a new and eventually utterly unbridgeable gulf, introducing into Middle Eastern societies a binary division between the 'traditional' and the 'modern'. As the cities became divided in terms of physical space between an old, traditional, shrinking and neglected kernel, with a population of declining social and political significance, and a rapidly expanding, increasingly prosperous modern urban environment, so did society reflect this division.[27]

For the European bourgeoisie of the nineteenth century, followed by the nationalist elites of the Middle East in the twentieth, the poor, the immoral and the criminal were linked, and the management and even eradication of the novel threat they represented required both repression and, especially, reform. There was, however, an additional dimension to the problem represented to local elites in the Middle East and North Africa by their own dangerous classes, a dimension resulting from the complications introduced by the intrusion and persistence of European imperial and colonial power. The marginal poor, the criminal and the merely disorderly offered sometimes similar but sometimes rather different challenges to European than to indigenous authority, and emerging nationalist and modernist discourses were obliged to configure the nature of the threat they posed within the context of a generalized critique of foreign domination. Prostitution, for example, a threat to the physical and moral health of society, became also a metaphor for national degradation and powerlessness against foreign sources of corruption. As the nation was ever more frequently symbolically depicted as a woman, who required protection from violent penetration by foreign powers, so the prostitute came to symbolize national and masculine humiliation and shame.

In these new 'modern' circumstances prevailing both in Europe and, slightly later, also in the Middle East, criminals, a straightforward threat to life and property, were an obvious danger. Crime itself came to be constructed as a class problem, committed by the poor against the better off. The most common type of crime was crime against property, often accompanied by violence, and was naturally most likely to be carried out by the poor, the line between the lowest levels of the working class and the so-called criminal class permeable and indistinct. The poor were not only adjacent to individual criminality but were also perceived as inclined to collective violence, the bread riot a universal, and often menacing, phenomenon. By the early twentieth century, the criminal class and the poor were joined by an entirely new category, an embryonic proletariat concentrated in its thousands in conditions of the utmost misery, with new and powerful weapons, for example the industrial strike, at its disposal. The ranks of the 'dangerous classes' were further swelled as a variety of the 'traditional' survival strategies of the poor were also criminalized. Begging, vagrancy, and prostitution, formerly tolerated, managed or ignored, were increasingly constrained by legal and police supervision and repression. Furthermore, not only were thieves, prostitutes and pimps to feel the weight of new legal and penal practices but they, along with beggars, vagrants, the idle, opium addicts, gangs of destitute children, fortune tellers and other elements deemed undesirable, and even socially pathological, by the rising elites, were to be reformed and moulded by education, sport and conscription into obedient citizens. A major prerequisite for the vanquishing of the backwardness and ignorance supposedly embodied in such representatives of the dangerous classes was the transformation of the physical environment and the creation of a new culture of modernity. From now on, not only would the poor and marginal be arrested by the police and imprisoned by the legal and penal processes, but the spaces they occupied, physical and cultural, would be denied them and they themselves made healthy, industrious and respectable.

This was an ambitious project. Everywhere, the implementation of such a modernist agenda required the state to develop massively enhanced coercive instruments. Most important of these instruments was a modern police force. It also required, perhaps even more importantly, a series of cultural offensives which would facilitate, indeed make unavoidable, an internalization of modernity on the social and on the individual psychological levels. People would be subject to modern institutions, but they would also look modern, wear modern clothes, behave in a modern way, with 'civilized' manners, and even experience appropriately modern emotions, arranging their family and personal relationships according to the new templates.

This project, when implemented in the Middle East and North Africa, has often been described as essentially colonial in character. Yet it was not only countries under direct European control, Egypt and French North Africa, which experienced this sometimes traumatic imposition of modernity. Still independent states, the Ottoman Empire and then the Turkish republic, and early Pahlavi Iran, untrammelled by fears of inauthenticity and assertive in their nationalisms, were perhaps even more aggressive than colonial authorities in reshaping their populations through the twin processes of repression and reform. Richard Keller's comment that representatives of the French *mission civilisatrice* often depicted their voyage into North African space 'as a regressive journey away from civilization into a foreign universe of misery, filth and infectious disorder', might be applied with equal force to the middle-class urban ideologues of Iranian and Turkish modernism as they contemplated the slums of their own cities.[28]

For the rising nationalist elites of the early twentieth-century Middle East, the transformation of public space and its control, in fact its policing, was a vital component of creating a modern 'civilized' society. Cities, especially capital cities most ostentatiously under the European gaze, were required to *look* modern, as an essential prerequisite of *being* modern. Remnants of the 'traditional', the 'oriental', the 'uncivilized', even occasionally the religious, had to be removed from sight, the streets and squares no longer the natural home of beggars, vagabonds, mendicant sufis, popular entertainers, flagellation processions, and so on. People and activities which had customarily been tolerated unless and until they became actually disruptive were now deemed an affront to modernity and criminalized. As well as offering unfortunate individuals a sometimes compulsory alternative, the modernist campaign came to imply a war of attrition against an entire urban subculture.

The result of this campaign was a veritable mania for institutionalizing the marginal. Criminals were to be confined to prisons, the insane to asylums, street children to orphanages, women of unconventional morality to red-light districts and brothels, beggars to poorhouses, the contagious sick to hospitals. Such institutions were advertised as modern, sharp contrasts drawn with the older and traditional dungeons and madhouses, and were based on overtly reforming impulses, especially the desire for rehabilitation. Even the names of the new institutions reflected this new agenda, destitute children in Ottoman cities, for example, being consigned to reformatories (*islahhane*).[29] Criminals might now be identified, apprehended and punished but also possibly reformed. Similarly the mentally ill, the physically disabled, and those with contagious diseases might be placed in institutions and again possibly cured. In any case, society would be protected from them.[30] Concealed behind high walls, they would no longer be allowed to impart a sense of sickness and backwardness to the streets of major towns and cities, where health and hygiene, of individuals but also, by extension, of society, had become a modernist obsession. Out of this panoply of panopticons gradually emerged the social sciences and the new profession of social work, while a growing interest in eugenics supposedly offered scientific possibilities for combating a feared racial degeneration.[31]

But it should not be assumed that the respectable classes themselves escaped the proliferating forms of confinement. New bureaucracies pioneered new discourses and practices of work. Binaries were established between work and leisure and between home and office, new anxieties were generated by the newly-discovered social and moral danger of laziness, and a fixed and lengthened working day was disciplined by electric lighting and clocks, while the young found themselves not only in schools but also in scouting organizations and, especially, in the barracks of the new armies.[32] Such profound and cumulative changes to the ways of life of the 'respectable classes' further emphasized and made visible the distance separating them from those remaining outside and even resistant to the world of modernity. Nonetheless, danger continued to lurk everywhere, indeed at the very heart of the modernist project. A too-ready adoption of European clothing produced, for example, the reviled 'dandy', while the emancipated woman harboured the potential not only for immorality but for undermining the very structure of family life and therefore of society.[33]

******

Part One of this book contains four chapters which discuss different categories of 'dangerous' women, and the impact of the modernist agenda upon them: prostitutes or sex workers, the rather more vaguely defined but almost equally problematic 'disorderly' women, and female petty criminals. All three categories carried with them a legacy of historical suspicion, but also generated particular modernist anxieties and demanded new types of action from the authorities.

From a conventional pre-modern point of view, women were, as such, intrinsically dangerous, their sexuality a cause of *fitna* (discord or disturbance), a source of potential corruption to both individual men and to society more generally. The answer traditionally given to the problem discursively presented by women, therefore, was their strict guardianship and control by men and, as far as possible, their seclusion, either literally, within the confines of the home, or symbolically, by the veil. Given the strict limitations imposed on women, and the ease and speed with which they might find themselves ejected from the world of family and kin-based respectability, it is unsurprising that prostitution or commercial sex work was a common feature of larger Middle Eastern and North African cities, especially ports, trading and pilgrimage centres. It was also highly diverse, encompassing highly paid 'courtesans' catering to the requirements of elite men, skilled entertainers, singers and dancers, who also offered sexual services, and abjectly poor and desperate women catering to the lowest end of the market.[34] It took place in or in the neighbourhood of brothels, taverns and coffee houses, which were usually subject to some sort of informal red-light zoning, but also, more discreetly, in private homes. The demarcation line between prostitutes and 'respectable' working class women, was often blurred. Further uncertainty arose from the 'professional', or alternatively casual and part-time possibilities, offered by the trade, from a legal failure to differentiate between fornication, adultery and prostitution, and from an inclination to equate the latter with a vague moral looseness.[35] A particularly knotty ambiguity arose in Iran from the practice of *muta* or pleasure marriage, a temporary union contracted for a limited period of time, and sometimes, though by no means invariably, amounting to little more than a legitimized form of prostitution.[36]

A pervasive attitude that prostitution was a necessary evil, a guarantee of social order and even facilitated the sharp gender segregation prevailing in respectable society, governed the behaviour of the authorities. Pragmatism, tinged with a degree of ambivalence was the order of the day, punctuated by bouts of sometimes harsh but always short-lived repression, should the trade become a public nuisance or should a ruler wish to demonstrate his piety to his subjects, to himself or to some recalcitrant clerics. Premodern states in the Middle East and North Africa, like their contemporaries across Europe regulated, taxed and zoned prostitution, at least as far as their limited capacities permitted. The encroachment of modernity, however, fundamentally disrupted this rough and ready equilibrium. From the late nineteenth century, a modern gender discourse emerged advocating the emancipation of women, their education and employment, and an end to veiling, seclusion, child marriage, polygamy and male repudiation, producing what was, perhaps, the most acute of all the anxieties of modernity, that of gender relations.[37] In this context, prostitution was transformed from a necessary evil and occasional localized nuisance into a vehicle for new and entirely modern fears. It became a symbolic representation of a nexus of social evils, a metaphor for national corruption and decline and a serious threat to the moral, physical and even racial health of society.

Anxieties about prostitution were both class and gender based. Female emancipation complicated older boundaries, between those of dubious morality and respectable women, between the poor and their presumed social superiors. This gave rise to profound uncertainty as to how this transition to modernity should be managed and what its consequences might be. How would the boundaries of respectability be preserved as women intruded ever more into male public space? How could the disruptive power of female sexuality be contained and family honour protected? Fears about the spread of prostitution and of disease, physical and social, also became closely bound up with concern about the rapidly changing morphology of Middle Eastern cities. Uncontrolled migration was inevitably accompanied by unemployment, vagrancy and crime among both men and women, and especially prostitution among women and young boys, while the inevitable disintegration of the stability of the old urban quarters brought with it a new anonymity and nightmares of subaltern policing.

The debates over prostitution which raged across the entire region in the nineteenth and early twentieth centuries seemed unable to resolve a conundrum about the essential nature of women in general and prostitutes in particular. Were they victims of a harsh fate and in need of protection, or were they morally deficient, addicted to pleasure, luxury and idleness, and willing choosers of a life of degradation? Could they be rehabilitated or should they be punished? Social commentators ceaselessly struggled with the riddle: were they in danger or were they dangerous?[38]

The most common initial response to the new fears about the impact of prostitution was to impose a modern system of regulationism which, unlike its medieval precursors, depended for its effectiveness on a state of considerable power and complexity, including bureaucratic, police, judicial and medical systems. Modern regulationism was of French origin, a theoretically comprehensive carceral system involving legally regulated brothels, clinics for medical supervision, and prisons for the recalcitrant.[39] Francesca Biancani, using a Foucauldian lens, describes the imposition of this system in Egypt after the British occupation, examining a number of inter-related practices, labelling, counting, spatial segregation or zoning, in state-licensed brothels, medicalization and detention. She also analyses the racialization of the system and its importance to the maintenance of the colonial order. Nonetheless she concludes that most sex work in Cairo actually succeeded in keeping below the radar of the authorities and outside the regulationist system.

In a second chapter on prostitution, Jairan Gahan looks at the much more ambiguous experience of Iran, where the new, post-1921, independent state vacillated between regulation and suppression (abolition). In Iran, as across the Middle East and North Africa, notions which underpinned regulationism, of prostitutes as a threat, to public and even racial health, as well as to morality, began increasingly to be challenged by more sympathetic views of 'fallen women'. Changing attitudes resulted from a range of causes including a greater understanding of the role of men in transmitting sexual diseases, the popularity of a cultural romanticism imported from Europe, and especially the newly audible voices of female reformers themselves. Indeed, organizations such as the Egyptian Feminist Union and the Iranian women's journal *Alam-i Nisvan* were crucial to popularizing the idea that prostitution was degrading not only to women but also and equally to men, and should not be tolerated, let alone managed, by a modern state and society.[40] For modernists across the region, what was required was a fundamentally new approach to sexual behaviour in particular and morality in general. Moral rectitude must now be based on individual responsibility, internalized sexual repression and self-control, instilled by education, rather than by physical seclusion and family supervision and control.[41] In a survey of the entire Pahlavi period, Gahan charts the course of the never resolved struggle between regulationist and abolitionist impulses in Iran, especially as epitomized by the tensions existing around the red-light district of Shahr-i naw, the emergence of the profession of social work and the increasing sublimation of the fight against prostitution into a 'rescue mission'.

Elite discourses on prostitution evolved during the twentieth century, but the basic parameters of the debate, regulationism versus abolition, remained and remained unresolved. Subaltern views, however, especially as articulated in popular mass cultural productions such as the commercial cinema and popular music tended towards more romanticized and broadly sympathetic narratives. The immensely popular pre-revolutionary Iranian genre of *filmfarsi*, for example, which featured heroic 'tough guys', sometimes featured such characters rescuing or reforming prostitutes.[42] Another example of the readiness of the Iranian lower classes to embrace morally ambiguous women is that of the entertainer Mahvash. Becoming a prostitute in Shahr-i naw after an unhappy childhood, sexual abuse and several unhappy marriages to abusive men, Mahvash, whose talents were recognized while she was still working in a brothel, became hugely popular as a singer of the despised *motrebi* genre, unwesternized popular urban music relating the hardships of the life of the poor and underprivileged. She appeared in many films and wrote an explicit autobiography, making no attempt to conceal, indeed even revelling in her past, and when she died in 1961 her funeral attracted perhaps a million or more mourners.[43]

The narrative of Mahvash's life illustrates the difficulty of penetrating beyond the dominant discourse on prostitution to uncover the authentic experiences of prostitutes themselves. Their voices are rarely audible at all, and when they are, tend to mimic elite understandings of their motivations, attitudes and behaviours. The woman lured into prostitution as the victim of unscrupulous male exploitation and deception, for example, is a common trope and was indeed Mahvash's own version of her 'fall'.

The mimicking by prostitutes of elite attitudes is again strikingly in evidence in Kamran Shirdel's documentary *Qal'ah* (The Castle), a subtle subversion of the official discourse of rehabilitation, shot in 1966 in Shahr-i naw and commissioned by the Women's Organization of Iran.[44] The women who relate their stories openly to camera, with no attempt to disguise their identity, typically blame their family, their parents or their husbands, for forcing or cheating them into a life of degradation. They present themselves as powerless and innocent, gullible, often child victims, sometimes tricked or even sold to brothels. Yet the versions of their own lives provided to Shahla Haeri by temporary *mut'a* wives (*sighehs*) in 1970s Iran, for example, demonstrates the real complexities and ambiguities of women's motivation.[45] Although unhappy marriages, male deception, divorce, and lack of education and employment opportunities figure prominently, yet these women are neither not totally destitute nor absolutely lacking alternatives.

The third chapter in this section is also concerned with anxieties about and fears of women in general and prostitution in particular but as expressed in a more diffuse way. Müge Telci Özbek discusses the alarm caused by young, single, working-class Muslim women who, having freed themselves from family and community ties and migrated to the city, moved at will through the urban spaces of early twentieth-century Istanbul. Vagrancy, of both men and women, had, by the late nineteenth century, become a quite specific concern to the authorities. As elsewhere, young, single, mobile men were considered a source of disorder or worse while vagrant women were a threat to morality and social order, and vagrants attracted a mass of legislation. As Özbek demonstrates, the intervention of the authorities to control supposed vagrants often affected populations far beyond the strictly homeless, acting as a disciplinary tool to be used against the urban poor more generally.

Özbek begins with a discussion of the significance of space for gender and class relationships, pointing out that since urban space was defined primarily as a male space, the very presence of women within it was profoundly problematic.[46] By the turn of the century, still small but socially salient numbers of single women were migrating to the Ottoman capital, either in search of a better life or in flight from an intolerable old one. Competing for the few low-paid jobs available, usually in situations where they might easily be compromised, such as domestic service, they often drifted into part-time prostitution, or perhaps only a promiscuous lifestyle or a more general vagrancy. Even were they to succeed in the unequal struggle to maintain their respectability, they could never escape elite views of the risk they supposedly represented to order and morality. Nonetheless, Özbek concludes that, despite the constant harassment of 'disorderly' women, late Ottoman Istanbul provided women with 'at least the hope of personal freedom and the ability to shape their own lives'.[47]

If prostitution was one answer to poverty and lack of other options, petty crime was another. Hanan Hammad describes the resort by poor women to theft in interwar urban Egypt. Indeed, as she points out, despite the scholarly interest in prostitution, in fact petty theft was the most frequent cause of the imprisonment of women in interwar Egypt. She again links perceptions of female pickpockets and shoplifters to the notion of honour. Regular employment as factory hands or domestic servants already violated class and gendered codes of respectability. Theft, she argues, offered the possibility of material gain to women who had little or nothing to lose in terms of status, such women already condemned by respectable society due to their inability to live up to the standards of *mastura*, being a morally and sexually protected member of society. For Hammad's Cairo, as for Özbek's Istanbul, the new scale of rural to urban migration is key to the social transformations of the late nineteenth to early twentieth century. Just as demographic changes led to larger numbers of the poor concentrated in urban slums, to a more intense struggle for employment and greater relative poverty, so urban modernization facilitated new forms of crime. Urban spaces provided a welcome anonymity for petty criminals, department stores offered tempting opportunities for shoplifters while pickpockets haunted the fleeting crowds passing through the new transport hubs.

The phenomenon of gendered crime links Parts One and Two of the collection. Hammad situated her study of petty crime in Cairo within an analysis of the conditions endured by and opportunities available to poor Egyptian women, both their own and society's perceptions of their actions governed by overarching and powerful gender codes. The four chapters in Part Two address another form of crime, that of banditry, which is not only in practice almost exclusively male but, with its codes of honour and performances of masculinity, also highly discursively gendered. All four chapters engage directly with Eric Hobsbawm's foundational text in the field of 'Bandit Studies'. The first chapter, by Stephanie Cronin, surveys the debates which were stimulated by Hobsbawm's thesis and asks why scholarship on the Middle East and North Africa has so far largely remained outside these debates. She asks in particular why there has been such a lack of interest in banditry when the phenomenon itself, and rural crime in general, was so widespread. Why are so few individual bandits celebrated or reviled? Why is there no Middle Eastern or North African counterpart to the Mexicans Emiliano Zapata and Pancho Villa, the Brazilian Lampiao, the Australian Ned Kelly, the Sicilian Salvatore Guiliano, or the Chinese Bai Lang, let alone to the female Indian 'bandit queen', Phoolan Devi. Cronin revisits the vexed question of the relationship between bandits and, on the one hand, the peasantry from whom they sprang, and, on the other, the landlords and local rulers into whose service they were often recruited. Using examples from diverse historical and geographical periods, colonial North Africa and Egypt, interwar Palestine, Kemalist Turkey and Pahlavi Iran, early modern Mediterranean corsairing and Morisco piracy, Cronin interrogates the notion of crime as a distorted form of social protest and wider issues of labelling and elite and popular perceptions.

The second chapter in this part continues the discussion of banditry as political resistance in a close case study of colonial Algeria. The treatment of the Algerian peasantry by the French authorities was exceptionally harsh as France was engaged in a particular settler-colonial project which required not just the exploitation of the indigenous population but their marginalization and substitution by European colonists. In his account, Antonin Plarier presents an analysis of the phenomenon of banditry within a very precise context: the rapid transformation of Algerian rural society by European colonization. Plarier begins by outlining the scale of the dispossession of the Algerian peasantry, both of land and of customary rights, and points out the synchronicity between the waves of expropriation and the rise of large-scale banditry. The bandits whom he describes were far from peripheral but rather emerged at the heart of rural societies and often constituted themselves as legitimate political authorities, their political claims reinforced by theatrical displays of tax collecting, demonstrations of generosity, and moments of violence, usually against members of local elites and collaborators. It was indeed the political potential of banditry, its possible role as the first stage in the development of an insurrection, which most alarmed the French authorities and at which they directed their main repressive measures. Plarier concludes that, notwithstanding the complexity of the bandit phenomenon, and the utility to the colonial administration of exaggerating the threat it represented, the history of Algerian banditry reveals important limitations on colonial power.

The final two chapters leave the colonial context to examine banditry in the independent states of late Qajar Iran and the early Turkish republic. The chapters in this section together illustrate strikingly the similarities between nationalist elites and colonial powers in their approach to the rural poor and to rural dissent, and in their preferred mechanisms for establishing their version of order in the countryside. As Selim Deringil has commented, the late nineteenth century was a time when the Ottoman elite itself adopted a colonial stance towards the peoples of the imperial periphery, combining a 'civilising mission' mentality taken directly from France with their own 'project of modernity', then adding a particular Ibn Khaldunian binary between the desert and the town, between nomads and civilization, the latter an essentially urban phenomenon.[48]

Mattin Biglari, in his study of southern Iran in the early twentieth century, begins by pointing out the deep-seated hostility felt by the constitutionalist and post-constitutionalist elites towards the nomadic tribes, a naturally 'dangerous class' and a disruptive force always liable to recruitment by foreign interests. He further argues that this hostility has survived within the historiography of modern Iran, banditry explained away with culturally essentialist references to a traditional tribal culture of raiding. Biglari, on the contrary, situates his discussion in a specific historical context, one of state formation, the commercialization of agriculture and the loss of customary rights, and presents banditry as a rational form of protest and survival and even of resistance. He also disputes the notion that banditry in Iran was necessarily a tribal phenomenon, but rather often involved settled villagers and even townspeople. Indeed, Biglari insists on the everyday practical connections between the rural and urban populations and the general impact on both of the revolutionary upheavals of the constitutional period and older subaltern political traditions in shaping popular understanding of such matters as legitimacy, authority, justice and popular rights and entitlements. It is only within this context, he argues, that the popular meaning and significance of banditry can be properly understood.

In a similar vein, the final chapter in this section presents banditry as one of a range of methods by which the peasantry in early Republican Turkey avoided or, *in extremis*, resisted, the demands of the new authorities. As Metinsoy points out, the experiences of the peasantry have been almost totally neglected by Western scholarship and the Turkish intelligentsia, both mesmerized by the Kemalist project. Like Biglari, Metinsoy also situates his study of Turkish rural crime within a particular context, in this case the profound economic, political and social change of the interwar decades, a period when the government's ambitious projects were often funded by an increase of the fiscal burden on the peasantry. Metinsoy describes the gradual escalation of peasant resistance, from a stubborn non-cooperation to smuggling, finally culminating in an epidemic of theft, robbery, physical attacks, arson, murder and banditry which plagued all of Anatolia. The targets of these attacks, tax collectors, district governors, gendarme officers, and especially village headmen, large landowners and usurers, indicate clearly the class rather than the ethnic nature of the conflict. Indeed Metinsoy points out explicitly that banditry was by no means peculiar to the Kurdish areas, nor was it much related to pastoralism, tribalism, or Kurdish nationalism. For the rural poor across Anatolia the road to banditry was neither long nor complicated, flight to the mountains often only to avoid reprisals after some hostile encounter with the authorities. Metinsoy ends by considering the long-term impact of peasant resistance on the Kemalist state and concludes that it was profound. Peasant intractability led not only to a limited land reform but also to the creation of a heartland in which would arise the conservative-religious politics of more recent decades.

The final part of the book contains three case studies of the dangers perceived in or represented by various kinds of social and individual intrusions onto the streets of Middle Eastern towns and cities. The food, or more specifically the bread riot was a common occurrence across the Middle East and North Africa, as it was in other parts of the non-European world and in Europe itself. Indeed, it was a major concern of premodern governments for whom social stability and political order was prized above the maximization of profit. The longevity and ubiquity, and even the rather ritualized character of the bread riot is striking. In medieval Cairo, early modern Damascus, across the Ottoman Empire and in Safavid and Qajar Iran, the urban poor frequently took collective action to assert their right to bread and to exert pressure of various kinds, sometimes peaceful, sometimes not, on the authorities to control excesses in the operation of the market. All invoked the concept of the 'just price', displayed suspicions of plots to hoard grain and manipulate prices and anger against merchants, millers and bakers, and demanded official intervention to regulate the grain trade. Till Grallert looks at the phenomenon of food riots in late Ottoman Syria, in the cities of Beirut, Damascus, Aleppo, Hama and Homs, using mainly the local press. He points out the limited correlation between food prices and riots, and then analyses in details the riots themselves. He concludes that food riots were neither particularly riotous nor predominantly concerned with food. Neither were they, he argues, particularly Islamic nor informed by a 'politics of notables'. Noting that these riots were rarely effective in producing cheaper food, he rather sees these riots as part of a 'repertoire of contention'. The demand for bread at affordable and established prices was largely symbolic and part of a larger negotiation of political legitimacy in times of internal and external crisis.[49]

For the final two chapters in the collection, the concept of the lumpenproletariat is key. Olmo Gölz uses the participation of *lutis* and *luti* bosses in the overthrow of the Iranian prime minister, Muhammad Musaddiq, in 1953 to shed light on the wider problems of comprehension presented by this liminal, highly gendered, social group. Although the nomenclature of *luti* and *lutigari* is specific to Iran, other countries of the Middle East, and Europe too, possess broadly similar phenomena, well-organized gangs of young men, illiterate and drawn from the urban poor. Such formations are indeed almost identical to the Italian *lazzeroni* specifically mentioned by Marx in his own list of lumpen elements. For the gangmember, physical strength and courage, 'manliness', were vital, as was honour, and a reputation for being ready to defend it with violence, on his own behalf, that of his quarter, and sometimes of the vaguely defined oppressed in general.[50] The importance of controlling and dominating the streets was well understood by all political tendencies in Iran, even the Tudeh deploying hoodlums for brawls with their opponents. In a micro-historical approach to the 1953 coup, Gölz investigates the role of *lutis* and *lutigari* in modern Iranian politics through an account of the lives of two famous *luti* bosses, Sha'ban Ja'fari and Tayyeb Hajj Reza'i. Through this analysis he also sheds light on the nature of Pahlavi modernity, which first, in a period of weakness, made use of the *lutis* but subsequently, after securing its ascendancy, marginalized them, either by transforming them into harmless folkloristic remnants of a constructed Persian ancient world or by criminalizing them.

The final chapter in the collection brings the story to contemporary Iran, with Maziyar Ghiabi's ethnographic discussion of another, particularly threatening element of the lumpenproletariat, the drug addict. Certainly drug use across the Middle East is by no means a modern phenomenon. A recent study of Iran, for example, concludes that drugs and other stimulants were widely available in pre-modern and early modern urban areas. Opium was used by both rich and poor, for medicinal and recreational purposes, and attracted little moral opprobrium.[51] However, although drug use itself is not modern, the figure of the addict is a different matter. The addict, a twentieth-century construction, Ghiabi argues, turned the poor, working-class, young, male user into a major threat, moral, social and physical, strikingly similar to that of the prostitute. Ghiabi first describes the conditions endured by the homeless addicts. Confined to particular desolate areas of the city, 'cleansed' from the streets and out of sight of the respectable Tehran middle class, addicts are then the prey of the dealers, a kind of order imposed by roughnecks employed by the boss of the *patoq* (hangout). He discusses the modernization of drug use through the twentieth and into the twenty-first centuries: the shift from opium smoking, anachronistic by the 1950s, to heroin, and most recently to metamphetamines, each of these substances producing, in turn, its own moral panic focused always on the addict. Ghiabi also traces the nomenclature of the Islamic Republic towards not only drug users/addicts but also towards the lower classes who produce them, showing how the post-revolutionary Fanonesque terminology of the *mosta'zafin* (the disinherited) has gradually been replaced, in the post-war era of reconstruction, by the derogatory term *arazel va owbash* (riff-raff). Although the Islamic Republic has adopted a more therapeutic approach to the problem of burgeoning drug use and addiction than some of its neighbours in the region, drugs remain strongly associated with milieux of sexual depravity, moral decadence and alcoholism. Lumpen addicts, conceptualized as a public order problem as well as a health threat, are still primarily dealt with by the police, while their middle-class counterparts avail themselves of extensive medical facilities in place to help overcome dependence.

******

Much of the literature on the 'dangerous classes' has focused on the late nineteenth and early twentieth century, it being generally assumed that the dangerous themselves and the environments which produced and succoured them would disappear with the triumph of modernity and its accompanying education, regular employment, and prosperity. The twenty-first century has, however, so far proved this assumption to be mistaken. On the contrary, such 'dangerous' environments appear to be proliferating.

The countries of the contemporary Middle East and North Africa have failed to resolve or sometimes even to address a number of interrelated problems which have produced an almost permanent sense of social crisis. A demographic bulge, the inadequacy and corruption of authoritarian governments in thrall to the International Monetary Fund, the dislocation arising from mass migration internally and overseas, the exacerbation of existing chronic inequalities, have led to the creation of a layer of unemployed or semi-employed young men, in Middle Eastern cities and, increasingly, of Middle Eastern origin in European cities, crippled by a pervasive sense of hopelessness, prone to petty crime and vulnerable to induction as footsoldiers into gangsterism and jihadism.[52] Such marginal young men now appear in various guises, migrants, petty criminals, drug addicts/pushers, and, perhaps that most dangerous of all the dangerous classes, terrorists. A modern lumpenproletariat, they demonstrate precisely that layer's typical political liminality but eventual propensity to mobilization by reactionary leaderships. Similarly, the conditions tending to give rise to prostitution, poverty, war, social collapse, forced as well as voluntary migration, rural to urban and increasingly transnational, continue to worsen. They are, furthermore, exacerbated by the appearance of novel forms of an older exploitation, the trafficking of women and girls on a truly modern scale and the more localized activities, such as the temporary marriages to Syrian refugees contracted by rich men from the Gulf. In these circumstances the old debates between regulationists, who argued that the legalization of prostitution offered the most realistic method for managing prostitution, and abolitionists, continue unresolved and unabated. Vagrancy has reappeared as homelessness, and from San Francisco to London the authorities are still trying to clear the streets of beggars without addressing the problems of poverty and housing.

Other of the phenomena addressed in this collection have also proved adept at reinvention, most notably that of banditry. Until recently, a discourse of modernism assumed that banditry was confined to the pathological margins of society and to the past. It has, however, shown itself to be capable of multiple reinventions and has reappeared across the Middle East and North Africa as smuggling and piracy, popular attitudes as ambiguous as ever.

The reconfiguration of the 'mob' or the urban crowd as a rational, and usually peaceful, actor, conscious of its own legitimacy, has been victorious in social history. The assumption of the literature which has proved mistaken, however, was that bread riots were a typical feature of the pre-modern economy. For E. P. Thompson himself, it was in pre-industrial societies that the market, and specifically the struggle over prices, and therefore the bread or food riot, was the primary arena of class struggle. As industrialization advanced the workplace, factory and mine, and the struggle over wages, would supersede this older conflict. Indeed, for much of the twentieth century, subaltern economic struggles were mostly conducted via formal organizations including political parties and trade unions. Over the last thirty years across the Middle East and North Africa, and indeed around the world, however, and quite contrary to earlier analyses, the food riot has reappeared as a result of neo-liberalism-induced austerity measures. Everywhere the removal of subsidies on staple foods, especially bread, has generated wave after wave of popular protest.[53] The reappearance of the food riot was perhaps most spectacularly announced by the massive protests which shook Cairo in January 1977 following the removal of state subsidies on staple foods as demanded by the World Bank and the International Monetary Fund. Modern *intifadat al-khubz* often bear a striking resemblance to the protests of the nineteenth and early twentieth centuries, with their near spontaneity and absence of identifiable leaderships, the role of women, and the central demand, for political intervention to modify the operations of the free market.

Thus prostitutes, now more usually described, in an attempt to avoid connotations of moral disapprobation, as sex workers, bandits, now gangsters and smugglers, and the desperate and hungry poor now battling not local merchants and landowners but global economic forces, each illustrates the reemergence, reinvention, resurrection or modernization of older 'dangers'. Thus the constantly evolving dangerous classes remain, still subject to elite policies formulated in the late nineteenth to early twentieth centuries, combining criminalization, medicalization, simultaneous concealment and surveillance, the dangerous kept out of sight but under close observation, and rehabilitation. These lives are the subject of this collection.

Part One

Dangerous Women

Disciplining Sex Work in Colonial Cairo

Francesca Biancani

In the last quarter of the nineteenth century, as Egypt's capital Cairo became an increasingly cosmopolitan city marked by the contradictions of globalization and colonialism, urban sex work changed dramatically. Anxieties about the influx of rural migrants, manumitted slaves and unattached foreign women engaging more or less overtly in the selling of sexual services haunted modern urban life in cosmopolitan Cairo. Mass free movement, the intermingling of socially disparate people and unsupervised physical contact between the sexes raised serious suspicions among the authorities: crowds and individual bodies were seen by the ruling elites as dangerous sites of moral degeneration and physical pollution that had to be actively monitored. The Egyptian authorities – and after 1882 the British colonial administrators – tried to implement a whole array of disciplinary techniques to ensure public order and health. After decades of loose administrative intervention by the Egyptian authorities, the British introduced a local version of French-inspired regulationism after they took power. Based on governmental sources, colonial archives, local and imperial narratives, and sexologist literature, this chapter presents a detailed analysis of sex work regulation as a specific type of colonial and biopolitical project. The term 'colonial' here carries two interrelated but distinct meanings. First, and primarily, it refers to the expanding capacity of state institutions to intervene and establish order and uniformity over societal processes. This was a self-strengthening policy Egyptian and colonial ruling elites alike adopted to discipline a marginal segment of the population: unruly women selling sex. Second, the adjective 'colonial' qualifies the historical case of imperial intervention in Egypt with its specific governmentality. Clearly, Egypt was not formally a colony during the period considered here, yet Egyptian politics were largely shaped by a set of hierarchical and extractive power relations imposed by an external power. The limited nature of Egyptian sovereignty, even after the declaration of independence and the formal end of the British protectorate in 1922, meant the country was in a situation of de facto colonial subordination.

In this context, the regulation of prostitution is seen as a distinct dimension of the modern 'power to colonize', to use Timothy Mitchell's famous expression.[1] It is a type of epistemology of power centred on the imperative of controlling individual embodied practices in such a way as to maximize their positive effects and minimize their potential dangers to collective well-being and productivity. Disciplinary logics and techniques came to 'colonize' human interactions, by defining normative and heteronormative racialized, classed and gendered subjectivities whose orderly production and reproduction were integral to modern biopolitical forms of governmentality.[2] In Egypt the antecedents of biopolitical concerns can be traced back to Muhammad Ali's modernizing efforts. They morphed into a self-conscious disciplinary project at the intersection between imperial and nationalist politics in and after 1882, when sex work regulation was introduced. This imperial policy was aimed at both protecting colonial troops from venereal diseases and preserving public order. The fascinating process by which sex workers were turned into a specific 'dangerous class' by the state[3] can be investigated at different levels. This chapter focuses on the process with a view of pushing the boundaries of Foucaldian governmentality and biopolitical theory beyond its Eurocentric focus.[4] The colony was a laboratory where imperial disciplinary strategies were tested and contested, interiorized, then manipulated and rearticulated by local hegemonic groups and ordinary people during the formulation of their own types of vernacular modernity. Egypt was the site of a subtle and complex interplay between a colonial power and a formally sovereign, yet de facto externally controlled, local form of rule, an emerging modernist and nationalist movement, and the problems arising from the existence of large numbers of non-local subjects protected by capitulary legislation. It therefore offers an interesting example of the provincialization of sex work regulation as a facet of typically Western imperial governmentality and its imagined order. In this chapter, I focus mainly on the prescriptive aspects of regulation, namely the techniques through which individual supervision extended to quite a comprehensive, if flawed, system of surveillance in Cairo in the last quarter of the nineteenth century. This regime consisted of a number of interrelated practices: labelling, zoning, medicalization, detention and racialization. The subjectification of sex workers as prostitutes constituted both the outcome and the necessary prerequisite of regulationism.

Labelling

As shown by Khaled Fahmy,[5] in Egypt the emergence of state interest in sex workers' activities can be traced back to Muhammad Ali's defensive modernization reforms[6]: in 1834 a ban on sex work expelled Cairo's prostitutes and performers – albeit temporarily – to Upper Egypt.[7] This was a decisive break from the previous Mamluk and Ottoman practices of de facto toleration, whereby sex work was treated as a profession and, despite being excluded from the guild system, taxed. Taxation was carried out by tax farmers and community leaders, who had free reign in adding or erasing women's names from their registers, often in return for a bribe.

The advent of regulationism in 1882 resulted in a dramatic qualitative change in the way sex work was managed in modern Cairo and signalled a momentous transformation in the relationship between the state and the people. By starting to regulate sex work directly, the state expanded its reach over society in an unprecedented way. The institutionalization of prostitution through the establishment of state-licensed brothels in designated urban areas where registered sex workers offered their services entailed the creation of a system of legal oversight. This was carried out by the brothel owners, who were responsible for making sure their employees underwent weekly medical checks, and by the so-called lock hospital, used for quarantining sex workers suffering from venereal diseases. This system was accompanied by a broad medical discourse on social hygiene, reflecting the emerging political priority of creating a normative knowledge corpus about the biological and the social.

The British introduced systematic regulationist policies – a local variant of the French-style state-licensed brothel system – immediately after their occupation of Egypt in September 1882.[8] At that time, the modular logic of individual confinement and regulation of abnormal social practices were turned into an expansive regulatory apparatus for reasons of sheer imperial governmentality. Based on a double standard for male and female sexualities, and on the Augustinian conception of prostitution as a 'necessary evil', this system of regulated prostitution understood prostitutes as a clear-cut, separate category of marginal social actors. Removed from the working class they originally belonged to, they were increasingly stigmatized as agents of moral corruption and physical contamination. The Malthusian logic of social productivity came to bear on this subaltern group in such a way that regulation was seen as the key method to transform these 'indolent', disorderly elements into disciplined workers, thus making their activity both socially and morally acceptable. Unlike France, Great Britain was not a regulationist country: the Contagious Diseases Act of 1864 was the closest it came to sex work regulation. The Act was repealed in 1883 due to vocal opposition from a variegated abolitionist front. Yet, regulationism was invariably put into place in the British colonies, where racist notions about the cultural inferiority and sexual primitivism of the native people were coupled with the paramount importance of colonial security. Utilitarian concerns about public order and the spread of venereal diseases among imperial troops made regulation mandatory, all the while 'offering a counterargument to the notion that British liberalism was largely responsible for the limited engagement with regulationist pratices'.[9]

The first law disciplining sex work was drafted in Egypt on 31 October 1882, i.e. only a month and a half after the British victory against the nationalist uprising led by Colonel Ahmad 'Urabi at Tell al-Kabir, which brought about the occupation of Egypt by 13,000 colonial troops. According to the Egyptian social historian 'Imad Hilal,[10] the British authorities forced the Egyptian government to adopt overtly racist discrimination against sex workers. Since the 'Orient' was commonly associated with images of sensuality, lust and unrestrained vice, the colonial imagination constructed local women as subhuman. As one Lieutenant Olliver, on duty on the HMS *Calypso* of the Mediterranean Fleet during the First World War, put it:

Perhaps people in England do not realize the effect that the immense inferiority of foreign women – compared to our own – has on men; more or less according to the meridian of longitude of the place so is the woman either a beast of burden, a chattel of her man, or more or less his equal. Tho' one may respect ones' equal, one has not the same feeling for the chattel of a man who is decidedly inferior to

oneself and who does not respect herself. And the whisky or vodka inside one
tends to take away the objection to her *dago* nationality or her yellow skins.[11]

Given the enthusiasm with which rank-and-file soldiers on leave tended to
patronize brothels and taverns throughout the empire, the authorities felt the need to
take measures to help prevent the physical degeneration of the occupying forces, in
later times steering towards abolitionism. Security reasons were combined with public
order and health considerations. According to N. W. Willis, an Australian author of
pamphlets on moral reform in the interwar years, Cairo had been reeking with violence
and disease before the arrival of the British:

> The Wazza [the Wassʻah, the Cairene area for licensed native prostitution, *mine*]
> bazaar was to be found a fearful death-trap of iniquity […] and the Egyptian police
> was afraid to enter [it] in response to the cries of the unfortunate who were being
> done to death. It was then – in the dark days of Egypt – quite a common thing to
> discover the mangled body of one of the poor unhappy women in the roadway
> at Wazza bazaar as the beneficent sun cast its morning rays on this plague-spot.
> Then, no man or woman was safe in such dens. Many went into the dark, dirty
> lanes and came out no more … this state of things has been abolished, until today
> the place is safe for a European to walk through as Piccadilly Circus or Leicester
> Square.[12]

In other words, according to Willis, the introduction of regulationism in Cairo
was tantamount to a philanthropic act, which not only benefitted the city's ordinary
residents but, most crucially, the sex workers themselves, as they could now ply their
trade in a safe environment. According to this narrative, sex work regulation in Egypt
was part and parcel of the British civilizing mission, and it was justified by the locals'
cultural backwardness.

The *manshur ʻamm*, or 'general decree', of 1882 profoundly changed the practice
of sex work in Egypt.[13] It formally established sex work as a profession by creating
a juridical difference between women who were legally authorized to exchange sex
for money in state-licensed brothels, and unauthorized clandestine prostitutes and
streetwalkers. Regulationism introduced a system of supervision consisting of the
brothel, where prostitutes worked under the control of the brothel owner (*badrona*), and
the inspection room (*maktab al-taftish*). Two inspection rooms managed by the central
Health Administration were opened in both Cairo and Alexandria. The prostitutes'
names had to be listed in special registers, together with the results of their medical
check-ups. If diagnosed with a disease, prostitutes would be hospitalized and could
resume work only after they were discharged from the lock hospital and issued with
a medical certificate. Prostitutes had to obtain licences as a proof of their professional
status; more importantly, third parties were granted the right to run brothels legally
by applying for a regular licence. According to Article 3 of the decree, every prostitute
(*imraʻah ʻahirah*) working in a locale known for prostitution was obliged to register
her name with the local police in the Bureau of Medical Inspection. She was given an
identification card that clearly showed her name, age, address, personal characteristics

and the name of the brothel owner she was working for. She had to undergo weekly sanitary inspections, and the results were reported on her card. The inspections took place on a daily basis, from 8.00 am to 1.00 pm in summer and from 10.00 am to 2.00 pm in winter. Doctors were prohibited from carrying out sanitary check-ups at the woman's domicile. The prostitutes who were unable to attend the weekly sanitary inspection due to illness had to send a doctor's certificate proving that their condition prevented them from being present at the medical inspection. The same provisions applied to female brothel owners, with the exception of women over fifty years of age. The effort to make the marginal status of prostitutes clear is evident in Article 13: every prostitute who wished to leave the trade as a result of marriage or repentance (*tawbah*)[14] had to produce two witnesses and apply to the Public Health Administration in order to have her name removed from the registration list. Pecuniary fines were applied to enforce the law: all women who failed to attend medical examinations or produce a doctor's certificate were subjected to a 50 piastres fine in the first instance, 100 piastres in the second and imprisonment from two to eight days thereafter.[15] The 1882 decree was followed by a number of legal texts elaborating upon its main provisions. In July 1885, for example, an ordinance on the medical inspection of prostitutes was promulgated by the Minister of Interior, 'Abd al-Qadir Hilmi Pasha.[16] It stipulated that the inspection bureaus of Cairo and Alexandria were to be staffed by one or two doctors, one nurse, a secretary with knowledge of Arabic and French, a police officer and a suitable number of guards. A comprehensive Law on Brothels (*La'ihah Buyut-al-'ahirat*) was finally issued on 15 July 1896.[17] This law marked the real beginning of licensed prostitution (*bigha' rasmi*, literally 'official prostitution') in Egypt, and it constituted the basis for the 1905 Arête. The latter was the ultimate legal text on state-regulated sex work and disciplined the activities of licensed prostitutes residing in brothels until the abolition of prostitution in 1949. Article 1 of the 1896 law defined brothel as 'the place where two or more women are living permanently or assembling temporarily for the purpose of prostitution'. According to Article 5, in order to open a brothel a written request had to be submitted to the Governorate, or the Provincial Administration, at least fifteen days prior to the proposed opening date. The request had to include the name, place of birth and nationality of each applicant as well as information about the location and number of rooms of the establishment, and details about the legal owners of the premises. The actual licence consisted of a certificate of inclusion in the brothels register. Both foreigners and locals could apply for a permit, provided they were not minors or interdicted. Those who had been convicted of a crime in the five years prior to the application, as well as commercial sex entrepreneurs whose establishments had been closed down by police authorities for not complying with the existing laws, were forbidden from applying for a license. The brothel owner had to supply a detailed list with the names of registered prostitutes and other people living and working in the house (e.g. servants) to the authorities. Prostitutes had to be at least eighteen years old. Every prostitute received a photo ID card from the police, which was to be renewed annually. Finally, according to Article 15 women had to submit to the weekly medical examination (*kashf tibbi*) described earlier on. In sum, the whole text was characterized by an emerging preoccupation with labelling prostitutes as such and marking them out as a specific sociological type.

Zoning

As Philipp Howell remarked, 'forms of regulation typically operated through a range of *spatial* projects designed to produce order and manageability, particularly in the Western city'.[18] Zoning, that is the spatial definition of specific areas of the city for the confinement of prostitutes, worked as the main tool of control and normalization of 'deviant behaviour' in the cityscape. As documented by an imposing corpus of literature about the interplay between spatial arrangements and colonial modes of power, segregation often took a cruder, coercive form in the empire.[19] Supported by racist ideology and unmitigated by any concerns about inalienable individual rights and self-cultivation, segregation sometimes took the form of collective displacement of prostitutes to peripheral areas outside the city walls. This move reflected what the human geographer Stephen Legg termed 'civil abandonment'.[20] This did not happen in colonial Egypt, where regulated prostitution was placed at the centre of the production of the colonial urban space, in both Cairo and Alexandria, figuratively and literally.[21] The main red-light district of Cairo was located in Azbakiyyah, a central area concentrating the trappings of *fin-de-siècle* cosmopolitan life: hotels frequented by hordes of international tourists during the winter months; foreign-owned large department stores such as Cicurel, Chemla, Rivoli and Tiring; the Cairo Opera; the Azbakiyyah Gardens (opened in 1872 and designed after Paris's Bois de Boulogne); local branches of the main European companies and societies; and the stock exchange.

Descriptions of Azbakiyyah and its 'red-light' district are easy to locate in old travelogues, as the area was considered a 'spectacle' of the city, a must-see spot for tourists visiting Cairo.[22] The Wagh-al-Birkah contained mostly foreign prostitutes – Greek, Italian and French women – with a licence. The street, with the Shari'al-Geninah and Shari' Clot-Bey appendages, was flanked by three-storey buildings in a Mediterranean style with wrought iron balconies stretching out onto the street. It was a very crowded tourist area, full of bars, taverns and cabarets, in which sex was offered as a commodity to throngs of westernizing local elites, foreign residents, imperial soldiers and international tourists in search for the 'Oriental experience'. The Wass'ah, instead, contained brothels staffed by local women. Russell Pasha, the former head (*hikimdar*) of Cairo's city police, recalled in his memoirs that a stroll through the area 'reminded one of a zoo, with its painted harlots sitting like beast of prey behind the iron grilles of their ground floor brothels, while a noisy crowd of low class natives, interspersed with soldiers in uniform and sight-seeing tourists made their way along the narrow lanes'.[23] Brothels could not have more than one door and had to be completely detached from other buildings, shops or public places in order to avoid causing grievances to respectable people. They also had to be far from churches and schools, so that religious sensibilities and the young generations' morals were not harmed. Prostitutes were required to avoid standing in the doorways or in the windows. From the Wass'ah, multiple alleys departed towards inner areas whereby the coexistence between illicit activities and 'respectable people' in everyday interactions was the norm rather than an exception, amid bursts of complaints by reform-minded individuals. In fact, in Cairo sex work was not spatially insular or confined to the licensed area: it permeated the entire urban fabric in its informal guise. Several historical sources reveal that sex work was far from being marginalized or removed from the eyes of the passers-by. Those who opposed the regulation of prostitution highlighted the physical proximity of vice to 'decent honourable families' and young generations.[24] Their newspaper columns show how prostitution was anything but carefully circumscribed or segregated in Cairo. According to a contemporary description:

> So familiar is the sight of brazen women, lost to all womanly feelings, lost to all shame and often perverted by a sexual lunacy into sexual monomaniacs; so common and so familiar is their presence, hanging from their windows almost in the nude, smoking, cursing, screeching like fiends or laughing like mocking devils; so accustomed have the inhabitants, young and old, become to all the signs of their business that they now pass, as a matter of fact, as something necessary for the use of man.[25]

On a similar note, Florence Wakefield, a British social worker from the British Association for Moral and Social Hygiene, wrote in a report on the British Army and prostitution regulation in Egypt:

> Children live in and frequent the segregated areas. I saw three little boys sitting down for the night against the wall of one of the narrow, crowded streets. Throngs of men, many of them at student age and appearance, saunter through the streets, when the women sit at their doors in scanty garments calling to each other and the passers-by. Some of them disappeared as we approached, some stood up respectfully and greeted the police officer as a trusted friend – as indeed he was […] The area impressed me as a sort of moral swamp, spreading contamination over the whole town.

Despite the existence of specific regulations aimed at spatially circumscribing prostitution, prostitutes were quite visible and navigated the public space. Brothels may have satisfied the regulations that required only one access door and fenced windows, but prostitutes would shout at potential customers from the balconies or thresholds and solicit on the streets.

Counting

Quantification was a different type of disciplinary technique, whose cumulative effects impacted the public opinion on prostitution no less than law enforcement. Over time, the production of statistics has proven to be a powerful governmentality tool, and it has been used to construct normative corpuses of knowledge in the social sciences. The importance of counting for the creation of a biopolitical system is obvious. Demographic statistics and censuses are key measures for the enhancement of the productivity and well-being of a people, by virtue of their capacity to study, understand and regulate patterns of reproduction, labour, residence, etc. The practice of counting has been inclusive as much as it has been exclusionary: it was used both to demarcate belonging and to circumscribe difference. Such statistical knowledge, a real tool of power, was constructed through the accumulation of large volumes of data and information.

Being a regulationist country from 1882 to 1949, Egypt produced a distinct type of documents concerning prostitution and its place in Egyptian society. Authorities tried to monitor and discipline sex work by turning it into a quantifiable phenomenon as much as possible. Police and sanitary officials were instructed to collect detailed information about the sex workers' social profiles, while brothel owners were requested to keep registers with their employees' names, provenance and age. Unfortunately, none of these materials are available to researchers today. What historians can make use of in an attempt to reconstruct the dimension of the phenomenon are aggregate data in the censuses (available for 1917 and 1927) and, more significantly, the yearly reports on public security and public health from the Egyptian Ministry of Interior (available for 1921 to 1946 inclusive). These sources have in fact been used and compiled in a number of publications on prostitution and venereal diseases, by abolitionist societies and public health experts, respectively.[26]

According to the 1917 census, there were 1,395 prostitutes in Cairo (with a greater concentration in Bab-al-sha'riyyah, Azbakiyyah and Sayyidah Zaynab). This number is much smaller than other contemporaneous estimates. For example Guy Thornton, chaplain of the Australian and New Zealand Army Corps garrisoned in Cairo during the First World War, writing in 1915, mentioned at least 2,300 native plus 800 European women registered as prostitutes, 'without considering clandestine prostitutes numbering in the thousands'.[27] Two years earlier, Major Frank Young, honorary secretary of the YMCA National Committee, told the *Egyptian Gazette* that 'with the increasing prices in all directions in Egypt, thanks to the popularity of the country as a tourist and a winter resort, one thing remains cheap: vice'.[28] It may be that a major 'purification campaign' carried out under martial law in 1916, during the First World War, had significantly reduced the numbers in the trade. However, without detailed information on this specific episode except for some media coverage, it may be safer to say that, despite the enforcement of state-licensed prostitution in Cairo, the actual numbers of women practising the trade can only be estimated. Moreover, it is commonly accepted that a decrease in licensed prostitution may reflect a significant increase in clandestine sex work: in other words, not a decrease in the actual number of sex workers but simply their 'going underground'. In the 1927 census, the first one listing prostitution as a separate professional category (i.e. separate from 'unproductive' activities such as begging and vagrancy), the registered female prostitutes numbered 749: 680 locals and 69 foreigners. Once again the numbers must be treated with great caution. In 1926, two years after a crackdown on clandestine prostitutes and procurers in the native quarter, the Cairo City Police reported the existence of 1,184 licensed women: 859 Egyptians and 325 Europeans. According to the report, 102 clandestine houses had been raided in 1926. In this case I was not able to verify the contemporaneous trend in clandestine sex work, which would give us a more comprehensive picture of the phenomenon. Contemporary observers described prostitution in Cairo as unabated and flourishing, thanks to relative post-war prosperity.[29] Moreover, according to Russell Pasha, head of the Cairo City Police, in 1931 the enforcement of state regulation on prostitution did not have any positive impact on public security, as the bulk of commercial sex trade was illicit and out of the authorities' reach. Russell Pasha stated that brothels catered for working-class customers and the 'baser kind of tourists', while '99% of respectable middle-class Egyptian men consorted with clandestine prostitutes'.[30] In fact, he maintained that the general standard of morality in the city was so low that 'there was no need for any but working-class men to cohort with licensed prostitutes because there was an ample supply of other complaisant girls'.[31] If we bear in mind that in the 1927 census, almost 400,000 people in Cairo figured as unpaid workers, the vast majority of them women, it is difficult to estimate how many of them clandestinely engaged in some form of sex work. The available data document only the expansion or contraction of the licensed sector, the relative presence of local as opposed to foreign women employed as prostitutes and the number of clandestine houses raided every year. They reflect the contours of the extent to which public security officials were able to scrutinize the trade, not what was really going on. The public health bureaus for sanitary inspection of licensed prostitutes recorded the numbers of licensed and unlicensed Egyptian sex workers they interacted with in the years 1921 to 1927, while yearly reports of Cairo's city police reconstruct trends in the trade between 1928 and 1946. These data are collated in the Table 1.1[32]:

Table 1.1 Number of Licensed and Unlicensed Prostitutes, 1921–46

Year	Number of Unlicensed Prostitutes Known to the Police	Number of Licensed Prostitutes
1921	906	1,210
1922	651	1,243
1923	840	1,070
1924	735	843
1925	884	718
1926	-	745
1927	723	641
1928	-	620
1929	-	628
1930	-	653
1931	-	338
1932	2,497 (Azbakiyyah area only)	726
1933	-	745
1934	2,278	848
1935	2,009	804
1936	2,899	821
1937	2,893	823
1938	-	699

Year	Number of Unlicensed Prostitutes Known to the Police	Number of Licensed Prostitutes
1939	-	582
1940	2,124	606
1941	-	742
1942	2,624	758
1943	4,319	631
1944	2,909	571
1945	3,772	555
1946	1,219	462

Source: Data from the records of the public health bureaus for sanitary inspection of licensed prostitutes 1921–27, and the annual reports of Cairo's city police 1928–46.

Between 1925 and 1946, the number of unlicensed sex workers found in clandestine houses or caught soliciting in the streets always exceeded the number of registered women. Looking at licensed prostitution data only, one could at first assume there was a decline in sex work. However, the data on clandestine prostitution reveal an entirely different picture, namely an upsurge in sex work in the 1930s and again during the Second World War, concentrated in the casual and informal sector. Women increasingly seemed to avoid licensed sex work. This was often because they did not want to comply with the compulsory medical inspections that severely affected their ability to work and earn a living if diagnosed with a disease. This was especially true at times when sex work was sustained by increased demand and, therefore, became a particularly interesting occupation. In 1943, for example, when thousands of soldiers were stationed in Cairo, the police detected 4,319 unlicensed prostitutes against 631 licensed ones. Two years later the number of unlicensed prostitutes was recorded at 3,772 as opposed to 551 licensed ones. This is undoubtedly useful information for the description of general trends, but it is far from indicative of the phenomenon. While there was a general agreement among experts on the fact that the clandestine sex trade was several times larger than its licensed counterpart, estimates of its actual volume differed. N. W. Willis argued that:

> To every licensed woman in Cairo or Alexandria there are at least ten, perhaps, twenty unlicensed, uncontrolled, women of every colour or nationality *except British and Americans* [my emphasis] [...] most of the women are French; next in numbers come Italians, and there are also Germans, Swiss, Greeks and Spanish.[33]

Dr Fikhri Mikha'il Farag, a prominent specialist on venereal diseases, gave the most disquieting estimates: he argued that the number of unlicensed prostitutes could be thirty-five to forty times that of registered women. Thus if in 1921 there were 906 licensed prostitutes, the number of unregistered sex workers would be around 35,000 to 40,000.[34] Finally, Louise Dorothy Potter, an abolitionist social worker active in Egypt in the 1930s, wrote in the leaflet *Egypt is awakening. Is it true?*:

Cairo has, it is officially stated, about five times as many 'secret' as 'registered' women. This is true in different degrees of every regulated city. In practice, therefore, vice is not confined by the system of licensed prostitution.[35]

As noted earlier, the data on licensed prostitution do not offer an accurate picture of the diffusion of sex work in Cairo. Key information, such as the actual number of clandestine sex workers, is not retrievable and it is bound to remain unknown. Moreover, the proliferation of haphazard and fragmentary data is interesting in itself, as it points to dominant anxieties and concerns about quantification and control.

Medicalizing

The Egyptian and colonial authorities claimed that one of the main reasons for the adoption of regulationist legislation was to prevent the spread of sexually transmitted diseases. According to this logic, only the containment of the brothels' inmates and strict supervision of their medical condition could prevent the transmission of syphilis and its degenerative effects on the entire society.

Of course the discourse on sanitary supervision of sex workers can be framed within the larger debate on public health, an integral facet of Egypt's defensive modernization project since the beginning of the nineteenth century. The link between scientific medical discourse and modern state-building has been studied extensively in order to show how under Muhammad Ali's rule modern clinical medicine was introduced and developed in Egypt as a tool of self-strengthening state reform.[36] By the 1820s, French consultants were hired to set up Qasr al 'Aini, the first modern medical school in Egypt, under the direction of the French doctor Clot-Bey. The four-year medical curriculum was modelled on the French one. Clot-Bey's reforms were not meant to frenchify Egyptian medicine but simply to introduce modern medical knowledge and practices. In other words, French doctors were to educate a native class of professionals to Western standards. The process of institutionalization of the medical profession went on under a different guise after the British occupation of 1882. In 1893, the Qasr al 'Ayni hospital was taken over by the British on the grounds of its supposedly poor management by the Egyptian government, and it was only returned to the Egyptian authorities in 1929. The anglicization of medicine in Egypt resulted in a dramatic decrease in the number of Egyptian doctors. The British administration introduced tuition fees and imposed English as the language of instruction, thus limiting access to a small elite of upper-class, English-speaking locals. Clearly, the British wanted to encourage the practice of medicine as a trade, not as a service for the benefit of the Egyptian population. Legal regulations, for example, privileged foreign practitioners: they could work in Egypt freely, as a medical diploma from any medical school in the world was the sole requisite for obtaining a licence in Egypt. More importantly, the Qasr al 'Aini curriculum was geared not towards specialization but the training of general practitioners for state healthcare facilities. Those who passed the final exams were referred to as 'graduates', not doctors.[37] At the same time, the top echelons of the profession became the domain of graduates of foreign institutions. As el-Azhary Sonbol reports,

> The number of Europeans working in Egypt rose from 109,725 in 1897 to 147,063 in 1907, an increase of 35 per cent in 10 years. The number of Greeks increased by 65 per cent; Germans, 35 per cent; Italians, 43 per cent; Swiss, 35 per cent; and Belgians, 33 per cent. In addition, a great number of Syrians and Armenians, all of whom were Ottoman subjects, settled in the country.[38]

Foreign doctors formed a powerful professional class catering to the needs of wealthy urban elites, while the sanitary needs of the vast majority of poor and rural Egyptians were almost completely ignored. Thus, the knowledge of Western medicine became not only a tool of social control but also constituted a form of power capital, jealously guarded by the colonial elites and their associates. Here we can see an interesting parallel between sex work regulation and the institutionalization of modern medicine and the medical profession under colonial domination. Although disciplinary techniques imported from the West had already been deployed in Egypt before the colonial period, their consolidation into self-conscious biopolitical regulative apparatuses, driven by the increasing scientification of local culture and based on racial hierarchies, was definitely a colonial endeavour.

With the increasing stratification of Egyptian society and the emergence of a nationalist elite, namely a specific group of self-identified agents of modernization, Egyptian doctors – often educated or trained abroad – started to act as mediators between local sensitivities, the imperatives of westernization and cultural imitation. In the 1920s – a century after the first encounter between European and local medicine – a group of Egyptian doctors established themselves as recognized specialists. This professional elite of upper-middle-class men began to question the predominance of European doctors and institutions and assert themselves as pioneers of a truly local, nationalist medical science at the service of the well-off members of the Egyptian population. Liat Kozma excellently explained how 'reformers and medical doctors who started writing about sex in Arabic, presented themselves as liberating their readers from the hold of customs and organized religion and thus situated themselves as the vanguard of a modern and enlightened East'.[39] Experts in reproductive health and sexology ('*ilm al-tanassuliyyat*, 'science of reproduction') clearly considered the rational management of sex work an issue of national interest. In 1924, the Berlin-educated dermatologist and self-proclaimed sexologist Fakhri Mikha'il Farag wrote that Egyptians needed to be taught about sexual health and reproductive matters exactly as they had been acquainted with technological innovations, such as the telegraph, one generation before. His tract on the spread of venereal diseases (*amrad tanassuliyyah* or *zahriyyah*) provides vital information on the medicalization of prostitution in early twentieth-century Cairo. Faraj described the three sanitary bureaus for prostitutes in Cairo: one in the Darb-al-Nubi, for sex workers active in Bab-al-Sha'riyyah and Azbakiyyah; one in 'Abbasiyyah; and one in Sayyidah Zaynab. He compared them to their counterparts in Berlin in an attempt to underline the serious shortcomings of sanitary policies in the Egyptian capital. In 1921, for example, 1,381 prostitutes were listed in the registers of the Darb-al-Nubi bureau. During that year, 390 women were struck off the list for various reasons: as a result, the actual number of prostitutes regularly inspected in the bureau was 991. As the clinic was open four days a week, and the total number of inspections that year was 29,208, this means 143 women were inspected per day.[40] Moreover, it is important to remember that the bureaus were only open from 10.00 am to 1.00 or 2.00 pm, and in addition to carrying out medical inspections the medical staff also had administrative responsibilities. Thus we may conclude that every medical check-up would last only a few minutes, instead of the sixty minutes necessary for a thorough internal and external examination and correct diagnosis of venereal diseases. The doctors themselves lamented that they were virtually unable to detect any infection under these circumstances. The regulations concerning the frequency of medical check-ups (once a week) were also evaded. Local women were checked twenty times a year (i.e. every eighteen days), while foreign women were subjected to medical examinations thirty times a year (i.e. every twelve days). Burtuqalis Bey, a gynaecologist specialized in the treatment of venereal diseases in Cairo during the 1900s, claimed that a medical inspection would take him at least thirty minutes, while in state-run bureaus a doctor would check tens of women in that time.[41] Foreign women were exempted from medical inspection if they were able to provide a certificate signed by a private practitioner: this resulted in frequent forgeries. If a foreign woman was diagnosed with a venereal disease, the doctors would notify her consul, who would then prohibit her from practicing the trade until recovery. Given that free clinics were not available, and European women were not obliged by law to seek treatment in venereal wards, foreign prostitutes were largely allowed to keep working provided they did so clandestinely and were not caught prostituting themselves in the *quartier réservé* or soliciting in the streets.

In addition, prostitutes resorted to a number of strategies in order to escape supervision. Some disinfected themselves prior to the check-ups or used special ointments to conceal the external manifestations of syphilis in the hope that they could deceive the doctors. Traditional barbers and midwives played an important role in these practices, as they had some knowledge of traditional medicine. In 1934, for example, a barber known for being a specialist in the camouflage of syphilis marks on the bodies of prostitutes was arrested in Alexandria. In time, a new practice was introduced: rich customers would pay for a private examination for the prostitutes they wanted to consort with, so as to be certain the women were not infected. For a considerable sum of money, a specialist would inspect the prostitute and sign a certificate stating she was free from infection, which was valid for 24 hours. Obviously, such medical inspections had no diagnostic significance. Women, Burtuqalis Bey wrote, were treated like fresh fish, to be consumed within one day after being bought.[42]

In 1904, a hospital for the treatment of native syphilitic prostitutes was opened in Sayyidah Zaynab. The hospital, called 'al-Hod al-Marsud' (haunted basin) contained two hundred beds. The hospital was staffed by only three doctors and the inmates stayed in crowded rooms with windows barred to prevent their escape. Any sex worker found infected with a venereal disease, whether during a routine medical inspection or while she was prostituting herself (in the streets or in a clandestine brothel), was confined to this lock hospital for treatment. The hospital was equipped for the diagnosis and treatment of venereal diseases throughout their different stages and in accordance with medical practices. For instance, large quantities of mercury and potassium permanganate were used to suppress the infections. Reports by public health authorities point out the constant increase in the number of patients; between 1925 and 1931 the number of women treated in al-Hod al-Marsud rose from 2,830 to 5,783.[43] As stated by Muhammad Shahin, the author of a treatise on the system of venereal clinics established across the country in the mid-1920s, the rise in the number of patients may have reflected a greater awareness of the necessity to cure infections promptly and in accordance with the correct sanitary practices. However, the high number of inmates who stopped treatment upon the disappearance of external symptoms, that is, without full recovery, does not corroborate Shahin's hypothesis.[44] In other words, the number of syphilitic patients was constantly on the rise. This means that regulationist policies did not curb the spread of sexually transmitted diseases, as patients evaded medical techniques of infection control whenever possible. In addition, Shahin's report states that between 1925 and 1932 on average 44 per cent of al-Hod al-Marsud patients at any one time had previously interrupted their treatment.[45] The reasons for this were manifold: not only was hospitalization perceived by the women as an unwanted form of confinement, restraining their freedom of movement, but it also severely affected their economic circumstances. Moreover, the treatment was not free: in 1918 inmates paid 47 millims per day, 50 millims in 1919, and 78 millims in 1920.[46] Brothel owners often advanced money to pay for the prostitutes' hospital fees, charging high rates of interest. We must also take into consideration the fact that a significant number of foreign practitioners were not subject to sanitary control and were thus left virtually free to prostitute themselves despite being infected. Moreover, the vast majority of sex workers in Cairo engaged in clandestine prostitution in an attempt to avoid state control. Sanitary officials considered the treatment provided at the clinic a medical failure; they were perfectly aware that for the majority of women, full recovery was not possible without several years of costly therapy. Secondary and tertiary syphilis, for instance, was to be treated with mercury and potassium permanganate tablets for three years. In addition, the patient was to be kept under observation for two years, with blood tests taken at regular intervals. In reality, though, patients were often discharged from the hospital after only a few days, or once their exterior symptoms disappeared.

Confinement

In theory, the Egyptian regulationist system was informed by principles of enclosure and hierarchical supervision. However, none of these requirements were respected in Cairo. As we have seen, the *quartier réservé* in fact only hosted a small share of the available establishments, since prostitution in Cairo was scattered across the entire urban fabric. The majority of licensed brothels were opened in the touristic and nightlife areas of Cairo – Azbakiyyah and the surrounding neighbourhoods – thus underlining how the expansion of prostitution was intertwined with the growing upper-middle-class purchasing power and global commerce. Nevertheless, sex work was practiced illegally all over the city. Despite specific regulations aimed at enhancing the enclosure system, sex work was not segregated. Due to a specific clause forbidding doctors from making house calls, medical check-ups did not take place in brothels. Thus Cairene prostitutes enjoyed liberty of movement to a degree unknown to sex workers subjected to the same regulationist system in other countries. There was certainly a hierarchy within the brothel, but nothing comparable to the French system; the madame was often a prostitute herself and the presence of men – whether husbands, pimps or paramours – was not exceptional. Clandestine establishments in particular were often akin to family businesses, with the owner's family and servants occupying one storey of the building, while sex workers and customers used the rest of the house. Hence, instead of a careful separation between prostitution and the domestic economy, sex work and family work overlapped. In the French system, the brothel owner was considered to be an agent of the central government, indeed the very antithesis of elusive procurers and pimps who evaded supervision and police control over their milieu.[47] In Cairo, by contrast, brothel owners allied with local pimps and bullies to evade state control. In some cases, police officers were known to have an understanding with brothel owners and prostitutes.[48]

Prostitutes caught soliciting in the streets or those failing to turn up for their medical check-ups were taken to the local police section (*qism*) to be sentenced and transferred to the relevant prison (*niyabah*). Unlike French prisons, Egyptian penitentiaries did not have a separate section for prostitutes. Close supervision was not enforced due to infrastructural constraints: in the *niyabah* of Bulaq, the isolation cell was designed to contain no more than fifteen people, but in reality it accommodated forty; in the penitentiary of Old Cairo, isolation cells contained no lavatories; in the 'Abdin *niyabah* there were no windows; in al-Khalifah's the isolation cell had a shattered roof.[49] The efficiency of Egypt's regulationist system was jeopardized, above all, by the very existence of unequal colonial power relations, such as those at work in the capitulary legal system. The dual system,[50] and the privileges granted to foreign communities by the capitulations, severely curtailed the capacity of both local and British police to enforce the law effectively. Since its inception, sex work regulation in Egypt applied differently to local women and foreign nationals. Such differences were based on the colonial logic behind the Cairene regulation of prostitution and the forms of local government more broadly.

Racialization and the colonial order

Prostitution in Cairo was described in contemporary sources as a two-tier trade with spatial, juridical and cultural distinction between European sex workers (*afrangi*) and their native counterparts. Discourses on the prostitutional milieu by Western puritan reformers and imperial authorities maintained that European prostitution in Cairo was mostly squalid and deplorable, but still civilized compared to the native, 'Oriental' abjection and filthiness. They subscribed to a fiction of imperial and racial superiority, while pointing to the necessity of correcting working-class female sexuality and moral weakness through metropolitan campaigns for moral purity and social regeneration. Many accounts routinely stressed this point: the aforementioned Russell Pasha wrote in his service memoirs that Wagh-al-Birkah, the Azbakiyyah area frequented by European prostitutes, was populated,

> With European women of all breeds and races *other than British* [my emphasis], who were not allowed by their consular authority to practice this licensed trade in Egypt. Most of the women were of the third class category for whom Marseilles had no further use, and who would eventually be passed on to Bombay or the Far-East markets, but *they were still Europeans* [my emphasis] and not yet fallen so low as to live in the one-room shacks of the Wass'ah which had always been the quarter for purely native prostitution of the lower class.[51]

In the Wagh-al-Birkah, European prostitutes did not offer a more edifying sight, at least not according to Douglas Sladen. He, however, does not seem to have been entirely immune to the fascination of the scene:

> Every floor has its balcony and every balcony has its fantastically robed Juliet leaning over. As the street, in spite of its glare, is not well lighted, you cannot see how displeasing they are; you get a mere impression of light draperies trailing from lofty balconies under lustrous night blue of Egypt, while from the rooms behind lamps with rose-coloured shades diffuse invitations.[52]

Like the Wass'ah, the nearby Harat-al-Ruhi contained many low-class brothels with a more diverse ethnic make-up. Here, Jewish women could be found next to Italians and Levantines. Prostitutes soliciting in the streets were described by travellers as rapacious, dangerous beings: 'wild-eyed, lithe creatures, human leopards' or 'night birds seeking whom they may devour'.[53] Local women were not considered morally degenerate but seen as devoid of any sense of morality. Rather than being seen as 'fallen women', a category later introduced by the activists of foreign benevolent societies and local feminist associations, Egyptian prostitutes epitomized widespread beliefs about the lasciviousness of uncivilized, backward Oriental peoples.

European observers were certainly more concerned with the presence of European women (mostly French, Italian, Greek and Austrian) selling themselves unabashedly to black, brown or white men, than with the plight of Egyptian sex workers, ordinarily described as beastly creatures or freaks. Both foreign and native sex workers were essentialized by the colonial gaze, although in distinct ways. European women were portrayed as victims of the 'white slave trade': mindless or retarded, typically low-class girls whose lack of sound moral judgement ultimately accounted for their present situation. In contrast, local women were often described as voluntary sex workers.[54]

Ethnicity and race were constructed as determinants of sex work practice by the very same institutions of colonial control. Yet, the efficiency of the regulationist system in Egypt was jeopardized above all by the colonial underpinnings of the legislation: its inherently racist logic. On the one hand, the existence of a dual legal system – with separate courts for local subjects and foreign nationals, legal privileges enjoyed by non-Egyptians and the notoriously lenient justice administered by consular courts – hindered the capacity of both local and colonial police to combat illicit sex work effectively. Colonial power relations allowed capitulary subjects in Egypt to profit from illicit activity in the country, boosting the consolidation of transnational networks trafficking in any merchandise, women included. Foreign women could receive medical examinations from private practitioners, instead of going to the local *maktab al-taftish*. If diagnosed with a disease, Egyptian subjects were confined to the al-Hod al-Marsud lock hospital, while foreign women were expected to notify their consular authorities and undergo medical treatment on their own initiative. Of course, this rarely happened. Infected foreign sex workers normally started working illegally or obtained false health certificates from complacent doctors. Thus the different treatment of local and foreign sex workers in relation to health checks made medicalization untenable. The closest Cairo came to the medicalization of European prostitutes was in 1915, when the 'European Bureau de Moeurs' and a dedicated lock hospital were opened in the predominantly Coptic area of Shubra as part of a major purification campaign carried out under martial law. The military authorities advocated a 'pragmatic approach' to regulation in order to curb the spread of venereal diseases among the troops. Consuls grudgingly agreed to these measures, provided they were temporary, as they feared that sex work regulations could call into question the whole system of privileges enjoyed by capitulary subjects in Egypt. This bespeaks the racial hierarchy constitutive of the imperial enterprise. The British introduced sex work regulation out of concerns for colonial governmentality. While the racial hierarchy at the core of the colonial order made sex work regulation completely inefficient, common evasion practices made possible by this racial hierarchy turned regulation into an apparently necessary method of social control.

Conclusion

As Cairo became a cosmopolitan global capital caught between the contradictions of an emerging nationalist political culture and the reality of colonial domination, the introduction of regulated sex work in 1882 marked an effort to mark out prostitutes – labelled as a new and distinct sociological type – and contain them through a dedicated disciplinary system. Egypt's regulationist policies reflected the expansion of biopolitical concerns from the metropolis to the colony and the ways in which these policies were negotiated in local power relations, cultural norms and the imperatives of colonial governmentality. British authorities enforced sex work regulation, as they did in other imperial domains, for both pragmatic and ideological reasons. Pragmatic considerations included the preservation of Cairo's public order and the well-being of British occupying troops. These were fundamental in motivating sex work regulation, but so was the racist orientalist ideology and the belief in a Western civilizing mission.

Egyptian regulationism was a colonial disciplinary project linking sex, gender, public health and order, based on principles of quantification, spatial segregation and medical supervision, which proved to be unclear and unsuccessful. Contemporary sources expressed the anxiety of the ruling elites about labelling and quantifying sex workers. While these testimonies are certainly interesting, they do not allow us to get a clear picture of the quantitative dimension of the phenomenon, given that the bulk of sex work in Cairo always managed to stay below the authorities' radar. The regulationist system was not inclusive enough. Egyptian prostitutes avoided regulation by practicing sex work informally, in clandestine houses, camouflaged in the urban fabric and often for limited periods of time. Foreign prostitutes, for their part, were shielded by capitulary legislation and consular protection. Consequently, they were mostly free to ply their trade undisturbed and outside the system of licensed brothels. In practice, both local and foreign women strenuously resisted pigeonholing by state authorities. In fact, it seems the more inclusive the regulation, the more it excludes, marginalizes and alienates the necessarily complex, fragmented and at times even contradictory forms of human agencies.[55] I believe the study of sex work regulation in colonial Egypt provides a lens for studying the complex ways in which difference and hybridity were essential to the colonial order as they legitimized the deployment of disciplinary mechanisms devised to consolidate, and thus normalize, an order based on difference. Regulated prostitution, in the imperial mind, buttressed the colonial order as one of the main tools for normalizing racial hierarchies through the management of marginalized women.

Governing Prostitutes between Fear and Compassion: Tehran's Red-Light District (1922–1970)

Jairan Gahan

Introduction

Tehran's red-light district, also called 'The New City' (Shahr-i naw), has a significant place in the collective memory of Iranians. It serves as a site for national, urban and religious myths, with proliferating rumours around it. Its residents are remembered in two seemingly opposing terms: as both subjects of compassion and targets of resentment. On the one hand, popular accounts of the twentieth-century political upheavals portray them as friends of ruffians and counter-revolutionary subjects, who are easily bought and sold. The role of prostitutes in the 1921 coup d'état, the 1932 protests against D'Arcy's Oil concession and the 1953 coup d'état against Mosaddeq's nationalist government is commonly presented in this way.[1, 2] The infamous photo of a pick-up truck packed with ruffians and a woman wearing a loose *chadur* standing next to them with a club in her hand circulates online as a proof of the vile nature of the red-light district women. On the other hand, there is a bevy of journalistic work dating back to the 1930s that portrays the district's prostitutes as victims of larger social inequalities, who were in need of rescue and care.[3] Kaveh Golestan's grotesque and striking black and white photographs depict prostitutes in dire living conditions, in run-down houses with threadbare mattresses, peeling wallpaper, broken tiles and mouldy basins. These portraits have fixed the image of prostitutes as victims in need of compassion and humanitarian aid. In short, the public has conceptualized and remembered the red-light district women as both dangerous and in danger. In this chapter, I demonstrate the inner solidarity between these two seemingly opposing views, and that together they informed the state's two-pronged policy of regulation and abolition of prostitution in the Pahlavi era (1924–1979).

The abolitionist approach considers sex work a practice inherently violent towards women and attempts to eradicate it completely. Regulationism perceives prostitutes as a threat to public health and hygiene, and typically includes policies that monitor their health through compulsory and invasive medical check-ups, and put them under rigorous surveillance.[4] These two models – continuously debated among feminists and governments throughout the twentieth and the twenty-first centuries – constituted the bedrock of state-sponsored humanitarianism in Iran during the Pahlavi era.[5]

The hyper-visibility of the figure of the prostitute in the cultural memory of Iranians stands in contrast with the absence of scholarly accounts of prostitution in the historiography of modern Iran. While the role of women in the state's nation-building project has been the focus of much historical research, scholars have paid little attention to marginal groups who were not included in the state's ideology, such as performers, café dancers and prostitutes.[6] In this chapter, I examine the governance of Tehran's red-light district to illustrate how marginal sites and subjects served as laboratories in which the state experimented with modern forms of governance – including bodily regimentation and rehabilitation – sovereignly, arbitrarily and indeterminately, with minimum expense and maximum ambition.[7] The chapter will investigate broader questions about the role of humanitarianism in the governance of subjects who cannot be fully integrated into the political system of the state and are placed at the threshold of legality.

Medicalization of prostitution

In the late nineteenth century, prostitutes were not spatially segregated in Tehran. During the Muzaffarī period (1896–1907) they were dispersed throughout the city. They were most commonly punished by eviction from their neighbourhood or the city, an act referred to as *nafi balad*. If prostitutes were involved in a public controversy, they were usually flogged and shamed publicly.[8] It was only in the 1910s, in the context of brisk urbanization, a sharp population increase and a rapid spread of venereal diseases that modern medicalized techniques of governance entered the analytics of controlling prostitution.

In urban centres in particular, fighting the spread of venereal diseases became a matter of urgency due to the government's concern about population decline. Government physicians predominantly framed prostitution as a medical problem and put prostitutes at the forefront of sanitary reforms. They emphasized that prostitutes were a primary source of venereal disease, as they described the prostitutes' body as a more potent site for infection and transmission.[9] Surin Tumaniyans, a Christian physician who wrote prolifically on the compatibility of Islam with microbiology, suggested that prostitutes were infertile due to the 'plenitude of the gonorrhoea microbe in their ovaries'.[10] He went so far as to claim that all prostitutes were sterile due to chronic gonorrhoea. Dr Dubshan, a physician in the Soviet Hospital (marizkhanah Shawravi) published a book on syphilis in which he asserted that prostitution was the main cause of syphilis.[11]

Concomitantly, nationalist sentiments and anxieties over foreign invasion exacerbated Tehran residents' bias against prostitutes, particularly because the latter catered to the Cossack soldiers. Residents voiced their discontent about the presence of prostitutes in their neighbourhoods and labelled them as sources of hygienic threat, moral pollution and foreign assault.[12] The newspaper *The New Iran (Iran-i naw)* was filled with reports of the Cossacks' reckless behaviour in the city. The Cossacks were commonly accused of 'violating (*daridah*) our women's honour and respectability', and the prostitutes were accused of facilitating this violation.[13] Regardless of the reliability of such accounts, these narratives contributed to the image of prostitutes as subjects who lack autonomy and boundaries. Against the backdrop of fear of foreign invasion (particularly British and Russian) and loss of control over Iran's national borders, the state's securitizing discourse slipped into medical discourse. Microbes of syphilis, gonorrhoea and chancre became emblematic of foreign enemies, sneaking under the nation's skin and threatening the foundation of the next generation. The state even launched awareness campaigns to 'wage a war' against venereal diseases.

Government physicians saw the prostitutes' bodies as the most vulnerable to microbe-enemies, their reproductive organs as infertile and their sense of morality as fundamentally corrupt. Prostitutes became emblematic of contact zones through which Iran encountered the world. They were under the spotlight of reformist, moral and religious literature, seen as the most vulnerable of penetrable bodies, without political or physical boundaries or a sense of morality.[14] Stories of prostitutes' pretence of love and subsequent betrayal sneaked into local newspapers (*havadis-i shahri*) that usually reported urban crimes. Ali Akbar Hakamizadah, editor of the monthly *Humayun*, warned against the 'venereal diseases and moral corruption' caused by prostitutes. He described prostitutes as 'flirtatious emotionless women who are all microbes from head to toe'.[15] The biweekly *Taqaddum* described prostitutes as women who are 'inferior in thought, morals, and nature' to other women and men.[16]

The prominence of the figure of the prostitute in the national memory of Iranians as a hireling who contributed to various political schemes is rooted in the convergence of the security discourse in politics with the medical discourse on public health.[17] It is with reference to this historical legacy that in 1950, Abul'hasan Ha'irizādah (1888–1972), a member of the parliament, described Iran as a prostitute who 'winks at the other [Russia], while signing a contract with Britain'.[18] Sexual labour folded into political labour as a sexual service in exchange for money was translated into national treason. Sex work throughout the twentieth century was loaded with broader political significance and negative value. The public imagined prostitutes as undesirable members of their imagined nation, undeserving of citizenship.

In March 1922, in what appears to be one of the earliest attempts to concentrate prostitutes in a single area in Tehran, the Ministry of Internal Affairs (vizarat-i dakhilah) with the cooperation of the Commissioner Office[19] displaced a number of prostitutes to an area just outside the city gates.[20] Shahr-i naw, was an emerging neighbourhood south of the Cossacks' military camp at the time, known for its green areas, gardens and large properties. With the government's forceful displacement of residents it was gradually established as Tehran's red-light district during the 1920s.[21] The formation of the district was an early (extra-)legal experiment with zoning practices. According to the First Amendment of the Iranian Constitution, 'no citizen could be expelled from their land, forcefully settled in a specific place, or forbidden from residing in a place unless in cases that are explicitly indicated in the law [i.e. codified law]'.[22] In the absence of any codified laws regarding prostitution, when law and its execution had collapsed, the state's action became the rule. For the next sixty years, the district continued to serve as an experimentation site for governing techniques, especially regulationism and medical governance.

The Public Hygiene Council, comprised of prominent physicians, was part of the state's regulatory apparatus for monitoring and supervising prostitutes. The Council implemented surveillance techniques that were mainly geared towards protecting citizens from the spread of venereal diseases, which was framed in terms of a national threat. The council members identified and reported ill prostitutes who were to be relocated to Shahr-i naw. For instance, on 1 February 1927, Dr De Lapouge, a French doctor and a member of the Council, reported a number of French women to the Ministry of Internal Affairs for spreading venereal diseases in Tehran.[23] According to his letter these women, who entered the city on a servant work permit (*tazkarah-yi khidmatkari*), resided at Café Lux in Lalizar Street, where they were working as prostitutes. The letter further noted that since they were 'causing the spread of venereal diseases', they had to be evicted from the city, transferred to Shahr-i naw and placed under medical supervision. Within a month, by 1 March 1927, the police displaced the eighteen women identified by De Lapouge to Shahr-i naw and sent them to a clinic for treatment.[24] This is an early instance of physicians directly orchestrating the state's 'fight against venereal diseases'. Gradually other large cities, including Mashhad, Isfahan and Shiraz, opened special health clinics and developed surveillance mechanisms such as mandatory health cards – through which clinics kept track of prostitutes' health condition and regular examination – medical check-ups and occasional detention to monitor prostitutes as the primary carriers of venereal diseases. In Isfahan, if prostitutes were diagnosed with a venereal disease, they were banned from working until they recovered.[25] In the name of caring for citizens and killing intruding microbes, the state developed regulatory mechanisms to monitor diseased female bodies.

In 1940, Dr Charles Oberlin (1895–1960), the first dean of the Faculty of Medicine at Tehran University, convinced the state to merge Tehran's Venereal Disease Hospital (Nahid) with the department of skin diseases at Sina hospital. In his proposal to the Ministry of Culture, Oberlin complained about the high cost of treatment at Nahīd. He criticized the management of the hospital: 'It seems relevant to mention how these women were treated there! They [i.e. government officials] had chosen a lavish house with a vast garden [for these prostitutes] and had turned it into a luxurious hospital … they [i.e. hospital personnel] even used the fancy method of blood testing to diagnose syphilis.' According to his post-merger diagrams, the new clinic treated triple the number of syphilis patients than Nahid and at a lower cost. The high number of patients that he included in his charts could have been a result of the misdiagnosis that would ensue in the absence of blood tests. Regardless of the accuracy of Oberlin's claims, this case reveals the hierarchal structure embedded in state medical programmes, premised on moral values and sensibilities in favour or against certain citizens. The questions of who needs the care of the state, how much care they deserve and how much the state cares were all interconnected and considered in designing public health policy. Dr Oberlin, as a state actor, considered prostitutes unworthy of lavish treatment and niche medical technologies. This attitude was based on a perceived moral devaluation of prostitutes, rooted in prior moral sensibilities and resentment of their proximity to venereal disease microbes. This attitude of providing only the minimum necessary care runs throughout later state policies and plans regarding the women of Shahr-i naw.

Humanitarianism in the red-light district: Between abolition and regulation

The medicalizing policies championed by the Public Hygiene Council ran in parallel with other, more compassionate approaches towards prostitutes, which became more prominent in the middle of the twentieth century. From its very beginning, Tehran's red-light district received sharp criticism from abolitionists, who condemned the legalization and regulation of prostitution.[26] Abolitionist attitudes rely heavily on a humanitarian discourse that equates prostitution with sex-trafficking and aspires to rescue prostitutes. In 1928, roughly seven years after the formation of Shahr-i naw, Mihrtaj Rakhshan, a women's rights activist, educator and a columnist in the women's journal *'Alam-i niswan*, published a tendentious article against Shahr-i naw.[27] She asked the state to shut down the district and establish a 'House of Hope' (*khanah-yi umid*) to 'rescue' the district's women from the 'forced crime' of prostitution. Referring to this rescue mission as 'the most sacred of national measures', she appealed to the readers' sense of compassion: 'Let us pity the vulnerable girl who once was dear to her parents and is now so embarrassed, scared, and ashamed that she sees no choice but to endure this dire life forever, despite her averseness [to this profession].' To make a distinction between prostitution and forced prostitution, she argued:

> I am not a fan of prostitutes. In fact, I hate them so much that even their breath scares me. However, I defend those wretched ones who have been deceived and are now awakened from their ignorance.[28]

In her article, she evoked a compassionate attitude towards vulnerable prostitutes while allowing for hostile responses to voluntary prostitution. In Rakhshan's vision, there is constant oscillation between resentment and compassion, which led to an unresolvable indeterminacy toward the figure of the prostitute. Since the line between forced prostitution and voluntary prostitution is blurred, the state officials as well as the public could never determinately decide whether prostitutes deserved compassion or hostility. How was this indeterminacy and ambiguity reflected in the governance of Shahr-i naw? How did the state decide what quality of life the district deserved and what healthcare services to provide for its prostitutes?

In the 1940s the fight against prostitution was fully sublimated into humanitarian rescue missions. Western medicine discovered penicillin as the definite cure for syphilis, which had previously been an incurable disease.[29] Due to the mass import of penicillin after the Second World War, venereal diseases ceased to be an urgent national threat. Concomitantly, Tehran expanded, enveloping the red-light district into the heart of the city. Shahr-i naw, originally conceived as a red-light district outside the city bounds, was now situated in the centre of the city. Prostitutes returned to the public eye, only this time the people's attention focused on their precarious living and working conditions. This compassionate impulse towards the figure of the vulnerable prostitute also prevailed in the press and in literary works, such as Hidayatullah Hakimilahi's *Come with Me to Shahr-i naw* (*Ba man bi Shaht-i naw biyayid*, 1945),[30]

Mirza Fereydun Nadiri's *I was Never a Prostitute* (*Man fahishah nabudam*, 1946), Jahangir Jalili's *I too Have Cried* (*Man ham giryah kardam*, 1949) and many works by Javad Fazil, including *The Prostitute* (*Fahishah*, 1953) and *The Innocent Lady* (*Banu-yi bi gunah*, 1952).[31]

Similar attitudes can be observed later in films: both features, such as *Kandū* (Firaydun Gulah, 1975), and documentaries, such as *Qal'ah* (Kamran Shirdel, 1965) and *The Other Side of Pleasure* (*An su-yi lizzat*, Davud Rustayi, 1977), the latter commissioned by the Tehran municipality as part of a campaign against addiction. In most cultural works, compassion for the figure of the prostitute is accompanied by disgust for her abject, diseased body.[32] For instance, Mahmūd Zand-Muqaddam – a journalist-ethnographer – described Shahr-i naw as an infected place: 'A step away from the gates of the fortress, into the district, rotten smells bombard your senses; the smell of urine and sludge; the suffocating smell of trash; rotten bodies; infected wounds; coagulated vomit.'[33] Grounded in humanitarian values, his investigation of the dire life of the Shahr-i naw women sublimated his disgust with and fear of diseased prostitutes into a compassionate impulse.

This shift in public attitudes was concurrent with the post-Second World War campaign of Muhammad Reza Shah's government, which increasingly foregrounded the compassionate efforts of the state. In the 1940s and 1950s there was a proliferation of state-sponsored welfare organizations in Iran.[34] Most of them were nominally led by women from the royal family, including the Shah's twin sister Ashraf, his elder sister Shams and Queen Farah.[35] In 1947, Muhammad Reza Shah appointed Ashraf vice-chair of the Royal Organization of Social Services. Farah Pahlavi inaugurated and led many charity and welfare organizations after her coronation as Muhamad Reza Shah's queen in 1959, most significantly the Farah Pahlavi Charitable Society (jam'iyyat-i khayriyyah-yi Farah Pahlavi). The Society later turned into a well-established, state-run welfare organization, today known as Bihzisti. Members of parliament addressed the three royal women as 'Angels of Benefaction' (*firishtigan-i nikukari*).[36] By the 1960s, in parallel with the top-down land reforms and modernization plans known as the 'White Revolution', the state increasingly self-identified as a 'service-giving' state (*dawlat-i khidmatguzar*) and sought to popularize its image as a welfare state providing care for its people.[37]

In line with this compassionate campaign, imposing care as a regulatory mechanism of population control moved to the forefront of state policies on prostitution. In the 1950s, the General Department of Public Health initiated a Plan for Fighting Sexually Transmitted Diseases (*tarh-i mubarizah ba bimariha-yi amizishi*) with the cooperation of the World Health Organization (WHO).[38] The Bimāristān-i Nijat was the main hospital tasked with the execution of this plan in Tehran. Even the name of this hospital (literally 'rescue hospital') shows that state was portrayed as the medico-moral saviour of the population. On 29 June 1953, with WHO assistance, the Nijat hospital officially opened a centre for fighting sexually transmitted diseases (STDs).[39] The centre established a clinic in Shahr-i naw. According to the clinic report, the centre in Shahr-i naw treated 9,000 patients with gonorrhoea or syphilis between June 1953 and March 1954.[40] Controlling Tehran's prostitutes was a priority for the hospital; the clinic staff even visited the homes of prostitutes to force treatment on them. By 1955, the plan for fighting STDs had expanded into other major cities in Iran, offering free medical and social services to prostitutes.[41] By 1957, the Nijāt clinic was administering mandatory biweekly shots of penicillin to prostitutes as well as holding monthly workshops and film screenings for them.[42]

Meanwhile, the state also developed and experimented with short-lived measures aimed at abolishing the district, as opposed to regulating it. In 1953 the city police attempted to restrict traffic to and from Shahr-i naw by surrounding it with brick walls and making entry possible only through two tall brown iron gates.[43] Subsequently the district came to be called the Ward (*Qal'ah*), and access was limited and monitored by two soldiers at the gates. Ordinary women and underage boys were officially barred from entry, but of course they snuck in. The police also announced that it would not allow new women to move there.

Simultaneously with the intensification of medicalized surveillance and regulationist policies, the state promised to allocate funds for the complete demolition of the district. After a detailed census in Shahr-i naw in 1957, the state allocated 20 million tomans to the Association for Fighting Prostitution for the 'rehabilitation and empowerment' of the district's prostitutes. The Association was a local grassroots organization formed in 1953.[44] It planned to build 'Houses of Salvation' (*khanah-yi rastigari*), similar to what the abolitionist activist Rakhshān imagined thirty years earlier. Members of the Association proposed that the district be bulldozed entirely and turned into a park (a plan only realized two decades after the Islamic Revolution, in the 1990s).

Later that year, on 15 October, the commissioner's office of petitions of the National Parliament held a meeting with the head of the police department, General 'Alavi, the mayor of Tehran, Musi Maham, and the Attorney General to discuss the strategy for the district. The meeting vividly reflects the state's indeterminacy in dealing with Shahr-i naw. General 'Alavi believed that it was impossible to eradicate the district since it had approximately two thousand residents. According to 'Alavi, the relocation of all the residents and businesses in the area would be too costly.[45] He also claimed that 'the presence of prostitutes in the society is like a safety valve for preserving public modesty and honour'. The parliamentarian agreed that prostitution responds to people's 'natural instincts' and therefore its complete abolition was unrealistic. However, he was critical of 'the state legally keeping prostitutes in a corrupted place'. The Attorney General noted that it was illegal to force prostitutes to evacuate and it was not possible 'to go against the law bluntly'. Here, the Attorney General is most probably referring to the First Amendment of the Iranian Constitution – mentioned earlier – which made it illegal to relocate or expel citizens from their residential households. He suggested that they block entry to 'the centre of corruption' (*markaz-i fisad*) by closing the gates, to implicitly force residents to evacuate without having to break the law.

Unlike the other attendees, who understood prostitutes as a potential cause of public unrest, Mayor Mahām stated that many of these women were 'wretched' and had no other choice, and expressed his concern for their well-being. He added that if the state provided him with sufficient funds, he would do his best to establish career centres and provide 'respectable' (*abirumand*) living conditions to help these women find other occupations – a plan in line with the Association's abolitionist vision. He estimated that 60 per cent of prostitutes would quit the profession if given other work. Interestingly, he was the only one present whose ultimate goal was the complete eradication of prostitution. Other members of the committee chose the pragmatic path of tacitly tolerating Shahr-i naw, while trying to find practical ways to regulate it and keep the neighbouring residents content.

The attendees eventually decided to: first, form a commission to pass an Act for Fight Against Prostitution; second, use municipal funds for the relocation of prostitutes; and third, give the police and the Attorney General more freedom to prevent the corruption of women. This last clause meant that the police would have an (extra-)legal status within the bounds of the district, where once again law and its execution could collapse. This decision was followed up with the establishment of a police station in the district in 1954.[46] It tacitly allowed the suspension of codified law and thus for police raids and brothel busting in the district. The fate of the residents was increasingly in the hands of the executive branch of the state, in particular the local police, who had permission to act sovereignly and indeterminately. Thus Shahr-i naw continued to serve as an (extra-)legal site ruled under a de facto state of exception.[47]

In the same year, Iran joined the UN Protocol to Prevent, Suppress, and Punish Trafficking in Persons.[48] This move can be read as a further step in the direction of abolitionism, which sees sex work only in the context of sex trafficking. In December, Mayor Maham wrote a letter to the National Parliament explaining that to shut down Shahr-i naw the municipality first had to prepare another place for the district's prostitutes.[49] However, no plan that could meaningfully change the women's life conditions or allow them to find other work had been proposed. In April 1959, the municipality and the district police (*kalantari*) shut the northern gate and closed all cafés and bars in the area, including the ones outside the gates.[50] The municipality also announced that it would shut down the other gate too, but this final step towards the closure of the district never happened.[51]

Not only did the state seek to limit the flow of people, alcohol, opium and cash into the district, it also restricted the availability of electricity and running water.[52] Most houses in Shahr-i naw did not have showers, and almost none of the old clay houses had electricity and water pipes. None of the streets were asphalted and running ditches were major sources of pollution. It was as if the district's lifelines were being cut off gradually. Nevertheless, the district stubbornly kept expanding. By the 1960s, Shahr'i naw was strategically located to the south of a military camp and the north of the central bus and railway station, a bustling inter-city transportation hub. Bars, cafes, restaurants and alcohol shops were back in business. With at least 1,180 female worker-residents, Shahr-i naw housed 753 merchants and 179 stores, including grocery stores, butcheries, thrift stores, barbershops and beauty salons. The district had its own entertainment units comprising two famous theatres, Hafiz and Shukūfah-yi naw, which ran shows all day long. The area was 13,500 square metres in size, with two main streets, Haj ʿAbdul Mahmud and Qavam Daftar, and thirty alleys, such as Kuchah Hamam, Kilidi, Shukuh and Urang, crossing them on a grid plan.[53]

Despite the rigorous public health campaign of the 1950s, the understaffed clinic in Qalamistan Street (immediately outside Shahr-i naw) – the only medical centre serving the district's women in the 1960s – could barely meet the demand.[54] The majority of prostitutes had few or no savings, many were in debt bondage and most had no access to social services and medical insurance, except for the mandatory venereal disease check-ups. However, despite the state's grand ambitions in the 1950s, the check-ups had turned into a matter of formality.[55] With the increasing number of higher class prostitutes outside the district (either working on their own or in private illegal brothels and *najibkhanah*), Shahr-i naw started catering to lower-middle-class men. By the 1960s, Shahr-i naw had turned into the second cheapest area for prostitution in Tehran.[56] Thus in spite of the government's compassionate campaign that imagined the prostitute as a vulnerable subject in need of rescue and care and deserving of public compassion, life conditions in Shahr-i naw became increasingly precarious. Why did this happen? And why did the abolitionist approach never realize its final vision for the district, i.e. its complete eradication and the rehabilitation of its women?

The economy of sovereign experimentation

Minimum funding allocation was at the heart of the plans for Shahr-i naw. In January 1968, Safi Asfiya,[57] director of the state's Management and Planning Organization (known as the father of liberal economy in Iran), annulled the 1958 promise of 20 million tomans for the development of a rehabilitation centre for prostitutes outside Tehran.[58] According to Asfiya, the centre was not in line with the government's Fourth Development Plan.[59] Instead, the state allocated 30 million tomans for the construction of accommodation for 100 homeless women and the creation of two working camps (*urdu-yi kar*), each with a capacity of 50 people, where female vagrants (*zanan-i vilgard*) would be taught crafts.[60] The head of the Association for Fighting Prostitution argued the scale of and funding for the new plan was insufficient. He had a point: over one thousand prostitutes resided in Shahr-i naw at the time, but despite the state's compassionate rhetoric, the new plan only aimed to provide shelter for one-tenth of that number. Nevertheless, the state decided to stick to Asfiya's plan.[61]

The value of state care for the prostitutes in Shahr-i naw was calculated at a level that barely met the residents' immediate needs. The correspondence between the Association and Asfiya includes a report on prostitution in Tehran prepared by 'specialists' in the Ministry of Labour. Even in this report there is a dual attitude of hostility and compassion towards the prostitutes. On the one hand, the report asserts that most women engaging in prostitution are underprivileged as they are 'slow, illiterate, or without any special skills'. But then it adds that some women are just 'greedy' (*tama'kar*) and enter the profession for financial gain. Here, we can see how the line that Rakhshān, the women's rights activist, attempted to draw between forced and voluntary prostitution in her newspaper article surfaced four decades later in a government report. The Head of the Health and Welfare Department in the Management and Planning Organization also noted this duality, stating that 'it is not clear whether the research aims at reducing prostitution or improving the prostitutes' conditions.'[62]

In 1968, concomitant with Asfiya's annulment of the fund allocation for the rehabilitation of prostitutes in Shahr-i naw, the state sponsored an in-depth study of sex work in Tehran by the Social Work Higher Education Institute (Amuzishgah-i 'ali-yi madadkari-yi ijtima`i).[63] The study focused on Shahr-i naw but also addressed different forms of urban prostitution, ranging from informal sex work at cafés and bars to street prostitution and private brothels. The study was published in 1970, with a print run of five hundred copies. A private publisher subsequently printed another three thousand copies. By authorizing the publication of this report, the state projected a compassionate image of itself. The report, the only publicly available study on Shahr-i naw, has consolidated this image in the collective memory of Iranians. Sattareh Farman-farma'iyan, the institute's founder, was entrusted with leading the study. The publication established her image as the main proponent of empathy for the Shahr-i naw prostitutes and of improvements to their living and working conditions.

However, the government's motivation behind funding the institute's research and social work was primarily to reduce state expenditure on dealing with prostitution in Shahr-i naw and Tehran more broadly. The Ministry of Internal Affairs claimed that 'the burden of arresting stray women [prostitutes outside the district]' put pressure on the police force. The Ministry further explained that since the law did not penalize prostitutes, the police arrested them as stray women (*zanan-i vilgard*), kept them at the station overnight and transferred them to women's prison the next day. They were then taken to court, where they mostly accepted their charges, which led to detention for no longer than ten days.[64] This vicious cycle of arrest, detention and release was wasting police resources (both human and spatial) with no tangible return. As such, the primary drive behind this social welfare experiment, which was used to showcase the state's compassionate face, was in fact economic.

Not surprisingly, the institute's programmes did not escape the duality towards prostitution that was present in the government's attitude as well as in public opinion. The 1968 report shows that the institute's efforts were pulled in two directions. Farman-farma'iyan recounted the institute's main goals as 'facilitating the emancipation, rehabilitation (*i'adah-yi haysiyyat*), and re-empowerment (*baztavani*) of prostitutes' as well as the 'prevention of the spread of prostitution'.[65] Thus even its goals were twofold: encouraging prostitutes to quit their jobs, while at the same time supporting them in their profession. The report concluded that despite the prostitutes' 'unfavourable' conditions (health issues, addiction, illiteracy and destitution) there was still hope for their 'rehabilitation'.[66] The conclusion refers to prostitution as an 'inevitable reality' and 'a disturbing phenomenon one needs to bear'.[67]

Significantly, the project was funded primarily as a pilot study. In order to gather data, Farman-farma'iyan established a social service centre in Shahr-i naw through which she conducted research about the capacity of social work in Iran; gathered data; and offered social services to prostitutes. The centre experimented with modes of compassionate regulation such as using madams – brothel managers – to monitor prostitutes medical check-ups and health condition; renewed health cards; referral services; and work camps. The staff's interviews with prostitutes may have amplified their voice in policy deliberations. However, ultimately, the interviews allowed the centre to estimate how many of these women were willing to quit prostitution and explore different ways of motivating them to do so. Furthermore, the centre experimented with placing a few women in work camps which had a dual work-learn (*amuzishi-tawlidi*) purpose. The centre's ultimate goal was to discover more effective regulatory mechanisms for Shahr-i naw. Also, the centre did not entirely escape the state's liberal economic logic. For instance, one of its recommendations was to use the female brothel managers' intimate ties with the prostitutes to monitor the latter's health. The implementation of such micro-techniques of governance above all, aimed at reducing state expenditure on public health.

However, the efforts of Farman-farma'iyan and her team cannot be reduced to regulationism and prohibitionism. Through the twenty thousand interviews conducted by its staff, the centre attempted to gain the trust of brothel managers and prostitutes and include them in the decision-making processes concerning the district. The centre lobbied the municipality to improve the social, health and economic conditions of the district's prostitutes. The municipality asphalted the two main streets and filled the filthy pools or turned them into fountains. It also assigned a street sweeper to clean the running ditches, promised to build three hygienic public washrooms and agreed to connect the district to the water and electricity grid.[68] In collaboration with the Nijat hospital, social workers identified prostitutes suffering from syphilis or gonorrhoea and convinced 569 of them to seek treatment. Interestingly, only 84 followed up and finished their treatments. The centre also sought to enable prostitutes to better navigate their everyday lives in the district. For instance, it obliged them to open bank accounts so that they would learn how to save money and thus work their way out of their debt bondage.[69] The centre continued to function until the Islamic Revolution. Shahr-i naw continued to dwell indeterminately somewhere between legitimacy and illegitimacy, as an improper part of Tehran. The district consistently received fewer resources, as the lives of prostitutes were considered less worthy than the lives of other citizens.

Conclusion

Looking at the state policies towards Shahr-i naw between the 1920s and the 1960s as a whole, it becomes clear that there was never a master plan for the district. Until the 1960s the state played the matter of Shahr-i naw by ear, taking measures one at a time, letting them unfold in the texture of the city. The funding promised for the regeneration of the district in 1958 never came through. Ten years later, after a preliminary research study conducted by Tehran University, the state started funding a social services centre in Shahr-i naw, not only to improve the prostitutes' lives but to also reduce the amount of resources wasted on them by the police. For the better half of the twentieth century, time and again, different state institutions failed to decide whether to allocate resources to improving the prostitutes' living conditions, or to eradicating the profession altogether. It was precisely this indeterminacy between regulation and prohibition – and inner solidarity between the two – that ran through the different stages of the government's policy-making regarding Shahr-i naw and hindered the full implementation of any finite plan for the district. The state executed plans that minimized expenditure while also trying new methods of humanitarian governance, ranging from medical check-ups to rehabilitation centres. In the absence of consistent execution of the codified law (which was passed shortly after the formation of the district and criminalized prostitution businesses), the state constantly oscillated between prohibitionist and regulationist policies. Without a consistent policy on prostitution, Shahr-i naw's fate was dictated by the state's economic rationale.

The deep incoherency in the state's management of Shahr-i naw does not mean that state institutions were ineffective. Rather, it reflects the sovereign and indeterminate experimentation at the heart of the modern state, in this case with the concept of 'good life' (which refers to the quality of citizens' life) and 'humanitarian governance' within the state's liberal economic policies. The treatment of Shahr-i naw was stuck between the regulatory and the eliminating power of the state. The ultimate sovereign act of the modern state was to arbitrarily oscillate between these two expressions of modern rule. The modern state's sovereignty is defined as the power that attempts to confine the outside and interiorize the excluded.[70] The metaphor is particularly powerful in describing the state's power in Shahr-i naw, as the government spatially included the district within the bounds of Tehran, while excluding it from the city by erecting walls around it. Shahr-i naw was never to be a well-regulated, legitimate part of Tehran. In effect, the district, as a space inhabited by citizens who were considered less worthy, served as an 'underfunded and overextended' laboratory of the modern nation-state, where the relations between the state and the citizens were constantly tested and shaped with 'minimum expense and maximum ambition'.[71]

'Disorderly Women' and the Politics of Urban Space in Early Twentieth-Century Istanbul (1900–1914)

Müge Özbek

Archival documents demonstrate that in the early 1900s and 1910s, the Istanbul police arrested a number of women for being 'disorderly' (*uygunsuz*). In most of the cases, the label 'disorderly' connoted a 'connection to' or 'potential for' prostitution. Frequently, the women arrested for being 'disorderly' were accused of 'prostituting here and there', 'soliciting in the streets' or 'behaving immorally'. However, the police refrained from calling these women 'prostitutes' and consistently used the label 'disorderly woman'. A closer look at early twentieth-century documents concerning 'disorderly women' reveals that the label was used to identify young, solitary, poor Muslim women who were not bound by customary family and community ties and who moved freely through Istanbul's urban space.

From the late eighteenth century onwards a small, though socially and economically significant, group of solitary women had joined the growing ranks of the poor in Istanbul. Without family support and control, they entered the city labour force unbound by traditional gender expectations and engaged in sexual behaviour considered illicit by the standards of the time. Because of their 'promiscuous' lifestyles, class origins and spatial mobility in an urban setting, they defied contemporary expectations of domesticity and models of proper womanhood. Middle-class perceptions of solitary, poor women who fell outside customary structures were negative: they were seen as prostitutes, or at the very least potential prostitutes.[1] Indeed, most of these women turned to prostitution as the most reasonable economic and social option to earn their livelihoods in the Ottoman capital. The female newcomers to the city competed for the few low-paid and low-status employment opportunities available to women, primarily in domestic service, cleaning, laundry and prostitution. Some also worked as street vendors, shop assistants, seamstresses, waitresses, singers, dancers and actresses. Many resorted to prostitution, some to supplement their limited earnings and others for their primary income.[2]

On 14 January 1884, the Ottoman State Council issued the Ordinance for the Sanitary Inspection of Some Private Houses within the Border of the Municipality of the Sixth District (*Altıncı Dâire-i Belediye Dâhilinde Bulunan Ba'zı Husûsî Hanelerin Hıdemât-ı Sıhhiyesine Dâir Ta'lîmâtnâme*). This first attempt at regulating prostitution in the Ottoman Empire was geographically limited to the sixth district (Beyoğlu) and only targeted non-Muslim women. The advocates of the new ordinance, led by Eduard Blaque, the renowned mayor of the district, presented the regulation as a pragmatic approach to maintain urban order and public health. According to these advocates, it was impossible to completely abolish prostitution in the area, but imposing an enrolment system that required prostitutes to undergo compulsory medical checks would severely restrict the harm that prostitution inflicted on society.[3] The regulation of prostitution in Beyoğlu was an experiment and a model. The district's specific religious, cultural and economic context justified a form of legislation that would be inappropriate in other parts of the city. Limiting enrolment to non-Muslim women was also critical for the justification of the ordinance. According to a widely accepted feminist view, the regulatory mechanisms were directed not only at prostitutes but at all poor women, a troublesome component of the urban poor in the ever-growing urban centres of the nineteenth century.[4] I contend that the establishment of a regulatory system in Beyoğlu was a milestone in the governmental approaches to poor women in the urban spaces of late Ottoman Istanbul.

However, a number of women remained beyond the scope of this initiative: women outside of Beyoğlu and Muslim women. Although the Ottoman government tried different methods for expanding their control over poor Muslim women it was not until 1915, with the Regulation for the Prevention of the Transmission of Contagious Diseases (*Emraz-ı Zühreviyenin Men-i Sirayeti Hakkında Nizamname*) issued by the Young Turk regime, that Muslim women were brought under the umbrella of a regulatory policy.[5] I argue that prior to 1915 the Ottoman government had pursued a policy centred on merely limiting the visibility and mobility of Muslim women in the streets of Istanbul. Young and poor Muslim women were excluded from Istanbul's urban space through deportation to provincial cities or through absorption into relief institutions. However, none of the efforts to control solitary, poor women in Istanbul had proven effective in the face of contemporary realities. This chapter will focus on the lives and experiences of solitary, poor Muslim women – the so-called 'disorderly women' – in late Ottoman Istanbul, along with governmental policies aimed at controlling their urban mobility, sexuality and labour.

From the mid-nineteenth century onwards, solitary, poor women associated with prostitution and vice became a great source of anxiety for the middle- and upper-class residents of Istanbul. Women were expected to remain in the private sphere of their homes, engaging in sexual activity only in the interest of procreation. The usual middle-class point of view associated solitary, working women with prostitution and saw them as contaminating respectable houses and the city as a whole with disorder, immorality and disease. Yet a number of sexually active women who lacked customary familial bonds and their own households increasingly appeared in the capital's newly expanding public spaces.

Importantly, the portrayal of these women by the middle class often related to broader anxieties related to the social, political and economic crises in the Empire in the nineteenth and early twentieth centuries. More often than not, solitary, poor women were depicted as symbols and symptoms of the decline of paternal authority, whereby the authority of the father or patriarch in the personal sphere was also imagined as and associated with the authority of the Empire in the public sphere. It was also a period in which gender, class, ethnic and religious identities were subject to negotiation and transformation. As Istanbul underwent a hasty urbanization, particularly in the second half of the nineteenth century, cultural constructions of gender and sexuality, family liabilities and paradigms of work changed as rapidly as the city itself. In this context, questions of national and gender identities and issues of public health, religious hegemony, urban security, social order and sexual politics were all played out in the public debate concerning solitary, poor women.[6]

The second half of the nineteenth century was also a critical period in which new approaches to urban population and urban space were formed and new institutions were created for the regulation and control of the 'dangerous classes.' I contend that the treatment of solitary, poor women in the second half of the nineteenth and early twentieth centuries in Istanbul was closely related to new conceptualizations of urban space, which redefined the boundaries of participation, security and visibility. From the mid-nineteenth century onwards, Ottoman governmental agencies tried to suppress the visibility of solitary, poor women in urban areas and control their sexual and vocational behaviour.[7]

The term 'disorderly' differentiated unregistered Muslim 'prostitutes' from their registered non-Muslim sisters. 'Disorderly woman' as a flexible term also provided the police and other government staff with the opportunity to include all solitary, poor Muslim women who were away from their families in this category whenever they wanted to interfere in their lives and existence in the city. While solitary non-Muslim women who were away from customary communities and households were more directly labelled – and frequently registered as –prostitutes, such Muslim women were referred to as disorderly and attempts were made to prevent them from prostitution.

In contemporary daily newspapers and periodicals, one can easily find traces of the perception that equated the female poor with prostitution and vice. For example, in an article published in *Sabah*, the author divided beggars into four subcategories, one of which were 'the children, young girls and unattended women'. He claimed that as young beggar girls frequently concealed their illicit activities behind begging, they should be treated as prostitutes and subjected to the relevant laws. According to the author, these female beggars were extremely harmful to the morality and chastity of society as well as to public health. He also suggested that '[male] child beggars' should be put to work in proper reformatories (*ıslahane*). Here the author emphasizes an idea widely accepted in the nineteenth century: the belief in the disciplinary power of work. He dwells on this belief and argues that providing disciplinary education would save these children from turning into criminals. What is most noteworthy is the different way that 'young female beggars' and 'young male beggars' are addressed. According to the author, though female beggars might be 'truly poor', they are also at risk of engaging in 'some immoral activities', clearly meaning prostitution. Moreover, the author warns that prostitution is not only a moral problem but that 'young female beggars' also pose a threat to public health and order, concluding that the police should deal with them. This is in sharp contrast to his recommended treatment for male beggars. In another article, the same author recommends fair treatment of female domestic servants, lest girls treated badly by their employers run away to live corrupted lives on the streets, which would be a grave moral and social threat to Istanbul's residents.[8]

I argue that the term 'disorderly woman' was the female equivalent of the male 'vagrant'. Like their counterparts, 'disorderly women' were poor, unskilled and away from home. However, solitary, poor women were the hardest-pressed component of the 'wandering poor' of Istanbul. They were restricted by a patriarchal economy predicated on their direct dependence on men and by the assumption that a woman's place was at home. Yet, because those systems were severely strained, poor and solitary women increasingly became more apparent in the public urban sphere. Moreover, they were finding unprecedented ways to survive, constructing new kinds of social, sexual and occupational relations as well as inventing new ways to use public spaces. Towards the late nineteenth century, the image of solitary, poor women in the Ottoman press oscillated between victims in danger and a dangerous threat to middle-class morality and family life. While non-Muslim women on the streets of Istanbul were officially registered as prostitutes, deciding what to do with their Muslim counterparts proved a problem. The issue was frequently discussed in the press, and the administrative authorities tried to find ways to remove solitary, poor women from the urban scene. Ottoman administers and middle-class commentators stressed that the removal of 'disorderly women' from Istanbul was vital in order to protect public morality, health and order. The question was how.

The police did not know what to do with Muslim women arrested while soliciting in the streets. In many cases, local neighbourhood police in Istanbul sent notes to the Police Directorate requesting advice following the arrest of 'disorderly/homeless' women. The police knew that if they released these women, they would immediately return to the streets, as they had no alternative. The police officers were also concerned that some of these women were 'contaminated' with venereal diseases.

Deportation to provincial cities

Police documents from the early 1900s reveals that the most frequently used method for the containment of 'disorderly women' was to send them out to the provinces. In 1903, for example, the Ministry of Police transported two women named Hayriye and Sadriye – arrested while soliciting in the streets of Istanbul – to Izmir for rehabilitation. According to the police, Hayriye's and Sadriye's presence in Istanbul was 'inconvenient and insecure' as they were 'of the disorderly sort' and had nowhere to stay and nobody to protect and supervise them in the capital. The governorship of Izmir was ordered to provide accommodation for these two women.[9]

Indeed, the practice of deporting prostitutes to the provinces was not a novelty. Yet, the anxieties and concerns that prompted the revival of this traditional practice in the early 1900s differed from the ones of earlier eras. In the eighteenth and early nineteenth centuries prostitution was usually seen as a local nuisance for neighbourhoods and small communities. Prostitutes were typically transported to remote islands to soothe irate local populations.[10] However, in the early twentieth century prostitutes who wandered unchecked in urban spaces were seen not as local nuisances but as a threat to the gendered and class-based order of the city. Their removal, then, was part of a conscious effort to impose a certain idea of society on the city.

The removal of such women, however, was not free of problems. With no means of earning a living, they usually fell deeper into extreme poverty. They often still resorted to prostitution, although it became harder for them to earn money in this way as they suffered more stringent police scrutiny in their new locales. The local authorities saw these women, who frequently knocked on their door for support, as a source of annoyance. They had to find shelter for these women, provide sustenance and eliminate 'the sexual and moral threats' they posed for local people. In many cases, provincial governorships strived to send deportees back to Istanbul, requested their transportation to other cities, or demanded money for providing their sustenance.

For example, the Kastamonu authorities returned a woman named Feraset, deported by the Ministry of Police for being 'disorderly', back to Istanbul. They noted that she continued her miserable conduct in Kastamonu and, according to her own statement, had property in Istanbul. Yet this did not convince the Ministry of Police, and Feraset was immediately sent back to Kastamonu. In an accompanying note, the Ministry of Police stated that she had nothing and no one in Istanbul. Her stay in the capital was declared 'inappropriate and unsafe'. The Ministry's note also included a warning: returning women who had been transported for being 'disorderly' when it was perfectly possible to provide for them in their new locations caused extra work and costs and was strongly discouraged.[11]

A similar example involves a woman named Nikdar and her two daughters, Dürdane and Suna, who were deported from Istanbul to Edirne. The family requested permission to return, claiming that they were originally from the capital. On 30 July 1904, the government of Edirne conveyed the family's petition to the Ministry of Police. The Ministry rejected the request. Although it was conceded that the women were indeed originally from Istanbul, their return was considered impermissible as they were of the 'inappropriate' sort and had no relatives in the capital.[12]

In another case, the Hüdavendigar governorship sent a telegram to the Ministry of Interior concerning the annoyance caused by ten female exiles in Bursa. The governorship stated that these women, deported to Bursa for being 'disorderly', had no relatives there, were unqualified for work in the city's factories or anywhere else, and had fallen into misery. They occupied the local police stations with regular demands to such a degree that the police said they were unable to find time to deal with other, more important issues. Hence the Hüdavendigar governorship requested a solution to the situation.[13] The Ministry of Interior forwarded the telegram to the Ministry of Police, stating that it was a police matter and that they had sent these women to Bursa in the first place. However, the telegram did not meet with much sympathy, the Istanbul police merely reiterated that these women had been found to be 'hazardous' in the capital and their return would lead to serious problems. The Ministry of Police requested that the Ministry of Interior remind the governorship of Hüdavendigar of these issues and order them not to allow the women to return to Istanbul. In a second telegram, the governor of Hüdavendigar informed Istanbul that the exiles' misery was causing inappropriate conduct in his jurisdiction and an urgent solution was required.

The Ministry of Interior also conveyed this telegram to the Ministry of Police and asked if it was possible to provide for the sustenance of these women. In response, the Ministry of Police repeated their concerns and stated that they had nothing to do or say regarding the subsistence of these women; the Ministry of Interior should decide what was best and/or possible and convey this to the authorities in Hüdavendigar.[14]

Sometimes young and poor women were transported to other cities for different reasons, such as begging, but the concern was similar. Urban administrators argued that young beggar girls frequently used begging as a front for illicit activities and should therefore be treated as prostitutes. Indeed, the Ordinance on Vagrancy stipulated that women convicted thereof were to be sent to their own cities if possible, or to another city where they could find a job. For example, three young women – Fatma, daughter of Muhammed Ali, Esma, daughter of Mehmet, and Esma, daughter of Ali – were accused and convicted of vagrancy by the Üsküdar Court. Depending on the Law of Vagrancy, the Court decided to send them to Izmit; in addition, they had to pay 800 kuruş of court fees.[15]

On 30 June 1909, the Kastamonu local government sent a woman named Dürdane back to the Ministry of Police. She was deported to Kastamonu because of 'inappropriate behaviour' and the fact that she had nobody to supervise her and nowhere to stay. However, the Kastamonu administration contested the decision, claiming that Dürdane was not from Kastamonu and that she had no one there either. The Kastamonu police found that she was originally from Edremit, a town in Hüdavendigar, where she had an uncle who worked in the Forestry Directorate and a sister named Fatma. The governorship of Kastamonu then requested that she be sent to Edirne. There is no clear explanation in the documents for why they chose Edirne as an alternative destination.[16]

On 2 September 1909, the Ministry of Police transported a woman known as 'Emine from Bursa' to Bursa. Emine had been observed not behaving in accordance with Islamic morals and had no one to supervise her in Istanbul, hence the Ministry considered her stay there 'hazardous'. However, the Hüdavendigar administration sent her back to Istanbul within five days, stating that according to their own investigation, Emine was actually from İnebolu, not from Bursa. The Ministry of Police then sent her to İnebolu on 11 September 1909.[17]

Şükriye was transported to Kastamonu because of her 'disorderly' behaviour. She claimed that she had been married to Boşnak Hacı Ömer, who lived in Üsküdar, and that six years previously he had petitioned the court for a divorce. The Kastamonu police requested that their Istanbul colleagues check whether the divorce had taken place. It was probably their intention to send Şükriye back to her husband in the event they were still married.[18]

Confinement in reformatories and poor houses

As the examples above demonstrate, deportation to other cities proved inefficient and costly. Most of the time the arrested women were sent back, much to the frustration of the police. What is more, they returned to the streets as soon as they were released.

Hence a discussion ensued in the press about possible alternatives to deportation that could help control the proliferation of 'lower-class' Muslim prostitutes. In a 1903 article in the *Sabah* daily newspaper, the author argued for the necessity of establishing a reformatory where young girls who occasionally resorted to prostitution would be kept and trained to earn their livelihood in an honourable way. The article dramatically described the miserable conditions these girls lived in and highlighted that most of them fell into misery at a very young age and were innocent victims of their immoral, ignorant parents. The author argued that everyone in the city was responsible for saving these innocent children from misery and for providing them with safe places to live. However, he warned, placing them in vocational schools along with 'completely' innocent girls (who had not 'fallen') would not be appropriate as it would be harmful for the latter. The best solution, in his opinion, was establishing reformatories specifically for young Muslim prostitutes. He also emphasized that police action was not a satisfactory solution. Although the police frequently brought in children soliciting around the Galata Bridge and Karaköy, they could not be held in jail indefinitely. And as soon as they were released, these children returned to the same habits. Thus, the author argued, establishing a reformatory was indispensable to solving the problem[19]

Such alternative methods for containing 'disorderly women' were also on the police agenda. Given the government's lack of funds, the establishment of special reformatories was not feasible. For a while, the police tried sending the arrested women to Darülaceze, a designated poorhouse.[20] On 10 October 1908, the Ministry of Police conveyed a request from the Istanbul Police Directorate to the Ministry of Interior regarding the many homeless women apprehended while prostituting in various parts of Istanbul and sent to the Police Directorate from local stations. The Directorate was in a quandary over what to do about these women. Releasing them did not solve the problem because they would only return to the streets. Moreover, some were suffering from various diseases and needed to be sheltered and cured. The issue was discussed in the Police Assembly with the conclusion that these women should be sent to Darülaceze (and the ill among them to hospitals, as was done in 'civilized' countries).[21] Yet, the Ministry of Police rejected this suggestion on the basis that sending homeless prostitutes to Darülaceze would be inappropriate.[22]

However, releasing these women would cause other kinds of trouble, and their misery needed to be alleviated. Therefore, the Istanbul Police Directorate requested that the Ministry of Interior order the municipal administration to allocate a place for these women.[23] The Ministry did as it was asked on 8 November 1908, but the municipality refused to grant the request.[24] It stated that there was no appropriate place it could allocate for this purpose and that in 'civilized' countries such women were kept in special wards in women's prisons, separated from other female prisoners. The police should therefore take care of this matter, as prisons were under their authority.[25] The police again replied that the responsibility for arranging a shelter for homeless prostitutes should lie with the municipal administration.[26]

Thus there was no consensus between the police and the municipality on policy, and the issue continued to be negotiated on a case-by-case basis. For example, the police seized a woman named Melek while she was prostituting herself in a hotel room in Derviş Street, Beyoğlu. During the police inquiry, Melek stated that she was originally from Arabia and had been brought to Istanbul by Şeyh Ibrahim, a slave commissioner, five or six years earlier. Immediately after her arrival, she was sold to Mustafa Rukneddin Bey, who died a few years later. She was then sold again, this time to Nazmi Bey, a notable from Edirne. Melek lived in his house in Edirne until 1908. After the Proclamation of Liberty in 1908, she was freed and decided to return to Istanbul. There she worked as a domestic servant in several houses. However, at the time of her arrest, she had not been able to find any work for fifteen days. Melek also claimed that she had been forced into that hotel room against her will. The Census Department had no record of her; she did not have any relatives in Istanbul or Edirne, and she did not know where exactly she was from. The police asked the management of Darülaceze to accept Melek, as they did not want to release her back onto the streets.[27]

On 16 January 1911, the Ministry of Interior sent the municipality a request to accept a woman named Hacer into Darülaceze. Hacer was originally from a town in Bulgaria. She had come to Istanbul eight or ten years earlier and had been a prostitute ever since. At the time of the request, she was housed in a women's prison. The Ministry stated that Hacer had no living relatives in her hometown, so it was not possible to send her back. On the other hand, it could be appropriate to find her employment in domestic service or send her to a philanthropic institution. In any case, the Ministry claimed, it was not possible to continue to keep her in the women's prison.[28]

Sending the women to their families was another alternative. For example, on 27 August 1910, the Istanbul police reported that on 13 August they had raided a hotel after a tip-off (*ihbar*). They arrested three women – Resmiye, Fatma and Ayşe– who were found in one of the rooms accompanied by two military officers and two vagrants. Resmiye was handed over to the Beyoğlu police as she resided in an imam's house behind the Tophane Barracks. Fatma was from Istanbul. Her father, Refik Efendi (an ex-officer in the Forestry Directorate), and her mother had died ten years earlier. Her only living relative was her brother, Muhammed Ragıp Efendi, who was working at the Russian Consulate. Fatma started prostituting herself after her parents' death but had quit two years earlier when she married Abdullah from Sivas, Divriği. At the time, Abdullah worked in a brickyard in Eyüp. A year into their marriage, Abdullah left his job in Istanbul and returned to Divriği, taking Fatma with him. However, he later sent her back to Istanbul. Ayşe was brought to Istanbul from Cide (in Kastamonu province) to work as a domestic servant. After working in several houses, she married Şeyh Hasan, an adopted child (*besleme*). However, when her husband died, she was left with no means of support and had been residing in the neighbourhood imam's house for ten days. Ayşe claimed that Feride and Fatma had tricked her into prostitution on the day she was arrested. Nonetheless, her parents were still alive in Cide. According to the police, releasing these two women would lead them to continue their immoral conduct, and the best solution would be to send Ayşe to Cide and Fatma to Divriği. However, the report stated that the Hasköy police could not afford the transport costs.[29]

In most cases finding the women's families was not possible. On 18 April 1910, the Public Security Directorate sent a note to the Trabzon Police Directorate, asking for the settlement of a woman named Hayrünisa. She was being sent to Trabzon for the second time, and the note requested that the Trabzon police prevent her return to

Istanbul. It was noted that the request was based on the Ministry of Interior order about preventing the return of women sent to provincial cities. Hayrünisa was a runaway domestic servant who had been working in a mansion belonging to the governor of İzmir, Mahmud Muhtar Bey. She was detained by the police while 'soliciting in the streets' of Istanbul after she had escaped from Mahmud Bey's residence. During her questioning, she stated that she had some relatives in Trabzon, and the police deported her there. However, the Trabzon police sent her back to Istanbul, stating that, contrary to Hayrünisa's own assertions, she had no family in Trabzon. In a note to the Public Security Directorate dated 7 March 1910, the Governor of Trabzon stated that settlement of this morally depraved woman in Trabzon, where she had no relatives to care for and supervise her, was improper.[30] However, this did not satisfy the Istanbul police and she was deported to Trabzon again.

Criminalization of prostitution

As the examples above illustrate, the police had trouble finding shelter for women arrested while engaging in prostitution. They could not detain these women, yet when they were released they returned to the streets. After 1908, the policing of the poor in Istanbul became more systematic. A new Vagrancy Law was adopted and put into practice in 1909, and the police also drafted a law criminalizing unregistered prostitutes.[31]

On 23 May 1910, the Public Security Directorate requested the Ministry of Interior add a paragraph to Article 113 of the Turkish Penal Code, to penalize women engaging in illegal prostitution. According to the police, these women were behaving repulsively in the streets and had impudent relationships with lower-class men. It was noted that this made a bad impression on public thoughts and feelings, violated the rules of religion and common decency, and harmed public morality and public health. The police therefore considered it necessary to prevent and limit the detrimental behaviour of such women to establish and maintain public order. The Directorate claimed it was doing its best to limit the harmful effects of the situation by whatever means possible, despite the lack of a legal framework for a permanent solution. The legal means at hand, such as fines or reprimands for resisting the police, were found to be insufficient. The police proposed a more serious punishment for these women: detention for up to ten days or a fine of one to five Ottoman liras.[32]

The Ministry of Interior approved the proposal and the police drafted the text and presented it to the Ministry on 28 June.[33] The draft law stated:

> Those who do not obey the instructions and warnings of the police or other public officers, those involved in any kind of mischievous conduct or circumstance that is determined by the police to be detrimental to public morals, the stability or security of the country, or discipline and order, in a way that threatens the people's peace and rest, will, in an effort to prevent the spread of contagious diseases, be sentenced to detention from 24 hours to 10 days and/or a fine of one half to five Ottoman gold liras.[34]

The Ministry of Interior sent the draft law to the Ministry of Justice on 2 July 1910. The accompanying note stated that the proposed draft was prepared in response to the needs of the Public Security Directorate. It was intended to put an end to the problem of clandestine prostitution throughout the residential neighbourhoods of Istanbul and to limit the various associated problems. The clandestine prostitution referred to in the documents related to Muslim women, because the police could force non-Muslim women to register. The Ministry of Interior also underlined the importance of the proposed law for the protection of public health and general security, and requested its inclusion in the Penal Code.[35]

On 28 November 1910, as no response had been conveyed to the police, the Public Security Directorate enquired about progress regarding the draft law and reminded the Ministry of Interior that the issue was urgent, as the problem increased with every passing day.[36] Three days later, on 1 December, the Ministry of Interior passed these considerations on to the Ministry of Justice and once more requested urgent inclusion of the draft law in the Penal Code.[37]

The Ministry of Justice rejected the draft on 19 December, pointing out that prostitutes were in fact victims of poverty who deserved protection, not criminals deserving punishment. Most of them were dragged down into prostitution because of poverty and the need for a livelihood; it was therefore the government's duty to protect these women by placing them into institutions designed to protect and provide for people in need, such as Darülaceze, or to provide for their livelihood by other means. While undesirable and annoying situations should be avoided, all these aspects should also be taken into account. Only then would the treatment of these women be fair. If some women still continued to behave in unchaste and indecent ways, despite the hand lent by the government, levying a fine would be a more effectual punishment as most of them suffered from poverty. And because such a penalty was already included in Article 251 of the Penal Code, the Ministry of Justice found adding a new article unnecessary.[38]

The Ministry of Interior forwarded the memorandum to the police on 24 December 1910. However, the police administration found this explanation unsatisfactory and on 22 January 1911, sent a letter to the Ministry of Interior requesting permission to act in accordance with the draft law. In its reply dated 28 January, the Ministry of Interior reiterated that the Ministry of Justice declared that Article 251 of the Penal Code already provided the necessary legal framework and ordered the police to act accordingly.[39]

To solve the problems caused by the proliferation of clandestine prostitution in the capital, on 13 September 1911, the Istanbul police proposed the application of Article 99 of the Penal Code to prostitutes and their associates. According to the police, the situation was alarming: some women rented houses in the residential neighbourhoods of Üsküdar, Beyoğlu and the old city, and used them to engage in prostitution. Many other 'unchaste' women often joined them there. The police further claimed that officers frequently received complaints from the respectable residents of these neighbourhoods, as the prostitutes' immoral behaviour offended common decency and public morality. However, the police was unable to act efficiently because, they said, they lacked a legal framework. First, as the Penal Code did not specify any punishment for such women and their associates, the police could not arrest or detain them. Second, the police could not raid these houses because their inviolability was assured by the Constitution. Therefore these women, who were free of any supervision and control, caused many scandals. Sometimes the honourable local residents, said the police, were provoked by these scandals and the comings and goings of many morally suspicious men in their neighbourhoods. Moreover, as these women were not registered and not subject to medical inspection, they spread contagious diseases.[40]

On 14 October 1911, the Ministry of Interior asked the Istanbul Police Directorate whether Article 80 of the Police Regulations, which covered the closure and prevention of brothels, was sufficient for dealing with the houses-turned-brothels in residential neighbourhoods. On 12 November 1911, the police replied that it had tried using Article 80, but to no avail. The article stipulated that if a house used as a brothel was not owned by the brothel-keeper, they were to be evicted. However, if the brothel-keeper owned the house, the police could not evict them. Furthermore, forcing the brother-keeper to leave was not a sufficient precaution since prostitutes and their associates were constantly on the move. When they realized they would be forced to leave one house, they could easily move to another, in a different part of the city, and even return to the same neighbourhood a few weeks later. Also, the women prostituting themselves in these houses generally resided elsewhere. Therefore, in many cases, Article 80 was not sufficient to prevent prostitution.

On 4 February 1912, the Police Directorate proposed another draft law on regulating prostitution to the Ministry of Interior, but their effort was futile.[41] On 29 March 1913, the Police Chief sent a slightly different proposal, this time describing the prostitutes as women in need of help and protection and suggested establishing a reformatory where they could be placed to gain new skills to earn a living. The document explained that prostitution in residential neighbourhoods provoked discomfort in honourable citizens and led to their complaints. Although the police tried hard to prevent these situations and often arrested the prostituting women, it was difficult to decide what to do with them afterwards.

The Police Chief explained that the officers were at pains to release these women back onto the streets. However, as the women were poor and had nowhere to stay and no one to supervise them, releasing them meant the continuation of not only their immoral behaviour and misery but also the problems they caused. On the other hand, the police were unable to find a safe place where these women could stay. This issue was also important for establishing public order and security, as these women caused many problems. The Police Chief pointed out that some of them were suffering from diseases and were a threat to public health. It was necessary for the government to take action to prevent these dilemmas and rescue these helpless women from poverty and misery. At this point, the Police Chief proposed the establishment of a reformatory for them. He informed the Ministry that he had contacted the Mayor about the issue and he had agreed to provide a pavilion for these women in Darülaceze. However, a monthly stipend of two liras per woman was needed from the government. The women would need a stipend only for a year, as the training they would receive would subsequently allow them to earn a living. The Police Chief argued this reformatory would prevent immoral situations, rescue many lives and end the misery of many women. He requested immediate authorization for the necessary actions.[42] On 5 April 1913, the Ministry delivered a copy of this letter to the Mayor, noting the Police Directorate's request for a place for unregistered prostitutes in Darülaceze.[43]

In his reply, sent on 8 April 1913, the Mayor admitted he had previously agreed to allocate a place for these helpless women in Darülaceze. However, he added that no appropriate place was available immediately; the government would have to allocate five thousand liras to construct a pavilion to accommodate them (in addition to providing a stipend of two liras per month for each woman).[44]

On 13 April 1913, the Ministry of Interior informed the Police Directorate of the Mayor's conditions and declared that it was impossible for the government to allocate such an amount of money to reforming unregistered prostitutes. It was impossible for the Ministry to even suggest such a project. The Ministry offered another solution, based on the fact that most of these women were not residents of the capital. Those suffering from a disease were to be sent to the hospital in Kastamonu and non-residents were to be sent to their hometowns. Those originally from Istanbul were to be placed in Darülaceze or in private employment, to save them from prostitution and misery. The police were advised to follow this directive going forward.[45]

Conclusion

Deliberations among the authorities as well as public discussions in the press continued without reaching a solution. All those discussions shared a particular conception of urban space, defined primarily as a male space. The women who ventured there, particularly solitary, poor women, were seen as endangering not only their own sexual reputation and sexual purity but also public morality, public health and security. Both the government authorities and public intellectuals believed that solitary, poor women should be excluded from Istanbul's urban public life. Like the streets of Istanbul, the police archives were overrun with 'disorderly' women and both the police and society as a whole struggled to contain them. 'Disorderly women,' seen as both victims of society and potentially dangerous outsiders, were ungrounded figures that disrupted the idealized gender regime upon which patriarchal authority depended. Their existence continued to provoke fear, anxiety, guilt and inadequacy in society as a whole.

There are no first-hand accounts of how lower-class women actually experienced urban life in its many forms. Most of our knowledge relates to the hardships and sexual dangers they faced. Isolation from kin and community left them vulnerable to sexual and other abuse. In addition, the absence of male breadwinners confined them to extreme poverty, as the job market in late Ottoman Istanbul provided only a limited range of poorly paid and exploitative choices for women lacking skills. However, from the available sources we know that many poor women tried to reach Istanbul to start a new life; they tried to return when they were deported; and they escaped from the households they worked for or from the houses of their fathers or husbands to establish a life on their own in the capital. From this we can conclude that Istanbul at least provided these poor women with the hope of personal freedom and the ability to shape their own lives. In the Ottoman capital, some found freedom from the constraints of custom and community, along with unprecedented opportunities for redefining and expressing themselves. Even the fear they provoked in the ruling elite and the middle class implies that late Ottoman Istanbul should be understood as an urban space offering new opportunities for everyday negotiation of self and identity.

Disreputable by Definition: Respectability and Theft by Poor Women in Urban Interwar Egypt

Hanan Hammad

On 10 May 1938, four women and a teenage boy took a train from Cairo to al-Mahalla al-Kubra. A police officer became suspicious of their movement between several textile shops because they left the boy outside every time they went into a shop. The policeman took them into the station, where a search of their items revealed that the women had snatched two large bundles (thirty-eight and thirty-two metres) of poplin fabric, three metres of a cheaper lightweight batiste fabric and a half metre of poplin.[1] The band consisted of Siddiqa Musa ʿEid, a 55-year-old laundry woman from Zaqaziq with nine recorded theft crimes; Naffusa Hassanal-Simbawi, a fifty-year-old married woman from Muski in Cairo with seven recorded theft crimes; Tafida Najib Maqqar, a forty-year-old dressmaker from Bulaq in Cairo; Saʿada Surur Ibrahim, a thirty-year-old margarine merchant from Bulaq in Cairo; and Muhammad Hassan Ibrahim Hilal, a thirteen-year-old boy who worked in a chair factory in Rud al-Farag in Cairo.

The batiste fabric was wrapped in paper from Amin al-Sihli's store and the small piece of poplin was wrapped in paper from ʿAbd al-Hayy Muhammad al-Qarʿ's store, among the biggest and best-known textile stores in the commercial district. When police called the owners, al-Sihli testified that the women paid for the batiste fabric but stole the thirty-eight metres of poplin bundle, which was worth 16.25 Egyptian pounds. Al-Qarʿ testified that the four women bought the small piece of poplin but stole the thirty-two metres, with a value of 13.5 Egyptian pounds. Three of the women had distracted shop assistants by bargaining to buy the fabric, while the fourth stole from the most expensive sections in each store. ʿEid and al-Simbawi had substantial criminal records for theft, so the judge sentenced them to a special reform institute for an unlimited period. The court sentenced the other two women to one year in jail with hard labour and acquitted the boy.[2]

Petty theft was the most frequent crime committed by imprisoned Egyptian women in the interwar period. Nevertheless, research on Egyptian women involved in illicit activities in the nineteenth and twentieth centuries has focused almost exclusively on prostitution and other sexual offenses.[3] Similarly, recent scholarly inquiry on crime in the first half of the twentieth century in Egypt has ignored women's non-sexual criminality.[4] Theft misdemeanours recorded in Ministry of Interior Affairs security reports more than doubled in Egypt between 1926 (47,944) and 1944 (109,968).[5] An official survey on Egyptian prisons in 1930 revealed that most convicted women and child inmates were in prison for theft and other misdemeanours.[6] Intensified policing, greater public vigilance, poverty, and population growth each in part explain the rise in thefts reported during this period.

Itinerant women working in groups or individually were active in shoplifting, as illustrated above, as well as in pickpocketing and other forms of non-violent theft. Women's petty thefts were usually isolated acts. Most women captured in state archives for committing theft were factory workers who stole or attempted to steal from their workplace. Others were domestic workers in urban middle-class homes, often migrants from rural parts of Egypt, who stole and resold their bosses' household items.

Most poor and working-class women who stole did so to cope with poverty in cities. I argue that poor and working-class Egyptian women who worked for pay already had difficulty meeting classed and gendered notions of reputation in urban contexts of dislocation, vulnerability and economic insecurity. Petty theft offered the possibility of material gain without great loss to social status for women with few material or social protections in urban Egypt. The popular term *satr* (feminine adj. *mastura*) captures the essence of the notion of Egyptian respectability. Satr is a multifaceted concept that literally means covering up or becoming invisible and idiomatically means sexual, moral and socio-economic respectability.[7] It was particularly important that girls and women maintain satr. Lawfully fulfilling basic needs such as food and shelter and preserving moral and sexual honour were essential to maintaining a respectable (mastura) status as a woman. Publicly violating social norms undermined respectability, and publicly conforming to norms in dress and behaviour sustained respectability. Even with the coercive integration of Egypt into the global economy and its rise as a modern state in the late nineteenth century, Egyptian respectability remained gendered, sexualized and class specific.[8]

Women's respectability depended on their family status, socio-economic material standing and sexual conduct. For upper-class women, respectability meant seclusion in order to be invisible to strangers. The ideal of female seclusion in order to prevent casual interactions between men and women affected lower-class women even though they could not afford to be restricted to their homes. Thus entire communities monitored poorer women as they crossed such boundaries. Such collective monitoring was more difficult with mass urbanization, making it easier for women committing theft to violate gendered standards of respectability in interwar urban Egypt. They engaged in theft because socio-economic changes made it harder for them to survive by simply relying on traditional methods such as marriage or work within family structures. Moreover, their material and institutional positions, as girls and women who had to work in mixed-gender contexts, making low wages that kept them poor and constituted them as low-status, meant that criminal behaviour offered the possibility of gain without great status loss.

I use unpublished court records, published police reports, official security statistics, and contemporary press to tell the story of women's participation in petty crime in Egyptian urban centres between the two world wars. The court records come from two major provincial towns, al-Mahalla al-Kubra, in the middle of the Nile Delta, and Tanta, a railroad hub in the Nile Delta.[9] Security sources include annual reports for the entire country published by the Department of Public Security at the Ministry of Interior Affairs, substantiating national patterns. I recognize that state sources are designed to serve state purposes and do not necessarily preserve the voices of the women involved in recorded incidents. As Mario Ruiz persuasively shows, the production of criminal statistics since the late nineteenth century in Egypt was part of an agenda to efficiently govern and manage crime.[10] Crime statistics were also integral to a broad effort to represent state bureaucracies as impartial. Police-affiliated researchers, moreover, adopted terminology that magnified the importance and potency of their work and explicitly demanded increases in their privileges and resources. Legal changes that criminalized more actions and categorized some misdemeanours as felonies also enlarged crime statistics.[11] Despite the reservations rightly raised by historians concerning criminal statistics in Egypt during the British colonial period between 1882 and 1952, relative poverty did increase, nonviolent and property crimes did rise in growing cities and women were involved in such crimes. While I do not contest state crime statistics in this chapter, I also do not take at face value their categorizations and labels.

The first section that follows discusses population growth and massive rural-to-urban migration that challenged extant social status systems and forms of class and gender control. These dynamics produced anxieties reflected in state policies, new forms of social control and reformist and media rhetoric. The second section focuses on the contradictions of life for poor and working-class women who worked in the urban legal economy. It was usually impossible for these women to earn enough money or maintain satr, since the very institutions that benefitted from their labour ensured their poverty and judged them as morally deficient for being desperate enough to work in low-status jobs. The third section uses archival material to discuss the range of women's activities as thieves and burglars in interwar urban Egypt.

Class inequality, dislocation and anxiety in growing cities

After achieving quasi-independence in 1922, the Egyptian state saw its supreme duties as recording social conditions and ameliorating the most unsavoury among them.[12] Rural-to-urban population shifts from the nineteenth century had already contributed to state anxieties about morality and public order.[13] People in towns including Port Said, Suez, Tanta and Mansura were subject to the 1908 Penal Code criminalizing individuals who lacked permanent residences or jobs, or who begged in public places.[14] The situation was so alarming that the state established the Ministry of Social Affairs in 1939 for the stated purpose of social rehabilitation to uplift the poor and promote social justice.[15]

Interwar policies, discourses and initiatives to contain and manage the lower classes in growing cities occurred against the backdrop of the nationalist struggle to achieve complete independence from the British by demonstrating economic modernization.[16] Cities attracted young people seeking education and employment in the ever-growing state bureaucracy as well as people from rural areas who moved to industrial and urban towns to escape acute poverty.[17] Women and children were among these rural-to-urban migrants. The population of Cairo increased by 52 per cent in the 1890s.[18] The 1907 census recorded that one-third of Cairo residents were born elsewhere.[19] Between 1917 and 1937, the population of Cairo increased by 66 per cent, from 790,929 to more than 1.3 million.[20] Egypt's population more generally grew 25 per cent between 1927 and 1937, from 12.2 to 15.9 million, but the urban population increased 56 per cent, from 1.9 to 2.9 million.[21] In 1947, 33 per cent of the total population of Egypt lived in urban areas.[22] These major dislocations inevitably made it difficult to sustain existing village-, city- and neighbourhood-based norms and relations that governed the behaviours of girls and women.

Modern transportation networks made it easier for men and women to travel between towns and villages and between rural areas and urban centres.[23] In the second half of the nineteenth century, the first lines of the growing national railroad connected Cairo and Alexandria with major cities in Lower and Upper Egypt. Narrow railways in the Delta as well as in Fayyum and Hilwan, allowed lower-class men and women to move between villages and towns, as did paved roads, tramways and buses that were part of decades-long urban development projects.[24] The tram alone accommodated up to 120 passengers in one trip in the early 1900s.[25] People from urban peripheries more easily and frequently travelled to and from city centres in Cairo, Alexandria, Port Said and Zifta. More people experienced work and leisure outside their homes, including enjoying urban modes of entertainment that attracted crowds.[26]

Pickpocketing (*nashl*), which increased after the First World War, took place mostly in crowded urban spaces and transportation hubs where perpetrators and victims were moving. Streetcars and tram stations attracted female as well as male pickpockets.[27] In 1902 the earliest security report documented a pickpocketing incident by two men from Zifta and Asyut who were labelled *nashshal*, professional pickpockets.[28] My analysis of annual security reports issued by the Ministry of Interior Affairs indicates that between 1926 and 1964, 238 women pickpocketed 978 times in Cairo, mostly on buses and trams (32 per cent of incidents), in streets (23 per cent), in houses (7.2 per cent) and in hospitals (6.6 per cent).[29] Police also arrested women in Cairo for pickpocketing in churches, stores, camps, parks and hotels. The first reported case of a female pickpocket in Cairo took place in 1926.[30] Women pickpockets were famous for their skill of quickly jumping in and out of moving vehicles. For example, thirty-year-old Wasila Wisal snatched a gold bracelet from Ihsan Muhammad Filfila while he was descending from a train. Because Wisal had a criminal record, the court sentenced her to three years in jail with hard labour.[31] The increase in pickpocketing and speculation that gangsters trained young children in this work invited intensive policing after the First World War.[32] The Ministry of Interior Affairs established the Department to Fight Pickpocketing Theft as well as a corps of secret police officers in plain clothes in 1923.

City wages were low, the cost of living was high and sustaining a life through legal employment was difficult. Immigrants from rural areas offered an abundant, disposable and exploitable workforce for urban industries. A 1930s survey of 16,900 people in 3,333 urban working-class families reported that the average family of five lived in 1.6 rooms.[33] Each family had 21.075 Egyptian pounds of annual income but spent 195 piasters every month (23.4 Egyptian pounds per year) on basic needs such as food, shelter and clothing. Every family thus had an average debt of 24 piasters. Although the study does not discuss how poor families covered the average gap between income and expenses, later scholarly speculation indicates the importance of begging and theft.[34] While living standards were miserable, it is unclear whether they were worse than in rural areas. Children who sold trivial items in urban areas, shined shoes or begged in the first half of the twentieth century were usually orphaned, abandoned or sent out by parents to earn a living despite 1908 legislation punishing waifs and strays with confinement in a juvenile reformatory.[35] Poverty and economic dislocation in cities forced most individuals, including girls and women, to participate in a wage-based economy and find other means of survival.

The Ministry of Interior Affairs made it obligatory for domestic workers to acquire a work licence in 1917.[36] Women with criminal records nevertheless got such jobs, which indicates that the rule was not always respected.[37] Indeed, previous arrests may have encouraged women to commit theft repeatedly, since criminal activity offered the possibility of material gain without staining a reputation further. In turn, middle-class urban families and men living alone in cities expected girls and women from the country and poor neighbourhoods to work as domestic servants. Many middle-class bachelors and married men left their village families because they had access to higher education or work as technocrats and bureaucrats in industry and government. This enlarged the market for domestic service by unskilled and uneducated women. Women's domestic work earnings were often a combination of wages and used household items donated as charity by employers. At the same time, female servants witnessed the higher living standard of their employers and during their workday had access to most of their employers' household materials, including cash and jewellery. Such accessibility tempted some women to commit theft, and they stole whatever they could trade for cash. According to police records, frequently stolen items included clothing and kitchenware, although domestic workers also stole cash, jewellery, perfume and silk handkerchiefs.[38] There are no documented cases of food theft, although foodstuffs must have been readily available. Employers may have overlooked food theft out of sympathy or due to its more trivial value. Other employers may have simply fired a maid rather than report her to the police. Circulation of stolen clothing and kitchenware in marketplaces indicates that many thefts were successful or unreported. Police documented several cases where the victims searched for the stolen items until they found them in the marketplace, in secondhand stalls or with the purchaser.[39]

The socially accepted focus of the state's core apparatuses became the production and enforcement of policies in the name of the 'common' social interest. As Omnia El Shakry argues, Egyptian social reformers targeted women and peasants in transformation projects that aimed to minimize class antagonisms even as they relied on the violence and coercion that already structured relations between cities and villages.[40] Reformers expected women to reproduce labour power and peasant men and women to be sources of labour extraction. The annual security reports from which some of the accounts discussed in this chapter are taken were printed and enjoyed limited circulation among officials, security forces and readers with an interest in police work or security procedures. Their authors highlighted the hard work of the security forces in fighting unusual criminal patterns and served an 'alerting' function for a perceived law-abiding public. Truthful or fabricated, these anecdotes reinforced the role of the police force as a protector of public security and order.

Many government initiatives and reports focused on increased crime in Egyptian cities between the 1930s and the 1960s. The government formed a committee to discuss the increase in peddlers roaming the streets, mostly rural immigrants in 1931. Chaired by the politician and pediatrician Hafiz 'Afifi, the committee recommended the government grant work licences to those convicted of petty theft.[41] It is not clear whether the government acted on this recommendation and, if so, whether it was effective. A general security administration report in 1938 pointed to a dramatic rise in incidents of banditry and armed robbery, linking them to the spread of poverty, political instability, increased defense expenses and cancellation of development projects.[42]

Reformers and pundits participated in such anxiety discourse, which communicated worries about urban disorder and disintegration as well as nationalist desires in a semi-colonial situation. In the 1930s newspaper columnists claimed that some of the unemployed poor preferred jail time because they at least did not have to worry about food and shelter in prison.[43] The Egyptian Society for Social Reform, chaired by the famous intellectual and politician Muhammad Husayn Haykal, held a conference in 1940 to address rural-to-urban immigration, a phenomenon considered the cause of multiple problems.[44] Rural children who roamed urban streets begging and stealing attracted some attention and contradicted reformers' hopes that all children in independent Egypt would go to school and master Western technology and sports.[45]

The 'marginal' population enlarged between the wars to incorporate many more people who had fallen in moral and material terms, underscoring the failure of urban centres to absorb migrants and intensifying elite anxieties. At the same time, higher city densities and transportation options facilitated anonymity, which made it easier for some women to violate respectability norms.

The impossibility of being poor and mastura in the city

After Egypt gained quasi independence in 1923, national commitments to education and a modern economy assumed that more girls and women would attend schools and work in factories. Many families, moreover, needed the income of girls and women who worked for pay. Girls attending school were cherished national commodities as long as they conformed to norms of public morality.[46] However, poor and working-class women who worked in mixed-gender settings such as factories, shops and homes already suffered from a sexualized form of stigma and low status that did not usually follow boys and men in the same occupations. Because factory work necessitated interaction between men and women and long hours away from community monitoring, some working-class families hid such work by daughters to protect family reputations and marriage prospects.[47] Poor women were always subject to losing satr in big cities, given their limited employment choices and the lack of material means for families to provide protective seclusion. These women, then, did not have to fear moving from respectable to disreputable on the status spectrum. With petty theft, they had little to lose in terms of status and much to gain materially.

Since escaping poverty in rural areas was the primary reason for emigration to cities for most people, assistance from home communities was not a practical expectation. Rural-to-urban women migrants often lost connections to community networks due to distance but they also escaped community surveillance. Many of these migrant domestic workers could not rely on familial support and protection anyway, because their families were too poor and too low in social status. Women migrants and their children were particularly vulnerable to weakened support networks after divorce or the death of a spouse.[48] Remaining respectable required women to find a lawful source of sufficient income to stave off starvation while preserving their moral sexual honour by living as a *mastura*. By definition, women working unsupervised in private homes in the city could not sustain rural or middle-class notions of respectability. Coming from poor families to live with and work for strangers, especially bachelors, compromised their respectability. Society categorized such women as disreputable because they were not under the guardianship of family members or their communities of origin.

Social responses to women engaged in theft differed. Based on my examination of hundreds of petty theft cases between 1924 and 1949, it appears that the legal system considered female criminals far less threatening and problematic than men. Men convicted of any theft crime faced jail sentences, while courts rarely sent to prison women convicted in similar cases. Judges often suspended the jail sentence or replaced it with a monetary fine, particularly when the defendant had no criminal record. As most women's violations were petty thefts, misdemeanour rather than criminal courts handled their cases. Judges in misdemeanour courts often expressed hope that women would reform and that the first offense would be the last, hoping to encourage a future straight path.[49] They warned women not to steal again. Courts recognized occasional thefts as motivated by temptation.[50] Judges in many cases treated female theft offenders with leniency, but they never acquitted them. Instead, they imposed fines on them or suspended their jail sentences to decrease the damage to their reputations, especially when convicts were unmarried or did not have a criminal record. Judges sometimes argued that avoiding jail time offered a woman a second chance to live respectably. One judge explicitly stated that leniency was necessary 'lest the jail corrupts her morality and destroys her future'.[51] Judges assumed that women in prisons would mingle with professional criminals who might corrupt them and that no respectable man would marry a woman with a prison history.

The lenient sentences and reformative gender rhetoric in the misdemeanour courts differed from Egyptian press discourse that held poor and working-class women responsible for moral disintegration, as illustrated by a number of campaigns in support of policing that targeted and condemned 'criminals from the gentle sex' and domestic servants in the 1930s.[52] Press reports denied the possibility of respectability for any female domestic worker and portrayed all maids as fallen women or thieves who took up domestic service as a cover. Incidents where maids committed offenses against their employers were used to generalize that all domestic servants were dangerous criminals. For example, an op-ed in the weekly *al-Siyasa* in 1928 accused all female maids of being 'ignorant about everything except stealing and causing troubles to respectable Egyptian families'.[53]

In contrast to the forgiving treatment of women criminals by Egyptian courts, European courts during the same period were more likely to assume that women convicted of crimes were irredeemable. British courts demonized female offenders and condemned women, especially unmarried and independent women, more harshly than male offenders because they viewed them as threats to the social order.[54] In fact, the Cesare Lombroso theory of the 'born criminal', dominant in European and American criminology in the late nineteenth and early twentieth centuries, claimed that criminal women were far more cunning and dangerous than criminal men.[55] Unlike the courts, this theory influenced the Egyptian popular press. Crime news sections (*akhbar al-hawadith*) employed Lombroso's approach to analyse violent crimes that captured public interest, as in the case of two sisters, Raya and Sakina, who were convicted of murder in 1921.[56]

Our knowledge of women's engagement in theft between the two world wars in Egypt is limited to what fragmented sources reveal. We can only speculate about the factors that escaped documentation. State documents follow a formula that does not reflect the views of women arrested for theft or provide the context for their decision making. We do not know what they thought about respectability norms, how they explained their work to themselves or the courts, or what their priorities were. They may even have constituted themselves as *mastura* because their crimes did not involve sexual exchange. It is unlikely that they made ideological statements about the lawfulness or righteousness of theft. They are more likely to have tried to justify their actions and ask for forgiveness. The notion of 'compelling circumstances' (*zuruf*) could be used as a justification for illicit behaviour in certain situations and to claim respect. We do know that while some professional tricksters took advantage of urban anonymity and mobility to pretend that they were domestic workers in order to rob middle-class homes, others went with the easy option of targeting homes in poor neighbourhoods, where their appearance would not raise suspicion or require explanation. Some women took up home robbery as a profession, subverting assumptions that organized criminality was the purview and inclination of men. The evidence regarding non-violent theft crimes in interwar Egypt indicates that gendered and classed standards of respectability were the least of poor and working-class women's concerns.

When crime does pay: Burglary and theft by women in interwar Egypt

Jewellers (*sagha*) frequently informed the police when they were suspicious that a woman was trying to sell stolen jewellery, particularly if they thought her too poor to own such expensive commodities.[57] Goldsmiths found it beneficial to cooperate with police because this guaranteed friendly connections and protection against thieves and hustlers, whose tricks ranged from shoplifting to exchanging real pieces of gold jewellery with fake ones.[58] In an interesting case, a goldsmith in al-Mahalla reported an eight-year-old maid from the village of Sunbat because she came alone to his store to shop for gold jewellery. Police learned she had stolen a five-pound bill from her employer. Due to her youth, the court surrendered her to her guardian, who guaranteed her future good behaviour.[59] Sixty-year-old 'Aziza Ahmad gave another young maid, ten-year-old Na'imaal-Dib, five pieces of candy and took a piece of gold jewellery al-Dib had stolen from her employer, Hidiya al-Shishtawi.[60] The court returned the child to her guardian and punished 'Aziza Ahmad with one month in jail. In other cases, parents took stolen money and items, or the children gave them to parents or other adult relatives because they did not know what to do with them.[61] As expected, police also searched the homes of maids based on false allegations of theft reported by antagonized employers.[62]

Breaking into people's homes was a violent business undertaken by the impudent and agile. Unlike men who robbed homes, women burglars did not resort to violence, intimidation or physical strength. Instead, they took advantage of expectations that women were weak and in need of protection. Women burglars perfected an approach that used wit, quick moves, trickery and clever language, committing their crimes during the daytime. I found no records of women robbing locations at night. Rather, women nimbly entered and escaped quickly after snatching valuable items. Women burglars understood well that the increasing anonymity of city life facilitated their work. They won sympathy and open doors for temporary accommodation by pretending to be lost in the big city with no means to get home. The following morning, a host would offer some cash to a stray female guest for her return home, only to find that she had taken jewellery and clothing.[63]

Cairo police reported the trajectory of an epic woman burglar, Khadra Alial Niklawi, between 1935 and 1939. Unfortunately, the records provide no information about her domestic life, origins or domicile. We know that she was a skilled actor with a talent for jumping in and out of buses and trains. In her five-year career, al Niklawi also committed a series of home thefts in several neighbourhoods across Cairo. Her stock-in-trade trick was to emotionally manipulate her victims by pretending to be desperate for a job. Once hired as a maid, she collected jewellery and cash and disappeared. She was successful repeatedly, adopting a different name each time. We do not know how many times she got away with stolen booty, but police arrested her and courts tried her in twenty such cases.[64] The al-Niklawi example indicates that state regulation of domestic servants was limited in its impact, as maids and employing families either ignored or were unaware of it. In raising awareness about the tricks used by professional women burglars in 1930s Egypt, a security expert warned that some pretended to sell perfume door-to-door. Instead of perfume, homemakers sniffed drug samples that knocked them unconscious while their homes were robbed.[65]

Successful female burglars left robbed houses with bulky spoils such as bundles of clothes and copper pots.[66] In some interesting cases recorded in the archives, an original owner recognized stolen clothes worn by someone who had purchased them.[67] Ihsan 'Abd al-Qawi Ibrahim, for example, recognized her stolen clothes on her coworker in a textile factory, Umm Khalil Ibrahim Farag. Ibrahim insisted on reporting the case to the police, and an investigation proved that Umm Khalil's father had purchased the stolen clothes at the marketplace. The vendor revealed the identity of the woman burglar who had sold the items to him. The thief had robbed clothing from two neighbouring houses in one day.[68] In a similar case, Fatima Muhammad Yusuf stole a copper pot from the house of Khadra Mustafa ʿAshur and sold it to Nazla Salim. ʿAshur recognized her pot while Salim was selling it in the coppersmith market.[69] These cases show the other side of urban anonymity, the nested communities of the urban poor. Many of these burglars operated on a short transactional circuit: they stole from the poor and working class, then sold the booty to vendors working in the resale market, who resold items to poorer customers in the same community.

Urban marketplaces and stores were the destinations of major local and national transportation lines. They were also sites of pricey fashion and classed consumption patterns. Department stores and textile and clothing shops mushroomed in Egyptian towns, signifying a rise in consumption and capitalist capacity.[70] Tracing the transformation of Egyptian consumerism and the emergence of department stores, Nancy Reynolds shows that conventional stores retained their appeal among the middle and lower classes and coexisted with new department stores, since consumption hailed all groups in society, including the very poor and the urban and rural working classes.[71] The small- and medium-sized conventional retail establishments dominated the commerce landscape, including in large cities such as Cairo and Alexandria, in the first half of the twentieth century, with the majority hiring four people or fewer.[72] Most stores did not have security staff to police customers. Shoplifters, who were almost exclusively girls and women, mixed among women shoppers. Their long voluminous robes (*galabiyyas*) and soft straw baskets (*quffa*) or big cloth sacks (*makhla*) afforded space to hide stolen items. Some women hid small pieces of fabric under clothing, in underwear, around their waists or inside their black overwrap (*milaya laff*).

I do not mean that middle- and upper-class women never shoplifted. Historians remind us that the concept of kleptomania emerged in the age of mass consumerism and retailing and saved well-to-do European shoplifters 'of good character' from being jailed like common criminals.[73] Middle- and upper-class shoplifting in Egypt might have escaped documentation because such women got away with theft; well-off families could have extricated arrested women and managers may not have wanted to risk incurring a lawsuit or losing business.

Professional shoplifters acted individually but also worked in groups that roamed stores to seem more innocent, since it was common for female relatives, friends and neighbours to shop for clothes together. As indicated by the account at the beginning of the chapter, shoplifting groups divided the work: one or two women kept the shop assistant busy while other women snatched and hid items in their baskets. Shoplifting groups travelled together from one town to another, accumulating work experience and skill. They also developed encrypted communication systems that translated into substantive criminal records.[74] Bands of shoplifters ventured into small stores, where shoplifting risks were higher and products were limited but where it was easier to distract a shop assistant with only one customer.[75] When caught committing theft, female shoplifters could accuse shop assistants of framing them because a negotiation over prices had failed.[76] On the other hand, shoplifters had to consider that other customers and bystanders might report them.[77]

Shoplifting became so frequent that big department stores hired women guards to conduct body searches of suspicious girls and women. Misr for Spinning and

Weaving Company, the largest textile manufacturer in Egypt, hired such guards and frequently pressed charges against shoplifters in its co-op store. The woman guard Asmahan 'Abd al-Latif was instrumental in catching shoplifters, searching their bodies thoroughly and sending them to court for small and large thefts.[78] Those caught by 'Abd al-Latif faced up to one month of prison with hard labour. These penalties were significant, since the same court often suspended jail sentences for women factory workers who stole pieces of cloth from their workplaces, provided they had no criminal record. A judge explained his leniency in one case: 'Lest jail time stain her future forever.'[79] When caught, some thieves offered police officers cash bribes for their freedom before reaching the police station. Reports were filed only when the policeman refused the bribe and reported it, adding one more charge against the arrested woman.[80]

Pharmacies, doctors' offices, and the goldsmith market also attracted creative women thieves who developed their expertise and tailored their techniques to the type of business they targeted. Annual security reports often highlighted the cases of women shoplifters with unique skills. For example, Nabawiyya Shahin Saqr was a highly confident and effective thief in Cairo in the late 1930s. In five reported cases, she pretended to have a sudden health crisis while waiting in a pharmacy or a doctor's office. Once the pharmacist or doctor rushed to provide medical aid, she would snatch cash or valuable items.[81]

Women involved in theft had to acquire skills and develop tricks to succeed. Police, in turn, developed particular tactics to find stolen items and catch the thieves. Migrant women villagers lacking social support and failing to act according to urbanite mores were easy targets for arrest because police treated them as inherently suspicious.[82] Patrolling police officers, including in plain clothes, sometimes arrested women perceived to be dressed beyond their means in public places. If an officer decided that a rural woman wore or carried clothes that someone like her could not afford, he could take her to the police station for interrogation.[83] In 1945, a patrol officer stopped two women on the road between al-Mahalla and the Hayatim village because he thought one of them was hiding a stolen live duck in her long, loose dress. The women were disturbed and confused and one of them refused to stop. At the courthouse, the defendant was offended that the officer labeled her a *ghagariyya* (gypsy woman), insisting to the judge that she was an Arab woman. She explained that she had been on her way to the pharmacy to buy medicine and did not steal a thing. The judge responded with poetic discourse in standard Arabic that mocked her: 'The weeping wolf reveals his identity.'[84] This phrase communicated that her behaviour, dress and statements did not match her 'true' positionality as a marginal member of society, a thieving wolf in sheep's clothing. As a man in a powerful position, the judge did not consider how encountering even a low-ranking police officer might terrify working-class men and women, whether or not they had violated the law. The wolf metaphor also hints at the judge's prejudice against a woman of foreign origin. Women typically identified themselves through kinship, locality and, to a lesser extent, profession but never ethnicity. The woman may have been one of the Palestinians who fled their homes during the Great Revolt of 1936 to 1939, and was resettled to that part of the Egyptian Delta. Oral histories I conducted with such Palestinian refugees indicate that they kept their identities, particularly in dress, until the 1970s, after which they mostly assimilated while maintaining contact with relatives in Gaza.

Some burglars, men and women, specialized in stealing clothes that hung on lines to dry. Laundry thieves developed tools to cut clotheslines on balconies from the street below. They chose a quiet moment with no passersby and moved fast. Capturing laundry on rooftops required physical strength and fitness to jump safely to the ground.[85] As with most domestic services, laundry work was almost exclusively a women's business. Many offenders were laundry women with easy access to a house.[86] To contain the surge of laundry theft, in 1936 the court equated trading in clothes known to be stolen with committing theft and convicted mostly women vendors who agreed to buy and sell clothes for less than a quarter of their value.[87] After arrest, a criminal record frequently revealed a history of theft. Either previous jail sentences provided no deterrence or laundry thieves had no option but to continue this source of income.[88] In addition to four previously recorded thefts, Fatima Sulayman al-Shaykh appeared in the misdemeanour court records twice in 1930. A married woman of between twenty-five and thirty years old, she was convicted of stealing copper pots from the house of Fatima al-Bastawisi al-Abyad and clothes from the house of 'Atiyya Ibrahim al-Nuwayhi. The court sentenced her to six months in jail with hard labour.[89]

While we should assume that many women got away with committing theft, when caught, they reinforced their marginal positionalities as poor and low status within the justice system and before shop owners and managers, homeowners, employers and others from whom they stole. Analogously, for their tactics to be effective, such girls and women often had to pass as respectable, which demonstrated the lack of substance behind gender- and class-based assumptions of respectability. Specifically, poor women planning illicit behaviour dressed for and acted out parts that allowed them to blend in with all the other righteous women.

Conclusion

Marginality for Egyptian women arrested for theft was a complex experience that extended beyond being legally and socially condemned. Capitalist consolidation of wealth and land, lack of investment in social needs, the semi-colonial status of Egypt and poverty delimited poor women's ability to choose gender-separated forms of work. Nor could they live lives of leisure supported by husbands, brothers or fathers, or take well-paid jobs that required education and connections. Many poor Egyptians had to leave villages to live and work in towns and cities between the two world wars. Migration from the countryside and population density in rapidly growing cities offered both less support for the poor and greater anonymity for poor women. Economic conditions were hardly better for the poor in cities. Male-dominated bourgeois society had already socially condemned poor and uneducated women who had to work for a wage outside the home, as did widely shared patriarchal values. Such women had little to lose in gendered respectability. Indeed, women who worked in theft and other illicit areas may have realized the impossibility of maintaining village standards of gendered respectability. The rise in women's involvement in theft crimes as indicated by arrests during the interwar period seems to indicate that respectability based on material and social 'protection' had less currency because it was impossible. To survive, these women took low-status jobs that women with more choices avoided. Guilty or innocent, moreover, poor women in cities were more likely to be subject to police surveillance and harassment. Poor and working-class women who engaged in theft had more to gain materially than lose in status or respectability. Since class and gender ideologies as well as socio-economic positionalities determined respectability, it was already less available to poor and working-class girls and women, especially if they worked for wages.

The biggest challenge in this research project was the lack of sources from the perspectives of the most marginalized in society. Illiteracy prevailed in the first half of the twentieth century, which makes it impossible to recover the voices and experiences of such women. In addition to serving the interests and reflecting the voices of state authorities and the privileged in society, male functionaries largely produced the documents I relied on, thus functioning to additionally silence women's voices. By drawing heavily on court records, security reports and state statistics, I showed that poor women in interwar Egyptian cities and towns resorted to condemned and illegal work without apology or concern for respectability norms that never offered them much protection in the first place. Hegemonic norms constituted girls and women who had to work for a wage as disreputable. Many questions remain that may be answerable with prisoners' records, confessions and testimonies as well as testimonies by medical experts and wardens. For example, did home and family remain central to the women who committed occasional theft or made a living through crime? To what degree did women use family rhetoric to explain their choices? Did any of the successful women translate theft into long-term social mobility?

Acknowledgements

I would like to thank Liat Kozma, Seçil Yılmaz, Simon Jackson, Camila Pastor de Maria y Campos and Francesca Biancani for their insightful feedback on the first draft of this chapter.

Part Two

Banditry and Crime

Noble Robbers, Avengers and Entrepreneurs: Eric Hobsbawm and Banditry in Iran, the Middle East and North Africa

Stephanie Cronin

Banditry, on land and sea, and allied trades such as smuggling, have been widespread and endemic across the Middle East and North Africa. That this is so is attested to by a variety of sources, some hostile and emanating from elite origins, state archives, court records, chronicles, accounts of European travellers, and some more sympathetic, popular song, poetry and folklore. Yet the Middle Eastern experience of banditry has thus far failed to receive sustained academic attention and the figure of the bandit has found fuller representation in literature, most notably in the novels of the Turkish author Yashar Kemal.[1] In particular, the debates stimulated by Eric Hobsbawm's thesis of social banditry has elicited only a few responses from scholars of the Middle East and North Africa, and those largely negative, failing to spark the kind of comparative and theoretical interest that has proved so productive for Latin America, China and southern Europe.[2]

The purpose of the survey which follows is two-fold. It is, firstly, to encourage a discussion within Middle Eastern and North African Studies of the social significance of crime in general, and specific phenomena such as banditry and smuggling in particular. Secondly, it hopes to provide some historical context for the startling re-emergence in the ungoverned spaces created by state collapse of types of actors and activities associated with banditry and smuggling and often thought of as belonging to the past. These include mafia-type gangs, militias/warlords sometimes with quasi-political ambitions, and smuggling, now of a wide variety of commodities, including people, weapons and drugs, on a massive scale across the Middle East and Northwest Africa. Finally, and particularly, the survey offers an explanatory framework for the profoundly ambiguous popular attitudes often displayed towards such figures and their behaviour.

The publication of Eric Hobsbawm's '*Bandits*' in 1969 was a foundational event.[3] Although criticized as methodologically unsound, theoretically flawed, empirically limited and latterly, after its influence had spread among scholars working on the non-European world, as Eurocentric, the book itself and its central notion of social banditry are still, several decades after its first appearance, compulsory referential starting points for any discussion of banditry, of premodern rural crime, indeed for the social history of crime in general. Even though the search for the social bandit often failed, the quest itself has offered productive ways of thinking about contested definitions of crime, the nature and scope of peasant resistance and the subaltern psychological world.

Hobsbawm's location of social banditry within a world of peasant resistance was originally part of a wider intellectual endeavour aimed at redefining the phenomenon of crime, the criminal no longer simply a pathological individual but criminal action a rational activity.[4] A further step was taken as crime came to be seen as, under certain conditions, a form of subaltern resistance, conscious or unconscious, and an embryonic form of social protest. Especially in the context of the arrival of modernity, exemplified by eighteenth-century England and entailing the disintegration of pre-capitalist social and economic structures and the ruthless consolidation of new 'modern' relationships enforced by harsh and novel legal, judicial and penal systems, lawbreakers and outlaws of every kind, food rioters, smugglers and poachers, along with bandits and pirates, were rehabilitated, emerging as crypto- or proto-rebels.

Hobsbawm's thesis of social banditry was a contribution to this wider historical revisionism. For Hobsbawm, this specific form of rural crime functioned as a manifestation of peasant protest, the designation of social bandit applying to peasant outlaws whom the authorities regarded as criminals, but who remained within their own peasant communities, and were 'considered by their people as heroes, as champions, avengers, fighters for justice, perhaps even leaders of liberation, and in any case as men to be admired, helped and supported'.[5] He insisted on the essential connection between the peasantry and social banditry, rejected modern forms of urban terrorism or gang activity as banditry, and clearly distinguished social banditry from both the professional underworld of common robbers and communities, such as beduin, for whom raiding was a normal economic activity. As well as the noble robber, Hobsbawm identified the avenger, who shared many of the characteristics of the noble robber, and was also a symptom of peasant discontent, but for whom to be 'terrifying and pitiless' was at least an important as being a friend of the poor.[6] A third type, the haiduk, largely a Balkan phenomenon, was rather more particular. In addition to living by robbery, the haiduk was also and equally a patriot, even a nationalist, and a fighter against foreign (usually Ottoman) oppression.

It should be noted, firstly, that Hobsbawm's social bandit was a rather conservative figure, his actions a form of protest against intolerable conditions, lacking any vision of social transformation and often aiming at a return to an idealized past. Only rarely, and under strictly circumscribed historical conditions, could such social bandits summon the potential to transcend the parochial limitations of peasant ideology and politics and assume a revolutionary role. Secondly, Hobsbawm, his conceptualization rather more subtle than his critics allowed, suggested social banditry only as one variant of banditry, and did not claim that all bandits or bandits in general fell into this category, this vulgarization of his original thesis later becoming rather widespread among his critics.[7] He particularly distinguished the social bandit from two quite separate categories of rural brigands, simple robbers or rural desperadoes, and bandit gentry or robber barons, warlords in contemporary Middle Eastern parlance.

Two lines of objection to the Hobsbawmian social bandit appeared immediately. The first and perhaps most obvious was his romanticization of the phenomenon, based on an uncritical use of the literature and legend of banditry. As he himself later conceded, very little about the historical reality of social banditry, let alone the careers of specific individual bandits, might actually be inferred from the songs sung and the stories told.[8] The second objection was to his equally uncritical acceptance of Balkan nationalist historiography for his construction of the haiduk.[9] The first charge against Hobsbawm was originally elaborated in an extremely influential article by Anton Blok.[10] Basing his critique on his research into the Sicilian mafia, Blok argued that any analysis of banditry must look at the actual behaviour and actions of bandits, not on their popular perception. Blok insisted that far from representing the grievances and incipient defiance of their own peasant communities, bandits rather developed connections to local elites, landlords and others, to whom they looked for political protection and for whom they actually acted as enforcers against the peasants, citing as evidence the Sicilian Giuliano Salvatore's attacks on communists and trade unionists just after the Second World War, and his contemporary, Luciano Leggio's reign of terror against peasants mobilizing to demand agrarian reform.[11] In addition, banditry offered the bandit social mobility and an escape from peasant life and, by siphoning off young unmarried men, the most combative elements of village society, removed potential footsoldiers of revolt. Far from challenging local power structures, Blok concluded that banditry contributed both materially and ideologically to weakening the capacities of peasants to resist.

The polarities offered by Hobsbawm and Blok were taken up and explored by scholars working within and across a range of disciplines and geographical regions to produce an increasingly sophisticated body of work on bandits and banditry. The taxonomic approach, sometimes reduced to the simple question of whether the social bandit existed or not, was soon superseded by inquiries into methodology and meaning. The distinction between bandit reality and bandit mythology quickly came to be generally acknowledged, including by Hobsbawm himself. It was not conceded, however, that this meant that the social bandit could be dismissed as a mere figment of the imagination. The almost universal existence of Robin Hood legends across the world suggested, on the contrary, their profound historical, political and social significance.[12] As a consequence, both sympathizers of the social bandit thesis and those sceptical of the thesis, and occasionally also of the politics behind it, began to take a closer and more contextualized look at the folklore itself, interrogating the production, transmission, transmutation, and, perhaps most importantly, reception, of stories of bandit heroics. A number of case studies painstakingly deconstructed bandit legends, tracing their manipulation within the strategic discourses of power-seeking elites, particularly an urban nationalist intelligentsia. Perhaps the most comprehensive such deconstruction was that of Balkan nationalism's romanticization of the bandit klephts and haiduks. Although preying ruthlessly on the peasantry and motivated largely if not exclusively by the prospect of booty, klephts and haiduks became the embodiment of anti-Ottoman freedom-fighting in Balkan nationalist historiographies, myths about brigand heroes manipulated by post-independence ruling classes.[13] Again, the Lithuanian popular cultural icon, Tadas Blinda, 'a leveller of the world', who was reputed to take from the rich and give to the poor, seems to have been in fact a horse-thief lynched by an angry mob who was transformed into a noble bandit by urban intellectuals first in the service of Lithuanian nationalism and later, in the Soviet period, as a progenitor of peasant class struggle.[14] Nonetheless such demolitions still failed to account for the origins of the myths in folk culture and their enthusiastic embrace by all manner of subalterns. The dynamics of myth-creation remain complex. Where and how the myth originates is as important, though harder to trace, as the way in which it is subsequently shaped. Popular responses to literary reworking of oral or folk history have, in their turn, their own impact on future cultural representation. The bandit himself may even strive to conform to the script. Far from reducible to a unilinear process whereby harsh peasant reality is appropriated and glamourized by a remote literati, subalterns as well as elites each make their own contributions to the profoundly contested meaning of bandit legends.[15]

Hobsbawm's own interest in banditry had originated in an interest in peasant discontent and resistance. The centrality of a focus on the meaning of banditry in peasant consciousness and the place of crime in class conflict was famously reasserted by Ranajit Guha in his study of colonial India published thirty years after Hobsbawm's book. Guha pointed out, firstly, that the peasant was typically prepared to tolerate, and 'often positively approve of a wide variety of crimes induced by poverty'.[16] Secondly, actual peasant revolt was preceded by a 'wave of "preliminary outrages"' – an increase in rural criminal activity which was often a feature of periods of immiseration and which signalled a lowering of the peasant's toleration of his conditions of existence.[17] Thirdly, such rural crime, including banditry, possessed an inversive function, symbolically or explicitly challenging social hierarchies and codes of deference, introducing a blurring within which peasants were increasingly enabled to invest rural lawbreaking and violence with new meanings, such code switching facilitated by the fact that the peasants' attitude towards activities labelled as crime in any case differed greatly from that of their class antagonists.[18]

Guha's direction of attention towards the necessity of interpreting sources differently in order to gain access to the consciousness of both peasant and bandit was made within the context of wider methodological debates.[19] Although Hobsbawm himself acknowledged the difficulties raised by his reliance on folklore and literature, his supporters countered that sceptics of the social bandit themselves often neglected to interrogate their own reliance on written texts emanating from elite sources, especially police and judicial records. Such sources, in addition to reflecting a tendency to conflate all types of rural lawbreaking into a single undifferentiated criminal category, were in particular hardly likely to reflect any popular perceptions or bandit self-images of legitimate resistance. Whereas state archives might be useful for chronologies of action, they say little, might even be profoundly misleading, about meaning. A single action, or category of activity, might appear to the authorities and therefore in the archives under the catch-all rubric of banditry, but might have been interpreted by the archivally silent lower echelons of rural society as invested with defiance, resistance or protest. Much work on banditry in the Middle East has indeed displayed a sometimes unconscious privileging of the written text, an assumption that elite-generated archival sources are relatively free of the subjectivity and bias which allegedly mars orally transmitted material. This approach has been particularly problematic where the events addressed are within living memory and popular voices thus easily accessible.

Another and quite novel line of criticism emerged when feminist scholarship began to try to gender Bandit Studies. This endeavour did not only involve the search for female bandits but examined such issues as the division of labour within peasant societies which might facilitate bandit activity, the role of extended households and domestic organization.[20] Gender studies particularly asked whether the continuing interest in banditry concealed a romanticized view of male violence.[21] Certainly for southern Europe and the Middle East and North Africa, deeply embedded cultural codes of honour and shame and notions of masculinity have been identified as important tropes in shaping popular sympathies for a range of picaresque figures on the margins of, or even outside, social and legal boundaries.

To what extent, then, does the recent work done in the wider field of Bandit Studies help to elucidate the experience of the Middle East and North Africa? Firstly, how can we explain the absence of the Middle East and North Africa from the historical controversies described above? Why has there been such a lack of interest in banditry when the phenomenon itself, and rural crime in general, was so widespread? Why are so few individual bandits celebrated or reviled? Why is there no Middle Eastern or North African counterpart to the Mexicans Emiliano Zapata or Pancho Villa, the Brazilian Lampiao, the Australian Ned Kelly, the Sicilian Salvatore Guiliano, or the Chinese Bai Lang, let alone to the female Indian 'bandit queen', Phoolan Devi.[22] What do we mean by banditry in the Middle Eastern context? Who became a bandit? Why and in what circumstances? What did bandits do and how was this perceived by elites and subalterns? What were the connections between bandits and peasants, and between bandits and the worlds of power? And, perhaps most importantly, who has written about bandits and what sources have they used?

Hobsbawm's elaboration of the concept of social banditry as a form of peasant protest was largely based on his analysis of European history. His central concept, however, proved particularly tempting to scholars working on the non-European world where both numerically preponderant peasant populations, and banditry itself, either still existed or were a very recent memory. This was particularly the case for parts of the world which had still living traditions of peasant populism, especially Latin America, or where peasants, and their fringe of bandits, had been allocated a politically salient historical role and their activities incorporated into a hegemonic discourse, most notably China.[23] Unfortunately, neither of these conditions held true for the Middle East and North Africa. Although in every country of the region the vast majority of the population was, until very recently, rural, national historiographies have been dominated by the politics of urban elites. In contrast to nationalisms elsewhere, Middle Eastern varieties have in general not valued the peasantry as the living reservoir of an authentic 'national' culture but have rather tended to exclude the rural areas and those who inhabited them from both actual political action and from the imagined historical community.

One reason for the lack of interest in banditry in the Middle East and North Africa and scepticism of social banditry in particular may, therefore, be found in the fact that, in general, bandits have not been incorporated as heroic figures into nationalist historiographies or state-building ideologies. A major exception is the Balkans under Ottoman rule, where a specific construction of banditry, Hobsbawm's klephts and haiduks, became central to an elite liberation discourse, and where, accordingly, scholarship followed. Another partial exception is French North Africa where the context of the anti-colonial struggle produced several candidates for the status of social bandit or *bandit d'honneur*. Indeed, only Algerian nationalism has truly embraced the bandit as a figure of political significance.[24] In relation to the central lands of the Middle East, however, banditry has been allocated rather the contrary role. Here state-building was often authoritarian and undertaken at the initiative of entrenched rulers and elites. With certain partial exceptions, for example colonial North Africa and mandatory Palestine, there was no place here for the revolutionary haiduk, let alone a Zapata. Across the Middle East, an anti-bandit discourse was appealing to indigenous elites and to colonial and imperial authorities alike, elite oppositional movements also sharing this perspective. Even the radical post-1967 Palestinian nationalist movement found peasant approbation of certain well-defined types of banditry somewhat embarrassing as a manifestation of backwardness.[25]

Nonetheless, a small number of scholarly engagements with the phenomenon of banditry in the Middle East have emerged. Three of the most significant are those of Nathan Brown on late nineteenth-century Egypt, of Karen Barkey on the seventeenth-century Ottoman Empire, and of Andrew Gould on nineteenth-century Anatolia. Yet all three reject the notion of social banditry and find the significance of banditry in its connection to the worlds of power, and more specifically to its role in state-building.[26] For both Brown and Barkey, for example, bandits were an unmitigated curse and a tool of oppression, perpetrators of violence against and exploitation of a helpless peasantry and in league with local power-holders of every kind. Brown goes even further than Anton Blok, stressing the complete self-interest of bandits, no more tied to the interests of notables than representing those of peasants.[27]

Brown's main interest is in the utilization of an anti-banditry discourse in the pursuit of an elite nationalist state-building project. In late nineteenth-century Egypt, the khedivial government, struggling to survive, based its resistance to the encroachment of British imperial power and its claims to legitimacy on its ability to maintain security in the countryside.[28] Indeed the Egyptian elite shared its fear of rural native defiance with Britain and was at least as concerned as the British about its own physical safety and the security of its property. Here, unlike the Balkans, no nationalist leadership unleashed the power of bandits across the vast rural hinterland in a challenge to foreign authority, nor did a nationalist intelligentsia celebrate the valour and deeds of brigand heroes. On the contrary, Brown shows how, in the 1880s, immediately after the British occupation, the khedivial authorities discovered, or perhaps invented, an unprecedented crisis of violent rural crime, deploying this imagined crisis for two purposes: to enhance their claims to sovereignty vis-à-vis the British, and to strengthen their control over their own peasantry, using the banditry 'crisis' as a justification for an ambitious state-building agenda, constructing new and strengthening existing disciplinary institutions, including a centralized police force, prisons and courts and national legal codes. The newly-established and draconian Brigandage Commissions failed and were abolished in 1889. But the British occupying authorities then appropriated the ideological weapon forged by the khedivial government and turned it against its creators, using the continuing rural insecurity to justify their own increasing presence within the Egyptian administration. Yet the discourse of order remained as central to the British as it had been to the Egyptian authorities, and the bandit continued as the symbolic representative of chaos and violence, a threat to life and property of Egyptians and British alike.

For Barkey, closely following Blok, bandits were certainly a feature of the drastic material deterioration in the Ottoman Empire typical of the global crisis of the seventeenth century, but their significance lay in their ambitions vis a vis the patrimonial Ottoman state, not in representing a rebellious peasantry.[29] Their proliferation was a direct consequence of Ottoman state-building, as they were recruited into new regular armies, trained in the use of weapons, but then casually demobilized. Cast adrift, they became mercenaries, either joining the retinues of local warlords or notables, or turned themselves into bandit gangs, becoming instruments of repression in the hands of landlords, officials, or warlord-rebels. The Ottoman government responded with a policy of bargaining and incorporation. Where possible, bandit gangs which became too menacing were suppressed by force. More frequently they were simply absorbed, their leaders offered state appointments, successful elite incorporation indeed, according to Barkey, the main objective of bandit activity.[30]

Certainly, as Brown and Barkey argue, banditry across the Middle East and North Africa, as elsewhere, was often not exclusively a subaltern activity. Bandits often possessed, as Blok noted in relation to Sicily, a symbiotic relationship with such rudimentary forces of law and authority as existed on the local level, collusion sometimes open, sometimes covert, bandits acquiring protection in return for a share of the loot. For the Middle East and North Africa, this was especially the case where tribal ties of kinship, real or fictive, linked bandits directly to local landowners or state officials. Banditry might even constitute a route of upward social mobility. Bandit figures often intruded into the politics of premodern Middle Eastern and North African states, thereby forcing themselves into the archives, but they resembled Hobsbawm's robber barons, not his social bandit. The offer of elite incorporation in return for submission was a central strategy of states for dealing with all troublesome or rebellious elements which were too powerful to suppress and bandit leaders and local warlords often graduated into legitimate and high-ranking official positions. Their performance of power notwithstanding, premodern Middle Eastern and North African governments and their armies were in reality small and weak, lacking the material means to enforce their will across large territories, and political survival depended on an ability to manipulate and accommodate a variety of interests with only the occasional application of exemplary force. Examples abound of negotiation with, and incorporation and utilization of, bandits and all manner of rural adventurers.[31] A classic case of the bandit-turned-governor is that of Sharif Mawlay Ahmad al-Raysuni in nineteenth-century Morocco.[32] Beginning as a cattle rustler and gun-runner, al-Raysuni progressed to kidnapping and ransoming Europeans, a particularly lucrative business, establishing himself as local strongman and warlord in north-western Morocco. He eventually obtained from the sultan of Morocco the governorship of the coastal town of Asila, from which position he went on to establish good relations with the emerging Spanish protectorate.

A case of a 'bandit elite,' rather than an opportunist individual, is that of the derebeys, local tribal rulers of Cilicia, in southeastern Anatolia.[33] The derebeys were among the last local rulers to resist the centralizing expansion of the nineteenth-century Ottoman state, surviving until the 1860s. They were notorious in Istanbul for their brigandage and a derebey was conventionally described in Ottoman documents as *shaki*, outlaw or brigand or possibly rebel. Their speciality consisted of presiding over gangs drawn from the local population, who held up caravans in mountain passes and raided villages on the surrounding plain, the derebeys becoming effectively 'lords of the bandits'.[34] The Ottoman government, wishing to bring the region under its direct control but lacking the resources, and perhaps the inclination, to confront the derebeys militarily, instead approached them as a ruling elite in their own right and offered them high positions and generous salaries in return for submission. The derebeys, sharing the culture and politics of patrimonialism and, perhaps reading the writing on the wall, acceded, leaving their tribespeople to cope alone with the collapse of their economy and forced settlement in the plain below their mountain home. Patrimonial strategies were reserved exclusively for local elites, including bandit leaders.

Hobsbawm conceded the prevalence of such connections, between bandits and the worlds of power, but his social banditry was a quite different phenomenon, and interesting insofar as it functioned, under certain circumstances, as an articulation of peasant discontent. Barkey's rejection of the social bandit was, on the contrary, crucially embedded in a denial of the very existence of strategies of rebellion among Ottoman peasants. In her view, the failure to rebel was certainly not the result of a lack of material distress, Ottoman peasants experiencing many of the hardships which produced rural revolts across Europe during the seventeenth century. It was rather the result of the existence of preferable alternatives to the risky strategy of open defiance, Ottoman peasants, apparently lacking the profound attachment to the land typical of peasant consciousness, preferring to leave the land rather than to fight for it, straightforward criminal banditry itself becoming a favoured survival strategy of vagrant ex-peasants in headlong flight from their villages.[35]

A broader general scepticism regarding peasant rebellion may thus constitute a further reason for the general unpopularity of social banditry in studies of the Middle East.[36] Much of the recent research into banditry in other areas of the world has been prompted by a more general interest in peasant resistance. As far as the Middle East and North Africa is concerned, the rise of Peasant Studies as a discrete field of research in the 1970s found comparatively little response. Since the region appeared to lack the large-scale uprisings characteristic of countries such as China or the politically significant peasant movements of Latin America, historians of the Middle East and North Africa tended to dismiss the countryside as uninteresting and the consciousness and agency of its inhabitants has been little investigated. If historians of the region have often been content to share Marx's characterization of peasants as so many potatoes in sacks, their view of nomads/beduin, often prime candidates for bandit gangs, has sometimes been actively hostile. Following the mediaeval scholar Ibn Khaldun, scholarship has tended to depict tribal nomads as mere instruments of their khans, any resistance from them merely a symptom of an eternal conflict between tribal chaos (the desert) and state-imposed order (the sown).[37]

Brown's dismissal of the social bandit in Egypt, and Barkey's in the Ottoman Empire, are based largely on close reading of official documents located in state archives. That a different methodology might produce different results can clearly be seen in Barkey who, when she turns to popular traditions, becomes more sympathetic to the possible existence of social banditry. State and elite-generated sources on rural dissent, indeed on crime in general, are replete with perennial problems of interpretation: generic labelling, the subsuming of widely differing types of rural violence under the heading of crime, the use of words with the connotation of banditry/brigandage as part of a search for legitimacy. The late nineteenth-century Egyptian banditry commissions, for example, lumped all rural violence together into a single undifferentiated category, the work of 'miscreants' (*ashqiya*').[38] Barkey's use of the term banditry applies to an even more diffuse phenomenon, the so-called Celali rebels of the seventeenth-century Ottoman Empire. The Ottoman government referred to all its armed opponents in the countryside, whether rebel bands numbering thousands or small groups of robbers, as Celalis, using this designation to delegitimize any and all rural unrest by identifying it with the traumatic rebellion of Sheyh Celal at the beginning of the sixteenth century.[39] In any case, for states such as the Ottoman Empire, banditry and robbery were indeed both a form of rebellion against its authority and the sources often deployed a colourful vocabulary of undifferentiated abuse, individual words containing the meaning of both brigand and rebel.[40]

The meta-language of official sources has therefore made it difficult to disentangle the different activities of different kinds of groups. Given the strong ideological imperatives embedded in the archival material it is extremely unlikely that bandit activity, or indeed any kind of rural violence, would appear in anything other than an extremely negative light. Egyptian and Ottoman archives are, naturally enough, replete with vivid accounts of the brutality of bandits and the suffering of the poor at their hands, including petitions and appeals to courts for justice by peasants themselves. Yet none of this evidence is unmediated, the petitions of illiterate villagers and supposedly verbatim statements by bandits surviving in court records having passed equally through the filter of scribal pens.[41]

Although most bandit activity in the Middle East and North Africa, as Hobsbawm pointed out regarding Europe, was simple robbery and extortion targeting the accessible and defenceless poor, yet the generic labelling for ideological purposes typical of official records renders invisible different and more complex stories. Perhaps the most famous appellation of the term banditry to an authentic case of peasant resistance is the British labelling of the 1936 revolt in mandatory Palestine. British officials and press reports routinely branded the rebel peasant fighters as outlaws, bandits, gangsters and highwaymen, as a ploy to discredit the uprising's nationalist aims, a linguistic practice continued by Israeli academia.[42] Another much earlier but similar contest over naming may be found in the case of the activities of post-*Reconquista* exiles (*manfiyyun*) in Andalusia. These Muslims and Moriscos, described as bandits in Spanish sources, have, on the contrary, been reclaimed by North African scholars as the last remnants of Moorish resistance to the *Reconquista*.[43]

The possibilities suggested by the deconstruction of contests over labelling and meaning are well illustrated in a study of colonial Algeria.[44] Here we find the invention, by French settlers, of the 'myth of Algerian banditry', a myth which was then utilized to delegitimize both Algerian claims to the land and indigenous resistance to dispossession.[45] This case provides a classic illustration of the social and political consequences of the revolutionary impact of capitalism on a pre-industrial economy. Across a forrested region near the city of Annaba (Bône) in northeastern Algeria, the local population maintained a precarious ecological equilibrium through a practice known as *kcar*, the controlled burning of the forest to obtain pastures and farmland. The arrival of increasing numbers of French colonisers after the conquest of Algeria in 1830 inaugurated first a struggle over concepts of land ownership and use leading to dispossession, then the criminalization of the customary practice of *kcar*, and finally the labelling of *kcar* as banditry and a symbol of political and especially religious resistance. The Algerians, although they conceded formal ownership of the forest to the Ottoman landlords, believed that they too, as those who worked it, possessed rights over it. In particular, they considered the areas they cleared through their own labour as their own property, an inheritance for their children. The French colonial authorities, on the other hand, disregarded the customary claims of the Algerians and embarked on a policy of the conversion of all of the forest into pure private property and its expropriation and concession to French businessmen for commercial exploitation, specifically the production of cork.[46] The Algerians' use of the forest was accordingly increasingly restricted, upon pain of punishment by large fines and collective responsibility. The Algerians responded using a variety of tactics, evading the forest guards, presenting petitions to the colonial authorities and, occasionally, deliberately burning the forest down.[47] The practice of *kcar* had always contained the possibility that fires might accidentally get out of control. The French, however, could not or would not distinguish accident from arson. They increasingly identified all *kcar* fires as arson and tried to ban the practice altogether, which for the Algerians represented a lethal assault on their way of life. The French were committed to the destruction of the indigenous political economy, and could neither recognize the legitimacy of, nor tolerate, resistance. Their solution to their dilemma, by which they made their own situation comprehensible, was to turn the Algerian resisters into bandits practising arson.[48]

Yet elite discourses were always capable of considerable plasticity. The case of Egypt demonstrates how the significance of activities which were, in times of political stability and elite consensus, mundanely relegated to the purely criminal might be transformed into resistance by the wider political context. The late nineteenth-century Brigandage Commissions had defined all rural violence as crime. In 1919, however, similar actions by peasants, the killing of village elders, attacks on police, theft of moveable property, food, cattle, sheep and fodder, especially that which had been hoarded by the wealthy during the war, were briefly reinterpreted as manifestations of a peasant revolt, part of a national struggle, indeed a revolution, directed against the British Protectorate and in favour of independence and led by the middle-class liberal nationalists of the Wafd Party.[49]

Prevailing ideologies of modernism continued in the twentieth-century Middle East to confine the bandit to the pathological margins of society, while the label was applied indiscriminately to a vast range of rural opposition. From the 1920s onwards, the new Turkish republic combined all manifestations of armed rural dissent, whether Kurdish nationalist, religious, peasant or robber, into a single category of bandit, this category then defined as a threat to the state and crushed. Mustafa Kemal's contemporary, Reza Shah of Iran, similarly deployed the discourse of the 'man of order' to establish the new state's physical control throughout the countryside, over rural criminals of all sorts, bandits, highway robbers and nomadic raiders, but also, and as part of the same process and often using the same justificatory vocabulary, over tribal khans and semi-autonomous local rulers and their agricultural-pastoralist populations.[50] For the nationalist elite of Pahlavi Iran, the suppression of banditry was a central trope in the wider transformation of troublesome pastoral nomads into settled productive farmers. Reza Shah's son, Muhammad Reza Shah, continued the project. Although tribal power had been decisively crushed, partly by military force but mainly by socio-economic transformation, a phenomenon defined as banditry reappeared. Just as in the Turkey of the 1960s and 1970s, the nomenclature of banditry was applied to Kurdish opposition in the rural areas, so in Iran, the designation bandit was applied to guerrilla movements who launched armed actions in the 1970s against the shah's regime.

The practice of nomad raiding, endemic across the premodern Middle East and North Africa, has also magnified uncertainties about the activities and identities of bandits. Hobsbawm himself specifically excluded communities for whom raiding was part of the normal way of life, such as nomads/beduin, from consideration as social bandits. But were such raiders, at least in their own eyes, even bandits? The literature has, in general, adopted the perspective of those who were the targets of such raiding. Yet what may be deduced regarding the perspectives of the raiders themselves? Across the Middle East, tribal nomads adopted, for example, the roles of paid protectors of caravans that carried people and goods along trade and pilgrim routes. This system, which appeared from the outside to be a kind of protection racket, was seen from the inside as legitimate recompense for the passage of strangers through tribal territories. It frequently broke down, with tribes attacking the caravans they had been paid to protect.[51] Such breakdowns were recorded by local authorities and European travellers as resulting from the nomads' instinctive preference for loot over obligation, or even from some atavistic nomad savagery, but certainly other factors were operative. A failure to pay the agreed sums, either in part or in full, for example, might sour relations between merchants and tribes, leading the latter to take what they considered themselves to have been cheated of. From the mid-nineteenth century on, state-sponsored changes in landownership and the loss of customary rights of pasturage might also prompt dispossessed nomads to compensate themselves through attacks on formerly secure trade routes, even though these routes were guaranteed by their own chiefs and khans. Beduin robberies of pilgrims on the Hajj road were notorious, although the beduin tribes, or rather their leaders, received subsidies from the Ottoman government to discourage raiding. The Ottoman sources were quick to attribute such robberies to a natural beduin inclination to crime.[52] Yet again the subsidy system frequently broke down, the beduin then obliged to take what was necessary to their survival.[53]

Bandits of this kind originated from within peasant and pastoral communities, especially those with a tribal organization and they remained in varying degrees of contact with local populations. This contact might be very close and supportive, especially where ties of kin existed, but might also be deeply antagonistic and exploitative. Both nomadic and settled communities often gave succour to bandits, but, where succour was denied, the bandits' treatment of 'hostile' villages might be extremely brutal. To some extent, Hobsbawm's distinction between nomadic raiding and banditry proper breaks down in the Middle Eastern context, the boundaries between nomads and peasants often fluid and permeable. Settled cultivators might be recently sedentarized former nomads, communities might be mixed cultivators and pastoralists, and peasants and nomads linked by tribal ties. Thus it is possible to see certain instances of nomadic raiding not as a phenomenon necessarily disconnected from and hostile to peasant life, but rather as an aspect of peasant economic activity, hardship and perhaps discontent. On the other hand, however, although they did not necessarily divide nomad from peasant, tribal ties might nonetheless impede as much as augment wider geographical or class-based bonds of solidarity, their privileging of vertical hierarchies and their fostering of inter-tribal violence often fatal to sustained rebellion.

Banditry has therefore been significant in both peasant and pastoralist strategies of survival in the Middle East and North Africa. This does not necessarily imply the presence of permanent bandit gangs. For many rural communities, a resort to banditry might not imply a way of life, involving an irreversible departure from peasant or pastoral origins, but might rather be a temporary activity, taken up in times of hardship and abandoned when the hardship passed, or might be seasonal or part-time, engaged in to supplement the inadequate rewards of agricultural or pastoral labour. Banditry might also be a strategy of the socially excluded, the marginal and the desperate, those with nothing to lose. Nineteenth-century Morocco gives us many stories of fugitive slaves becoming highway robbers. The escaped slave Bilal, for example, gathered a band around him and pillaged travellers, moving from one tribe's territory to another whenever he felt threatened, his career lasting ten years. Other slaves operated in both northern and southern Morocco, always, interestingly, in association with free people.[54] Such slaves typically became bandits after some interruption to their slave career. Often having been bodyguards or otherwise familiar with weapons, they simply struck out on their own when opportunity offered.[55] Another figure, more truly an outlaw than the peasant or nomad robber, was the military deserter, possessing the advantage of military knowledge and training and sometimes also weapons. Demobilized soldiers have perennially provided bandit material. Rapid and chaotic demobilization produced waves of Celalis in the seventeenth-century Ottoman Empire, while the imposition of modern conscription in the nineteenth and twentieth centuries created many fugitives from enlistment and especially deserters. Deserters might have any of a range of motives, political opposition, personal antagonism, a simple wish to avoid military service, the need to leave the army to return home for family reasons or even merely to help with the harvest. Once outside the law, the deserter often linked up with civilian bands of robbers. By the 1920s in countries where military service was considered a pillar of the new state, such as Iran and Turkey, the deserter, from both the gendarmerie and the army and with some military experience, had become a specific and serious threat to rural security.[56]

Middle Eastern banditry, like crime in general, is often assumed to have been not only endemic but unchanging, its supposedly final elimination a consequence of modernization in general and the successful creation of rural police forces or gendarmeries in particular. Yet is it possible, on the contrary, to detect in the Middle East and North Africa epidemics of banditry reflecting 'the disruption of an entire society, the rise of new classes and social structures, the resistance of entire communities or peoples against the destruction of its way of life'?[57] A rise in the incidence of banditry is generally and naturally associated with an increase in rural immiseration and pauperization and periods of economic crisis, thus constituting a strategy of survival. But given the much greater availability of source material, the late nineteenth and early twentieth centuries seem to demonstrate not only an increase in banditry but to suggest that this increase may be a direct consequence of, and form of resistance to, accelerating political and economic change, sometimes called modernization, including political centralization and the development of capitalism and its penetration into the rural areas.

The late nineteenth/early twentieth-century Middle East certainly possessed the two conditions proposed as necessary for the emergence of social banditry: class conflict producing communal solidarity in the countryside, and an absence of institutionalized mechanisms, such as political parties and peasant unions, for expressing and managing this conflict.[58] The rapid commercialization of agriculture as the region was drawn into the global economy, the resulting criminalization of customary rights to the land for peasants and to pasturage for nomads producing dispossession and impoverishment in the countryside, combined with authoritarian political systems, whether colonial or independent, to deprive the rural poor of viable alternatives to illegality.

The connection between modernization and banditry has been concretized in relation to late nineteenth-century Ottoman state-building. The Ottoman road-building programme, for example, was intended to improve security, enhance trade and knit the empire together. The new roads, however, were not only an instrument of state power, but also provided space and opportunity for contesting that power.[59] Not only were the new roads a product of Ottoman modernization, but so too were the highway robbers who infested them. These robbers included a variety of fugitives from new state institutions and policies, nomads fleeing compulsory sedentarization, peasants forced off the land by the spread of private ownership and impoverished by the commercialization of agriculture, rogue gendarmes, deserters from the army and evaders of conscription. In Egypt too, an increase in banditry seems to have resulted from similar changes initiated by the khedivial state, the collapse of the older subsistence economy and the replacement by production of cash crops grown for export, rural indebtedness, and the ever heavier hand of the state itself, with its demands for service in the army and forced labour. Organic connections between peasant resistance and banditry in the new Turkish republic, for example, may be discerned in the low-level violence endemic in the rural areas during the interwar period. Such violence was a last resort of the peasantry in the face of social and economic crisis and state policies, this violence taking the form of individual attacks on tax officials, gendarmes, village headmen, moneylenders, and the violation of the property rights of landowners and monopoly companies.[60]

The contemporary period in Iran saw the introduction of similar policies with similar results. Here too a determined assault on the way of life of the rural poor had begun in the nineteenth century with the twin processes of the integration of Iran into the global economy and the deepening penetration of capitalist relations into the countryside. In 1927 the newly-consolidated Iranian monarchy launched an accelerated programme of unprecedented legislative radicalism, introducing a number of measures – conscription, land laws leading to the loss of customary cultivation and pasturage rights, dress laws aimed at the destruction of tribal culture, nomadic settlement and monopolies on opium and tobacco production – which had an immediate and devastating impact on the rural population, both peasants and pastoralists. The results were exactly the proliferation of outrages identified by Guha as precursors of rebellion in India, successive waves of rural violence which began in the mid-1920s with increasing lawlessness and robbery, duly reaching a crescendo in 1929 with outbreaks across the country of nomad and peasant risings of an intensity which threatened the very survival of the regime. After the suppression of these risings, the rural areas reverted to lawlessness and banditry, serious insecurity continuing for several years. At the core of this violence were rebellions by the still armed and mobile nomadic tribes, accompanied by peasant discontent, many peasants in fact sedentarized former pastoralists with tribal links to the nomads. Widespread banditry was also an integral feature of these uprisings, again by elements with tribal connections. The actions of the tribal insurgents and bandit gangs were indistinguishable, as indeed were the two groups themselves, but both occasionally displayed a striking sensitivity to their wider base of support worthy of a social bandit. For example, the opium monopoly, which drastically reduced the income from poppy cultivation, had been the state policy, above all others, which had unified the opposition of the disparate elements of the rural poor across southern Iran. When tribal rebels took control of a small town in eastern Fars, they drove out the government officials and took possession of the government stores of opium. They then returned the opium to the cultivators for sale on the open market, less 10 per cent, the equivalent of the government tax, which they kept for themselves. A similar story came from further north, in the region of Isfahan. Here one of the largest bandit gangs, together with tribal rebels, again captured the government opium store, took out the government percentage of 10 per cent, and returned the remainder to the peasants, taking receipts.[61]

In the late nineteenth to early twentieth century, modernization, as well as stimulating banditry, also produced modernized types of crime, and led to further innovations in the panoply of subaltern avoidance and resistance. As new states consolidated their control over national territories, imposed controls and taxes on the movement of goods and people, and established borders of theoretical and legal impermeability, smuggling erupted on a massive scale. Across the Middle East and North Africa, as elsewhere, smuggling and banditry were closely allied, bandits engaging in smuggling and vice versa. Both, but especially smuggling, were directly related to state policies. Wherever restrictions were imposed, and especially where those restrictions were deemed illegitimate, individuals and entire communities devised ways of evading them.

Smuggling, like banditry, might be a means of survival in hard times, an economic opportunity, or a form of resistance to authority. The outbreak of a veritable war in the late Ottoman Empire between a French-owned tobacco company with a newly-granted monopoly, the Régie, and local growers abetted by smuggling rings, demonstrates the presence of all three motives.[62] For the professional and well-organized smuggling rings, the Régie's efforts to control the production and sale of tobacco represented an opportunity to make fortunes, perhaps as much as half the tobacco grown escaping Régie control.[63] For the peasant cultivators, smuggling became a way of compensating for the reduced income resulting from the operation of the monopoly. Selling to smugglers also meant avoiding the government taxes and, if the cultivator was a sharecropper, handing over any portion to the landlord.[64] It was not only the producers who were complicit in the smuggling, but consumers also, who willingly purchased tobacco from smugglers going from door to door in villages. Even representatives of the Ottoman state, officials and gendarmes, turned a blind eye to smuggling, or even participated in it.

For the peasant cultivators, smuggling was a strategy of both survival and resistance. But its success depended on its being embedded in a sympathetic environment where it was widely perceived as legitimate and even, insofar as it hampered and frustrated the Régie, as a social good. The general population and even the Ottoman government itself resented the encroachment on sovereignty represented by the increasing foreign presence throughout the empire and the Régie's lack of legitimacy contributed to a general readiness by wide layers of Ottoman society to evade and resist the company's monopoly.

Smuggling was a covert, but very effective, means of undermining the Régie. It was one aspect of a broader struggle against the monopoly which combined legal and recognized traditions of protest, such as demonstrations and presenting petitions to the Sultan, with violent defiance, rioting and the stoning of Régie offices and attacks on Régie troops.[65] The struggle between the Régie and the smugglers was indeed both bitter and violent. According to one Ottoman report, in the first fourteen years of the company's operation, not less than two thousand people every year had lost their lives in this struggle.[66] Such resistance harried the operations of the Régie on the ground but it failed to offer any broader challenge to the continuation of the foreign monopoly. It remained scattered and sporadic, confined to the countryside and small towns, and almost completely subaltern in character. Its limitations are revealed by its contrast to neighbouring Iran, where a mass urban movement led by a powerful coalition of ulama, merchants and reformist intellectuals forced the cancellation of a similar tobacco monopoly. Although the Régie strained every nerve to suppress the illegal trade, in the end the company learned to live with it and the Ottoman government to live with the company. The Régie survived all the vicissitudes of revolution and war until it was finally nationalized by the new Turkish republic in 1925, the Kemalist authorities rejecting foreign control but retaining a monopoly as part of their étatiste economic policies. The smuggling continued.

Most smuggling was not, of course, either on the scale, nor possessing the overt political significance of the Ottoman tobacco war. Nonetheless, smuggling everywhere, like banditry but perhaps to an even greater extent, required the active collaboration of elements among the larger local community. Both, but again especially smuggling, were extremely difficult to suppress. Prescribed penalties might be severe but their application depended on apprehending the elusive malefactors. Since proof against the accused, and even the accused themselves, might be hard to find, the authorities often resorted to collective punishments, fixing blame on villages in the vicinity of the crime, local peasants being ready scapegoats.[67] Subsequent scholarship might debate the existence and character of the relationship between bandits and peasants but the Ottoman authorities were in no doubt regarding their mutually supportive links. In Iran too collective punishment, especially against nomads in the form of the authorized plundering of tents, was common, and often resulted in the generation of further banditry by the impoverished and vengeful tribal communities.[68]

Both banditry and smuggling might also be carried out at sea as well as on land and contemporary authorities made a similar assumption about the existence of close and friendly connections between local coastal communities and sea-bandits or pirates. Villagers might provide pirates, who prowled along the coast, waited and watched just outside harbours and hid in coves and bays, with news of approaching ships, as well as food and shelter.[69] One example comes from the early eighteenth century when an Ottoman court ruled that local villagers on the Aegean coast must recompense the owner of a tobacco shipment looted by pirates as it had been proved that one of the villagers had passed information about the cargo to the pirates. As not only the pirates themselves, but even the villager who had alerted them escaped, it was the remaining villagers who paid the price.[70]

As in the case of land banditry, both scholarly and popular interest in sea-banditry, especially in the Mediterranean, has adopted an elite perspective. Regarding the Barbary corsairs in the western Mediterranean from the sixteenth to the early nineteenth century, for example, we know a great deal of their place in interstate relations, in naval warfare, and the strategic, economic, and legal dimensions of their activities, of corsairing's role in the slave trade and Muslim-Christian relations as seen through the prism of the ransoming of captives.[71] Of the pirates or corsairs themselves, however, and of pirate crews, we know very little. This is in stark contrast to our knowledge of the 'Golden Age' of Atlantic piracy in the late seventeenth to early eighteenth century where we find studies both of the lives of individual pirates and of piracy as a collective response to the brutalities of naval life.[72]

Yet corsairing in the western Mediterranean, both Muslim and Christian, may also be approached from a subaltern direction, tracing not only the macroeconomic and political roles of the corsairs, but also something of their background, their motivation and the character of their activities. The Barbary corsairs, from the point of view of their own societies, seem to resemble very closely Hobsbawm's 'avenger'. Indeed, as *kursan* they are quite clearly differentiated in Arabic from ordinary sea-robber (*liss al-bahr*). The Barbary corsairs were the sea-borne counterparts of the Morisco bandits of sixteenth-century Andalusia. At the beginning of the seventeenth century, Spain had begun the mass expulsion of the Moriscos, Spanish Muslims who had converted to Christianity after the *Reconquista* but who remained objects of suspicion. The numbers deported by ship and abandoned on North African shores amounted to at least half a million, and possibly many more. Hundreds of thousands of these Moriscos settled where they had been forced to disembark from the Spanish galleys, in North African coastal towns. Dispossessed and exiled, they devoted themselves to harrying their former compatriots, launching what became known in Arabic sources as a seaborne jihad, the corsairs described by Arabic sources as *ghazi* (religious warrior). The 'Corsair Republic' of the port of Salé was populated largely by expelled Moriscos, some of whom became famous. These corsairs found representation in elite biographical and polemical literature, but also in popular poetry and song, where they took on the quality of Hobsbawm's avenger, memorializing injustice and offering hope of retaliation.[73]

The phenomenon of the Barbary corsairs, so terrifying to early modern Europe, may thus be related directly to the catastrophe which befell the Spanish Moriscos and their individual and collective strategies of revenge and compensation. In general, major waves of piracy, like banditry, were not a perennial and random hazard but rather arose from social dislocation and military conflict. As Celalis were produced by the military mobilizations of the seventeenth century, and swarms of deserters by twentieth-century conscription, so pirates proliferated in times of, and especially after the end of, large-scale naval conflict. The Mediterranean east of Malta, for example, witnessed an explosion of Greek piracy in the 1820s linked to the Greek war of independence. Again, these Greek pirates may be seen as the exact counterparts of the mainland klephts and were romanticized accordingly, by both Greek nationalists and philhellenic sentiment in Western Europe.

Corsairing, like certain types of banditry, was an integral element of premodern local and regional economies throughout the Mediterranean, Christian as well as Muslim, both sides combining material benefit with religious justification. It was distinguished, at least theoretically, from piracy proper by the stipulation that its legitimacy depended on its being carried out under the auspices of a recognized authority, who shared by right in the booty.[74]

In practice corsairing activity exactly resembled piracy, the only distinction being the formal possession of the patronage of a recognized ruler. It was thus extremely easy, and almost inevitable when times were hard, for legitimate corsairs to turn into pirates. Maltese seamen, for example, accumulated centuries of experience under the patronage of the Knights of Malta.[75] Although their activities were theoretically limited to the traditional enemies of Christianity, Maltese corsairs would often, when legitimate prey ran short, close their eyes 'to the fussy terms of their letter of marque', and attack friendly and unfriendly shipping alike, even though this actually turned them into pirates, subject to the death penalty.[76] When corsairing was legally abolished at the end of the eighteenth century, these coastal communities were left without the means of making a legitimate living. Many complied with the new legal prohibition, some ceased corsairing but took up other seaborne crime, especially smuggling, some emigrated to North Africa taking their skills with them, and some simply continued as before, their activities now purely criminal. Many narratives of their activities, their capture and their fates may be found in the archives of the Vice-Admiralty Court established in Malta by the British.

Sea-banditry or piracy and smuggling were closely connected and were as endemic to the waters of the Middle East and North Africa as robbery was to the land. Just as pastoral nomadism lent itself easily to banditry, so the economic activities of coastal communities, fishing and sea-faring, might similarly slide, almost imperceptibly, into illegality, smuggling and sea-banditry. Mediterranean piracy was often on a small scale, the crews made up of ordinary fishermen or local seamen, their vessels small boats powered by oars,[77] the picture they presented far from the images of galleons armed with cannon familiar from the popular imagination of Caribbean piracy. In this sense they may also be seen as connected to peasant strategies of survival and resistance. Towns along the North African coast, for example, which had earlier played a role in the corsair economies, seem to have adapted to seaborne smuggling particularly easily.[78]

Sea-banditry or piracy and smuggling in the eastern Mediterranean also allow a glimpse of the smugglers and pirates themselves. To some extent, outlaw life offered an inherent challenge to existing hierarchies. The little that we know of the precise composition of Middle Eastern and North African bandit gangs or pirate crews seems to indicate the fluidity of social, religious and ethnic boundaries officially depicted as rigid and impermeable. This may hint at the irrelevance of these boundaries to those sharing outlaw status, or perhaps at a deliberate challenge to convention, or it may be evidence of an actual plebeian indifference to and disregard of such boundaries typical of lower-class life. Marinos Sariyannis has noted the remarkably mixed religious and ethnic character of urban criminal gangs in seventeenth-century Istanbul and the linguistically and religiously mixed pirate crews.[79] Although Andalusian exiles were a dominant force in Barbary corsairing, a single crew might include not only Spanish and Moroccan Muslims but also renegades and Christians, Greeks, Russians, French, Dutch and so on.[80] They were indeed motley crews. Piracy even appeared to offer opportunities for, or at least held out the hope of, rapid changes in individual fortune, even a kind of social mobility, an Ottoman pirate novel of the late seventeenth century, a rare surviving specimen of popular literature, telling the tale of a slave becoming a pirate commander.[81]

The case of North Africa also highlights particularly the connections between Christian and Muslim subalterns in the nexus of extra-legal seaborne activities. Malta, as a result of its earlier role as a hub of corsairing and piracy, had become by the nineteenth century the centre of Mediterranean smuggling, of slaves (after the abolition of the trade), weapons and gunpowder, tobacco and spirits, and the Maltese its principal practitioners.[82] Poor European migrants settled in the port cities, especially the experienced and extensively networked Maltese, played a key role in connecting Mediterranean suppliers of smuggled commodities with the North African interior, such smuggling again usually on a small, domestic scale with women closely involved in the hiding and selling of goods.[83]

What we know of premodern, and even modern, Middle Eastern land and sea bandits comes from two quite separate and contradictory categories of sources, on the one hand official reports, court records and the rarely independent and always elite press, on the other hand folk stories, poems and songs. The former invariably emphasize the anarchic violence of bandits and their threat to life and property, primarily of the rich, although peasant suffering is also sometimes mobilized. Folk stories and songs, on the other hand, conform very closely to their cultural counterparts elsewhere, making sense of the bandit phenomenon from the point of view of those at variance with the prevailing political, social and economic order, turning the bandit sometimes into a picaresque hero triumphing over the authorities against the odds, sometimes into an avenger of injustice.[84] Much attention has focused on trying to explain these contradictory narratives and to reconciling them, in other words to establishing the 'truth' about bandit activities. But it is perhaps more useful to regard them as symptomatic of fundamentally opposed worldviews, of those who prospered under the status quo, and those who did not. Rather than reconciling them, they might be decoded, to glimpse, not an accurate picture of what bandits did, but rather how the lower classes perceived them and, perhaps more importantly, how the lower classes perceived the authorities, the common enemies of themselves and the bandits.

To what extent, then, does Middle Eastern folk culture really allow us access to the subaltern psychological world? Despite the reinvention of bandits by Balkan nationalists and Turkish Marxists, it seems that much Middle Eastern popular bandit mythology has genuinely popular origins. The folk tales emerged and crystallized within an oral tradition. They were spread by professional story-tellers who were free to improvise, thus shaping their narratives in response to the demands of their audiences. More generally, popular attitudes towards authority and legitimacy, justice and resistance, are crucial to understanding the ways in which bandit narratives were constructed and incorporated into popular discourses. Folk stories often contained an element of rudimentary class consciousness, contrasting a worthless and stupid king with a poor man seeking justice and true happiness, concluding with the triumph of the latter.[85] Hints at subaltern subversions of elite notions of crime and criminality may be found in Ottoman folk stories in which crimes are frequent but any sort of disapproval rare.[86] Executed robbers might find admiration from the poor of Istanbul because of their 'manliness and gallantry', and there seems to have been some popular sympathy for prisoners and attacks on jails were common features of Istanbul revolts.[87]

Many of the admirable traits bestowed by folklore on the bandit-hero may be traced to a broader popular cultural consensus, reinforced by the glamour of the picaresque and local codes of honour and masculinity. This combination of attitudes may be seen very powerfully in an urban context in relation to the *qabadayat* of Ottoman cities, the Iranian *lutis*, and possibly also the Egyptian *futuwwat* or *baltagiya*.[88] These well-organized gangs of young men, illiterate and drawn from the urban poor were important features of pre-modern Middle Eastern cities.[89] Both their actual activities and attitudes towards them recall the social bandit story. Physical strength and courage, 'manliness', were vital to the gangmember, as was honour, and a reputation for being ready to defend it with violence, on his own behalf, that of his quarter, and sometimes of the vaguely defined oppressed in general.[90] A code of chivalry was important, and the protection of women and children emphasized. Attitudes towards these gangs were as varied as towards bandits. Elite descriptions stress their thievery, idleness and troublemaking, while their own self-image seems to have been largely accepted and perpetuated by the urban poor, from whose ranks they were drawn, although even here they retained their marginal, even sometimes deviant, status. Although often posing as popular leaders of their quarter, many gangs also had actual connections to local notables and especially to religious figures, for whom they would provide muscle in conflicts, with other urban quarters, hostile notables or the government.

Such gangs had no necessary political inclination or affiliation. *Lutis*, for example, were to be found on both sides during the Iranian constitutional revolution.[91] Although their plebeian origins and their self-proclaimed role as defenders of the poor might appear to make them candidates for the patronage of the Left, in fact during the twentieth century the links between the gangs and political tendencies of a more or less reactionary character became more overt, and the gaps between gang mythology and the actual roles they played became wider, the similarities with Anton Blok's mafia emerging more strongly. *Lutis* were key mobilizers of the crowd which provided support on the Tehran streets for the overthrow in 1953 of the nationalist prime minister Dr Muhammad Musaddiq, and even more recently the Egyptian *baltagiya* were identified as the prime instigators of the violence against anti-Mubarak protesters in Tahrir Square during the Egyptian uprising in 2011.

Such bandit biographies as have emerged in the Middle East and North Africa must then be read within the context of these preexisting scripts. One of the earliest and most famous bandit-heroes whose actual existence is more or less certain is the sixteenth-century Ottoman Koroglu. The Ottoman records make it difficult to distinguish his social banditry from his straightforward robbery, but it seems that he either actually did, or quickly attracted a reputation for, attacking officials singled out as oppressors of the poor.[92] Within a generation, Koroglu had become a favourite subject of storytelling, transformed from a coarse but amusing trickster into an avenger against tyranny. Commemorated in verse as 'the people's sword', he became a hero, reputedly calling on the peasants to take up arms against the sultan in the quest for justice.[93]

More recent history allows the contours of bandit figures, and even social bandits, to emerge somewhat more reliably.[94] The French colonial presence in North Africa, like foreign domination elsewhere, appears to have provided particularly fertile ground for the emergence of social bandit legends, the colonial authorities and the local populations having a mutual interest in the manufacture of bandit stories. While colonial or imperial authority labelled resistance as banditry, local opinion appropriated banditry as resistance.

A wave of banditry, or at least violence, swept the Algerian countryside following the 1871 uprising in Kabylia, a mountainous coastal region in the north of the country, and its suppression by the French. It flared up again in the 1880s to 1890s, producing the famous story of Muhammad Abdun.[95] Unjustly accused of murder and imprisoned on Devil's Island, Muhammad Abdun escaped and, after a series of extraordinary adventures, returned to exact vengeance. Whether the local population supported Abdun or merely feared him is unclear, nor can his robbery be easily distinguished from his rebelliousness, but his activities led to a spreading attitude of non-cooperation with the French authorities, especially a refusal to pay taxes or to accept office as French-appointed village headmen or to join the police. The French certainly believed themselves to be facing the beginnings of a revolt and responded accordingly.

A neghbouring region of Algeria produced the better-known 'bandit of honour' Messaoud Ben Zelmat, active in the Aurès beween 1917 and1921.[96] The story begins in 1915 when Ali Ben Zelmat, a shepherd, was denounced for theft and sentenced to prison, escaped, returned to kill the man who had denounced him and then took to the forest. He joined a group of army deserters and they established themselves in the mountains. In 1917, after government forces attacked the band, Ali was found dead. His brother, Messaoud, took command of the remnants of the band and vowed to avenge his brother, and he and his men carried out a series of robberies and murders, operations taking place within a context of serious local tension. The First World War, in which the Ottomans and French were on opposing sides, was unpopular, and conscription into the French army was especially hated and resisted, a situation which gave Messaoud Ben Zelmat's activities a sheen of political significance and genuine local support and even admiration. According to a report by a French gendarmerie officer, the bandits were able to rely on local people for everything they wanted, food, ammunition, shelter and information.[97] Eventually Messaoud Ben Zelmat's luck ran out and, betrayed by local shepherds, in 1921 he was killed by native Algerian soldiers.

Massaoud Ben Zelmat's reputation rests on two local sources, songs sung by local women, and the reminiscences of a rather marginal European who had befriended him, Jean-Baptiste Capeletti, this material shaped into a story of social banditry, although not national resistance, in an article by Jean Déjeux. Capeletti had spent most of his long life in the Aurès mountains, where he made a living as a miller and married a local Berber woman. In 1975, at the age of one hundred, Capeletti gave a description of his great friend, Messaoud Ben Zelmat, bestowing on him the title of a bandit of honour, whose main aim was to protect the 'little people' against the local notables who exploited the poor and weak, Capaletti confirming both Messaoud's popularity among his own people and the fear in which he was held by the army and especially by the notables.[98] Another important element in the creation of the Messaoud legend was the repertoire of songs composed about him and sung by local women. Using the imagery of love poetry, these songs celebrated Messaoud's bravery, chivalry, generosity, protection of the poor, and contempt for material possessions. Conforming closely to generic bandit narratives, the songs marvel at his miraculous powers and mourn his death through betrayal, using poetic conventions to incorporate Messaoud into widely shared folk traditions.[99]

Messaoud Ben Zelmat, however, remained a figure of only local legend, and was never incorporated into the genealogy of Algerian nationalism. Indeed Middle Eastern and North African Zapatas are rare. Iran, however, does provide one example of a bandit turned revolutionary who still occupies an important place in collective memories of the popular struggle for justice.[100] Sattar Khan was a one-time bandit and *luti* who became a renowned fighter in the constitutional revolution of early twentieth-century Iran. Sattar's reputation, still alive and fostered in the Islamic republic, is largely the result of the work of populist Iranian intellectuals who have glorified him and his activities, this perspective triumphing over that of elitist historians writing in the Pahlavi period who were have been much more sceptical, insisting on his being nothing more than a bandit.[101] Born in 1868, Sattar's youth included periods of imprisonment punctuated by both brigandage, in which trade he followed his elder brother who had been executed, and service in the local gendarmerie. Sympathetic biographers, however, subsequently provided him with a version of his early life more appropriate to a *luti* as a righteous, if violent, defender of the oppressed. The constitutional revolution which broke out in Iran in 1905, and especially the civil war of 1908 to 1909 between constitutionalists and supporters of the shah, which centred on Sattar's home, the northern city of Tabriz, gave him the opportunity to emerge as a national figure and he became, and was recognized internationally as, a leading fighter of the constitutionalist forces. His is one of the earliest Middle Eastern examples of mythologizing through photography, images of him as the archetypal bandit-hero, draped in bandoliers, disseminated widely through the press and as postcards. Probably understanding little of the national political objectives of the constitutional movement, and possibly motivated by a desire for revenge against the authorities who had executed his brother, Sattar's new role was predicated on his *luti* background. His familiarity with weapons, his need to maintain his reputation for courage and manliness and his status as defender of his quarter, made him a natural militia leader and he soon came to be credited by local opinion with the possession of magical powers, the protection of a saint and invulnerability to bullets.[102] Perhaps more Pancho Villa than Zapata, Sattar's later political failures and personal weaknesses, much in evidence after the constitutionalist victory, did nothing to tarnish his reputation, rather his humble origins, his illiteracy, his reputation for piety (deserved or not) and as a defender of the poor, made him an icon for the revolutionary movement of the 1970s.[103]

The Middle East and North Africa has experienced every type of banditry imaginable. It has seen bandit-kings and warlords presiding over extensive raiding networks, entire communities, Turkish and Iranian nomads, desert beduin, integrating banditry and smuggling as essential elements into their precarious local economies, 'everyday' banditry as a last resort of pauperized peasants and pastoralists in the face of economic catastrophe and social marginalization, banditry as a form of rural resistance and even, occasionally, bandits as revolutionaries. Banditry on land and sea has occupied a key place in elite discourses and has also spawned a vast repertoire of popular iconography, these contrasting and entirely irreconcilable interpretations revealing an often submerged but perennial ideological war between state and subaltern. If Robin Hood has been hard to find on the ground, the avenger has exercised an extraordinary power over the popular imagination.

A widespread scepticism about the capacity of Middle Eastern peasantries for collective action, an inclination to interpret peasant violence as tribal or religious rather than economically motivated and class-based, a lack of interest in peasant resistance, an outdated and unsophisticated methodological approach which privileges elite textual sources and takes little or no account of advances in oral history and memory studies, have combined to produce an emphasis in Middle Eastern scholarship on the relationship between bandits and the worlds of power. A different approach, however, provides different answers. In particular, close attention to the deconstruction of the language of existing elite sources, the semiotics of banditry, the adoption of a microhistorical perspective, and the incorporation of perspectives derived from non-elite sources, can tease out subaltern stories. In particular, the perspectives discernible within folk culture might be not accepted uncritically but treated with equal seriousness to those found within state archives. Stories about bandits may be myths, but whose myths are they? Ballads and poems about Greek or Bulgarian haiduks may have been appropriated by local nationalist elites, but they were originally genuinely popular creations, produced by the rural communities themselves who clung to them. The songs about the Algerian 'bandit d'honneur', Messaoud Ben

Zelmat, were sung by local women before they were picked up by French intellectuals, while the seventeenth-century Anatolian bandit Koroglu achieved his fame across the Turkish and Persian-speaking worlds by oral repetition and popular shaping of the legends surrounding him.

Banditry has constantly reinvented itself in response to state policies and especially to modernization. In the classical sense it did decline across the Middle East and North Africa in the decades after the Second World War, as the peasantry itself shrank rapidly or found new, if muted, representation in radical regimes with programmes of land reform. Strong states, with powerful armies and gendarmeries and modern infrastructure, reduced the scope for rural crime while the 'mobile margin' of peasant society,[104] disaffected young men, found opportunities in education and expanding economies and massive migration to the cities and abroad. Yet smuggling became more profitable than ever, and urban crime offered new opportunities, especially in the drug trade.[105] Since the invasion of Iraq in 2003, banditry has indeed, together with its partners, smuggling and piracy, recently experienced a massive resurgence in the ungoverned spaces, on land and sea, created by the collapsing states of the modern Middle East and North Africa. In many of the countries of the region, militias now occupy the ambiguous space once filled by bandits. Just as demobilized Ottoman soldiers of the seventeenth century joined bandit gangs, so Iraqi troops, suddenly turned out after the US invasion of 2003, provided much of the personnel for the mushrooming militias. The meta-language of terrorism now obscures a complex reality, as did once a similar meta-language of banditry. Vast fortunes are being made smuggling the same commodities as in the nineteenth century: cigarettes and drugs across the Sahara to North Africa and then into Europe, people across the Mediterranean and weapons everywhere. Piracy is now a multi-million-dollar industry in the seas off the Horn of Africa, causing the cost of maritime insurance to rocket and, as in the seventeenth and eighteenth centuries so once again, people captured for ransom are as valuable as cargoes. Yet, in addition to the ruthless egoism of the people-smugglers of the Mediterranean, often refugees themselves, the contemporary Middle East also suggests instances of such activities as representative of political protest and resistance, the smugglers of the Gaza tunnels a striking example. Banditry, as economic opportunity, survival, and perhaps occasionally rebellion, is once again endemic across the region.

Acknowledgements

The author is grateful to Roshan Cultural Heritage Institute and its president, Dr Elahé Omidyar Mir-Djalali, for funding the fellowship which enabled her to work on this article.

Rural Banditry in Colonial Algeria (1871–1914)*

Antonin Plarier

Banditry in Algeria was an object of fear and fascination among the French colonial population and the subject of a considerable volume of written commentaries. The colonial authorities sought to impress the significance of the problem upon the public. In 1892 the General Council of Algiers confidently estimated the number of bandits roaming the country at 1,300.[1] Meanwhile, newspapers and the administration relayed the message, already circulating as a rumour, that 900 Algerians sentenced to forced labour in French Guiana had escaped and returned to Algeria.[2] The bandits' possible transformation into a menacing army was the stuff of nightmares for the European colonists. This fear led them to exaggerate the severity of the phenomenon of banditry.[3] The figures put forward by the General Council of Algiers may have been fanciful, yet Arezky el Bashir's band of thirty-five individuals, which enjoyed a large support base in the rural regions, was not to be underestimated.[4]

The social phenomenon of banditry was present throughout Algeria's colonial history. Scholars of the Maghreb and the Middle East have used and debated the theoretical model of the social bandit derived originally from the work of Eric Hobsbawm.[5] Historian Jean Déjeux has readily applied the concept of social banditry to Algeria,[6] whereas David Hart has criticized its use, arguing that it relies too heavily on the imagery of bandits found in folklore.[7] Alain Mahé, using the term 'bandits of honor', argues that bandits endorsed the 'cardinal values of virility and honor' and were therefore early champions of the values defended by the National Liberation Army.[8] He thus endorses Mahfoud Kaddache's thesis that bandits of honour were Algeria's first 'patriots'.[9] His thesis subsuming the history of colonial social conflict within a narrative of the development of the national movement is, however, potentially reductive and demands interrogation.[10] This chapter aims to shed new light on the phenomenon of banditry in rural societies transformed by colonization.

The colonial conquest of Algeria in 1830 triggered a vast movement of expropriation that eventually affected the whole country. From 1830 to 1870, hundreds of thousands of hectares of land were transferred from their Algerian owners to the hands of the

* I wish to thank Joseph La Hausse de Lalouvière (Harvard University) for his careful reading and constructive criticism.

settlers, colonial companies or the state. The Europeans appropriated land through various means, including sequestration, the ordinances of 1844 and 1846, and the *senatus-consulte* of 1863.[11] This process reached its peak in 1871 when the colonial administration oversaw a massive sequestration in response to an insurrection..[12]

The multifaceted process of dispossession offers a gateway to understanding banditry. The term 'banditry' needs to be carefully defined, however, since the colonial administration used it not only to describe but also to denigrate. Not relying on the colonial authorities' definition, this chapter returns to Hobsbawm's original concept of the bandit as a member of 'a group that uses violence and practices armed robbery', one who acts outside the law and is pursued by its enforcers.[13] The bandit's resilience depends on their connection to the rural environment from which they emerged.

The conditions for the emergence of banditry

The insurrection of 1871 led by El Moqrani spread across a third of Algeria's territory.[14] The suppression of this movement prompted the adoption of a broad policy of economic sanctions. The authorities imposed collective fines on the insurgents and carried out individual and collective sequestrations of the insurgents' land. Some of the land sequestrated collectively could be bought back by its owners at one-fifth of its value.[15] However, the authorities prevented the repurchase of lands deemed important for colonization. Former owners were permitted to occupy those lands until the colonial administration had sufficient means to allocate them to settlers, usually within the framework of settlement villages. These sequestrations restarted the official process of settlement which turned over 643,546 hectares of land to settlement villages.[16] More than a third of this land (36.9 per cent, 234,375 hectares) came from the sequestrations of 1871.[17] The act of sequestration preceded, often by several years, the eventual foreclosure on the properties and eviction of their original owners. The settlement village of Yakouren in Kabylia was only opened in 1888, several years after the creation of the neighbouring villages of Fréha and Mekla and seventeen years after the sequestration was announced. The Yakouren settlement was based on 408 hectares of seized land plus a nearby cork oak forest that was incorporated into the colonial *domaine*, as explained below. All of the land allocated to this village came from the sequestration of 1871. The state's land grab policy contributed to the rise of banditry, and it is striking how much the two processes went hand in hand. Arezky el Bachir's band appears to have sprung up when the settlement process was at its most intensive – at the time when Yakouren was created – and grew in numbers until the beginning of 1894, when the majority of its members were either eliminated or arrested during a major military campaign.[18]

Land dispossession was accompanied by increasing restrictions on customary rights. As in the case of land, a purely legalistic approach is not sufficient to fully appreciate the extent of the problem. For example, forests were an integral part of the rural economy as they provided the rural population with a significant share of the resources needed for breeding livestock, producing handicrafts, cooking and construction.[19] Colonization led to disputes over the use of forests because the colonial authorities, interpreting the so-called 'Muslim' law, treated the forests as vacant land which under the regency of Algiers had belonged to the bey. The statute of 16 June 1851 enshrined this approach in law.[20] The state then used the designation of vacant land to claim ownership of the forests and impose restrictions on or abolish the preexisting rights of use. However, this law remained inoperative until the forests were delimitated and a forest authority created. The creation of a forest administration extensive enough to modify the structures of rural life was a relatively slow, faltering process, occasionally subject to sudden progress. The Forestry Service, established in 1838, still had only thirty-four members in 1843.[21] It was pioneering in the sense that its members were committed to surveying Algeria's forest resources and to classifying them. The delimitation of these resources, a condition for the state's real ownership and hence intervention, did not begin before the 1850s. This enormous task – the total forest area was estimated at more than 2 million hectares – took several decades. By 1870, 1,750,000 hectares of forest were delineated and a further 550,000 hectares by 1880. By 1888 the demarcated forest area encompassed 3,247,692 hectares but more than 1 million hectares had not yet been delimited and therefore belonged to the state only in theory, as asserted by the law of 1851.[22]

This progress in forest delimitation after 1871 corresponds to what André Nouschi calls the 'triumph of the strongest men',[23] a period in Algerian history when the forest management and surveillance apparatus grew noticeably stronger. From 1872 to 1886, the number of officers increased from 30 to 80, the number of agents from 171 to 373, and the number of native guards from 96 to 200. The overall number of forestry personnel increased by 119 per cent over fourteen years. The increase was most marked in areas populated by cork oaks. In 1891, 275 forest rangers guarded 275,000 hectares of cork oak forests – one for every 1,000 hectares – whereas only 740 guarded the remaining 1,479,000 hectares – one for every 2,000 hectares.[24]The colonial state prioritized the protection of the forests designated for colonization and invested not only in personnel but also infrastructure in doing so. More forest guard stations were constructed in the cork oak areas than elsewhere. With more stations, the guards were better placed to get to the scene of an incident quickly, so the service was more efficient overall. The construction of forest guard stations in the areas under the Forestry Service jurisdiction was therefore one of the key stages in the Service's evolution.

This development of the forestry system fostered rural discontent and banditry. Disputes over grazing, a central component of customary rights in forest areas, were a key stimulus for rural discontent. Under the regency of Algiers, the Beylik theoretically owned the forests but in practice did not restrict their use, with the minor exception of those needed for the naval industry.[25] The colonial administration, along with new landowners and concessionaires, promoted a new approach which turned those lands into state, communal or private property. Customary rights were not, however, systematically suppressed. The colonial authorities could not simply abolish them, neither in law nor in practice. Successive laws reaffirmed and increasingly restricted the ability of the rural population to maintain and enforce their customary rights vis-à-vis the new landowners. This legislative process reached its height with the Forestry Law of 9 December 1885, in which article 1 affirmed the entitlement of forest owners to dispense with the existing rights of use. This law was the handiwork of the forestry lobby, which had the legislators' ear. The law put in place an industrial and commercial policy designed to make forest resources more profitable. 'Without the suspension of user rights and suppression of (cultivated) enclaves there can be no industrial exploitation of the forests,'[26] affirmed M. Étienne, a parliamentarian in Algeria and an owner of a great fortune in France. The forestry administration enforced these changes. The resulting restrictions on or suppression of customary rights were the cause of considerable conflict.

The number of crimes reported by the forest department increased sharply from 7,883 in 1881[27] to 21,250 in 1902.[28] The increase did not, however, accurately reflect the extent of criminality since, according to the general government, the forest department recorded only 10 per cent of offenses.[29] The nature of the recorded infractions did not change much during those two decades. Two-thirds of the reports concerned illegal grazing, just over 10 per cent illicit clearing of crops or forest and the remainder tree felling. The fines for these offences were a significant source of profit for the forest owners (including individual proprietors).[30] Conversely, they were a real burden for the rural populations living in or near the contested forests. 'It is in this way that the forestry administration keeps 800,000 natives down,' said the indignant senator Jules Ferry, 'making them kneel and tremble before it, and extracting from their poverty a heavy annual tribute which in 1884 amounted to 1,265,312 francs of financial penalties, fines, damages and expenses; in 1885, 1,321,307 francs; in 1888, 1,119,652 francs; in 1890, 1 658 958 Fr.'[31]

In this context, certain forest areas became the theatre of a war of attrition,[32] or, in E. P. Thompson's term, a 'forest war'.[33] Reports by forest agents and conservators complained about it repeatedly. For instance, in a note to the Governor General, the Directorate of Agriculture and Forestry referred to:

> Devastation in the forests of the Azazga chiefdom. Grave and constant depredations, which the forestry service is powerless to repress. Some indigenous tribes are in a latent rebellion against the authorities. Those cutting down trees illegally in the State forests escape prosecution thanks to the complicity of the tribe chief who opposes both the administrative authorities and the forest department by inertia or by concealing the identity of the perpetrators.[34]

However, this conflict was not present on all of Algeria's territory, as it depended on the relations between the local population and the forest department in any given administrative district. From this point of view, the pace and pattern of the department's growth based on the areas' estimated wealth were decisive. In some parts of the Aures, forest rangers only established themselves from 1905 onwards and even then imperfectly and precariously.[35]

These conflicts were certainly connected with banditry, although the two phenomena were distinct and had different dynamics. A particularly interesting case is that of Ahmed Chabbi from the Beni Salah tribe, who was convicted of murdering a *garde-champêtre*[36] guarding Amédée Rebattu's cork oak concession. The Beni Salah tribe, based in the east of Algeria in the Seybouse valley, suffered various forms of dispossession after the French conquest. Sequestration was imposed in 1852 following a revolt[37] and again in 1871[38] and 1877[39] as a result of forest fires deemed to be of criminal origin. Some the state's cork oak forests were allocated to very wealthy people as concessions.[40] Amédée Rebattu managed a concession of 2,258 hectares. He hired a garde-champêtre and a native guard. In 1876 Ahmed Chabbi murdered the *garde-champêtre*. Even without knowing the precise circumstances of this murder, one can piece together a plausible picture from the facts gleaned from the archives. Concessionaires and forest owners were well organized in defending their interests and complained constantly about the preservation of customary rights and certain agricultural enclaves within their land, which they regarded as an unbearable constraint on their enjoyment of the property. Customary rights were the cause of conflict on the Beni Salah territory too after the sénatus-consulte was implemented in 1869.[41] Branded as 'indigénophile' by its detractors, the sénatus-consulte constituted a stage in the delimitation and formalization of the property of the tribes.[42] The question of customary rights, however, reappeared periodically through the actions of individual forest rangers. In the Souk Ahras province, just south of Beni Salah, a ranger connected to the concessionaire Lambert was accused of multiplying the number of reports for pasture. These reports reached an extravagant total of 88,555 francs in the space of a few months of verbalization.[43] There is no evidence that similar extravagance occurred on the property managed by Amédée Rebattu but, nevertheless, his complaints to the general government, in which he defended the need to expropriate the owners of enclaves, indicated that a conflict had taken place. Ahmed Chabbi murdered the *garde-champêtre* most likely because of this conflict. After his arrest, Chabbi managed to escape[44] and he became a 'fearsome bandit' in the eyes of the French authorities.[45]

In the case of the Arezky's band, the establishment of the settlement village followed the construction of a forest ranger station for a ranger and an indigenous guard in an adjacent *gourbi*.[46] This served to strengthen law enforcement, particularly with regard to the prohibition of charcoal manufacture. To produce charcoal, people collected wood from the forests and burned it under a layer of soil to starve it of oxygen. This became a commercial activity, and the colonial authorities sought to tax it by issuing manufacture licences. The colonists involved in this trade often sought increased state surveillance to enforce the prohibition. Illicit charcoal production became the subject of regular conflicts and occasional police reports (when the perpetrators were identifiable). Hadj Ali, one of the bandits close to Arezky, was wanted for the murder of a family of Italian charcoal makers in the Yakouren forest. Furthermore, with his band he ransomed 'especially forest rangers, who fear[ed] him very much'.[47] Hadj Ali's murder of the Italian charcoal makers can be interpreted as related to the conflict over customary rights in forests.

The process of colonization or, more precisely, of dispossession and privatization of the commons, was an essential condition for the emergence of banditry. The poet Si Mohand ou M'hand illustrates it with these verses:

'The rules are now perverted,
It is thus established
The vile men have taken the upper hand.

All well-born men have taken to the forest
Braving the torments of adversity.'[48]

Banditry: A phenomenon of protest at the heart of rural society

Banditry cannot be understood outside the social environment that gives rise to it and that accommodates it. The social environment is fundamental to the bandit's existence, and their resilience depends on understanding this fact. One should thus read banditry not as a marginal phenomenon[49] but as one that emerged at the heart of rural societies. In this way, Eric Hobsbawm's notion of a 'social bandit' takes on full significance.

The administrative authorities in charge of keeping bandits in Algeria under surveillance and repressing them considered this anchoring the main danger. They believed the removal of this anchoring would put an end to banditry. Bouguerra ben Belkacem, the leader of a bandit group operating in the Philippeville region from 1875 to 1878, was accused of thirteen murders and multiple thefts. At the trial, his judges claimed he was free to carry out these acts because during his four years as band leader there were no 'voices to denounce him'.[50] Similarly, the sub-prefect of Tizi-Ouzou considered Arezky el Bashir's band to be practically untouchable due to the support it had among the population, including among the Europeans 'forming pacts' with the band, 'by spirit of opposition'[51] to the administration. These conflicts were fought over the 'monopoly on the legitimate use of physical force'[52] by the competing authorities. The loose character of the colonial administrative network as well as its lack of political hegemony left a vacuum filled by bandits, who presented themselves as a rival political power. Faced with a colonial authority that was certainly powerful but distant from their daily life in the countryside, European settlers sometimes reached an agreement with bandits, whose authority was more immediate and visible. Bouzian el Kalaï, the famous bandit of the Oranais in the 1870s, counted among his supporters at least one European, Jean-Baptiste Graillat, who was accused of 'having furnished weapons, ammunition, instruments of crime, housing, a place of retreat, and a meeting place to an organized criminal association against persons and property'.[53] Graillat's situation was representative of a section of the colonists. Tucked away on an isolated farm that he struggled to make prosperous, his relations with the local Algerians were out of reach of the central authorities' prying eyes. The transcript of his defence during his trial in 1876 clearly establishes the existence of relations between the colonists and the bandits. The latter visited Graillat at his home several times. Reports differed, however, as to the nature of their exchanges. Graillat denied that he sold arms to the bandits. By contrast, the testimony of Bouzian, of Bouzian's companion Si Kaddour and of Graillat's servant Antonin Macias affirmed that Graillat had sold arms. Even more compromisingly, the *brigadier de gendarmerie* Théry Charlemagne accused him of having knowingly given false information on at least two occasions. The transcript of the trial contains no evidence in favour of the accused. The close relations between bandits and colonial settlers were possible because the main seats of the colonial authorities were so far removed from where the settlers lived. The *gendarmerie* was several hours' ride from Graillat's home and his nearest European neighbour was five kilometres away. It seems likely that good relations were in the best interests of both the bandits and the settlers. The ammunition purchased by Bouzian and his companions was overpriced, which was understandable considering the relative precariousness of Graillat's situation.[54] This type of relationship outside the framework of the 'colonizer' and the 'colonized' occurred regularly during the period when the three most famous bands of Algeria's colonial period were active. This contributes to making the phenomenon of banditry in a colonial situation more complex than it first appears.

Bandits adopted certain practical methods that traditionally belonged to a legitimately if not legally constituted political authority. For instance, they collected taxes from the local population: 'the bandits demanded money from all the people who properly served the administration and who would not submit to them'.[55] Arezky was even accused of 'levying fees on market routes'.[56] Bouzian el Kalaï devised his own particular form of taxation by stealing directly from the *caïd* (a village chief nominated by the colonial administrator) and the *douar* tax collector Ouled Saïd. The *caïd* was robbed on his way to Mascara (the district capital), while he was transporting the taxes of his constituents.[57] Besides capturing the revenues collected by the legally constituted authority, the bandits also sought to assert their charismatic authority. They sometimes organized large festivals on religious occasions. These expensive festivals, where guests often numbered in their hundreds, were an opportunity to demonstrate the bandits' gratitude to their social environment but also to emphasize the people's obligations and loyalty to them. For example, Arezky el Bashir organized a *diffa* (feast) to celebrate his son's circumcision.[58] Mohammed Saïd ou Abdoun too organized a *diffa* which one thousand guests attended. Their ability to organize such events without the knowledge – or at least without the interference – of the authorities reveals how bandits were anchored in and respected by the local community. The bandits' centrality in social life is also attested by the fact that people continued to take care of their land and cattle even when they were away from the village. In this way, the property belonging to Abdoun, who was at one time a companion of Arezky el Bashir, was 'managed and administered by relatives'.[59] The shared management of their land and livestock enabled these men to generate the income needed to procure services. The nicknames that journalists or administrators gave Arezky, such as 'the king of the forest'[60] or 'the chief of the Sebaou'[61] were not simply expressions of an Orientalist imagination but also an acknowledgment of the political reality.

This political power expressed itself by the use of violence. An analysis of its targets allows us to interpret some of the bandits' motivations[62]:

The data in Figure 6.1 are an imperfect reflection of the bands' activities. Thefts from rural Algerians are under-represented because they were less likely to result in conviction. The first council of war of the Oran division did not take into account the innumerable 'rapine acts committed daily to support the existence [that the band of Homati] led'.[63] Despite being under-represented in the official figures, ordinary Algerians were still the bandits' most frequent target. These figures reveal the complexity of the banditry phenomenon. The wealth of the Algerian victims was regularly cited as the crime motive, revealing the socio-economic hierarchy within the colonized society. European victims were less numerous but still significant – 17 per cent of all convictions. Crimes against Europeans were often perpetrated by well-established bands with several months or years of experience, who were consequently

Crimes repartition of banditry

Crimes against authorities 15%

Robberies against merchants 9%

Crimes against informers 15%

Robberies against rural Europeans 24%

Robberies against rural Europeans 37%

- Robberies against merchants
- Robberies against rural Europeans
- Robberies against rural Europeans
- Crimes against informers
- Crimes against authorities

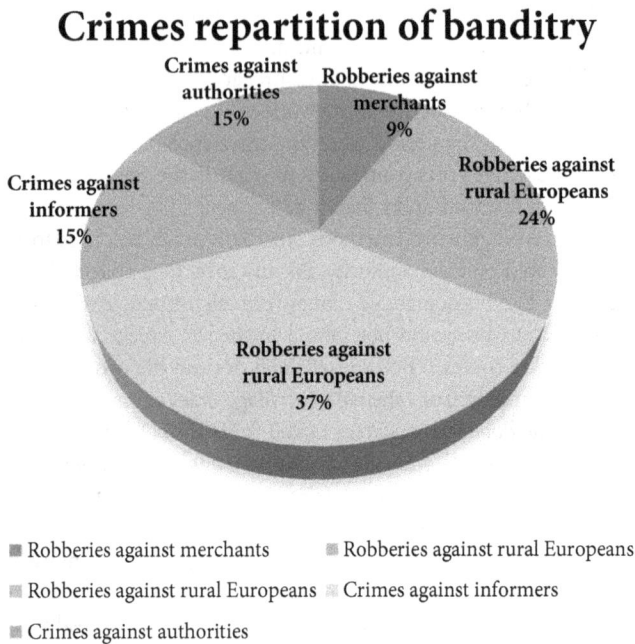

Figure 6.1 Targets of violent crime in banditry-related convictions (Algeria, 1871–1914)

more confident in their actions. However, some of the better-known bands, such as Arezky el Bashir's band, managed to consistently avoid this kind of confrontation. Bashir only targeted the Algerian representatives of the colonial authorities when seeking vindication. Attacks on merchants, who were often portrayed as Kabyle or Jewish, made up 10 per cent of the banditry-related crimes that resulted in conviction. The bandits thus understood and used social stratification to get rich quickly. The sums extorted from merchants on market routes were large relative to rural people's other sources of income. The evidence suggests that bandits worked almost exclusively as labourers, farmers or charcoal-burners. The term 'farmer' refers to peasants managing their own land. The farmers' standard of living is difficult to quantify, but labourers and charcoal-burners were undoubtedly poorly paid. A labourer earned on average 1 to 1.50 francs per day. In the case of the Beni Salah band, convicted in 1883 by the Assize Court of Bone, three of their robberies had reportedly yielded 1,030 francs, 725 francs and 5,000 francs.[64] These were extraordinary sums compared to the labourers' daily income. Finally, the specific dynamics of banditry help explain the last two groups targeted by bandits. The first consists of members of the colonial administration in charge of gathering intelligence on bandits or actively suppressing them. These were the Algerian agents of the colonial administration (*amins, spahis*). Occasionally, however, a European gendarme or forest ranger was found among the targets. The second group comprised Algerians who informed on the bandits, who account for 15 per cent of the convictions handed down by the assize courts or councils of war. The bandits sought to incite fear in those who might be tempted to give information to the authorities.

Theatricality was part of the political dimension of the bandits' violent acts. Bouzian el Kalaï first became a bandit when he refused to pay his taxes, the main manifestation of state authority. The caïd who sought to impose the tax upon him was slapped and then ridiculed. The bandits then completed the caïd's humiliation by stripping him and leaving him naked some distance away from his douar.[65] The purpose was to undermine his authority and manliness by means of symbolic violence, a strategy that bandits used frequently. Representatives of the authorities would also often fall victim to these measures, as in the case of a forest ranger abducted and 'put in a state of complete nudity'.[66] Showing the vulnerability of official authority in this way helped establish the authority of the bandits in counterpoint. Theatricality was also a feature of the great diffas the bandits organized. At one of them, in a symbolic battle, 'the guests made tricks about the French authorities'. The liveliest member of the band snuck out past their comrades, then came back in, shouting: 'The administrator! The gendarmes! And sat back to their place having provoked peals of laughter and *lazzi* from the few hundred natives who surrounded them'.[67] This spectacle of the oppressed, where statements usually kept private erupted into the public sphere, was deeply disturbing to the colonial authorities, who never succeeded in eradicating this kind of behaviour.[68]

Eradicating banditry: The limits of the colonial state

In addition to the scenes already described, the very existence of bandits as a rival political power served to deride the colonial authorities. Administrators' reports constantly expressed an association between this rival authority and the apprehension of an imminent revolt. Camille Sabatier, who successively served as a judge in Blida, an administrator of a *commune mixte* in Kabylie, then an MP for Oran and finally a commissioner of the general government on prison matters,[69] clearly expressed this opinion:

> It is among the gangs of thieves and criminals that they recruited the most vigorous agents of the insurrections; and it is also with the resurgence of crimes and offenses against individuals that the beginnings of an insurrectionary period can be detected.[70]

Public speeches on 'insecurity' thus not only include a sharp condemnation of attacks on property[71] but also a politicized fear that the situation would degenerate into insurrection. The colonial authorities sought to crush banditry precisely because they recognized it was the earliest stage in the evolution of an insurrection. But they faced a dilemma: how could the colonial state exert repressive force without experiencing a failure that would in fact reveal its weaknesses? Despite their best efforts, the colonial authorities regularly failed to crush banditry. The unequal balance of power frequently compelled bandits to evade the colonial authorities rather than seek open confrontation with a larger and better-equipped force. When seeking to evade the gendarme patrols, the spahis or the army, bandits made use of their own intelligence network. The colonial officials lacked access to this subaltern information network and complained constantly that they were thwarted in their efforts to intervene. 'The natives do not seem to be loyal to us, and the information I receive does not seem to me sufficiently clear to enable us to act effectively,'[72] reported the administrator of the commune mixte of Azazga before the beginning of a military campaign to eradicate banditry in Kabylia. The French colonial officers did not fully trust their own indigenous agents. Compulsory transfers, revocations or even trials for cooperation with bandits happened regularly. Following the assault on two gendarmes in the Blida area in 1906, the city police chief reported that he was 'unable to obtain information, including from the indigenous personnel'.[73] In this way bandits managed to avoid capture and punishment, sometimes for many years. In the defined corpus, it took in average two years and eight months to suppress a bandit – measured from the time of his first infraction to his effective arrest – but bandits were at large from anywhere between a few days and nine years.

The colonial authorities took two distinct but complementary tactics in liquidating bandit bands. First, they sought to isolate the bandits socially. There were special surveillance procedures for targeting the milieu presumed to be supporting bandits. Through these non-judicial procedures, the administrator of a *commune mixte* could request the resettlement of these people to a new, distant place of residence.[74] The colonial administration used this procedure consistently in banditry cases. The administrator of the commune mixte of Zerizer used this weapon in 1881 in order to eradicate the bandits who sowed 'terror in this country'.[75] He deported seventy-one people suspected of supporting a band, only four of whom were convicted of banditry by the Assize Court in Bone. The number of bandits among the deportees gives an indication of how well embedded they were in society. The deportees experienced a sad and constrained exile as well as terrible poverty and few means of escaping from it. Such conditions were often fatal; at least sixteen of the seventy-one people deported by the Zerizer official did not survive their deportation.[76] While trying to deprive the bandits of support and access to intelligence, the colonial administration also sought to obtain information. They routinely offered bounties for the denunciation or capture of bandits, with the size of the reward increasing gradually. The colonial authorities took advantage of the population's general poverty to lure in informants. In the 1870s, 1,000 francs were promised to 'the native or the detachment'[77] who will succeed in capturing the bandit Bouziane El Kalaï. The bounties were relatively effective so long as the informants remained protected, but the amounts grew steadily over time precisely because the informants' safety could not be guaranteed.[78]

In addition to social isolation, military intervention was the second major tool of repression. Military campaigns were rare but revealed the colonial administration's political fear of banditry. Of the nineteen bands mentioned above, four were liquidated through military intervention. In two cases it took multiple campaigns for the authorities to achieve their objectives. The first military campaign against the Arezky band failed partly because of its lack of understanding of the social environment as well as geographical conditions. The state only resorted to military campaigns in cases when the civil authorities were unable to eradicate a given band. Nonetheless, social isolation was still a necessary first step to any successful military intervention. The colonial military force was much greater than that of any bandit group. The military manoeuvers involved sealing off a territory and then scouring it thoroughly. Stations were established at intersections and passes and travel routes were restricted. Between these stations, patrols or mobile groups coordinated with each other to prevent bandits from moving between territories. These operations employed military personnel as well as the civilian population forced to serve under the supervision of the administrator or sub-prefect in charge. In November 1893, 310 men were mobilized in the military campaign in Kabylie, half of them *tirailleurs*. The authorities preferred to deploy Senegalese riflemen recruited in French West Africa, relying on their reputation for violence and cruelty in order to incite fear among the rural population.[79]

The troops lived off the local population. The sub-prefect of Tizi Ouzou defended this approach as follows:

> Although I am in principle an enemy of collective responsibility, since it is undeniable that the natives, whether through fear or for any other reason, give their support to the bandits, the troops employed in the repression of banditry might live off the *douars* during the occupation, with the amounts to be requisitioned to be determined in advance.[80]

It was therefore also a way of making rural people pay for the support they have given to the bandits. Feeding a military unit of several dozen men (several hundred were distributed among a number of *douars*) was a considerable economic burden for the local population. The use of the term 'collective responsibility' by the sub-prefect of Tizi-Ouzou was not innocent. It echoed the colonial debates of the time and the prevailing opinion that colonized people should not benefit from the principle of individuality of punishment. Although during other campaigns the troops were supposed to cover their own costs, the existence of written complaints by rural people as well as the authorities' repeated insistence on the rule indicates that the army often did not follow it in practice. In addition to imposing a financial burden, the colonial administration pursued a policy of terror towards the rural population during these military campaigns. Complaints from the rural population testify to the humiliations and violence they suffered. Complaints relating to several incidents were preserved in the archives despite the many obstacles to their redress. In a 1904 case of brigandage that led to investigations in the Hessounat *douar*, the indigenous deputy complained to the Justice Minister about the violence he had suffered and his wives' humiliation at being made to strip naked while the security forces searched their house.[81] The purpose of the campaigns was not only to defeat the bandits but also to impose political control over the local population in the never-ending battles between the authorities and the bandits over legitimacy. These campaigns, coupled with the social isolation of bandits, ultimately succeeded in breaking up the bands they targeted. Nevertheless, the phenomenon of banditry reappeared regularly in different regions of Algeria, even experiencing something of a revival during the First World War.[82]

Conclusion

The first salvo of critiques against Hobsbawm focused on his use of oral or literary sources to document the history of banditry and not the history of its representations. This critique is now generally accepted, including by the pioneer historian himself.[83] Does this mean that the notion of social banditry is no longer meaningful? The romantic view of banditry must be treated sceptically or interpreted as a historical representation in itself. Yet social banditry remains a relevant concept when understood as a phenomenon that was not marginal but central to the societies in which it emerged. To shed light on the reasons behind the emergence of banditry, attention should be paid to large-scale social transformations within rural societies. Understanding dispossession on a global as well as local scale is central to shedding light on the appearance, spread and life cycle of banditry. Dispossession was part of the reason why bandits received support in their social environment. Other factors – including family ties, relationships between or within tribes, the values of the so-called 'traditional societies' – were also relevant but probably less so. The colonial state nevertheless remained outside the bounds of these relations and thus struggled to understand the phenomenon of banditry and bring it under control. Fearful of potential risks to its authority, the colonial administration tended to overestimate the numerical scale, if not the political significance, of banditry. There were two main reasons behind the authorities' exaggeration of the problem. First, the prospect of an imminent insurrection was a source of constant preoccupation for the colonial administration. Second, the exaggeration of the phenomenon served to legitimize the expansion of law enforcement mechanisms and weld colonial public opinion around the government by stirring up fears of the 'native bandit'. The latter function of state responses to banditry should not be underestimated as case studies on Algerian banditry tend to show a complex phenomenon regularly transgressing the imported categories of the 'colonized' and the 'colonizers'. In any case, the colonial state's different responses to banditry stemmed from the basic aim of annihilating this form of resistance to the state authority. Ironically, the history of the colonial administration's struggle with banditry reveals important limits of its power.

A State of 'Tribal Lawlessness'? Rural and Urban Crime in Fars Province (*c.* 1910–15)

Mattin Biglari

A Qashqai said to me … that in modern Persia the rifle is a sceptre and that every rifleman is a Shah

Arnold Wilson.[1]

As has now been well established, Iran's modernizing elites in the late nineteenth and twentieth centuries saw overcoming the country's supposed 'tribal problem' as crucial for national salvation.[2] Central to the 'myth of the saviour' built around the person of Reza Shah was his ability to suppress the tribes after a period of so-called 'disintegration' between 1911 and 1921, following the Constitutional Revolution.[3] This was unquestionably partly due to the power possessed by the large tribal confederations that had the potential to undermine central authority. But it was also because on a more local level these pastoral nomadic groups seemed to represent the absence of authority, especially by virtue of their association with banditry on the country's main trade routes.[4] By their very nature, tribes were seen as a 'dangerous class' on the margins of society, culturally imbued with criminality.[5] Indeed, such perceptions shared many similarities with the concept of a 'criminal tribe' existing elsewhere, which assumed tribespeople were habitually or even hereditarily inclined to a life of crime.[6]

Such a view has been reproduced in historiography, meaning banditry in modern Iran has often been explained away with culturally essentialist references to a supposedly traditional tribal culture of raiding, leaving little or no room for other contributing factors. For example, Mansoureh Ettehadieh, in her study of criminality in the late Qajar period, asserts:

> We see that most of the robbery and looting was done by tribes, which was probably as much a way of life as due to economic circumstances. The worst affected areas were not necessarily those suffering most from economic regression.[7]

Granted, there had been a long-established culture of raiding amongst the tribes in Iran, as there had been across most of the Middle East and North Africa. Yet there are several problems with solely relying on this fact in explanations of banditry.

Eric Hobsbawm's work on 'social banditry' has been greatly influential in showing how, far from only being the result of a supposedly inherent propensity to steal, banditry could be a rational activity carried out as a form of survival or even social protest.[8] Although there have been some powerful critiques concerning both Hobsbawm's methodology and the content of his thesis, and indeed he himself made revisions to his own argument, the social banditry thesis has opened up a discussion allowing historians to point to the changing socio-economic and political factors behind banditry, especially in societies experiencing oncoming modernization. Moreover, like broader works on crime and society, it has revealed how subalterns viewed so-called criminal activities as legitimate – what historians have labelled 'social crime' – even when not explicitly framed as resistance.[9] As historians in this field have shown, the very characterization of an act as a 'crime' delineates points of inequality and alternative notions of justice throughout history. For instance, Muir and Ruggiero argue: 'what societies label crime usually represents perceived ruptures or breaks in the ties that bind people together, the little deaths of social life'.[10] Crime, then, should be viewed as a 'shifting moral concept' largely – though not exclusively – defined by those in power.[11]

As Stephanie Cronin has pointed out, although the social banditry thesis has been a subject of much discussion concerning various geographical areas, it has been of little interest or value to historians of the Middle East and North Africa region examining it in the rural context.[12] As regards the Middle East, historians have mostly stressed bandits' links to state networks of power and their plunder of defenceless peasants, for example Karen Barkey on the Ottoman Empire or Nathan Brown on Khedival Egypt.[13] Thus, they have tended to agree much more with Anton Blok's famous critique of Hobsbawm's social banditry thesis.[14] Blok argued that far from being a form of peasant resistance or 'primitive rebellion', banditry primarily preyed on and suppressed the peasantry. The association of pastoral nomadic tribes with banditry in the Middle Eastern context would, on the surface, seem to support such a view: tribes certainly were important in the maintenance of state power – especially in Qajar Iran – and they did predominantly live away from villages.[15] Even Hobsbawm himself made a distinction between banditry proper and the raiding of nomadic tribes such as those of the Bedouin, suggesting the latter could never be seen as legitimate by the peasantry.[16]

In this chapter, however, by focusing on the southern Iranian province of Fars in the years between 1910 and 1915, I argue that banditry could be a rational form of protest or survival, and cannot be sufficiently understood solely with reference to the tribal culture of raiding. I show that banditry was not necessarily a tribal phenomenon but rather involved a variety of actors, including settled villagers, townspeople and even those charged with fighting crime. Such fluidity belies the notion of a static 'dangerous class', stemming instead from shared and similar lived experiences – especially destitution, dearth and disaster, all of which were becoming increasingly common. Even if one were to accept that tribal raiding had always been a conscious response to such phenomena, we must be aware of the qualitatively different scale of change in living conditions experienced at this liminal moment, shaped by a vibrant revolutionary and post-revolutionary political culture as well as Iran's increasing integration into the world economy.[17] To focus on raiding culture alone diverts attention away from such historicity, meaning we are not able to understand why banditry was apparently increasing so rapidly at this time. It would also overlook many important concurrent processes such as state formation, the commercialization of agriculture and the loss of customary tribal rights.

These processes should not be taken to conceptualize banditry as symptomatic of a great divide between state and society. Such a view would seem to assume that rural society exists as an autonomous obstacle to statecraft, which, as scholars of the Middle East and North Africa region have warned, would lead us on the mistaken quest to uncover the lost perspective of the liberal humanist subject.[18] As has been established, the agency of the popular classes in Qajar Iran was realized within the framework of the existing polity not externally in opposition to it.[19] Nevertheless, as this chapter will show, although we need not romanticize banditry as a bastion of premodern resistance, its prevalence can still be understood as a survival strategy in response to the accelerating processes of modernization – especially when its near-universality is taken into account.

At the same time, it is necessary to understand how, more than being a mere survival strategy, banditry could potentially serve as a form of political protest. As John Chalcraft argues, it is too teleological to argue that capitalist development or socio-economic modernization determined the nature of protest in the Middle East and North Africa.[20] Rather, we should look to the agency and creativity of people to frame the forms of opposition that cannot be neatly explained by the context.[21] I argue that, especially when understood alongside contemporary forms of articulation in the urban protests of the Qajar period, banditry could be linked to ideas of social justice. It was at this time that, distinct from the traditional notions of raiding, banditry increasingly functioned as a weapon against new state-imposed forms of justice. Modernization did not determine this outcome, but it helped undermine the existing system of consent and negotiation that had marked Qajar Iran, and it was this moment of 'hegemonic contraction' that enabled new forms of political articulation and a refashioning of old ones.[22]

To be sure, historians have acknowledged the political nature of banditry in the Iranian case. Stephanie Cronin reveals the fluidity of banditry and its links to forms of protest against the processes of modernization in the Bakhtiari lands around Isfahan, especially in the 1920s and 1930s, while Khazeni's study on the same tribal confederation reveals some links between the notions of justice and highway robbery at the turn of the twentieth century.[23] Concerning the Qashqai confederation in Fars, Lois Beck goes as far as arguing that 'theft on the trade routes … was not a "tribal" problem', while Safiri's thesis on the South Persia Rifles draws some attention to the phenomenon of settled villagers taking to banditry.[24] Finally, Nouraei and Martin provide a broader account of the rise of banditry across the country in this period and link it to the problems of scarcity and tribal notions of justice.[25]

In this chapter I build on these studies with a more micro-historical focus on criminality in Fars during a shorter period, especially in the final section examining the case of Kazerun. A micro-historical methodology, particularly in the way of *Alltagsgeschichte* (the history of everyday life), can provide a more qualitative picture of the anonymous 'multitudes in their workaday trials and tribulations'.[26] It shifts attention to the *lived* experiences of everyday life where subaltern agency is realized. As Lefebvre argues, the everyday is the site in which forces of quotidian praxis 'modify' apparent structures in 'perpetual movement'.[27] It is this coming together of 'noneveryday eventfulness' with the repetition of the everyday that allows us to understand how participants were simultaneously 'objects of history and its subjects'.[28]Adopting a micro-historical approach does not mean we are confined to telling a bounded, narrow story. Rather, micro-history enables one to demonstrate how spatial localities, far from being rigidly fixed, are constantly constructed by a plurality of material practices between the local and the global.[29] As Jefroudi points out, it is the site of the local that is the setting in which even some of the most global processes, such as the development of capitalism, can be best discerned.[30] I also argue that such fluidity of space also existed between town and country, which makes rural banditry understandable only in relation to practices in urban areas. Farzin Vejdani has successfully demonstrated how a micro-historical focus on crime in the Iranian context can map out the connection between social relations, space and daily practices, not just within a city but also its vicinity.[31] In adopting a similar focus on crime 'from below', I aim to show how a micro-history of banditry in Fars can offer a bottom-up perspective of crime in Iran more generally, complementing recent informative studies on the views of Iranian authorities and intellectuals.[32]

Trade, tribes and banditry on the Bushehr-Shiraz Road

Because of its proximity to the Persian Gulf, Fars had long been one of Iran's main trade regions. As early as 1763 Karim Khan Zand signed a treaty with the East India Company giving Britain a trade monopoly on woollens in the country as well as the sole right to have a trading station at Bushehr. As a result, trade along the road between Bushehr and Shiraz greatly increased, especially after the advent of steam navigation in the Persian Gulf and the creation of the Suez Canal in the second half of the nineteenth century made Iran's southern ports much more accessible.[33]

The increase in trade along the road also provided opportunities for loot for those living in its vicinity. Thus there was a rise in robberies reported by many foreign firms at that time, so much so that a road toll system known as *rahdari* was developed to ensure safe passage of caravans along the route: this was levied at different toll stations and entitled each caravan to a night watchman and an escort of guards up to the next station.[34] But as Beck points out, the continued delegation of authority along the road in the late nineteenth an early twentieth centuries saw the *rahdari* system become increasingly unregulated. Those responsible for collecting tolls competed against each other by raising the rate, often by way of organized robbery to artificially inflate the price of guards.[35] In this context, *rahdari* increasingly operated as a form of blackmail, levied with the veiled threat of robbery if not paid.

Indeed, those who were tasked with guarding the road were often the ones accused of organizing the robberies that occurred along it. These were often the tribal chieftains of the Qashqai confederation, which many British traders considered to be the 'most troublesome ... of the bandit tribes'.[36] Ever since 1865, when Qashqai nomads cut several miles of telegraph wire, British authorities had condemned the 'lawlessness' of the confederation.[37] In 1893 Edward Browne claimed an Armenian traveller had also warned him:

> The only people that I have seen worse than the Lurs … are the Kashkais, for though the former will usually rob you if they can, and would not hesitate to murder you if you refused to give up your possessions to them, the latter, not content with this, will murder you even if you make no resistance, alleging that the world is well quit of one who is such a coward that he will not fight for his own.[38]

Nevertheless, British traders and authorities relied on the Qashqai khans – especially the head of the confederation, the *ilkhani* – to enforce order within the tribe to ensure security on the roads.[39] By 1904 Isma'il Khan Sowlat al-Dowleh established himself as the *ilkhani* and all those possessing local authority for sections of the road, even if not members of the Qashqai, were nominally answerable to him.[40]

Yet under Sowlat's authority, security on the road deteriorated, especially during the Constitutional Revolution. Already as early as 1909 the British firms Messrs Ziegler and Co. and Dixon and Co. complained to the Board of Trade that 'in recent years, caravan robberies on a large scale have taken place, and certain tribes have made a regular and profitable business of stopping and robbing caravans'.[41] This correlated with an increase in *rahdari* rates: they rose dramatically from 3.7 krans per mule in 1907 to 11.15 in 1910.[42] Such was the state of the road, and such were the security issues associated with the tribes, that the British embassy issued the so-called 'British Note' in October 1910. The note complained that 'the principal channels through which British trade used to pass to the interior of the country are now practically closed by the depredations of tribesmen, who appear to be completely beyond the control of the central Government'.[43]

The rise in robberies also coincided with the reported increase in arms distributed throughout the province. In 1892 the Qashqai were said to be in possession of two hundred Martinis, but by 1900 this number was estimated to have risen to two thousand, increasing even more by 1910.[44] When *The Times* correspondent Arthur Moore visited in 1909, he claimed that 'every town possesses stores of rifles, and the bazaars are full of Mausers, Winchesters, Martinis, Mauser pistols, and Belgian Brownings, exposed for sale to any purchaser who will pay'.[45] A major factor behind this trend was the growth in arms smuggling from Muscat, while many weapons were also acquired through robbing the caravans of foreign companies. British political officer Arnold Wilson, who was 'impressed by the large supplies of arms and ammunition in the hands of the tribes between the coast and Shiraz', found upon close inspection the majority of the arms seemed to have arrived in the area through arms trafficking by French firms.[46]

Yet despite the continued increase in robbery throughout the whole province as the Constitutional Revolution came to a close, it was *rahdari* along the Bushehr-Shiraz road that was consistently the main grievance of British authorities. Indeed, *rahdari* rates would go on to jump to 28.12 krans per mule by 1912.[47] Thus, although many other tribes – such as the Khamseh Confederation (the other main tribal confederation in Fars) as well as smaller independent ones such as the notorious Boir Ahmadi –

were associated with robbery, it was the Qashqai who continued to figure as the most dangerous in the minds of British companies and authorities by virtue of Sowlat's nominal control of the roads. Moreover, increasing *rahdari* rates was only possible due to the prevalence of robberies along the road, which was attributed to Qashqai raids and Sowlat's unwillingness or inability to maintain security.

Iranian observers were equally damning of the tribes' role in creating chaos. The pages of *Vaqaye'-e Ettefaqiyeh* – a collection of daily reports on Fars written by the Iranian staff at the British consulate in Shiraz – are replete with numerous episodes of banditry and complaints about the state of wickedness/villainy (*sherarat*) prevailing in the countryside because of the tribes, especially the Qashqai. For example, one report claimed that the Qashqai 'rob everywhere without any regard for the states around Fars' and for a month had established a situation of 'disorder (*eghteshash*) and theft (*dozdi*), the severity of which worsens day by day'.[48] By 1910, such views were becoming increasingly common in constitutionalist discourse, linking the 'lawlessness and anarchy' in the country to the power of the regional tribal leaders.[49]

A culture of raiding?

However, attributing this so-called lawlessness to the tribes and to a traditional, habitual culture of raiding would not be particularly helpful. First, it diverts attention from some of the many ongoing processes at the time that might have been crucial to the rise in banditry, especially the change in people's access to subsistence. Since the mid-nineteenth century, both Iran's increasing integration into the world market and the depreciation of its silver currency had caused a great shift in agricultural production from the growing of wheat – the country's main subsistence crop – to more profitable cash crops for export, such as tobacco, opium and cotton.[50] This 'commercialization of agriculture' also exacerbated the rise in food insecurity: land was increasingly transferred from state ownership into the possession of profit-seeking landlords who usually forced the predominantly share-cropping peasantry to produce cash crops instead of subsistence crops.[51] As the value of land continued to rise, sharecroppers became increasingly indebted and unable to pay rents. As a result, the period saw a higher degree of stratification within villages, including the rise in the number of landless peasants forced to either seek wage labour in the village or to move to nearby towns.[52] In addition, as grain started to function more as a form of currency, many merchants periodically took to hoarding it and thus contributing to the dearth of foodstuffs.[53] The commercialization of agriculture was particularly pronounced in Fars province because it was a key region for producing cash crops, especially opium and tobacco. This helps explain why the province – especially Shiraz – had been one of the most politically volatile parts of the country.[54]

As has been well established, there is a strong connection between banditry and dearth once rural populations become unable to meet their own subsistence needs.[55] In the Iranian case, many settled villagers took to banditry as early as the great famine of 1871 to 1872, while there was an increase in tribal plunder because of the severe loss of fodder for nomads' animals at the same time.[56] In the post-constitutional period, then, it is hardly surprising that robberies should be so common in a region experiencing severe dearth, as sources indicate. In February 1911, for instance, one Western traveller reported that 'in the last two years more than one quarter of the total corn-land of Fars has gone out of cultivation'.[57] By 1913 the situation had apparently not improved, with the Shiraz consul reporting that 'a general scarcity of grain of every kind prevails already all over the province, with correspondingly high prices'.[58]

As a result of such scarcity in the province, many settled agriculturalists evidently took to banditry. We see in various reports that whole villages were sometimes abandoned. Moir, for example, was struck on his return to the once 'prosperous village' of Mahyar to find that seven years since his last visit it was 'practically deserted', as were Maqsud Beik, Aminabad and Shurjestan.[59] Whether this was a direct consequence of the commercialization of agriculture or mainly a response to increased plunder remains unclear, but it was unquestionably a rising trend correlating with the prevalence of dearth. And it is certain that these settled agriculturalists, once 'peaceful villagers', were now themselves 'taking to brigandage as the only means of earning a living'.[60] For example, in 1911 the settled Kordshulis had suddenly turned to cutting telegraph wires and blackmailing passing caravans at Tange-ye Bolaghi.[61] In fact, in a list of claims made by British firms concerning robberies between 1908 and 1911, 'villagers' were recorded as the attackers on no less than fourteen occasions (in addition to settled tribes such as the Kordshulis, who were excluded from this category).[62] The prevalence of robberies committed by non-nomadic elements explains Arthur Moore's 1914 observation that 'Fars is full of masterless men who have cast off, or never had, any tribal allegiance, and live by plunder'.[63] That the majority of British authorities and company officials should mistake these people for tribesmen is testament to their conflation of banditry with the 'tribal problem', but this was far from reality.

Even when we do come across instances of banditry committed by tribal nomads, its nature hints at wider processes of change. One notable phenomenon in Fars at the time is the existence of inter-tribal bandit gangs. In the attack on the gendarmerie captain Eckford on 11 December 1912, for example, it was reported that a band of some two to three hundred tribesmen comprising Boir Ahmadis, Mamasanis and Kashkulis (the latter being a Qashqai sub-tribe, or *tireh*) was responsible.[64] But why members from different tribes should work together can only be understood in the context of the eroding vertical relationships of tribal authority at the time. As Stephanie Cronin shows in her comprehensive account of the Bakhtiari confederation, the period following the Constitutional Revolution was marked by increasing intra-tribal stratification between more senior khans and junior khans as well as between these figures and more subaltern tribesmen under their authority. As senior tribe members came to buy and assert their right to land and be drawn more into urban politics, junior khans and subaltern tribesmen began to resist the inequalities in wealth and loss of customary rights.[65] This was symptomatic of a wider process of 'hegemonic contraction', whereby the existing systems of consent and forms of authority were becoming undermined by the prevailing trends of modernization and integration into the world economy.[66]

Several sources testify to the hegemonic contraction within the Qashqai and Khamseh tribal confederations at the time. According to the Shiraz consul, Walter Smart, for instance, the Khamseh were reported to be in 'a chronic state of insubordination'. Even Qashqai tribesmen – traditionally more coherent and loyal to their *ilkhani* – were said to be becoming 'more and more insubordinate', with *kalantars* (chiefs of tribal unites responsible for liaising with the *ilkhani*) creating 'for themselves a position of independence against which no *ilkhani*, under present conditions, can successfully assert himself'.[67] One of the notable figures leading the wave of defection from Sowlat within the Qashqai at this time was Muhammad ʿAli Khan Kashkuli, hence the Kashkulis were operating independently or with other tribes and often directly against the interests of Sowlat. Thus, in contrast to the traditional function of raiding to secure vertical bonds of authority, these inter-tribal bandit robberies can be interpreted as evidence of linkages along more horizontal lines in opposition to senior tribal leadership.[68]

In addition, many robberies at that time reveal a struggle over inequalities in wealth, especially discernible when one examines reports of 'plunder' against landowners. In a report of 28 May 1912, for example, the Shiraz consul wrote that a number of landowners had 'been threatening to take refuge in Consulate' to protest the government's inability 'to protect their properties against tribesmen'.[69] Such attacks were sometimes directed even against one's own tribal leader: the Khamseh were said to not only be ignoring their *ilkhani*, Qavam al-Molk, in his 'injunctions against their freebooting exploits', but also going so far as to plunder his own estates.[70] Furthermore, it is evident that the label of 'plunder' used in official sources could sometimes conceal acts of land expropriation. Occasional slippages in the sources reveal that far from being about the raiding for booty that the term 'plunder' would suggest, attacks on wealthy landowners' property were in reality about controlling subsistence. For example, one report states that most landowners had seen their properties 'pillaged' by tribesmen that had in many cases 'actually taken possession of the land'.[71] Such acts can be read as attempts to tackle inequalities in access to subsistence, either by staying to cultivate land or deny its cultivation to others – much like the famous peasant uprisings in Gilan during the Constitutional Revolution.[72]

To be sure, plunder was still regularly committed against poorer villagers, who sometimes fought back. But, as has been shown, settled populations could also turn to plunder; as Cronin points out, there was no rigid boundary between sedentary and nomadic life in Iran, especially not in Fars because of the agricultural opportunities offered by the Zagros Mountains.[73] Thus, in contrast to Hobsbawm's view, plunder was not necessarily a tribal phenomenon targeted against the peasantry but rather it could be an endogenous aspect of peasant survival.[74]

Urban crime: Theft, protest and justice in Shiraz

If we situate banditry within a wider context of criminality by shifting the focus to urban crime in this period, we begin to see that theft could serve as a form of social protest, especially as sources covering the urban context provide greater voice to subaltern grievances.

Shiraz had long been considered a town full of disorderly elements.[75] In the nineteenth and early twentieth centuries it experienced a huge number of protests and uprisings in which supposedly criminal figures played a key role. They mostly comprised *lutis* – gangs of young men who undertook various prominent activities in public life, such as leading religious ceremonies or protecting neighbourhoods.[76] Their ability to enforce their will outside the law and their supposedly disorderly and improper behaviour made them a potential source of danger and criminality in the view of many authorities and foreign onlookers.[77] Yet the *lutis'* self-declared concern for social justice and their frequent involvement in protests meant they were often lauded by the popular classes as champions of the people against tyranny and injustice.[78] Central to the *luti* ethos was a value system combining the Islamic concept of chivalry (*javanmardi* or *futuvvat*) with Iranian heroic mythology.[79] For many urban poor, this justified the acts of theft that *lutis* were so often implicated in, even if in reality they might target the poor from outside their neighbourhoods or be used by the authorities to crack down on popular protest.[80] Thus, in their idealized form, encapsulated most famously in the figure of Sattar Khan during the Constitutional Revolution, *lutis* can be considered urban versions of Hobsbawm's mythologised social bandits, stealing and fighting in the name of people's justice, much like the popular conceptions of '*ayyaran* in earlier times.[81]

In Shiraz during the period under study, British onlookers frequently attributed protests to the *lutis'* opportunism and criminality. According to the British consul in Shiraz in 1910, the presence of a large number of *lutis* 'who depend on the more or less prolonged agitations which … furnish not only a daily wage, but an opportunity for pilfering cartridges, making petty extortions, etc.' was the 'root cause' of unrest in the town.[82] Such conceptions understood the *lutis* as devoid of any genuine political motive or value system that might legitimize their actions; in other words, they were seen as nothing more than petty criminals using protest as a source of income. As recent works have shown, such perceptions were simplistic; although *lutis* were often paid to agitate and steal on behalf of the ulema or even the government authorities, they saw those actions as compatible with their own ethical code and sense of justice.[83]

It is also evident that the legitimacy of theft could extend to other actors and groups involved in popular protest. In reports on political demonstrations of the time we find regular incidences of looting existing side by side with articulations of dissent. In one Moharram procession of 1910, for example, it was reported that a large crowd went around the town singing constitutional songs, while at the same time 'pilfering on the way'.[84] Although the exact social composition of such crowds is rarely specified, research on protest in Qajar Iran has demonstrated the large number of non-*lutis* involved; women in particular often played a leading role.[85] Large-scale looting also periodically targeted minorities, especially Jews: the famous pogrom in the Jewish quarter in October 1910 is a case in point.[86] These incidents, all of which were centred on a major grievance, suggest that, far from being the preserve of opportunistic professional criminal gangs, theft could be used by the population as a political weapon. Of course, just like rural banditry, it might also be used against the most vulnerable. But as Martin finds, theft could be compatible with ideas of justice ('*adl*), balance (*al-mizan*) and order (*nezam*), which were so central to protests in Qajar Iran.[87] These ideas were especially important in a town like Shiraz, where the political culture and discourse had been so vibrant during the Constitutional Revolution.[88]

The compatibility of such ideas with theft in popular opinion is further supported by the fact that even those tasked with preventing theft (especially soldiers) could be implicated in it. According to the British consul, in 1910, soldiers were 'doing a lot of thieving in the town', even being so bold as to target the house of an agent of the foreign firm Ziegler.[89] Similarly, the soldiers who had been ordered to put down the pogrom in the Jewish quarter later that year were said to have soon joined the looting.[90] Such acts were unquestionably linked to the destitution the soldiers in Shiraz were suffering at the time, nearing starvation as their pay was often months in arrears. This is perhaps why the soldiers who had taken part in looting often took sanctuary (*bast*) immediately before or after. For example, on 11 March 1911, soldiers took *bast* in the Shiraz telegraph office demanding to be paid, yet they had fought with the townspeople and pillaged some shops in the bazaar just before that.[91] As Vejdani argues, taking *bast* often accompanied crimes because it offered a legal 'space of exception' to delay or avoid punishment.[92] In this sense, it directly appealed to public opinion and popular understandings of justice as an informal means of exoneration.[93] Thus *bast* had to have at least some element of protest to justify one's actions, especially as it had been such an important form of contestation during the Constitutional Revolution.

The timing of such incidents over the years, particularly in periods of dearth, suggests that the soldiers' willingness to maintain order was linked to authorities' capacity to provide subsistence for them.[94] For instance, in May 1902 there was a severe grain shortage that meant most bakeries across Shiraz had to close. Large crowds of up to two hundred people scrambled for bread outside the few bakeries that were open, sometimes so frantically that several individuals were trampled and children were pushed onto bakery hot plates. On one occasion during this shortage, a soldier had quarrelled with a townsperson outside a bakery by Masjed-e Vakil and was subsequently hit, before retaliating by bringing his regiment to fight the locals and loot the local shops.[95] The records mention a number of similar episodes, which suggests that attitudes to theft were not rigidly defined. If the very people responsible for preventing theft were themselves stealing because of their poverty, then theft could be entirely justified by one's circumstances. Moreover, as Vejdani highlights, in late Qajar Iran what was considered a crime depended more on particular socio-spatial relations: for example, what neighbourhood someone came from or whether they had vertical relations to higher-status individuals.[96]

Thus, as the state's imposition of justice was becoming increasingly formalized from the beginning of the Constitutional Revolution, it faced active opposition on a large scale. In Shiraz artefacts of state justice, such as gallows, were targets of attacks and robbery, building on a tradition of opposition to secular punishment.[97] But whereas previously such opposition had targeted local law enforcement authorities, now it was also being levelled at the depersonalized justice system emanating from the central government. It was at this time, after all, that the Ministry of Justice ('*adlieh*) became popularly known as *zolmiyeh* (or the House of Oppression) across the country.[98] Evidence of such sentiment can be observed in Shiraz too, such as in November 1910 when a crowd stormed and sacked the Courts of Justice, taking away or destroying all the legal documents in its archive.[99]

The meaning of such acts can be better understood in the context of the changing nature of law. As Enayat points out, up until the Constitutional Revolution, acts defined as one of the 'four crimes' – murder, assault, rape and theft – were outside the domain of *shariʿah* courts. They were instead dealt with in the secular customary (*ʿorf*) courts, which were unstructured and informal and subject more to the decisions of local authorities than a codified law (not unlike *shariʿah* courts in this sense but with less popular authority).[100] Thus, depending on one's connections, one could escape punishment. After the Constitutional Revolution, however, the Ministry of Justice took over the responsibility for such matters through local courts and state-appointed judges.[101] Theft was criminalized through the formal codification of the penal law. Popular opposition to the Ministry of Justice, then, can perhaps in part be read as a widely felt disregard for the state's formal criminalization of theft – especially so, as Martin argues, given that theft had been a matter people would take into their own hands as it was outside the parameters of *shariʿah* law.[102] Indeed, there was a great deal of debate about the role of *shariʿah* and *ʿorf* law during the Constitutional Revolution, which continued to be unresolved during the period in focus.[103] During the decade after the revolution, several statesmen debated about what defined crime and how it should be punished, resulting in various abandoned attempts at passing a penal code.[104] Even the very definitions of 'theft' and 'thief' were matters for public debate well into the 1920s, becoming, for instance, a topic of a running essay competition in the *Shefaq-e Sorkh* newspaper.[105]

The contemporaneous wave of rural banditry in Fars must be understood in this context. Rural Iran was not shut off from the ideas of justice that so animated the political discourse in the towns, with there being much movement between urban and rural areas. Peasants and semi-pastoralists would regularly come to Shiraz to sell their produce and were exposed to the public life of the street and bazaar. Ordinary tribesmen were perhaps even more exposed to protests, as they were often brought into the town by their leaders to prevent them, for example by denying access to the British consulate to would-be *bastis*. However, sometimes tribesmen participated in *bast* themselves.[106] In turn, urban actors, especially members of the ulema, travelled to the countryside to agitate the rural population. The communications infrastructure, particularly the telegraph system, was also important in disseminating ideas. At various places along the telegraph line people protested in ways similar to those in towns, making the same appeals for justice. For example, in February 1913, 250 villagers took *bast* in the telegraph office in Dehbid, while in March a group of muleteers did the same in Borazjan, leaving two thousand mules without oversight.[107] It was by such communication means that constitutionalist urban politics, revolving around the creation of the *majles*, was transmitted to the countryside, allowing peasants to rearticulate and improve their rights (*hoquq*).[108]

This fluidity between town and country helps explain why the actions of rural bandits may be framed as a form of protest. Certainly, by their very status as outlaws, the bandits opposed any attempts to formalize the justice system. Even the country's most notorious bandit, Nayyeb Hossein Kashi, went out of his way to attack the Ministry of Justice building in Tabbas in 1913 as protestors had done in Shiraz in 1910, setting fire to the local judge's dossiers and taking away his seals.[109] Of course, bandits did steal from both the poor and the wealthy, but they also justified some of their actions by appealing to social justice. As Nouraei and Martin highlight, the nomads engaged in highway robbery, distinguished between plunder (*gharati*) and stolen goods, with the former seen as a legitimate means of restoring equality, especially when exacted from foreigners and the wealthy.[110] Similarly, in his study of the Bakhtiari, Khazeni finds that tribesmen considered banditry a legitimate form of resistance to 'oppression and unjust exaction' by the government.[111] Such conceptions of justice may have also derived in part from the bandits' own rural traditions: for example, tribal custom or, for non-tribal bandits, the notions of collective responsibility and 'moral economy' evident in many peasant societies (and traditionally articulated in the form of the 'Circle of Justice' in the Iranian context).[112] Nevertheless, the bandits' actions and values should not necessarily be seen as inherently opposed or external to the state's authority even if they were against particular policies or failings. Rather, they should be viewed as appeals to the state authorities to restore justice and the balance that had underpinned the 'Qajar Pact'.[113] After all, the discussion on justice in the countryside had been animated by the constitutionalist project. This political culture, combined with increasing state encroachment and the commercialization of agriculture, constituted a moment of hegemonic contraction that did help spur new forms of articulation, but they took place within the existing hegemonic framework.[114]

To be sure, even if it is clear enough that banditry was commonly accepted as a legitimate means of survival, the links between banditry and protest were not always articulated explicitly. Sources on the rural areas do reveal instances of protest but not to the same extent as in the cities. Thus, although for some individuals banditry was clearly a means of protest, it is difficult to generalize given the dearth of sources. Nevertheless, the next case study, on the town of Kazerun and its vicinity, will demonstrate that where sources allow, a micro-historical approach can elucidate a clearer link between theft and political protest in a rural location.

The fluidity of criminality: The case of Kazerun

Located approximately halfway along the Bushehr-Shiraz road, Kazerun county is situated in a large fertile valley in the southern Zagros mountains. This setting provided abundant opportunities for the production of grains, beans, fruits (especially oranges), tobacco and opium.[115] The area was suitable for a sedentary lifestyle, having been host to the ancient Sasanian city of Bishapur. In 1912 it was home to a total population of 20,000 (12,000 in the city of Kazerun). Its location in the *garmsir* (warm zone), excellent grazing land and agricultural possibilities also drew pastoral and semi-pastoral nomads, especially during winter months. In particular the Kashkuli Qashqais, who Arnold Wilson described as 'extensive agriculturalists', spent a great deal of time in the area and were heavily involved in local politics.[116] Overall, the boundaries between sedentary and nomadic life were especially porous.

The whole population was dependent on the trade flowing through the Bushehr-Shiraz road. As eyewitness accounts testify, many people settled along the road evidently seeking to earn a living from it. This could be through various means, such as employment as a muleteer or road guard; Kazerun was often cited as being notable for its large populations of muleteers. But one might also choose to take advantage of the situation by engaging in blackmail or robbing the passing caravans. Being a *tofangchi* – a gun-owner – enabled one to have flexibility of choice in such matters. There are many reports of instances when road guards suddenly turned to robbing or blackmailing the very caravans they had been paid to protect.

Rahdari proved to be especially lucrative, with the rates increasing rapidly in 1911 and 1912. Such was its value that competition for nominal control over the road and the right to levy the road tax could be fierce, leading to the emergence of several rival groups in the area. Around 1905, the *kalantar* of Kamarej, Haidar Khan, took control of the road to Kazerun by force. When Haidar Khan died in 1909, power passed to his 'black confidant', Khorshid.[117] In spring 1911, Muhammad 'Ali Khan Kashkuli, with the support of governor general Nezam al-Soltaneh, attacked Khorshid in Kamarej and took control of Shahpur and Rahdar (north of the 'no-man's land' of Tange-ye Torkan),[118] which were important strategic positions for the control of *rahdari*.[119] After Khorshid re-established authority in Kamarej itself, he formed an alliance with Kazerun against the Kashkulis, resulting in a highly anarchic and unstable situation for the passing traffic, marked by an increase in attacks and robberies.[120] But there were also other means to undermine rivals: in 1911 the Kashkulis began diverting traffic from the Tange-ye Torkan via Shahpur to Shiraz, bypassing Kazerun altogether and denying its population profits from the passing caravans. In response Khorshid and the Kazerunis avoided Kashkuli territory by directing caravans along a 'very precipitous route' from Kamarej to Kazerun through the mountains. Due to this state of uncertainty caravans needed additional protection, causing *rahdari* rates to rise even more and, in turn, further fuelling competition for the right to levy it.[121]

Muhammad 'Ali Khan Kashkuli in particular profited from this situation. His *ilkhani*, Sowlat al-Dowleh, had been expected to reap the greatest rewards from the attack on Kamarej, but Muhammad 'Ali defected from him soon after. This was no doubt in part because of Sowlat's uncompromising levying of the *maliyat* tax whose rate he kept increasing, which caused widespread loss of support from other Qashqai *tirehs*. Sowlat's redirection of the caravan route from Kazerun to Jirreh in 1910, denying the Kashkulis income from the road, also caused resentment.[122] In October 1911, once Sowlat had been stripped of the title of *ilkhani*, Qavam al-Molk granted Muhammad 'Ali Khan nominal control of the Bushehr-Shiraz road.[123]

It was in this context that Muhammad 'Ali Khan engaged in a sustained campaign of banditry against both the local population and the passing caravans from late 1911 to 1913. This included regular attacks on and looting of Kazerun, the capturing of various villages in the area as well as the building of forts. By 1913 he was said to have attained 'such an influential position that he had made himself practically master of large areas north and north-west of Shiraz', and one of his letters reveals his intention to become the master of Mamasani county.[124] Local resistance to his activities did occasionally occur. Sometimes villagers and townsmen attempted to fight off Muhammad 'Ali's men; in other instances they protested at the local telegraph office, appealing to higher authorities for action.[125] But it would be wrong to assume that there was a strict town-tribe divide. Sedentary townsmen or villagers sometimes decided to take up arms and join Muhammad 'Ali's bandit gang; the most notable person to do so was 'Ali Muhammad Kamareji, who achieved notoriety among British authorities as a 'brigand' and 'outlaw' for his deeds on behalf of the Kashkuli khan.

Muhammad 'Ali Khan's gang often targeted foreigners, a trend that can be understood within the wider context of growing xenophobia and anti-imperialism in the area. There were many reports of robbery committed against European travellers throughout 1912 and 1913, in conjunction with allegations of harassment at the hands of the Iranian road guards. The villages in the Konar Takhteh plain were said to be 'particularly notorious for the ill-treatment of caravans, extortion, general turbulence and insulting behaviour to Europeans'.[126] Similarly, according to the Shiraz consul, Walter Smart, the attitude of 'roadguards, especially at Rahdar, towards European travellers is disgraceful. Apart from being heavily blackmailed, European travellers must expect to be treated with violent discourtesy, even threatened with pointed rifles, by these servants of the Kashkuli Khans'.[127] Indeed, Smart himself became the victim of an attack in December 1911, when eight hundred of Muhammad 'Ali's men – reported to have been led by 'Ali Muhammad Kamareji – ambushed him and his accompanying troops from the Thirty-Ninth Central Indian Horse regiment near Kazerun. It is clear that although Smart was quickly given shelter by Muhammad 'Ali himself, the attack was fuelled by xenophobia, especially against Indians. In Muhammad 'Ali's exchanges with Smart, he characterized Smart's Indian companions as 'black idolaters' who had no right to be involved in policing the road because they were inferior to the Qashqais.[128]

But it is evident that Muhammad 'Ali Khan also especially resented the British presence. Muhammad 'Ali was reported to have told a German merchant robbed by his gang that 'after the blood which had been shed, it was lucky for him that he was not an Englishman'.[129] This cohered with a wave of anti-British feeling that was sweeping the countryside, largely moving from urban centres to rural areas. In Bushehr and Shiraz the ulema had already organized a boycott against the increased British incursion into the country.[130] Soon some mullahs were travelling into rural Fars in order to mobilize local opposition: for example, Sheikh 'Ali Dashti went from Bushehr to Borazjan in January 1912.[131] Such ideas were also transmitted via the telegraph, with messages lauding the Kashkulis' recent actions against the British sent to Muhammad 'Ali Khan even from Tehran.[132] The effect of such agitation is apparent in the crucial role that local villagers played in the attack on Smart, when 'every village and tower' along the retreat to Kazerun contributed riflemen to open fire on the foreign troops.[133] Thus as far as banditry committed against foreigners was concerned, there was a great deal of local support.

Furthermore, this support could also extend to resisting the state's attempts to bring the roads under control. After the threatening 'British Note' of October 1910, the Iranian government agreed to create a gendarmerie to enforce law and order on the roads, but this was not realized in Fars until the summer of 1912.[134] The gendarmerie was given the task of enforcing new governor general Mokhber al-Soltaneh's policy of abolishing *rahdari*, but British intelligence at the time suggested that this would face popular opposition. For example in July 1912 Smart claimed that *rahdari* could be moderated but not abolished because 'any attempt to abolish *rahdari* entirely and immediately would mean that the gendarmerie would be faced by the hostility of both the Kashgais and the settled population along the road', rendering 'the task of the gendarmerie quite impossible'.[135] Similarly the British Resident Sir Percy Cox asserted that despite the insecurity caused by *rahdari*, 'a large part of the sedentary population along the road is vitally interested in the maintenance of the present condition of affairs'.[136]

Such claims were soon proven true: gendarmes were regularly attacked when attempting to apprehend prominent bandits. In one particularly notable incident in November 1913, gendarmes endeavoured to capture the now notorious ʿAli Muhammad Kamareji. They encircled his gang at the Tul-e Kolah fort but ʿAli Muhammad and his companions managed to escape. When the gendarmes pursued the bandits to Kazerun, many villagers from along the way flocked into the town to attack them, soon followed by ʿAli Muhammad and his gang, who had been hiding in the neighbourhood.[137] Meanwhile, those from other settlements such as Kamarej also began rising against the gendarmes: even a gendarme officer at the Rahdar caravanserai defected to ʿAli Muhammad.[138] It was reported by the Kazerun signaller that 'all prominent local people are in favour of ʿAli Muhammad', who had evidently framed his efforts as part of a national struggle by sending out letters all over the country that incited people to oppose the gendarmerie.[139] Thus, there could have been some political purpose behind the actions of this so-called 'bandit', even if he so often engaged in stealing from the local poor. That he had popular support on this issue is testament to the depth of *rahdari*'s popularity and legitimacy in the eyes of many local people. Crucially, they also framed its defence as part of an anti-imperialist struggle; according to Safiri, the Kazerunis justified the attack of November 1913 by claiming the gendarmerie represented British interests.[140] It can be argued, therefore, that in the area around Kazerun, the bandits seeking to defend *rahdari* shared similarities with Hobsbawm's social bandits, insofar as they were conscious upholders of popularly held values against the social injustices of modernization, especially imperialism.

This, too, was certainly aided by the absence of commonly accepted legal boundaries criminalizing banditry in an abstract sense. As has already been pointed out, there was a great deal of fluidity between guarding and robbing the passing caravans in the area. Perhaps the greatest indicator of the ambiguity of law was shown in the way even gendarmes could move between the two. In February and March 1914, gendarmes and their hired *tofangchis* clashed with the locals again but on this occasion also took to looting parts of Kazerun for several days. Even the chief army instructor in Fars, Colonel J. N. Merrill, testified that he witnessed most gendarmes engaging in widespread pillage and rape, especially targeting the Jewish neighbourhood.[141] This soon spread outside Kazerun, and there were many reports of gendarmes stealing mules from muleteers in the town's vicinity.[142]

Although these gendarmes were in opposition to the local population by virtue of their official posts, their disregard for law and lack of concern for criminality can, in fact, be considered symptomatic of the feelings held widely among the locals. This is because, in Fars at that time at least, gendarmes were largely recruited locally. Since 1912, Major Siefvert had led a recruitment drive for the gendarmerie in villages along the road to Bushehr.[143] In addition, many gendarmes complained about arrears in pay and also lack of food, making the same appeals to justice that we find in other protests at the time. Their actions in Kazerun, then, should be understood within the context of local protest and socially accepted means of responding to destitution and starvation.

Despite the resistance to the abolition of *rahdari*, by late 1914 the practice had virtually stopped on the Bushehr-Shiraz road. The Gulf Residency Administration report from the end of the year states:

> The last six months of the year have shown the province to be in a state of tranquillity, unparalleled any time these past five years. On the Bushire-Shiraz road, *Rahdari* has ceased, caravans and travellers have passed practically unmolested and credit must be given to the Gendarmerie for having brought about, for the moment, this satisfactory state of affairs.[144]

This had been helped by the British government offering the Iranian government £100,000 in 1913 for the maintenance of the gendarmerie in Fars.[145] Not only did this money go towards recruiting and maintaining more troops, it also was used to pay subsidies to the khans holding authority along the road as a compensation for the loss of *rahdari* income. Another factor was the return of Sowlat al-Dowleh to the position of *ilkhani*; with the backing of the new governor general, he launched a campaign against the dissidents within his confederation, especially the Kashkulis.[146]

Nevertheless, such was the depth of anti-British feeling that when the First World War broke out, a large section of the population in Fars supported the German war effort by renewing attacks and robberies on British troops. This was accompanied by a wave of anti-imperialist agitation calling for the defence of both nation and Islam, spread in the region especially through telegraphs and newspapers.[147] Both Muhammad 'Ali Khan Kashkuli and 'Ali Muhammad Kamareji evidently took part in this struggle. The latter continued his attacks until his death in 1915, and was subsequently remembered locally as an anti-imperialist fighter.[148] According to the local nationalist newspapers of the time, the former was said to have joined the nationalist cause against the British, making 'protestations of patriotism' and expressing his 'desire to guard Islam'.[149] Although his later switch of allegiance to the British towards the end of the war may cast doubt on the genuineness of his anti-imperialist feelings, his connection to the nationalist struggle problematizes his designation as a mere 'bandit' or 'outlaw' living on the margins of society. Rather, both of these figures, much maligned in British sources, demonstrated an awareness of wider social sentiments and appealed to these to gather support; whether they did so instrumentally or not, their acts of theft and robbery had wider popular legitimacy, challenging any normative judgments regarding their criminal status.

Conclusion

Many of the themes that characterized the Fars province at the time can be observed in Kazerun on the micro-level. These include the fluid and temporary nature of criminality; the connection between banditry and socio-economic and political processes; the breakdown of tribal authority; the blurring of legal boundaries; as well as the link between theft, protest and concepts of justice. Although there were local particularities in the Kazerun context, the parallels between this county and the wider province concerning banditry and theft can be explained in part by comparable levels of dearth, destitution and disempowerment resulting from state encroachment and the commercialization of agriculture. Added to this was a vibrant political discussion on justice during the Constitutional Revolution, which spread as a result of modern infrastructure and means of communication. Overall, Kazerun, like Fars and the rest of the country, was experiencing a moment of 'hegemonic contraction' that undermined the existing system of consent and authority. This meant that not only was theft becoming a survival strategy for an increasing portion of the population but it was also allowed to become part of new forms of political articulation. It was increasingly framed with reference to the social injustices perpetrated by the state and the imperial powers.

References to primordial cultural traditions, in this case tribal raiding, do not help us illuminate the changing context. That is not to argue that tribal politics did not figure at all in the prevalence of banditry in Fars; as has been shown, the rivalries between and within tribes, especially for control of the Bushehr-Shiraz road, were often very important in the outbreaks of banditry. But tribes are not static, unitary entities; rather, their politics are realized within a particular spatial environment and historical moment.[150] In certain spatial-temporal moments, even an old tribal practice such as raiding could attain relatively new meanings and practitioners.

Above all, banditry was not a practice confined to a particular 'dangerous class' exogenous to 'society'. Banditry was not committed *against* the peasantry or townspeople. To hold such an opinion would presuppose that banditry existed in an inherent opposition to law-abiding society. But in practice banditry had no normative attachment to law on the popular level; rather, it could be contingently legitimate in a given moment. It was in this sense that banditry was truly 'social', unlike the activities of the famous bandits discussed by Hobsbawm. Although we can detect Robin Hood-like traits in some Fars-bandits, the reality presents a more complicated picture that defies the romantic ideal of the 'noble robber': bandits did defend popular values against the authorities and yet still also frequently targeted the most vulnerable.[151] In truth, banditry was most often a 'weapon of the weak' used against the weak, even if wealthier landlords and merchants occasionally fell victim to it or some notable bandits emerged to capture romantic imagination.[152] Similarly, in this case we cannot point to a 'straight world' against which an 'underworld' of 'antisocial crime' can be defined – a distinction Hobsbawm makes in his cases of social banditry.[153] In reality Iranian society was made up of many different groups with potentially conflicting attitudes towards crime. Thus we have to be open to the possibility that even when committed against the poor, crime may not have been just a means of survival for its perpetrators but also potentially a form of protest. When we speak of 'social crime', then, we must be aware of its potential to oppress other groups.

This raises the question as to whether we can delineate between 'good' and 'bad' crime at all and points to the related discussion concerning the possibility that *all* crime might hold the potential for protest, which Hobsbawm himself has addressed.[154] It is clear by now that we should not view the law as a mere instrument for the ruling class to maintain power and only criminalize activities that directly threaten it. As Stuart Hall and Phil Scraton have remarked:

> The undoubted role of the law in maintaining a particular set of economic relations, in establishing class hegemony and legitimating a system of power, does not adequately account for the real, historical complexity of its functioning. The 'rule of law' is a contradictory social relation, an arena of struggle. It is something which the poor and the oppressed have struggled *against*, struggled *within*, and sometimes struggled *for*.[155]

Not only may laws be popularly consented to, they might even be used by the poor for personal gain.[156] It is for this reason that the law must be studied in its particular historical moment rather than treated as a static, 'silent constant'.[157] Ultimately, however, only those with a certain degree of power have the ability to define acts as 'crime' in the legal sense. Thus it is easy enough to see how some illegal acts could be popularly viewed as direct forms of protest. It also means, more significantly, that illegal acts that were less obviously framed as protest could still be a form of defiance as they indirectly challenged the ruling authority. In this sense, although John Rule is correct to stress that the most important aspect of 'social crime' is the element of popular approval and legitimacy rather than protest, we should also acknowledge that the degree to which an illegal act is consciously a form of protest does not necessarily affect its subversive impact on the established order.[158]

For this reason banditry and theft in places such as Fars influenced wider nationalist discourse in Iran. By the end of the Constitutional Revolution, their prevalence across the spectrum of the disempowered popular classes presented a problem for the formalization of law and order. Even for the former democrat of the Constitutional Revolution, Hassan Taqizadeh, the masses were nothing more than 'thieves and self-interested people'.[159] For the modernizing elites, theft was something that could only be remedied through a reform of the people's character and mind. For them, democratic politics could no longer be entrusted to the population. Rather, what was needed was a turn towards discipline, governmentality and authoritarian control. Among the 'dangerous classes' of society supposedly responsible for lawlessness, the tribes were to be one of the central targets in Reza Shah's efforts to control the country, whether through means of suppression or co-option.[160] The abstract rule of law, after all, demanded a legible and detectable population – something that the tribes seemed to inherently defy by their very existence. The 'tribal problem', then, would continue to live on in elite discourse until much later in the twentieth century.

Rural Crimes As Everyday Peasant Politics: Tax Delinquency, Smuggling, Theft and Banditry in Modern Turkey

Murat Metinsoy

Up to the 1990s, the peasantry had been so predominant in Turkey that Eric Hobsbawm wrote, 'Only one peasant stronghold remained in or around the neighbourhood of Europe and the Middle East – Turkey, where the peasantry declined but in the mid-1980s, still remained an absolute majority.'[1] As is well known, this was partially due to the structural limitations of the Turkish modernization even at its zenith during the 1920s and the 1930s. As this chapter reveals, another important but less-known reason was the peasants' struggle to survive and the resulting social conflicts that further delayed the dissolution of the peasantry and the modernization process.

Using new sources and drawing on a history-from-below approach, this chapter scrutinizes the everyday and informal means by which the Anatolian peasants survived, protected themselves and made their voices heard by the authorities during the first two decades of the Turkish republic. It shows how political exclusion drove the peasants to adopt more subtle and everyday forms of resistance short of rebellion that manifested itself in rural crimes. It also shows how and to what extent peasants influenced Turkish politics and modernization, albeit indirectly and unintentionally. Contrary to existing studies that portray peasants as hapless, intimidated opponents or archaic groups doomed to extinction, this chapter points out their key role in the formation of modern Turkey.

After the foundation of the Republic of Turkey in 1923, the single-party state, led by Atatürk and his Republican People's Party (RPP), embarked on a series of extensive political, cultural, legal and economic reform programmes to create a modern nation-state during the interwar period. State centralization and economic, legal and cultural modernization processes gained new momentum. Comprehensive modernization schemes were accompanied by the state's growing control over the population. The development of a Muslim-Turkish commercial class and the unification of local markets into a national market were among the primary goals of the new regime. The ruling elite, in close association and overlapping with business circles, gave impetus to economic modernization through the policy of state capitalism. In particular, the lack of basic industries led the new rulers to pursue state-led industrialization schemes.

In these years, peasants formed 80 per cent of Turkey's society and the agricultural sector was the mainstay of the economy, so the new regime had no other choice than funding its projects with rural resources. Hence, despite the abolition of the tithe (*aşar*) in 1925 and the ruling circles' populist rhetoric – embodied in Atatürk's famous saying 'the peasant is the master of the nation' (*köylü milletin efendisidir*) – the costs of creating a modern state weighed heavily on the lower echelons of the peasantry. The new taxes, monopolies, the commercialization of the rural economy as well as the industrialization schemes brought further exploitation and oppression. The poor peasants were squeezed between agents of the state (tax collectors, factory officials, gendarmes) and local power holders (village headmen and large landowners). The Great Depression further worsened the already unfavourable conditions in rural areas.

These aspects of Turkish history are all well known from historical studies. What is less known and equally important, however, is the peasants' experience of these extraordinary conditions, particularly their struggle for survival and rights. Surprisingly, although peasants constituted the majority of the population, their relations with the state and the local power holders have not been explored in depth. Scholars have mostly focused on state economic policies and agricultural structures.[2] The absence of organized peasant rebellions, except for a few well-known religious, tribal and Kurdish uprisings, led them to presume that the peasants simply succumbed to the increasing state intervention in their lives and the growing social injustice.[3] Historians of modern Turkey have barely examined everyday forms of the peasants' struggle for survival.[4] Rather, their focus on the ruling elite's populist discourse and the abolition of the tithe led them to argue that the new republic eased the peasants' economic conditions at the expense of industrialization.[5] They have also seen the small land holding as a static land tenure system, as if it had been free from the greed of large landowners (*ağa*s) and state capitalism. This postulation led historians to underestimate the intra-village struggles in which smallholders strove to keep their farms from falling under the large landowners' control.[6] This interpretation has also underpinned the peasant passivity thesis. Historians, whether critical or nationalist, have mostly considered rural crimes – such as livestock theft, smuggling and banditry – as peculiar to tribalism or Kurdish nationalism in eastern Anatolia.[7] Studies on Kurdish rebellions paid attention to rural crimes in the Kurdish provinces as long as they were tied with the Kurdish nationalist movement; other rural crimes were excluded from the narrative of 'the Kurdish awakening' or labelled as primordial acts of the peasants.[8]

However, given the broader definition of politics as a struggle for the allocation of economic resources and rights, the peasants' actions labelled as crime by the authorities can in fact be considered an extension of their politics in the form of anonymous resistance.[9] This resistance took various forms, ranging from tax avoidance, smuggling, and the theft of crops and livestock, to fights, physical attacks and finally banditry when avoidance was impossible. Along with other reasons, the accumulation of all these acts compelled the government to soften the obligations imposed on the peasantry or to ease the conditions that induced them to illegal actions and aggression. Thus they deserve close attention as the infra-politics of national politics.

Tax delinquency

Minimizing losses by avoiding heavy taxes was perhaps the peasants' main means of survival. Disputes over taxes were endemic in the Anatolian countryside and were the primary cause of rural crimes from evasion to violence.

The new republic relied on agriculture as the backbone of the economy to fund its extensive modernization schemes. Direct or indirect taxes on crops and livestock were the most common way of capturing agricultural surplus. Therefore, despite the abolition of the tithe in 1925 other agricultural taxes and tax burdens on the peasants gradually increased until the early 1930s. By doing so, the government attempted to compensate for the loss of tithe revenues.

The peasantry faced three major direct taxes in this period: the land tax, the livestock tax and the road tax. The land tax was imposed on all privately owned lands regardless of whether marshy, fallow, infertile or cultivated. The government gradually increased the land tax rates during the 1920s.[10] Under these circumstances, only big landowners who were able to produce on a large scale with greater input had enough cash to pay it. This tax therefore aggrieved primarily small- and middle-scale farmers, who were not able to cultivate all of their lands due to a lack of adequate agricultural equipment, irrigation and labour. As a result, they were often compelled to sell their land or run into debt.[11]

The livestock tax was one of the most important sources of revenue for the government from the beginning of the Independence War, with the rate increasing fourfold during the war. Between 1923 and 1929, and especially right after the abolition of the tithe, the government further increased its rate several times and extended the scope of the tax from sheep and goats to cows, oxen, donkeys, pigs, horses and camels.[12]

The road tax was another source of distress for peasants and low-income city dwellers. The National Assembly first imposed it in the Road Obligation Law of 1921, to finance the Independence War. This annual tax required each male between the ages of eighteen and sixty (except for the handicapped) to pay four days' income or provide three days' labour on road construction. In 1925, the law was amended to increase the tax. The tax amount was changed again in 1929 to a flat rate of 10 liras. The labour equivalent of the cash payment was also increased to twelve days working on road construction (at a maximum of twelve hours' distance from the taxpayer's domicile). This allowed the government to benefit from an unpaid labour force made up of low-income people, most of whom were poor peasants.[13]

Furthermore, the government imposed a wheat protection tax on mills in 1934 to create a fund for wheat purchases. The fund aimed to inhibit fluctuations in wheat production and prices.[14] Although in theory levied only on town mills, the tax also adversely affected peasants living near towns.

All these taxes weighed heavily on small peasants. Compounded by agricultural prices pushed down due to the economic crisis and by the government officials' red tape, malfeasance and mistakes, these taxes caused widespread discontent that culminated in tax avoidance and even protests in rural areas.

Petitions and letters to government offices and newspapers were an important, mostly formal, strategy for coping with the tax burden. Hundreds of thousands of peasants sought tax reduction, tax amnesty or redress for wrongdoing or abuse by tax collectors in this way. Letters from peasants complaining about agricultural taxes inundated the national press and the central authorities, especially during the Great Depression. The majority of petitions were by individuals, yet there was also a considerable number of collective petitions and letters penned by small or large groups of peasants. Rather than using anti-government or seditious language, the peasants used a rhetorical pose by praising the new regime in order to present their demands and complaints as legitimate and to invite the leaders to live up to their commitments and the RPP's principle of populism.[15]

When their demands were not met, peasants resorted to tax evasion. As David Burg writes in his comprehensive study on tax revolts, 'avoidance, although perhaps not overtly insurrectionist, has been a significant act of resistance to taxation'. In this period, Turkish peasants undertook several subtle avoidance strategies such as not declaring or undervaluing their property and hiding their income and taxable assets.[16]

As the prominent expert of agricultural economy Ömer Lütfi Barkan documented and Finance Ministry reports confirmed, the peasants either did not report or under reported their land holdings. There were also many who did not register their lands under their own names in order to escape the land tax.[17]

Likewise, peasants also tried to evade the livestock tax by under reporting or not declaring their animals. Many hid their animals in bedrooms, forests, hills or caves when tax officials came to their village. Livestock tax evasion was rampant especially in the distant mountainous eastern provinces, where animal husbandry was the main livelihood. Therefore there were always great gaps between the real numbers of livestock and the number taxed. For instance, whereas according to the official records there were 5,000 sheep in the centre of Bitlis, the real number was up to 40,000. Likewise, in Siirt the peasants declared only 12,000 sheep but the true number was 25,000.[18] In Dersim the number of declared and officially recorded farm animals was 68,875, but the peasants actually had around 170,000 farm animals. That is to say, the Dersim peasants managed to shelter about 100,000 animals from the livestock tax during the 1930s.[19] Many peasants managed to mislead tax officials by declaring that their sheep and goats were missing or else below the taxable age.[20] Indeed, the number of animals recorded and taxed by the state decreased sharply throughout the country after the tax increase.[21]

The most widespread tax avoidance method was to disappear whenever the tax officials came to the village. A peasant in Ardahan told Lilo Linke, a foreign journalist who toured Anatolia extensively in 1935: 'The peasants have nothing for themselves. They are so poor that they disappear into the mountains when the tax-collector comes near them.'[22]

In some villages, the peasants set up alarm systems to detect approaching tax collectors. In Diyarbakır, for instance, when the Kurdish shepherds caught sight of a tax collector, they spread the encoded news among the peasants by saying, 'the wolf is coming!' (*vêr gamê vêr* in Zazaki Kurdish).[23] In the villages of Balıkesir, the peasants began to stand watch on the roads to escape probable raids by the gendarme after they heard that the security forces started to detain those who did not fulfil their road tax obligations.[24]

Although corruption of the tax collectors was a significant problem, it did sometimes create an opportunity for the peasants to evade taxes. Tax collector salaries were low, and many were willing to accept bribes in the guise of a gift. Many peasants managed to avoid paying higher sums by bribing the tax collector with about a quarter (sometimes even less) of the tax amount owed or foodstuffs such as cereals, meat, eggs, milk or honey.[25]

When avoidance was not possible, the peasants did not hesitate to confront the tax collectors and the accompanying gendarmes, neither of whom they considered sympathetic. The peasantry always considered tax collectors a threat to their economic well-being; they were agents of the urban elite who transferred the peasants' daily bread to the well-off city dwellers. Whenever a tax collector dropped in, the villagers would say, 'The masters in the cities cannot eat stone!'[26] As is obvious from their ciphered message 'the wolf is coming!', for the Kurdish peasants, the tax officials were as dangerous as wolves. As foreign journalist Bernard Newman noted, in a large part of Anatolia the peasants regarded the tax collector as 'an agent of the devil'.[27] Yıldız Sertel, a contemporary sociologist who conducted a field study in Anatolian villages, wrote in her memoir that the peasants had deemed the state and its tax collectors 'the angel of death'.[28]

Such negative perceptions often led to aggressive action towards the tax officials. When there was no other way out, the peasants did not hesitate to raise their objections directly. Individual protests were a widespread pattern, but collective tax protests in front of the offices of the local authorities also happened occasionally. The wave of peasant women's protests that spread throughout central Anatolia in 1934 stands as a striking example of collective action. On 10 June 1934, fifteen women chanted slogans against the wheat protection tax in front of the government office in Kayseri. The security forces prosecuted some of them.[29] One month later, in July 1934, two other protests occurred: poor elderly peasant women in the İskilip district of Çorum and the Mudurnu district of Bolu rallied in front of government offices. According to the official who reported the events, 'the women made a great fuss in the streets and created uproar'. The protesters, complaining of poverty, demanded that the local government decrease the wheat protection tax.[30] In July 1934, a group of small flour mill owners from several villages around Ankara gathered in front of the Finance Ministry and expressed their objections to the tax burden imposed on them by the district governors.[31]

As a last resort, tax resistance took the form of attacks on tax collectors. Attacks when the tax collectors were on the road or even in a village, especially during or after tax collection, were the most frequent pattern of violence against them. Newspapers of the time are replete with stories about unfortunate tax collectors who were beaten, stabbed, shot or robbed by peasants.[32]

Sometimes the peasants confronted the tax collectors and security forces openly. For instance, in May 1929 peasants in a village near Urfa opposed a livestock census. Their quarrel with the tax collectors, escorted by gendarmes, led to a serious fight, at the end of which some livestock owners managed to escape with their animals.[33]

In April 1930 in the Girlavik village near Birecik, a peasant with a tax debt attempted to flee his home as soon as he realized that a tax official accompanied by gendarmes had arrived in the village. When the gendarmes surrounded him, the peasant shot a gendarme and the tax collector dead, and then managed to escape. Thenceforward, he lived in the mountains as the famous bandit Girlavikli Hino.[34]

Such armed clashes were not peculiar to eastern Anatolia. In June 1934, some peasants from the Botsa village in Konya attacked the tax collectors and gendarmes who had expropriated their untaxed livestock, and retook their animals. Another gendarme battalion then raided the village and beat the peasants, who in turn sued the tax officials and gendarmes.[35] Another incident of armed resistance occured in the Manavgat district of Antalya at midnight on 3 June 1937, when a group of peasants attacked a gendarme battalion and killed one officer. Livestock tax evasion was the main cause behind the incident.[36]

In eastern Anatolia, tax-related armed attacks on tax collectors and gendarmes sometimes grew into local uprisings. Since tribal community ties were used to mobilize support from other peasants, these uprisings have mostly been explained with reference to Kurdish nationalism or tribalism. Undoubtedly, Kurdish nationalists engineered several rebellions during this period. However, a closer look reveals that the peasants' subjective economic experiences and motivations played a more important role than nationalist motivations or the efforts of Kurdish organizations.

The Buban Rebellion is an example of how economic struggle underpinned the conflicts between state and society in the Kurdish provinces. In 1934, some villages in the Mutki district of Siirt (today the area of Bitlis) rebelled against the government. This incident, referred to as the Buban Tribe Rebellion, is usually considered to have been engineered by Kurdish nationalist groups. However, as in many other instances of peasant resistance in the region, this insurrection had not been motivated by any ideological hostility to the Turkish state but rather by state control over the local order.[37] The peasants first objected and then rose up against the government when the tax collectors and the gendarmes attempted to collect the road tax and to force those who could not pay to work on road construction sites. In addition, the state's policy of disarming the peasants left them defenceless against attacks by outsiders in the dangerous uplands. This also helped stoke the insurgence, which lasted about a year before the gendarme put it down.[38]

Less than one year later, in April 1935, Kurdish peasants in the Sason district of Siirt rose up against the government officials and security forces. Again neither Kurdish nationalism nor foreign powers were behind this insurgence. The conflicts broke out due to the growing tension between the tax collectors and the poor peasants who subsisted on animal husbandry and illegal tobacco farming. The annual census of taxable animals in spring always caused quarrels between the peasants and the tax collectors. The peasants frequently hid their animals; refused to report them or prevented the officials from counting them by sometimes driving the tax officials out of their villages. The intervention of the monopoly officials in the peasants' tobacco cultivation also fuelled local anxiety.[39] As a result of the pervasive non-cooperation, tax evasion and smuggling in the mountain villages in Sason, the local governor, accompanied by the *müftü* (official Muslim scholar and community leader) visited them to persuade the peasants to cooperate with the government. During a dinner given in his honour, a furious fight between the officials and the peasants broke out over tax matters. The fight escalated into an armed clash in which the district governor was killed and the *müftü* severely injured. The peasants were accused of the murder and hid in the mountains to defend themselves against the security forces. News of the events, labelled by the government as a rebellion, spread to other villages in Sason, which then also turned to armed resistance against tax collectors and monopoly officials. Hence peasant resistance was transformed into a local uprising, which attracted many other peasants in the region facing similar problems.[40]

Peasants spread their views and aspirations and communicated with each other through rumours. The peasants made use of this informal medium to produce and spread manipulative information in order to hearten disobedience by others, legitimize their own actions or provoke a government reaction against the tax collectors. When taxes increased and the tension between peasants and tax collectors rose, rumours about tax officials or the government sprang up. In January 1939, a few months after President Atatürk's death, a rumour alleging that a tax official had fired his gun into the air to celebrate the president's death and chanted anti-regime slogans swept through the villages in Kars. However, an investigation revealed this rumour had been put into circulation to set the local government against the tax collector because he had pressured peasants who avoided paying tax.[41] Also in January 1939, a peasant from a village in the Trabzon province refused to pay his taxes; to mobilize other peasants to join his disobedience, he spread a rumour of a military plot in Ankara.[42] Another rumour alleged that the new president İnönü had killed three tax collectors during his tour of Kastamonu in December 1938. Rumour had it that based on a widespread denunciation of a tax collector, İnönü wanted to investigate the situation; when the accused tax collector and two of his colleagues attacked the president, he shot them in self-defence.[43] It was not possible to ascertain the source of the rumour, however, it is reasonable to think that peasants had sought to justify their hatred of and resistance to tax collectors by fabricating this rumour.

The effects of tax resistance

Peasant resistance, along with other factors, obliged the government to reduce the rates and scope of taxation during the 1930s. Facing widespread land tax evasion and without an accurate land registry or cadastral information, the government left land tax revenues to the local governments and cut the rate by about 35 per cent.[44] In addition, widespread discontent and tax avoidance as well as a fall in livestock prices due to the Great Depression resulted in successive reductions in the livestock tax rates in 1931, 1932, 1936 and 1938, nearly halving them and removing horses and donkeys from the list of taxable livestock.[45] Similarly, in 1931 resistance to the road tax in both rural and urban areas forced the government to lower the rates by around 50–65 per cent and to adjust the labour equivalent accordingly.[46] Finally, in May 1935, in view of the widespread complaints and protests against the wheat protection tax, all village wheat mills, including those near urban centres, were exempted. Furthermore, the government forgave some outstanding agricultural tax debts in 1934 and 1938.[47]

However, the peasants' struggles with taxes did not end here. Public and private monopolies meant indirect taxation. The monopoly system also brought about the commercialization of rural resources and restricted the peasants' access to them. Peasants resisted the monopolies through smuggling.

Social smuggling: Coping with monopolies

Smuggling, or what I prefer to call 'social smuggling', was the daily illegal production and trade by small producers and consumers of the basic consumer goods monopolized by the government. Rather than the lucrative transactions carried out by smuggling bands, the main purpose of this kind of smuggling was to avoid the restrictions on production and trade and the high prices imposed by the monopolies. This made smuggling another form of peasant resistance to the government's intervention in the local economy.

In the Ottoman era, monopolies constituted a major source of revenue on which the government relied to finance its economic and administrative modernization projects or to repay foreign loans. The Turkish republic resorted to monopolies more systematically than the Ottoman administration had done in order to finance the modernization and state-making schemes. The production and trade of goods such as salt, tobacco, cigarettes, cigarette paper, alcoholic beverages, sugar, matches and lighters were monopolized during the first two decades of the republic. By heavily taxing or leasing out the production or trade of these commodities to a limited number of public and private enterprises, the government generated enormous revenues. Monopolies were the second largest source of income for the state budget after taxes. The tobacco monopoly alone generated about 10 to 14 per cent of the government's revenue during the 1923 to 1943 timespan.[48]

Indirect taxation through monopolies, imposed alongside direct taxes, drove down the standard of living in the countryside. The monopoly system hit a large number of small traders, producers or consumers of the monopolized goods. The introduction of the tobacco monopoly, for instance, meant the removal of livelihood from many tobacco farmers and itinerant tobacco merchants of peasant origin. The government did not permit peasants to cultivate and sell tobacco, produce cigarettes, make use of salt mines and lakes, produce and sell alcoholic beverages, or cut timber in the forests without a licence. For low-income peasants getting a licence meant an additional cost. Consequently, such restrictions encouraged smuggling. Thus, conflicts between peasants and monopoly officials (backed by the security forces) were a phenomenon of rural life, albeit not so harsh and bloody as in the Ottoman Empire.[49]

Smuggling was so widespread that the government promulgated the Law on the Prohibition and Prosecution of Smuggling in 1927.[50] When it proved to be ineffective, more comprehensive and harsher anti-smuggling laws were passed in 1929[51] and 1932.[52] According to the preamble of the 1932 law, smuggling had gained a momentum that threatened the country; therefore its causes and antidotes required more serious reconsideration.[53]

The ruling circles considered smuggling so subversive and dangerous that in 1931, the RPP deputies suggested re-establishing the Independence Tribunals (*İstiklâl Mahkemeleri*), which had operated from the Independence War to the mid-1920s to quickly prosecute deserters, traitors, and rebels.[54] Instead, the Justice Ministry set up specialized courts to deal with smuggling in provinces where it was most rampant.[55] The government also launched a strong propaganda campaign that equated smuggling with treason. However, neither punitive measures nor extensive propaganda were able to cope with the smuggling epidemic.

The main characteristics, actors and dimensions of social smuggling

Many reasons drove peasants to smuggling. The restriction on production, high licence fees and taxes, the maze of regulations and frequent malfeasance by monopoly officials all pushed agricultural producers and traders to shift to a 'black economy'. As producers and traders, peasants strived to protect their traditional economic rights by resisting state control over their age-old everyday transactions. As compared to their astronomical prices, the poor-quality commodities produced and sold by the monopolies increased the demand for smuggled goods, as did the price difference between smuggled and taxed goods.

Smuggling therefore stands out largely as a loss-minimizing strategy for the peasants as producers, traders and consumers in a repressive tax regime that favoured a small number of national monopolies protected with high tariff rates. Peasants compensated for the unfavourable prices the monopolies offered by means of smuggling.

In this sense, smuggling was not peculiar to large bands. In fact, it was a widely recognized activity largely diffused to the grassroots. Low-income people considered smuggling a legitimate and even glorified job, whereas the ruling circles categorized it as crime against property and even against the nation. The ruling authorities were right in their concern about the effect of smuggling on the state monopolies: it indirectly increased the bargaining power of small producers and consumers by providing cheaper alternatives. Therefore, it spread throughout Anatolia during the economic crisis that made the peasants' life much harder.

Social smuggling was carried out by low-income people, especially poor peasants in rural areas or frontier zones that made cross-border transactions or escape from law enforcers easier. As noted by an observer, the smugglers in rural areas were all poor people striving to make ends meet.[56] The press, though it criticized smuggling, frequently pointed out that many low-income people depended on their moderate earnings from smuggling. Court cases demonstrate most smugglers were small dealers living from hand to mouth. For example, in a smuggling trial in April 1935, two defendants from villages near Istanbul alleged that they had to get involved in smuggling because of poverty, which was accepted as true both by the court and the press commenting on the trial.[57]

Forests, mountains, lakes and rivers, caves, graveyards, farmhouses and cottages were often used to conceal smuggled items. Both consumers and traders hid the smuggled items inside their socks, shirts, pants, secret compartments in their bags or in their homes under beds or in cupboards called *yüklük*. They also used a coded language to confuse the authorities; for instance, shredded tobacco was referred to as 'ayınga' and tobacco smugglers 'ayıngacı'.[58]

The scale of smuggling is hinted at in the historical records, most of which are reports on smugglers captured by security forces. Successful smugglers left little or no trace of their activities; therefore the evidence available, albeit in huge quantity, is only the tip of the iceberg. The press often ran stories on smuggling; the *İkdam* newspaper, for example, reported several cases of smuggling to draw attention to its prevalence across the country in the late 1920s. Increasing state intervention in the economy during the 1930s accelerated smuggling, which also meant it featured more frequently in the press. For example, on 1 April 1932, a newspaper wrote that the specialized court for smuggling in İstanbul alone ruled on eleven cases a day. In June 1932, the gendarmes arrested four hundred smugglers just in Muğla, sixteen of whom received inprisonment. The specialized court in Gaziantep was choked with thousands of cases; it reportedly ruled on 4,250 cases in 1934 alone.[59]

Despite the state's immense efforts to stamp it out, in 1938 a contemporary observer noted that 'smuggling maintains its dominance and triumphs despite the struggle of the state institutions that costs millions of Turkish liras'.[60] For one thing, the government failed to gain the people's support in this struggle. The state propaganda labelled smugglers as 'traitors' and 'degenerates' and invited citizens to denounce them immediately. However, the poor and smallholding peasants, especially in the eastern provinces, saw smuggling as their main livelihood given the high cost of living and the provisioning problems the government was unable to solve.[61]

An official report on smuggling from October 1933 states that some smugglers also engaged in banditry for reasons of self-defence: one way to cope with the security forces was to fend them off, and smugglers sometimes resisted capture by opening fire.[62] In one instance among many, in December 1931 in the Tepeköy village near Kütahya, seven armed smugglers were ambushed and captured with 250 *okka*s of cut rag tobacco.[63] As reported by the Trabzon governorship, the tobacco smugglers did not hesistate to fire back on the government forces.[64]

The state pressure on the peasants who produced unlicensed tobacco or salt often led them to take up arms against monopoly officials and security forces. Throughout the eastern provinces – Dersim, Muş, Siirt, Bitlis, Urfa and Diyarbakır – the peasants continued to produce tobacco without a licence on their few *dönüm*s of land and sell it clandestinely to neighbouring tribes, towns or traders.[65] This caused never-ending fights between the security forces and villagers involved in illegal tobacco production and trade. These clashes, usually interpreted as ethnic conflicts by Turkish and Kurdish scholars, were in fact related to economic conflict over scarce resources.[66]

The monopoly administration (*inhisarlar idaresi*) exerted considerable effort to conquer the markets in the Kurdish provinces in the east. Economic life in these distant mountainous provinces had remained more autonomous, with strong ties to cross-border markets, since the Ottomans. However, the new state aimed to create a unified market within the national borders. The monopoly administration, managed by the bureaucratic elite and working hand in hand with business circles, thirsted for the profits expected to flow from these places. This was another reason behind the state's brutality in the Kurdish provinces.[67] Consequently, the vicious cycle of social injustice, illegal economic transactions, state violence and further injustice engendered serious tensions and armed conflicts.

In one incident in 1933, the monopoly administration officials raided Halikan and Harabak, two villages near Sason whose economies relied on tobacco and livestock farming. The monopoly administration officials, accompanied by gendarmes, attempted to destroy the illegal tobacco farms but were confronted by the peasants.[68] The tension remained under control until the government took harsher action against illegal tobacco cultivation in 1935. Along with the above-mentioned conflict caused by the livestock tax, the officials' attempt to dismantle the tobacco farms spurred a widespread peasant uprising referred to as the Second Sason Insurgency. The uprising in Sason has widely been considered an extension of Kurdish or tribal resistance, but it was essentially related to the peasants' effort to prevent the spread of the state-imposed market regulations that undermined their livelihood.[69]

Salt was another vital resource for peasants, used as a key ingredient in animal husbandry, leather processing and daily food. Upon nationalizing the salt mines and lakes, the government levied high monopoly taxes on salt production and trade. This resulted in a concominant increase in salt prices, which aggrieved both livestock owners and consumers.[70] The soaring prices of salt led some peasants and traders to continue extracting salt from nearby mines and lakes clandestinely. For example, the peasants near Lake Seyfe, an important salt lake in Kırşehir, would shovel the salt from the lake and load it on their donkeys secretly in the darkness of night, sometimes having to confront monopoly officials. The use of contraband salt was so widespread in Anatolian villages that peasants kept the salt they owned a secret to avoid being suspected of illegally extracting it.[71]

The conflict over access to salt, concurrent with other conflicts between the government and locals, escalated into revolts. For instance, in the Baykan district of Siirt, a dispute between the monopoly officials and peasants over the latter's use of salt mines and lakes without official permission grew into a local uprising with Kurdish and Islamic overtones. The Şeyh Abdürrahman Rebellion (named thus by the state) that broke out in 1926 is one such incident. Although the government claimed the right to all salt mines in the region, the peasants persisted in using them illegally. The theft of a huge amount of salt from the salt depots of the monopoly administration in the Melekhan subdistrict triggered the revolt. When the gendarmes attempted to arrest Abdürrahman, a local livestock owner, and his fellows as the suspected thieves, he and his tribe rose up against the gendarmes. The uprising spread to nearby villages and subdistricts, including Mollaşeref, Merijan and Navalan, and the government had to seal the area off to quell the rebellion.[72]

The effects of smuggling

The government initially responded to smuggling with punitive measures and propaganda, neither of which was to be successful. In the mid-1930s the government began to turn to economic measures to eliminate the economic conditions that paved the way for smuggling. In the mid- and the late 1930s leading politicians, including Prime Minister İnönü, began to push for discounts on goods that often featured among contraband items such as sugar, salt, tobacco, cigarettes, rakı and cotton textiles.[73] Thus smuggling increased the consumers' bargaining power by prompting the government to take action against the soaring prices of monopoly goods.

Moreover, smuggling, undermining the status of monopolies, created an informal duopoly that enabled the consumers to choose the better alternative. Therefore, people in Anatolia, especially the peasants, did not give up illegal economic transactions in the first two decades of the republic. Uncontrolled tobacco smuggling was among the factors that obliged the government to officially allow many of the peasants who had been banned from tobacco cultivation to grow it again. A careful look at the zones where tobacco cultivation was forbidden reveals that a considerable portion of the arable land was reopened to tobacco farming between 1930 and 1938. In practice this meant many illegal tobacco farms regained their legal status.[74]

Monopoly products remained expensive despite the fall in the prices of raw materials due to the economic crisis. Given the high profit margins of the monopoly goods, smuggling, along with the economic depression, likely played a role in the significant drop in monopoly income – from 41 million liras in 1930 to 32 million liras in 1935. That meant the incomes the government obtained for its modernization projects through monopolies fell behind the levels it had expected.[75]

Theft, robbery, and violence

When it was unavoidable, the peasants did not hesitate to violate the property or lives of people who were oppressive and corrupt, such as tax collectors, district governors, gendarmes, village headmen, large landowners and moneylenders. The peasants' repertoire of action ranged from theft, intimidation and physical attacks to robbery and banditry. Turkey's authoritarian system did not allow poor peasants to pursue their rights through legal political participation, and these acts, considered criminal by the ruling circles, were their last resort for self-help and self-defense. For this reason, taking politics in its wider sense as a struggle for survival and scarce economic resources, I propose abandoning an absolute distinction between the notions of political acts and crimes commited in self-defence against the overlapping exploitation and oppression by the state and local power holders. When the peasants' misery and ill-treatment reached a level so unbearable that they could do nothing but violate the law, they tried less drastic acts first: stealing, robbery, arson, fighting or physical attacks. Only some took things a step further and resorted to armed resistance, that is, banditry, when push came to shove.

Violation of property: Theft of crops and livestock

Struggles over livestock and crops, which could be lifted easily, did not necessarily generate open confrontation. The main threat directed towards the livestock and crops belonging to big farmers was theft. Livestock theft was so widespread that in the early 1930s many farmers began to stand guard with their rifles day and night.[76] The epidemic proportions of livestock theft were behind the 1929 amendment of the Law on the Elimination of Livestock Theft, which dated from 6 April 1923. This law, incapable of preventing livestock theft, was once again discussed in the National Assembly in December 1933. During the parliamentary session, a Samsun MP argued that almost all peasants in this province had turned into thieves of animal and crop.[77]

The İzmir RPP provincial congress held in 1936 noted that 'agricultural security' (*zirai asayiş*) was not good in the districts. According to the minutes of the congress, many shepherds were stealing crops and animals from farmers.[78] This was not unique to İzmir; many poor shepherds and herders stole the livestock of their *ağas* and then pretended to have been raided by robbers.[79]

A newspaper reported in 1932 that horse theft in the Çukurova region (one of the most important agricultural centres) had increased so much in the preceding few years that the number of stolen horses exceeded five hundred a year.[80] Similarly, in April 1932 an article titled 'Livestock Theft in Aydın' in the same paper reported that cattle rustling had begun to torment the farmers of the region. It mentioned an incident when seven poor peasants from an Aydın village had stolen a farmer's cows, slaughtered them and sold the meat and hides at the Aydın bazaar.[81] In October 1936 it was reported from Karaman that the nearby villages were full of livestock thieves.[82]

An official report by Hulusi Alataş, the then health and social aid minister, argued that landlessness was a major reason why poor peasants, especially in the eastern provinces, engaged in theft, robbery or arson in order to survive. Livestock theft in particular was plaguing the eastern countryside and the minister called on the government to urgently distribute arable land to the landless peasants to cure this epidemic.[83]

Attacking and murdering village headmen, landowners and state officials

Often the peasants' objections to anything they perceived as injustice, whether due to disputes over land, livestock or taxes, turned into a fight to the death. Angry peasants found themselves in direct confrontation with their oppressors. Accordingly, the crime rates, including injuries, murders as well as theft, were on the rise in rural areas, especially during the late 1920s and early 1930s. As stated in official reports, security could not be effectively maintained in the Anatolian countryside. Despite the relative economic recovery in the mid-1920s, the Great Depression and heavy taxes worsened living standards again, which boosted the number of crimes.[84]

Conflicting claims over scarce resources such as land and water often ended in fights and even murder. As documented by Barkan, who examined the court files of 1,279 murder cases from Kocaeli, Bursa, Denizli, Konya, İçel, Rize, Malatya and Sivas, about 40 per cent of these murders were closely connected to disputes over land and other agricultural resources.[85] Likewise, a contemporaneous politician and forensic medicine expert Fahri Ecevit wrote a report for the *Police Periodical* on the causes of the crime boom in rural areas during the 1930s. In contrast to the politicians' oversimplifications ascribing the problem to alcoholism and love affairs, he argued that the majority of the crimes committed by peasants stemmed from land disputes.[86]

Oppressive village headmen, landowners and tax collectors were the groups primarily vulnerable to peasants' attacks. Poor peasants and smallholders especially hated village headmen, who mostly came from or were manipulated by influential families. What is more, the village headmen functioned as intermediaries between the state and the peasantry by liaising with state officials, taking care of public and even private property, reporting crimes and criminals, and even determining the amount of tax owed by the peasants. They even had the right to levy a village tax (*salma*) to meet the cost of public works in the village. For these reasons, peasant discontent with state policies and social injustice often turned into acts of violence directed at village headmen.

For instance, in the Burhaniye village near Adapazarı, the village headman pressured the peasants to pay a tax he levied to fill the village fund. When some of the peasants objected, a squabble ensued, three peasants started fighting with the headman and one of them shot and killed him.[87] In another incident in a village near Balıkesir, a peasant named Mustafa first shot the village headman and then cut his throat. Such horrible page-three stories appeared in the press regularly during this period.[88]

State officials, especially tax collectors, debt enforcement officials and gendarmes, were also at a risk of peasant attacks. In one instance, a debt enforcement official accompanied by a gendarme officer confiscated the money and property of a poor peasant named Adem Pehlivan from the Akça village in Balıkesir for failing to pay the road tax. Adem Pehlivan, aided by two angry friends armed with rifles, ambushed and killed the gendarme officer, took all the confiscated money and ran away.[89] Other similar cases included the murder of a tax collector named Akif Fikri in Düzce in 1931;[90] the killing of a tax collector named Raşid in 1936[91]; and the shooting of a tax collector in a village near Muğla, also in 1936.[92] All of these crimes were committed by poor peasants. These were not sporadic examples but part and parcel of daily life in the Anatolian countryside.

As mentioned above, peasants, especially in the eastern Kurdish provinces, were capable of long-lasting collective resistance. For example, in April 1934 the peasants living in a village near Mutki joined forces to prevent both the tax officials and the gendarmes from entering their village.[93] Likewise, in June 1935 peasants in Sason stood up to the state officials pressing them to pay taxes, which led to an armed uprising.[94]

Land was the main cause for which peasants were willing to run the risk of committing murder or being murdered. Fights due to land disputes between peasants were common and often ended in murder. In the Yomra district of Trabzon, where many peasants were in debt to moneylenders, for instance, a poor peasant named Kamil killed Mustafa Ağa who had attempted to take his land.[95] In one Anatolian village, one peasant shot another because of a quarrel over the ownership of a vegetable garden.[96] Likewise, in August 1931 a fight over land and irrigation water between two peasants in the Hacılar village near Kayseri ended in murder.[97] Such fatal incidents were so widespread in villages that during İnönü's tour of Kastamonu in 1938, the peasants complained about the high number of murders caused by disagreements over land.[98]

Peasants sometimes resisted the enclosure of collectively used lands for private use. Upon the Uşak municipality's decision to assign a pasture of about 100 *dönüms* in Akse village to a sugar factory in 1932, the peasants came to blows with the gendarmes accompanying the municipality officials who came to the village to fence off the land. Armed with sticks and stones, the peasants attacked the factory staff and descended on the factory building to intimidate the administration. After this incident, the mayor of the Uşak province, accompanied by gendarmes, went to the village to enclose the land. The peasants again rose up. The brawl turned into a gunfight in which four peasants were seriously wounded, and many were prosecuted afterwards.[99]

Local administrators were so overwhelmed by such land-related conflicts that some admonished the government to urgently sort out the land problem. For instance, the Diyarbakır governor, Cemal Bardakçı, reported that there were more than 3,500 inmates in the Diyarbakır prisons in 1926, most of whom were smallholders who had refused to surrender their small plots to large landowners. He strongly recommended the government to distribute vacant lands to the landless poor peasants to prevent the soaring crimes.[100]

Taking to the hills: Banditry

Clausewitz's idea that 'war is an extension of politics by other means' is true not only for relations between states but also for the relations between states and their citizens or between social groups.[101] Banditry – i.e. the waging of an armed struggle against security forces or local adversaries by hiding out in mountains – though a regular way of life for many robbers and killers, was generally the last resort for peasants resisting injustice. Banditry was no stranger to Anatolian society since the Ottoman Empire.[102] As elsewhere in the world, during the Ottoman era banditry and political brigandage emerged in connection with the social effects of wars, economic crises, the decline of state authority or poor administration. Bandits sprung up also as a response to increasing state intervention, modernization or market forces that damaged people's livelihood.[103]

The long war years extending from the Balkan Wars through the First World War to the Independence War had turned Anatolian society upside down and created a power vacuum that the outlaws exploited in the first years of the republic. The new Turkish state exerted great effort to impose its authority. However, the attempt to build a modern central administration and penetrate social, economic and cultural life generated new conflicts that fed banditry. The Great Depression further damaged the social balance. Thus, banditry, albeit in decline compared to the early 1920s, did not disappear during the interwar years.

Banditry and struggles between bandits and gendarmes were so common in the interwar years that the *Köroğlu* newspaper serialized a short novel titled *Candarma Bekir Eşkıya Peşinde* (Gendarme Bekir in Pursuit of Bandit, first published on 30 January 1932).[104] The phenomenon of banditry also left its mark in the literary works penned by Turkey's most prominent novelists. Banditry featured in the masterpieces of Yaşar Kemal, Kemal Bilbaşar and Kemal Tahir, all of whom were keen observers of rural life during the early republic. The hero of Yaşar Kemal's magnum opus *İnce Memed* was a famous good bandit who waged a war against a greedy *ağa* in the 1930s. Bilbaşar's *Memo* was another figure who rose up against a cruel *ağa* in the same period. On the other hand, Tahir presented bandits who were manipulated by *ağas* or had ill intensions.[105] Despite the existence of vicious bandits, as a contemporary eyewitness wrote in *Ülkü* (*Ideal*, the most popular official periodical released by the Ankara People's House), there were many good bandits who stood up to social injustice and whom the peasants respected.[106]

Bearing in mind that banditry was a last resort in the struggle against social injustice, the actions of most of the bandits during the interwar years fit the notion of 'social banditry'[107] if we define the term more broadly than Hobsbawm did. Admittedly there were also oppressive and criminal-minded bandits who cooperated with the dominant groups or who did not differentiate among their targets. However, most bandits were not ruthless outlaws who wanted to make a fortune by robbing people from all classes indiscriminately. On the contrary, they were, for the most part, oppressed, exploited, and abused peasants who strove to survive. Although they struggled only for their own causes and did not champion social reform, they mostly targeted their specific oppressors, exploiters and state agents who mistreated their families or the well-off propertied classes. This distinguished them from criminal-minded outlaws. Consequently, they were sometimes admired and aided by poor peasants and became the subjects of popular songs and poems.

The road to banditry was not very long or complicated and did not require much planning or organization. All the above-mentioned individual events of theft, fight and murder could open the doors into banditry. Some peasants who committed these acts had no choice but to flee to the mountains to defend themselves. This not only provided them with an escape from their enemies but also with an opportunity to take revenge by robbing, frightening or attacking them.

Moreover, contrary to the general assumption, banditry was not peculiar to the Kurdish provinces. Nor was it much related to tribalism or Kurdish nationalism. It would be an oversimplification to attribute such a widespread social phenomenon only to these factors. Above all, it was the peasant discontent with sharp social injustice and domination that gave rise to banditry as a coping mechanism.[108] Undoubtedly, collective reactions in the form of insurrection developed wherever tribal and ethnic ties made mobilization of the peasant community more feasible. Furthermore, due to the very unequal distribution of land, lack of state and judicial authority, proximity to frontier zones, mountainous topography as well as Kurdish or tribal idendities, large bandit groups were much more noticeable in eastern Anatolia than in any other region of Turkey. However, other regions of Anatolia were also replete with bandit groups, both small and big.

In other words, as Hobsbawm underlines, banditry had to do with peasant aggression caused by the deterioration of living standards, growing inequality, economic crisis, increasing state intervention and rural oppression.[109] Indeed, as Scott points out, peasants could become more aggressive when the prices of their crops dropped sharply, exploitation became more intense and their moral economy, based on mutuality, solidarity, fairness and justice, was broken by market forces.[110] Indeed, by intimidating, attacking and robbing state agents, rich merchants and greedy large landlords, the bandits stood for a sort of peasant resistance to the growing rural pauperization and oppression.

A brief overview of the petitions complaining of bandits gives insight into the nature of banditry and its targets. The authors of these petitions were generally rich and powerful peasants, as is clear from the properties they lost to the bandits, and their nicknames and titles such as '*muhtar*', '*hacı*', '*ağa*', '*hacı ağa*', '*efendi*', '*tüccar*' and '*eşraf*'. Merchants and company managers travelling along intercity highways were also targeted frequently. In 1934, for example, Hacı B. from Ünye complained that a group of bandits seized 1,500 liras from him. Haşim Efendi, also from Ünye, complained of widespread robbery and murder by bandits in the region. In a similar vein, a merchant named Hüdaverdi Efendi from Elaziz demanded the government compensate him for a lorry stolen by bandits. Likewise, Ali Efendi, a livestock merchant in the Erciş district of Van, claimed damages for seven hundred sheep extorted by bandits.[111] These are a few cases among many.

Disputes over land and other rural resources were one of the causes pushing disadvantaged peasants to banditry in order to defend their small properties and their rights to use common fields. The rampant banditry in the Kadirli district of Adana in the late 1920s and early 1930s, for example, was closely related to the disputes over a large uncultivated area known as Akçasaz. The story of some of the bandits might shed light upon what fuelled banditry in that region. In 1927 a peasant named Remzi, aggrieved by corrupt officials and the *ağa* who tried to seize his land, objected to them. To silence him, the public prosecutor issued an arrest warrant. As soon as he heard of this, Remzi fled into the mountains and became a bandit to fight against his oppressors.[112] Hacıveli's story was somewhat similar. He was a farmer from the same district who became a bandit to fight against the *ağa* who had seized his land. Safiye Mehmet, a popular bandit in Kadirli, had also taken to the hills to challenge an *ağa* for taking his beloved horse.[113]

Similar economic conflicts pushed the peasants to mountains in all parts of Anatolia. Cello was another famous bandit in the early 1930s. He had been a poor young peasant who herded the cattle of his *ağa* in the İncedere village of Kayseri. When the *ağa* had not paid him for a long time, Cello stole one of the *ağa*'s donkeys and sold it to buy a gun. He then left the village to become a bandit and robbed mail cars in order to survive in the mountains.[114]

Alo, a well-known bandit of the 1930s, had been a poor shepherd working on the farm of Demiroğlu Molla Hüseyin Ağa in the Keklikoluk village of Maraş. Alo resented the *ağa* as the latter cheated and exploited him on several occasions. Well aware of Alo's resentment, the *ağa* decided to punish him by alleging that Alo and his mother had stolen a lamb from his farm, then he had Alo's mother beaten in the village square so severely that she died. After this, Alo obtained some rifles, took to the Taurus Mountains and joined Kara Paşo, who was another good bandit with the reputation of targeting greedy *ağas*. Aware of the peasants' covert support of Alo, Demiroğlu began to terrorize them and sent his armed men to the mountains to kill Alo. The latter shot about twenty of them dead and took revenge by raiding Demiroğlu's cottage and killing him.[115]

Another example involves Alim, a young peasant boy from Afyon, a western Anatolian wheat and opium centre. He was reputed to be a brave *efe* (as bandits were called in the Aegean region) in the 1930s. A dominant family prevented Alim's family from cultivating their own lands in Dinar district and fights gradually broke out between the two families. Alim killed one member of the rival family and severely wounded two others. To escape prosecution and probable reprisal, he headed for the hills. The gunfights between him and the rival family continued until Alim was killed in the 1950s.[116]

Some peasants took shelter in the mountains and became bandits after a confrontation with state officials. The case of Girlavikli Hino, mentioned above, is a good example. The Kurdish-populated eastern highlands were full of peasants like him. Such individual or communal resistance to the state's assault on local economic relations occasionally became politicized, adopting ethnic-tribal tones to mobilize the neighbouring peasant communities.

Highway robbery and raids on houses or farms were perhaps the most common crimes committed by bandits both in order to survive in the mountains and to intimidate their foes. Bandits stopped and robbed cars, buses and lorries, whether civilian or military, which generally conveyed rich merchants, tax officials and bureaucrats. Newspapers of the time were full of news about banditry even after the single-party state had consolidated its power during the 1930s. In December 1935, for instance, it was reported that two bandit leaders named Kucaklı Hasan and Siverekli Ramazan had been robbing rich peasants and passengers in the Urfa region since 1926. They had many supporters among poor peasants. Their bands had killed eight people, including four gendarmes, in nine years.[117] It is possible to identify traces of similar robberies in the western countryside. For example, a bandit named Muradoğlu Vahid held sway over Düzce and its surrounding region from 1933 to May 1935, hijacking well-off passengers and raiding influential individuals' farms and homes until the gendarmes killed him in a confrontation.[118]

A limited number of bandits were much closer to Hobsbawm's notion of a social bandit, helping the indigent peasants in some ways. Some attempted to dispense justice in order to save the poor peasants from the law courts as they were open to manipulation by local power brokers. Serving as more efficient, quicker and mobile 'moral law courts' sympathetic to the poor, bandits aimed to gain popular support. For example, imitating the late and well-known bandit Çakırcalı Mehmet Efe, Gezik Duran stormed through the Adana region during the 1920s raiding rich peasants' houses and robbing or killing many. The peasants actively supported and aided him,[119] and some folk songs expressed grief after his death at the hands of Kel Kadı Osman, a killer with a bad reputation whom the peasants hated.[120]

In another case, a group of bandits began attacking rich and oppressive estate owners in Kozan (Adana) in June 1931. Their first attack was on the Alçalı village, where they robbed a village grocer of 400 liras. What is more unusual, they attempted to replace the government authority and laws with their own, which they considered more practical and moral. For this reason, they even visited villages to settle disputes between peasants.[121] As reported by a newspaper in July 1933, some poor peasants admired and aided such bandits.[122]

Concluding remarks: Dangerous politics in dangerous conditions

Under authoritarian state capitalism, peasant politics in Turkey took everyday and informal forms. The mostly illiterate poor people's misery, grievance and struggle for survival took the form of self-protective and loss-minimizing acts, which often fell into the category of what the state and local power-holders labelled crime. Looking at the issue in the context of social conflict, I propose considering the bulk of rural crimes as the everyday and informal politics of poor peasants, devised to cope with their oppressors and exploiters. The main point I wish to make is that social injustice was the main force fuelling rural crimes. Assault on their age-old lifestyles and basic livelihood as well as exclusion from official politics under an authoritarian polity left the peasants with no option other than defending themselves through familiar illegal means.

Undoubtedly the peasants never targeted the social and political order directly, nor did they envisage an alternative order. They sought rather to secure their existing livelihood and rights. However, their daily informal politics were not inconsequential. It created a covert negotiation process and, notwithstanding the lack of any profound change, forced the state to revise its policies. It is possible to say that the peasants' everyday politics, in addition to other considerations – such as creating stability in the Kurdish regions through resettlement policies – was behind the state's attempts at land reform, which resulted in a – albeit limited and intermittent – distribution of land to landless peasants and smallholders. The peasants' intractability may have been part of the reason behind the ruling elite's decision to establish village institutes in the early 1940s to educate and subdue them.

Above all, the peasants' everyday politics constituted a great obstacle to the state's access to rural surpluses for financing its modernization projects. In other words, not only infrastructural weakness to transform the countryside but also peasants' struggle for survival must also have played a role in the sluggish nature of Turkey's transformation from a rural to an urban society. The concomitant predominance of the peasantry and agriculture as the chief sector of society and the economy also left its mark on social, cultural and political life. It would create a fertile ground for the rise of conservative religious politics in the following decades. Along with other factors such as neoliberal policies and globalization, which eroded the welfare state and civic national identity, the prevalence of a rural society based on traditional and religious bonds can be held responsible for the rise of political Islam in Turkey.

Political violence and banditry is also part of the legacy of peasant politics, especially in the Kurdish provinces. It strongly influenced the strategies that the Kurdish political movement adopted in the following decades. The Kurdish peasants' resistance to social injustice and the state control created conditions in which the Kurdish political movement could gain mass support. Indeed, the popular bandits of the 1920s and 1930s, even though most of them did not have any ideological agenda, served as a model of armed resistance for the next generations, who saw no other way out in the face of Ankara's militarist policies.

Perhaps the most important conclusion to be drawn from this study is that people under dangerous conditions that disenfranchise them socially and politically adopt dangerous politics. This is evident also from the wave of violent attacks and political turbulence that have engulfed Turkey, the Middle East and other parts of the world. There must be no doubt that the poverty and social injustice accompanied by political exclusion and oppression suffered by the growing masses of urban poor, ethnic and religious minorities and hapless migrant groups will make them feel they have no way to survive other than violating the law. Gradually, such acts may take an ideological or organized form and create the social ground for greater political turmoils as has been experienced in Turkey.

Part Three

Dangerous Streets

Urban Food Riots in Late Ottoman *Bilad al-Sham* as a 'Repertoire of Contention'

Till Grallert

On 21 August 1908, less than four weeks after the restoration of the constitution in the Ottoman Empire, the daily newspaper *Lisan al-Hal* from Beirut published the following article:

> Large crowds of the poor and destitute gathered the morning before yesterday [19. August] (*ijtama'a* [...] *jumhur kabir min al-fuqara' wa arbab al-ayyal*) in front of the government Serail in Beirut. [There] they cried for help, lamented the current situation and called for the prices of flour and bread to be lowered to ease their suffering and that of all the poor; [...] most flour merchants and oven and bakery owners tyrannise them and profit from [the sale of] sunflower bread in clear breach of all laws and regulations (*jami' al-qawanin wa-l-shara'i'*) to the extent that a *ratl*[1] of bread was sold at more than 7.5 piastres (Ps).[2] This is unjust (*hadha mi-ma ta'bahu al-'adala*) and unacceptable.
>
> The protesters grew increasingly vocal until the vigorous Anis Efendi Ramadan, inspector of the police, went out to meet them and soothed their minds with a speech full of courtesy and refinement. He assured the protesters that the authorities were directing their zeal and efforts to the lowering of the prices of foodstuffs and they withdrew gratefully.
>
> Their agreement lasted until they were met by another group of the poor (*jama'at min amthalihim arbab al-'ayyal wa-l-fuqara'*) and joined them on their way to protest at the customs office. They scattered the flour [found there] on the floor [in an attempt to] prevent its export from the province and chased away everyone who tried to stop them. They only stopped when the director of the

This paper is based on a presentation titled 'Women in the streets! Urban food riots in late Ottoman *Bilād al-Shām*', which I delivered at the conference 'The "Dangerous Classes" in the Middle East and North Africa', St Antony's college, University of Oxford, 26 January 2017. I thank all participants for their valuable comments. All data sets and visualizations are openly available at: https://doi.org/10.5281/zenodo.1008999.

police assured them again of the seriousness [of the government's efforts] to secure the necessary funds to reduce food prices. He explained it would take less than ten days for the serious flour shortage (*qadiyyat al-tahin*, "flour calamity"), as well as all other problems they were complaining of, to ease. Thus they were appeased.

Yesterday [20. August] the poor gathered again and decided to repeat their demonstrations (*muzaharat*) and thus today they roamed wheat stores and all other places where flour is sold. They also protested against the high prices of meat etc.[3]

Despite the officials' promises and explanations, the 'flour calamity' continued: grain prices in Beirut remained high throughout August, at 60 to 62 piastres (Ps) for a *kile* (bushel)[4] of best-quality wheat and Ps 35 to 42 for lower-quality wheat from the Hawran.[5] Some three weeks after the food riot, on the occasion of Sultan 'Abdülhamid II's birthday on 16 Sha'ban 1326 (=15 September), unspecified 'poor people' of Beirut approached the governor general (*vali*) Nazim Pasha – already the third person in this post since the August incidents – with a call to rein in the merchants and to adopt sufficient measures against the high prices of flour and bread. The merchants responded by claiming that their suppliers in the neighbouring province of Syria were the ones to blame. Thus, Nazim Pasha contented himself with establishing an inquiry and appealing to the merchants to lower prices once the inquiry had come to a conclusion. The last available newspaper report on this matter states that the governor general is still waiting for an answer from Damascus.[6]

The incident is puzzling: poor people, suffering from high prices of flour and bread, repeatedly took to the streets in a rather orderly fashion to demand lower prices. They gathered at the seat of the local authorities, complained about greedy merchants and called for effective price controls. They did not resort to looting, despite flour and wheat being readily available in the city. Even when breaking into warehouses (at customs) they did not seize the food they claimed to be unable to afford. Instead, they scattered it on the floor to prevent its export from the city since they identified exports as one of the main causes of high grain prices. Finally, they failed to achieve any immediate price reduction despite the authorities' promises to the contrary. The main question is thus twofold: why did the protestors opt for this particular form of contentious action even though it proved unsuccessful and why did they not seize the food available in the market?

This chapter tries to answer this question by presenting a first analysis of a sample of nineteen food riots in Aleppo, Beirut, Damascus, Hama, Homs, Jaffa and Jerusalem at the end of Ottoman rule, between the mid-1870s and 1918 (Figure 9.1). The phenomenon of food riots in the Middle East preceding the 'IMF riots' of the 1970s and 1980s (named after the International Monetary Fund, whose policies were deemed responsible for igniting the protests) has not yet received sufficient systematic scholarly attention. This chapter represents the first foray in this direction.

The first part of this chapter focuses on price data and their potential correlation with food riots. Focusing on wheat prices as the only available measure, we will see only a limited correlation between high food prices and the occurrence of food riots.

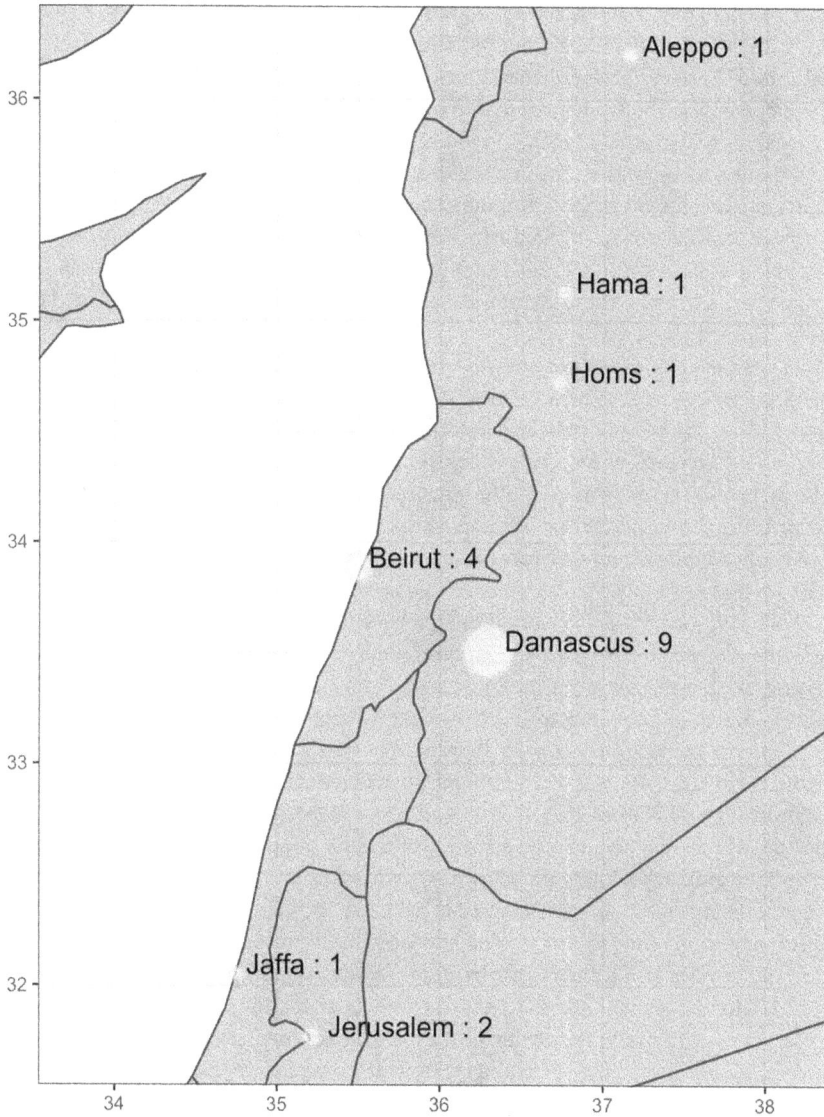

Figure 9.1 Food riots in *Bilad al-Sham*, 1874–1916.

First, while riots occurred only in times of severely elevated prices, high prices did not necessarily result in riots. Second, food riots had no discernible short-term effect on food prices. The second part presents a comparative analysis of the food riots. Noting the apparent failure of food riots to immediately lower food prices and the relatively rare instances of looting (that also did not commonly target food stores), this chapter posits that food riots were neither particularly riotous nor predominantly concerned with food. I argue that the demand for bread had a largely symbolic value and that these contentious performances shared claims and forms to the extent that allows us to speak of a shared and, for the period under study, stable 'repertoire of contention' or 'a limited set of routines that are learned, shared, and acted out through a relatively deliberate process of choice'.[7] Protestors could resort to this repertoire in negotiations over political legitimacy within the existing political order, based on the provision for just rule and safety of life. Presenting the components of this particular repertoire of contention, I will also show that it was neither particularly Islamic nor informed by a 'politics of notables'.

This chapter employs a systematic reading of five Beiruti and two Damascene newspapers and takes occasional recourse to various other newspapers and journals from Beirut, Cairo, Damascus, Istanbul and Jerusalem between 1875 and 1918.[8] Almost all detailed accounts of food riots stem from the contemporaneous local news press. The press also regularly carried information on local retail and wholesale prices (see below). The price information was augmented through foreign archival material such as British, American and German consular reports, including the files of the German military and its supply chains in *Bilad al-Sham* during the First World War.

Following Charles Tilly's work, I use the term *food riot* to refer to a particular type of contentious collective action: a group of people assembling in a public place and raising the demand for lower food prices vis-à-vis another group of people.[9] All food riots in my sample conform to this basic definition of a specific *form* of action as well as a specific contentious *claim*. It then follows that food *riots* were not necessarily riotous or violent, nor was their main purpose necessarily the immediate supply with (affordable) *food*. Rather, I argue, *food* and *access to food* at *fair prices* had a symbolic and discursive function: the demand for affordable food gained its power from its inherent legitimacy within any political system based on the minimal consent of the ruled to being ruled. As such food riots were part of the negotiations over political legitimacy *within* the Ottoman political order. I nevertheless retain the terms 'bread riot' and 'food riot' in tribute to the existing literature on this phenomenon.

Contemporaneous sources did not use a single or specific term to label the events under study. The Arabic denominator for the series of food riots across North Africa and the Middle East in the 1970s and 1980s (IMF riots), namely *intifadat al-khubz*, had not yet been coined in the early twentieth century. The common term for reporting food riots in the press was thus the generic 'incident' (*haditha*).[10] When food riots turned violent, witnesses referred to a battle (*ma'raka*), such as the one in Aleppo in 1910,[11] or even *thawra* (rebellion, revolt)[12] and *fitna* (strife),[13] as in Hama and Homs the same year; these were loaded terms that clearly marked the events as illegitimate.[14] Yet, Beirut's *Lisan al-Hal* acknowledged that the violent food riot and looting in Homs was 'a rebellion of empty stomachs' (*thawrat al-butun al-faghira*).[15]

My argument is informed by the existing scholarship on food riots in other parts of the world in the wake of E. P. Thompson's seminal work on the 'moral economy of the crowd' in eighteenth-century England and Louise Tilly's work on eighteenth-century France. Both Thompson and Tilly agree that food riots, instead of being a spontaneous expression of hunger, were inherently political movements – tactics employed by the lower urban classes to achieve well-defined political aims vis-à-vis a more powerful ruler or ruling class.[16] They showed how food riots became particularly important during a paradigmatic shift in the political economy of both England and France. They argued that food riots 'marked the nationalization and politicization of the problem of subsistence, and [were] based on a conscious popular model of how the economy should work'.[17] Faced with the new model of market economy, the crowds called on the authorities to obey the 'paternalist model', or the 'moral economy of provision' of old, in which market inspectors would supervise direct marketing from the rural producers to the urban consumers and enforce the 'just price'.[18] Noting the almost complete failure of food riots to immediately lower prices, Thompson argued that the threat of riots functioned as a general check on bread prices in the long term; in order for the anticipation of riots to trigger relief measures, such anticipation had to be occasionally sustained by actual riots.[19] The occasion thus became a tactical choice.

Thompson's original contribution led to a sustained debate about the beliefs and imaginations of the protestors and whether the reactionary adherence to a 'moral economy' could and should be seen as a conclusive explanation of food riots in general.[20] A large body of scholarship on food riots in market economies emerged in the wake of the so-called 'IMF riots' that took place in most countries of south America, Africa (including every north-African country with the exception of Libya), and south Asia as well as in Turkey and Iran between 1976 and 1992 and that further underlined the nature of food riots as inherently political actions. Scholars noted that such riots did not occur in times of extreme scarcity but in reaction to a highly uneven distribution of available food. As such, the argument runs, food riots document an entitlement gap between popular expectations and realizable supply.[21]

Scholars also tried to explain why the 'initiators of the [early modern] riots were, very often, the women',[22] with arguments ranging from their almost natural disposal towards mutiny, to being more involved in face-to-face marketing, to women being regarded as the embodiment of disorder, which in turn caused men to dress up as women in a symbolic performance.[23] After the disappearance of food riots and the exclusion of women from the emerging public sphere of formal politics, female food riots resurfaced in industrial societies in the twentieth century.[24]

With regards to the Middle East, crowds, collective action and popular contentions have become the focus of scholarly scrutiny as well as political and public discourses since the beginning of the ill-labelled Arab Spring in 2011.[25] Historical studies have mentioned urban food riots in the Middle East in passing,[26] including some of the riots studied in this chapter.[27] Yet, the genealogy of popular participation and urban popular contentions in the Middle East remains largely obscure on the empirical as well as the analytical level.[28] Thirty years ago, Edmund Burke III presented the first foray into a systematic study of collective action in the Middle East over the *longue durée*. He followed the lead of E. P. Thompson and Charles Tilly in abolishing the old cliché of mindless and spontaneous mobs and put forward three broad claims in his attempt to apply Tilly's 'repertoire of contention' to historical Middle Eastern societies: first, that the contentious repertoire *remained* Islamic as 'movements invariably began in the chief mosque of the city',[29] where contentious claims were discussed among the crowds before '*ulamā*' emissaries were sent to the rulers for negotiations and before the crowds marched onto the seat of the authorities; second, that the crowds targeted stores and barns; and third, that food riots were absent from the protest forms of the nineteenth century.[30] All three claims are proven wrong by the case studies presented in this chapter.[31]

Food prices and food riots

Reliable historical economic data for Middle Eastern societies is difficult to come by. This is not so much due to a shortage of sources but the larger academic trend of moving away from quantitative economic micro-history and the tedious nature of the compilation process. Export statistics from various ports in the Eastern Mediterranean can be gleaned from consular reports[32]; records of the grain exchange in Istanbul are available for scholarly scrutiny; and most newspapers regularly published articles about staple goods and their prices. It seems, however, that only Donald Quataert's seminal thesis on agriculture in Anatolia undertook the task of compiling and publishing detailed time-series on grain prices.[33] Others either published edited consular sources[34] or provide only very limited quantitative data.[35]

It is beyond the scope of this chapter to describe the price sampling methodologies, the resulting sample and my analysis in detail. A short overview must suffice. The time-series of price data were compiled from local newspapers and supplemented with information from American, British and German archival documents. While newspapers regularly published prices, the frequency of such information varied between locations and over time and is largely unpredictable. Prices were published for different purposes and audiences: lists of wholesale prices were published for the benefit of merchants and without comment; imperial authorities published price lists for tenders to supply the army; local authorities issued threshold prices for basic necessities; and authors included information on prices in their reports from across the region. Therefore, information on wholesale commodity prices and especially grain prices is more frequently available for the port city of Beirut than for the inland cities of Damascus or Jerusalem. Lists of wholesale prices the authorities were willing to pay are more commonly available for Damascus, the seat of an imperial Army Corps. Finally, journalists and local authorities tended to focus on prices only when they deviated from the long-term trend, leading to more data points on inflated prices. The only meaningful time-series with sufficient data to actually analyse long-term developments thus compiled are the prices of a *kile* of wheat (Figure 9.2).[36] This set of qualitative price information can be further complemented and validated by qualitative statements on the prices of foodstuffs and changes thereof, which were also frequently published in the press (Figure 9.3).

Relying predominantly on wholesale prices of wheat for evaluating the relation between changes in food prices and the occurrence of food riots is a fruitful endeavour because of the particularities of the food economy in *Bilad al-Sham*. First, although information on consumption is scarce, a sketch of the general pattern is possible. The majority of townspeople was poor and lived mainly on vegetarian provisions, with

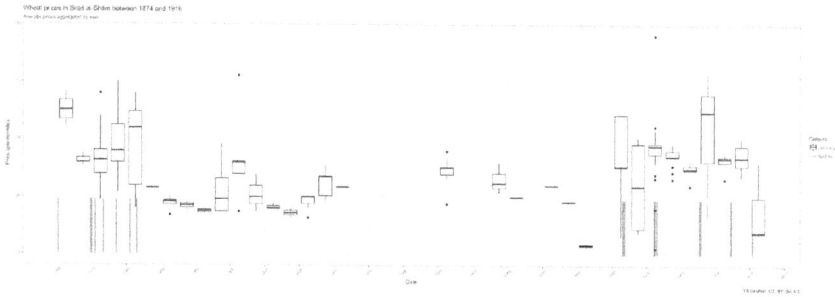

Figure 9.2 Wheat prices in *Bilad al-Sham*, 1874–1916 (average prices aggregated by year).

Note: This box plot represents the distribution of daily average wheat prices aggregated by year. The size of the boxes is determined by the first and third quartile; the bar inside the box represents the median. Food riots are indicated by red vertical lines.

cereals as their main source of nutrition. They preferred white bread made from wheat – a rule from which they diverted only in times of want, when brown and even black bread became the only options. In accordance with European patterns, the demand for bread, which accounted for half of people's normal diet – approximately 1/4 *ratl* per day – was highly inelastic (i.e. unresponsive to a change in price) and would even reach 90 per cent in times of want (because all available funds would be spent on bread).[37] Second, complaints about expensive or unaffordable bread commonly provided wholesale wheat prices, thus linking the two. Third, the relation between a volume of wheat and a weight of bread does not change considerably, save for changes in the recipe. Fourth, the vast majority of townspeople had neither an oven nor the means to buy large quantities of grain immediately after the harvest when prices were low and to safely store them for several months. Thus, they relied on the local neighbourhood ovens-cum-bakeries for their daily bread.[38] In this regard it does not matter whether bakeries operated independently from millers and wholesale grain merchants or not:

Figure 9.3 Qualitative information on prices of food stuffs, 1874–1916 (showing qualitative price information).

Note: This plot shows the clustering of qualitative price information. Each coloured dot represents a source providing one of the five qualitative price information listed on the left.

Wheat prices in Bilād al-Shām between 1874 and 1916

Annual cycle of average prices aggregated by month

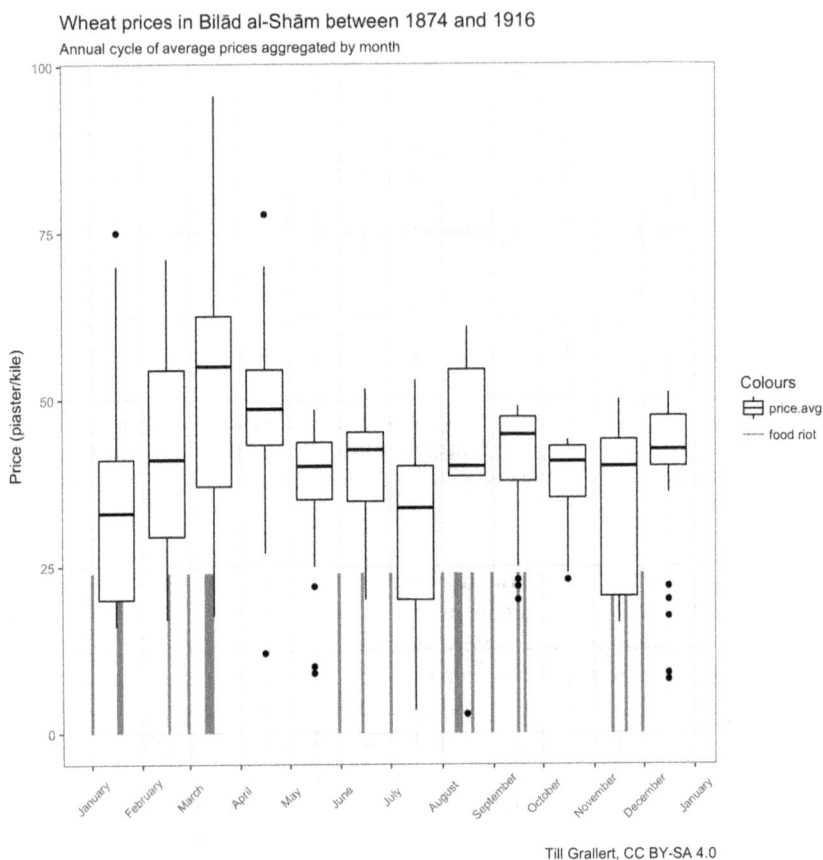

Till Grallert, CC BY-SA 4.0

Figure 9.4 Annual cycle of wheat prices in *Bilad al-Sham*, 1874–1916.

the townspeople were completely dependent on the availability and constant supply of *sufficient* amounts of bread and therefore grain at *affordable* prices in a money-based market economy.

Figure 9.2 shows the highly uneven distribution and fluctuation of wholesale wheat prices and food riots in *Bilad al-Sham* between the mid-1870s and the end of 1916 (when, due to the First World War, prices skyrocketed to an extent that would distort the plot). Prices fluctuated widely year-on-year, in addition to the annual cycle of rising prices during the spring, before the new harvest reached the market in June (Figure 9.4). In years of abundant harvests, such as 1882, 1884, 1905 or 1906, prices would fall below the long-term average of Ps 20 to 25 per *kile*[39] to Ps 17 and even Ps 14. When calamities such as locusts and insufficient winter rains threatened failing harvests, prices reached Ps 60 per *kile* and more. This data does not mirror the trend of falling grain prices between 1876 and 1905 followed by a sharp increase of some 25 per cent between 1906 and 1908, observed by Donald Quataert in Anatolia. Since the 1876 to 1905 decrease was partially due to American wheat flooding the world markets, it is not surprising that it cannot be observed in Bilad al-Sham, which relied on local crops. While average grain prices in Istanbul fell from approximately Ps 25"20 per *kile* to Ps 18"20, Ps 25 was considered the normal price in Damascus in good years.[40] The inflation and fluctuation of exchange rates between the gold lira and the silver piaster are of no importance in this context since prices were always quoted in piastres only.[41]

The comparison of the time-series of wheat prices across *Bilad al-Sham* with the temporal distribution of food riots (marked by vertical red lines in the plots) allows for two observations. On the one hand, we see only limited and certainly no simple causal relations between high food prices and the occurrence of food riots. Food riots coincided with periods of elevated food prices as measured in wholesale prices of wheat. But this cannot be said of the opposite – high food prices did not necessary result in food riots. Thus, while high food prices coincided with food riots in the late 1870s, 1908 and 1910, extensive archival research has not brought up any report on food riots in 1891 or 1898.[42] The broader context of the Ottoman Empire may help explain this. During the late 1870s and from 1909 onwards, the empire's institutions were weakened by wars, resulting in increased conscription among the poor and thus a prolonged absence of men from *Bilad al-Sham*, state bankruptcy in 1876, the introduction of paper currency (*kaime*) subject to high inflation rates, and the state's inability to pay salaries in conjunction with forced subscriptions among officials to finance the war effort. In addition, during both periods the empire underwent rapid political transformations: the proclamation of the Constitution in 1876 and its restoration in 1908 were both framed by revolutionary discourses of general equality and liberty. Further research on food riots during other historical periods is necessary to substantiate this argument but the concurrence of these major crises and food riots seems a promising track to follow.

There were, of course, local factors that contributed to the decision on whether to engage in a food riot or not. The summer of 1910, which saw a series of food riots in Aleppo, Damascus, Hama and Homs (see below), is a case in point. In all four cities, newspapers reported high prices, the suffering of the poor and criticized hoarding merchants and adulterated bread as well as idle authorities. Similar reports were coming from Beirut, but despite bread prices reaching the same threshold of Ps 7"20 as in August 1908 (see above),[43] this time there was no food riot. This absence even served as an argument against the ban of flour exports from Beirut to Damascus at the time: the province of Syria argued that orders to send all available flour to Damascus should be upheld since there had been no food riot in Beirut and thus it could not possibly be worse off than Damascus.[44]

On the other hand, the comparison of prices with the occurrence of food riots reveals the inherent failure of these contentious performances in bringing about lower food prices in the short term. We will return to this point in the next section of this chapter.

The repertoire of the food riot

If food prices cannot explain the timing of food riots and if food riots have no discernible short-term effect on food prices, one has to look at the specific events for the reasons why protestors opted for this specific contentious form and claim and why they did so at these particular times. The sample of nineteen food riots in Aleppo, Beirut, Damascus, Hama, Homs, Jaffa and Jerusalem share enough structural characteristics and the reports thereon display enough narrative commonalities to argue that the 'food riot' was indeed a 'repertoire of contention'. Charles Tilly's idea of a repertoire as learned and of shared routines as readily available contentious performances, can help us make sense of the protestors' seemingly paradoxical choices. They protested in times of destitution, expending calories without being able to eat sufficiently; they protested despite the threat of violent repercussion; and complaining about hoarding merchants, the protestors addressed authorities with the demand to enforce threshold prices despite the authorities' apparent inability to prevent such protest or to enforce such prices.

The repertoire of the food riot in late Ottoman *Bilad al-Sham* can be broken down into a sequence of events that occurred in three phases: a prologue of artificially high prices and 'inspiring' events conducive to popular protest; the food riot itself that never lasted through the night but could be repeated over some days and which rarely involved the looting of foodstuffs; and the immediate aftermath of not more than a month during which the authorities tried to contain the anger through (largely symbolic) investigations and administrative measures.

The prologue

All food riots were preceded by extended periods of hardship and elevated food prices during which a discourse on *artificially* high prices surfaced in the written sources. The timing of the contentious collective action itself then depended on local circumstances.

Artificially high prices

Prohibitive prices of bread and grain were commonly portrayed as artificially high and blamed on greedy wholesale merchants seeking undue profits from either exporting or hoarding cereals and thus draining the local market. In the case of Damascus and Beirut, exports were usually destined for foreign markets, but in inland towns, such as Hama and Homs, Damascus as the provincial capital was the main export destination deemed responsible for the price hikes.

At the time of increased and rising prices, some (unnamed) people would begin to criticize (*shaka*) those responsible as evil-doing hoarders and monopolists (*muhtakirun*).[45] Newspapers went to some lengths to emphasize the sinister machinations of the grain merchants, addressing them as the 'lords of greed' (*arbab al-matami* ')[46] conspiring to form monopolies (*ista 'thara*[47]) and cartels (*i 'tasaba*[48]). When reporting on the riots, many sources emphasize that criticism of the merchants' illegal actions had been raised before anything of a violent nature happened and through established channels, such as a petition.[49]

Thus for example in the summer of 1910, Aleppo suffered from extremely high prices of wheat in early June and hoarding merchants were blamed for the calamity. When the price of wheat fell from a height of Ps 57–64 per *kile* to Ps 27–30, some merchants began to buy up all the grain in the market in order to push prices up again. Newspapers singled out 'Abd al-Rahman Efendi Jasir, a merchant who still held a large quantity of wheat from the previous year's harvest, for having caused an increase to Ps 40 per *kile* with this tactic.[50]

Prices were also high and grain was all but unavailable to the poor in Hama and Homs during the summer of 1910 due to a cartel (*i'tisab*) of grain merchants hoarding and exporting cereals to more profitable locations. In Hama, all available reports[51] blamed greedy wholesale merchants and their attempts to profit from the unrest in the Hawran and the resulting high grain prices in Damascus by exporting all available cereals to the provincial capital. Some if not all grain merchants in Homs closed their stores, arguing that they could not afford to sell at the price imposed by the authorities.[52] Two weeks before the food riot in Homs on 13 August, the common people (*al-'amma*) had addressed a petition to the authorities, explaining their suffering from obscene prices of grain and calling on the officials to intervene and show consideration for the poor. But the government did not find a means to satisfy their demands, despite ample wheat being available in the granaries.[53]

An advantageous moment

Once the stage was set and merchants' responsibility for the suffering of the poor was established, protestors seemingly had to make a tactical decision as to the timing of the contentious collective action: one that would ensure high visibility of the protest, draw larger crowds of protestors, avoid violent retribution and cause maximum embarrassment to the authorities. People usually took to the streets on Fridays, when towns were crowded with worshippers and shoppers; in close temporal proximity to religious and state holidays, when towns were the stage for large, state-sponsored and affirmative public rituals that displayed a model *of* and *for* society based on the circle of justice and good governance[54]; and after changes in administrative personnel, when a new governor (*mutasarrif*) or governor general (*vali*) was less likely to be able to rely on local networks of support or command the full loyalty of the local garrison.

Thus, the Beirut food riot of August 1908 took place at a time of political turmoil. The Young Turks had just staged their coup and reinstated the Constitution of 1876. Their followers and the Committee of Union and Progress (CUP) tried to quickly seize power on all levels of the state administration and across the whole empire, bringing a quick succession of appointments and dismissals of officials and large-scale public celebrations. When protestors took to the streets on 19 August, Beirut had seen daily popular celebrations and the second governo general in the course of a month had already submitted his resignation.[55] By the time the poor raised the matter of high food prices again, on the occasion of the Sultan's birthday on 15 Sha'ban 1326 aH (= 15 September), at least two other people had been appointed to the post.[56]

In March 1878 Cevdet Pasha, the governor general of Syria, was new to Damascus and all but one battalion of the 5th Army were absent from the city, fighting in the Russo-Ottoman War. Upon the public reading of his *firman* of appointment on 8 March, he announced the beginning of an era of the rule of law and just government.[57] Food riots began on 12 March and continued to intensify until their culmination on 16 March, which happened to be the day of *mawlid nabawi* (the Prophet's birthday), on 12 Rabi' I 1295 aH. Thirty-two years later, another food riot took place in Damascus one day before *mawlid nabawi* 1331 aH, on 17 February 1913.[58]

Similar arguments can be made about the 1910 food riots in Aleppo, Damascus, Hama and Homs. Protestors pushed their negotiating power by exercising their constitutional rights to assemble and protest and by employing the new symbolic repertoire of popular rallies and demonstrations – commonly staged in support of the authorities and against foreign enemies[59] – against the authorities themselves in close temporal proximity to official celebrations of the second anniversary of the restoration of the Constitution on 24 July (the food riots took place in mid-June in Aleppo, on 2 July in Damascus, on 11 August in Hama and two days later in Homs). In addition to this larger context, a new director of police, Nafidh Efendi, had arrived in Damascus the day before the demonstration, while the entire municipal council had stepped down on 15 June over a fiscal scandal surrounding the project to supply the city with water from 'Ayn Fija.[60]

The food riot itself

The actual food riot was a bounded event commonly lasting only a few hours. It could be repeated on successive days or within a week's time but it never continued through the night. Its main characteristics were that (1) large crowds of protestors targeted the authorities in a mostly peaceful manner, calling for the enforcement of *fair* prices (*as'ar mu'atadila, ta'dil al-as'ar*), and (2) in the rare cases when violent looting took place, the crowds predominantly targeted non-food items.

Good examples of the above sequence of events include the food riot in Beirut in 1908, outlined at the beginning of this chapter, and the food riots in Damascus, Hama and Homs in 1910. It is worth looking at them in some detail. On the morning of 2 July 1910, criers roamed the streets of Damascus, calling on the people to join a demonstration against high bread prices at Marja Square and in front of the New Serail.[61] Within an hour, the streets were packed with people marching towards Marja Square. The crowds were headed by a vanguard of women howling and shouting their disgust about the authorities' failure to provide bread at fair prices.[62] The marchers united at Marja Square, where women, many of them carrying children and infants, took the lead again and noisily demonstrated under the windows of the New Serail, which was located off Marja Square on the banks of the Barada River.[63] Officials in the various offices around the square became wary and called on the 5th Army, headquartered in the city, to send in troops for their protection. The army complied and imperial troops dispersed the demonstrators with threats of violence, beating and by sloshing them with water from fire engines. The agitated crowds scattered through the city in search of grain traders, all the while chanting insults and abuse of hoarders, calling on God to deliver them from the tyranny of the monopolists.[64] Yet no looting seemed to have followed the incident. By the evening, the city was quiet again and the governor general, Isma'il Fadil Pasha,[65] delivered a talk on his recent journey to the southern districts of Kerak and the Hawran at the local CUP branch.[66]

A month later, in Hama, a demonstration against high bread prices escalated into a violent food riot on Thursday, 11 August 1910.[67] That day, a large crowd of poor men, women and children marched to Governor Nazim Bey's Serail on the eastern banks of the Orontes river.[68] There they demonstrated peacefully against the merchants' high profits from the trade of foodstuffs and against all exports to Damascus. Nazim Bey directed the crowd's anger to the municipality (*belediye*) at the opposite, Western, end of the street leading to the Serail. He called upon the *belediye* to enforce sufficient price control measures. However, the governor and the municipality could not agree upon their respective responsibilities; dissatisfied by the official response, the crowds dispersed and began to attack stores in three different locations.

At first, the protestors tried to enter al-Mashnuq's store. When they failed to break into the warehouse, they resorted to throwing stones. They then turned onto Mahmud al-Farra, the merchant whom they identified as the main culprit behind their misery. They located al-Farra at the slaughterhouse and threatened him with murder. He managed to lock himself inside and later escaped.

The crowd then split in two. One group went to the railway station to the south-west of the city, where large quantities of grain destined for export to Damascus were stored. The protestors forced the gates of some of the surrounding warehouses open and looted some six hundred bags of grain without touching any of the railway carriages full of wheat that were waiting on a siding. The stationmaster, a certain Nabih Efendi, apparently managed to convince the crowd that the station, its stores of lentils and onions, and all coaches were property of the state and that the Hijaz Railway as such was a pious Muslim endeavour and therefore should be protected from their wrath – he also allegedly managed to take the photo of the protestors with their loot that was later used for identification. After successfully seizing the grain, the crowds broke into one of al-Farra's warehouses at the station. It turned out to hold skins and empty bags, which they looted. According to *al-Muqtabas*, the crowds then began shouting: 'By God, onto al-Barudi, onto al-Barudi'.

At the western square, they looted the stores of Ahmad al-Samsam, Ibn al-Habiyan and al-Barudi, and took all the rice, sugar and coffee they could find. Finally, they looted Aswad and Sharrah's warehouse in the al-Jisr quarter and took all the grain stored inside.

The crowds roamed the streets for two-and-a-half hours without any intervention by the authorities and were finally dispersed by a small detachment of motorized imperial troops (fifteen men). *Al-Muqtabas* mentioned the honourable but futile attempt of a single mounted policeman, a certain Khudr Efendi, to disperse the crowd. The newspaper also polemically mocked the commander of the gendarmerie as having said in Ottoman Turkish 'My dear, what can we do?' (*canım ne yapalım*) upon his arrival at the scene, after which he retreated with his men.[69]

Two days later, on the morning of Saturday, 13 August 1910, an agitated crowd comprising thousands of poor and destitute people – 'among them old and young, the shaykh, the young, the woman, and the infant'[70] – gathered in the Suqs in the eastern part of Homs and then moved northwards in the direction of the Serail and the *belediye*.[71] They gathered without weapons but – some claimed – with the intent to loot and plunder the grain stores. Ahmad Kurd 'Ali, the brother of Muhammad Kurd 'Ali and co-editor of his newspaper *al-Muqtabas*, was on a journey to the north and quickly travelled to the location of the incident, from where he filed a number of lengthy reports. According to him, the food riot began with a certain Yusuf 'Abyan who:

> Wanted to buy flour in the quarter of Bab Tadmur to the east of Homs. But what he wanted could not be obtained because the city had been devoid of this item according to some papers. The man took off his shoes, put both of them on a stick, and began to run and yell: 'oh poor, I am your father. I sacrificed my life for your sake' (*ayyuha al-fuqara' fa-ana abukum afadi bi-hayati fi sabilikim*).[72]

Despite numerous long reports in the press, the sequence of events that followed is not entirely clear. However, demonstrations and looting occurred in at least four different locations: the square in front of the Serail, the warehouses near the municipal garden, the Tripoli-Homs coach station and the railway station on the Damascus-Hama line.[73]

Reports agree that the first confrontation between the protestors and the authorities took place in front of the Serail.[74] According to *al-Ittihad al-'Uthmani*'s final report on the incident, the crowds marched through the streets and directly onto the Serail, 'shouting slogans, swearing and cursing (*ma 'nahu al-sibb wa-l-shatm*) at everybody not marching with them'.[75] There they held a demonstration and called on the authorities to rein in the merchants and prevent them from exporting grain from the city. They were confronted by the *kaymakam* (local sub-governor), 'Ata Allah Bey al-Ayyubi, accompanied by three or four gendarmes and policemen.[76] He delivered a speech, threatening, pleading, cautioning and promising to decrease the price to Ps 3 for a *ratl* of flour.[77] According to Ahmad Kurd 'Ali, the crowds rejoiced at the *kaymakam*'s announcements and would have left had it not been for some riff-raff among them.[78] A certain T. M. reported in *al-Ittihad al-'Uthmani* how some of the nobles and officials began to disperse the crowds after the *kaymakam*'s speech. This initiated a skirmish during which the demonstrators started to throw stones, realized their strength and then began to attack warehouses.[79] However the violent confrontation might have begun, the *kaymakam* gathered all the gendarmes he could muster – about ten men – and ordered them to shoot into the air to disperse the protestors. Many of the protestors fled then but at least three groups remained: one went on to loot warehouses in town, one engaged the gendarmerie at the coach road station and the third attacked the railway station.[80] Meanwhile the *kaymakam* requested reinforcements from Hama and Damascus.

The first group of looters targeted the stores of Mustafa 'Abbas, Najib Latif and Mustafa Efendi Arslan, all in the vicinity of the municipal gardens adjacent to the Serail.[81]

The second group went to the Tripoli-Homs coach station and attempted to break into the warehouses there.[82] They encountered the gendarme Tawfiq Efendi al-Atasi, attacked him with stones and wounded him on the forehead. The *kaymakam* arrived with three gendarmes, but they were also met with showers of stones and he had to retreat to the Serail with the gendarmerie commander. From there they tried to rescue al-Atasi again by threatening to use firearms. This stopped the crowd and the protestors dispersed.[83]

The third group went to the railway station in the south-west of the city,[84] where they began looting some sixteen wagons[85] filled with grain, fat and manufactured goods from Hama and Homs, all destined for export. When three gendarmes and some volunteers – the already wounded Tawfiq Efendi al-Atasi, Badawi Efendi al-Sibaʿi, Ahmad al-Sibaʿi and the municipal bailiff (*jawish*) Ahin Ibn Diyab – arrived at the scene, the looters abandoned the wagons and went to the warehouses in search of grain. A vanguard of the protestors had already forced their way into the stores located near the station and looted the Khan al-Salmuniyin, Khan Bayt al-Tayf, Makhzan Bayt Badrita, Makhzan Bayt Talimat, Makhzan Farkuh and a number of other warehouses not identified by name.[86] According to one report, the crowd insulted the gendarmes during the altercation and gave them a severe beating (again). At some point the gendarmes even had to surrender their arms, although they were later returned.[87] In another version of the story, the station officials defended themselves by the same means as the protestors, i.e. by throwing stones at the looters. A Circassian called Idris drove his horse into the crowd in order to relieve the defenders, but he was repelled with showers of stones.[88]

Looting and violent attacks continued sporadically into the evening, with groups of agitated people roaming the streets and inciting speeches delivered across the town. The crowds only dispersed after dark.[89]

The narratives about these incidents are fascinating and deserve a study of their own – what, for instance, is the political agenda behind *al-Muqtabas*' mocking polemic of the gendarmerie commander in Hama, providing a most probably unsubstantiated quote in Ottoman only? However, here we are concerned with food riots as contentious performances and with establishing a set of features that are common to most, if not all.

The formation of a crowd

Food riots invariably commenced with the gathering of a crowd of townspeople – usually described as consisting of the poor. Sometimes authors emphasize the inclusive character of the crowd by mentioning men, women and children, old and young, etc. At least in Damascus, women were portrayed as leading the crowds or even as constituting the majority of participants. Unfortunately the identities of protestors cannot be established beyond such generic descriptions. The only exception is the above-mentioned Yusuf ʿAbyan from Homs.

The terms used to label the crowds of protestors were mostly derivatives of the roots *j-m-ʿ* and *j-m-h-r* – i.e. *tajamhara*,[90] *ijtamaʿa*,[91] *tajammaʿ*[92] and *jamʿ/jumuʿ*[93] and *jumhur*[94]/*jamahir*.[95] As such, they do not carry a moral judgement. Reports commonly emphasized the needy state of the protestors. Thus, we are informed about the gathering of 'a large crowd of the poor' (*jamm ghafir min al-fuqara*')[96] and 'crowds of poor inhabitants' (*jumu' al-fuqara' min al-ahali*).[97] The presence of women further underlined the neediness of the protestors: in Damascus 'a crowd of poor women gathered' (*ijtama'a jami' al-fuqara' min al-nisa*')[98] in March 1878; also in Damascus, 'crowds of women banded together [...] in front of the Serail' (*kaththarat jumu' al-nisa*')[99] some thirty-two years later, in July 1910, 'carrying small boys and infant girls in their arms'[100] 'until the streets were congested; women leading and the men behind them as the main force' (*hata ghassat al-shawari' wa-l-nisa' fi al-muqaddima wa-l-rijal min wara'ihin ka-quwwat al-zahr*)[101]; and in February 1916, 'the town hall was packed with poor women' (*izduhimat ams dar al-baladiyya bi-l-faqirat al-nisa*')[102]; in Aleppo, 'poor Muslims, women and men, gathered together' (*tajamhara [...] fuqara' al-muslimin nisa'an wa-rijalan*)[103] in June 1910; 'Umar Safi reported from Homs two months later that those looting the grain stores were unarmed since the crowd was made of 'the poor, women, and children'.[104] This pattern of explicitly stating the all-encompassing character of the protest was not limited to food riots; a report on the Algerian refugees' protest in front of the Serail in Beirut in January 1910 read: *tajamma' 'adad wafir bayn rijal wa-nisa' wa-awlad min al-muhajirin al-jaza'irin al-fuqara*'.[105]

The gathered people were described in neutral terms – such as *al-qawm* (groups of people),[106] *al-'amma* (the commoners)[107] or *al-sha'b* (the populace)[108] – unless the food riot turned violent. Then the reports immediately switched to terms denouncing the crowds' actions as illicit. Violent protestors were portrayed as rebels (*tha'irun*[109] or *thuwwar*[110]) and the crowds were denounced as a mob of riff-raff (*al-ra'a'*[111] and *al-ghawgha*'[112]).

Peaceful demonstration

In most cases the crowd gathered at or marched onto the seat of the local government, be it the municipality or the seat of the district or provincial authorities. There they peacefully raised their complaints about hoarding merchants and their demands for the authorities' intervention to ensure affordable bread and grain, namely the enforcement of a *just price*. What sets food riots apart from other forms of contentious performance, such as soldiers' mutiny or inter-communal violence, is that the protestors took recourse neither to an Islamicate repertoire nor to the 'politics of notables'. We do not have a single report of crowds assembling at a central mosque or of notables acting as intermediaries between the populace and the ruling authorities.[113] The importance of the latter point cannot be overstated. In the wake of Hourani's seminal article, the importance of a class of local intermediaries – commonly referred to as *'ayan* – for the governance of *Bilad al-Sham* and the Ottoman ancien régime has become a given in scholarly literature.[114] The extent of this phenomenon is such that Dana Sajdi lamented the prevalence of ''ayan-ology' among scholars of the modern Arabic-speaking provinces of the Ottoman Empire in the eastern Mediterranean, even though they lacked an 'agreement on how this category is constituted'.[115]

Dissolution of the crowd or escalation into a riot

Once the protestors made their complaints to the authorities, representatives of the state attempted to appease the gathered crowds. They acknowledged and affirmed the inherent legitimacy and justness of the people's demands and tried to dissolve the potentially dangerous gathering through a combination of promises, threats and violence. In some cases, the crowds gathered not in front of the highest political authority but at the most prominent square in town, which could be near the *belediye* or the *kaymakam*'s office. In those instances, the lower officials tried to redirect the crowd's anger to the higher authority – the governor or governor general.

The authorities' initial reaction was the decisive factor in determining whether a peaceful demonstration turned into a violent riot and looting. If they failed to dissolve the crowd, the agitated demonstrators began roaming the streets to search for other targets. It seems as if the original threat of violence had to be backed up by real violence if the authorities showed contempt for the protestors.

(Optional) Rioting and looting

The crowds finally turned against the merchant class, identified by both the protestors and the authorities as responsible for the general calamity. Groups of people violently looted warehouses and stores. They targeted warehouses at railway and coach stations in particular, as they were part of the vilified export trade. However, in all but one case, when the grain stores at the Homs railway station were looted, the looters targeted anything but food and thus seem to have been bent on inflicting harm on their oppressors rather than satisfying their demand for food. The local authorities, already tainted by their earlier failure, were often portrayed as utterly helpless and incompetent during the violent part of the collective action.

Successful intervention of the highest representative of the central authorities

Peace and tranquillity as the defining basis of Ottoman political legitimacy – *asayiş-i 'umumi* or *al-raha al-'ummumiyya* – were finally re-established by the intervention of the highest representative of the central authorities, namely the governor or governor general, with the help of imperial troops or the gendarmerie.

The aftermath

The aftermath of a food riot commonly saw two diametrically opposed developments. On the one hand, the press published long eulogies for the central authorities, represented by the governor general, for punishing the hoarders and for enforcing fair maximum prices. On the other hand, no factual reports of falling food prices can be found.

Official investigation

After violence had been quelled or after the peaceful demonstration had been dissolved, the highest representative of the central authorities commonly engaged in a flurry of activities demonstrating the empire's energetic intervention to restore justice. Committees were set up to investigate the (pre-established) cause for high prices, namely the hoarding merchants; exports of grain were (again) banned; wholesale merchants were reprimanded for the artificial price hikes; some grain was confiscated from the hoarding merchants (but not redistributed); and official maximum prices for grain, flour and bread were again published by the municipalities. Only in a single instance, when the protestors looted grain stores in Homs in 1910, did the authorities prosecute them. Otherwise, protestors went unpunished (but not necessarily unhurt), which was both an affirmation of the protest's legitimacy (in form and content) and a tacit acknowledgement of the impossibility of effective law enforcement.

The events of 1910 shall again serve as an example. For a number of days after the riots in Aleppo in June, soldiers patrolled the al-*Jalum* quarter to preserve safety and public order. The authorities arrested ʿ*Abd al-Rahman* Efendi *Jasir*, the merchant deemed responsible for the price increase, seized his grain and sold some of it in a public auction. The governor general counselled all other grain merchants to immediately sell a large quantity of wheat. In addition, he prohibited the export of grain from the province.[116]

Two weeks later, on 3 July, in Damascus, the governor general invited the leading notables and dignitaries of the city, the *imams* of the quarters and their *mukhtars* for separate meetings at the Serail and severely reprimanded them over the previous day's demonstrations. He explained that while the people had a legal right to gather and petition the authorities, the events were outright illegal as they inflicted harm upon the homeland. As the notables and heads of the land (*bilad*) they had the duty to counsel the people in comprehensible language that such actions were not advisable.[117] In addition, provincial authorities wrote to the districts of Hama and the Hawran as well as the neighbouring province of Beirut, imploring them to send whatever supplies of wheat they had to Damascus. In Damascus itself, the municipality set the maximum price for a *ratl* bread of good quality at Ps 3"30 and took unspecified measures against the merchants suspected of hoarding.[118] One week after the food riot, *al-Bashir* reported that the provincial administrative council had investigated the high prices of wheat and come to the conclusion that hoarding merchants were the sole culprits. Consequently, the council banned this practice.[119]

In the aftermath of the food riot in Hama on 11 August 1910 (called *hadithat Hama*[120] and *fitna*[121]), the authorities set up an investigative committee to establish the reasons behind the price hikes and identify the looters. Both the governor of Hama and the governor general of Syria issued orders against inflated prices and banned exports from Syria. But while the press called for the punishment of all monopolists, reports on falling prices are nowhere to be found.

In Homs, the *kaymakam* and the small number of gendarmes under his command began conducting door-to-door searches for looted goods after an uneasy but quiet night on 14 August 1910. Those found in possession of stolen wheat were arrested. At noon, an official investigation was set up with the participation of the gendarmerie, the province's public prosecutor, who had arrived from Damascus for this purpose, and the local authorities.[122] In the evening a company (*bölük*) of imperial troops arrived from Damascus as a reinforcement to prevent further rioting and to help recover the loot.[123]

That night the looters tried to get rid of the stolen grain in anticipation of retribution. Some buried it in their homes, some hid it underneath legitimate grain, but many threw the cereals into the streets, the moat of the citadel and into sewers.[124] The following day, the *kaymakam* and the *kaza's* public prosecutor continued the door-to-door searches and arrests. Within a week about one hundred people were sentenced but only forty-nine were arrested for their participation in the looting (i.e. more than half of those sentenced were never apprehended).[125] The recovered foodstuffs were brought to the Serail.[126] The merchants gathered and called upon the authorities to either surrender the confiscated grain or pay the official price, as was their right under the law.[127]

Finally, the local authorities tried to enforce lower prices. Municipal criers walked the streets of Homs under orders of the head of the *belediye*, Muhiyi al-Din Efendi Shams al-Din, announcing the prohibition of grain exports to destinations outside the province. They stated that those found guilty of breaching these orders would be punished and their grain would be seized.[128]

No reports on falling grain prices

Ultimately, despite all the praise of successful interventions by the central authorities, food prices did not fall in any significant way in the immediate aftermath of food riots. In many instances, they even continued to rise until the arrival of new harvests caused the usual cyclical decrease.

According to a generic note in *al-Bashir*, the measures undertaken by the authorities in Aleppo were successful and the price of grain fell,[129] but in early July 1910 a *kile* of wheat was still sold at Ps 64[130] – the same as the maximum price at the onset of the events. In mid-August Ahmad Kurd ʿAli reported from Aleppo that false rumours of locusts destroying the harvests were used to justify the continually high prices. He complained that a *kile* of wheat still cost Ps 30 to 39.[131]

In Damascus, the price of wheat fell to Ps 53 per *kile*[132] on 2 July 1910, the day of the riot. Two months later prices had hardly improved. The *belediye* convened a meeting of bakers and millers on 29 August and announced new maximum prices: Ps 40 to Ps 57 for a *wazna* of flour, and Ps 3 to Ps 3"35 for a ratl of bread, depending on the quality[133] – which is almost the same price as the Ps 3"30 for a ratl of good bread imposed on the day of the riot.

Two weeks after the food riot in Damascus, on 17 February 1913, *al-Muqtabas* reported a 30 per cent drop in the price of a *wazna* of flour from Ps 6"0 to Ps 4"20.[134] A day later, on 3 March, the *belediye* set a new maximum price for a *ratl* of bread at Ps 4.[135] However, on 6 March, *al-Muqtabas* stated that against all hopes the price of grain had not fallen.[136] The MP for Damascus, Shukri al-'Asali, lobbied for easing the price of wheat through lifting all import customs for the duration of two months[137] but at the end of March wheat was still sold at Ps 59 to 65 per *kile*, because up to three-quarters of all millers did not adhere to the prices established by the *belediye*. Therefore a meeting of millers and flour merchants was convened at the municipality on 30 March[138]; the merchants claimed they could not possibly buy wheat at lower prices and that they would have to sell at even higher prices in consequence.[139] A week later, prices reached up to Ps 80 per *kile* of wheat.[140]

Conclusion

This chapter has presented the first systematic attempt to study food riots in Bilad al-Sham during the final decades of Ottoman rule. A brief foray into a time-series of wheat prices across the entire region has shown the limited explanatory power of food prices for the occurrence of food riots. On the one hand, periods of high food prices did not necessarily result in food riots and, on the other, food riots were never successful in bringing about lower food prices. Turning to micro-studies of individual food riots, I put forward the observation of the significant structural similarities among the riots that can be broken down into three different phases and a sequence of bounded events common to (almost) all food riots.

I argued that such a shared and learned repertoire can serve to answer the question why protestors did engage in food riots even though they constantly proved unsuccessful in achieving their stated goal and why the protestors did not usually seize food by force. The demand for bread at *affordable* and *established* prices was largely symbolic – as attested by the constant failure of the protest in securing this demand – and part of the larger negotiation of political legitimacy in times of internal and external crisis. In line with the 'moral economy' of English and French crowds in the seventeenth century, protestors called on the rulers to obey the ancien régime of paternalist obligations towards the ruled. The demand for bread was chosen because it was (and is) inherently legitimate. The protests were accompanied by a discourse on greedy merchants who were ultimately to blame either for the enforcement of an *unfair* market economy, governed by the forces of supply and demand, or for sabotaging the fair negotiation of prices through the formation of cartels and hoarding. The protestors offered the authorities a way forward: rein in the merchants, re-establish your authority over public affairs and win our continued loyalty as Ottoman subjects.

The Dangerous Classes and the 1953 Coup in Iran: On the Decline of *lutigari* Masculinities

Olmo Gölz

Introduction

'Hegel remarks somewhere that all great world-historic facts and personages appear, so to speak, twice. He forgot to add: the first time as tragedy, the second time as farce.'[1] With these words Karl Marx opens his seminal analysis of the French coup d'état of 1851, *The Eighteenth Brumaire of Louis Bonaparte* (written in 1852), in order to introduce his diagnosis that the repetition of history is but reactionary. Faced with the events of the 1953 coup in Iran, what would Marx have said? Probably: *I told you so!*

Indeed, the coup d'état of 19 August 1953 appears to be a replication of the processes witnessed by Marx in the French context in two ways: first, the coup that brought Mohammad Reza Shah Pahlavi (1919–80) back to power can be seen as a conservative reaction against a political system which back then had been perceived as progressive and suitable to the global post-war order – all discussions about the involvement of foreign powers or the actual constitution of Premier Mohammad Mosaddeq's (1880–1967) government aside. Second, the prominent participation of the social class that Marx would have described as lumpenproletariat – or the 'dangerous classes'[2] – is as evident as in the French coup d'état on 2 December 1851.

This is true of the actual coup of 28 Mordad (= 19 August 1953) as well as of its rehearsal in February the same year, the 'proto-coup'[3] of 9 Esfand (= 29 February 1953). Apart from all the fiery scholarly and popular disputes revolving around the causes of the appearance of thugs and hoodlums in these events, the fact that they significantly contributed to both incidents is uncontested. This chapter focuses on the participation of these elements of society in Iranian politics during the first phase of the reign of Mohammad Reza Shah Pahlavi between 1941 and 1963. With regard to the 1953 coup culminating in the toppling of Mosaddeq for the benefit of the Shah, the involvement of the dangerous classes became a crucial factor at the beginning of the year. On 9 February a crowd of protestors gathered in front of Mosaddeq's residence in order to prevent the Shah's departure to Europe – a journey that would probably have led to his exile. The Foreign Broadcast Information Service of the CIA committed the Persian broadcast of 1 March to paper the next day:

When some active officers, in and out of uniform, a number of retired officers headed by some known thugs went toward the Premier's house and started their attacks and aggression [...] the security officials not only did not prevent the attack of these individuals on the Premier's house, but one of the active officers, accompanied by a notorious thug riding military jeep No. 15, 195, attacked the doors of Dr. Mossadeq's residence.[4]

Sha'ban Ja'fari (1921–2006) was the most prominent member of this heterogeneous group as well as its instigator and leader. He was also the 'notorious thug' who drove the jeep that rammed the barred gate – a story he himself proudly confirmed in a biographical interview in 2002.[5] He claimed to have gathered a mob of five thousand people, composed of his followers from *zurkhaneh* circles (i.e. wrestlers from the Iranian 'houses of strength'), some peons from the bazaar (the majority of the established *bazaris* still supported Mosaddeq at that time) and a bunch of discharged soldiers and officers.[6] In sum, a group that seemingly affirms the classical Marxian definition of the composition of the dangerous classes or, to use the Persian term, *lutis*.

In *The Eighteenth Brumaire*, Marx defines the lumpenproletariat as 'the whole indefinite, disintegrated mass, thrown hither and thither' and provides a list of examples including vagabonds, discharged soldiers, ragpickers and the like.[7] Hence, Karl Marx and Frederick Engels used the term lumpenproletariat for those members of society who do not produce and are not integrated in society's production processes.[8] According to Marx, the lowest classes are nothing but a source of danger for society for two reasons: first, the lumpenproletariat is a hotbed of criminality, immorality and licentiousness[9]; and second, in consequence of their economic existence, members of the lumpenproletariat 'follow a politics of non-commitment which at the end may work against the interests of the producing classes', as Asef Bayat puts it.[10] Hence, the lowest classes are not only dangerous in a merely material sense, depriving manufacturers of their legitimate earnings. They are also dangerous from the point of view of historical materialism, since their unpredictability challenges the communist project. Paradoxically, due to their anachronistic appearance they also challenge the reactionary order they may help bring to power, as will be shown here.

The intention of this chapter is twofold. First, the juxtaposition between the political role of the dangerous classes during the resurrection of the Pahlavi monarchy in 1953 and the public discourses on the masculinity ethos of *lutigari* in Iran will show the validity of the Marxian view of the dangerous classes as reactionary and poisonous. By participating in the processes leading to the actual coup d'état, the *lutis* have not only 'betrayed' the communist cause at the time but their participation also entailed a distinct menace for the order they helped bring to power: their anachronistic character challenged the legitimacy of the Shah's reign until the revolution of 1978/79. I argue that the decline of *lutigari* masculinities in Pahlavi Iran has to be read against this background. The pejorative depiction of the participating men as members of the lumpenproletariat (Pers. *lompan*) or as representatives of a 'traditional, folkloristic Iran' (Pers. *luti* or *javanmardi*, i.e. 'young-manliness') can be seen as a marginalization strategy deploying the perception of lumpenproletariat as politically dangerous. Second, the focus on two well-known and ambiguous individuals – thugs or *lompan* for leftists and Marxists, *lutis* or *javanmardan* for conservatives – will show that the classical Marxian class theory needs clarification concerning the composition of the lumpenproletariat and the role of specific actors associated with this social class. Building on the work of Max Horkheimer and Theodor Adorno, the two leading theorists of the Frankfurt School, this chapter introduces the theoretical terms of rackets and racketeers to the analysis of the 'dangerous classes' both in the Iranian context and more broadly.

In order to attain this objective, this chapter focuses on the life stories of the two most famous *lutis* in the second Pahlavi period (i.e. the reign of Mohammad Reza Shah Pahlavi, 1941–79), whose performances oscillated between those of heroic political figures and those of mere thugs and brutal racketeers: Tayyeb Hajj Reza'i (1912–63) and Sha'ban Ja'fari. After discussing the *lutigari* ethos in a broader sense, I shall demonstrate the extent of the enormous political influence these two gang leaders of the urban poor wielded during the crucial year of 1953 as well as their marginalization in the aftermath of the coup. This will be juxtaposed with Horkheimer's and Adorno's racket theory.

The ambiguities of terms – *luti* and *lutigari*

It is impossible to talk about the concept of the dangerous classes in Iran without referring to the *luti* phenomenon. Despite its prominence in common parlance in modern Iran, there is no consensus about all its meanings and connotations. In order to define a Weberian ideal type, one's range would have to include 'dervish-like entertainers', 'urban Robin Hood-type bandits', roughs and knife-wielders, and the like.[11] Notably, Willem Floor made a great effort to trace the term and excavate all its linguistic and historical meanings back to the tenth century.[12] However, Vanessa Martin's synopsis is sufficient for the purpose of this chapter:

> The name *lūṭī* was given to people in a variety of occupations in urban centres for many centuries in Iran. It could indicate their cultural values, their economic standing, usually among the poorer social groups, and their political role. In a word, *lūṭīs* could be the socially conscious leaders of the poor, whose heroic values inspired them, and they could be every sort of thug, rogue and thief.[13]

That said, the connotation depends on one's viewpoint: the term can both glorify and condemn. As a result of this ambiguity, the *luti* has often been conceptualized as analogous to Eric Hobsbawm's 'social bandit'.[14]

However, the lowest common denominator of all definitions lies in the assertion that the *luti* represents a social configuration of the *urban* poor deeply entrenched in Iranian traditions. Thus, in contrast to the social bandit, the *luti* is neither a manifestation of rural interests in opposition to the political centre, nor is he a social figure dependent on a specific historical configuration of change – the two defining criteria of Hobsbawm's social bandit. On the contrary, the *luti* is associated precisely with the *urban* centres of Iran. Also, the discourse on the *luti* culture and tradition shows that, apart from its relational connotation and endogenous ambiguities, the term does not have much in common with the concept of the social bandit.

As contrasted with Hobsbawm's social bandit, one does not become a *luti* through a specific act of initiation comparable to an act of banditry that ipso facto defines the bandit. Rather, the term is better explained as a way of living. Whatever one perceives to be the main attributes of a *luti* – positive or negative – being a *luti* is a *choice*. Most importantly, the *luti* is always a man. Therefore we have to speak of the *luti* as a man perceived by the community as living his life according to a configuration of masculinity in an Iranian context which champions the enforcement of alternative orders on the local level in an urban environment.[15]

The term *lutigari* defines this specific configuration of masculinity idealizing strength, honour, action and the capability to protect areas, families or disciples – in short, being able to stand one's ground. It is a configuration formulated in opposition to state structures and elitism and hence it is mostly anti-intellectualist. The concept may also – but does not have to – include religious references,[16] whereby piety is seen as a sign of ideal manhood. In addition, the term *lutigari* not only legitimizes deviant and insubordinate behaviour through its idealization of alternative orders but rather *expects* actions in opposition to rules and norms. Accordingly, the *luti* does not play by the rules of the state, he creates and enforces his own order – while allegedly only respecting the traditions of his environment and the *luti* concept itself.

The cases of Tayyeb Hajj Reza'i and Sha'ban Ja'fari correspond to this. The former was a traditional athlete, wrestler and a renowned leader of ruffians. He was jailed on numerous occasions for street brawls and even murder. In 1947, he opened a fruit store in the main fruit and vegetable market of southern Tehran and became its self-appointed chief and protector, respected for his display of Islamic virtues but feared due to his propensity to violence. Accordingly, the anthropologist Fariba Adelkhah used his example to explain the meaning of the concept of *javanmardi* in modern Iran.[17] In other words, he is presented as a model of *lutigari*; the *javanmard-e bozorg* (the great ideal man), as he is described in his most recent biography.[18]

The second *luti*, Sha'ban 'The Brainless' Ja'fari, was born in Tehran in 1921 and dropped out of school after the fourth grade. He was around fourteen years old when he began frequenting Tehran's traditional athletics clubs, the *zurkhaneh* ('the house of strength').[19] At the age of fifteen he was arrested and imprisoned for the first time for his role in a street brawl. He later became an important symbolic figure for the south Tehranian ruffians attracted by the homosocial milieu of the *zurkhaneh*, the 'traditional place for the development and spiritualization of manly prowess, and the strongest locus of the *luti* ethos'.[20] Sha'ban Ja'fari insisted on being known as a *shirinkar* (lit. 'sweet-doer', an honorific title for athletes able to lift the heaviest stones and iron bows) early on.[21] Accordingly, as early as 1943 he became the national champion in two traditional *zurkhaneh* strength exercises. He described himself as a patriot, a family-oriented person, a man with a deep sense of honour who fought several times for the glory of his neighbourhood and was devoted to defending the honour of his *mahalle's* women.[22]

To sum up, in the early 1950s both Tayyeb Hajj Reza'i and Sha'ban Ja'fari were enforcing their own order on a local level and were regarded as *lutis*. In addition, they both came from a poor family background and established their position as the most important gang leaders of the urban poor, i.e. of the dangerous classes, in Tehran; one cannot speak about the political role of the lumpenproletariat in the 1953 coup without mentioning these two actors. However, both Reza'i and Ja'fari had become wealthy and influential by that time, so it is unclear whether they themselves can still be categorized as members of the lumpenproletariat. The answer to this question can only be given drawing on the racket theory, as will be discussed below. For the time being we will treat the dangerous classes in modern Iran as inseparable from the *luti* milieu.

The *lutis* and the state

The cases of Tayyeb Hajj Reza'i and Sha'ban Ja'fari also have to be put into a historical context evaluating the past and future of the *luti* ethos. Although their lives took different directions in the aftermath of the coup, their mark on the concepts of *lutigari* and *luti* can be felt to this day. The two concepts are not immutable, but they are mutually dependent and have been shaped in the public consciousness by well-known figures seen as role models. Indeed, Tayyeb and Sha'ban can in many ways be seen as such defining figures, as had *their* own role models been back then.

During the Constitutional Revolution (1905–1911), the most famous *lutis* were the horse dealer Sattar Khan[23] (1868–1914) and the stone mason Baqer Khan[24] (1861–1916), who led the constitutionalist forces from Tabriz against the royalists in Tehran.[25] Their story is remarkable and became common knowledge in the cultural memory of Iran. When the leading revolutionary intellectuals where forced to flee Tehran and go into exile in 1907, Tabriz became the new centre of national resistance to Mohammad 'Ali Shah's (1872–1925) dictatorship.[26] The royalist forces initially took over parts of the city but were run out of town by local groups headed by Sattar Khan and Baqer Khan, and Tabriz then resisted the royalists for nine months. The resistance in Tabriz started with a remarkably heroic episode: when fighting broke out in Tabriz, Sattar Khan and his men went into the streets to protect their neighbourhood against the government troops. In contrast to Baqer Khan who, after nearly two weeks of heavy fighting in the city, hoisted a white flag to signal his surrender, Sattar Khan held his ground. It is said that he personally rode through the city on 17 July 1908 and tore down all the white flags.[27] This courageous act emboldened the people of Tabriz to continue their resistance against the Shah's troops. Eventually, large heterogeneous groups of revolutionaries marched from the west, north (headed by the two *luti*) and south towards Tehran in 1909, conquered the capital in the name of the constitutionalist cause and forced Mohammad 'Ali Shah to abdicate. This cemented the status of Sattar Khan and Baqer Khan as national heroes.[28]

To sum up, the example of these two famous revolutionary leaders, originating from the lower classes and adhering to the *luti* values and virtues, forged a notion of *lutigari* which put strong emphasis on political action and legitimized questioning the state – and actually opposing it when the community under the *lutis'* protection is endangered. In the post-war period, these heroic examples from the Constitutional Revolution offered an image of an ideal manhood that does not encourage respect for the state in general but rather for ad hoc political action in the form of street politics. The leadership of Tayyeb Hajj Reza'i and Sha'ban Ja'fari relied in great part on the discourses shaped by the examples from the Constitutional Revolution.

Regarding the actions of the main *luti* protagonists of the Constitutional Revolution and the coup d'état, Marx would again have said: the first time is a tragedy, the second is a farce. Sattar Khan and Baqer Khan, the two national heroes of the Constitutional Revolution, were excluded from the new government and died an unworthy death shortly afterwards – this being the tragedy. The second time – the farce – is represented by the contribution of the *lutis* to the 1953 coup when they saw their deeds as reflecting the tradition of their constitutional era predecessors.

According to Marx, the reactionary French coup d'état of 1851 had only been successful because Louis-Napoléon Bonaparte managed to establish himself as the chief of the lumpenproletariat, whilst this 'scum, offal, refuse of all classes' was the only class upon which he could rely unconditionally.[29]

Over one hundred years later, Mohammad Reza Shah sent a telegram from Rome to Tehran on 20 August 1953, addressing the Iranian people. The preceding days had seen a failed coup on 16 August, some brawls the day after – a communist escalation probably triggered by agent provocateurs employed by the CIA[30] – and finally a huge riot by the dangerous classes on the morning of 19 August.[31] In his telegram, sent one day after the successful coup d'état, the Shah presented the coup as a *qiyam-e melli*, a people's revolt: 'In the name of God Almighty, I thank the Iranian people for supporting me and defending the Constitution.'[32]

To whom does the Shah express his thanks here? The 'Iranian people' who gathered on the crucial morning of 19 August mostly comprised of segments of the dangerous classes, as the CIA report on the events suggests. Following the issue of a royal decree dismissing premier Mosaddeq, pro-Shah groups started assembling in the bazaar area but lacked leadership.[33] This gap was filled by the *lutis*. Fakhreddin Azimi wrote: '[The royalist segments] enjoyed the backing of truck-loads of club-wielding and rampaging thugs who had been mobilized by mob leaders. With the aim of demoralizing government supporters they swiftly and indiscriminately attacked passers-by in the center of Tehran while chanting "long live the Shah".'[34] In doing so, the *lutis* provided the 'sound effect'[35] for the subsequent military coup.

The fiery scholarly debates on the coup have in recent years focused mostly on the question of who instigated the leaders of the dangerous classes. Does their emergence have to be explained against the background of a conspiracy by the CIA and the British Secret Intelligence Service (SIS)?[36] Should the coup be seen as a follow-up to a spontaneous popular uprising in response to a perceived communist threat?[37] Are high-ranking Shi'i clerics the 'missing link'?[38] However, there is no question about the fact that a group of *lutis* actually *did* play a leading role in the events.

Tayyeb Hajj Reza'i was one of the leading *luti* figures at the time. In the years before the coup, Tayyeb had not only managed to become successful in the shady world of Tehran's fruit and vegetable market[39] he also established himself in the logistics business, owning several lorries.[40] Obviously, he was the one who provided the 'truck-loads of club-wielding rampaging thugs' during the coup. Ali Rahnema reports an interview where Tayyeb Hajj Reza'i 'recalls "I immediately sent for the purchase of ten truck-loads of sticks (*dah bar-e choob kharidam*), we already had a few machetes and knives, we gathered all the boys and came to town in trucks and jeeps." Tayyeb boastfully tells his interviewer that "you know what we did that day or rather everyone knows what happened and what did not happen [on 28 Mordad]".[41] Rahnema concludes: 'Most of Tayyeb's group on 28 Mordad [...] were well known in the circle of roughnecks, athletes and unruly gallant knife-wielders'.[42] Basically, Tayyeb used his influence to trigger action on the street, so that the *lutis* from southern Tehran could prevail over the crowd of Mosaddeq and *Tudeh* sympathisers; the military forces, loyal to the Shah, only joined later.[43] As a result, the Shah himself conferred the honorific '*taj-bakhsh*' (kingmaker) on Tayyeb and rewarded him with the Second Class Medal of Rastakhez (resurgence).[44]

Although it is widely believed that Sha'ban Ja'fari also played a prominent role on the morning of 19 August,[45] this is not true. He was imprisoned after the events of 28 February and was only released at noon on the day of the coup, when a group of protesters gathered in front of the jail and demanded his release.[46] However, due to his loyalty during the February 'proto-coup' as well as his participation in the events of 19 August immediately after getting out of prison, he too was rewarded with the honorific *taj-bakhsh*.[47]

To sum up, when the Shah sent his thanks to the Iranian people and when he later rewarded the leading *lutis* with honorifics, he showed his gratitude to the dangerous classes who had been vital to the coup, which Rahnema describes as the product of thugs, turncoats, soldiers and spooks, as per the subtitle of his book. According to leftist thinking, at this point the Shah had declared himself the chief of the lumpenproletariat.

This applies even to recent Iranian publications, such as historian Mojtaba Zadeh-Mohammadi's *Lompan-ha dar siyasat-e 'asr-e pahlavi* (The lumpenproletariat in Pahlavī Politics) where the author declares that the *lutis* of 1940s and 1950s Iran were degenerate subjects who had lost contact to the roots of *javanmardi* and *lutigari* and became *lompan* in a purely Marxian sense.[48] In doing so, Zadeh-Mohammadi transferred the 'scum and rubbish'-rhetoric of Marx and Engels to the case of the Iranian *lutis*, as the publications of the communist Tudeh party have done ever since the 1953 coup.[49] The leftists' frustration with the emergence of the *lutis* precisely at a time when the communist project in Iran stood on the threshold of victory is evident. In their view, the dangerous classes acted in line with Karl Marx's warning that the lumpenproletariat may turn against the interests of the people and suspend the course of history determined by historical materialism.

However, the interpretation of the *lutis'* role in the coup d'état against Premier Mohammad Mosaddeq in August 1953 as a farce is not exclusive to leftist analyses. On the contrary, the prominent role of the *lutis* during this episode has often been used to illustrate the anachronistic character of the coup. Especially for secular nationalists, the contribution of the dangerous classes to the events serves as evidence of foreign conspiracy to this day. However, this anachronism is a problem for the state as well, since its reliance on the 'traditional' *lutis* contradicts the modernizing agenda of Iran in the late 1950s and 1960s.

The state and *lutigari*

Describing the state's dependency on the dangerous classes, Zadeh-Mohammadi states that after the invasion of Iran by the allied troops in 1941 'every individual, as well as every political party or group had to exploit violent vagabonds and hoodlums in order to enforce its political objectives'.[50] This implies that *all* factions, regardless of their political tendencies or affiliation to societal strata, had to rely on troublemakers from the lower classes as their muscle. In effect, Zadeh-Mohammadi says that even the Shah was *forced* to trust actors whose political action took the form of violent street fights.[51]

The coup d'état of 1953, while by far not the only example of this in Iran in the 1940s and 1950s, is the most significant one. However, although the Shah – and consequently the state – profited from the service of the *lutis,* this dependency was naturally in conflict with state interests as well as with the concerns of ruling elites. Therefore, while the leftist reaction to the role of the lumpenproletariat in the coup was unambiguous, the state had to be strategic.

The sociologist Georgi Derluguian used the word 'taming' to describe the state's relation to alternative power centres, which he identifies as chieftaincies: 'Chieftains seek to expand and realize statehood, whereas states emerge in the main by taming and incorporating chieftaincies'.[52] Thus, on the one hand he observes that alternative power structures pose a threat to the system they themselves helped to establish; on the other hand he hints at a solution to this problem: these alternative power structures have to be physically and discursively demolished and deconstructed step by step.

Such discursive deconstruction usually turns first to configurations which champion other sources of the right to rule than the state. We have defined *lutigari* in 1950s Iran as a notion of masculinity based on opposition to superior power structures, glorification of local order and face-to-face action, and which legitimized the questioning of the state. Accordingly, we could expect a discursive contestation of this notion by the Pahlavi state.

Indeed, the deconstruction of the underlying configurations of masculinities has been pivotal in the recommendations for Iran based on modernization theory. For example, while discussing the relation between 'ingenuity cultures' and 'courage cultures' (obviously nothing more than a racist discrimination between the West and the rest of the world), David Riesman states in his introduction to Daniel Lerner's *The Passing of Traditional Society. Modernizing the Middle East* in 1958: 'My own impression is that the ingenuity needed to escape the all-too-evident impasses of the Middle East can neither be imported nor be locally engendered without a lessening of the dominant male values, what the Spanish term "*machismo*".[53]

This quote is not used here as a rehash of old-fashioned modernization theory but to show that the discursive deconstruction of specific configurations of masculinities and their relation to modernity was a topic of discussion at the time. Leonard Binder, another representative of modernization theory, picked the topic up in 1964. He explicitly uses the term *lutigari*, which he defines as 'a colloquial term for a kind of chivalric friendship involving the doing of mutual favors'.[54] Binder identifies this ethos of masculinity as the glue that holds together groups which otherwise show 'little common effort for a common objective',[55] an interpretation which clearly indicates that *lutigari* has to be regarded as an agent of backwardness.

Daniel Lerner saw modern media outlets as the key weapon against these configurations of masculinities: 'The male vanity culture which underlay traditional institutions has proved relatively defenceless against inroads of the mass media, particularly the movies.'[56] However, this assertion proved dramatically wrong in Iran's case: the country's dynamic cinema industry produced numerous tough-guy movies in the 1950s and 1960s, and the genre proved popular.[57] At the same time, as Hamid Naficy shows in his *A Social History of Iranian Cinema*, some contemporaries were critical of the genre:

> According to [one critic], tough-guy movies glorified the lives of the lumpen, who were not engaged in meaningful social production but led a shiftless, degenerate, and 'parasitical life'. The toughs and their women eked out a marginal existence in debased professions, exhibited antisocial behavior, and involved themselves in criminal schemes. Their lives included the vending of seasonal foods, gofering, rabble-rousing, knife-wielding, pimping, spying, singing and dancing, smuggling, stealing, and prostitution."[58]

Nevertheless, tough-guy movies remained popular in Iran.[59] Their continued production in the 1950s and 1960s may, according to Naficy, be seen as resistance by independent filmmakers to the government strategies to 'hail and subjugate Iranians and to turn them into consumers of cheap, debased Western entertainment and products'.[60]

The state against the *lutis*

The growth of the tough-guy movie genre is an example of how complicated the discursive deconstruction of a well-known configuration is – not only for the regime back then but also for researchers interested in excavating the regime's strategies. It is much easier to determine the conditions and dominant configurations at a given time than to trace how they were shaped by specific discursive strategies. For instance, in her study *Religion, Culture and Politics in Iran*, Joanna de Groot convincingly argues that in the 1960s 'young men's street activities did not replicate the *luti* presence of the earlier times, but refigured gender and generation in the new settings of modern streets and migrant neighbourhoods'.[61] In this regard, it was first and foremost the rapid change in society – the expansion of bureaucracy, education, migration, emancipation or diversification – that helped to unmask the *lutigari* ethos as anachronistic and outdated precisely in the way the advocates of modernization theory had hoped for, with the Shah himself being its main advocate ever since he announced the 'White Revolution' in 1963 – a development programme which explicitly propagated new gender configurations.

However, in order to trace the state strategies towards *lutigari* masculinities in particular, it helps to focus again on the lives of the main representatives of this challenged configuration in post-coup Iran. One can argue that if the concept of *lutigari* is mediated to the public by role models, they must be demolished and deconstructed in order to contaminate the ethos itself. This can be done either by corrupting and marginalizing these role models and implicitly the principles and values they stand for, or by criminalizing and prosecuting them in order to demonize their values and virtues. The stories of Sha'ban Ja'fari and Tayyeb Hajj Reza'i are paradigmatic examples of these strategies.

Sha'ban Ja'fari is an example of successful corruption – or 'taming', to use Derluguian's term – of a former representative of an alternative power structure. His transformation from a local power broker to a mere folkloristic representative of an ancient Persian world is a striking example of the strategic marginalization of the *lutigari* ethos in 1950s and 1960s Iran. Prior to the coup, he was one of the most powerful figures in Tehran's street politics. In July 1952, when the power struggle between the Shah and Mosaddeq escalated for the first time, Sha'ban supported the premier (until January 1953 he regarded himself as a supporter of Mosaddeq[62]) and managed to gain control over the streets. Mohsen Mobasser, the police commander in the bazar district at the time, remembers in his interview with the *Harvard Iranian Oral History Collection* that it wasn't he and his forces who controlled the streets, rather, it was Sha'ban Ja'fari who was in command.[63] Until he got detained during the incident of 28 February 1953, he was a major factor in Tehran politics.

After the August 1953 coup, the Shah personally gave permission for the opening of the bashgah-e Sha'ban Ja'fari, a sports club named after and run by Ja'fari, close to the main city park.[64] Publicly honoured by the Shah and rewarded with a sports club, Sha'ban Ja'fari 'retired' from politics and from questioning the state. He became a '*luti* in retirement' and a folkloristic attraction instead. Seemingly every foreign celebrity staying in Iran had to pay a visit at the bashgah-e Sha'ban Ja'fari, as attested by numerous photographs depicting celebrities from all over the world – including Muhammad Ali, Jawaharlal Nehru and Gina Lollobrigida.[65] Although he gained some credit by keeping the Iranian *zurkhaneh* tradition alive,[66] his marginalization as a *luti* was complete by the mid-1960s. In the end he became a farce – first when he lost access to the court in the early 1970s and then again when he tried to mobilize his disciples in support of the Shah in 1978, but failed terribly. He fled the country in January 1979.[67]

While Sha'ban Ja'fari was lucky enough to just become marginalized, Tayyeb Hajj Reza'i's life took a different direction. As a successful and influential businessman in the late 1940s and early 1950s, and by the same token deeply embedded in the *luti* culture as one of its leading figures, he was not easy for the regime to undermine. One attempt occurred in 1959, when the Shah's wife gave birth to the heir apparent. In gratitude for his support during the coup some years earlier, the Shah decided to honour Tayyeb by having the delivery take place in a hospital located in one of Tehran's poor southern neighbourhoods that was known to be under Tayyeb's protection. However, this turned out to be the beginning of the end for Tayyeb Hajj Reza'i. After a public confrontation with Ne'matollah Nasiri (the then police governor of Tehran) about the number of police units in Tayyeb's *mahelleh*, things went south for the famous *luti*.[68] The police made life so hard for him that he first lost his monopoly on the banana trade and later ran up debts. In 1963 he took the side of the ascending Ayatollah Khomeini and was accused of organizing a mob on his behalf on 5 June, during the riots nowadays remembered as *Qiyam-e Panzdahom-e Khordad* (seen by the Islamic republic regime as a turning point on the road towards the Islamic Revolution of 1978–79), and later executed.[69] Today, common knowledge in Iran claims that Tayyeb had to die because of his refusal to denounce Ayatollah Khomeini as the hidden hand behind the riots.[70]

Even though Tayyeb Hajj Reza'i is remembered in a positive light due to the steadfastness he showed up until his death, what matters is the effect his execution had at the time. The *luti* Tayyeb Hajj Reza'i died and with him a configuration that threatened the state. Therefore the cases of Sha'ban Ja'fari and Tayyeb Hajj Reza'i show how the strategies of marginalization and prosecution led to the decline of *lutigari* masculinities in Pahlavi Iran. Ashgar Fathi's essay about the political role of the rebels during the Constitutional Revolution, written in the mid-1970s, attests to this decline:

> Looties have been disappearing in recent years in Iran owing to the expansion of urbanization and its accompanying style of life. They belonged to an informal association with a long-standing tradition. These simple men, mostly in their twenties or early thirties, were found in every township and more specifically in every town district over the country.[71]

In addition, Joanna de Groot observes the emergence of a pejorative meaning of the term *luti*, which can only be an effect of the aftermath of the coup d'état of 1953, since until then the *luti* heroes of the Constitutional Revolution had been symbols of morality: 'The term *luti*, which incorporated ideas of popular morality, decency and protectiveness, was often used at moments of popular disorder to stigmatise the violent, immoral and unrespectable character of protesters.'[72]

A theoretical corrective: The racket theory

As stated at the beginning of this chapter, in Iran the concept of the dangerous classes is inseparable from the phenomenon of the *lutis*. By the same token, my study has shown the enormous importance of the leading *luti* figures not only on historical dynamics but also on the *lutis* as a social group: first, due to their sheer power as the leading figures of the milieu itself and, second, due to their influence on the underlying configuration of masculinity, i.e. the *lutigari* masculinity. It is obviously not convincing to categorize these rich and influential men as members of the lumpenproletariat in the classical Marxian sense, since they were not thrown 'hither and thither' and, without a doubt, belonged to the producing classes. If one intends to follow the Marxian class theory while dealing with dialectical challenges to the concept of the lumpenproletariat, one needs to introduce a theoretical corrective when confronted with the cases of the prominent members of this social stratum. In order to do so, I propose to consider the racket theory, formulated by Max Horkheimer and Theodor W. Adorno.

The racket theory was first promoted by the exiled members of the Frankfurt School during the early 1940s. In order to explain the emergence of the Nazis in Germany and in particular the movement's internal contentions on the way to power and as it consolidated its position, the members of the *Institut für Sozialforschung* (then located in New York) developed a theory of domination based on protection. The theory is admittedly only fragmentary (only three short essays by Horkheimer and Adorno deal with it directly[73]), however, the idea that the 'racket is the basic principle of domination'[74] formed the intellectual basis of the two authors' famous *Dialectic of Enlightment.*[75] Horkheimer defines rackets as follows: 'A racket is a conspiratorial group which enforces its collective interests at the expense of the society.'[76] Therefore, the term characterizes a 'privileged complicity' whose stability is conditioned by the 'informal ties and the intensity of the linkages to state structures as well as economic, legal *and illicit* structures of the society'.[77] At first glance, the members' class affiliation is of lesser importance, because they would always try to work in the interest of the racket they are affiliated with. In this regard, Adorno observes that the same class affiliation does not imply the same direction of action, as conformity might seem more logical to the individual.[78] Consequently, cliquishness defines the actions of individuals and competing rackets are always struggling to achieve monopoly in their respective fields of interest. Therefore we can see history as a succession of gang fights, cliques and rackets.[79]

By the same token, the racket functions as a form of protection. It protects its members in return for their respect for internal hierarchies, driving out internal competitors as well as fighting external threats.[80] In this regard the racketeer works in the way Charles Tilly has coined later: 'Someone who produces both the danger and, at a price, the shield against it is a racketeer.'[81]

However, the purpose in formulating the racket theory was not to replace the Marxian class theory but to refine it. The racket theory 'provides an account of group loyalties which are more particularistic than those of classes but retains the close connections with material interests which characterize class theories'.[82] Hence, the emphasis on the importance of racketeering and cliquishness accompanies the Marxian class theory and enriches its strict 'horizontal' thinking with a 'vertical' element. As Peter Stirk puts it: 'The point of referring to rackets, and not just to ruling classes, was that the idea of a racket contains the suggestion of coercion and coercion was the common denominator of domination. From this perspective, history, which Marx had described as the history of classes, was a history of domination.'[83]

This dynamic theoretical corrective makes it possible to talk about men like Sha'ban Ja'fari and Tayyeb Hajj Reza'i – who maintained links to the highest political circles and even personally to the Shah – and regard them as the leaders of their respective rackets or as members of the royalist clique (or racket) and at the same time to acknowledge them as members of their *luti* milieus. They were powerful and wealthy racketeers belonging to the dangerous classes. This theoretical configuration offers an explanation of the role of figures like Sha'ban and Tayyeb that classical Marxian class theory does not provide. By the same token, their highly dynamic use of street politics in the struggle with their political enemies, can be attributed to both class consciousness *and* personal interest. A person can fight for both their racket and their class – or, as in Sha'ban and Tayyeb's case, in accordance with the *luti* ethos – at the same time. In addition, the marginalization and execution of these actors can be explained through the logic of rackets: internal competitors have to be driven out either through discursive deconstruction or physically.

Conclusion

To sum up, the coup d'état of 1953 has proven a farce in all aspects. It left in its wake a demolished secular-nationalist project, a disillusioned communist movement, a discredited monarch, a deep scar on Iran's foreign relations and a general atmosphere of suspicion. Even the rise of political Islam, embodied by the ascending Ayatollah Khomeinī, had to wait until the three leading Ayatollahs – Kashani, Behbahani and Borujerdi – passed away between 1961 and 1963. The discussions about the importance of their contributions to the events aside, all three had undoubtedly played a role in the events of 1953. However, it was the distinct configuration of masculinity glorifying the enforcement of alternative orders – the ethos of *lutigari* – that suffered the hardest blow.

Much has been written about the involvement of foreign powers in the coup d'état of 28 Mordad. Ali Rahnema puts an end to all doubt in his thoroughly researched book *Behind the 1953 Coup in Iran* when he writes that the events of 19 August were not 'impromptu or unprepared, but carefully and intelligently thought out, revised and planned by the key foreign and domestic masterminds who gathered at the American Embassy'.[84] Consequently, he concludes: 'That the events of 28 Mordad were a spontaneous mass movement, a national resurgence, a popular uprising, a legal counter-coup, a backlash of the people's discontent, even a jihad against atheism and Communism orchestrated by religious leaders, cannot be demonstrated or supported by historical facts.'[85]

It was not the task of this chapter to challenge this view. On the contrary, with the controversy over who is to blame for the coup resolved, it is now feasible to focus on the micro stories. In this regard, I have presented the cases of two famous *lutis*, Sha'ban Ja'fari and Tayyeb Hajj Reza'i, who both played prominent roles in the coup as well as in its aftermath, in order to shed light on the political role and significance of the dangerous classes in the 1953 coup in Iran. Consequently, I boldly claim that the emergence and participation of the dangerous classes in the coup served as a defining moment for all parties. For the leftists, the Marxian idea of the unreliability of the lumpenproletariat was proven right. For secular nationalists, the participation of these groups epitomized the immorality of the foreign powers which orchestrated the actions of the poor. For the royalists, the power of the racketeers associated with the dangerous classes became obvious. In this regard, these racketeers became a menace to the order they themselves helped to establish and had to be driven out of the bigger, royalist racket.

My assumption was that the processes and dynamics of the coup had been triggered by a configuration of masculinity that exalts the idea of alternative orders on a local level. In this chapter, I was not interested in the question of whether the *luti* leaders acted on someone else's orders or on their own initiative, in order to achieve political or individual goals – although the latter would be consistent with racket theory. Here

I merely wanted to shed light on the relation between the Iranian concept of *lutis* and the Marxian category of the dangerous classes through the lens of the 1953 coup. By the same token, the focus on the life stories of two famous *lutis* shows the decline of the *lutigari* ethos. My observation is that this decline followed the dialectical logic of the lumpenproletariat: the dangerous classes not only represent a threat for the 'course of history' as dictated by historical materialism, they also threaten the reactionary cause. According to Marxian thinking, the unreliability of the lumpenproletariat is not a one-way street. In the end, *lutigari* – a configuration of masculinity that idealizes strength, honour, deed and action, and the capability to protect areas, families or disciples, as defined at the beginning of this chapter – had to be deconstructed. On the left side of the political spectrum this deconstruction followed the logic of the 'scum and rubbish' rhetoric that depicts *lutis* as members of the lumpenproletariat. As the examples of Sha'ban Ja'fari and Tayyeb Hajj Reza'i have shown, on the other side of the political spectrum this deconstruction was accomplished through turning the actors into representatives of folkloristic symbols of an earlier era or through criminalizing and persecuting them.

The 'Virtual Poor' in Iran: The Dangerous Classes and Homeless Life in Capitalist Times

Maziyar Ghiabi

Introduction: Agency in garbage economics

Homeless life in Tehran is increasingly visible to the public eye.[1] Temporary shelters, offering refuge from the capital's cold winters or its exploitative housing market, host competing groups of the urban poor. These include lumpen workers (i.e. casual workers with low pay); rural migrants settled on the urban fringes; Afghan immigrants or Afghans resettled in Iran but with unrecognized status; and individuals suffering destitution for health, social and/or economic reasons, who all subsist on the waste and leftover commodities of middle-class urban dwellers. This is visible in south Tehran, where the poor and rural migrants have traditionally been concentrated (notably around the Great Bazar). It is also increasingly apparent in north Tehran, for example in the middle-class district of Farahzad, although homeless men and women usually try to be inconspicuous to avoid complaints from the residents or confrontations with the police. Many of these individuals come from rural communities on the Iranian plateau but they no longer look – or want to look – like rural migrants. In worn-out clothes – often found in the street and featuring slogans in English, flags of Western countries and fake brands – they gather plastic bottles, iron waste, copper, etc. for sale to wholesalers. Thus the garbage economy provides them with at least a small income.

Vagrancy, homelessness and drug consumption are not modern phenomena in Iran. They have long held a codified place in popular culture, with Islamic ethics and jurisprudence encouraging charity and the sheltering of beggars and other altruistic actions. There was wide tolerance for opiate use in Iran up until the 1950s, with apothecaries and folk doctors providing prescriptions.[2] Homelessness and drug use have often been used interchangeably in the public discourse, for instance in reference to vagrant derviches (*darvish*). However, with the turn of the twentieth century – and the modernization of the Iranian state – a shift occurred in both the government's and the people's attitude towards the homeless and, concomitantly, drug consumption. Today, this attitude can be seen in the layout of the *mahalleh* in Tehran's Shemiranat district, one of the city's oldest, where the Emamzadeh Davoud is positioned at one end and a shelter for homeless drug users is at the other.

The new modernizing state was more concerned with public intoxication rather than intoxication as such. Laws regulating the use of narcotic substances were first introduced in Iran in the 1910s. The controls on illicit drugs that are in place today originated at the international meetings in Shanghai (1909) and The Hague (1912). There, world powers and opium producers – including Iran (then Qajar Persia) – agreed to control the administration of narcotic substances and to limit domestic consumption. The authorities in Tehran envisaged adopting measures that were more Catholic than the Pope: Iran was the first opium-producing country to introduce penalties for opium consumption, a highly popular habit embedded in people's everyday lives. These measures, however, discriminated against the poor through a legal device that has remained a feature of Iran's drug policy from then on. The 1918 drug law referred to *tajahor* (an Arabic term meaning 'to publicly manifest something'). Thus the newly established legal framework did not focus on eradicating narcotics consumption as such. Rather, it aimed to remove the proletarian (and lumpen) consumers from public spaces, as opium could only be consumed in private homes. The poor, who often had very restricted or no living quarters, thus sought out illegal coffee houses designated for opium rituals, which remained in business until the 1950s. The underground (and therefore legendary) *shirehkesh-khaneh*, the smoking houses for *shireh* (a powerful derivate of opium residue), were another option. Between the 1900s and the 1940s, there were 175 *shirehkesh-khaneh* in Tehran alone.[3]

What later came to be known internationally as the 'War on Drugs' (after Richard Nixon's expression in 1971) has in practice been an 'exercise in xenophobia' towards the poor, the stranger, the migrant and the marginal.[4] Condemnation of drug users is almost uniformly legislated across the globe today, although the means of repression differ. For instance, European countries have adopted limited tolerance and welfare-oriented measures towards drug addicts, with some notable exceptions such as the crackdown on drug users among minority groups (Africans and Arabs) in the low-income housing projects (*banlieues*) in France. Other countries – notably the United States but more recently also the Philippines, most Arab countries and authoritarian states such as Russia and China – have adopted militaristic strategies and heavy repression.[5] The Islamic Republic of Iran has embraced draconian measures against drug dealers combined with compassionate welfare services for what it calls 'addicts'. The line in between these two approaches is thin and the category of plebeians, 'dangerous classes' and the virtual poor plays a key discriminant. All three categories belong to the popular classes and the borders between them are fluid. The term 'plebeian' refers to individuals or collectives belonging to the populace who are subaltern to a propertied class and whose place is not at the core of the institutional order. In this chapter I use it in reference to individuals or groups, often with a rural background but living in urban settings, with insecure and low-paid jobs. The expression 'dangerous classes' (called the lumpenproletariat by Marx and Engels), denotes those who have fallen out of the working classes into the lower depths of the urban social environments and who survive there by their wits and by various 'amoral', 'disreputable' or criminal strategies.[6] Finally, I use the definition of the virtual poor that sees them as living on the verge of poverty, or in a situation where poverty seems an imminent outcome of the present. This chapter highlights the thin and permeable border between these categories – as perceived by the state and the social and moral order – and those in danger.

In modern times, street drug consumers have included people from all three categories: lumpen, plebeians and the virtual poor. This group is the object of structural violence produced by capitalist forms of government and exploitation.[7] This violence is first and foremost physical: it operates through mass incarceration,[8] police killings and large-scale substance abuse. It is also symbolic, manifested through the ideology of 'individual achievement and free market efficiency' that marks them out as inefficient, parasitic elements.[9] Spatial segregation, in the form of a prison or a ghetto, impedes human development through the exclusion of the working class and the undeserving poor from the mainstream economy. In addition, ideological exclusion condemns them to virtual oblivion through a process of lumpenization, driven by multiple factors connected to the illegal, informal economy, including that of drugs. Petty drug dealing, drug consumption, prison, 'addiction' and drug violence become part of the drug assemblage.[10]

Lumpenization is productive for capitalist exploitation. Criminal charges against drug users (or 'abusers' according to this logic) – have lowered the wages of everyone else in the working class. The moral stigma of drug use, too, has discouraged many from joining trade unions.[11] Thus the 'War on Drugs' has in fact been a war on poor drug users. The mass of minimum-wage workers, often with substance abuse disorders and/ or criminal records, enables the procurement of cheap labour. The McDonald's staff are an epitome of this trend in the West. In Iran, where McDonald's does not operate, it is the unskilled daily labourers, garbage collectors, street vendors, deliverymen and those with a criminal and/or drug abuse history who accept minimum-wage employment. This goes hand in hand with the depoliticization of unruly urban subjects living at the city's edges or, in the words of Iranian director Rakhshan Bani Etemad, 'under the skin of the city'.[12] People with criminal records struggle to find employment in general but for those with drug offences the task becomes virtually impossible. This process of lumpenization of the plebeian classes does not differ across the East–West divide.

One cannot speak of drug users as a 'class'. The category is an invention of a political machine that considers certain substances and plants exceptional (e.g. poppy/opium, coca/cocaine, cannabis/marijuana) but regulates others (e.g. tobacco, alcohol) in a flourishing capitalist market.[13] The drug 'addict' – in the lexicon of the twentieth-century drug wars – is neither part of the economic system of production nor of the moral order. Addicts are seen as parasites par excellence, because in the popular imagination they are useless. They rely on illegal income or charity and are therefore a liability in the political economy of development. Yet, the addict is also an avid consumer, drug use being tied with chronic drug consumerism and the unending search for money to support it. This inescapable drive for consumption is what makes the so-called 'addicts' an essential identity and product of capitalist times. Therefore, 'addicts' are not a class but a category that cuts across social classes. This is instrumental in discriminating against the poor and the marginal.

There is no distinction between proletariat and lumpenproletariat in my analysis because the experience of living under drug prohibition brings the wage labourers of factories, farms and industries closer to the life of the wageless, the so-called people of the 'informal economy'. Michael Denning argues that 'we must insist that "proletarian" is not a synonym for "wage labourer" but for dispossession, expropriation and radical dependence on the market'; one may also include the illegal market in this definition.[14] In the world of drug consumption, this market dependence defines the life of users in structural ways. In a system where those consuming certain substances are the object of police repression, the wage labourer exists as what Marx defined as 'a virtual pauper',[15] for whom poverty is a reality in waiting, likely but not necessarily inescapable.

Based on this rationale, the figure of the 'addict' – and particularly the homeless addict – is a preeminent example of a 'dangerous class'. This group has been systematically regarded as distinct, with its own ecology, with its peculiar forms of economic sustenance and bearing danger, disorder and 'irrational violence'. Its perceived dangerousness is manifested through concerns over criminality, health, morality and middle-class prosperity. The danger, however, is binary: seen as socially dangerous political misfits, addicts are also in danger, because their life – qualifying as 'bare life' (*zoê*, as opposed to *bios*) in Agambian terms[16] – is disposable, precarious, wasteful and contaminated.[17]

This overlapping of medical, social, criminal and political concerns is a side effect of the medicalization of politics vis-à-vis deviancy. The Italian physician (and 'physiognomist') Cesare Lombroso was among the founders of this approach. He sought to separate, on shaky medical grounds, the healthy from the fool (*i mattoidi*)[18]; an expedient to protect the status quo and middle-class sensibilities amidst the plebeian revolts of the nineteenth century. Despite being confuted by science, his theories have left their mark on the nexus between medicine and criminology, of which drugs policy is a special field (though I have no knowledge about Lombroso's fame among Iranian scientists). In this medico-political frame, medical understanding enables moral and political judgement, which in turn bestows a classist character upon scientific definitions (such as mental disorder, addiction, etc.). The rigid categories of medical sciences enmesh with the more ambiguous ones of human knowledge in a classist plot clothed in neutral, *technical* language. The state's adoption of criminological labels when engaging with homeless drug users is, in the words of the British psychiatrist R. D. Laing, 'a social fact which in turn is a political event'.[19]

Through an 'in-depth' description of lumpen life, this chapter invites the reader to observe how categories borne out of sociological analysis in other times and spaces can be at work in new contexts. The intent is not simply to add new historical cases to our body of knowledge but to give anthropological depth to our understanding of the lumpen and dangerous classes, the plebeians and virtual poor. In this vein, the chapter is a ethnographic history of modern Iranian society.

Ethnographic vignette: A homeless encampment and a drug hotspot

In the Farahzad district in northern Tehran, close to a Shi'a shrine, there is a shelter for homeless drug users who do not want to sleep rough in the valley that separates the Farahzad blocks from the more traditional, village-like neighbourhood around the shrine. However, most drug users prefer to spend the night in the open, where hundreds – sometimes thousands – of people gather around bonfires. An open-air market of heroin (*gart*) and methamphetamine (*shisheh*) creates a feast of the underworld, which members of the middle class, especially younger ones, attend out of adventurism, curiosity and convenience. For the homeless, alternating rough sleeping with shelter beds is also a convenient option. The food provided at the shelter complements their daily diet of large amounts of bread with a warm dish of *gheimé* (split peas stew) or *adasi* (lentil soup) and a few cups of very sweet tea.

Most of those frequenting this *patoq* (hangout)[20] do not live in the neighbourhood, although there are locals who spend their evenings here. Better prices, steady availability and less oscillation in the quality of drugs guarantee a better consumer experience even in the face of the sheer degradation of the surroundings. The Farahzad valley (*darreh-ye Farahzad*), where the shelter is located, has become a notorious site of drug use and open drug dealing in the last decade following arrests and clampdowns in other areas of Tehran. Journalists have named it 'The Autonomous Area of Farahzad.' Police attempts to bust Said Sahné, the drug lord of Farahzad (and allegedly one of the biggest in town), have been unsuccessful.[21] The police operations clamping down on drug users' gatherings in more visible areas of the city have driven them to this traditional neighbourhood. In turn, the area has become a successful market for narcotics and stimulants, connecting the traditional criminal and drug-dealing districts of the south with the westernized bourgeois north.

In reality, Farahzad Valley's drug scene is made of numerous *patoqs*. The one closest to the shrine – *Chehel Pelleh* (Forty Steps) – sits at the bottom of an old staircase once made of forty steps, today mostly just crumbling bricks and clay. It is known as the area's main hotspot. There is a continual bustle; some people arrive via the main road from the nearby residential complex and others from the shrine's neighbourhood. Strategically located, *Chehel Pelleh* is isolated from the main roads and therefore from the police, and it operates in an economy of its own.

The *patoq*'s 'high street' is located on flat ground surrounded by trees and water streams. On one of the dirt paths into the valley, a man sells different cuts of aluminium paper and various models of lighters at a homemade wooden desk. These paraphernalia of heroin smoking are available for the modest price of 1,000 or 2,000 tuman (*c.* £0.50 in 2016). On the other side, there is the *tarazudar* (weight-scaler) – the person in charge of drug dealing, especially of quantities larger than one dose. The *tarazudar* sells heroin and methamphetamine; the former has been in vogue in Tehran since the late 1950s, the latter is a new drug increasingly popular since the mid-2000s. The local boss hides the main drug stash in several places, I'm told. In case of a police raid – not an improbable occurrence – the main dealer has the option of running away (he usually has a means of escape in place, for example, a motorbike or a hide-out in the neighbourhood) or of hiding in the crowd of drug users. In the latter scenario, he risks being arrested but avoids being recognized as a dealer and facing the draconian penalties for dealing, which in Iran included capital punishment up until 2017.

Inside the *patoq*, security is guaranteed by a number of *gardan kolofts* (roughnecks), who act as vigilantes. They carry clubs and knifes but no guns. The *patoq* boss pays them a daily wage for their services, mostly in the form of drugs they can resell or a small amount of money, or a combination of both. Strangers are often suspected of being undercover cops or informants and thus dissuaded from passing through the *patoq*. At times this also applies to humanitarian groups, for example outreach activists providing clean needles, condoms and primary health care. On one occasion, following a police raid in the area, one of the vigilantes threw a heavy wooden club at me, shouting '*boro gomsho ****!*' ('get lost, ****!'). Diffidence towards strangers is the rule, a fact that undermines health initiatives among drug users, especially injectors.

The reason why HIV prevention activities are often rejected is, in the words of one of the bosses, 'because here in *Chehel Pelleh*, we don't have them! *Tazriq nadarim*, we don't have injecting drug users, we don't want them, they are dirty. We are clean. This is a clean space!'. Perplexed by my question, he added 'Go to the *patoq* Mohammad Deraz [*Mohammad the tall*], you can give this stuff [clean needles, etc.] away there, *unà tazrighian*, they're injectors!' Yet HIV is rampant on these sites and mobility between different hotspots increases the chances of disease transmission, whether through shared injecting paraphernalia or sexual encounters. Many drug users approach healthcare volunteers to obtain a few clean syringes and condoms and to be tested for HIV and hepatitis, although they prefer to do so inconspicuously.

There is a social and ethical stratification among the patoqs. About twenty minutes' walk from *Chehel Pelleh* there is the *Mohammad Deraz patoq* (*Mohammad the tall*), named after a local dealer who, according to a local myth, was very tall. The atmosphere in this patoq is more relaxed; there are men and women from different social backgrounds, and the average age is lower. The enclave also functions as an illegal camping site for homeless people. It is there that I encountered Fereshteh and her boyfriend.

A young couple covered in dirt, with grey faces, sit in front of a small blue tent. I met them around 10.00 am while they were smoking heroin on a piece of aluminium. They had just woken up and were preparing their breakfast explained Hamid, who introduced me to them. Fereshteh welcomed me with a big smile. Her lips are dark from the heroin smoke and her face swollen. She cannot be older than twenty-five. After the mutual introductions she offers me an apple; in keeping with the Iranian custom and regardless of the destitution in which she and most others there live, she insists that I must have something while we sit together. So we split the apple in two and we eat it; her boyfriend declines to share it out of courtesy. 'We have less than nothing and that is all I can offer you', says Fereshteh and, taking up the aluminium, adds, 'Not to be impolite: *befarma!* Help yourself if you please!' I decline her kind offer of heroin, saying that I'm okay with the apple. She asks me whether I am a recovered addict, because 'you look good', 'you're healthy' and 'it's evident you're in a good state'. Then she adds, 'Wow, I haven't talked to a non-addict for such a long time, it is so nice to speak to people who are not addicts. Here everyone is an addict; everyone uses drugs or is in recovery or used to be addicted. All NGO workers, too, are former addicts, they all hung out here with us until recently [nodding towards Hamid].' She inhales the smoke – a process historically knwon as 'chasing the dragon' – through a tube and concludes, 'I haven't spoken to anyone who is not an addict for three years.'

Fereshteh has tried to 'get clean' several times. Earlier in the year she signed up at a methadone clinic, which happened to be just up the hill, near the shrine, managed by a philanthropic doctor who provides his services free-of-charge. She felt awful and thought of dying, because her drug of choice is not heroin – she claims while holding some in her hand – but *shisheh*. Methadone, the legal substitute for opiates, did not work for her: 'I need energy and speed, otherwise I'll starve.' She says heroin helps her relax, have a sound sleep (*mesl-e takh bekhabam*) and take away her body pain (*dardam bicharam kard*). She takes heroin when she wakes up and before she goes to sleep. *Shisheh* keeps her going while she is working and hustling, and she also takes it 'for pleasure'.[22]

She has lived in the tent with her boyfriend for more than a year, hence their pitiful appearance. They are not married but they live together. Their existence parallels the so-called 'white marriages' of many young urban couples who, not ready for the formalities and commitments (including financial and housing) of *de jure* marriage, opt for informal arrangements, living under the same roof. This option nonetheless remains illegal and subject to – albeit haphazard – repression by the state authorities.[23] For Fereshteh this is the least of her troubles. Her boyfriend sells used mobile phones and does petty dealing around town. He has been in and out of the treatment centre but with no success. Fereshteh collects garbage – one of the few female collectors I met – and when desperate she begs. 'We want to get back our lives and return to society. Pray for us! Three years ago I was studying at a school and now I'm in this ….' She is suddenly interrupted by her boyfriend: 'Careful! You're on fire!' Her hood had caught fire from the jet lighter's powerful flame while she was lighting up some heroin. Fereshteh looks at me for a second or two, evidently on a heroin high, smiles and replies while taking off the hood of her jumper, 'puff, if I were at home I would be screaming like crazy here and there. Here, it doesn't matter, it's like this, we live like this, it's normal. We set ourselves on fire!'

A few metres away, later that day, I encountered an old man – or perhaps a forty-year-old who looked seventy – whose tent had burnt down. His response to the fact that all of his possessions had literally gone up in smoke was emblematic of lumpen life in the street and in the valleys: 'It doesn't matter, it's a *sadaghe-ye khoda*, an offering to God, it saved my life, had I been asleep in the tent, I'd be dead now.'

In Tehran alone there are around fifteen thousand homeless people, with the number fluctuating according to the seasonal movements of vagrants from the Iranian hinterland. There is a strong link between homelessness and drug addiction. The number of homeless people addicted to illicit substances (heroin, meth, alcohol, morphine, black market methadone, etc.)[24] reached 42,000 nationwide in 2016 – more than 80 per cent of the homeless population.[25] A high incidence of HIV/AIDS and other venereal disease has also been revealed. The homeless remain largely invisible in Tehran's cityscape, concentrating in the popular districts of the south, the valleys and caves in the north, the desert lands under highway bridges and recently also the suburban graveyards. They are called *kartonkhab* (cardboard-box sleeper), *velgard* (vagrant) or *bikhaneman* (homeless). However, the police refers to them as *mo'tadan-e porkhatar* (dangerous addicts), a term that sums up the government's approach to this section of the population.

The *Barzakh*: State, policing and street life

Iran's first drug law of 1909 has been updated and amended on many occasions, for example, the Opium Monopoly (1925), the Opium Prohibition (1955), the Opium Regulation (1969), Total Prohibition (1980) and its updates in 1988, 1997, 2005, 2010, 2013, etc. The phenomenon of drug use and addiction has witnessed several shifts. Once the opium-smoking dens were closed down in the mid-1950s, heroin (and morphine) gained popularity. *Kerak* (crack, named after its cocaine base) appeared in Iran at the turn of the millennium, at the same times as in the United States. A few years later, around 2005, the drug scene saw the appearance of *shisheh* (methamphetamines), which marked an epochal change in Iranian drug culture. Whereas opium, heroin and *kerak* are narcotics (opiates) that diminish pain, *shisheh* is a powerful stimulant that produces a lack of sleep as well as arousing sexual desire.

Each of these trends engendered a new 'moral panic' focusing on the 'addicts' and their a volatile actions. Since the start of drug prohibition, the media – a 'daily bulletin of alarm and victory'[26] – have regularly reported on the crimes committed by the 'dangerous class' of drug users. The culprits are mostly poor or impoverished men who have acquired a taste for drugs, usually opium or heroin, and who commit crimes, often cruel, to secure money to buy them. Most of them are wageless or in desultory employment, often in the illegal/informal market, which is an equal-opportunity employer. They tend to come from the newly urbanized masses that moved to Tehran during Shah Mohammad Reza Pahlavi's 1960s modernization programmes. This mass migration resulted in the ruralization of the cityscape in southern Tehran and the urbanization of village culture; previously rural communities were suddenly exposed to the 'dangerous lives' of the urban lumpenproletariat.

In the decades following the Islamic Revolution of 1979, the authorities have used the derogatory term *arazel va owbash* to refer to the unruly residents of these suburbs. Its meaning is vague, but Shahram Khosravi suggests that since 2007 it has been used as an opposite to the romanticized image of the *louti*, a gallant delinquent of the traditional neighbourhoods surrounding the bazaar.[27] The etymology of *arazel* can be traced back to the Arabic root 'R-DH-L', which indicates something 'low' or 'abject'; *awbash* stands for 'riff-raff'. Both words are of Koranic origin and carry a very negative meaning. Based on this, *arazel va owbash* can be translated with the Marxist term 'social scum', 'rotting mass' or 'disintegrated mass'; Marx's 'lumpen' may indeed be the best translation.

Politicians and law enforcement officials of the Islamic Republic have remained vague on who exactly belongs to this multifarious group of dangerous individuals. Those arrested for being *arazel va awbash* are also regularly accused of being involved in drug dealing and/or being addicts. In the official discourse, being connected to drugs triggers an association with a milieu of sexual depravity, moral decadence, alcoholism, Satanism and *zurguyi* (bullying).[28] Thus drug addicts could destabilize the moral order on which the Islamic Republic rests its legitimacy. The lumpen people, unable to adapt to the engaged and modernizing momentum of the post-Iran-Iraq-War era (1989 onwards), risk contaminating its body politic. Their physical and psychological deviancy, i.e. addiction, is seen as an internal source of contamination. In addition, addicts are seen as part of an external 'imperialist plot' (*toute' este'mari*), aimed at undermining the Islamic Revolution through the diffusion of a westernized decadent lifestyle.[29]

This targeting of the plebeian classes emerged out of the shift in the political economy and governing cadres after the end of the Iran-Iraq War (1980–88). In the first years after the revolution, when Ayatollah Khomeini's authority remained unchallenged, the Koranic term *mosta'zafin* (disinherited) was used as an opposite to the capitalist, westernized class of the *mostakbarin* (the arrogant). Policies in favour of the poor and the urban proletariat were legitimized as part of the social transformation to which many had pledged support in 1979, amidst the revolutionary fervour.[30] This Fanonian legacy lasted until the early 1990s, when the necessities of reconstruction led to the shelving of the populist love for the wretched of the earth in favour of developmental goals, investment and capital accumulation. Populist policies enjoyed a brief revival during Mahmud Ahmadinejad's presidency from 2005 to 2013.[31]

The Islamic Republic has hardly regarded addicts as deserving of its compassion. Their psyche and body are at odds with the moral purity praised by the clerical establishment. Yet, by the mid-2000s, a vast system of public health services had been put in place for people seeking medical assistance to rid themselves of their drug habit. These benefitted not the poor and disenfranchised but the middle class. The poor remained at the mercy of the imperatives of public order and moral decency. Using the same logic that governed the first drug laws in the early twentieth century, policing operations kept on arresting – the Persian term used for these mass arrests is *jam'avari* (collecting) – 'dangerous addicts' (*mo'tadan-e porkhatar*) in parks, alleys and under bridges. The coexistence of welfare and punishment is an established trait of contemporary anti-narcotics policy around the globe. But the mass scale of police operations in Iran turned the 'addicts' into disposable items of police management and economy.[32] Javad Sorkhé's story is testimony to this.[33]

Javad is a 32-year-old man. His family left their village in the Central Region (*Ostan-e Markazi*) for Tehran in the early 1970s; Javad was born in Islamshahr, on the outskirts of Tehran. He is the oldest of five brothers and two sisters. Having dropped out of school in his teens, he has worked as a taxi driver in Shahr-e Rey, a bus driver's assistant on the Tehran-Qom line and a petty drug dealer over the last fifteen years. Opium was a formative element in his life. His father and mother were both heavy opium users, and by the age of sixteen Javad himself had acquired a taste for opium, hashish and, later, with his friends, heroin. His story is similar to that of many young men in the lumpen city. Unemployment, illegal employment, family crisis, prison, disease, violence and drug abuse. All of this, he reiterates, impeded his attempts to get married: 'no girl wanted the son of an addict', 'no girl wants someone without a future', 'all the girls look out for the rich kids', 'if you marry someone from here [the neighbourhood] they are bound to be from a desperate family; [and] I got enough desperation myself'. His father's death put further pressure on him to sustain the family: 'it was enough *for our hand to reach our mouth*, but drugs need money and we, *mashallah*, are all [drug] consumers!'

Unable to get a job legally because cheap unskilled manual labourers were available due to the influx of Afghan migrants in the 1980s, Javad was thrown into the informal market of smuggled goods and petty dealing: 'I had a job, it was working out, then I got into some troubles with the man running the business and I was kicked out; then I got another job but *hammash khomar budam*, I was always high, couldn't get my shit together', 'it was dangerous but I made enough to have my stuff and help my mom'. After a couple of years, 'I got caught because some of the kids reported my name to get one year instead of five, that's how it works'. On this line, he cites *Hich Kas*, the Iranian rapper he knows I listen to, in the song *Ekhtelaf* [Difference/Disagreement/Conflict]:

inja jangalé, bokhor ta khordé nashi.
(Here is the jungle, eat not to be eaten!).

His words triggered in my mind the song's next two lines, which I thought described the situation more closely:

Ekhtelaf-e tabaqati inja bi-dad mikoné, bu-ye mardom-e zakhmi adamo bimar mikoné.
(Class difference oppresses this place, the smell of wounded people sickens.)

When I met Javad, he was smoking heroin and *shisheh*. The first is a downer (opiate), the other a powerful stimulant, an upper. His meth habit has resulted in greater mobility in the city, new encounters, a more efficient work/rest balance but has also increased his paranoia and made his relationships more volatile. His reactions, he confessed, had become more aggressive and he had lost the capacity 'to wait'.[34] Javad would purchase a few *suts* (1/10 of a gramme) and smoke it while on a stroll around town. In his own words, he is a *flâneur* of the modern city.[35] He would take out his glass pipe and torch lighter, inhale with a deep breath, holding in, blowing out, before putting everything back in his pocket. 'My body is used to morphine, *tarkib-am morfini-é*, I have an affinity for morphine but this [*shisheh*] turns on my brain. Otherwise I'm lost.' With meth, he felt motivated to stroll across the city, beyond his usual neighbourhood. On the back seat of his friends' motorbikes, on public transport, he and his friends reasserted their presence in the areas outside their class-based domain. Newspaper accounts of *shisheh* smokers acting unpredictably mushroomed throughout the 2010s. The general public as well as state officials reacted by starting a moral panic about the so-called *shisheh crisis*.[36]

Javad has ended up in prison on several occasions. Twice for petty dealing and once for thuggery. Meanwhile he has developed a taste for heroin, which he smokes with 'the kids' (*bacche-ha*), while killing time in southern Tehran. In prison, he needed heroin to avoid the heavy withdrawal symptoms, so he resorted to sharing it with other inmates through a self-made pump. 'Thank God, I did not get AIDS! But I had no other solution there', he confesses while we walk around Harandi Park. Once out of prison he failed to find a stable dwelling and spent time wandering from parks to friends' flats to the compulsory treatment camps. Treatment always came against his will, following police arrests that were part of the policy of collecting homeless drug users and the *arazel*.

'Why did the police arrest you? They keep saying "addiction is a medical issue", "the addict is a person with a disease", "we provide treatment for the addicts" and then someone like you gets caught every two months,' I ask in a purposefully naïve tone. His response is telling of the lumpen's awareness of how violence is reproduced within the machine of the state:

> You know how the police works. Every now and then, the commander of some police unit decides that the statistics of crime are low, so the police captain comes to the office and says, 'today I want 100 criminals'. The easiest way to get this number is to raid a *patoq* and you can get as many as you like. They test you [for addiction] and then send you to a [treatment] camp for one, two, three months ... The addict is easy to get, so you know it's convenient for them. Newspapers talk about us. The rich feel more secure. The shop owners sell more. The treatment centres get their subsidies. Even the dealers take a break so the price goes up. And us? *Khob*, well, *we* get fu****!

Clear evidence of the systematic use of addicts as a useful expedient to improve policing statistics is difficult to obtain. But a quick look at the number of people incarcerated or referred to state-run treatment centres (for mandatory treatment) over the last three decades provides a telling picture. In 1989, the number of drug offenders in prison totalled 60,000. Ten years later, in 1999, it reached 210,000 and in 2001 around 250,000.[37] This steady increase is only partly justified by the more efficient enforcement of anti-narcotics measures by the Iranian police. Javad's arrest preceding his last prison term did not entail any specific crime, such as drug dealing or smuggling illicit goods, only being a 'dangerous addict'. He recollects being taken to *Shafaq*, a notoriously violent mandatory treatment camp, on at least four occasions.

> You get arrested together with a hundred other people and you end up in a place where you are 'detoxified' for a few weeks. Some people are happy about this, especially when it gets colder in December and January. You get a warm place to stay for a few weeks and then you can go back to your place, the park, anywhere, after Nouruz [the Iranian new year on 21 March].

Incidents of homeless drug users – or simply poor vagrants – freezing to death in Tehran's cold winters are common. During my fieldwork in the Farahzad *patoq*, there were several reports of homeless users falling asleep in the valley and freezing to death. Death in a *patoq* is only noted as a contribution to public statistics. It is a circumstantial event on the homeless journey from *bare life* to *bare death*.[38] This overlapping of life and death is presented as justifiable on the grounds of ineligibility: many homeless drug users, especially those from faraway rural regions or belonging to ethnic minorities, for example Afghan migrants, lack proper identification. Inability to provide an ID card means finding oneself without access to basic services, such as healthcare, education, housing and welfare. This is the case for many children of immigrants (especially from Afghanistan) but also for many homeless people who have lost track of their papers due to their unsettled existence. With no identification their compulsory treatment or incarceration can be extended for longer periods.

The homeless person (*bi-khaneh* or *kartonkhab*) exemplifies a case of *khanemansuzi*. It means 'burning one's house down' and it captures the status of the homeless drug users accurately, namely their abandonment by and disconnection from family and the resulting loss of social integration. The drug users who have lost their home are equivalent to illegal immigrants; people *sans papiers* who cannot be recognized by the state and whose identity is unclear. They must pursue a life outside the formal order to avoid incarceration or deportation. In line with the *khanemansuzi* metaphor, homeless drug users live their lives in *kharabat* (ruins), the image used in Persian poetry to describe wine taverns, bandits' nests, a sacred refuge or the wreck of a soul.

Metaphors are abundant in lumpen life and they often bear empirical value. 'We are in *Barzakh*' says Hamid, another 'experienced' (his words) drug user from Darvazeh Ghar. 'They take us, set us free, re-take us, it's like a game.' *Barzakh* indicates the Islamic Limbo, the place where men and women await the end of time and God's judgement. Limbo, however, has its material equivalent: *graves*. In November 2016, a shocking article in *Shahrvand* showed more than fifty homeless drug users living and sleeping in the graveyards of Nasirabad, on the Tehran-Saveh highway. They occupied around twenty graves, spreading around piles of carton, plastic bags and wood. Two to four people lived in each tomb, burning wood to warm up in the freezing cold of the Iranian plateau. *Gurkhabi* (sleeping in graves) became a new term for the homeless, stirring piety and compassion around Iran. The Oscar-winning director Asghar Farhadi even wrote a letter to President Hassan Rouhani demanding urgent government intervention.[39]

Living in graves is indeed a powerful image in the public eye. Homeless users turn sacred, spiritual places – such as the shrine in Farahzad or even graveyards – into profane sites of human decadence. The cemetery can no longer act as a place of quiet meditation where ordinary people bring their sorrows. It is now a space of destitution, with the graves of the dead inhabited by precarious homeless people. Yet, as a man in treatment in Shahr-e Rey explained, graves are good for 'avoiding the police and the cold'. This is not an Iranian oddity. In Cairo, for instance, the dwellers in the *ashawiyyat*, the informal residences in the city's huge cemetery, enjoy better conditions than those living in the city's crowded suburbs. Better access to facilities, connection to the city centre and insularity from state encroachment guarantees a safer existence. Although the 'gravesleepers of Nasirabad' did not establish informal settlements like their Cairene equivalents, they too found themselves in safer – albeit precarious – conditions than the homeless users living in parks or under bridges.[40] However, following the *Shahrvand* article on rough sleepers in the cemetery, the police intervened, rounded up all the homeless drug users residing there and sent them to a compulsory treatment camp. Once out, almost all of them relapsed into drug use. In many cases, the deserts surrounding Nasirabad became their new residence.[41]

Subjected to systemic violence that denies them a place to exist, homeless drug users live in a political economy of their own, consisting of charity, hustling and sharing.

The economics of doing good and bad: Philanthropic piety and capitalist opportunism

Darvazeh Ghar is the centre of gravity of philanthropic endeavours targeting the urban proletariat and homeless drug users. This area took shape towards the late nineteenth century, during Nasser al-Din Shah's (1831–96) reign. Nasser al-Din ordered the building of a new city gate that connected Tehran to the then city of Ray (today absorbed in Greater Tehran). Its name has a mysterious allure: it is said to derive from an episode in which one of the sons of the Imam Musa al-Kazem, the seventh Shi'a Imam, took refuge in a cave (*ghar* means 'cave' in Persian) while fleeing the government officials who were chasing him and, as is often the case with Shi'a leaders, disappeared.[42] In the twentieth century, informal settlements dug in the ground (called *gowd*) formed the most populated quarters of the area. The *gowds* hosted mostly brick makers who, given the lack of building land, created their homes digging into the ground. In the 1980s, these *gowds* were targeted by Iraqi air raids, because Baghdad thought these settlements hid weapon factories. In the 1990s, under the Rafsanjani government, the *gowds* were removed to make space for new urban projects. The *gowd-e ma'sumi* became Harandi Park; *gowd-e arab-ha*, Baharan Garden; *gowd-e anvari*, Khajavi Kermani Park; and *gowd-e Khalu Qanbar* was replaced by Haqqani Park.[43]

The four parks together form the centre of gravity of lumpen drug use in Tehran. The presence of unruly, disorderly subjects in these public spaces also embodies the politico-economic effect of lumpen lives in the city. The parks and green spaces, carefully promoted by the Tehran municipality, have become 'no-go zones' for children and families, at least according to public reports. Shops and traders in these areas protest against the presence of homeless people, which transforms 'decent neighbourhoods' into lumpen citadels. 'We don't sell anything except *nakh 'oqabi* [single sticks of *Winston Red*, popular brand for homeless and hashish smokers],' lamented a shop owner in Darvazeh Ghar. He added 'Even mothers who come here buy just half a kilo of lentils; no yogurt, no milk. Here, *harf-e avvalo e'tiyad dare*! ['addiction runs the place!']'

Lumpen life has long been a feature of the neighbourhood, which in recent years has also seen an increase in philanthropic activity. Civil society groups have become active in the area; public attention peaked in autumn 2015, when several groups of volunteers, humanitarian groups and philanthropic citizens started to bring cooked meals and clothes to the park and distribute them among the drug users. Well-dressed women attending charitable events in the area would often bring large pots of rice and stew and distribute them in the park. This provoked skirmishes and fights among the numerous homeless people in the park attempting to secure a warm, often sophisticated, meal. Some of the women were baffled by the violent scenes and would soon walk – if not run – out of the park. Despite these incidents, the area witnessed a steady increase of charitable activity. A few months later, a charity organization started to paint 'walls of kindness' (*divar-e mehrabani*) in Tehran and later in other cities.

The project encourages the residents to donate warm clothes, food and other essential items to those in need.

The provision of food and clothes has also become the subject of satire. Detractors hold that 'the drug addicts are no longer satisfied by bread and egg or bread and cheese, but they expect sophisticated food and are spoiled for choice'. Others claim that public attention is driven by sentimental piety and is not grounded in a real understanding of the complexities of drug addiction, especially in the Harandi area. In the words of a *Sharq* columnist, this humanitarian approach was a type of 'addict-nurturing [*mo'tadparvari*]'.[44] One public official cynically suggested that the provision of food might well be a stratagem used by treatment centres to attract drug users towards their facilities and, at the same time, attract public funding towards their organizations.

On 9 October 2015, I was invited to attend the 'First Marathon of Recovered Female Drug Addicts', organized by the House of Sun (*khaneh-ye khorshid*) and crossing the four parks of Harandi, Razi, Baharan and Shush. The House of Sun has been active in the southern corner of Harandi Park for over two decades, providing free-of-charge services and support to female drug users and women seeking refuge (called *run-away girls* in Iran). This supposedly sporting event drew a large crowd of women (and some men). Two players from the Iranian women's national football team led a collective gymnastics session, a symbolic way to recover the park from the sight of widespread destitution. The event turned out not to be a marathon – not even close – but rather a public demonstration that brought together more than a thousand (mostly) women to march through the park in the middle of a drug users' gathering that included dozens of women. The term 'marathon', I thought, was probably used to avoid making the event look too political in the eyes of the municipal officials; a women-led march against drugs would probably not have received their approval.

Many of the women who took part in the march had previous experience of life in the park and were acquainted with people still living and using there. The event slogans included 'Our Iran is paradise! Don't smoke, it's not nice! [*Iran-e ma beheshté, dud nakonid ke zeshté*]'; they were interspersed with prayers for the souls of the drug addicts, and many of the participating women would approach the people lying on the grass to try to connect with them and dissuade them from using drugs. I witnessed a man approach an older woman and beg her to stop chanting against drug use, 'because we are feeling ashamed and embarrassed in front of you'. Others would cover their faces or shout aggressively at the many photographers trying to take their picture.

The event resonated strongly in the drug policy community, but it also manifested some of the profound changes that Iranian society had experienced in the course of the 2010s. Women who had a history of drug abuse openly participated in the event without hiding their 'immoral' past and marched in the parks where they once spent their time taking drugs. In doing so, they also directly addressed the drug users in the parks and invited them to give up. The associations participating in this march were not the usual collection of anti-drug campaigners but an array of humanitarian groups, user-led organizations and people with a history of drug use who were openly discussing addiction as a contemporary reality in Iran. Leila Arshad (aka Lily), the main organizer of the event and director of the House of Sun, has long been working in this neighbourhood.[45] While the attendees were gathering in the non-governmental organization's (NGO) courtyard, she told them: 'one of our objectives is to attract the attention of the officials and the public towards your problems: the lack of employment, housing, insurance, treatment, respect and social inclusion'.[46]

A few weeks after the marathon, a group of forty men raided the informal camp in Harandi Park, set on fire several tents and attacked a number of homeless drug users with sticks and clubs. The municipality declared that the attack was perpetrated 'by the people', denying any responsibility. Others hinted at the lack of response by the police. This occurrence notwithstanding, the attitude of Iranians towards charity has changed significantly over the years. Begging and petty vending is accepted less *for God's sake* and more in exchange for merchandise or services.[47] Philanthropy itself has transmuted; it has lost its Islamic framework and became more market-oriented. This reminds one of the Italian psychiatrist Franco Basaglia, who noticed the following advertisement on the New York subway:

> Which of these human tragedies do you prefer? Vietnam, Biafra, the Arab-Israeli controversy, the black ghettos, hunger in India … ? Choose yours and help, helping the Red Cross.[48]

Despite the rise of philanthropy targeted at homeless people, including drug users, the lumpen economy does not rely exclusively on charity. To get by, most homeless users find creative and painful ways of earning a living, as Reza's case demonstrates.

Reza comes from a well-off family, but he has been expelled from his wife's house because of his morphine addiction. He now resides in a small rented room in the south of Tehran, where he carries on using morphine and also smoking meth. Recently he signed up to a methadone substitution programme and he is now trying to get off both drugs. He speaks frankly with me (while I often found him lying to the NGO workers with whom he sometimes volunteers): 'I still do *shisheh* when I visit some old friends; now I'm selling some used stuff that I barter with a guy. It's a good deal, I'm happy.' Most of the time, he repairs old watches, lighters and mobile phones and resells them in the informal markets across Tehran or to other drug users he encounters along his path. His line of business complies with the ruthless rules of capital. 'Hey *dash Reza*! What's up? Did you make enough money from ripping me off the other day? You came and took my watch when I was lying on the ground half-alive, didn't you?' shouts a man while we walk in one of the parks. Reza walks straight ahead, without paying attention to the man, and explains: 'he begged me to buy it, now he regrets? *Be man ché*, why should I care?' Drug users on a high or with heavy withdrawal symptoms can be good sellers due to their euphoria or desperate need. Reza's mind works quickly and he is always busy doing something, whether handling some tech product or calling people to set up meetings, reunions and barter sessions. His economic existence, like that of many other impoverished drug users, fits in the category of 'jobs without definition'.[49] Yet it falls under the category of work, not charity or theft (although stolen goods are part of this economy).

Chemical calibration is an expedient Reza uses to be more productive. Mobility and focus help him not to get lost in the low ends of narcotic dependence. The practice, a *leitmotif* in my discussions with homeless users, is also common in other types of employment. Female drug users face a higher risk in the illegal drug market. Their bodies serve as an exchange product when monetary capital is absent. Similarly, many sex workers use methamphetamine (and to a lesser extent heroin) to provide a better sexual experience for their clients. Sometimes the client requires the sex worker to consume the drug before their sexual intercourse. Meth is a powerful sexual stimulant and it triggers a sexual impulse where desire is absent or recalcitrant. The stories of sex workers familiar with the drug and/or forced to use it, or actively seeking drugs or alcohol to sustain their working life, are common and rich in details. Drugs help coping with the pain and danger of sexual commerce and thus sex work is likely to pave the way to heavy addiction.[50] Ali Cheraq-qovveh (Ali 'Torch'), another young man whom I interviewed during my fieldwork, discussed drugs and sex while also telling me about his attempts at recovery:

> I learnt a lot because of my drug use, I went to many places, I met many girls whom I otherwise wouldn't have been able to meet. They didn't have money and were ready to give themselves in exchange for drugs, or did not have a place where to use and since I had a room, they would ask me to let them come there to use and spend time with me. I didn't have much money, but I had a place and drugs. At the time, a lot of heroin passed through my hands and I got some cuts on it, *posht-am garm bud*, I was on the safe side. But I never dared to take advantage of these girls, I used to tell them, 'if you don't have money, come and use with me, but don't sell yourself, I can share with you'. It was nice to have some female company anyway so I didn't mind.

Mohsen had a similar attitude. His kindness was perhaps a way to keep his reputation clean with me, but his narrative holds water:

> I always thought of God, even during the period when I was using drugs, when I would beg to get the money, I would still share the drugs with those who couldn't afford them. I was a boy, I could collect rubbish, I could beg, but a girl, can she collect rubbish? Can she beg for money without risk? In these times of ours, a girl who asks someone for money can be taken away, don't you know?

The gendered dimension of lumpen life puts female drug users from poor backgrounds in the open market for sex and drugs. In this context, sharing is caring and may imply sexual concessions or friendship, whether to avoid the risk of using in public (when one's safe space is limited) or to extract enough capital to sustain one's consumption. Sharing, however, is part of the political economy of drug use – establishing lasting reciprocal bonds but also increasing the risk of contracting diseases such as hepatitis and HIV. Sharing one's drugs with a companion who lacks the means to buy any or is physically impaired means that the favour may be called in on a rainy day.

Consisting of daily expediences, such as barter, repairs, collecting abandoned objects, selling small items, begging and drawing on charity, lumpen economy is a diverse ecosystem that changes according to personal and structural conditions. Philanthropy is just one side of its everyday flow.

Conclusions. Methodological encounters with homeless life

If you want to know what it means to be poor, you have to get involved and mix with the poor, if you want to know what it means to be an addict, you have to mix with them. If someone doesn't know about drugs, take him to the meetings of *NA* [Narcotic Anonymous] for a month, or to a treatment camp. *Sir ta piazesho bebin.* Mazi, you've got this work on the addicts, you come from Oxford, you're cool and know all the numbers. Now you want to understand how desperate people live? You need to get destroyed in it [*khurd besham*] to understand a desperate addict's life.

Mohsen's incitement to immerse myself in the discourse of homeless addiction, poverty and a dangerous life was a powerful piece of advice that seconded my theoretical approach 'from below' and my choice of ethnographic history. This perspective debunks the knowledge gathered from elite interviews and epidemiological interpretation of homeless life and intoxication. Top-down approaches, albeit articulated and linear, eventually reproduce bourgeois images and tropes and their panic vis-à-vis lumpen life. Lumpen life as seen from below reassesses the categories of 'dangerous' and 'marginal'. It is through an engaged perspective that one's analysis captures – or aims to capture – violence at the lumpen level, classist xenophobia and everyday agency at work in the precarious existence of people *in danger*. This chapter reviewed these aspects by letting the voices of the interviewees from my fieldwork 'speak' about their daily occurrences, desires and expedients. Imprecise, messy and disorderly, lumpen narratives – I believe – add some meaning to the theory of class struggle. By showing how this group lives and who is part of it, the argument has focused on the structural violence homeless people are subjected to. Their lives revolve around their shanty dwellings – valleys, parks, graves – and the institutions of internment – prison, rehab and morgue. Finally, the chapter described the economic activities that sustain lumpen life by exploring the combination of agency and philanthropy in Tehran. This panoramic view offers the reader an inductive approach to knowledge, which is in part a function of the ethnographic method that drives the analysis. There is still space for a final theoretical consideration.

A caricature published in response to the Iranian Ministry of Health's statement that 'nine addicts pass away in Iran every day' shows two homeless drug users sitting in a park. One of them says, 'I don't understand why we must always get to near-extinction for them to decide to do something [about us].' There is a level of animalization of human life at play here. The considerations of confining health danger and preserving middle-class decorum have become paramount in the government's approach to homeless drug users. The 'target population', in the policy jargon, is rendered less visible or invisible through focused policing (special centres, arrest quotas, prison, seclusion in confined areas). When homeless people cannot be removed from the public sphere, their presence is managed through periodical 'sanitary' interventions or it is concentrated in proletarian areas away from the middle-class gaze, such as

Darvazeh Ghar. Does this approach differ in any substantial way from public order measures vis-à-vis stray dogs?

The Governor of Tehran warned people that 'in Tehran there are no hungry people … those you see are addicts. Their case is different.'[51] Popular resentment of 'addicts' is expressed aloud. On numerous occasions, people I encountered said, 'Why don't we get all of them and kill them? So the problem is solved. These people *adam nemishan*, they cannot become human!' This chapter helps reveal the fault lines and rationales that, *in praxis*, govern the way the state exercises its prerogatives towards those whom the capitalist system of production render vulnerable.

Capital is a spectre that hunts lumpen life, which in turn fantasizes about its persecutor.

Notes

Introduction

1 Eric Hobsbawm, *Bandits* (London: Weidenfeld and Nicolson, [1969] 2000).
2 E. P. Thompson, 'The Moral Economy of the English Crowd in the Eighteenth Century', *Past and Present* 50, no. 1 (1971): 76–136.
3 Louis Chevalier, *Labouring and Dangerous Classes In Paris During the First Half of the Nineteenth Century*, trans. Frank Jellinek (Princeton, NJ: Princeon University Press, 1973).
4 Karl Marx, 'The Eighteenth Brumaire of Louis Napoleon', in *Surveys from Exile*, trans. and introduced by David Fernbach (Harmondsworth: Penguin, 1973), 146–249, 197.
5 Charles Loring Brace, *The Dangerous Classes and Twenty Years' Work Among Them* (New York: Wynkoop & Hallenbeck, 1872). The phrase is however most associated with Honoré Antoine Frégier, whose book, *Des Classes Dangereuses de la Population Dans Les Grandes Villes, Et Des Moyens De Les Rendre Meilleures ...*, was published in Paris in 1840.
6 See Chapter 10, in this volume.
7 Marx, 'The Eighteenth Brumaire', p. 197.
8 C. E. Bosworth, 'Banū Sāsān', *Encyclopaedia Iranica* 3, no. 7 (1988): 721–722; *The Mediaeval Islamic Underworld: the Banu Sasan in Arabic Society and Literature* (Leiden: Brill, 1976). See also A. Sabra, *Poverty and Charity in Medieval Islam: Mamluk Egypt, 1250–1517* (Cambridge: Cambridge University Press, 2000), 32–67.
9 S. Wild, 'Jugglers and Fraudulent Sufis', Rundgren (ed.), *Proceedings of the VIth Congress of Arabic and Islamic Studies*, Visby 13–16 August, Stockholm 17–19 August 1972, 58–62.
10 Wild, 'Jugglers and Fraudulent Sufis', 58.
11 Ibid., 60–61.
12 Sabra, *Poverty and Charity*; C. E. Bosworth, 'Begging', *Encyclopaedia Iranica* 4, facs. 1 (1989): 80–84.
13 See Chevalier, *Labouring Classes and Dangerous Classes*.
14 Hasan Mir'Ābedini, 'Moshfeq-e Kazemi, Sayyed Mortaza', *Encyclopaedia Iranica*, 2011. Available online: http://www.iranicaonline.org/articles/moshfeq-kazemi (accessed 4 July 2019).
15 Cyrus Schayegh, 'Criminal-Women and Mother-Women: Socio-Cultural Transformations and the Critique of Criminality in Early Post-World War 11 Iran', *Journal of Middle East Women's Studies* 2, no. 3 (2006): 1–21.
16 Nurçin İleri, 'Between the Real and the Imaginary: Late Ottoman Istanbul as a Crime Scene', *Journal of the Ottoman and Turkish Studies Association* 4, no. 1 (2017): 95–116.
17 İleri, 'Between the Real and the Imaginary', 111–114.

18 Shaun Lopez, 'Madams, Murders, and the Media: *Akbar al-Hawadith* and the
    Emergence of a Mass Culture in Egypt', in *Re-Envisioning Egypt 1919–1952*, eds
    Arthur Goldschmidt and Amy J. Johnson (Cairo: American University in Cairo
    Press, 2005). See also Mary Nefertiti Takla, 'Murder in Alexandria: The Gender,
    Sexual and Class Politics of Criminality in Egypt, 1914–1921' (PhD thesis, UCLA,
    2016). Available online: https://escholarship.org/uc/item/4r35401h (accessed 4 July
    2019).

19 Cyrus Schayegh, 'Serial Murder in Tehran: Crime, Science and the Formation of
    Modern State and Society in Interwar Iran', *Comparative Studies in Society and
    History* 47, no. 4 (2005): 836–862.

20 See Chapter 4, in this volume.

21 Hooshang Amirahmadi, *The Political Economy of Iran under the Qajars: Society,
    Politics, Economics and Foreign Relations, 1796–1926* (London: I.B. Tauris, 2012), 19.

22 Ferdan Ergut, 'Policing the Poor in the Late Ottoman Empire', *Middle Eastern Studies*
    38, no. 2 (2000): 149–164.

23 Liat Kozma, 'Wandering About as She Pleases: Prostitutes, Adolescent Girls, and
    Female Slaves in Cairo's Public Space, 1850–1882', *Journal of Women of the Middle
    East and the Islamic World* 10 (2012): 18–36, 19.

24 Timothy Mitchell, *Colonising Egypt* (Cambridge: Cambridge University Press,
    1988); Eckart Ehlers and Willem Floor, 'Urban Change in Iran, 1920–1941', *Iranian
    Studies* 26, nos 3–4 (1993): 251–275. See also Khaled Fahmy, 'Modernizing Cairo:
    A Revisionist Narrative', in *Making Cairo Medieval*, eds Nezar AlSayyad, Irene A.
    Bierman, Nasser Rabat (Lanham, MD: Lexington Books, 2005), 173–199.

25 Baron Hausmann was responsible for a massive programme of urban reconstruction
    in Paris in the mid-nineteenth century. His project was motivated by concerns about
    public health, aesthetics, and political security. Bourgeois observers in the first half of
    the nineteenth century had perfectly articulated fears about the relationship between
    urban design and the dangerous classes, the overcrowded medieval quarters of Paris
    harbouring a population believed to be prone to the interconnected evils of poverty,
    disease, crime and political unrest. For Hausmann, the destruction of the slums
    clustered in the centre of the city and the building of wide boulevards and parks
    would make the city more beautiful, would allow the provision of clean water and
    sewage facilities, but would also prevent the Parisian poor from engaging in urban
    insurrection, with its riots and barricades, and would permit the easy movement of
    troops through the city.

26 Ehlers and Floor, 'Urban Change in Iran', 259.

27 G. J. Breyley and Sasan Fatemi, *Iranian Music and Popular Entertainment: From
    Motrebi to Losanjelesi and Beyond* (Abingdon: Routledge, 2016).

28 Richard C. Keller, *Colonial Madness: Psychiatry in French North Africa* (Chicago:
    University of Chicago Press, 2007), 22.

29 Nazan Maksudyan, 'Orphans, Cities, and the State: Vocational Orphanages
    ("Islahhanes") and Reform in the Late Ottoman Urban Space', *International Journal of
    Middle Eastern Studies* 43, no. 3 (2011): 493–511.

30 Firoozeh Kashani-Sabet, 'The Haves and Have Nots: A Historical Study of Disability
    in Modern Iran', *Iranian Studies* 43, no. 2 (2010): 167–195.

31 See Cyrus Schayegh, *Who is Knowledgeable is Strong: Science, Class, and the
    Formation of Modern Iranian Society, 1900–1950* (Berkeley: University of California
    Press, 2009); '"A Sound Mind Lives in a Healthy Body": Texts and Contexts in the

Iranian Modernists' Scientific Discourse of Health, 1910s-1940s', *International Journal of Middle East Studies* 37, no. 2 (2005): 167–188.

32 Melis Hafez, 'The Lazy, the Idle, and the Industrious: Discourse of Work and Productivity in Late Ottoman Society' (PhD thesis, UCLA, 2012). Available online: https://escholarship.org/uc/item/3pj7009t (accessed 4 July 2019).

33 Cyrus Schayegh, 'Criminal Women and Mother-Women: Sociocultural Transformations and the Critique of Criminality in Early Post-World War II Iran', *Journal of Middle East Women's Studies* 2, no. 3 (Fall 2006): 1–21.

34 Rudi Matthee, 'Prostitutes, Courtesans, and Dancing Girls: Omen Entertainers in Safavid Iran', in *Iran and Beyond: Essays in Middle Eastern History in Honor of Nikki R. Keddie*, eds Rudi Matthee, Beth Baron and Nikki R. Keddie (Costa Mesa, CA: Mazda Publishers, 2000), 121–150, M. Willem Floor, *A Social History of Sexual Relations in Iran* (Washington, DC: Mage Publishers, 2008).

35 James E. Baldwin, 'Prostitution, Islamic Law and Ottoman Societies', *Journal of the Economic and Social History of the Orient* 55 (2012): 117–152. The literature on prostitution in the Middle East and North Africa is now extensive. See, inter alia, Mark David Wyers, *Wicked Istanbul: The Regulation of Prostitution in the Early Turkish Republic* (Istanbul: Libra Kitapçılık ve Yayıncılık, 2013); Francesca Biancani, *Sex Work in Colonial Egypt: Women, Modernity and the Global Economy* (London: I.B. Tauris, 2018); Liat Kozma, *Global Women, Colonial Ports: Prostitution in the Interwar Middle East* (Albany: State University of New York Press, 2017); Fariba Zarinbaf, *Crime and Punishment in Istanbul*, 1700–1800 (Berkeley: University of California Press, 2010), 86–111; Elyse Semerdjian, '*Off the Straight Path*': *Illicit Sex, Law, and Community in Ottoman Aleppo* (Syracuse, NY: Syracuse University Press, 2008), 94–137; Hanan Hammad, *Industrial Sexuality: Gender, Urbanization, and Social Transformation in Egypt* (Austin: University of Texas Press, 2016), 141–208; Khaled Fahmy, 'Prostitution in Nineteenth-Century Egypt', in *Outside In: On the Margins of the Modern Middle East*, ed. Eugene Rogan (London: I.B. Tauris, 2002), 77–103; Bruce W. Dunne, 'French Regulation of Prostitution in Nineteenth-Cetury Colonial Algeria', *Arab Studies Journal* 2, no. 1 (1994): 24–30; 'Sexuality and the "Civilizing Process" in Modern Egypt' (PhD thesis, Gergetown University, 1996).

36 Shahla Haeri, *Law of Desire: Temporary Marriage in Iran* (London: I.B. Tauris, 1989).

37 Palmira Brummett, 'Dogs, Women, Cholera, and Other Menaces in the Streets: Cartoon Satire in the Ottoman Revolutionary Press', *International Journal of Middle East Studies* 27, no. 4 (1995): 433–460.

38 Judith R. Walkowitz, *City of Dreadful Delight: Narratives Of Sexual Danger In Late-Victorian London* (Chicago: University of Chicago Press, 1992); Timothy J. Gilfoyle, 'Prostitutes in History: From Parables of Pornography to Metaphors of Modernity', *American Historical Review* 104, no. 1 (1999): 127.

39 Gilfoyle, 'Prostitutes in History'.

40 See Kozma, *Global Women, Colonial Ports*.

41 For similar attitudes in the context of the conflict over veiling, see Stephanie Cronin, 'Introduction: Coercion or Empowerment? Anti-veiling Campaigns: A Comparative Perspective', in *Anti-Veiling Campaigns in the Muslim World: Gender, Modernism and the Politics of Dress*, ed. Stephanie Cronin (Abingdon: Routledge, 2014), 1–36.

42 Hamid Naficy, *A Social History of Iranian Cinema: Volume 2, The Industrializing Years, 1941–1978* (Durham, NC: Duke University Press, 2011), 266–290.

43 H. E. Chehabi, 'Voices Unveiled: Women Singers in Iran', in *Iran and Beyond: Essays in Middle Eastern History in Honor of Nikki R. Keddie*, eds Beth Baron and Rudi

Matthee (Costa Mesa, CA: Mazda Publishers, 2000), 151–166; Kamran Talatoff, *Modernity, Sexuality, and Ideology in Iran: The Life and Legacy of a Popular Female Artist* (Syracuse, NY: Syracuse University Press, 2011).

44   This film, sometimes known as *The Women's Quarter*, is available online, as are Shirdel's *Women's Prison* and *Iran is the Capital of Tehran*. Shirdel's technique, in all three films, is to use stark images of reality to critique the official narrative. For a discussion of Kamran Shirdel's films, see Naficy, *A Social History of Iranian Cinema*.

45   Haeri, *Law of Desire*.

46   For further discussions of fears arising from gendered transgressions of public space, see Shirine Hamadeh, 'Mean Streets: Space and Moral Order in Early Modern Istanbul', *Turcica* 44 (2012–13): 249–277; Kozma, 'Wandering About as She Pleases'.

47   See Chapter 3, in this volume.

48   Selim Deringil, '"They Live in a State of Nomadism and Savagery": The Late Ottoman Empire and the Post-Colonial Debate', *Comparative Studies in Society and History* 45, no. 2 (2003): 311–342, 311, 317.

49   For a discussion of the conflict between the moral economy and the free market in nineteenth-century Iran see Stephanie Cronin, 'Bread and Justice in Qajar Iran: The Moral Economy, the Free Market and the Hungry Poor', *Middle Eastern Studies* 54, no. 6 (2018): 843–877.

50   Vanessa Martin, *The Qajar Pact: Bargaining, Protest and the State in 19th-Century Persia* (London: I.B. Tauris, 2005), 113–132.

51   Rudi Matthee, *The Pursuit of Pleasure: Drugs and Simulants in Iranian History, 1500-1900* (Princeton, NJ: Princeton University Press, 2005), 293.

52   A particularly interesting variant of this phenomenon is the appearance in Morocco of *Tcharmils*, marginal young men organized into gangs who engage in theatrical displays of violent crime and parade themselves on social media.

53   John Walton and David Seddon, *Free Markets and Food Riots: The Politics of Global Adjustment* (Oxford: Blackwell Publishers, 1994), 171.

Chapter 1

1   Timothy Mitchell, *Colonizing Egypt* (Berkeley: University of California Press, 1988), IX.

2   Here I am obviously looking at prostitution regulation through a Foucauldian lens; on the relationship between biopolitical power, the making of social marginality and prostitution see Michel Foucault, *Discipline and Punish, the Birth of the Prison* (New York: Vintage Books, 1985); *The History of Sexuality*, vol. 1, *An Introduction* (New York: Vintage Books, 1980); Michel Foucault, *Society Must be Defended. Lectures at the Collège de France, 1975–1976* (New York: Picador, 2003) and Michel Foucault, *The Birth of Biopolitics: Lectures at the Collège de France, 1978–1979* (Basingstoke: Palgrave Mamillan, 2008).

3   In this article, as in my broader reflection on the topic, I use the term sex worker with the purpose of going beyond the reductionism implicit in the term 'prostitute' while at the same time claiming the centrality of rationality and agency in all cases when women (often with radically different degrees of autonomy and independence) resorted to transactional sex to earn a living. See Francesca Biancani, *Sex Work in Colonial Egypt: Women, Modernity and the Global Economy* (London: I.B. Tauris, 2018), 16.

4   This article feeds into a discrete corpus of literature on colonial regulationism
     in multiple settings as widely discussed by Philip Howell in 'Race, Space and the
     Regulation of Prostitution in Colonial Hong Kong', *Urban History* 31, no. 2 (2004):
     229–248, 231; see also Stephen Legg, 'Beyond the European province: Foucault and
     postcolonialism', in *Space, Knowledge and Power. Foucault and Geography*, eds Jeremy
     W. Crampton and Stuart Elden (Aldershot: Routledge, 2007), 265–288.
5   Khaled Fahmy, 'Prostitution in Nineteenth Century Egypt', in *Outside In: on the
     Margins of the Modern Middle East*, ed. Eugene Rogan (London: I.B. Tauris, 2002), 77
6   By the term 'defensive modernization' I refer to a set of reforms aimed at expanding
     both the productive and military capacities of the state vis-à-vis increasing European
     encroachment by selectively incorporating Western-like institutions and techniques.
7   The reasons for the ban have been extensively discussed in existing literature. See
     Fahmy, 'Prostitution in Nineteenth Century Egypt', 81; Judith E. Tucker, *Women
     in Nineteenth Century Egypt* (Cambridge: Cambridge University Press, 1985), 151.
     Hanan Kholoussy in her article 'Monitoring and Medicalising Male Sexuality in
     Semi-colonial Egypt', *Gender & History* 22, no. 3 (2010): 677–691, 679 reconsidered
     the 'civil society' argument, according to which Muhammad Ali responded to
     popular distaste for foreign influence. Fahmy in particular reconsidered the 'public
     opinion argument' according to which the sex workers' ban was a response to
     people's dislike for the Pashas' westernizing reforms, or widespread protest against
     the power of state officials such as the Copt Antum Tuma, who were in charge of sex
     work taxation.
8   Also known as the French system, sex work regulation was firstly theorized by
     the Parisian Doctor Parent in J. B. Parent-Duchâtelet, *De la prostitution dans la
     ville de Paris: considérée sous le rapport de l'hygiéne publique, de la morale et de
     l'administration*, 2 vols (Paris: J.-B. Baillière, 1836). For essential references on
     the history and logic of regulation in France see Alain Corbain, *Women for Hire,
     Prostitution and Sexuality in France after 1850* (Cambridge, MA: Harvard University
     Press, 1996) and Jill Harsin, *Policing Prostitution in Nineteenth Century Paris*
     (Princeton, NJ: Princeton University Press, 1985).
9   Philip Howell, *Geographies of Regulation, Policing Prostitution in Nineteenth Century
     Britain and the Empire* (Cambridge: Cambridge University Press, 2009), 9; and Philip
     Howell, 'Historical Geographies of the Regulation of Prostitution in Britain and the
     British Empire', University of Cambridge, 24 March 2014. Available online: http://
     www.geog.cam.ac.uk/research/projects/prostitutionregulation/ (accessed 1 May
     2017).
10   'Imad Hilal, *al-Baghayya fi-Misr, Dirasah Tarikhiyyah wa Igtima'iyyah* (al-Qahira:
     Dar al-'Arabi, 2002), 65; Bruce W. Dunne, 'Sexuality and the Civilizing Process in
     Modern Egypt' (PhD thesis, Georgetown University, 1996), 141–142. Hilal and
     Dunne both agree on the fact that the first mention of this document, of which no
     original version remains, is made in Fillib Jallad, *Qamus al-Qada' wa al-Idarah*,
     vol. 3 (al-Iskandariyyah: Lagoudakis, 1906), 240, 245. Here it is said that a decree
     of the Ministry of Interior dated 11 November 1882 referred to a previous 'law',
     promulgated by the British-appointed Sanitary Commission to address the most
     urgent matters of public health such as 'the medical examination of female prostitutes
     to prevent the spread of venereal disease'.
11   WL, 3/AMSH/B/07/05.
12   N. W. Willis, *Anti-Christ in Egypt* (London: Anglo-Eastern Pub. Co, 1914), 35–36.
13   Jallad, *Qamus*, 240, 245.

14   The concept of repentance (*tawbah*) seems to be connected to that of *islah-i-nefs* (self-reform or self-discipline), appearing in a number of Ottoman legal cases from the nineteenth century. According to Elyse Semerdijan, this practice was established already in the seventeenth and eighteenth centuries, when prostitutes could express formal regret of their past misdeeds and promise not to engage in prostitution anymore. The practice had a religious undertone, symbolizing a turn to the 'straight path'. A prostitute's repentance was registered in court and she was allowed reintegration into society. See Elise Semerdijan, *Off the Straight Path: Illicit Sex, Law, and Community in Ottoman Aleppo* (Syracuse, NY: Syracuse University Press, 2008), 202–204. In modern times the language of religion seems to have given way to that of redemptive productive work in the ideology of modern reformist institutions such as the poorhouse and refuge.

15   *La'ihah Maktab al-Kashf 'ala al-Niswah al-'Ahirat*, article 14.

16   *al-Qarrarat wa al Manshurat al-Sadirah sanat-1885*, al-Matba'ah al-Amiriyyah bi-Bulaq, 1886, 153–157; *Nizarah al-Dakhiliyyah, Idarah 'Umum al-Sahhah, Dikritat wa Lawa'ih Sahhiyyah* (Cairo: al-Matba'ah al-Amiriyyah bi-Bulaq, 1895), 54–56.

17   *Nizarah al-Dakhiliyyah, al-Qawanin al-Idariyyah wa al-Jina'iyyah, al-Juz' al-Rabi' al-Qawanin al-Khususiyyah* (Cairo: al-Matba'ah al-Amiriyyah bi-Bulaq, n.d.), 430–435.

18   Philip Howell, 'Race, Space, and the Regulation of Prostitution in Colonial Hong Kong', *Urban History* 31, no. 2 (2004): 229–248, 233.

19   Phillippa Levine, 'Modernity, Medicine and Colonialism: the Contagious Diseases Ordinances in Hong Kong and the Straits Settlements', *Positions* 6, no. 3 (1998): 675–705, 683. On cantonment as a major device of spatial surveillance see Stephen Legg, 'Governing Prostitution in Colonial Delhi: From Cantonment Regulations to International Hygiene (1864–1939)', *Social History* 34, no. 4 (2009): 447–467, 452. The martial character of colonial regulation was particularly evident in French colonies, where the French regulationist model was applied to the fullest. See Christelle Tharaud, *La Prostitution coloniale in Algérie, Tunisie, Maroc, 1830–1910* (Paris: Payot, 2003) and 'Colonialist Regulationist Prostitution in the Maghreb and the Struggle for Abolition', in *Trafficking in Women, 1924–1926, The Paul Kinsie Report for the League of Nations*, vol. 2, eds Jean-Michel Chaumont, Magaly Rodriguez Garcia and Paul Servais (Geneva: United Nations, 2017), 126–132; Driss Maghraoui, 'Gendering Urban Colonial Casablanca: the Case of the Quartier Resérvé of Bousbir', in *Gendering Urban Space in the Middle East, South Asia and Africa*, eds Martina Rieker and Kamran Asdar Ali (New York: Palgrave Macmillan, 2008), 17–44; Jean-François Staszak, 'Planning Prostitution in Colonial Marocco: Bousbir, Casablanca's Quartier Réservé', in *(Sub)urban Sexscapes: Geographies and Regulation of Sex Industry*, eds Paul J. Maginn and Christine Steinmetz (New York: Routledge, 2015), 175–196.

20   For a major introduction to the racial construction of space in global modern cities see Charles H. Nightingale, *Segregation: A Global History of Divided Cities* (Chicago: University of Chicago Press, 2014); Stephen Legg, *Prostitution and the Ends of Empire, Scales, Governmentality, and Interwar India* (Durham, NC: Duke University Press, 2014), 41.

21   In this regard, Cairo seems to recall other imperial settings characterized by a high degree of cosmopolitanism, such as Hong Kong, both in terms of the centrality of the sex work area and the racial profiling of establishments within it. See Howell, 'Race, Space and the Regulation of Prostitution in Colonial Hong Kong', 246.

22 Douglas Sladen, *Oriental Cairo, the City of the Arabian Nights* (London: Hurst & Blackett, 1911); Thomas Russell Pasha, *Egyptian Service 1902–1946* (London: John Murray, 1949); Willis, *Anti-Christ in Egypt*; Guy Thornton, *With the Anzacs in Cairo, the Tale of a Great Fight* (London: H.R. Allenson, 1916).

23 Russell Pasha, *Egyptian Service*, 80.

24 See an instance Mahmud Abu-al-'Uyyun, 'Chastity Screams', in *Al-Ahram*, 8 December 1923, n.p. which opened a series devoted to the issue of licensed prostitution and the state of morals in Egypt.

25 Willis, *Anti-Christ in Egypt*, 44.

26 See for example Duktur Fakhr Mikha'il Faraj, *Taqrir 'an Intishar al-Bigha' wa al-Amrad al-Tanassuliyyah bi-l- Qutr al Masri wa ba'd al-Turuq al-Mumkin Ittiba'iha li-Muharibah* (Cairo: al-Matba'ah al-'Asriyyah, 1924); Muhammad Farid Junaydi, *al-Bigha', Bahth 'ilmi 'amali* (Cairo: Matba'at al-Nasr, 1934); Mahmud Abu al-'Uyun, *Mushkilah al-Bigha' al- Rasmi* (Cairo: Matba'at al-Hilal, 1933); Burtuqalis Bay, *al-Bigha' aw Kathir al-'ahara fi-l-Qutr al-Masri* (Cairo: Matba'ah Hindiyyah, 1907).

27 Thornton, *With the Anzacs in Cairo*, 59. As a prominent evangelist and puritan abolitionist, Thornton could have had reasons to exaggerate the numbers in order to create panic and alarmism.

28 Frank Young, 'The Cheapest Thing in Egypt', *Egyptian Gazette*, 7 October 1913.

29 WL, 4/IBS/6/024, The International Bureau for the Suppression of Traffic in Women and Children, *The Case for the Abolition of the Government Regulation of Prostitution* (Cairo: Nile Mission Press, 1939).

30 Ibid.

31 WL, 4/IBS/6/025, Personal communication of Russell Pasha to Mr Sempkins, secretary of the National Vigilance Association (hereafter NVA), 23 February 1931. Russell Pasha's judgement certainly sounds profoundly classist and moralistic, and his claim about the number of Cairene middle-class men patronizing clandestine prostitutes is hyperbolic and doesn't have any statistical value. As a consequence, Russell Pasha was in favour of closing down the licensed quarter in the city centre and transferring the brothel area to the outskirts of the city. The same point of view had been advocated in his 1926 Cairo City Police Report: 'I would maintain a purely native licensed prostitution quarter on the outskirts to meet the demand of the native population until what time that education and civilization made it possible to do away with licensed prostitution altogether.' WL, 4/IBS/5/2/40, Cairo City Police Report, 1926.

32 Data for the years 1921 to1927 were taken from *Taqrir Sanawi 'an 'Amal Taftish Sahhat al-Qahirah li-sanawat 1922, 1925, 1927*, al-Matba'ah al-Amiriyyah bi-l-Qahirah. Data for the period 1928 to 1946 were taken from Wizarat al-Dakhiliyyah-Bulis Madinat al-Qahirah, *Taqrir Sanawi-al-'am 1930*, al-Matba'ah al-Amiriyyah bi-Bulaq, 1931; Wizarat al-Dakhiliyyah – Bulis Madinat al-Qahirah, *Taqrir Sanawi al-'am 1933*, al-Matba'ah al-Amiriyyah bi-Bulaq, 1934; Wizarat al-Dakhiliyya-Bulis Madinat al-Qahirah, *Taqrir Sanawi al-'am 1935*, al-Matba'ah al-Amiriyyah bi-Bulaq, 1936; Wizarat al-Dakhaliyyah -Bulis Madinat al-Qahirah, *Taqrir Sanawi al-'am 1937*, al-Matba'ah al-Amiriyyah bi-Bulaq, 1938; Wizarat al-Sahhah al- 'Umumiyyah, *Taqrir Sanawi 'an A'mal Taftish Sahhat- al-Qahirah li-'am 1936*, al-Matba'ah al-Amiriyyah bi-Bulaq, 1939; Wizarat al-Sahhah al-'Umumiyyah- *Taqrir Sanawi 'an sanat-1937*, Dar al-Tiba'ah al-Fayyada, al- Qahirah, 1939; Wizarat al-Dakhiliyyah – Bulis Madinat al-Qahirah, *Taqrir Sanawi li-sanatay 1942–1943*, al-Matb'ah al-Amiriyyah bi-l-Qahirah, 1944; Wizarat al-Dakhaliyyah – Bulis Madinat al-Qahirah, *Taqrir*

824222642222242222224222222222222

Sanawi li-sanat- 1944, Matba'ah al-Amiriyyah bi-Bulaq bi-l-Qahirah, 1944; Wizarat al-Sahhah al-'Umumiyyah, *Taqrīr Sanawi li-sanat 1946*, Matba'ah al-Amiriyyah bi-Bulaq bi-l-Qahirah; Wizarat al-Sahhah al-'Umumiyyah, *al-Taqrir al-Sanawi al-'amm li-sanat 1943*, Matba'ah al-Amiriyyah bi-Bulaq bi-l-Qahirah.

33   Willis, *Anti-Christ in Egypt*, 40.

34   Fakhr Mikhail Faraj, *Taqrir 'an Intishar al-Bigha' wa al-Amrad al-Tanassuliyyah bi-l-Qutr al-Masri wa ba'd al-Turuq al-Mumkin Ittiba'iha li-Muharibah* (Cairo: al-Matba'ah al-'Asriyyah, 1924), 40–41.

35   WL, IBS/6/033.

36   See also LaVerne Kuhnke, *Lives at Risk: Public Health in Nineteenth Century Egypt* (Berkeley: University of California Press, 1990), 3–4, 334; Amira el-Azhary Sonbol, *The Creation of a Medical Profession in Egypt* (Syracuse, NY: Syracuse University Press, 1991), X and 27–35; Serge Jagailloux, *La Médicalization de l'Egypte au XIXe siècle, 1798–1918* (Paris: Editions Recherches sur les Civilizations, 1986); Nancy E. Gallagher, *Egypt's Other Wars: Epidemics and the Politics of Public Health* (Syracuse, NY: Syracuse University Press, 1990). On similar dynamics in other Middle Eastern contexts see Nancy E. Gallagher, *Medicine and Power in Tunisia, 1790–1900* (Cambridge: Cambridge University Press, 1983); Ellen J. Amster, *Medicine and the Saints. Science, Islam, and the Colonial Encounter in Marocco, 1877–1956* (Austin: University of Texas Press, 2014); Cyrus Schayegh, *Who is Knowledgeable is Strong: Science, Class, and the Formation of Modern Iranian Society, 1900–1950* (Berkeley: California University Press, 2004).

37   el-Azhary Sonbol, *Creation*, 114.

38   Ibid., 112.

39   Liat Kozma, "'We, the sexologists … '": Arabic Medical Writing on Sexuality', *Journal of the History of Sexuality* 22, no. 3 (2013): 432. Again, this happened in the context of the global circulation of Western sexological ideas which, from the late nineteenth century onwards, played an increasingly important role in shaping vernacular modern identities beyond Europe, see Chris Waters, 'Sexology', in *Palgrave Advances in the Modern History of Sexuality*, eds H. G. Cocks and Matt Houlbrook (Basingstoke: Palgrave Macmillan, 2006), 41–63.

40   Faraj, *Taqrir 'an Intishar*, 46. In the 'Abbasiyyah Bureau, sixty-five women were inspected each day, while in the Sayyidah Zaynab Bureau the number was fifty-five.

41   Burtuqalis Bey, *al-Bigha' aw Khatar 'aharah fi-l- Qutr al-Misri*, tarjamah Dawwud Barakat (Cairo: Matba'ah Hindiyyah 1907), 26.

42   Ibid., 33.

43   Muhammad Shahin, *Taqrir min-Mukafahat-al-Amrad al-Zahriyyah bi-l-Qutr al-Masri* (Cairo: n.p., 1933), table 1. Muhammad Shahin was the representative of the Ministry of Interior for Health Affairs.

44   Ibid., 2.

45   Ibid., 9.

46   Faraj, *Taqrir 'an Intishar*, 60–61.

47   Corbain, *Women for Hire*, 11.

48   Yunan Labib Rizq. 'Safety First', *al-Ahram Weekly Online*, 6–12 December 2001, no. 563. Available online: http://weekly.ahram.org.eg/2001/563/chrncls.htm (accessed 1 May 2017).

49   *Al-Taqrir al-Sanawi li-Bulis Madinat-al-Qahirah 'an-Sanat- 1933*, 6.

50   From 1875 to 1947, Egypt had a dual judicial system. Foreign consular courts, in which foreigners were judged according to the laws of their respective countries,

existed alongside Egyptian national courts for Egyptian subjects. The summary way in which law was enacted in consular courts explains why foreign citizens in Egypt were virtually free to engage in any illicit activity. For a good overview see Mark Hoyle, *Mixed Courts of Egypt* (London: Graham and Trotman, 1968).

51 Russell Pasha, *Egyptian Service*, 179.
52 Sladen, *Oriental Cairo*, 60.
53 Ibid., 109.
54 WL, IBS/6/031- El-Garbya case. Note by Sister Margaret Clare, note by Mr Hughes (parquet), 1 folder, 1923–24.
55 The more effectively regulationism is deployed, the more inclusive it is, as it is able to control, monitor and check its targets, i.e. prostitutes. Their inclusion within the dominant order as 'docile' objects of control, though, works through exclusion, as prostitutes are projected as 'marginals'. In short, the more 'marginalized' marginal groups are as such, the more they are in fact included and incorporated within the dominant order.

Chapter 2

1 The conception of the prostitute as a counter-nationalist force is not exclusive to Iran. Similar conceptions can be seen across the Middle East including in Egypt, Turkey, Syria and Iraq. See for example Liat Kozma, *Global Women, Colonial Ports: Prostitution in the Interwar Middle East* (Albany: State University of New York Press, 2017); Emine Ö. Evered and Kyle T. Evered, "'Protecting the National Body'": Regulating the Practice and the Place of Prostitution in Early Republican Turkey', *Gender, Place & Culture* 20, no. 7 (2013): 839–857; Margot Badran, *Feminists, Islam, and Nation: Gender and the Making of Modern Egypt* (Princeton, NJ: Princeton University Press, 1995).
2 Iskandar Dildum, La'l Shakiri, Mustafa and Hadi Vakili, Nagsh-i ruspiyan-i Shahr-i naw dar Coup du-ta-yi 28 Murdad-i 1332', *Ganjinah-yi Asnad* 26, no. 1 (Bahar 1395 [Spring 2016]): 60–81.
3 For a few examples, see Zakariyya Hashemi, Tuti (Tehran: Hadaf, 1969); Mahmoud Zand-Muqaddam, *Qal'ah* (Tehran: Maziyar Publishing House, 1958); Hidayat Hakimilahi, *Ba man bi Shahr-i naw bi-yayid*, vol. 2 (Tehran, 1947); Hidayat Hakimilahi, *Ba man bi Shahr-i naw bi-yayid*, vol. 1 (Tehran, 1946).
4 Today, there are three different legal approaches to prostitution: criminalization (based on abolitionism), legalization (based on regulationism) and decriminalization. For rich debates on criminalization and its harmful implications for sex workers in global and national contexts, see Kamala Kempadoo, 'The Modern-Day White (Wo) Man's Burden: Trends in Anti-Trafficking and Anti-Slavery Campaigns', *Journal of Human Trafficking* 1, no. 1 (2015): 8–20; Kamala Kempadoo, Jyoti Sanghera and Bandana Pattanaik, *Trafficking and Prostitution Reconsidered: New Perspectives on Migration, Sex Work, and Human Rights* (Boulder, CO: Paradigm Publishers, 2005); Annie George, Sawmya Ray and U. Vindhya, 'Sex Trafficking and Sex Work: Definitions, Debates and Dynamics – A Review of Literature', *Economic and Political Weekly* 45, no. 17 (2010): 64–73; Kamala Kempadoo, 'Freelancers, Temporary Wives, and Beach-Boys: Researching Sex Work in the Caribbean', *Feminist Review* 67, no. 1 (2001): 39–62; Kamala Kempadoo, 'The War on Human Trafficking in

the Caribbean', *Race & Class* 49, no. 2 (2007): 79–85; Jo Doezema, 'Ouch!: Western Feminists' "Wounded Attachment" to the "Third World Prostitute"', *Feminist Review*, no. 67 (2001): 16–38; Saskia Sassen, 'Women's Burden: Counter-Geographies of Globalization and the Feminization of Survival', *Journal of International Affairs* 53, no. 2 (2000): 503–524; J. K. Anarfi, 'Ghanaian Women and Prostitution in Cote d'Ivoire', in *Global Sex Workers: Rights, Resistance, and Redefinition*, eds Kamala Kempadoo and Jo Doezema (New York: Routledge, 1998).

5   In this chapter, I employ Miriam Ticktin's definition of humanitarianism as 'an ethos, a cluster of sentiments, a set of laws, a moral imperative to intervene, and a form of government'. Miriam Ticktin, 'Transnational Humanitarianism', *Annual Review of Anthropology* 43, no. 1 (2014): 273–289.

6   There is only one scholarly book chapter written directly on prostitution during the early modern period, by Rudi Matthee, 'Prostitutes, Courtesans and Dancing Girls: Women Entertainers in Safavid Iran', in *Iran and Beyond: Essays in Middle Eastern History in Honor of Nikki R. Keddie*, eds Beth Baron and Rudi Matthee (Costa Mesa, CA: Mazda Publishers, 2000). Ida Meftahi aptly points out that Shahr-i naw, together with the cluster of entertainment centres in the south of Tehran, including the cafes and cabarets of Lālahzār street, constitute a 'negative space' in the cultural history of Iran. See *Gender and Dance in Modern Iran: Biopolitics on Stage* (New York: Routledge, 2016).

7   Throughout this chapter, I draw on Giorgeo Agamben's notion of sovereignty, which he defines as the power of the state to expand its rule over what it officially excludes. Through the exercise of sovereign power, the state normalizes exceptional suspensions of law, perpetually and indeterminately. The process of normalization of arbitrary rule was at play in the red-light district of Tehran from the very beginning of its formation. For a more detailed discussion on the sovereign rule of the modern state see, Giorgio Agamben, *Sovereign Power and Bare Life*, Homo Sacer 1 (Stanford, CA: Stanford University Press, 1998), 17–19.

8   Ensiah Rezaei and Shahla Azari, *Guzarish-ha-yi nazmiyyah az mahallat-i Tehran: rapurt-i vaqayi`-i mukhtalifah-yi mahallat-i dar al-khilafah*, vol. 1 (Tehran: Iran National Archive Organization, [1377] 1999).

9   For a few examples see Surin Tumaniyans, *Chira suzak wa syphilis mu`alijah nimishavand* (Tehran: Baradaran-i baghirzadah, [1309] 1930), 12, 16, 23, 75; Dubshan, *Syphilis wa Mukhtassat-i intishar-i an dar Iran* (Tehran: Matba'a-yi majlis, 1930), 17.

10   Tumaniyans, *Chira suzak wa syphilis mu`alijah nimishavand*, 75.

11   S. Dubshan, *Syphilis wa mukhtasat-i intishar-i an dar Iran* (Tehran: Matba'ah-yi majlis, [1319] 1930).

12   There are numerous instances of petitions against prostitution in Tehran, beginning in the 1910s. For local petitions that residents submitted to the parliament against the residency of prostitutes in their neighbourhoods before the formation of Shahr-i naw, see 'Tajammu' va i'tirāz-i yiki az mahallah-ha-yi Tajammu` wa i`tiraz-i yiki az mahallah-ha-yi Tehran, 1912, 293/4757, National Library and Archives of Iran; 'Raji' bi man'-i fahsha wa isti'mal-i taryak, 1951-1957 [1330-1336], sin2/22210/405/1/21 Library, Museum and Document Centre of Iran Parliament; '[Namah-ha-yi muti`addid az sakinin-i Tehran] raji` bi [Muzzir budan-i favahish [khanah-ha] va marakiz-i fisad [wa taqaza-yi bastan-i an-ha]', 1957–1960 [1336–1339], 19/35/11/4/20, Library, Museum and Document Centre of Iran Parliament.

13   'I`lan', *Iran-i naw* 3, no. 20 (18 April 1911): 4.

14   See end note 1.

15   Akbar Hakamizadah, 'Ranj-i bihūdah: guftar-i haftum', *Humayun* 1, no. 10 (Tīr 1314
      [June 1935]): 26.
16   'avamil-i taraqqi va inhitāt', *Taqqadum* 1, no. 7 (1307 [1928]): 403–408, 407.
17   For examples of such narratives see Mahmud Zand Muqaddam, *Shahr-i naw, Qal'ah-
      yi Zahidi 1348: Hamrah ba du didar az mujtami'-i bihzisti 1368*, Chap-i nukhust
      (Gothenberg: Khanah-i hunar wa adabiyat; Kitab-i Arzan, [1391] 2012); Muhammad
      Tulu'i, *Pidar wa Pisar: Naguftah-ha az zindagi wa ruzgar-i Pahlavi-ha* (Tehran:
      Intisharat-i 'ilmi, 1993); Iskandar Dildum, La'l Shakiri, Mustafa; and Hadi Vakili,
      'Naqsh-i ruspiyan-i Shahr-i naw dar Coup du-ta-yi 28 Murdad-i 1332', *Ganjinah-yi
      Asnad* 26, no. 1 (2016): 60–81; Ja'far Shahri, *Tehran-i qadim*, Chap-i 4, vol. 3, 5 vols.
      (Tehran: Mu'in, 1383 [2004]).
18   Abulhasan Ha'erizadah, *Mashruh-i muzakirat-i majlis*, dawrah 16, Majlis-i shawra-yi
      milli, jalasah 117 (Bahman 26, 1329 [16 February 1951]), 6.
19   In 1914, Tehran was divided into ten police districts, each of which was run by its
      own commissioner. Shahr-i naw – which was a newly developed neighbourhood –
      became the 10th district. For more detailed information on zoning of Tehran in
      1914, see Tafrishī, *Pulis-i khafiyyah-yi Iran: mururi bad rukhdad-ha-yi siyasi wa
      tarikhchah-yi shahrbani (1299–1320)*.
20   Popular narratives attribute an earlier organized attempt for concentrating
      prostitution into a single district to the chief of Tehran's police, the Austrian
      Conte de Monte Forte, who apparently displaced prostitutes to Chalah Silabi. This
      account mainly stems from a Tehran folk song about the Conte and his daughter
      who supposedly was abducted to work in Chalah Silabi. However, such accounts
      are closer to urban legends and do not provide any substantial information about
      the logistics of the plan. For the folk song see Tafrishi, *Pulis-i khafiyyahyi Iran*. For
      government correspondence on moving prostitutes to Shahr-i naw see, 'Malikin-i
      khanah-ha-yi Shahr-i naw, shikayat az ra'is-i jadid-i kumisariya-yi Shahr-i naw ki dar
      sadad-i muzahimat wa mudakhilat-i qair-i qanuni dar amlak-i an-ha bar amadah
      ast', 4 February 1922, 4/30/16/2/59, Library, Museum and Document Centre of Iran
      Parliament.
21   For the state of Shahr-i naw in its earlier years see Tafrishi, *Pulis-i khafiyyah-yi Iran*,
      49.
22   'Mutammam-i qanun-i asasi', Asl 14, Mihr 15, 1286 [8 October 1907], *Paygah-i
      ittila'at-i qavanin wa muqarrarat-i kishvar*. Available online: http://www.dastour.ir/
      brows/?lid=1734 (accessed 10 June 2017).
23   'Intiqal-i chand tan az zanan-i taba'a-yi faransah bi Shahr-i naw', 1305 [1926],
      293/873, Iran's National Archives.
24   'Nashriyah (Sihhi-yi kull-i majlis hifz al-sihha) Surat majlis, jalasah-yi 9', Isfand 1306
      [March 1927], 297/34336, Iran's National Archives. Other present members of the
      council included Nasrullah Khan Saif (saif al-attiba), Muhammad Khan Shaikh (ahya
      al-mulk), Partaw A'zam (Hakim A'zam), Muhammad Hasan Khan Luqman Adham
      (Hakim al-dawlah), Yunis Khan Afrukhtah and Said Khan Malik (Luqman al-Mulk).
25   'Guzarish-i 'amaliyyat-i chand mahah-yi marizkhanah-yi Khurshid', 1319 [1930],
      293/7664, Iran's National Archives.
26   For instance, in 1932, Zandukht (1908–1952), the owner and editor of the women's
      journal *The Daughters of Iran* (*Dukhtarān-i Iran*, 1920–1922) advocated complete
      abolition of prostitution in Iran. See Zandukht Shirazi, 'Natayij-i ara-yi nisvan
      chah budah? wa 'avaqib-i shirkat-i an-ha dar idarat-i dawlati chah mibashad?',
      Dukhtaran-i Iran 2, no. 7 (Azar 1311 [December 1932]): 9.

27　Badr al-Dujji Mihrtaj Rakhshan, graduated from the American School in Tehran
　　during the Constitutional Revolution and established one of the earliest public
　　schools for girls in Tehran called 'Umm al-Madaris'. She was an active figure during
　　the Constitutional Revolution and mobilized many women to join street rallies. See
　　Huma Sarshar, Chi kasi bi yad-i khanum mudir ast?', in *Nihzat-i nisvan-i sharq*, eds
　　Qulam Riza Salami and Afsaneh Najmabadi, Chap-i 1, Majmūʻah-yi mutaliʻat-i
　　zanan 2 (Tehran: Shirazah, 1384 [2005]), 313–329.

28　Qulam Riza Salami and Afsaneh Najmabadi, eds, *Nizhat-i nisvan-i sharq*, Chāp-i 1,
　　Majmuʻah-yi mutaliʻat-i zanan 2 (Tehran: Shirazah, 1384 [2005]), 310.

29　Although penicillin was discovered as the cure for syphilis in the 1920s, it only began
　　to be mass-produced and used as the main treatment for syphilis and malaria in the
　　1940s, during the Second World War. See Sinan Yıldırmaz, *Politics and the Peasantry
　　in Post-War Turkey: Social History, Culture and Modernization*, Library of Ottoman
　　Studies 46 (London: I.B. Tauris, 2017); John Parascandola, *Sex, Sin, and Science:
　　A History of Syphilis in America*, Healing Society–Disease, Medicine, and History
　　(Westport, CT: Praeger, 2008).

30　Hidayatullah Hakimilahi was a professional muckraker journalist and activist, born
　　in 1917, and educated in Oxford, UK. He actively wrote letters to the Department
　　of Justice, targeting different government offices, including the Office of the Prime
　　Minister and the National Bureau of Planning and Budget. In his journalistic career
　　he wrote prolifically throughout the 1940s to 1960s and turned most of his serialized
　　publications into independent books. His account of the red-light district of Tehran
　　called *Come with Me to Shahr-i naw* (*Ba man bi Shahr-i naw biyayid*) belongs to
　　his series of exposés – a collection depicting his visits to various sites of crime and
　　poverty in Tehran – which includes the following books: *Come with Me to Shahr-i
　　naw* (*Ba man bi Shahr-i naw bi-yayid*, 1946), *Come with Me to the Mental Asylum* (*Ba
　　man bi dar al-majanin biyayid*, 1947), *Come with me to Tehran* (*Ba man bi Tehran
　　biyayid* 1947), *Come with Me to the Military* (*Ba man bi artish biyayid*, 1948) and
　　Come with Me to Schools (*Ba man bi madaris biyayid*, 1948).

31　For a detailed analysis of the literature on prostitution in the twentieth century,
　　see Jairan Gahan, 'Intimating Tehran: Affective Narrativization in Iranian
　　Popular Literature on Prostitution, 1920–1960', in *Iranian Literary Modernity and
　　Historiography*, eds Hamid Rezaie-Yazdi and Arshavez Muzzafari (Abingdon:
　　Routledge, 2019).

32　For a more detailed discussion on the relation between disgust and compassion in
　　this literature see Jairan Gahan, 'Intimating Tehran: The Figure of the Prostitute
　　in Iranian Popular Literature', in *Persian Literature and Modernity: Production and
　　Reception*, eds Hamid Rezaei Yazdi and Arshavez Mozafari, Iranian Studies 37
　　(Abingdon: Routledge, 2019).

33　He first published his journalistic semi-ethnographic piece in the *Didaniha* journal
　　in 1973. Later he published a standalone book called *Qalʻah* (Tehran: Maziyar
　　Publishing House, 1978). A new edition of the book was recently republished as
　　Shahr-i naw, Qalʻah-yi Zahidi 1348: Hamrah ba du didar az mujtamaʻ-i bihzisti 1368.

34　A few examples include: the Royal Organization of Social Services (Sazman-i
　　shahnshahai-yi khatamat-i ijtimaʻi, 1947) and its dependent institutions including
　　the Farah Pahlavi Hospital (1962), the Reza Pahlavi Hospital (1961) and Ashraf
　　Pahlaviʼs Nursing Institution (1949); womenʼs organizations (*Sazman-i zanan*, 1966);
　　the Center for the Fight against Tuberculosis (Markaz-i mubarizah ba sil, 1956); and
　　the Foundation for the Regeneration of Rural Areas (Bungah-i ʻumran-i dihat, 1974).

For more information see Rahnama-yi mu'assisat-i ijtima`i wa khairiyya *dar Iran* (Tehran: Bashgah-i bain al-milali-yi zanan-i Iran, n.d.).

35 Ashraf was appointed head of the Organization for Social Services. She frequented Iran's provinces for the inauguration of public clinics and other welfare centres. Farah also inaugurated the Farah Charitable Society *'Jam'iyyat-i khayriyah-yi Farah'* in 1953.

36 Ra'īsī, Parliament Proceedings, Meeting no. 144 (Day 9, 1352 [1973]).

37 Specifically, the Cabinet of Huvaida and Mansūr was addressed as 'the service-giving government of Mansur's and 'the service-giving government of Huvaida' in the parliament. For a few examples see Asifi, Parliament Proceedings, Meeting no. 356 (Urdibihisht 19, 1346 [9 May 1967]); Muhazzab, Parliament Proceedings, Meeting no. 187 (Khurdad 25, 1344 [15 June 1965]); Rahnavardi, Parliament Proceedings, Meeting no. 143 (Bahman 3, 1343 [23 January 1965]).

38 'Guzarish-i `amaliyyat-i sal-i 1334 [Idarah-yi kul-i bihdasht]' (Tehran: Vizarat-i bihdari, Idarah-yi kul-i bihdasht, 1334 [1955]), Library, Museum and Document Centre of Iran Parliament, 22.

39 It is highly probable that this clinic is the same as the clinic that Sattarah Farman-farma'iyan mentions in her reports. If so, the clinic was located next to Shahr-i naw, outside the gates, on Qalamistan Street.

40 'Guzarish-i kumisiun-i bihdasht-i sazman-i barnamah', 1332 [1953], 220/9970, Iran's National Archives.

41 'Guzarish-i 'amaliyat-i sal-", 1334, 22.

42 'Guzarish-i sah salah-yi qismat-i bihdasht va umur-i 'umumi-yi sazman-i barnamah az Mihr 1334 ta Mihr 1337 (Tehran: Sazman-i barnamah, 1337 [1958]), 24.

43 'Mahsur shudan-i Shahr-i naw', 1344 [1965], 340/234, Iran's National Archives.

44 '[Namah-ha-yi muti'addid az sakinin-i Tehran]', Letter no. 922.

45 '[Namah-ha-yi muti`addid az sakinin-i Tehran]'.

46 'Khulasah-yi parvandah-yi favahish-i mahall-i Shahr-i naw'.

47 I borrow the term 'The state of exception' from Agamben, who redefines Carl Schmitt's initial concept of it. He demonstrates that states of exceptions are at the heart of modern state rule and allow the state to expand its reach. They are the mechanisms through which the state expands and perpetuates its power in suspension of the law. Famously he refers to Nazi camps as sites that were ruled under the 'state of exception'. See, Giorgio Agamben, *State of Exception*, Homo Sacer (Chicago: University of Chicago Press, 2005).

48 'Qanun-i ijazah-yi ilhaq-i dawlat-i Iran bah purutukul-ha-yi islahi man`i fahsha', (1337 [1958]), 97/339/257, Iran's National Archives.

49 '[Namah-ha-yi muti`addid az sakinin-i Tehran]', (Day 3, 1337 [24 December 1958]), Letter no. 23964.

50 There were two different zoning systems in Tehran in the 1960s. According to the police zoning system, Shahr-i naw was in District Twenty (*barzan bist*). According to the municipal zoning system, Shahr-i naw was in District Ten (*bakhsh-i dah*). See Murtiza Tafrishi, *Pulis-i khafiyyah-yi Iran*.

51 Some of the archival material about the governance of Shahr-i naw in this chapter is in the National Archives. It includes documents from 1967 and 1968, such as a preliminary report on prostitution in Tehran, the official correspondence of the Management and Planning Organization of Iran and its Hygiene and Welfare Department, and other documents such as letters about the budget for establishing work camps for prostitutes. Many of the letters and other documents lack full

identification information. Throughout this chapter, whenever I use documents from this collection, I include the record number and the date, if available. If there is no record number, I refer to the collection. For documents on the shutdown of the northern gate of Shahr-i naw in 1959, see '[Namah-ha-yi muti'addid az sakinin-i Tehran]', Letter no. 26416. Also see, Farman-farma'iyan, *Piramun-i ruspigari dar shahr-i Tehran*, 13.

52   Farman-farma'iyan, *Piramun-i ruspigari dar shahr-i Tehran*, 221.
53   Most of the details about Shahr-i naw and the everyday living conditions of its residents in the late 1960s are extracted from Sattarah Farman-farma'iyan's thorough report commissioned by the Tehran police. Farman-farma'iyan was a social worker and the founder of the Higher Education Institution of Social Work in Tehran (amuzishgah-i 'ali-yi khadamat-i ijtima'i). See Sattārah Farman-farma'iyan, *Piramun-i ruspigari dar shahr-i Tehran*, 2nd edn. (Tehran: Amuzishgah-i 'ali-yi khadamat-i ijtima'i, 1970), 13.
54   Farman-farma'iyan, *Piramun-i ruspigari dar shahr-i Tehran*, 213.
55   Farman-farma'iyan, *Piramun-i ruspigari dar shahr-i Tehran*, 214, 215.
56   By the 1960s, prostitution had become classed as there were different forms of female sex work (both formal and informal) all around Tehran. There were women who solicited independently on the streets, women who worked in the informal sector, with 'server licenses' (*khidmatkari*) issued by the city police at bars and cafes, women who worked in private brothels in the city and women known as ditch-residents (*gawdnishinan*) who worked in the slums of southern Tehran, or in motels on the way to the then suburban area of Karaj. The Shahr-i naw prostitutes charged the least after the slum workers. According to Farman-farma'iyan's survey in 1968, even street workers outside the district charged more than women in Shahr-i naw. This shows the low wages and life conditions of the Shahr-i naw prostitutes compared to other sex workers. For a more detailed account on different kinds of sex work in Tehran, see Sattarah Farman-farma'iyan, *Piramun-i ruspigari dar shahr-i Tehran*, 18–21.
57   Safi Asfiya (1916–2008) is best known for implementing a liberal economy in Iran through Muhammad Reza Shah's development plans. He initiated the practice of the state opening its development projects to private companies for bidding. He became a faculty member at Tehran University's Department of Mining Engineering in 1939 and served as the director of the Management and Planning Organization of Iran from 1962 to 1968. Known as 'the technocrats' technocrat', he became the deputy prime minister in charge of the state's development plans. For more information on his life see Abbas Milani, *Eminent Persians: The Men and Women Who Made Modern Iran, 1941–1979* (New York: Persian World Press, 2008), 92–95.
58   'Mutali'at wa masayil-i fahsha wa ishtiqal az su-yi guruh-i bihdasht ca rifah-i ijtima'i-yi sazman-i barnamah', 1357–1346 [1967–1968], 220/18603, Iran's National Archives.
59   Muhammad Reza Pahlavi's White Revolution consisted of a five-step development plan. The fourth development plan (1968–1972) focused on 'housing construction: architectural styles, building materials, and planning and implementation of apartments and other types of complexes'. For more information, see Pamela Karimi, *Domesticity and Consumer Culture in Iran* (New York: Routledge, 2013), 143.
60   Interestingly, the letter further notes that the Association has no executive power. Hence, matters regarding Shahr-i naw needed to be addressed to the Ministry of Internal Affairs rather than the Association. A series of letters between the Association for Fighting Prostitution and the Management and Planning

Organization of Iran follow this one. All of those letters further emphasize that the Association, established in the 1950s, lacks authority.

61 'Mutali'at wa masayil-i fahsha wa ishtiqal az su-yi guruh-i bihdasht ca rifah-i ijtima'i-yi sazman-i barnamah'.

62 'Mutali'at wa masayil-i fahsha wa ishtiqal az su-yi guruh-i bihdasht ca rifah-i ijtima'i-yi sazman-i barnamah'.

63 The institute itself was the first of its kind. Sattarah Farman-farma'iyan, who belonged to a powerful royal family that had close ties to the state, studied social work in the United States in the 1940s. Upon her return she opened a centre to train social workers. Using her ties with the royal family, she visited Muhammad Reza Shah and convinced him to partially fund her centre. For more information see Sattarah Farman-farma'iyan, *Dukhtari az Iran*, trans. Maryam A`layi (Tehran: Nashr-i Karang, 2004).

64 Farman-farma'iyan, *Piramun-i ruspigari dar shahr-i Tehran*, 207.

65 Ibid., 13.

66 Ibid., 128.

67 Ibid., 224.

68 Ibid., 216, 217.

69 Unfortunately there are no detailed accounts of these training activities in the report. However, the idea of using banks as educational tools to teach saving could be the subject of more detailed analysis.

70 Agamben, drawing on Carl Schmitt, argues that 'the sovereign is at the same time outside and inside the juridical order'. The legitimacy of sovereign power is further defined above the law – for it cannot be absolute sovereignty if it is confined and limited by law. See Agamben, *Sovereign Power and Bare Life*, 15.

71 Gyan Prakash argues that colonies served as laboratories of modernity, where authority was instituted with 'minimum expense and maximum ambition'. Similarly, the space of the Shahr-i naw district was a subaltern space in relation to Tehran proper. See Gyan Prakash, *Another Reason: Science and the Imagination of Modern India* (Princeton, NJ: University Press, 1999), 13. While his formulation reinstates a sense of lack regarding modernity in colonies, I still find the idea of a laboratory useful.

Chapter 3

1 By middle class, I mean the 'middling' ranks consisting of professionals, lawyers, physicians, military officers, manufactures, merchants, tradesmen and their families. While emphasizing middle-class anxieties, discourses and representations, my point is not that these views were not shared by people from upper or lower ranks of society. 'Middle-class discourses' were defined by a fear of downward mobility.

2 For histories of poor women and female children in the Ottoman Empire see: Fariba Zarinebaf-Sharh, *Crime and Punishment in Istanbul, 1700–1800* (Los Angles: University of California Press, 2010). Fariba Zarinebaf, *Women on the Margins: Gender, Charity and Justice in the Early Modern Middle East* (Istanbul: ISIS Press, 2014). Shirine Hamadeh, 'Mean Streets: Space and moral Order in Early Modern Istanbul,' *Turcica* 44 (2013): 249–277. Nazan Maksudyan, *Orphans and Destitute Children in the Late Ottoman Empire* (New York: Syracuse University Press, 2014).

Yahya Araz, *Osmanlı Toplumunda Çocuk Olmak (16. Yüzyıldan 19. Yüzyıl Başlarına)* (İstanbul: Kitap Yayınevi, 2013). Anastasia Falierou Köksal Duygu, ed., *A Social History of Late Ottoman Women: New Perspectives* (Leiden: Brill, 2013). Ebru Boyar, 'An Imagined Moral Community: Ottoman Female Public Presence, Honour and Marginality', in *Ottoman Women in Public Space*, eds Kate Fleet and Ebru Boyar (Leiden: Brill, 2016). Elif Mahir Metinsoy, *Ottoman Women During World War I: Everyday Experiences, Politics, and Conflict* (London Cambridge University Press, 2017).

3   Osman Nuri Ergin, *Mecelle-i Umûr-ı Belediyye*, 9 vols, vol. 6 (İstanbul: İstanbul Büyükşehir Belediyesi Kültür İşleri Daire Başkanlığı Yayınları, 1995), 3297.

4   Judith R. Walkowitz, *Prostitution and Victorian Society: Women, Class and the State* (Cambridge: Cambridge University Press, 1996).

5   Halim Alyot, *Türkiye'de Zabıta: Tarihi Gelişim ve Bugünkü Durum* (Ankara: İçişleri Bakanlığı Yayınları, 1947), 570–586.

6   In Ottoman historiography, there is a growing literature gendering the issues of national and ethnic identities, family, public health, religious hegemony, urban security and social order, and sexual politics, see Beth Baron, *Egypt as a Woman: Nationalism, Gender, and Politics* (Berkeley: University of California Press, 2005), Nikki R. Keddie and Beth Baron, *Women in Middle Eastern History: Shifting Boundaries in Sex and Gender* (New Haven, CT: Yale University Press, 1991), Alan Duben and Cem Behar, *İstanbul Haneleri: Evlilik, Aile ve Doğurganlık, 1880–1940* (İstanbul: İletişim Yayınları, 1996), Nazan Maksudyan, ed., *Women and the City, Women in the City: A Gendered Perspective on Ottoman Urban History* (New York: Berghahn, 2014), Kate Fleet Ebru Boyar, ed., *Ottoman Women in Public Space* (Leiden: Brill, 2016), Elizabeth Frierson, *Mirrors Out, Mirrors In: Domestication and Rejection of the Foreign in the Ottoman Women's Magazines* (New York: State University of New York, 2000), Elizabeth B. Frierson, 'Unimagined Communities: Women and Education in the Late-Ottoman Empire, 1876–1909', *Critical Matrix, The Princeton Journal of Women, Gender, and Culture* 9, no. 2 (1995): 55–90, Zafer Toprak, *Türkiye'de Kadın Özgürlüğü ve Feminizm* (Istanbul: Tarih Vakf ı Yurt Yayınları, 2014).

7   For studies on urban policing and social policy in Istanbul in the second half of the nineteenth and early twentieth centuries, see Ferdan Ergut, 'Policing the Poor in the Late Ottoman Empire', *Middle Eastern Studies* 38, no. 2 (2002): 149–164, Ferdan Ergut, *Modern Devlet ve Polis: Osmanlı'dan Cumhuriyet'e Toplumsal Denetimin Diyalektiği* (İstanbul: İletişim Yayınları, 2004), Noemi Levy and Alexandre Toumarkine, eds, *Osmanlı'da Asayiş, Suç ve Ceza, 18. -20. Yüzyıllar* (İstanbul: Tarih Vakfı Yurt Yayınları, 2007), Noémi Lévy-Aksu, *Osmanlı İstanbulu'nda Asayiş 1879–1909*, trans. Serra Akyüz Gönen (Istanbul: İletişim Yayınları, 2017), İlkay Yılmaz, *Serseri, Anarşist ve Fesadın Peşinde: II. Abdülhami Dönemi Güvenlik Politikaları Ekseninde Mürur Tezkereleri, Pasaportlar ve Otel Kayıtları* (İstanbul: Tarih Vakfı Yurt Yayınları, 2014), Nadir Özbek, *Osmanlı İmparatorluğu'nda Sosyal Devlet: Siyaset, İktidar ve Meşruiyet (1876–1914)* (İstanbul: İletişim Yayınları, 2002), Maksudyan, *Orphans and Destitute Children in the Late Ottoman Empire*. Also for the eighteenth and early nineteenth centuries, see Zarinebaf-Sharh, *Crime and Punishment in Istanbul, 1700–1800*, Betül Başaran, *Selim III, Social Control, and Policing in Istanbul at the end of the Eighteenth Century* (Leiden: Brill, 2014), Hamadeh, 'Mean Streets: Space and Moral Order in Early Modern Istanbul', 249–277.

8   Nadir Özbek, "'Beggars" and "Vagrants" in State Policy and Public Discourse During the Late Ottoman Empire: 1876–1914', *Middle Eastern Studies* 45, no. 5 (2009): 783–801, 787.
9   BOA, ZB, 400/101, 1320.Eylül.22 (5 October 1904).
10 During the late eighteenth and early nineteenth centuries the Ottoman governments frequently deported prostitutes to Ottoman islands such as Cyprus, Sakız, Limni and Bozcaada. BOA, C.ZB, 3139, 1233.Za.4.1233 (7 September 1818). BOA, C.ZB, 402, 1162.B.6 (22 June 1749). BOA, C.ZB, 1236, 1150.L.12 (2 February 1738), BOA, C.ZB, 200, 1134.Ş.18 (3 June 1722), ibid.
11 BOA, ZB, 437/68, 1320.Teşrinievvel.23 (5 November 1904).
12 BOA, ZB, 400/69, 1320.Teşrinievvel.21 (3 November 1904).
13 BOA, DH.MKT, 2868/26, 1327.C.17 (6 July 1909).
14 Ibid.
15 BOA, DH.EUM.THR, 3/17, 1327.S.25 (18 March 1909).
16 BOA, ZB, 496/40, 1325.Haziran.24 (7 July 1909).
17 BOA, ZB, 497/60, 1325.Teşrinievvel.29 (11 November 1909).
18 BOA, ZB, 486/17, 1324.Ağustos.31 (13 September 1908).
19 'Sokak Kızları', *Sabah*, No. 4277, 3 October 1900.
20 Darülaceze was the first 'modern' poorhouse of the Ottoman Empire established in 1896, during the rule of Abdülhamid II. See Özbek, *Osmanlı İmparatorluğu'nda Sosyal Devlet*.
21 BOA, DH.MKT, 2632/61, 1326.N.21 (17 October 1908).
22 Ibid.
23 BOA, DH.MKT, 2653/24, 1326.L.15 (10 November 1908), BOA, ZB, 327/113, 1324.Teşrinievvel.22 (4 November 1908).
24 BOA, DH.MKT, 2653/24, 1326.L.15 (10 November 1908).
25 BOA, DH.MKT, 2695/3, 1326.Z.05 (29 December 1908).
26 BOA, DH.MKT, 2653/24, 1326.L.15 (10 November 1908).
27 BOA, DH.EUM.THR, 34/70, 1326.Mayıs.15 (28 May 1910).
28 BOA, DH.ID, 47–1/11, 1320.M.15 (24 April 1902).
29 BOA, DH.EUM.THR, 50/61, 1328.N.17 (22 September 1910).
30 BOA, DH.EUM.THR, 96/7, 1328.R.07 (18 April 1910).
31 Meclis-i Meb'u^sa ^ n Zabıt Cerideleri (MMZC), I:31/C:1, 18 Feb. 1909 (5 S¸ubat 1324).
32 BOA, DH.EUM.THR, 58/48, 1328.Z.23 (31 December 1910). BOA, DH.EUM.KADL, 7/15, 1329.S.08 (8 February 1911).
33 BOA, DH.İD, 76/22, 1331.Ca.07 (14 April 1913).
34 BOA, DH.EUM.KADL, 7/15, 1329.S.08 (8 February 1911).
35 BOA, DH.İD, 76/22, 1331.Ca.07 (14 April 1913).
36 Ibid.
37 Ibid.
38 Ibid., BOA, DH.EUM.THR, 58/48, 1328.Z.23 (31 December 1910).
39 BOA, DH.İD, 76/22, 1331.Ca.07 (14 April 1913).
40 Ibid.
41 Ibid.
42 Ibid.
43 Ibid.
44 Ibid.
45 Ibid.

Chapter 4

1   Tanta Criminal Court Records 1938, file 7439, case 1328.

2   Ibid.

3   ʿAbdal-Wahab Bakr, *Mujtamaʿ al-Qahira al-Sirri, 1900–1951* [Cairo's Underground
     Society, 1900–1951] (Cairo: al-ʿArabi lil-Nashr wa al-Tawziʿ, 2001); Khaled Fahmy,
     'Prostitution in Nineteenth-Century Egypt', in *Outside In: On the Margins of the
     Modern Middle East*, ed. Eugene Rogan (London: I.B. Tauris, 2002), 77–103; Hanan
     Hammad, 'Between Egyptian National Purity and Local Flexibility: Prostitution
     in al Mahallaal-Kubra in the First Half of the Twentieth Century', *Journal of Social
     History* 44, no. 3 (2011): 751–783; Imad Hilal, *Al-Baghaya fi Misr: Dirasa Tarikhiyya
     Ijtimaʿiyya, 1834–1949* [Prostitutes in Egypt: A Sociohistorical Study, 1834–1949]
     (Cairo: al-ʿArabi lil-nashr wa-al-tawziʿ, 2001); Liat Kozma, 'Girls, Labor, and Sex in
     Precolonial Egypt, 1850–1882', in *Girlhood: A Global History*, eds Jennifer Helgren
     and Colleen A. Vasconcellos (New Brunswick, NJ: Rutgers University Press, 2010),
     344–362, *Policing Egyptian Women: Sex, Law, and Medicine in Khedival Egypt*
     (Syracuse, NY: Syracuse University Press, 2011).

4   ʿAbdal-Wahab Bakr, *al-Shawariʿ al-Khalfiyya: al-Jarima fi Misr fi al-Nisf al-Thani
     min al-Qarn al-ʿIshrin* [The Backstreets: Crimes in Egypt in the First Half of the
     Twentieth Century] (Cairo: Dar al-Wathaʿiq al-Qawmiyya, 2005); Amina Hijazi,
     al-Jarima fi Misr, 1919–1939 [Crime in Egypt, 1919–1939] (Cairo: Dar al-Wathaʿiq
     al-Qawmiyya, 2014).

5   I extracted figures for both years from reports on the state of public security in Egypt
     published in Cairo by the Public Security Department in Ministry of the Interior
     Affairs.

6   Muhammad Shahin, *Kifah al-Jarima* [Fighting Crime] (Cairo: al-Matbʿa al-
     Mutawasita, 1936).

7   el-Sayed El-Aswad, 'Thaqafat al-Satr wa Dilalatiha al-Ramziyya fi al-hayyah al-
     Shaʿbiyya al-ʿArabiyya' [Covering-Up Culture and Its Symbolic Meaning in Arab
     Popular Life], *Al-Maʾthurat al-Shaʿbiyya*, 8–27 July 2004.

8   Kozma, *Policing Egyptian Women*, xxii.

9   The records are stored in Dar al-Mahfuzat al-ʿUmumiyya (National Archive) in the
     Cairo Citadel.

10   Mario M. Ruiz, 'Criminal Statistics in the Long 1890s', in *The Long 1890s in Egypt:
     Colonial Quiescence, Subterranean Resistance*, eds Marilyn Booth and Anthony
     Gorman (Edinburgh: Edinburgh University Press, 2014), 141–166.

11   Nathan Brown, "Brigands and State Building: The Invention of Banditry in Modern
     Egypt," *Comparative Studies in Society and History*, 1990, 32:2: 258–81.

12   Mine Ener, *Managing Egypt's Poor and the Politics of Benevolence, 1800–1952*
     (Princeton, NJ: Princeton University Press, 2003), 100.

13   Mine Ener, 'Prohibitions on Begging and Loitering in Nineteenth-Century Egypt',
     Die Welt des Islams, n.s., 39, no. 3 (1999): 319–339.

14   Kamil Al-Misri, ed., *Qanun al-ʿUqubat al-Ahli Mudhayyal bi-Ahkam al-Mahakim al-
     Ahliyyah li-ghayat 1930* [The Penal Code with Verdicts of the National Courts until
     1930] (Cairo: al Maktaba al-Tujariyya al-Kubra, 1931), 161–164.

15   Amy J. Johnson, *Reconstructing Rural Egypt: Ahmed Hussein and the History of
     Egyptian Development* (Syracuse, NY: Syracuse University Press, 2004), 52.

16   Beth Baron, *Egypt as a Woman: Nationalism, Gender, and Politics* (Berkeley: University of California Press, 2005), 52; Hanan Hammad, *Industrial Sexuality: Mechanization, Sex, Gender, and Social Transformation in Modern Egypt* (Austin: University of Texas Press, 2016), 146; Hanan Kholoussy, 'Monitoring and Medicalising Male Sexuality in Semi-Colonial Egypt', *Gender & History* 22, no. 3 (2010): 677–691; Omnia El Shakry, 'Peasants, Crime, and Tea in Interwar Egypt', *ISIM Review* 21 (2008): 44–45.

17   For the connection between rural immigration and the formation of the Egyptian urban working class, see Joel Beinin and Zachary Lockman, *Workers on the Nile: Nationalism, Communism, Islam, and the Egyptian Working Class, 1882–1954* (Cairo: American University in Cairo Press, 1998), 24–31.

18   Hilmi Ahmad Shalabi, *Fusul fi Tarikh Tahdith al-Mudun* [Chapters on Modernizing Cities] (Cairo: al-Hayy'a al-Misriyya al-'amma lil-kitab, 1988), 74.

19   Ministry of Finance, Statistical Department, *Population Censuses Conducted in Egypt 1907* (Cairo: Government Press, 1909).

20   Ministry of Finance, Statistical and Census Department, *The Census of Egypt Taken in 1937* (Cairo: Government Press, 1941).

21   Ibid.

22   Ministry of Finance, Statistical Department, *Population Censuses Conducted in Egypt 1947* (Cairo: al-Matba'a al-amiriyya, 1953).

23   Fatima 'Alam al-Din 'Abd al-Wahid, *Tatawural-Naqlwaal-Muwasalatal-Dakhiliyya fi Misr fi 'ahd al-Ihtilal al-Britani 1882–1914* [The Development of Domestic Transportation in Egypt under the British Occupation, 1882–1914] (Cairo: al-Hay'a al-Misriyya al-'Amma lil-kitab, 1989).

24   Nancy Reynolds, *A City Consumed: Urban Commerce, the Cairo Fire, and the Politics of Decolonization in Egypt* (Stanford, CA: Stanford University Press, 2012), 45.

25   On Barak, *On Time: Technology and Temporality in Modern Egypt* (Berkeley: University of California Press, 2013), 157.

26   Ibid.

27   Ibid., 157.

28   Bakr, *al-Shawari' al-Khalfiyya*, 127.

29   Unfortunately, there is no available breakdown for marital status of these girls and women.

30   Sayyid 'Uways, 'Dhahirat Jara'im al-Nashl fi Muhit al-Nisa' fi Muhafazat al-Qahira' [The Pickpocketing Phenomenon among Women in the Cairo Province], *Al-Majalla al-Jina'iyya al-Qawmiyya* 8, no. 1 (1965): 67–94, 68.

31   Al-Mahalla Misdemeanour Court Records (hereafter MCR) 1943, file 6865, case 2697.

32   Husayn Muhammad Ali, 'Al-Nashl: Asalibahu wa Mawasimahu fi Madinat al-Qahira' ['Pickpocketing: Its Methods and Seasons in Cairo']. *Majallat al-Amn al-'Amm*, April 1959; Alexander Borgzanoa, *Asrar al-Nashshalin wa ma Yutakhaz Limukafahatihim* [The Secrets of Pickpockets and What Is Done to Fight Them] (Cairo: Matba'at Misr, 1927).

33   Charles Issawi, *Egypt at Mid-century: An Economic Survey* (Oxford: Oxford University Press, 1954), 87–89.

34   Bakr, *al-Shawari' al-Khalfiyya*, 67.

35   Ener, *Managing Egypt's Poor and the Politics of Benevolence*, 115.

36   Dar al-Watha'iq al-Qawmiyya, Abdin Archive, Mahfaza 523, document dated April 12, 1917.

37 MCR 1942, file 6792, case 2256.
38 MCR 1944, file 6920, cases 2498 and 2984. See also MCR 1945, file 7793, case 1977.
39 MCR 1942, file 6791, cases 1220 and 1132. See also MCR1945, file7793, case 1790 and file 7795, case 3654.
40 Omnia El Shakry, *The Great Social Laboratory: Subjects of Knowledge in Colonial and Postcolonial Egypt* (Stanford, CA: Stanford University Press, 2007), 10.
41 Cairo Police, *Annual Report 1931* (Cairo: al-Matb'a al-Amiriyya, 1932).
42 Idarat 'Umum al-Amn al-'Amm, *Taqrir 'an Halat al-Amn al-'Am bil-Mamlaka al-Misriyya* [Public Security Department: A Report on the State of Public Security in the Egyptian Kingdom] (Cairo: al-Matb 'a al-amiriyya bi-Bulaq, 1938).
43 Sami Georgy, 'Ziyadat al-Jara'im: Asbabiha wa 'Ilajaha' [The Increase in Crimes: Its Causes and Solutions], *al-Murshid*, 28 September 1936; Husayn Lutfi, 'Asbab Kathrat Hawadith al-Sariqa' [Causes of the Increase in Theft], *Al Muqattam*, 26 June 1939.
44 Muhammad Husayn Haykal, 'Hijrat al-rif ila al-mudun' [Rural Immigration to Cities], *Al Siyasa al-Usbu'iyya*, 20 April 1940.
45 Heidi Morrison, *Childhood and Colonial Modernity in Egypt* (New York: Palgrave Macmillan, 2015), 72–84; Muhammad Nabih Al-Tarabulsi, *Al-Mujrimun al-ahdath fi al-qanun al-Misri wa al-Tashri' al-Muqaran* [Child Criminals in the Egyptian Code and Comparative Law] (Cairo: Dar al-fikr al'Arabi, 1948).
46 Marilyn Booth, 'Disruptions of the Local, Eruptions of the Feminine: Local Reportage and National Anxieties in Egypt's 1890s', in *The Press in the Middle East and North Africa, 1850–1950: Politics, Social History, and Culture*, eds Anthony Gorman and Didier Monciaud (Edinburgh: Edinburgh University Press, forthcoming).
47 Hammad, *Industrial Sexuality*, 87; Taha Sa'd Uthman, 'Kifah 'Ummal al-Nasij, Mudhakkarat wa-watha'iq min tarikh 'ummal Misr: Kifah 'ummal al-nasij, 1938–1947 [Memoirs and Documents from the History of Egypt's Workers: The Struggle of Textile Workers, 1938–1947] (Cairo: Maktabat Madbuli, 1983), 205.
48 Ener, *Managing Egypt's Poor and the Politics of Benevolence*, 2.
49 MCR 1940, file 6861, case 2315; MCR1944, file 6917, case 505; MCR 1945, file 7792, case 1195.
50 Hammad, *Industrial Sexuality*, 95–96.
51 MCR1945, file 7792, case 1016; MCR 1945, file 7793, case 2002; MCR 1945, file 7794, case 2780; MCR 1945, file 7794, case 2819.
52 *Al-Dunya al-Musawara* campaigned against women criminals and venerated the 'struggle' of the police, see *Al-Dunya al-Musawara*, 'Jihad al-Bulis fi Mukafahat al-Mujrimin min al-Jins al-Latif' [The Police Struggle against Criminals of the Gentle Sex], 20 March 1930. See also al-Ahram's campaign against domestic servants on 13 and 18 October 1931.
53 Muhammad Tawfiq Diyab, 'Mushkilatal-Khadimat fi Misr' [The Problem of Maids in Egypt], *Al-Siyasa al-Usbu'iyya*, January 1928.
54 John Hostettler, *A History of Criminal Justice in England and Wales* (Sherfield on Loddon: Waterside, 2009), 254.
55 Cesare Lombroso and Guglielmo Ferrero, *Criminal Woman, the Prostitute, and the Normal Woman*, trans. Nicole Hahn Rafter and Mary Gibson (Durham, NC: Duke University Press, 2004), 263–264.
56 *Majallat Ra'msis*, 'Al-Insan al-Mujrim' [The Criminal], December/January 1920/21, 640–642.
57 MCR 1942, file 6792, case 3008.

58 MCR 1940, file 6861, case 1506.
59 MCR 1944, file 6920, case 2498.
60 MCR 1940, file 6861, case 1176.
61 MCR 1941, file 6788, case 517; MCR 1942, file 6792, case 1220.
62 MCR 1930, file 418, case 2116; MCR 1983, file 6775, case 85.
63 MCR 1942, file 6790, case 63.
64 Ministry of Interior, *Bolis Madinat al-Qahira: al-Taqrir al-Sanawi li-sanat 1939* [Cairo Police: Annual Report for 1939] (Cairo: al-Matba'a al-Amiriyya, 1940).
65 Shahin, *Kifah al-Jarima*, 104.
66 MCR 1943, file 6863, case 915.
67 MCR 1943, file 6791, case 1132.
68 MCR 1943, file 6863, case 894.
69 MCR 1943, file 6862, case 91.
70 See, for example, Mona L. Russell, *Creating the New Egyptian Woman: Consumerism, Education, and National Identity, 1863–1922* (New York: Palgrave Macmillan, 2004).
71 Reynolds, *A City Consumed*, 132.
72 Nancy Reynolds, 'Sharikat al-Baytal-Misri: Domesticating Commerce in Egypt, 1931–1956', *Arab Studies Journal* 7, no. 2–8 (1999–2000): 75–107, 79.
73 Kerry Segrave, *Shoplifting: A Social History* (Jefferson, NC: McFarland, 2001), 7–9.
74 Tanta Criminal Court Records 1938, file 7439, case 1328.
75 Tanta Appeal Court Records 1947, vol. 11, file 7553, case 4712.
76 MCR 1942, file 6792, case 2878.
77 MCR 1938, file 6776, case 2321; MCR 1941, file 6789, case 2708.
78 MCR 1938, file 6776, case 2321; MCR 1941, file 6789, cases 2222 and 2300.
79 MCR 1937, file 6773, case 3262; MCR 1938, file 6777, case 1808; MCR 1938, file 655, case 6775; MCR 1945, file7792, case 662; MCR 1945, file 7792, case 1016; MCR 1945, file 7794, case 2833; MCR 1945, file 7795, case 3404; MCR 1945, file 7795, case 3445.
80 MCR 1941, file 6789, case 2446.
81 Ministry of Interior, *Bolis Madinat al-Qahira*.
82 MCR 1942, file 6792, case 2256.
83 MCR 1942, file 6792, case 2954.
84 Ibid.
85 Ibid.
86 MCR 1943, file 6864, case 2377.
87 MCR 1936, file 6767, case 3075.
88 MCR 1930, file 4178, case 378.
89 MCR 1930, file 4178, case 378; MCR 1930, file 4180, case 1650.

Chapter 5

1   See, most notably, Yashar Kemal, *Memed, My Hawk*, trans. Edouard Roditi (London: Harvill Press, 1990). The possible existence of the social bandit has received more attention very recently. See the articles in this collection and also, for example, Abolhassan Hadjiheidari, 'Nāyeb Ḥoseyn Kāšī, Strassenräuber oder Revolutionär?: eine Untersuchung zur neueren Iranischen Geschichte (1850–1920)' (Berlin: Klaus Schwarz Verlag, 2011); Mohammed Saaid Ezzeldin, 'History and Memory of Bandits in Modern Egypt: The Controversy of Adham al-Sharqawi', MA thesis,

Georgetown University, 2013. Available online: https://repository.library.georgetown.
edu/bitstream/handle/10822/709716/Ezzeldin_georgetown_0076M_12481.
pdf;sequence=1 (accessed 27 June 2019).

2   The literature on social banditry, for and against, in these areas is very substantial.
     For Latin America, see, inter alia, Gilbert M. Joseph, 'On the Trail of Latin American
     Bandits: A Reexamination of Peasant Resistance', *Latin American Research Review*
     25, no. 3 (1990): 7–53, and the subsequent debate in that journal. See also Richard
     W. Slatta, ed., *Bandidos; the Varieties of Latin American Banditry* (New York:
     Greenwood, 1987). On China, see Patrick Fuliang Shan, 'Insecurity, Outlawry and
     Social Order: Banditry in China's Heilongjiang Frontier Region, 1900–1931', *Journal
     of Social History* 40, no. 1 (2006): 25–54; Robert J. Antony, 'Peasants, Heroes, and
     Brigands: The Problem of Social Banditry in Early Nineteenth-Century South China',
     Modern China 15, no. 2 (1989): 123–148. Tibet is discussed by Tsering Shakya, 'Ga
     rgya 'gram nag: A bandit or proto-rebel? The question of banditry as social protest in
     Nag chu', in *Trails of the Tibetan Tradition: Papers for Elliot Sperling* (Dharamshala:
     Amnye Machen Institute, 2014). For India, see David Arnold, 'Dacoity and Rural
     Crime in Madras, 1860–1940', *Journal of Peasant Studies* 6 (1979): 140–167; Kim
     A. Wagner, 'Thuggee and Social Banditry Reconsidered', *Historical Journal* 50, no.
     2 (2007): 353–376. For Southeast Asia see Greg Bankoff, 'Bandits, Banditry and
     Landscapes of Crime in the Nineteenth-Century Phillipines', *Journal of Southeast
     Asian Studies* 29, no. 2 (1998): 319–339; Boon Kheng Cheah, *The Peasant Robbers
     of Kedah, 1900–1919: Historical and Folk Perceptions* (London: Oxford University
     Press, 1988). For Africa, Allen Isaacman, 'Social Banditry in Zimbabwe (Rhodesia)
     and Mozambique, 1894–1907: An Expression of Early Peasant Protest', *Journal
     of Southern African Studies* 4, no. 1 (1977): 1–30; Donald Crummey, 'African
     Banditry Revisited.' Available online: https://www.brunel.ac.uk/__data/assets/
     pdf_file/0018/110736/Donald-Crummey,-African-Banditry-Revisited–an-essay.pdf
     (accessed 27 June 2019). The literature on social banditry in Europe is very extensive.
     For a recent account, see Shingo Minamizuka, *A Social Bandit in Nineteenth Century
     Hungary: Rósza Sándor* (Boulder, CO: East European Monographs, 2008). For a
     recent consideration of Balkan banditry see Frederick F. Anscombe, 'Albanians
     and "mountain bandits"', *Princeton Papers: Interdisciplinary Journal of Near Eastern
     Studies* 13 (2006): 87–114, reprinted in Frederick F. Anscombe, ed., *The Ottoman
     Balkans, 1750–1830* (Princeton, NJ: Markus Wiener Publishers, 2006), 87–113.

3   Eric Hobsbawm, *Bandits* (London: Weidenfeld and Nicolson, [1969] 2000).

4   Stanley Cohen, 'Bandits, Rebels or Criminals: African History and Western
     Criminology', *Africa: Journal of the International African Institute* 56, no. 4 (1986):
     468–483.

5   Hobsbawm, *Bandits*, 20.

6   Ibid., 67.

7   See Joseph, 'On the Trail of Latin American Bandits', note, 41, p. 38; Anton Blok,
     The Mafia of a Sicilian Village, 1860–1960: A Study of Violent Peasant Entrepreneurs
     (Oxford: Basil Blackwell, 1974), note 10, p. 101.

8   Hobsbawm, *Bandits*, 182.

9   Ibid., p. 182.

10   Anton Blok, 'The Peasant and the Brigand: Social Banditry Reconsidered',
     Comparative Studies in Society and History 14, no. 4 (1972): 494–503.

11   Ibid., 499.

12   Graham Seal, 'The Robin Hood Principle: Folklore, History and the Social Bandit', *Journal of Folklore Research* 46, no. 1 (2009): 67–89.

13   John S. Koliopoulos, *Brigands with a Cause: Brigandage and Irredentism in Modern Greece, 1821–1912* (Oxford: Clarendon Press, 1987); Maria Todorova, ed., *Balkan Identities: Nation and Memory* (New York: New York University Press, 2004), 21; Alice Blackwood, 'Criminal or Nationalist? The Social Purposes and Results of the Creation of a "Social Bandit" Mythos in the Balkans', *Balkan Folklore*, 1–11. Available online: https://www.academia.edu/4457176/Criminal_or_Nationalist_The_Social_ Purposes_and_Results_of_the_Creation_of_a_Social_Bandit_Mythos_in_the_ Balkans (accessed 27 June 2019).

14   Tomas Balkelis, 'Social Banditry and Nation-Making: The Myth of a Lithuanian Robber', *Past and Present*, 198, no. 1 (2008): 111–145.

15   See Seal, 'The Robin Hood Principle'.

16   Ranajit Guha, *Elementary Aspects of Peasant Insurgency in Colonial India*. Foreword by James Scott (Durham, NC: Duke University Press, 1999), 91.

17   Ibid., 83.

18   Ibid., 93; Joseph, 'On the Trail of Latin American Bandits', 20–22.

19   For a full discussion, see Joseph, 'On the Trail of Latin American Bandits'.

20   Joseph, 'On the Trail of Latin American Bandits', 34–35.

21   Donald Crummey, 'Introduction: "The Great Beast"', in Donald Crummey, ed., *Banditry, Rebellion and Social Protest in Africa* (London: Currey, 1986), 12.

22   For bandit biographies and (semi-)autobiographies, see, for example, Billy Jaynes Chandler, *The Bandit King: Lampiao of Brazil* (Austin: Texas A&M University Press, 1978); Phoolan Devi with Marie-Therese Cuny and Paul Rambali, *I, Phoolan Devi: The Autobiography of India's Bandit Queen* (New York: Little, Brown and Company, 1996).

23   Such incorporation has been important in assisting the collection of material. See for example the assiduous research carried out under official auspices in China into the bandit Bai Lang and his movement in Elizabeth J. Perry, 'Social Banditry Revisited: The Case of Bai Lang, a Chinese Brigand', *Modern China* 9, no. 3 (1983): 355–382, note 3, p. 379.

24   See, for example, Hasina Amrouni, 'Les bandits d'honneur d'Algérie'. Available online: https://www.memoria.dz/sep-2016/dossier/les-bandits-dhonneur-dalg-rie (accessed 27 June 2019); Settar Ouatmani, 'Arezki L'Bachir Un « bandit d'honneur » en Kabylie au xixe siècle', *Revue des mondes musulmans et de la Méditerranée*, 136 (2014): 187–202.

25   Ted Swedenburg, *Memories of Revolt: The 1936–1939 Rebellion and the Palestinian National Past* (Minneapolis: University of Minnesota Press, 1995), 94–96.

26   Nathan Brown, 'Brigands and State Building: The Invention of Banditry in Modern Egypt', *Comparative Studies in Society and History* 32, no. 2 (1990): 258–281; Karen Barkey, *Bandits and Bureaucrats: The Ottoman Route to State Centralization* (Ithaca, NY,: Cornell University Press, 1994).

27   Brown, 'Brigands and State Building', 263.

28   This account is drawn from Brown, 'Brigands and State Building'.

29   Barkey, *Bandits and Bureaucrats*. The notion of a generalized crisis of the seventeenth century was first proposed by Eric Hobsbawm in two articles published in *Past and Present* in 1954. For a recent assessment of the state of the debate and the literature thus generated see the articles collected in the *American Historical Review* 120, no. 4 (October 2015).

30 Barkey, *Bandits and Bureaucrats*.
31 David M. Hart, *Banditry in Islam: Case studies from Morocco, Algeria and the Pakistan North West Frontier* (Wisbech: Menas Press, 1987), 7. Such strategies were not confined to the Middle East and North Africa. Indeed the 'poacher turned gamekeeper' is probably a universal phenomenon.
32 Hart, *Banditry in Islam*, 19–26.
33 This account of is drawn from Andrew G. Gould, 'Lords or Bandits? The Derebeys of Cilicia', *International Journal of Middle East Studies* 7, no. 4 (1976): 485–506.
34 Ibid.
35 Barkey, *Bandits and Bureaucrats*, 9.
36 Ibid., 86. Brown's reluctance to accept the notion of social banditry stems from a perspective which sees both rebellion and banditry as symptomatic of the relations of power rather than as authentic peasant political activism. For a discussion of forms of peasant political activity in Egypt see Nathan Brown, *Peasant Politics in Modern Egypt: The Struggle Against the State* (New Haven, CT: Yale University Press, 1990). The supposed absence of peasant rebellion has been theorized. See Farhad Kazemi and Evand Abrahamian, 'The Nonrevolutionary Peasantry of Modern Iran', *Iranian Studies* 11, no. 1 (1978): 259–304.
37 Ibn Khaldun, *The Muqaddimah: An Introduction to History*, eds N. J. Dawood, and Franz Rosenthal (London: Routledge and Kegan Paul in association with Secker and Warburg, 1967).
38 Brown, 'Brigands and State Building', 260.
39 Barkey, *Bandits and Bureaucrats*, 153–154.
40 For a discussion of this vocabulary see Marinos Sariyannis, '"Mob", "Scamps" and Rebels in Sevententh Century Istanbul: Some Remarks on Ottoman Social Vocabulary', *International Journal of Turkish Studies* 11, nos 1–2 (2005): 1–15; Leslie Peirce, 'Abduction with (Dis)honor: Sovereigns, Brigands, and Heroes in the Ottoman World', *Journal of Early Modern History* 15 (2001): 311–329, 320.
41 Suraiya Faroqui, *Coping with the State: Political Conflict and Crime in the Ottoman Empire, 1550–1720* (Istanbul: Isis Press, 1995), 148.
42 Swedenburg, *Memories of Revolt*, 94–96.
43 Hart, *Banditry in Islam*, 2–3.
44 David Prochaska, 'Fire on the mountain: resisting colonialism in Algeria', in *Banditry, Rebellion and Social Protest in Africa*, ed. Donald Crummey (London: Currey, 1986), 229–252.
45 This account is drawn from Prochaska, 'Fire on the mountain'.
46 Prochaska, 'Fire on the mountain', 231–233.
47 Ibid., 237.
48 Ibid., 239–247.
49 Ellis Goldberg, 'Peasants in Revolt – Egypt 1919', *International Journal of Middle East Studies* 24, no. 2 (1992): 261–280.
50 Touraj Atabaki and Eric Jan Zürcher, eds, *Men of Order: authoritarian modernization under Atatürk and Reza Shah* (London: I.B. Tauris, 2003).
51 Fulya Ozkan, 'Gravediggers of the Modern State: Highway Robbers on the Trabzon-Bayezid Road, 1850s–1910s', *Journal of Persianate Studies* 7, no. 2 (2014): 225.
52 Faroqui, *Coping with the State*, 183.
53 Ibid., p. 182. For a most enlightening study of Ottoman 'colonial' attitudes towards the peoples of its own periphery, see Selim Derengil, '"They Live in a State of

Nomadism and Savagery": The Late Ottoman Empire and the Post-Colonial Debate', *Comparative Studies in Society and History* 45, no. 2 (2003): 311–342.

54 Mohammed Ennaji, *Serving the Master: Slavery and Society in Nineteenth-Century Morocco*, trans. Seth Graebner (Basingstoke: Macmillan, 1999), 50.

55 Ibid., 49–51.

56 For an account of one such deserter, see Stephanie Cronin, *Tribal Politics in Iran: Rural Conflict and the New State, 1921–1941* (Abingdon: Routledge, 2007), 107.

57 Hobsbawm, *Bandits*, 27.

58 Pat O'Malley, 'Class Conflict, Land and Social Banditry: Bushranging in Nineteenth Century Australia', *Social Problems* 26, no. 3 (1979): 271–283.

59 Ozkan, 'Gravediggers of the Modern State', 225.

60 Personal communication. I am grateful to Murat Metinsoy for this information.

61 Cronin, *Tribal Politics in Iran*, 128.

62 This account is drawn from Donald Quataert, 'The Régie, Smugglers and the Government', in *Social Disintegration and Popular Resistance in the Ottoman Empire, 1881–1908, Reactions to European Economic Penetration* (New York: New York University Press, 1983).

63 Ibid., 21.

64 Ibid., 24.

65 Ibid., 20.

66 Ibid., 34.

67 Ozkan, 'Gravediggers of the Modern State', 244.

68 Mansoureh Ettehadieh (Nezam-Mafie), 'Crime, security and insecurity: socio-political conditions of Iran, 1875–1924', in *War and Peace in Qajar Persia: Implications Past and Present*, ed. Roxane Farmanfarmaian (Abingdon: Routledge, 2008), 179.

69 Eyal Ginio, 'Piracy and Redemption in the Aegean Sea during the First Half of the Eighteenth Century', *Turcica* 33 (2001): 137–138.

70 Ibid.

71 See, for example, Alan G. Jamieson, *Lords of the Sea: A History of the Barbary Corsairs* (London: Reaktion Books, 2012); Catherine Wendy Bracewell, *The Uskoks of Senj: Piracy, Banditry, and Holy War in the Sixteenth-Century Adriatic* (Ithaca, NY: Cornell University Press, 1992).

72 Marcus Rediker has attempted the rehabilitation of Atlantic pirates rather as Hobsbawm did for bandits. See Marcus Rediker, *Outlaws of the Atlantic: Sailors, Pirates and Motley Crews in the Age of Sail* (London: Verso, 2014); *Villains of All Nations: Atlantic Pirates in the Golden Age* (London: Verso, 2004).

73 Daniel J. Vitkus, ed., Introduced by Nabil Matar, *Piracy, Slavery and Redemption: Barbary Captivity Narratives from Early Modern England* (New York: Columbia University Press, 2001), 11–12.

74 Corsair is an Italian loanword, adopted into Arabic in order to mark the distinction with pirate, known as *liss al-bahr* (sea-robber). J. B. Kelly, C. H. Imber, and Ch. Pellat, 'Kursān', *Encyclopaedia of Islam*, 2nd edn. (Leiden: Brill, 1960–2004).

75 Giovanni Bonello, 'Pirates in the Early British Era: The Malta Connections', *The Malta Historical Society*, 2010. Available online: http://www.mhs.eu.pn/60/60_21.html (accessed 27 June 2019).

76 Ibid.

77 Ibid.

78 Julia Clancy-Smith, *Mediterraneans: North Africa and Europe in an Age of Migrations, c. 1800–1900* (Berkeley: University of California Press, 2010), 171.

79 Marinos Sariyannis, '"Neglected Trades": Glimpses into the 17th Century Istanbul Underworld', *Turcica* 38 (2006): 155–179, 162.

80 'Kursān', *Encyclopaedia of Islam*.

81 Marinos Sariyannis, 'Images of the Mediterranean in an Ottoman Pirate Novel from the Late Seventeenth Century', *Journal of Ottoman Studies* 39 (2012): 189–204.

82 Clancy-Smith, *Mediterraneans*, 177.

83 Ibid., 172–173.

84 The capacity of an individual story simultaneously to possess absolutely contradictory meanings for the state and its elites on the one hand, and the poor on the other, is strikingly illustrated by the life of Adham al-Sharqawi, an Egyptian bandit of the early twentieth century. Whether al-Sharqawi emerges as a tyrant terrorizing the countryside or as a noble robber defending the oppressed from landlords and colonial officials, depends entirely on whether the sources used are newspaper and police reports or the *mawawil* (ballads) of the peasantry. Ezzeldin, 'History and Memory of Bandits in Modern Egypt'.

85 Jiři Cejpek, 'Iranian Folk Literature', in *History of Iranian Literature*, ed. Jan Rypka (Dordrecht: D. Reidel, 1968), 654–655.

86 Sariyannis, '"Neglected Trades"', 172.

87 Ibid., 172–173.

88 The ideological similarity between social bandit and luti tropes has been examined by Asghar Fathi, 'The Role of the "Rebels" in the Consitutional Movement in Iran', *International Journal of Middle East Studies* 10, no. 1 (1979): 55–66; Anja Pistor-Hatem, 'Sattār Khan', *Encyclopaedia Iranica*, 2009. Available online: http://www.iranicaonline.org/articles/sattar-khan-one-of-the-most-popular-heroes-from-tabriz-who-defended-the-town-during-the-lesser-autocracy-in-1908-09 (accessed 27 June 2019); 'The Iranian Constitutional Revolution as lieu(x) de mémoire: Sattar Khan', in *Iran's Constitutional Revolution: Popular Politics, Cultural Transformation and Transnational Connections*, ed. H. E. Chehabi and Vanessa Martin (New York: I.B. Tauris, 2010).

89 For the lutis in Iran see Vanessa Martin, *The Qajar Pact: Bargaining, Protest and the State in Nineteenth-Century Persia* (New York: I.B. Tauris, 2005), 113–132; for the *qabadays* see Phillip S. Khoury, 'Abu Ali al-Kilawi: A Damascus Qabaday', in *Struggle and Survival in the Modern Middle East*, eds Edmund Burke and David N. Yaghoubian (Berkeley: University of California Press, 2006), 152–163; Rebecca Joubin, 'The Politics of the Qabaday (Tough Man) and the Changing Father Figure in Syrian Televsion Drama', *Journal of Middle East Women's Studies* 12, no. 1 (2016): 50–56, for the *futuwwat*, see Hanan Hammad, *Industrial Sexuality: Gender, Urbanization, and Social Transformation in Egypt* (Austin: University of Texas Press, 2016); for a discussion of the *baltagiya* in contemporary Egypt, see Salwa Ismail, *Political Life in Cairo's New Quarters: Encountering the Everyday State* (Minneapolis: University of Minnesota Press, 2006), 139–145.

90 Martin, *The Qajar Pact*.

91 Fathi, 'The Role of the "Rebels"', 57.

92 Barkey, *Bandits and Bureaucrats*, 181–182.

93 Ibid., p. 181; Judith M. Wilks, 'The Persianization of Köroğlu: Banditry and Royalty in Three Versions of the Köruğlu "Destan"', *Asian Folklore Studies* 60, no. 2 (2001): 305–318. For an interesting example of the role of intellectuals in the production

of bandit myths, see Alexander Chodzko, *Specimens of the Popular Poetry of Persia: As Found in the Adventures and Improvisations of Kurroglou, the Bandit-minstrel of Northern Persia and in the Songs of the People Inhabiting the Shores of the Caspian Sea* (London: Printed for the Oriental Translation Fund of Great Britain and Ireland, 1842); Jean Calmard, 'Chodźko, Aleksander Borejko', *Encyclopaedia Iranica* 5, no. 5 (1991): 502–504.

94 Amrouni, 'Les bandits d'honneur d'Algérie; Ouatmani, 'Arezki L'Bachir'. Arezki has found his way into film, see *Arezki l'indigène* (dir. Djamel Bendeddouche, 2007).

95 The story of Abdun is drawn from Hart, *Banditry in Islam*, 37–40. See also Emile Violard, *Le Banditisme en Kabylie* (Paris: A. Savine, 1895).

96 Jean Déjeux, 'Un Bandit d'Honneur dans l'Aurès, de 1917 a 1921', *Revue de l'Occident musulman et de la Méditerranée* 26 (1978): 35–54. Ben Zelmat's story is summarized by Hart, *Banditry in Islam*, 42–45. see also Fanny Colonna, *Le Meunier, les moines et le bandit: Des vies quotidiennes dans l'Aurès (Algerie) du XXe siècle* (Paris: Sindbad, 2010).

97 Cited by Déjeux, 'Un Bandit d'Honneur', 42.

98 Ibid., 45.

99 For examples see ibid., 46–49.

100 For Sattar Khan see Pistor-Hatem, 'Sattār Khan', *Encyclopaedia Iranica*; 'The Iranian Constitutional Revolution as lieu(x) de mémoire'.

101 Reza Afshari, 'The Historians of the Constitutional Movement and the Making of the Iranian Populst Tradition', *International Journal of Middle East Studies* 25, no. 3 (1993): 477–494.

102 Fathi, 'The Role of the "Rebels"', 62–63.

103 For a further discussion of the role of bandits and desperadoes in the political turmoil of the constitutional years, see the recent study of Na'ib Husayn Khan Kashi and his gang. Hadjiheidari, 'Nāyeb Ḥoseyn Kāšī, Strassenräuber oder Revolutionär?'

104 Hobsbawm, *Bandits*, 35.

105 Ryan Gingeras, 'Beyond Istanbul's "Laz Underworld": Ottoman Paramilitarism and the Rise of Turkish Organised Crime', *Contemporary European History* 19, no. 3 (2010): 215–230; Judith Scheele, *Smugglers and Saints of the Sahara* (Cambridge: Cambridge University Press, 2015). For a recent discussion of smuggling and the interrelationships of smugglers, bazaaris and state agents in the context of the Islamic Republic of Iran see Narges Erami and Arang Keshavarzian, 'When Ties Don't Bind: Smuggling Effects, Bazaars and Regulatory Regimes in Postrevolutionary Iran', *Economy and Society* 44, no. 1 (February 2015): 110–139.

Chapter 6

1 See Alain Mahé, *Histoire de la Grande-Kabylie* (Paris: Bouchene, [2001] 2006), 218.

2 Alain Sainte-Marie, *Réflexions sur l'histoire du grand-banditisme* (Oran: CRIDSSH, 1984).

3 Corey Robin, *Fear, The History of a Political Idea* (Oxford: Oxford University Press, 2004).

4 Parquet du procureur général, 6 mars 1894, Archives Nationales (hereafter AN), Paris, BB-18-1968.

5   Eric Hobsbawm, *Bandits* (London: Weidenfeld and Nicolson, [1969] 2000); see Chapter 5 in this volume.

6   Jean Dejeux, 'Un Bandit d'honneur dans l'Aures, de 1917 à 1921', *Revue de l'Occident musulman et de la Méditerranée* 1, no. 26 (1978): 35–54.

7   David M. Hart, *Banditry in Islam: Case Studies from Morocco, Algeria and the Pakistan North West Frontier* (Wisbech: Menas Press, 1987).

8   Mahé, *Histoire de la Grande-Kabylie*, 218.

9   Mahfoud Kaddache, *Histoire du nationalisme algérien* (Alger: EDIF, 2000; Paris: Méditerranée, 2003), vol. 1, 25.

10   Frederick Cooper, *Colonialism in Question* (Berkeley: University of California Press, 2005).

11   The ordinances of 1844 and 1846 enabled French authorities to confiscate sections or entire plots of Algerian-owned land. The *senatus-consulte* delimited Algerian landed property which finally reinforced a regime of private landownership in Algeria that favoured European proprietors. See André Nouschi, 'La dépossession foncière et la paupérisation de la paysannerie algérienne', in *Histoire de l'Algérie à la période colonial*, ed. Abderrahmane Bouchène, Jean-Pierre Peyroulou, Sylvie Thénault, Ouanassa Siari Tengour (Alger: Barzakh; Paris: La Découverte, 2012), 190. John Ruedy, *Land Policy in Algeria* (Berkeley: University of California Press, 1967), 115.

12   Mohamed Brahim Salhi, 'L'insurrection de 1871', in *Histoire de l'Algérie à la période coloniale*, eds A. Bouchène et al. (Alger: Barzakh; Paris: La Découverte, 2012), 110.

13   Hobsbawm, *Bandits*, p. 28.

14   Charles Robert Ageron, *Les Algériens musulmans et la France (1871–1919)* (Saint-Denis: Bouchène, [1968] 2005), vol. 1, 24.

15   André Nouschi, *Enquête sur le niveau de vie des populations rurales constantinoises* (Saint-Denis: Bouchène, [1961] 2013), 329.

16   Henri Peyerimhoff, *Enquête sur les résultats de la colonisation officielle* (Alger: Imprimerie Torrent, 1906).

17   Ibid., p. 74.

18   Antonin Plarier, 'Banditisme et dépossession foncière en Algérie', in *Propriété et Société en Algérie contemporaine*, ed. D. Guignard (Aix-en-Provence: IREMAM, 2017), 194–205.

19   Nouschi, *Enquête sur le niveau de vie des populations rurales constantinoises*, 100.

20   Loi du 16 juin 1851 *in* M. Boutilly, *Recueil de la législation forestière algérienne* (Paris: Berger-Levrault Editeurs, 1904).

21   Diana K. Davis, *Resurrecting the Granary of Rome: Environmental History and French Colonia Expansion in North Africa* (Athens: Ohio University Press, 2007).

22   Ageron, *Les Algériens musulmans et la France (1871–1919)*, 123.

23   Nouschi, *Enquête sur le niveau de vie des populations rurales constantinoises*.

24   H. Marc, *Notes sur les Forêts en Algérie* (Paris: Larose, 1930).

25   Ageron, *Les Algériens musulmans et la France (1871–1919)*.

26   Cited by Davis, *Resurrecting the Granary of Rome: Environmental History and French Colonia Expansion in North Africa*, 145.

27   Ageron, *Les Algériens musulmans et la France (1871–1919)*, 126.

28   Gouvernement Général de l'Algérie, *Exposé de la situation de l'Algérie* (Alger: Imprimerie Juillet-Saint-Lager, 1904), 276.

29   Gouvernement Général de l'Algérie, *Exposé de la situation de l'Algérie* (Alger: Imprimerie Juillet-Saint-Lager, 1902), 236.

30 Jules Ferry, *Rapport fait au nom de la commission chargée d'examiner les modifications à introduire dans la législation et dans l'organisation des divers services de l'Algérie*, 1892, Archives Nationales d'Outre Mer (hereafter ANOM), 8X166.
31 Ibid.
32 Ageron, *Les Algériens musulmans et la France (1871–1919)*, 122.
33 E. P. Thompson, *Whigs and Hunters, the Origin of the Black Act* (London: Allen Lane, 1975).
34 Direction de l'agriculture, du commerce de la colonisation, Note pour le gouverneur général, 22 janvier 1909, Alger, Archives Nationales (hereafter DZAN), 12E-2082.
35 Jean Morizot, *L'Aurès ou le mythe de la montagne rebelle* (Paris: L'Harmattan, 1992).
36 A *garde-champêtre*, literally 'rural guard', combined the roles of forest ranger, game warden and police officer. Unlike forest rangers who were hired by the state, gardes-champêtre served rural communes and private land owners alike. Forest rangers were better paid and had greater powers to punish forest delinquency. Neither should be confused with indigenous or native guards who assisted gardes-champêtre and forest rangers, mostly serving as interpreters.
37 Conseil de Gouvernement, Séance du 17 février 1869, Délimitation du territoire de la tribu des Beni Salah, ANOM, 3F61.
38 Conseil de Gouvernement, Séance du 25 avril 1878, Incendies survenus pendant le mois d'août 1877 dans le nord est du département de Constantine, ANOM, P62.
39 Ibid.
40 Marc, *Notes sur les Forêts en Algérie*.
41 Conseil de Gouvernement, Séance du 17 février 1869, Délimitation du territoire de la tribu des Beni Salah, ANOM, 3F61.
42 Didier Guignard, 'Conservatoire ou révolutionnaire ? Le sénatus-consulte de 1863 appliqué au régime foncier d'Algérie', *Revue d'histoire du XIXe siècle* 41 (2010) : 81–95.
43 Au sujet de la situation politique du cercle de Souk Ahras, Lettre du chef du bureau arabe au général commandant la subdivision, 1er décembre 1876, ANOM, 24KK22.
44 Lettre du chef du bureau arabe de Souk Ahras au général commandant la subdivision de Bône, 15 septembre 1876, ANOM, 24KK24.
45 Rapport au sujet de la première partie de la conférence de 1880 sur la frontière tunisienne, 15 mai 1880, ANOM, 25H21.
46 Procès-verbal des séances des 9 et 10 août 1885, Commission des centres, 1885, ANOM, 26L87.
47 Rapport sur la répression du banditisme présenté par M. le sous-préfet de Tizi-Ouzou au préfet d'Alger et au gouverneur général, 1894, ANOM, 1F33.
48 Younes Adli, *Si Mohand ou Mhand (Alger:* EDIF, [2000] 2001).
49 Bernard Vincent, ed., *Les Marginaux et les exclus dans l'histoire* (Paris: Union Générale d'Edition, 1979).
50 Avis du conseil d'administration, séance du 22 mai 1878, AN, BB-24-2046-1.
51 Rapport du sous-préfet de Tizi Ouzou, 1895, ANOM, 1F33.
52 Max Weber, *Weber's Rationalism and Modern Society* (New York: Palgrave Macmillan, 2015).
53 Cour d'assises d'Oran – 1re session extraordinaire de 1876 – Présidence de M. le conseiller Perriné retranscrit *in* L'Echo d'Oran, 19 mai 1876.
54 Ibid.
55 Rapport sur la répression du banditisme présenté par M. le sous-préfet de Tizi-Ouzou au préfet d'Alger et au gouverneur général, 1894, ANOM, 1F33.

56   Ibid.

57   Cour d'assises d'Oran – 1re session extraordinaire de 1876 – Présidence de M. le
     conseiller Perriné retranscrit *in* L'Echo d'Oran, 19 mai 1876.

58   Ibid.

59   Ibid.

60   Jacques Francoeur, 'Le roi de la forêt', *La Revue algérienne illustrée*, 2e trimestre, 5, no.
     10 (1893) : 134–137.

61   Rapport sur la répression du banditisme présenté par M. le sous-préfet de Tizi-
     Ouzou au préfet d'Alger et au gouverneur général, 1894, ANOM, 1F33.

62   These data are the result of a systematic study of banditry sentences in Algeria in this
     period as well as related petitions for mercy. There are forty-nine cases in the BB24
     file of the French archives nationales in Pierrefitte. Out of these cases, nineteen fall
     within what we have defined as banditry. The criteria used here to define banditry
     are the multiplicity of the acts committed, the fact that one of these acts resulted in
     a prosecution which the person or group of persons being sued evaded by 'taking to
     the forest' and continuing their legally reprehensible activities. These 19 cases involve
     77 defendants and encompass 134 sentences. They do not represent the whole reality
     of banditry for several reasons. In order to be included in this file, a case had to
     include at least one death sentence that was carried out. Moreover, the charges are
     not necessarily exhaustive or representative of the bandits' activity. Their inclusion
     in the case depended on the capacity of the prosecution to generate testimonies that
     could lead to conviction. Many acts therefore escaped judgement.

63   Ministère de la justice, Direction des affaires criminelles et des grâces, dossier n°2772
     S.75, AN, BB24-2041.

64   Ministère de la justice, Direction des affaires criminelles et des grâces, dossier n°2848
     S.83, AN, BB24-2053.

65   N. Bendedouche, *Bouzian el Kalaï*, Manuscrit (1977), 67.

66   s.n., coupure de presse, 2 juin 1894, conservé par le sous-préfet de Tizi-Ouzou,
     ANOM, 1F33.

67   Rapport sur la répression du banditisme présenté par M. le sous-préfet de Tizi-
     Ouzou au préfet d'Alger et au gouverneur général, 1894, ANOM, 1F33.

68   James C. Scott, *Domination and the art of resistance* (New Haven, CT: Yale University
     Press, 1990).

69   Sylvie Thénault, *Violence ordinaire dans l'Algérie coloniale* (Paris: Odile Jacob, 2012),
     51.

70   Camille Sabatier, *La Question de la sécurité, insurrections, criminalité: les difficultés
     algériennes* (Alger: A. Jourdan, 1882), 6.

71   Ageron, *Les Algériens musulmans et la France (1871–1919)*, 240.

72   Lettre de l'administrateur M. Bouchot au sous-préfet de Tizi-Ouzou, 28 novembre
     1893, ANOM, 1F33.

73   Lettre du commissaire de police à Blida au préfet d'Alger, 11 octobre 1906, ANOM,
     1F34.

74   Thénault, *Violence ordinaire dans l'Algérie coloniale*, 123.

75   Sous-préfet de Bône à Monsieur le Préfet, 7 octobre 1881, ANOM, B3-294.

76   Requête des Beni Salah adressée au préfet de Constantine, 13 septembre 1883,
     ANOM, B3-294.

77   Correspondance entre le ministre de la Guerre et le ministre de l'Intérieur, 30
     décembre 1874, ANOM, F80-1683-A.

78 After the First World War, these bounties could reach the phenomenal amount of 10,000 francs. Administrateur adjoint de Batna, novembre 1920, ANOM, 1F33.
79 See Diaire des Pères blancs de Médina, 10 octobre 1914, Rome, Société des Missionnaires d'Afrique, D-OR-35.
80 Rapport du sous-préfet de Tizi Ouzou, 1894, ANOM, 1F33.
81 Procureur général près la cour d'appel d'Alger à Monsieur le Garde des Sceaux, Alger, 7 mars 1904, AN, Paris, BB18-2275.
82 Antonin Plarier, *Le banditisme en Algérie pendant la Première Guerre mondiale* (Paris: Karthala, forthcoming).
83 Eric Hobsbawm, *Les Bandits* (Paris: Zones, [1969] 2008), 9.

Chapter 7

1 Arnold Wilson, *SW. Persia: A Political Officer's Diary 1907–1914* (London: Oxford University Press, 1941), 189.
2 Stephanie Cronin, *Tribal Politics in Iran: Rural Conflict and the New State, 1921–1941* (London: Routledge/Taylor & Francis Group, 2007); Kaveh Bayat, 'Riza Shah and the Tribes: An Overview', in *The Making of Modern Iran: State and Society under Riza Shah, 1921–1941*, ed. Stephanie Cronin (Abingdon: Routledge, 2003), 213–219.
3 Oliver Bast, 'Disintegrating the "Discourse of Disintegration": Some Reflections on the Historiography of the Late Qajar Period and Iranian Cultural Memory', in *Iran in the 20th Century: Historiography and Political Culture*, ed. Touraj Atabaki (London: I.B. Tauris, 2009), 55–68; cf. Stephanie Cronin, *The Army and the Creation of the Pahlavi State in Iran, 1910–1926* (London: I.B. Tauris, 1996).
4 See, for example, the public discussion about tribes during the Constitutional Revolution in Afsaneh Najmabadi, *The Story of the Daughters of Quchan: Gender and National Memory in Iranian History* (Syracuse, NY: Syracuse University Press, 1998).
5 The term 'tribe' is used here as a translation for various Persian terms commonly referring to nomadic pastoralist groups such as 'ashayer or *ilat*. As such, I employ it differently to its function as a designation of primordial racial difference in wider British colonial discourse and administration, which is beyond the scope of this study.
   I use the term 'dangerous class' here not so much in the classic sense of a being a feature of urban poverty and mass urbanization as set out famously in Louis Chevalier, *Labouring and Dangerous Classes in Paris during the First Half of the Nineteenth Century*, trans. Frank Jellinek (London: Routledge & Kegan Paul, [1958] 1973). Rather, I use it metaphorically to refer to a social group seen to be highly or necessarily susceptible to criminality, similar to Marx and Engels's idea of the lumpenproletariat, but less specifically concerned with an underclass of the urban working class; see Robert L. Bussard, 'The "Dangerous Class" of Marx and Engels: The Rise of the Idea of the *Lumpenproletariat*', *History of European Ideas* 8, no. 6 (1987): 675–692.
6 The term 'criminal tribe' emerged in colonial British India to refer to certain tribes that the authorities believed to be naturally inclined to crime, even from birth; see Anand A. Yang, 'Dangerous Castes and Tribes: The Criminal Tribes Act and the Magahiya Doms of Northeast India', in *Crime and Criminality in British India*, ed. Anand A. Yang (Tucson: University of Arizona Press, 1985), 108–127; Stewart N.

Gordon, 'Bhils and the Idea of A Criminal Tribe in Nineteenth-Century India', in *Crime and Criminality in British India*, ed. Anand A. Yang (Tucson: University of Arizona Press, 1985), 128–139. For a powerful critique of the discursive concept of 'criminal tribe' see David Arnold, 'Dacoity and Rural Crime in Madras, 1860–1940', *Journal of Peasant Studies* 6 (1979): 140–167.

7   Mansoureh Ettehadieh, 'Crime, Security, and Insecurity: Socio-Political Conditions of Iran, 1875–1924', in *War and Peace in Qajar Persia: Implications Past and Present*, ed. Roxane Farmanfarmaian (London: Routledge, 2008), 181.

8   Eric J. Hobsbawm, *Bandits*, new edn. (London: Abacus, [1969] 2001); cf. Eric J. Hobsbawm, *Primitive Rebels: Studies in Archaic Forms of Social Movements in the 19th and 20th Centuries* (Manchester: Manchester University Press, 1959).

9   Douglas Hay, Peter Linebaugh, John G. Rule, E. P. Thompson and Cal Winslow, *Albion's Fatal Tree: Crime and Society in Eighteenth-Century England*, rev. edn. (London: Verso, [1975] 2011); and E. P. Thompson, *Whigs and Hunters: The Origin of the Black Act* (New York: Pantheon Books, 1975) have been especially influential in this field. The concept of 'social crime' has been subject to much critical historical debate; for an overview see Paul Knepper, *Writing the History of Crime* (London: Bloomsbury Academic, 2016); and Paul Lawrence, 'The Historiography of Crime and Criminal Justice', in *The Oxford Handbook of the History of Crime and Criminal Justice*, eds Paul Knepper and Anja Johansen (London: Oxford University Press, 2016), 17–37. For more recent attempts to defend the concept see John Rule, 'Social Crime in the Rural South in the Eighteenth and Nineteenth Centuries', in *Crime, Protest, and Popular Politics in Southern England, 1740–1850*, eds John Rule and Roger A. E. Wells (London: Hambledon Press, 1997), 153–168; and John Lea, 'Social Crime Revisited', *Theoretical Criminology* 3, no. 3 (1999): 307–325.

10   Edward Muir and Guido Ruggiero, eds, *History From Crime* (Baltimore: Johns Hopkins University Press, 1994), 226.

11   Florike Egmond, *Underworlds: Organized Crime in the Netherlands, 1650–1800* (Cambridge: Polity Press, 1993), 19.

12   See Chapter 5, in this volume. Notable exceptions in the Middle East and North Africa context are David Prochaska, 'Fire on the Mountain: Resisting Colonialism in Algeria', in *Banditry, Rebellion and Social Protest in Africa*, ed. Donald Crummey (London: James Curry, 1986), 229–252; and David M. Hart, *Banditry in Islam: Case Studies from Morocco, Algeria and the Pakistan North West Frontier* (Wisbech: Middle East & North African Studies Press, 1987). For a discussion of the social banditry thesis in relation to Latin America see Richard W. Slatta, ed., *Bandidos: The Varieties of Latin American Banditry* (New York: Greenwood Press, 1987). For Australia, see Pat O'Malley, 'Social Bandits, Modern Capitalism and the Traditional Peasantry. A Critique of Hobsbawm', *Journal of Peasant Studies* 6, no. 9 (1979): 489–501. For the USA, see Richard White, 'Outlaw Gangs of the Middle Border: American Social Bandits', *Western Historical Quarterly* 12, no. 4 (October 1981): 387–408. For China, see Robert J. Antony, 'Peasants, Heroes and Brigands: The Problems of Social Banditry in Early Nineteenth-Century South China', *Modern China* 15, no. 2 (April 1989): 123–148. For a Southeast Asian example, see Boon Kheng Cheah, *The Peasant Robbers of Kedah, 1900–1919: Historical and Folk Perceptions* (London: Oxford University Press, 1988). For numerous examples in sub-Saharan Africa see essays in Donald Crummey, ed., *Banditry, Rebellion and Social Protest in Africa* (London: James Curry, 1986). And for India see the essays in Anand A. Yang, ed., *Crime and Criminality in British India* (Tucson: University of Arizona Press, 1985); and Kim

A. Wagner, *Thuggee: Banditry and the British in Early Nineteenth-Century India* (Basingstoke: Palgrave Macmillan, 2007).

13   Karen Barkey, *Bandits and Bureaucrats: The Ottoman Route to Centralization* (Ithaca, NY: Cornell University Press, 1994); Nathan Brown, 'Brigands and State Building: The Invention of Banditry in Modern Egypt', *Comparative Studies in Society and History* 32, no. 2 (April 1990): 258–281; a more nuanced account is provided in Fulya Ozkan, 'Gravediggers of the Modern State: Highway Robbers on the Trabzon-Bayezid Road, 1850s–1910s', *Journal of Persianate Studies* 7 (2014): 219–250. Suraiya Faroqhi perhaps goes furthest to explain the socio-economic and political dimensions of banditry in the Ottoman Empire, including the motivations of bandits themselves; see Suraiya Faroqhi, *Coping with the State: Political Conflict and Crime in the Ottoman Empire, 1550–1720* (Istanbul: Isis Press, 1995); cf. Chapter 8, in this volume.

14   Anton Blok, 'The Peasant and the Brigand: Social Banditry Reconsidered', *Comparative Studies in Society and History* 14, no. 4 (September 1972): 494–503.

15   On the role of tribes in Iranian governance, see Richard Tapper, 'The Tribes in Eighteenth and Nineteenth Century Iran', in *The Cambridge History of Iran*, vol. 7, eds Peter Avery, Gavin Hambly and C. P. Melville (Cambridge: Cambridge University Press, 1991), 506–541. On the importance of tribes in state formation in the Middle Eastern context more generally see the essays in Philip S. Khoury and Joseph Kostiner, eds, *Tribes and State Formation in the Middle East* (Berkeley: University of California Press, 1990).

16   Hobsbawm, *Bandits*, 20.

17   It has been long acknowledged that raiding, at least against sedentary populations, could be an economic necessity for survival in times of difficulty. For example see Louise E. Sweet, 'Camel Raiding of North Arabian Bedouin: A Mechanism of Ecological Adaptation', *American Anthropologist* 67, no. 5 (October 1965): 1132–1150.

18   John Chalcraft, 'Engaging the State: Peasants and Petitions in Egypt on the Eve of Colonial Rule', *International Journal of Middle East Studies* 37 (2005): 303–325; Kyle J. Anderson, 'The Egyptian Labor Corps: Workers, Peasants, and the State in World War I', *International Journal of Middle East Studies* 49 (2017): 5–24. On the perils of uncovering the liberal humanist subject in subaltern studies see Rosalind O'Hanlon, 'Recovering the Subject: Subaltern Studies and Histories of Resistance in Colonial South Asia', *Modern Asian Studies* 22, no. 1 (1988): 189–224. For a related discussion concerning resistance in a Middle Eastern context see Anne Clément, 'Rethinking "Peasant Consciousness" in Colonial Egypt: An Exploration of the Performance of Folksongs by Upper Egyptian Agricultural Workers on the Archaeological Excavation Sites of Karnak and Dendera at the Turn of the Twentieth Century (1885–1914)', *History and Anthropology* 21, no. 2 (June 2010): 73–100; Lila Abu-Lughod, 'The Romance of Resistance: Tracing Transformations of Power Through Bedouin Women', *American Ethnologist* 17, no. 1 (February 1990): 41–55; Timothy Mitchell, 'Everyday Metaphors of Power', *Theory and Society* 19, no. 5 (October 1990): 545–577; and Saba Mahmood, *Politics of Piety: The Islamic Revival and the Feminist Subject* (Princeton, NJ: Princeton University Press, 2012).

19   Vanessa Martin, *The Qajar Pact: Bargaining, Protest and the State in Nineteenth-Century Persia* (London: I.B. Tauris, 2005).

20   John T. Chalcraft, *Popular Politics in the Making of the Modern Middle East* (Cambridge: Cambridge University Press, 2016), 15.

21   Ibid. On the creativity of protest in late Qajar and early Pahlavi Iran, especially see
     Stephanie Cronin, *Soldiers, Shahs and Subalterns in Iran: Opposition, Protest and
     Revolt, 1921–1941* (Basingstoke: Palgrave Macmillan, 2010).

22   As Chalcraft explains in reference to Gramsci, hegemonic contraction involves
     the eroding of existing forms of consent previously underpinning the authority of
     elites, as well as elites' inability to subsequently find new sources of legitimacy; see
     Chalcraft, *Popular Politics in the Making of the Modern Middle East*, 36–39.

23   Cronin, *Tribal Politics in Iran*; Khazeni, *Tribes & Empire on the Margins of
     Nineteenth-Century Iran*.

24   Lois Beck, *The Qashqa'i of Iran* (New Haven, CT: Yale University Press, 1986), 127;
     Floreeda Safiri, 'The South Persian Rifles' (PhD Thesis, University of Edinburgh,
     1976).

25   Morteza Nouraei and Vanessa Martin, 'Part II: The Karguzar and Security, the Trade
     Routes of Iran and Foreign Subjects 1900–1921', *Journal of the Royal Asiatic Society*
     16, no. 1 (April 2006): 29–41.

26   Alf Lüdtke, 'Introduction: What Is the History of Everyday Life and Who Are Its
     Practitioners?', in *The History of Everyday Life: Reconstructing Historical Experiences
     and Ways of Life*, ed. Alf Lüdtke, trans. William Templer (Princeton, NJ: Princeton
     University Press, 1995), 4.

27   Henri Lefebvre, *Critique of Everyday Life: The One-Volume Edition* (London: Verso,
     2014), 453. Cf. Michel de Certeau, *The Practice of Everyday Life*, trans. Steven F.
     Rendall (Berkeley: University of California Press, 1984).

28   Lüdtke, 'Introduction: What Is the History of Everyday Life and Who Are Its
     Practitioners?', 6. In this argument I am, of course, also drawing on E. P. Thompson,
     The Making of the English Working Class, rev. edn. (London: Penguin, [1963] 2013).

29   For a theoretical discussion on the interaction between the local and the global in the
     construction of space, see Doreen Massey, *For Space* (London: Sage, 2005).

30   Maral Jefroudi, 'The Opening-Up of the Past and the Possibilities of Global History
     for Iranian Historiography', in *Iran in the Middle East: Transnational Encounters and
     Social History*, eds Houchang Chehabi, Peyman Jafari and Maral Jefroudi (London:
     I.B. Tauris, 2015), 235–248.

31   F. Vejdani, 'Illict Acts and Sacred Space: Everyday Crime in the Shrine City of
     Mashhad, 1913–1914', *Journal of Persianate Studies* 7 (2014): 22–54.

32   On the attitudes of Iranian elites and intellectuals towards crime see, for instance,
     Cyrus Schayegh, 'Serial Murder in Tehran: Crime, Science, and the Formation of
     Modern State and Society in Interwar Iran', *Comparative Studies in Society and
     History* 47, no. 4 (October 2005): 836–862; Darius M. Rejali, *Torture & Modernity:
     Self, Society, and State in Modern Iran* (Boulder, CO: Westview Press, 1994); and Hadi
     Enayat, *Law, State and Society in Modern Iran: Constitutionalism, Autocracy, and
     Legal Reform, 1906–1941* (Basingstoke: Palgrave Macmillan, 2013).

33   Charles Philip Issawi, *The Economic History of Iran, 1800–1914* (Chicago: University
     of Chicago Press, 1971), 152–205.

34   Pierre Oberling, *The Qashqa'i Nomads of Fars* (The Hague: Mouton, 1974), 84.

35   Beck, *The Qashqa'i of Iran*, 90.

36   Ibid.

37   Ibid., 83.

38   Edward G. Browne, *A Year Amongst the Persians* (London: Adam and Charles Black,
     1893), 192–193.

39 For a brief summary of the role of the *ilkhani* and the structure of hierarchy within the Qashqai confederation, see Oberling, *The Qashqa'i Nomads of Fars*, 21–25; for a more thorough account, see Beck, *The Qashqa'i of Iran*, 163–234.

40 Beck, *The Qashqa'i of Iran*, 91.

41 Messrs Ziegler and Co. and Dixon & Co. to Board of Trade, 29 December 1909, L/PS/10/163, India Office Records (hereafter IOR).

42 Memorandum by Chick enclosed in telegram from Cox to Grey, 15 December 1912, L/PS/10/299, IOR.

43 Barclay to Persian Government, 14 October 1910, L/PS/10/163, IOR.

44 'Report on Fars by Captain A T Wilson, Indian Political Department', p. 39, L/PS/20/7, IOR.

45 Arthur Moore, *The Orient Express* (London: Constable & Company, 1914), 121–122.

46 Wilson, *SW. Persia: A Political Officer's Diary 1907–1914*, 191.

47 Memorandum by Chick enclosed in telegram from Cox to Grey, 15 December 1912, L/PS/10/299, IOR.

48 'Ali Akbar Sa'idi Sirjani, *Vaqaye'-e Ettefaqiyeh: Majmu'eh-e Gozareshha-ye Khafiyeh Nevisan-e Inglis Dar Velayat-E Jonubi-ye Iran Az Sal-e 1291 Ta 1322* (Tehran: Entesharat-e Novin, 1362), 712, 2 Jomada Avval 1321 [27 July 1903].

49 Janet Afary, *The Iranian Constitutional Revolution, 1906–1911 : Grassroots Democracy, Social Democracy, & the Origins of Feminism* (New York : Columbia University Press, 1996), 269.

50 Hooshang Amirahmadi, *The Political Economy of Iran under the Qajars: Society, Politics, Economics and Foreign Relations, 1796–1926* (London: I.B. Tauris, 2012), 23; John Foran, 'The Concept of Dependent Development as a Key to the Political Economy of Qajar Iran (1800–1925)', *Iranian Studies* 22, no. 2–3 (1989): 5–56, esp. 25–28; Issawi, *The Economic History of Iran, 1800–1914*, 18; Ahmad Seyf, 'Commercialization of Agriculture: Production and Trade of Opium in Persia, 1850–1906', *International Journal of Middle East Studies* 16, no. 2 (May 1984): 233–250.

51 Ann K. S. Lambton, *Landlord and Peasant in Persia: A Study of Land Tenure and Land Revenue Administration* (London: Oxford University Press, 1953), 152–153; Amirahmadi, *The Political Economy of Iran under the Qajars*, 23.

52 Amirahmadi, *The Political Economy of Iran under the Qajars*, 23; Foran, 'The Concept of Dependent Development', 31. For a more detailed outline of the stratification of villages, see Amirahmadi, *The Political Economy of Iran under the Qajars*, 51–54; Eric J. Hooglund, *Land and Revolution in Iran, 1960–1980* (Austin: University of Texas Press, 1982), 10–35; and Farhad Kazemi and Ervand Abrahamian, 'The Nonrevolutionary Peasantry of Modern Iran', *Iranian Studies* 11 (1978): 259–304.

53 Ranin Kazemi, 'Of Diet and Profit: On the Question of Subsistence Crises in Nineteenth-Century Iran', *Middle Eastern Studies* 52, no. 2 (2016): 335–358. The connection between the commercialization of agriculture and political protest in late nineteenth-century Iran has also been examined in Stephanie Cronin, 'Bread and Justice in Qajar Iran: The Moral Economy, the Free Market and the Hungry Poor', *Middle Eastern Studies* 54, no. 6 (2018): 843–877.

54 Idem, 'The Tobacco Protest in Nineteenth-Century Iran: The View from a Provincial Town', *Journal of Persianate Studies* 7 (2014): 251–295.

55 This was identified by Hobsbawm himself in *Bandits*. For a forceful articulation of this point, see Ranajit Guha, *Elementary Aspects of Peasant Insurgency in Colonial India* (Delhi: Oxford University Press, 1983).

56   Nouraei and Martin, 'Part II: The Karguzar and Security', 31; Beck, *The Qashqa'i of Iran*, 84.

57   Report by Moir enclosed in telegram from Smart to Barclay, 3 February 1911, L/PS/10/163, IOR.

58   Extract from Shiraz Diary, No. 40, for the Week Ending 4 October 1913, L/PS/10/404, IOR.

59   Report by Moir enclosed in telegram from Smart to Barclay, 3 February 1911, L/PS/10/163, IOR.

60   Ibid.

61   Ibid.

62   Knox to Barclay, 6 November 1911, FO 228/1036, The National Archives of the United Kingdom (hereafter TNA).

63   Moore, *The Orient Express*, 122.

64   'Report on Fars by Captain A T Wilson, Indian Political Department', p. 31, L/PS/20/7, IOR.

65   Cronin, *Tribal Politics in Iran*. This view was also put forward by Arnold Wilson in his reflections on his travels in Iran, writing that by *c.* 1911, 'government by tribes and great families was at an end: the system had broken down' in Wilson, *SW. Persia: A Political Officer's Diary 1907–1914*, 187.

66   For an account of hegemonic contraction resulting from such processes in the Middle East and North Africa region more generally see Chalcraft, *Popular Politics in the Making of the Modern Middle East*.

67   For Khamseh quote see 'General Situation in Fars', Smart to Townley, 24 June 1912, FO 248/1057, TNA; for the quote by Qashqai, see 'Review of General Situation in Fars During the Past Six Months', report by Smart enclosed in telegram from Cox to Government of India, 14 November 1912, L/PS/10/357, IOR.

68   On the traditional relationship between vertical tribal authority and raiding, see Richard Tapper, 'Raiding, Reaction and Rivalry: The Shahsevan in the Constitutional Period', *Bulletin of the School of Oriental and African Studies* 49, no. 3 (October 1986): 508–531, esp. 526, 529; and Pierre Oberling, 'The Tribes of Qaraca Dag: A Brief History', *Oriens* 17 (December 1964): 60–95, esp. 60–64.

69   Telegram by Smart, 28 May 1912, FO 248/1057, TNA.

70   'General Situation in Fars', Smart to Townley, 24 June 1912, FO 248/1057, TNA.

71   Diary of Shiraz Consulate for the Week Ending 21 December 1912, FO 248/1057, TNA.

72   On the peasant rebellions in Gilan see Afary, *The Iranian Constitutional Revolution*, 154–162.

73   See Cronin in this volume. A similar point is made by Faroqhi in relation to the Anatolian Steppes in Faroqhi, *Coping with the State*, 158.

74   Mirzai has shown how slavery could have a similar function in times of destitution in Iran; see Behnaz A. Mirzai, *A History of Slavery and Emancipation in Iran, 1800–1929* (Austin: University of Texas Press, 2017).

75   Martin, *The Qajar Pact*, 49.

76   On the roles of *lutis* in public life, see Reza Arasteh, 'The Character, Organization and Social Role of the Lutis (Javan-Mardan) in the Traditional Iranian Society of the Nineteenth Century', *Journal of the Economic and Social History of the Orient* 4, no. 1 (February 1961): 47–52.

77   Martin, *The Qajar Pact*, 115. Bell has recently made a convincing case for the overlap of gender and sexuality in the criminalization of *lutis* as deviant, dangerous subjects

on the margins of society; see Robert Joseph Bell, 'Luti Masculinity in Iranian Modernity, 1785–1941: Marginalization and the Anxieties of Proper Masculine Comportment' (MA thesis, City University of New York, 2015).

78   See Cronin in this volume. Cf. Martin, *The Qajar Pact*, 113–132; and Asghar Fathi, 'The Role of "Rebels" in the Constitutional Movement in Iran', *International Journal of Middle East Studies* 10, no. 1 (February 1979): 55–66.

79   Martin, *The Qajar Pact*, 113.

80   Ibid., 122. For a thorough account of the complicated role of *lutis* in urban politics more generally, see Willem M. Floor, 'The Political Role of Lutis in Iran', in *Modern Iran: The Dialectics of Continuity and Change*, eds Michael E. Bonine and Nikki R. Keddie (Albany: State University of New York Press, 1981), 83–95.

81   See Cronin in this volume; Fathi, 'The Role of "Rebels"', 57. For a discussion concerning whether Sattar Khan can be considered a 'social bandit', see Anja Pistor-Hatam, 'The Iranian Constitutional Revolution as Lieu(x) de Memoire: Sattar Khan', in *Iran's Constitutional Revolution: Popular Politics, Cultural Transformations and Transnational Connections*, eds H. E. Chehabi and Vanessa Martin (London: I.B. Tauris, 2010), 33–44. The existence of bandits in the 'Robin Hood' mould goes far back in Persian tradition in the form of *'ayyaran*. Some have argued for the origins of the phenomenon in pre-Islamic society; for example, see Mohsen Zakeri, *Sasanid Soldiers in Early Muslim Society: The Origins of 'Ayyaran and Futuwwa* (Wiesbaden: Harrassowitz Verlag, 1995). The noble robber depiction of *'ayyaran* in popular Persian romances of the medieval period such as *Samak-e 'Ayyar*, which were probably based on oral tradition, perhaps reveals the popularity and legitimacy of social banditry in wider society at the time in some form and stands in contrast to the authorities' largely negative conceptions of *'ayyaran*. For an overview of these depictions see Ameneh Gazerani, 'Thugs, Thieves, Tricksters or Popular Heroes? A Comparative Look at the Phenomenon of *'Ayyari*' (MA thesis, Ohio State University, 2003); and Claude Cahen and William L. Hanaway, Jr., "'Ayyar", *Encyclopaedia Iranica*. Available online: http://www.iranicaonline.org/articles/ayyar (accessed 7 August 2018).

82   Bill to Barclay, 26 March 1910, FO 248/1003, TNA.

83   For a recent, nuanced analysis of *lutis* and their relationship to conceptions of justice, see Farzin Vejdani, 'Urban Violence and Space: *Lutis*, Seminarians, and *Sayyids* in Late Qajar Iran', *Journal of Social History* 52, no. 4 (2019): 1185–1211; cf. Chapter 10 in this volume.

84   Shiraz News for Week Ending 2 February 1910, FO 248/1003, TNA.

85   Martin, *The Qajar Pact*, 95–112.

86   Vejdani argues that minority neighbourhoods, especially Jewish quarters, were legal 'spaces of exception' where the law was suspended insofar as the looting of these so-called 'morally polluted' areas was widely considered legitimate, helping explain why theft here was especially prevalent; see Vejdani, 'Urban Violence and Space'.

87   Martin, *The Qajar Pact*, esp. 124; cf. Vejdani, 'Urban Violence and Space'; Rejali, *Torture & Modernity*, 30.

88   For an overview of Shiraz's local politics and discussion during the Constitutional Revolution, see Vanessa Martin, *Iran between Islamic Nationalism and Secularism : The Constitutional Revolution of 1906* (London: I.B. Tauris, 2013), 147–168.

89   'News', report by Smart, 6 August 1910, FO 248/1003, TNA.

90   Smart to Barclay, 9 November 1910, FO 248/1003, TNA.

91   Shiraz News for Week Ending 11 March 1911, FO 248/1035, TNA.

92   Vejdani, 'Urban Violence and Space', 5.
93   This is evident in the genealogy of sanctuary-taking in Iranian history, see Peyman Eshaghi, 'Quietness beyond Political Power: Politics of Taking Sanctuary (*Bast Neshini*) in the Shi'ite Shrines of Iran', *Iranian Studies* 49, no. 3 (2016): 493–514.
94   For an analysis of the connection between concepts of justice and dearth in this moment of hegemonic contraction, especially with reference to the waning of food provisioning and legal changes in authorities' supervision of markets, see Cronin, 'Bread and Justice in Qajar Iran'. Cronin also reveals that on some occasions hungry soldiers sided with food protests in the 1890s.
95   Sa'idi Sirjani, *Vaqaye'-e Ettefaqiyeh*, 672, 8 Safar 1320 [16 May 1902].
96   Vejdani, 'Urban Violence and Space'.
97   Rejali, *Torture & Modernity*, 30. Many instances of similar attacks on state artefacts of justice can be found in Martin, *The Qajar Pact*.
98   Willem M. Floor, 'Change and Development in the Judicial System of Qajar Iran (1800–1925)', in *Qajar Iran: Political, Social and Cultural Change*, eds Clifford E. Bosworth and Carole Hillenbrand (Edinburgh: Edinburgh University Press, 1983), 132.
99   Smart to Barclay, 9 November 1910, FO 248/1003, TNA.
100   Enayat, *Law, State and Society in Modern Iran*, 33.
101   Ibid., 71.
102   Martin, *The Qajar Pact*, 127.
103   Martin, *Iran between Islamic Nationalism and Secularism*, 205–206.
104   For an overview of these attempts see Enayat, *Law, State and Society in Modern Iran*, 105–109.
105   See, for instance, '*Dozd Kist?*' ['Who is a Thief?'], *Shefaq-e Sorkh* 11 (9 April 1922).
106   Martin, *Iran between Islamic Nationalism and Secularism*, 163.
107   For Dehbid, see Diary of the Shiraz Consulate for the Week Ending 6 February 1913; for Borazjan, see Diary of the Shiraz Consulate for the Week Ending 22 March 1913, FO 248/1077, TNA.
108   Martin, *Iran between Islamic Nationalism and Secularism*, 205.
109   Enayat, *Law, State and Society in Modern Iran*, 71. Nayeb Hossein Kashi and his followers, although relatively little discussed in Anglophone historiography, remain greatly contested in Iranian scholarship. On one side are those who, using a combination of memoirs and local oral tradition, champion the *Nayebiyan* as upholders of ordinary people's justice and even of constitutional values; notable examples include Muhammad Reza Khosravi, *Toghiyan-e Nayebiyan Dar Jariyan-e Enqelab-e Mashrutiyat-e Iran* (Tehran: Beh Negar, 1368); A. Yaghmaei, *Hamase-ye Fathname-ye Nayebi* (Tehran: Esparak, 1368); and Amir Hushang Aryanpur, *Hamase-ye Toghiyan: Barresi-ye Jonbesh-e Nayebiyan-e Kashan Bar Asas-e Asnad* (Tehran: Ketab-e Ameh, 1388). However many historians have criticized such works and disputed any link to social banditry; see, for example, Kaveh Bayat, 'Toghiyan Bar Zed-e Tarikh', *Nashr-e Danesh* 10, no. 3 (1369): 32–37; Hassan Naraqi, *Kashan Dar Jonbesh-e Mashrute-ye Iran* (Tehran: Entesharate Iran, 1364); and Seyyed 'Ali Al-Davud, *Nayeb Hossein Kashi Dar Khur Biabanak* (Tehran: Ketabkhaneh, Muzeh va Markaz-e Asnad-e Majles-e Shura-ye Eslami, 1394). One reason for the ongoing contestation is the relative abundance of documentary evidence on offer that presents contrasting images of the group. See, for example, the large collection of complaints made by ordinary people on the subject in 'Abdolhoseyn Navaei and Muhammad Baqaei Shireh-Jini, *Nayebiyan-e Kashan*

(*Bar Asas-e Asnad*) (Tehran: Sazman-e Asnad-e Melli-ye Iran, 1379). For recent, nuanced analyses that make use of this published collection, see Seyyed Mahmud Saddat, Morteza Nouraei and Hoseyn Mir Ja'fari, 'An Analysis of the Performance of Nayebi Exiles to Kashan (Causes and Factors of the Occurrence and Continuance of Their Rebellion)', *Interdisciplinary Journal of Contemporary Research in Business* 5, no. 1 (May 2013): 113–130; and Abolhassan Hadjiheidari, "'Nayeb Hoseyn-e Kasi Straßenräuber Oder Revolutionar?" Eine Untersuchung Der Iranischen Geschichte 1850–1920' (PhD thesis, University of Tübingen, 2008).

110   Nouraei and Martin, 'Part II: The Karguzar and Security', 30.

111   Khazeni, *Tribes & Empire on the Margins of Nineteenth-Century Iran*, 95.

112   The concept of moral economy was first developed by E. P. Thompson in reference to the popular values of the English peasantry in the eighteenth century; see the essays on moral economy in E. P. Thompson, *Customs in Common: Studies in Traditional Popular Culture* (New York: New Press, 1993); cf. the famous adoption of the concept as applied to Southeast Asian peasant societies in James C. Scott, *The Moral Economy of the Peasant: Rebellion and Subsistence in Southeast Asia* (New Haven, CT: Yale University Press, 1976). Linda Darling has identified the moral economy in the Middle Eastern context (and especially in Iran) in the form of the 'Circle of Justice', which stressed the importance of cooperation between kings and subjects, so that peasants were protected by an army in return for taxation and economic productivity, and demands made of subjects were relaxed in times of disaster. Darling demonstrates the persistence of this idea through time and that, despite its explicit appearance waning in sources of the modern period, it shared many similarities with ideas of justice, law and constitution prevailing at the turn of the twentieth century; see Linda T. Darling, *A History of Social Justice and Political Power in the Middle East: The Circle of Justice from Mesopotamia to Globalization* (New York: Routledge, 2013).

113   Martin, *The Qajar Pact.*

114   Chalcraft, *Popular Politics in the Making of the Modern Middle East.*

115   Administration Report of the Persian Gulf Political Residency for the Year 1911, p. 16, R/15/1/711, IOR.

116   'Report on Fars by Captain A T Wilson, Indian Political Department', p. 69, L/PS/20/7, IOR.

117   Administration Report of the Persian Gulf Political Residency for the Year 1911, p. 14, R/15/1/711, IOR.

118   Tange-ye Torkan was frequently referred to a 'no-man's land'. See, for example, Administration Report of the Persian Gulf Political Residency for the Year 1911, p. 14, R/15/1/711, IOR.

119   Smart to Townley, 15 July 1912, FO 248/1057, TNA. This is corroborated by Iranian governmental documentary evidence; see letter from Nezam al-Soltaneh to Muhammad 'Ali Khan Kalantar Kashkuli and Nur Muhammad Khan Kalantar, undated, No. 98/293/212, Sazman-e Asnad-e Melli-ye Iran (National Archives of Iran).

120   Smart to Townley, 15 July 1912, FO 248/1057, TNA.

121   Smart to Townley, 15 July 1912, FO 248/1057, TNA.

122   Oberling, *The Qashqa'i Nomads of Fars*, 106–107.

123   Telegram by Knox, 24 October 1911, FO 248/1036, TNA.

124   Administration Report of the Persian Gulf Political Residency for the Year 1913, p. 19, R/15/1/711, IOR.

125   For incident of fighting, see 'Diary of the Shiraz Consulate for the Week Ending 25 January 1913'; for example of protest, see telegraph by Smart, 28 April 1913, FO 248/1077, TNA.

126   Memorandum by Chick enclosed in telegram from Cox to Grey, 15 December 1912, L/PS/10/299, IOR.

127   'General Situation in Fars', Smart to Townley, 24 June 1912, FO 248/1057, TNA.

128   Smart to Barclay, 8 February 1912, FO 248/1057, TNA.

129   Memorandum by Chick enclosed in telegram from Cox to Grey, 15 December 1912, L/PS/10/299, IOR.

130   H. Lyman Stebbings, 'British Imperialism, Regionalism, and Nationalism in Iran, 1890–1919', in *Iran Facing Others: Identity Boundaries in a Historical Perspective.*, eds Abbas Amanat and Farzin Vejdani (New York: Palgrave Macmillan, 2012), 162.

131   Telegram from Minister of Interior of the Persian Government to the Governor of Bushehr, 13 January 1912, FO 248/1057, TNA.

132   Telegram by Knox, 14 January 1912, FO 248/1057, TNA.

133   Telegram by Knox, 7 January 1912, FO 248/1057, TNA.

134   For a comprehensive outline of the development of the gendarmerie, see Cronin, *The Army and the Creation of the Pahlavi State in Iran, 1910–1926.*

135   Smart to Towney, 15 July 1912, L/PS/10/197/2, IOR.

136   Memorandum by Chick enclosed in telegram from Cox to Grey, 15 December 1912, L/PS/10/299, IOR. On local support for *rahdari* and opposition to gendarmerie, cf. Cronin, *The Army and the Creation of the Pahlavi State in Iran, 1910–1926*, 22–24.

137   Administration Report of the Persian Gulf Political Residency for the Year 1913, pp. 24–25, R/15/1/711, IOR.

138   Smart to Knox, 23 November 1913, enclosures 8 and 9, L/PS/10/404, IOR.

139   Ibid.

140   Safiri, 'The South Persian Rifles', 44.

141   Report by Merrill enclosed in telegram from O'Connor to Knox, 13 May 1914, L/PS/11/79, IOR.

142   Ibid.

143   Smart to Towney, 15 July 1912, L/PS/10/197/2, IOR.

144   Administration Report of the Persian Gulf Political Residency for the Year 1914, p. 9, R/15/1/711, IOR.

145   Oberling, *The Qashqa'i Nomads of Fars*, 121.

146   Ibid., 120.

147   See, for instance, Lyman Stebbings, 'British Imperialism, Regionalism, and Nationalism in Iran, 1890–1919', 162–163. In Fars, the German agitation against the British was famously led by Wilhelm Wasmuss, who became known as the 'German Lawrence' for his exploits; for an account of the role he played as well as the wider anti-British struggle in Fars during the war, see Beck, *The Qashqa'i of Iran*, 113–118. On the place of Iran in the First World War more generally, see Touraj Atabaki, ed., *Iran and the First World War: Battleground of the Great Powers* (London: I.B. Tauris, 2006).

148   See, for instance, '*Yek Sadomin Salgard-e Shehadat-e Qahreman-e Nashenakhteh va Sardar-e Mobarez 'Ali Muhammad Kamareji dar Jang-e Jahani-ye Aval beh hame-ye Vatanparastan-e Iran Tabrik Gofteh Mishavad*', 26 March 2016. Available online: www.iranfarskamarej.blogfa.com/post/49 (accessed 7 August 2018).

149 Extract from article in *Neda-ye Haq*, 13 Rabiʿ Avval 1335 [7 January 1917], 209r, L/ PS/10/612, IOR.

150 Rada Dyson-Hudson and Neville Dyson-Hudson, 'Nomadic Pastoralism', *Annual Review of Anthropology* 9 (1980): 15–61.

151 This often has been found the case by others exploring social banditry in other contexts; see, for example, the conclusions drawn in Slatta, *Bandidos*.

152 By 'weapon of weak' I do not necessarily mean a form of conscious everyday peasant as set out famously in J. C. Scott, *Weapons of the Weak: Everyday Forms of Peasant Resistance* (New Haven, CT; Yale University Press, 1985). Rather I refer to a means for the poor to realize agency in the tumults of everyday life in the face of inequality and injustice.

153 The very validity of the term 'underworld' has come under historical scrutiny; see Heather Shore, 'A Brief History of the Underworld and Organised Crime, c. 1750–1950', in *The Oxford Handbook of the History of Crime and Criminal Justice*, eds Paul Knepper and Anja Johansen (London: Oxford University Press, 2016), 170–191.

154 The distinction between 'good' and 'bad' crime was famously criticized in the preface of Hay et al., *Albion's Fatal Tree*. Hobsbawm addresses the debate in the postscript of the more recent edition of Hobsbawm, *Bandits*, 172–182. For an overview of the debate, see Knepper, *Writing the History of Crime*.

155 Stuart Hall and Phil Scraton, 'Law, Class and Control', in *Crime and Society: Readings in History and Theory*, eds Mike Fitzgerald, Gregor MacLennan and Jennie Pawson (London: Routlege & K. Paul, 1981), 492. E. P. Thomson had famously articulated a similar view before in Thompson, *Whigs and Hunters*, 262. Such a conception of the law also coheres with Antonio Gramsci's concept of hegemony; see Antonio Gramsci, *Selections from the Prison Notebooks of Antonio Gramsci*, trans. Quintin Hoare and Geoffrey Nowell-Smith, repr. (London: Lawrence and Wishart, 2007).

156 See, for example, Peter King, *Crime, Justice, and Discretion in England, 1740–1820* (Oxford: Oxford University Press, 2000). A similar argument can unquestionably be made for the Iranian case.

157 Markus D. Dubber, 'Histories of Crime and Criminal Justice', in *The Oxford Handbook of the History of Crime and Criminal Justice*, eds Paul Knepper and Anja Johansen (London: Oxford University Press, 2016), 609; cf. Hall and Scraton, 'Law, Class and Control', 494.

158 See Rule, 'Social Crime in the Rural South in the Eighteenth and Nineteenth Centuries'.

159 Quoted in Afary, *The Iranian Constitutional Revolution*, 299.

160 This is dealt with extensively in Cronin, *Tribal Politics in Iran*.

Chapter 8

1 Eric Hobsbawm, *Age of Extremes: A History of the World, 1914–1991* (New York: Vintage Books, 1994), 291.

2 There are specific village monographs based on field studies conducted between the 1930s and the 1960s. Undoubtedly, these pioneering studies presented a vivid picture of social life in Anatolian villages but did not problematize peasant politics. See

Niyazi Berkes, *Bazı Ankara Köyleri Üzerine Bir Araştırma* (Ankara: Uzluk Basımevi, 1942); Mediha Berkes' village monographs published in *Yurt ve Dünya* (Country and World) journal; Paul Stirling, *Culture and Economy: Changes in Turkish Villages* (Huntingdon: Eothen, 1993); İbrahim Yasa, *Hasanoğlan Köyü'nün İçtimaî-İktisadî Yapısı* (Ankara: Doğuş Ltd. O. Matbaası for Türkiye ve Orta Doğu Amme İdaresi Enstitüsü, 1955); İbrahim Yasa, *Sindel Köyü'nün Toplumsal ve Ekonomik Yapısı* (Ankara: Türkiye ve Orta Doğu Amme İdaresi Enstitüsü, 1960); Joseph Szyliowicz, *Political Change in Rural Turkey: Erdemli* (The Hague: Mouton, 1966); Mehmet Ali Şevki, *Kurna Köyü (Kocaeli Yarımadası) Monografisinden Üç Makale* [Articles published in *Siyasi İlimiler Mecmuası*, nos. 77–79 and 90], 1939; Pertev Naili Boratav, 'Mudurnu'nun Abant-Dibi Köyleri Üzerine 1940 Yılında Yapılmış Bir İncelemeden Notlar', *Sosyoloji Konferansları, On Yedinci Kitap*, no. 446 (İstanbul: İstanbul Üniversitesi İktisat Fakültesi Yayını, 1979): 94–122. In addition, folkloric studies by prominent folklorists such as Mehmet Enver Beşe, Pertev Naili Boratav, İlhan Başgöz and Mehmet Halit Bayrı, published in the periodical *Halk Bilgisi Haberleri* (People's Bulletin of Folklore), give important information about everyday life in Anatolian villages.

3   Çağlar Keyder, in his pioneering work based on an analytical historical-sociology approach to the relations between the state and classes, considered the peasantry a passive mass in the face of economic policies and conditions. Çağlar Keyder, 'Türk Demokrasisinin Ekonomi Politiği', in *Geçiş Sürecinde Türkiye*, eds Irvin Cemil Shick and Ertuğrul Ahmet Tonak (İstanbul: Belge Yayınları, 1998), 50.

4   The Anatolian peasants' daily struggles have been briefly examined in a few studies. See Şevket Pamuk, 'War, State Economic Policies, and Resistance by Agricultural Producers in Turkey, 1939–1945', in *Peasants & Politics in The Modern Middle East*, eds Farhad Kazemi and John Waterbury (Miami: Florida International University Press, 1991), 125–142; Elif Akçetin, 'Anatolian Peasants in the Great Depression, 1929–1933', *New Perspectives on Turkey* 23, no. 23 (Fall 2000): 79–102; Murat Metinsoy, *İkinci Dünya Savaşı'nda Türkiye: Savaş ve Gündelik Yaşam* (İstanbul: Homer Kitabevi, 2007; 2nd edn. İş Bankası Kültür Yayınları, 2016). The first two pioneering articles presented brief snapshots of the peasants' economic tactics to survive during the first years of the Second World War and the Great Depression, respectively. A special chapter in my book deals with the peasant resistance to wartime taxes, labour obligations, impoverishment and food scarcity.

5   Çağlar Keyder and Faruk Birtek have implied the existence of an alliance between the state and middle farmers in the 1930s. Faruk Birtek-Çağlar Keyder, 'Agriculture and the State: An Inquiry into Agricultural Differentiation and Political Alliances: The Case of Turkey', *Journal of Peasant Studies* 2, no. 4 (1975): 447–463.

6   Again, it has been generally argued that income differentiation within village communities is not important for understanding peasant politics. Çağlar Keyder, 'Türk Tarımında Küçük Meta Üretiminin Yerleşmesi (1946–1960)', in *Türkiye'de Tarımsal Yapılar*, eds Şevket Pamuk and Zafer Toprak (Ankara: Yurt Yayınevi, 1988), 163–174. See İzzettin Önder, 'Cumhuriyet Döneminde Tarım Kesimine Uygulanan Vergi Politikası', in *Türkiye'de Tarımsal Yapılar*, eds Şevket Pamuk and Zafer Toprak (Ankara: Yurt Yayınevi, 1988), 113–133.

7   Bilâl N. Şimşir, *Kürtçülük II, 1924–1999* (Ankara: Bilgi Yayınevi, 2009), 322–323; Cemşid Bender, *Genelkurmay Belgelerinde Kürt İsyanları* (İstanbul: Kaynak Yayınları, 1992); Safiye Dündar, *Kürtler ve Azınlık Tartışmaları: Tarih, Kimlik, İsyanlar, Sosyo-Kültürel Yapı, Terör* (İstanbul: Doğan Kitap, 2009), 159.

8   David McDowall, *A Modern History of the Kurds* (London: I.B. Tauris, 2004), 202–
    211; Martin van Bruinessen, *Kürdistan Üzerine Yazılar* (İstanbul: İletişim Yayınları,
    2002), 340; Wadie Jwaideh, *Kürt Milliyetçiliğinin Tarihi: Kökenleri ve Gelişimi*, 5th
    edn. (İstanbul: İletişim Yayınları, 2008), 403–433. Perhaps one exception to this is
    a very insightful contemporary account by Hikmet Kıvılcımlı, *Yol/İhtiyat Kuvvet
    Milliyet (Şark)* (İstanbul: Yol Yayınları, 1979).
9   For a broader definition of politics as a struggle for allocation of economic sources,
    see Harold D. Lasswell, *Politics: Who Gets What, When, How?* (Cleveland, OH: World
    Pub. Co., 1958). James C. Scott conceives politics as a two-dimensional phenomenon.
    High politics, one of these dimensions, is underpinned and deeply shaped by another
    dimension he calls 'infrapolitics', which takes place in everyday life as a struggle over
    scarce economic resources and rights. James C. Scott, *Domination and the Arts of
    Resistance: Hidden Transcripts* (New Haven, CT: Yale University Press, 1990). Joel
    S. Migdal also underscores the state and society interactions in everyday life and
    how the people reshape or thwart the state's plans and projects through a constant
    and covert negotiation process. See Joel S. Migdal, *State in Society: Studying How
    States and Societies Transforms and Constitute One Another* (Cambridge: Cambridge
    University Press, 2001); Joel S. Migdal, *Strong Societies and Weak States: State-
    Society Relations and State Capabilities in the Third World* (Princeton, NJ: Princeton
    University Press, 1988).
10 Önder, 'Cumhuriyet Döneminde Tarım Kesimine Uygulanan Vergi Politikası'; and
    Yorğaki Effimianidis, *Cihan İktisad Buhranı Önünde Türkiye* (İstanbul: Kaadçılık
    ve Matbaacılık Anonim Şirketi, 1935–1936), 278. According to Hershlag, the land
    tax constituted 13.7 per cent of the annual revenue of the government by 1929. Z.
    Yehuda Hershlag, *Turkey: The Challenge of Growth* (Leiden: E. J. Brill, 1968), 51.
11 Şevket Raşit Hatipoğlu, *Türkiye'de Ziraî Buhran* (Ankara: Yüksek Ziraat Enstitüsü,
    1936), 77. The peasants in a village near Ankara with whom Niyazi Berkes talked, for
    instance, had argued that the tithe was more favourable. Berkes, *Bazı Ankara Köyleri
    Üzerine Bir Araştırma*, 43. See the report of Bursa Deputy Şefik Lütfi (9 February
    1931), BCA CHP (Prime Ministry Republican Archive. Catalogue of the Republican
    People's Party) [490.1/729.478.1], 16 March 1931.
12 Cezmi Emiroğlu, *Türkiye'de Vergi Sistemi: Vasıtasız Vergiler* (Ankara: Damga
    Matbaası, 1932), 110–111; Hatipoğlu, *Türkiye'de Ziraî Buhran*, 77–79.
13 Afet İnan, *Yurt Bilgisi Notlarımdan: Vergi Bilgisi* (İstanbul: Devlet Matbaası, 1930),
    95–98; Isparta Mebusu Kemal Turan, *Yeni Vergi Kanunları'nın Tatbiki Mahiyeti ve
    Tediye Kabiliyeti Hakkında Tahliller* (İzmir: Hafız Ali Matbaası, 1931), 97.
14 The government purchased wheat through the *Ziraat Bankası* (Agriculture Bank)
    at stable prices between 1932 and 1938. Until 1935 it was aimed to protect peasants
    from sharp price declines, but the prices offered after 1935 remained below the
    recovered market prices.
15 Peasants poured out their complaints about taxes to newspapers through letters.
    'Halk Sütunu', *Köroğlu*, 10 July 1929; '960 Kuruş İçin', *Köroğlu*, 16 December 1929;
    'Köylünün Şikâyet Ettiği Vergiler-Tahsildar Meselesi-Yol Vergisi', *Cumhuriyet*, 22
    November 1930; 'Vergiler Hakkında Anket: Arazi Vergisi Aşar Vergisine Rahmet
    Okutacak Kadar Ağırdır', *Cumhuriyet*, 27 December 1930; Eşref, 'Haymana Halkı
    Neler Yapılmasını İstiyor?' *Vakit*, 10 October 1934; 'Fakir Kasaba Halkı Yemeklik
    Undan Vergi Alınmaması İçin Hükümetten Rica Ediyorlar', *Köroğlu*, 4 August, 1934;
    'Un Vergisi', *Köroğlu*, 8 December 1934; 'Yol Parasını Vermiyen Borçlulara Dair',
    Köroğlu, 28 February 1934; 'Çok Haklı Bir Sorgu: Safranbolu Köylülerinden Bir

Çok Mühür ve İmzalı Bir Mektup Aldık', *Köroğlu*, 29 August 1934; 'Haksızlık Olur mu Ya!' *Köroğlu*, 28 March 1936. In addition to the letters sent to the newspapers, the petition lists in the *TBMM Yıllık*s (Grand National Assembly of Turkey Annals) were full of petitions complaining of the tax rates and tax collectors. The peasants demanded also tax amnesty and reduction in tax rates. See *TBMM Yıllık 1929* (Ankara: TBMM Matbaası, 1929); *TBMM Yıllık 1931* (Ankara: TBMM Matbaası, 1931); *TBMM Yıllık 1934* (Ankara: TBMM Matbaası, 1934); *TBMM Yıllık 1935* (Ankara: TBMM Matbaası, 1935); *TBMM Yıllık 1936* (Ankara: TBMM Matbaası, 1936); *TBMM Yıllık 1939* (Ankara: TBMM Matbaası, 1939).

16   David F. Burg, *A World History of Tax Rebellions: An Encyclopedia of Tax Rebels, Revolts, and Riots from Antiquity to the Present* (New York: Routledge, 2004), ix.

17   Ömer Lütfi Barkan, "'Çiftçiyi Topraklandırma Kanunu" ve Türkiye'de Zirai Bir Reformun Ana Meseleleri', in *Türkiye'de Toprak Meselesi: Toplu Eserler 1*, ed. Ömer Lütfi Barkan (İstanbul: Gözlem Yayınları, 1980), 509.

18   Necmeddin Sahir Sılan, *Doğu Sorunu: Necmeddin Sahir Sılan Raporları (1939–1953)* (İstanbul: Tarih Vakfı Yurt Yayınları, 2010), 74; M. Reşat Mimaroğlu, *Gördüklerim ve Geçirdiklerim'den: Memurluk Hayatımın Hatıraları* (Ankara: T. C. Ziraat Bankası Matbaası, 1946), 105–114.

19   Faik Bulut, *Dersim Raporları* (İstanbul: Evrensel Basım Yayın, 1992), 254.

20   Refet Aksoy, *Köylülerimizle Başbaşa* (Yozgat: Yozgat İlbaylık Basımevi, 1936), 81.

21   According to the livestock statistics collected in 1946, the number of taxed sheep decreased from 13,632,000 in 1927 to 10,180,000 in 1929 and remained at about 10 million until the sharp reduction in the livestock tax rates in 1935. From then on, the numbers began to climb. T. C. Başbakanlık İstatistik Genel Müdürlüğü, *Hayvanlar İstatistiği 1944* (İstanbul: Hüsnütabiat Basımevi, 1946), 2.

22   Lilo Linke, *Allah Dethroned* (London: Constable & Co. Ltd., 1937), 130.

23   Orhan Miroğlu, *Hevsel Bahçesinde Bir Dut Ağacı: Canip Yıldırım'la Söyleşi* (İstanbul: İletişim, 2005), 53.

24   'Gözcüler', *Orak Çekiç* 9 (20 July 1936): 2.

25   BCA CHP [490.1/696.365.1], 19 February 1935. About the tendency of Turkish officials towards bribery under the guise of a gift (*bahşiş*), see the memoirs of the first US Ambassador to Turkey, Joseph Grew, *Atatürk ve Yeni Türkiye (1927–1932)* (İstanbul: Gündoğan Yayınları, 2002), 127, 175.

26   Mediha Esenel, *Geç Kalmış Kitap: 1940'lı Yıllarda Anadolu Köylerinde Araştırmalar ve Yaşadığım Çevreden İzlenimler* (İstanbul: Sistem Yayıncılık, 1999), 109.

27   Bernard Newman, *Turkish Crossroads* (London: Robert Hale Ltd., 1951), 187.

28   Yıldız Sertel, *Ardımdaki Yıllar* (İstanbul: İletişim Yayınları, 2001), 118.

29   BCA MGM (Prime Ministry Republican Archive, Catalogue of the General Directorate of the Transaction of the Prime Ministry) [30.10/104.676. 24], 14 June 1934.

30   BCA MGM [30.10/104.676.24], 8 July 1934.

31   'Köy Değirmenlerinden Alınacak Muamele Vergisi', *Vakit*, 31 July 1934.

32   Here are a few examples among many cases. In January 1931, for instance, unknown persons murdered and robbed the tax collector Tahsin Efendi, who had collected a sum of money in one Anatolian village that day. He was attacked on the way to town, most likely by a group of poor peasants from whom he had collected payments. 'Maliye Tahsildarı Öldürdü', *Köroğlu*, 24 January 1931. In June 1931, unknown persons attacked and murdered a tax collector named Ali Fikri Efendi on his way from collecting the taxes of Düzce villages. BCA BKK (Prime Ministry Republican

Archive, Catalogue of the Cabinet Decrees) [30.18.1.2/21.43.5.], 17 June 1931. Another tax collector, Raşid Efendi, was also killed on duty by unknown persons after tax collection in the villages of an Anatolian province in 1936. BCA BKK [30.18.1.2/62.17.17], 2 March 1936. In another instance, a peasant shot a tax collector through the head in Muğla in 1936. 'Tahsildarı Vuran Asıldı', *Köroğlu*, 23 May 1936. A tax collector who had collected about 550 liras in a village was robbed on duty, while he was taking a nap under a tree on his way to town. 'Tahsildar Uyumaz!' *Köroğlu*, 20 May 1936.

33   BCA MGM [30.10/127.914.14], 26 May 1929.
34   BCA MGM [30.10/105.684.13], 8 April 1930.
35   BCA MGM [30.10/128.923.7], 21 March 1935.
36   BCA MGM [30.10/105.686.2], 14 June 1937.
37   The peasants in the Kurdish mountainous villages resembled societies that avoid being organized in the form of a state, as Scott examines in the case of South Asian upland communities free from any state intervention. James C. Scott, *The Art of Not Being Governed: An Anarchist History of Upland Southeast Asia* (New Haven, CT: Yale University Press, 2009).
38   A. Cenani Gürbüz, *Mondros'tan Milenyuma Türkiye'de İsyanlar* (İstanbul: Bilge Karınca Yayınları, 2006), 92.
39   Ibid., 93.
40   'Sason Kaymakamı Nasıl Vuruldu?' *Köroğlu*, 12 June 1935. In addition, see Reşat Hallı, *Türkiye Cumhuriyeti'nde Ayaklanmalar (1924–1938)* (Ankara: Genelkurmay Harb Tarihi Başkanlığı, 1972), 156.
41   İBA (Interior Ministry Archive) [12212–4], 24 January 1939.
42   İBA [12212–4], 11 January 1939.
43   İBA [12212–4], 16 February 1939.
44   *CHP 1936 İl Kongreleri* (Ankara: n.p., 1937), 12.
45   Turan, *Yeni Vergi Kanunları'nın Tatbiki*, 79–84. Asım Us, *Asım Us'un Hatıra Notları: 1930'dan 1950 Yılına Kadar Atatürk ve İsmet İnönü Devirlerine Ait Seçme Fıkralar* (İstanbul: Vakit Matbaası, 1966), 247. *Hayvanlar Vergisi Dökümanları* (Ankara: T. C. Ziraat Vekâleti Birinci Köy ve Ziraat Kalkınması Kongresi Yayını, 1939). 'İnen Hayvan Vergileri', *Köroğlu*, 13 November 1935; 'Hayvan Vergisi Kanunu Kabul Edildi', *Son Posta*, 14 January 1936.
46   Turan, *Yeni Vergi Kanunları'nın Tatbiki*, 82.
47   Bilsay Kuruç, *Belgelerle Türkiye İktisat Politikası*, vol. 2 (Ankara: Ankara Üniversitesi Siyasal Bilgiler Fakültesi Yayınları, 1993), 327; Güneş Çetin, 'Vergi Aflarının Vergi Mükelleflerinin Tutum ve Davranışları Üzerindeki Etkisi', *Yönetim ve Ekonomi* 14, no. 2 (2007): 177.
48   Monopoly revenues, especially from the tobacco monopoly, were the major financial source for the building of railways. Kuruç, *Belgelerle Türkiye İktisat Politikası*, 251. Indeed, the documents of the tobacco monopoly directorate confirm this. The director-general also underlined the crucial importance of the tobacco monopoly revenues for the government's railway projects and argued that tobacco smuggling was a serious threat to their implementation. See *Tütün İnhisarlar İdaresi, Muharreratı Umumiye Mecmuası*, IV, (1929), 79, quoted in Fatma Doğruel and A. Suut Doğruel, *Osmanlı'dan Günümüze Tekel* (İstanbul: Tekel & Tarih Vakfı Yurt Yayınları, 2000), 150–151.
49   In the last decades of the Ottoman Empire, smuggling and armed conflicts between the smugglers and the security forces, especially the armed guards of the Régie, the

foreign institution that was granted a tobacco monopoly, had turned the Anatolian countryside into a bloodbath. According to Salih Zeki, the death toll due to the conflicts between smugglers and the Régie guards reached 60,000. Salih Zeki, *Türkiye'de Tütün Ziraat, Sınaat ve Ticareti* (İstanbul: Cumhuriyet Matbaası, 1928), 16–17.

50 Kaçakçılığın Men-i ve Takibi Hakkında Kanun, no. 1126, 10 July 1927, *Düstur III*, vol. 8, p. 1783.

51 Kaçakçılığın Men ve Takibi Hakkında Kanun, no. 1519, 15 April 1929, *Düstur III*, vol. 10, p. 1798.

52 Kaçakçılığın Men ve Takibine Dair Kanun, no. 1918, 7 January 1932, *Düstur III*, vol. 13, p. 57.

53 Fahri Çoker, *Türk Parlamento Tarihi: TBMM IV. Dönem (1931–1935)*, vol. 1 (Ankara: Türkiye Büyük Millet Meclisi Vakfı, 1996), 334.

54 *Akbaba*, 23.10.1931, quoted in Birgün Ayman Güler, ed., *Açıklamalı Yönetim Zamandizini, 1929–1939* (Ankara: Ankara Üniversitesi Basımevi, 2007), 293.

55 Askeri ve İhtisas Mahkemeleri Hakkında Kararname, *Resmi Gazete*, 26 January 1932.

56 Barbro Karabuda, *Goodbye to the Fez: A Portrait of Modern Turkey*, trans. Maurice Michael (London: Denis Dobson Books, 1959), 79.

57 For instance see 'Kaçak', *Köroğlu*, 13 April 1932; 'Ağır Bir Duruşma', *Son Posta*, 10 April 1935.

58 Sabri Yetkin, *Ege'de Eşkıyalar* (İstanbul: Tarih Vakfı Yurt Yayınları, 1997), 84.

59 'Sigara Kâğıdı Kaçakçıları', *İkdam*, 24 January 1926; 'Bursa'da Yakalanan Kaçakçılar', *İkdam*, 13 November 1927; 'Kaçakçılık', *Son Posta*, 1 April 1932; 'Muğla'da Mahkûm Olan Kaçakçılar', *Son Posta*, 2 June 1932. There are many similar examples.

60 Ali Enver Togsoy, 'Cenub Hudutlarımızda Kaçakçılık', *Resimli Ay* 28 (June 1938): 20.

61 Kıvılcımlı, *İhtiyat Kuvvet Milliyet (Şark)*, 51.

62 BCA MGM [30.10/105.684.33], 16 October 1933.

63 Hasan Basri Erk, *Kaçakçılık İşleri* (İstanbul: Cumhuriyet Matbaası, 1946). The newspapers were also replete with the stories of smugglers caught by the gendarme. 'Çorum'da Kaçakçılar', *Köroğlu*, 24 July 1929; 'Tabur Tabur Kaçakçılar', *Köroğlu*, 14 March 1931; 'Kaçakçılar', *Köroğlu*, 10 December 1931; 'Kaçakçılık Yapan Üç Muhtar', *Son Posta*, 14 May 1932; 'Kızılbaş Bekir Dede!' *Köroğlu*, 25 April 1934; 'Merzifon'da Bir Kaçakçılık Vakası', *Son Posta*, 8 January 1935; BCA MGM [030.10/105.685.9], 15 April 1936; 'Bir Haftada 53 Kaçakçı', *Köroğlu*, 29 July 1936.

64 BCA MGM [30.10/65.433.4], 24 July 1935.

65 Gürbüz, *Mondros'tan Milenyuma*, 93.

66 'Bitlis Civarında 460 Bin Kaçak Cigara Kağıdı Ele Geçirildi', *Son Posta*, 9 April 1932. For crimes committed during the last six months in Mardin during the first half of the 1936, see BCA MGM [030.10/40.239.11].

67 The memoirs of the gendarme lieutenant Cemal Madanoğlu, who took part in the military operations against the Kurdish smugglers, bandits and rebels in the Sason district during the 1930s, give a detailed picture of how and why the conflicts between gendarmes and peasants occured in these years. Here he emphasized the monopoly administration's efforts to control the local markets in the Kurdish provinces by setting up monopoly factories and stores. One day, his uncle, the director-general of the monopoly administration, Behçet Günay, had spoken to the economy minister, Celal Bayar, of his desire to establish monopoly factories in the eastern provinces. Cemal Madanoğlu, *Anılar (1911–1938)* (İstanbul: Çağdaş Yayınları, 1982), 135–136. Indeed, the government established two tobacco and

cigarette factories in the region, the first in Malatya in 1939, and then in Bitlis in 1940. Naturally, these attempts encountered peasant resistance.

68   See also Gürbüz, *Mondros'tan Milenyuma*, 93.

69   Ibid.

70   Bilsay Kuruç, *Belgelerle Türkiye İktisat Politikası*, vol. 1 (Ankara: Ankara Üniversitesi Basımevi, 1988), 231–232.

71   İsmail Yağcı, 'Tuz, Tahta Kaşık Kaçakçılığı ve Yol Parası'. Available online: http://m. turkiyegazetesi.com.tr/yazarlar/ismail-yagci/338738.aspx(18.07.2007).

72   Gürbüz, *Mondros'tan Milenyuma*, 89.

73   Behçet Günay, 'Şeker', *Ülkü* (September 1935): 79. See the Law on the Sugar Consumption Tax and Tariff Rate (*Şeker İstihlak ve Gümrük Resimleri Hakkında Kanun*), *Resmi Gazete*, no. 2785, 17 June 1935 (enactment date: 12 June 1935). Şevket Raşit Hatipoğlu, *Türkiye'de Zirai Buhran*, 57; *CHP 1936 İl Kongreleri*, 119. The Law on the Salt Price (*Tuz Fiyatı Hakkına Kanun*), no. 2752, 5 June 1935, Düstur, III, vol. 16, p. 1281. See also Summaries of the Reports of the Deputies Who Visited Their Election Districts in 1935, BCA CHP [490.1/725.481.1].

74   Compare the Tobacco Monopoly Law, no. 1701, 9 June 1930 (*Resmi Gazete*, 28 June 1930) and the Tobacco and Tobacco Monopoly Law, no. 3437, 10 June 1938 (*Resmi Gazete*, 25 June 1938).

75   Effimianidis, *Cihan İktisad Buhranı Önünde Türkiye*, 275.

76   Trakyalı Ali Galip, 'Köylü', *Ülkü* (November 1933): 327–328; 'Gediz'de Hayvan Hırsızları', *Köroğlu*, 31 October 1936.

77   'Hayvan Hırsızlığının Önüne Geçilmesi Hakkındaki Kanunun Bazı Maddelerinin Değiştirilmesi Üzerinde Görüşmeler', see Kuruç, *Belgelerle Türkiye İktisat Politikası*, vol. 2, 99.

78   *CHP 28/12/936 Tarihinde Toplanan Vilâyet Kongresi Zabıtnamesi*, 31, 50.

79   'Hayvan Hırsızlığının Önüne Geçilmesi Hakkındaki Kanunun Bazı Maddelerinin Değiştirilmesi Üzerinde Görüşmeler'; see Kuruç, *Belgelerle Türkiye İktisat Politikası*, vol. 2, 100.

80   'Yakalanan At Hırsızları', *Son Posta*, 10 September 1932.

81   'Aydın'da Hayvan Hırsızları', *Son Posta*, 3 April 1932.

82   'Karaman'da Hırsızlar', *Köroğlu*, 24 October 1936.

83   BCA MGM [30.10/123.879.10], 16 February 1938.

84   BCA MGM [30.10/64.432.2], 26 July 1930; see also 'Adliye İstatistiklerine Göre Memleketimizde Cürümler ve Mücrimler', *Polis Dergisi* 10 (1 May 1940): 31.

85   Barkan, 'Çiftçiyi Topraklandırma Kanunu', 513.

86   Fahri Ecevid, 'Suçluluk Bakımından Köylümüzün Ruhi Yapılışı', *Polis Dergisi* 3–4 (October 1938): 49–50.

87   'Köy Sandığı Parası İçin Muhtarı Vurmuşlar', *Köroğlu*, 7 October 1936.

88   'Muhtarı Vurdular', *Köroğlu*, 17 October 1936.

89   'Bir Jandarma Askeri Görevi Başında Şehit Edildi', *Son Posta*, 29 August 1932.

90   BCA BKK [30.18.1.2/21.43.5], 17 July 1931.

91   BCA BKK [30.18.1.2/62.17.17], 2 March 1936.

92   'Tahsildarı Vuran Asıldı'.

93   Gürbüz, *Mondros'tan Milenyuma*, 92.

94   'Sason Kaymakamı Nasıl Vuruldu?' *Köroğlu*, 12 June 1935.

95   Kıvılcımlı, *Yol/İhtiyat Kuvvet Milliyet* (*Şark*), 290.

96   'Bostan Yüzünden Bir Köylü Diğerini Saçma İle Yaraladı', *Köroğlu*, 10 September 1938.

97 *Cumhuriyet*, 10.08.1931, quoted in Kıvılcımlı, *Yol/İhtiyat Kuvvet Milliyet* (*Şark*), 145.
98 Mustafa Eski, *İsmet İnönü'nün Kastamonu Gezileri* (İstanbul: Çağdaş Yayınları, 1995), 48.
99 'Toprak Yüzünden Bir Facia', *Son Posta*, 8 September 1932; 'Kabahat Köylüler de Mi?' *Son Posta*, 9 September 1932.
100 See Cemal Bardakçı, *Toprak Dâvasından Siyasî Partilere* (İstanbul: Işıl Matbaası, 1945), 33–37.
101 Teodor Shanin, 'Peasantry As a Class', in *Peasants and Peasant Societies*, ed. Teodor Shanin (Oxford: Blackwell, 1987), 259.
102 For major studies on banditry during the Ottoman era, albeit with different approaches, see Mustafa Akdağ, *Türk Halkının Dirlik ve Düzenlik Kavgası* (Ankara: Bilgi Yayınları, 1975); Karen Barkey, *Bandits and Bureaucrats: The Ottoman Route to State Centralization* (Ithaca, NY: Cornell University Press, 1994); Sabri Yetkin, *Ege'de Eşkıyalar* (İstanbul: Tarih Vakfı Yurt Yayınları, 1996); Halil Dural, *Bize Derler Çakırca: 19. ve 20. Yüzyılda Ege'de Eşkıyalar* (İstanbul: Tarih Vakfı Yurt Yayınları, 1999).
103 For a recent analytical account of rural crimes such as banditry and piracy in the Middle East and North Africa, see Cronin's chapter in this volume.
104 See 'Candarma Bekir Eşkıya Peşinde'. The first instalment is titled 'Karakol Kumandanı Bekir Çavuş Cin Ali'yi Nasıl Bastı?' *Köroğlu*, 30 January 1932.
105 See Yaşar Kemal, *İnce Memed* (İstanbul: Çağlayan Yayınları, 1955); Kemal Bilbaşar, *Memo* (İstanbul: Tekin Yayınevi, 1969–1970); Kemal Tahir, *Rahmet Yolları Kesti* (İstanbul: Düşün Yayınevi, 1957).
106 Trakyalı Ali Galip, 'Köylü', 328. Note, the People's Houses were the main ideological apparatus of the republican state during the early republic. See M. Asım Karaömerlioğlu, 'The People's Houses and the Cult of the Peasants in Turkey', *Middle Eastern Studies* 34, no. 4 (1998): 67–91.
107 Eric Hobsbawm, *Bandits* (New York: Pantheon Books, 1981). Many historians of rural resistance and rural outlaws have criticized Hobsbawm's notion of 'social banditry' by arguing that very few cases fit the model. Yet, some researchers have argued that because of the social and economic causes behind banditry, many bandits – regardless of their intention – can be labelled social bandits despite lacking some of the criteria (such as championing social reform and freedom). I agree with the latter. For the discussion, see Richard White, 'Outlaw Gangs of the Middle Border: American Social Bandits', *Western Historical Quarterly*, no. 12 (4 October 1981); 387–408; Pat O'Malley, 'Social Bandits, Modern Capitalism and the Traditional Peasantry: A Critique of Hobsbawm', *Journal of Peasant Studies* 6, no. 4 (July 1979): 489–501 ; Anton Blok, 'The Peasant and the Brigand: Social Banditry Reconsidered', *Comparative Studies in Society and History* 14, no. 4 (September 1972): 494–503. I think it is unreasonable to disregard the banditry as an unconscious reaction of the ignorant peasants without taking into account their own experiences. Again it was not sensible to expect what is called social or good bandit to meet all of Hobsbawm's criteria or to measure them according to a strict scale.
108 Local notables, such as those with the titles *ağa*, *seyyit* or *şeyh* in the eastern provinces, were used to being obeyed as long as they supported the peasants under their patronage. However, once peasants failed to pay taxes and tributes to their *ağas* or the *ağas* failed to support them, especially due to the commercialization of the economy, an economic crisis or state centralization, tensions within the

village or tribal community tended to increase. For intra-village relations of power, patronage and economic exploitation in the Kurdish villages, see especially Kıvılcımlı, *Yol/İhtiyat Kuvvet Milliyet (Şark)*; İsmail Hüsrev (Tökin), *Türkiye Köy İktisadiyatı* (İstanbul: Matbaacılık ve Neşriyat Türk Anonim Şirketi, 1934), 177–179; İsmail Beşikçi, *Doğu Anadolu'nun Düzeni* (İstanbul: İsmail Beşikçi Vakfı, 2014).

109   Hobsbawm, *Bandits*, 22, 67.
110   James C. Scott, *Moral Economy of the Peasant: Rebellion and Subsistence in South Asia* (New Haven, CT: Yale University Press, 1976), 120.
111   See *TBMM Yıllık 1934*, 251, 287, 297, 370, 381; *TBMM Yıllık 1936* (Ankara: TBMM Matbaası, 1936), 315.
112   Cezmi Yurtsever, *Kadirli Tarihi* (Osmaniye: Kadirli Hizmet Birliği Kültür Yayınları, 1999), 259–261.
113   Ibid.
114   Mehmet Bayrak, *Öyküleriyle Halk Anlatı Türküleri* (Ankara: Özge Yayınları, 1996), 461.
115   Ibid., 558.
116   Ibid., 616. There is another version of the story, emphasizing love and family affairs. See Ayfet Aytaç, *Alim Efe* (Afyon: Tuna Yayınları, 2011).
117   'Başbelası Bir Çete Reisi Gebertildi', *Son Posta*, 1 December 1935.
118   'Muradoğlu Geberdi', *Köroğlu*, 8 May 1935.
119   'Gezik Duran', *Köroğlu*, 26 June 1929.
120   Mehmet Bayrak, *Eşkiyalık ve Eşkiya Türküleri: İnceleme, Antoloji* (Ankara: Yorum Yayınevi, 1985), 188–190.
121   'Bir Çete Türedi', *Köroğlu*, 24 June 1931.
122   'Eşkıya Yatağı', *Köroğlu*, 26 July 1933.

Chapter 9

1   Across *Bilad al-Sham* the basic weight was the *uqqa* of 400 *dirham*, roughly equalling 1.282 kg. For food items such as bread and flour, the *ratl* (pl. rutul, artal) of two *uqqa* was the common weight; Deutsches Handelsarchiv (henceforth Handelsarchiv) 15 November 1878 (#1878, Teil 2): 489, 27 August 1880 (#1880, Teil 2): 233, NACP RG 84 Damascus Vol. 8 Damascus 85, Meshaka to Bissinger, *Weights and Measures*, 22 November 1889, Halil İnalcık, 'Introduction to Ottoman Metrology', in *Studies in Ottoman Social and Economic History* (London: Variorum Reprints, 1985), 338–340; Chambre de Commerce Française de Constantinople, ed., *Poids, mesures, monnaies et cours du change dans les principales localités de l'Empire ottoman à la fin du 19e siècle* (Istanbul: Isis, [1893] 2002), 5–7, 53.
2   One Ottoman gold *lira* (£T) was nominally divided into 100 silver piasters (Ps, *kuruş/qurush*) and 400 copper *para* (bara) since the introduction of the bimetallic standard in 1844. Prices of everyday items and foodstuffs were commonly cited in piaster. The silver *mecidiye* coin of Ps 20 was the basis of most transactions. Due to the falling prices of silver in the world market, the Ottoman Empire devalued the *mecidiye* for the purpose of tax payments from Ps 20 to 19 in 1880. The official exchange rate between gold *lira* and silver piaster was set to Ps 123 in May 1883 for

the same reason. Local rates in *Bilad al-Sham* varied widely across time and place, but the piaster coin continued to devaluate.

3   *Lisan al-Hal* (henceforth *Lisan*) 21 August 1908 (#5795): 3. For a map of Beirut indicating the main locations see https://github.com/tillgrallert/p04b832f0/blob/master/maps/map_beirut.geojson (accessed 9 July 2019).

4   The *kile* (bushel) was the basic unit of the cereals trade (grain, flour and dough) in the Ottoman Empire and across *Bilad al-Sham*. The *kile* was divided into 2 *madd* and also referred to as *jift* (Ottoman *çift*: pair). The efforts to establish an imperial standard bushel (*Istanbul kilesi* or new *kile*) of 40 litres were not successful. In *Bilad al-Sham* a *kile* equalled about 36.8 litre. A less common volume was the *shunbul*, which equalled 3 *kile* in Aleppo and 2.25 *kile* in the ports of Tripoli and Acre; *Lisan* 31 January 1884 (#645), NACP RG 84 Damascus Vol. 8 Damascus 85, Meshaka to Bissinger, *Weights and Measures*, 22 November 1889, NACP RG 84 Damascus Vol. 8 Damascus, Meshaka to Bissinger, 16 December 1889, HCPP Cd. 6005–189; Devey, *Commercial Report Damascus 1911*; Jamal al-Din al-Qasimi and Khalil al-ʿAẓm, Qamus al-sinaʿat al-shamiyya, vol. 2, ed. Zafir al-Qasimi (Paris: Mouton & co., 1960), 291; İnalcık, *Introduction to Ottoman Metrology*, 333; Chambre de Commerce Française de Constantinople, *Poids et mesures*, 6–7.

5   *al-Bashir* (henceforth *Bashir*) 3 August 1908 (#1869), 17 August 1908 (#1871), 31 August 1908 (#1873).

6   *Lisan* 21 September 1908 (#5820):1, *Thamarat al-Funun* (henceforth *Thamarat*) 21 September 1908 (#1691), p. 4.

7   Charles Tilly, 'Contentious Repertoires in Great Britain, 1758–1834', *Social Science History* 17, no. 2 (1993): 264.

8   The newspapers are (dates in brackets indicate the periods consulted): *Hadiqat al-Akhbar* (1881–1888, semi-official weekly), *al-Bashir* (1878–1882, 1887–1910, weekly), *al-Janna* (1883–1884, weekly), *Thamarat al-Funun* (1875–1895, 1898–1900 and 1902–1908, weekly) and *Lisan al-Hal* (1877–1914, biweekly, since 1894 daily) from Beirut and the official gazette *Suriye* (1882–1888, 1899–1902, weekly) and, with changing titles, *al-Muqtabas* (1908–1914, daily) from Damascus. The journals are *al-Jinan*, *al-Mahabba* and *al-Hasna*ʾ from Beirut; *al-Haqaʾiq* from Damascus; *al-Muqtataf* in Beirut and later Cairo; *al-Muqtabas* in Cairo and later Damascus; and *Servet-i* Fünun, *The Levant Herald* and *Konstantinopler Handelsblatt* from Istanbul. The newspapers *al-Ittihad al-ʿUthmani* and *al-Iqbal* from Beirut and *al-Quds* from Jerusalem were consulted for periods of a few weeks surrounding individual food riots.

9   Charles Tilly, 'The Analysis of Popular Collective Action', *European Journal of Operational Research* 30, no. 3 (1987): 227.

10 E.g. *Bashir* 25 June 1910 (#1969), *al-Muqtabas*, the newspaper (arab. jarida, henceforth *Muqtabas* (j)) 14 August 1910 (#447), *al-Ittihad al-ʿUthmani* (henceforth *Ittihad*) 16 August 1910 (#583), *Lisan* 19 August 1910 (#6408), *Muqtabas* (j) 21 August 1910 (#453):1–2, *al-Iqbal* (henceforth *Iqbal*) 22 August 1910 (#361), *Ittihad* 22 August 1910 (#588).

11 *Lisan* 23 June 1910 (#6359), *Muqtabas* (j) 25 June 1910 (#405).

12 *Muqtabas* (j) 14 August 1910 (#447), *Ittihad* 16 August 1910 (#583), 19 August 1910 (#586), *Lisan* 19 August 1910 (#6408), *Ittihad* 22 August 1910 (#588).

13 *Iqbal* 15 August 1910 (#360), *Ittihad* 16 August 1910 (#583).

14 See Helga Rebhan, *Geschichte und Funktion einiger politischer Termini im Arabischen des 19. Jahrhunderts, 1798–1882* (Wiesbaden: Harrassowitz, 1986), 110ff, Ami

Ayalon, 'From Fitna to Thawra', *Studia Islamica* 66, no. 66 (1987): 145–174; for the historical semantics of both terms. On the Ottoman preference for *fitna* as a term for open rebellion against the state see Palmira Brummett, 'Classifying Ottoman Mutiny: The Act and Vision of Rebellion', *Turkish Studies Association Bulletin* 22, no. 1 (1998): 93, 102; Maurus Reinkowski, *Die Dinge der Ordnung: eine vergleichende Untersuchung über die osmanische Reformpolitik im 19. Jahrhundert* (Munich: Oldenbourg, 2005), 242; Marinos Sariyannis, '"Mobs", "Scamps," and Rebels in Seventeenth-century Istanbul: Some Remarks on Ottoman Social Vocabulary', *International Journal of Turkish Studies* 11, nos 1–2 (2005): 9–10.

15   *Lisan* 19 August 1910 (#6408).

16   Edward Palmer Thompson, 'The Moral Economy of the English Crowd in the Eighteenth Century', *Past and Present* 50, no. 1 (1971): 76–136; Louise A. Tilly, 'The Food Riot as a Form of Political Conflict in France', *Journal of Interdisciplinary History* 2, no. 1 (1971): 23–57.

17   Ibid., 26.

18   Thompson, *Moral Economy*, 83, 85–86, 117, 136.

19   Ibid.,120–126.

20   For example, John Bohstedt, *Riots and Community Politics in England and Wales 1790–1810* (Cambridge, MA: Harvard University Press, 1983); Jim C. Scott, *Weapons of the Weak: Everyday Forms of Peasant Resistance* (New Haven, CT: Yale University Press, 1985); Timothy Mitchell, 'Everyday Metaphors of Power', *Theory and Society* 19, no. 5 (1990): 545–577; John Bohstedt, 'The Moral Economy and the Discipline of Historical Context', *Journal of Social History* 26, no. 2 (1992): 265–284. A lot of the debate focuses on the sustainability of hegemonic ideas, or the ideas of the ruling classes, through persuasion or coercion. See also George Rudé's work on the formation of popular ideologies as an always specific amalgam of inherent and derived ideologies and the 'the circumstance and experience which, in the final analysis, determined the nature of the finale mixture'. George F. E. Rudé, *Ideology & Popular Protest* (Chapel Hill: University of North Carolina Press, 1995), 29.

21   Amartya Sen, *Poverty and Famines: An Essay on Entitlement and Deprivation* (Oxford: Oxford University Press, 1981); John Walton and David Seddon, *Free Markets & Food Riots* (Oxford: Blackwell, 1994), 39–40; Raj Patel and Philip McMichael, 'A Political Economy of the Food Riot', *Review-Fernand Braudel Center for the Study of Economies, Historical Systems, and Civilizations* 32, no. 1 (2009): 9–35; see also Claude Liauzu, 'Crises urbaines, crise de l'état, mouvements sociaux', in *État, ville et mouvements sociaux au Maghreb et au Moyen-Orient: actes du colloque C.N.R.S.-E.S.R.C. Paris, 23–27 mai 1986*, ed. Kenneth L. Brown (Paris: L'Harmattan, 1989), 23–41; Edmond III Burke, 'Towards a History of Urban Collective Action in the Middle East: Continuities and Change 1750–1980', in *État, Ville et Mouvements Sociaux au Maghreb au Moyen-Orient: Actes du Colloque C.N.R.S.-E.S.R.C. Paris, 23–27 Mai 1986*, ed. Kenneth L. Brown (Paris: l'Harmattan, 1989), 42–56; and other contributions in the same volume.

22   Thompson, *Moral Economy*.

23   For a summary of these arguments see John Bohstedt, 'Gender, Household and Community Politics: Women in English Riots 1790–1810', *Past and Present* 120 (1988): 88–122.

24   Cf. Lynne Taylor, 'Food Riots Revisited', *Journal of Social History* 30, no. 2 (1996): 483–496. On the emergence of the idea of women as housewives and mothers of the nation in Mount Lebanon, see Akram Fouad Khater, '"House" to "Goddess of

the House": Gender, Class, and Silk in 19ᵗʰ-Century Mount Lebanon', *International Journal of Middle East Studies* 28, no. 3 (1996): 325–348.

25   Cf. recent monographs such as Charles Tripp, *The Power and the People: Paths of Resistance in the Middle East* (New York: Cambridge University Press, 2013); and John Chalcraft, *Popular Politics in the Making of the Modern Middle East* (Cambridge: Cambridge University Press, 2016).

26   These include a female food riot in Acre in 1816 (Thomas Philipp, *Acre: The Rise and Fall of a Palestinian City, 1730–1831* [New York: Columbia University Press, 2001]), eighteenth-century food riots in Aleppo (Jean-Pierre Thieck, 'Décentralisation ottomane et affirmation urbaine à Alep à la fin du XVIIIème siècle', in *Mouvements communautaires et Espaces urbains au Machreq* [Beirut: CERMOC, 1985], 117–168), Cairo (Gabriel Baer, 'Popular Revolt in Ottoman Cairo', *Der Islam* 54, no. 2 [1977]: 213–242), and Damascus (James Grehan, 'Street Violence and Social Imagination in Late-Mamluk and Ottoman Damascus (Ca. 1500–1800)', *International Journal of Middle East Studies* 35 [2003]: 228–229, 232; James Grehan, 'Smoking and 'early Modern' Sociability: The Great Tobacco Debate in the Ottoman Middle East (Seventeenth to Eighteenth Centuries)', *The American Historical Review* 111, no. 5 [2006]: 1368; James Grehan, *Everyday Life and Consumer Culture in 18th-Century Damascus* [Seattle: University of Washington Press, 2007]).

27   These include the 1878 food riot in Damascus (James A. Reilly, 'Origins of Peripheral Capitalism in the Damascus Region, 1830–1914' [PhD diss., Georgetown University, 1987]: 89; James A. Reilly, 'Women in the Economic Life of Late-Ottoman Damascus', *Arabica* 42, no. 1 [1995]: 102; Butrus Abu-Manneh, 'The Genesis of Midḥat Pasha's Governorship in Syria 1878–1880', in *The Syrian Land: Processes of Integration and Fragmentation; Bilād al-Shām from the 18th to the 20th Century*, eds Thomas Philipp and Birgit Schaebler [Stuttgart: Franz Steiner Verlag, 1998], 253), the 1910 food riot in Homs (James A. Reilly, 'Inter-Confessional Relations in Nineteenth-Century Syria: Damascus, Homs and Hama Compared', *Islam and Christian-Muslim Relations* 7, no. 2 [1996]: 222) and the 1914 food riots in Beirut (Melanie Schulze Tanielian, 'Feeding the City: The Beirut Municipality and the Politics of Food during World War I', *International Journal of Middle East Studies* 46, no. 4 [2014]: 737, 742).

28   Cf. Seven Ağir, 'The Evolution of Grain Policy: The Ottoman Experience', *Journal of Interdisciplinary History* 43, no. 4 (2013) 591, for similar observations.

29   Burke, Urban Collective Action, 46.

30   Ibid., 45–51.

31   Burke's misjudgement was mainly due to the sample upon which he built his case, and which was limited to urban riots in Cairo and Damascus between 1750 and 1830. The sample was outlined in an earlier publication; Edmund III Burke, 'Understanding Arab Protest Movements', *Arab Studies Quarterly* 8, no. 4 (1986): 339. Nevertheless, Burke repeatedly reiterated these claims; for example, Edmund Burke III, 'Collective Action and Discursive Shifts: A Comparative Historical Perspective', Working Paper, 26 February 2004. Available online: http://escholarship.org/uc/item/40p248x1 (accessed 2 May 2013).

32   See, for instance, the annual trade statistics for each consular district published in the Parliamentary Papers of the British House of Commons, which are available online through ProQuest.

33   Donald Quataert, 'Ottoman Reform and Agriculture in Anatolia, 1876–1908' (PhD diss., University of California, 1973).

34 For example, Charles Issawi, *The Fertile Crescent 1800–1914: A Documentary Economic History* (Oxford: Oxford University Press, 1988).
35 For example, Sarah D Shields, 'Regional Trade and 19th-Century Mosul: Revising the Role of Europe in the Middle East Economy', *International Journal of Middle East Studies* 23, no. 1 (1991): 22, provides a table of only fourteen data points based on British consular reports.
36 As far as the relationship between local volumes was known, they have all been normalised to *kile*. All data sets and visualizations are openly available at https://doi.org/10.5281/zenodo.1008999.
37 HCPP C.635; Jago, *Condition of Industrial Classes in Syria*, 394–395; Levant Herald 22 December 1877 (vol.IX, #250):2, HCPP C.2285; Jago, *Commercial Report Damascus 1878*, 615; PRO FO 195/2024 Damascus 25, Richards to Currie, 13 May 1898, *Lisan* 2 July 1906 (#5137), *Bashir* 9 July 1906 (#1761), 22 July 1907 (#1815); Fritz Grobba, *Die Getreidewirtschaft Syriens und Palästinas seit Beginn des Weltkrieges* (Hannover: H. Lafaire, 1923); Thompson *Moral Economy*, 91–92; Linda Schilcher, 'The Grain Economy of Late Ottoman Syria and the Issue of Large-Scale Commercialization', in *Landholding and Commercial Agriculture in the Middle East*, eds Keyder Çağlar and Faruk Tabak (Albany: State University of New York Press, 1991), 174; Grehan, *Everyday Life*, 66–69.
38 This plot shows the clustering of qualitative price information. Each coloured dot represents a source providing one of the five qualitative price information listed on the left.
39 Cf. Handelsarchiv 22 November 1878 (#1878, Teil 2):501–522, PRO FO 195/2097 Damascus 26, Richards to O'Conor, *Quarterly Report*, 6 April 1901; Julius Zwiedinek von Südenhorst, *Syrien und seine Bedeutung für den Welthandel* (Wien: A.Hölder, 1873), 23–26.
40 See Quataert, *Ottoman Reform and Agriculture*: 187ff, 367ff; *Bashir* 2 May 1898 (#1331[a]), PRO FO 195/2097 Damascus 26, Richards to O'Conor, *Quarterly Report*, 6 April 1901.
41 Prices in other currencies, such as those in US Dollar or British Pound Sterling reported by the consuls to London or Washington, DC, are not currently included in the price data.
42 I have argued elsewhere that the prevailing view on the Ottoman Empire before 1908 as being able and willing to rigorously implement restrictive press censorship even across remote regions is part of the nation-building narratives after 1908 and particularly the Turkish and Arabic nationalist movements after the First World War. According to my data set of warnings to and suspensions of periodicals across *Bilad al-Sham*, neither 1891 nor 1898 were particularly oppressive years. Till Grallert, 'To Whom Belong the Streets? Property, Propriety, and Appropriation: The Production of Public Space in Late Ottoman Damascus, 1875–1914' (PhD diss., Freie Universität Berlin, April 2014), 86–94; cf. Ebru Boyar, 'The Press and the Palace: The Two-Way Relationship Between Abdülhamid II and the Press, 1876–1908', *Bulletin of the School of Oriental and African Studies* 69, no. 3 (2006): 417–432; the data set is available at https://doi.org/10.5281/zenodo.1063484.
43 *Lisan* 5 Jul 1910 (#6369), 6 Jul 1910 (#6370), *Iqbal* 18 Jul 1910 (#356).
44 *Bashir* 30 July 1910 (#1974).
45 For example, *Muqtabas* (j) 3 July 1910 (#412), *Lisan* 5 July 1910 (#6369), *Bashir* 9 July 1910 (#1971), *Muqtabas* (j) 14 August 1910 (#447), *Iqbal* 15 August 1910 (#360), *Ittihad* 15 August 1910 (#582).

46   For example, *Lisan* 23 June 1910 (#6359).

47   For example, *Lisan* 19 August 1910 (#6408).

48   For example, *Muqtabas* (j) 6 April 1910 (#337): 3, *Ittihad* 16 August 1910 (#583).

49   For example, *Lisan* 19 August 1910 (#6408).

50   *Lisan* 23 June 1910 (#6359), *Bashir* 25 June 1910 (#1969), *Muqtabas* (j) 25 June 1910 (#405). Prices were originally provided per *shunbul* and normalized to *kile*: 1 *shunbul* = 3 *kile*.

51   The following account of the food riot is based on *Lisan* 13 August 1910 (#6403), p. 2, *Muqtabas* (j) 14 August 1910 (#447), p. 2, *Iqbal* 15 August 1910 (#360), p. 6, 7, *Ittihad* 15 August 1910 (#582), p. 3, *Muqtabas* (j) 16 August 1910 (#449), p. 3, *Bashir* 20 August 1910 (#1977), p. 3, *Muqtabas* (j) 20 August 1910 (#452), p. 3, *Iqbal* 22 August 1910 (#361), p. 8.

52   *Muqtabas* (j) 14 August 1910 (#447), *Ittihad* 16 August 1910 (#583), 18 August 1910 (#585), 19 August 1910 (#586).

53   *Lisan* 19 August 1910 (#6408).

54   Clifford Geertz developed the idea that cultural patterns or systems of symbols simultaneously provide both a 'model of' and a 'model for' society. James Gelvin applied this idea to Fayşal's Arab Government; Clifford Geertz, 'Religion as Cultural System', in *The Interpretation of Cultures: Selected Essays* (n.p.: Fontana Press, [1966] 1993), 93; James L. Gelvin, 'Demonstrating Communities in Post-Ottoman Syria', *Journal of Interdisciplinary History* 25, no. 1 (1994): 30; James L. Gelvin, *Divided Loyalties: Nationalism and Mass Politics in Syria at the Close of Empire* (Berkeley: University of California Press, 1998), 226–228.

55   Muhammad ʿAli Bey Efendi arrived on 27 July and his successor ʿAli Akram Bey Efendi submitted his resignation within two days of his arrival on 16 August; *Lisan* 27 July 1908 (#5773), *Thamarat* 27 July 1908 (#1683), *Bashir* 17 August 1908 (#1871), *Iqbal* 17 August 1908 (#260), *Thamarat* 17 August 1908 (#1686).

56   Another ʿAli Akram Bey was appointed and replaced with Farid Pasha as acting governor general until the arrival of Nazim Pasha on 7 September; *Iqbal* 24 August 1908 (#261), 31 August 1908 (#262), *Lisan* 7 September 1908 (#5808), 8 September 1908 (#5809).

57   *Lisan* 14 March 1878 (#43), PRO FO 226/197 Damascus Political 5, Jago to Earl of Derby, *State of Affairs in Damascus*, 27 March 1878; William Smith Cooke, *The Ottoman Empire and its Tributary States (Excepting Egypt) With a Sketch of Greece*, repr. (Amsterdam: Grüner, [1876] 1968), 14, 31, 57–58.

58   *Muqtabas* (j) 18 Febuary 1913 (#1119).

59   After the Young Turk Revolution of 1908, the empire saw the emergence of a new symbolic repertoire of public rituals, namely the 'popular' demonstration against foreign adversaries of the empire – the novelty being the active participation of the population in these demonstrations in addition to their traditional role as spectators. Austria-Hungary's annexation of Bosnia and Herzegovina in 1908–1909, Greece's intervention in Crete in 1910, the Italian occupation of Tripoli in Libya in 1911–1912 or the Balkan War of 1912–1913 all provided occasions for these demonstrations; for more details on this argument, see Grallert, *To Whom Belong the Streets?*, 323–325, 342. For reports on demonstrations against Greece during the Cretan crisis in 1910, see *Muqtabas* (j) 24 May 1910 (#378):3, 25 May 1910 (#379), p. 3, 26 May 1910 (#380), p. 3, *Iqbal* 30 May 1910 (#349), pp. 5–6, PRO FO 618/3 Damascus Draft 18, Young to Lowther, *Monthly Report*, 10 Jun 1910, *Lisan* 18 June 1910 (#6355), p. 2, *Iqbal* 20 June 1910 (#352), p. 5, *Lisan* 20 June 1910 (#6356), 2.

60 *Muqtabas* (j) 16 June 1910 (#398), PRO FO 371/1002 Damascus 28, Devey to Lowther, *Quarterly Report*, 12 July 1910, *Muqtabas* (j) 23 July 1910 (#429), *Lisan* 23 July 1910 (#6385), *Muqtabas* (j) 25 July 1910 (#430).

61 For a map of Damascus indicating the main locations see https://github.com/ tillgrallert/p04b832f0/blob/master/maps/map_damascus.geojson (accessed 9 July 2019).

62 *Muqtabas* (j) 3 July 1910 (#412), *Lisan* 5 July 1910 (#6369).

63 Ibid.

64 Ibid. PRO FO 371/1002 Damascus 28, Devey to Lowther, *Quarterly Report*, 12 July 1910 just mentioned the bread riot in passing without providing any details.

65 Isma'il Fadil Pasha was of Cretan origin. After the restoration of the constitution, he was supervisor of the military academy in Istanbul and commander of the troops at Izmir. He was governor of Syria from September 1909. Due to the outbreak of the revolt in Karak he was recalled on 31 December 1910 and succeeded by 'Ali Ghalib Pasha. According to the British consul, he spoke only Turkish and no Arabic; *Bashir* 20 September 1909 (#1929), *Lisan* 21 September 1909 (#6126), PRO FO 618/3 Damascus Draft 50, Devey to Lowther, *Quarterly Report*, 4 October 1909, PRO FO 618/3 Damascus Draft 2, Devey to Marling, *Quarterly Report*, 3 January 1911, PRO FO 618/3 Damascus Draft 18, Devey to Lowther, *Quarterly Report*, 15 April 1911.

66 *Muqtabas* (j) 3 July 1910 (#412).

67 The account of the food riot is based on *Lisan* 13 August 1910 (#6403), p. 2, *Muqtabas* (j) 14 August 1910 (#447), p. 2, *Iqbal* 15 August 1910 (#360), p. 6, 7, *Ittihad* 15 August 1910 (#582), p. 3, *Muqtabas* (j) 16 August 1910 (#449), p. 3, *Bashir* 20 August 1910 (#1977), p. 3, *Muqtabas* (j) 20 August 1910 (#452), p. 3, *Iqbal* 22 August 1910 (#361), p. 8.

68 For a map of Hama indicating the main locations see https://github.com/tillgrallert/ p04b832f0/blob/master/maps/map_hama.geojson (accessed 9 July 2019).

69 *Muqtabas* (j) 14 August 1910 (#447), p. 2.

70 *Ittihad* 16 August 1910 (#583), p. 1.

71 For a map of Homs indicating the main locations see https://github.com/tillgrallert/ p04b832f0/blob/master/maps/map_homs.geojson (accessed 9 July 2019).

72 *Muqtabas* (j) 21 August 1910 (#453), pp. 1–2.

73 Some early and generic reports also mentioned the looting of flour and bread from bakeries; *Muqtabas* (j) 14 August 1910 (#447), *Bashir* 20 August 1910 (#1977), *al-Quds* (henceforth *Quds*) 26 August 1910 (#172), p. 2. This, however, is not corroborated by the more detailed accounts of events.

74 *Ittihad* 16 August 1910 (#583), 19 August 1910 (#586), *Lisan* 19 August 1910 (#6408), *Ittihad* 22 August 1910 (#588).

75 Ibid.

76 Homs was devoid of imperial troops since the local battalion had been removed to Damascus in the aftermath of the Young Turk Revolution. Only some gendarmes and a small detachment of cavalry remained stationed in the old barracks. Some of them were stationed at the Serail, two at the Ottoman Bank and three at the prison; *Ittihad* 16 August 1910 (#583).

77 Ibid., *Muqtabas* (j) 17 August 1910 (#450), *Lisan* 19 August 1910 (#6408), *Ittihad* 22 August 1910 (#588).

78 *Muqtabas* (j) 21 August 1910 (#453).

79 *Ittihad* 22 August 1910 (#588).

80 *Ittihad* 16 August 1910 (#583), *Lisan* 19 August 1910 (#6408).

81   *Muqtabas* (j) 17 August 1910 (#450), p. 3, 21 August 1910 (#453), *Ittihad* 22 August 1910 (#588).

82   *Muqtabas* (j) 21 August 1910 (#453), pp. 1–2 reported from Homs that the attack on the coach station occurred when the crowds could not at first reach the square of the Serail.

83   *Muqtabas* (j) 17 August 1910 (#450), p. 3, 21 August 1910 (#453), pp. 1–2.

84   *Ittihad* 16 August 1910 (#583), *Muqtabas* (j) 17 August 1910 (#450), p. 3, *Ittihad* 19 August 1910 (#586), *Muqtabas* (j) 21 August 1910 (#453), *Ittihad* 22 August 1910 (#588).

85   *Ittihad* 19 August 1910 (#586), *Muqtabas* (j) 21 August 1910 (#453), pp. 1–2. Earlier accounts had reported much larger but gradually decreasing numbers of wagons: *Ittihad* 16 August 1910 (#583) counted thirty wagons, *Muqtabas* (j) 17 August 1910 (#450), p. 3, with reference to *Lisan al-Sharq* from Hama, provided twenty-one and with reference to private sources only eighteen wagons.

86   Ibid., 3.

87   *Ittihad* 16 August 1910 (#583).

88   *Muqtabas* (j) 21 August 1910 (#453), pp. 1–2.

89   *Ittihad* 16 August 1910 (#583), *Muqtabas* (j) 17 August 1910 (#450), p. 3, *Lisan* 19 August 1910 (#6408).

90   *Bashir* 25 June 1910 (#1969), *Muqtabas* (j) 13 August 1910 (#446), p. 2, 16 August 1910 (#449), *Bashir* 20 August 1910 (#1977).

91   *Lisān* 23 June 1910 (#6359), *Muqtabas* (j) 3 July 1910 (#412), 4 July 1910 (#413), *Iqbal* 15 August 1910 (#360), *Ittihad* 15 August 1910 (#582).

92   *Iqbal* 22 August 1910 (#361).

93   *Muqtabas* (j) 3 July 1910 (#412), *Lisan* 5 July 1910 (#6369) *Ittihad* 16 August 1910 (#583), *Muqtabas* (j) 17 August 1910 (#450):3, *Lisan* 19 August 1910 (#6408).

94   *Lisan* 23 June 1910 (#6359).

95   *Muqtabas* (j) 21 August 1910 (#453): 1–2.

96   *Muqtabas* (j) 18 Febuary 1913 (#1119), cf. *Muqtabas* (j) 25 June 1910 (#405), *Ittihad* 16 August 1910 (#583).

97   Ibid.

98   Thamarat 21 March 1878 (#151).

99   *Muqtabas* (j) 3 July 1910 (#412). This aspect was also reported in *Iqbal* 11 July 1910 (#355), p. 5, *Muqtabas* (j) 1 March 1916 (#1837), p. 2.

100   *Lisan* 5 July 1910 (#6369), p. 2.

101   *Muqtabas* (j) 3 July 1910 (#412).

102   *Muqtabas* (j) 1 March 1916 (#1837),p. 2.

103   *Bashir* 25 June 1910 (#1969).

104   *Ittihad* 16 August 1910 (#583).

105   *Muqtabas* (j) 10 January 1911 (#570), p. 3, citing *al-Mufīd* from Beirut.

106   For example, *Lisān* 5 July 1910 (#6369). For this meaning of *al-qawm* see Butrus al-Bustani, *Kitab muhit al-muhit: Qamus mutawwal li-l-lugha al-ʿarabiyya*, vol. 2 (Bayrut, 1286 aH [1869–1870]), p. 1777.

107   For example, *Lisan* 19 August 1910 (#6408).

108   For example, Ibid.

109   For example, *Lisan* 23 June 1910 (#6359).

110   For example, *Ittihad* 18 August 1910 (#585), *Lisan* 19 August 1910 (#6408).

111   For example, *Muqtabas* (j) 14 August 1910 (#447), *Ittihad* 19 August 1910 (#586), *Muqtabas* (j) 21 August 1910 (#453):1–2, *Ittihad* 22 August 1910 (#588).

112 For example, *Muqtabas* (j) 20 August 1910 (#452): 3, 21 August 1910 (#453), pp. 1–2.

113 This directly contradicts Burke's characterization of the repertoire of contention in nineteenth-century Middle Eastern societies; see above.

114 Originally, Albert Hourani, 'Ottoman Reform and the Politics of Notables', in *The Modern Middle East: A Reader*, eds Albert Hourani, Philip S Khoury, and Mary C Wilson (Berkeley: University of California Press, [1968] 1993), 90, had introduced the a᾽yān as one of the three sub-groups of his 'secular' notables, alongside ᾽ulamā᾽ and leaders of local garrisons. See also Philip S. Khoury, *Urban Notables and Arab Nationalism: The Politics of Damascus, 1860–1920* (New York: Cambridge University Press, 1983); Ruth Michal Roded, 'Tradition and Change in Syria during the Last Decades of Ottoman Rule: The Urban Elite of Damaskus, Aleppo, Homs and Hama, 1876–1918' (PhD diss., University of Denver, 1984), 73–99; Linda Schatkowski Schilcher, *Families in Politics: Damascene Factions and Estates of the 18th and 19th Centuries* (Stuttgart: Steiner-Verlag-Wiesbaden, 1985); Ruth Michal Roded, 'The Syrian Urban Notables: Elite, Estates, Class?' *Asian and African Studies* 20 (1986): 146–171; Philip S. Khoury, 'The Urban Notable Paradigm Revisited', *Revue Des Mondes Musulmans Et de La Méditerranée* 55–56 (1990): 215–228. The application of 'ancién regime' as coined by Tocqueville to the Ottoman context was suggested by Ariel Salzmann, 'An Ancien Regime Revisited: "Privatization" and Political Economy in the Eighteenth-Century Ottoman Empire', *Politics Society* 21, no. 4 (1993): 393–423; Ariel Salzmann, *Tocqueville in the Ottoman Empire: Rival Paths to the Modern State* (Boston: Brill, 2004), esp. 11, 24–28; see also Yahya el-Ghoul, 'Bled et beldi, kbâr et a᾽yân: aspects linguistiques et historiques', *IBLA: Revue de l'Institut des Belles Lettres Arabes* 60, no. 179 (1997): 46; Nora Lafi, *Une ville du maghreb entre ancien régime et réformes ottomanes: Genèse des institutions municipales à tripoli de barbarie, 1795–1911* (Paris: l'Harmattan, 2002); Nora Lafi, 'Introduction', in *Municipalités méditerranéennes: les réformes urbaines ottomanes au miroir d'une histoire comparée (Moyen-Orient, Maghreb, Europe méridionale)*, ed. Nora Lafi (Berlin: Klaus Schwarz Verlag, 2005), 11–34; Nora Lafi, 'The Ottoman Municipal Reforms Between Old Regime and Modernity: Towards a New Interpretative Paradigm', in *First International Symposium on Eminönü*, ed. Fatih Sadırlı (Istanbul: Eminönü Belediyesi, 2006), 348–355.

115 Dana Sajdi, 'Peripheral Visions: The Worlds and Worldviews of Commoner Chroniclers in the 18th Century Ottoman Levant' (PhD diss., Columbia University, 2002), 3–13, 9.

116 *Muqtabas* (j) 25 June 1910 (#405), *Bashir* 25 June 1910 (#1969).

117 *Muqtabas* (j) 4 July 1910 (#413).

118 *Muqtabas* (j) 3 July 1910 (#412), *Lisan* 5 July 1910 (#6369), *Iqbal* 11 July 1910 (#355).

119 *Bashir* 9 July 1910 (#1971).

120 *Muqtabas* (j) 14 August 1910 (#447), *Iqbal* 22 August 1910 (#361).

121 *Iqbal* 15 August 1910 (#360).

122 *Muqtabas* (j) 17 August 1910 (#450), p. 3, *Ittihad* 18 August 1910 (#585).

123 Ibid. According to *Lisan* 19 August 1910 (#6408) the troops had arrived from Hama.

124 *Ittihad* 18 August 1910 (#585), *Muqtabas* (j) 21 Aug 1910 (#453).

125 Ibid., pp. 1–2. Similar low numbers of arrests were reported eight months later, when sixteen men – eleven of them in absentia – were sentenced to three years in

prison; *Muqtabas* (j) 29 May 1911 (#689): 3. Only one of the arrested was named: Ibn al-Mashita, having swallowed a piece of paper upon his arrest, caused a long investigation into what might have been written on this paper; *Lisan* 30 August 1910 (#6417).

126   *Ittihad* 18 August 1910 (#585), *Muqtabas* (j) 21 August 1910 (#453), *Lisan* 30 August 1910 (#6417).
127   *Ittihad* 18 August 1910 (#585).
128   *Muqtabas* (j) 21 August 1910 (#453), *Ittihad* 22 August 1910 (#588).
129   *Bashir* 25 June 1910 (#1969).
130   *Bashir* 9 July 1910 (#1971). Prices were originally provided per *shunbul* and normalized to *kile*: 1 *shunbul* = 3 *kile*.
131   *Muqtabas* (j) 16 August 1910 (#449), p. 3.
132   *Muqtabas* (j) 3 July 1910 (#412), *Lisan* 5 July 1910 (#6369).
133   *Muqtabas* (j) 30 August 1910 (#461).
134   *Muqtabas* (j) 2 March 1913 (#1128), p. 3.
135   *Muqtabas* (j) 4 March 1913 (#1130), p. 3.
136   *Muqtabas* (j) 6 March 1913 (#1132), p. 3.
137   *Muqtabas* (j) 25 March 1913 (#1148), p. 3.
138   *Muqtabas* (j) 29 March 1913 (#1151), p. 3.
139   *Muqtabas* (j) 31 March 1913 (#1153), p. 3.
140   *Muqtabas* (j) 7 April 1913 (#1159), p. 3.

Chapter 10

1   Karl Marx, 'The Eighteenth Brumaire of Louis Bonaparte', *Die Revolution*, no. 1 (1852): 5. Available online: https://www.marxists.org/archive/marx/works/download/pdf/18th-Brumaire.pdf (accessed 26 October 2017).
2   The German term Lumpenproletariat was translated as 'dangerous classes' in the early English version of the *Manifesto of the Communist Party* of 1848. The translation of Marx's other works use the German term. From a classical Marxian standpoint the terms lumpenproletariat and 'dangerous classes' are regarded as synonyms.
3   Fakhreddin Azimi, 'The Overthrow ofs the Government of Mosaddeq Reconsidered', *Iranian Studies* 45, no. 5 (2012): 697.
4   Teheran, Iranian Home Service, 'Mar. 02, 1953', in *Foreign Broadcast Information Service (FBIS): Iran* (Central Intelligence Agency, 1953), 1.
5   Homa Sarshar, *Sha'ban Ja'fari*, 2nd edn. (Los Angeles: Nab, 1381 h. sh. [2002]), 126–127.
6   Ibid., 125; See also Ali Rahnema, *Behind the 1953 Coup in Iran: Thugs, Turncoats, Soldiers, and Spooks* (Cambridge: Cambridge University Press, 2015), 38.
7   Marx, *The Eighteenth Brumaire of Louis Bonaparte*, 38: 'Alongside decayed roués with dubious means of subsistence and of dubious origin, alongside ruined and adventurous offshoots of the bourgeoisie, were vagabonds, discharged soldiers, discharged jailbirds, escaped galley slaves, swindlers, mountebanks, lazzaroni, pickpockets, tricksters, gamblers, *maquereaux* [pimps], brothel keepers, porters, literati, organ grinders, ragpickers, knife grinders, tinkers, beggars — in short, the

whole indefinite, disintegrated mass, thrown hither and thither, which the French call *la bohème*'.

8   Although Frederick Engels did not use the term lumpenproletariat explicitly, he depicts the same phenomena in his evaluation of the working class in England. Cf. Frederick Engels, *The Condition of the Working-Class in England in 1844*, trans. Florence Kelley Wischnewetzky (London: The Project Gutenberg eBook, 2005). Available online: http://www.gutenberg.org/files/17306/17306-h/17306-h.htm(accessed26October2017).

9   Cf. ibid., 93. Engels's statement in regard to the Irish in England who constituted the majority of the poorest classes at the time: 'Drink is the only thing which makes the Irishman's life worth having, drink and his cheery care-free temperament; so he revels in drink to the point of the most bestial drunkenness. The southern facile character of the Irishman, his crudity, which places him but little above the savage, his contempt for all humane enjoyments, in which his very crudeness makes him incapable of sharing, his filth and poverty, all favour drunkenness. The temptation is great, he cannot resist it, and so when he has money he gets rid of it down his throat.'

10 Asef Bayat, 'From "Dangerous Classes" to "Quiet Rebels": Politics of the Urban Subaltern in the Global South', *International Sociology* 15, no. 3 (2000): 536.

11 Cf. Willem M. Floor, 'Luṭi', *Encyclopædia Iranica*. Available online: http://www.iranicaonline.org/articles/luti (accessed 30 October 2017). See also M. C. Bateson, J. W. Clinton, J. B. M. Kassarjian, H. Safavi and M. Soraya, 'Ṣafā-yi Bāṭin: A Study of the Interrelations of a Set of Iranian Ideal Character Types', in *Psychological Dimensions of Near Eastern Studies*, eds Leon C. Brown and Norman Itzkowitz, Princeton Studies on the Near East (Princeton, NJ: Darwin Press, 1977), 266. Batson gives a list of ideal types ranging from a negative pole (thugs and ruffians) to a positive pole (chivalrous heroes and champions).

12 Floor, 'Luṭi'; Willem M. Floor, 'The lūṭis: A Social Phenomenon in Qājār Persia: A Reappraisal', *Die Welt des Islams* 13, nos 1–2 (1971): 103–120; Willem M. Floor, 'The Political Role of the Lutis in Iran', in *Modern Iran: The Dialectics of Continuity and Change*, eds Michael E. Bonine and Nikki R. Keddie (Albany: State University of New York Press, 1981), 83–95.

13 Vanessa Martin, 'The Lutis – The Turbulent Urban Poor', in *The Qajar Pact: Bargaining, Protest and the State in Nineteenth-Century Persia*, International library of Iranian studies 4 (London: Tauris, 2005), 113.

14 'The point about social bandits is that they are peasant outlaws whom the lord and state regard as criminals, but who remain within peasant society, and are considered by their people as heroes, as champions, avengers, fighters for justice, perhaps even leaders of liberation, and in any case as men to be admired helped and supported.' Eric J. Hobsbawm, *Bandits*, rev. edn. (New York: Pantheon Books, 1981), 17.

15 Cf. Floor, 'The Political Role of the Lutis in Iran', 88: 'Within their own districts *lūṭīs* aimed at making a reputation for themselves as generous men or *javanmards*, protecting the poor and weak in the neighbourhood as well as by opposing too grasping government officials – for which the population gratefully remembered them. To sustain their activities they demanded money from the rich in their district.'

16 Cf. John R. Perry, 'Ḥaydari and Neʿmati', *Encyclopædia Iranica*. Available online: http://www.iranicaonline.org/articles/haydari-and-nemati (accessed 30 October 2017).

17   Fariba Adelkhah, *Being Modern in Iran*, trans. Jonathan Derrick (London: Hurst & Co. in association with the Centre d'Etudes et de Recherches Internationales Paris, 1999), 30–52.

18   Geruh-e farhangi-ye Shahid-e Ebrahimhadi, *Tayyeb: Zendeginameh va khaterat-e Horr-e nehzat-e Imam Khomeyni Shahid-e Tayyeb-e Hajj Reza'i* (Tehran: Nashr-e Aminan, 1392 h. sh. [2013]), 11–13.

19   Rahnema, *Behind the 1953 Coup in Iran*, 304–305.

20   Bateson et al., 'Ṣafā-yi Bāṭin', 265.

21   Sarshar, *Sha'ban Ja'fari*, 27.

22   Ibid., 31.

23   Anja Pistor-Hatam, 'Sattār Khan', *Encyclopædia Iranica*. Available online: http://www.iranicaonline.org/articles/sattar-khan-one-of-the-most-popular-heroes-from-tabriz-who-defended-the-town-during-the-lesser-autocracy-in-1908-09 (accessed 30 October 2017).

24   Abbas Amanat, 'Bāqer Khan Sālār-e melli', *Encyclopædia Iranica*. Available online: http://www.iranicaonline.org/articles/baqer-khan-salar-melli (accessed 30 October 2017).

25   Cf. Ashgar Fathi, 'The Role of the "Rebels" in the Constitutional Movement in Iran', *International Journal of Middle East Studies* 10, no. 1 (1979): 56–57.

26   Janet Afary, *The Iranian Constitutional Revolution, 1906–1911: Grassroots Democracy, Social Democracy, & the Origins of Feminism,* The History and Society of the Modern Middle East (New York: Columbia University Press, 1996), 6.

27   Anja Pistor-Hatam, 'Sattār Khan'.

28   'Most famous of all Iranian *lutis* were Sattar Khan and Baqer Khan who led the constitutionalist forces in Tabriz against the royalist forces. As the last constitutionalist bulwark in the country, together with the forces from Rasht and the Bakhtiyari tribesmen, they forced Mohammad Ali Shah to abdicate in 1909. Because of their courageous resistance and leadership, both lutis became national heroes.' Floor, 'The Political Role of the Lutis in Iran', 91:

29   Marx, *The Eighteenth Brumaire of Louis Bonaparte*, 38.

30   Donald N. Wilber, *[CIA-files] Overthrow of Premier Mossadeq of Iran: November 1952 – August 1953* (CIA, [written 1954] 1969), Clandestine Service History, 63.

31   For detailed analyses of the processes see the newest contributions of Ervand Abrahamian and Ali Rahnema: Ervand Abrahamian, *The Coup: 1953 the CIA and the Roots of Modern U.S.-Iranian Relations* (New York: The New Press, 2013); Rahnema, *Behind the 1953 Coup in Iran*.

32   Gholam Reza Afkhami, *The Life and Times of the Shah* (Berkeley: University of California Press, 2009), 184.

33   'On 19 August, as soon as the city was awake, early risers could see photostats of type-set copies of the firman in the papers *Setareh Islam, Asia Javanan, Aram, Mard-i-Asia, Mellat-i-Ma* and the *Journal de Tehran*. […] Somewhat later in the morning the first of many thousand broadsheets which carried a photostatic copy of the firman and the text of the Zahedi statement appeared on the streets. Although each of these newspapers had a normal circulation of restricted size, the news they carried was undoubtedly flashed through the city word of mouth, for before 0900 hours pro-Shah groups were assembling in the bazaar area. Members of these groups had not only made their personal choice between Mossadeq and the Shah, but they were stirred up by the Tudeh activity of the preceding day and were ready to move. They

needed only leadership.' Wilber, *Overthrow of Premier Mossadeq of Iran*, Clandestine Service History, 65.

34   Azimi, 'The Overthrow of the Government of Mosaddeq Reconsidered', 703.
35   Michael Axworthy, *Revolutionary Iran: A History of the Islamic Republic* (London: Allen Lane, 2013), 121.
36   Cf. Azimi, 'The Overthrow of the Government of Mosaddeq Reconsidered'; Mark J. Gasiorowski, 'The Causes of Iran's 1953 Coup: A Critique of Darioush Bayandor's *Iran and the CIA*', *Iranian Studies* 45, no. 5 (2012): 669–678; Mark J. Gasiorowski, 'The 1953 Coup d'État against Mosaddeq', in *Mohammad Mosaddeq and the 1953 Coup in Iran*, eds Mark J. Gasiorowski and Malcom Byrne, 1st edn., Modern Intellectual and Political History of the Middle East (Syracuse, NY: Syracuse University Press, 2004), 227–260; Moyara de Moraes Ruehsen, 'Operation "Ajax" Revisited: Iran, 1953', *Middle Eastern Studies* 29, no. 3 (1993): 467–486.
37   Fariborz Mokhtari, 'Iran's 1953 Coup Revisited: Internal Dynamics versus External Intrigue', *Middle East Journal* 62, no. 3 (2008): 484.
38   Darioush Bayandor, *Iran and the CIA: The Fall of Mosaddeq Revisited* (Basingstoke: Palgrave Macmillan, 2010).
39   See Fariba Adelkhahs description of the milieu: 'This fruit and vegetable market is a very important place for the people of Tehran. [...] Probably [the] importance of vegetables and fruit in the diet of Tehran's citizens was even greater in the 1950s than today, because consumption of meat and rice was reserved for feast days. This means that considerable sums of money changed hands in the fruit and vegetable market – especially as that place, by its central position, also became the nodal point of trading networks that extended over the principal parts of the country, some goods being immediately forwarded to other cities. Conflicts, sometimes bloody, broke out among the "roughnecks" who tried to control the business. In addition, that market was the place where three categories of vendors interacted: the producers the middlemen and the traders, including itinerant traders. Negotiations were often rough. The harshness of the place was further emphasised by its lack of hygiene, rubbish and dropping of draught animals, mud and dust. The *meydun* never became a place where people could go in a family group to do shopping'. Adelkhah, *Being Modern in Iran*.
40   Geruh-e farhangi-ye Shahid-e Ebrahimhadi, *Tayyeb*, 37.
41   Rahnema, *Behind the 1953 Coup in Iran*, 160
42   Ibid.
43   Geruh-e farhangi-ye Shahid-e Ebrahimhadi, *Tayyeb*, 70
44   Rahnema, *Behind the 1953 Coup in Iran*, 304. See also Geruh-e farhangi-ye Shahid-e Ebrahimhadi, *Tayyeb*, 73.
45   See, for example, the false presentation of the events by Moyara de Moraes Ruehsen: 'With the streets finally clear, the following day (19 August) Shaban "the Brainless" Jafari and two to three hundred large men with bulging biceps from the zurkhaneh (a traditional wrestling and body building club) led a large, rowdy demonstration from southern Tehran to the city's central square. Instead of quelling the riots, this time the police participated.' Moraes Ruehsen, 'Operation "Ajax" Revisited: Iran, 1953', 480.
46   Cf. Sarshar, *Sha'ban Ja'fari,*, 159–163.
47   Geruh-e farhangi-ye Shahid-e Ebrahimhadi, *Tayyeb*, 73.
48   Mojtaba Zadeh-Mohammadi, *Lompan-ha dar siyasat-e 'asr-e pahlavi*, 3rd ed. (Tehran: Nashr-e markaz, 1392 h. sh. [2013]), 6–8.

49   F. M. Khwashir, *Tajrobe-ye bist-o-hasht-e mordad* (Tehran: Entesharat-e Hezb-e
     Tudeh-ye Iran, 1359 h. sh. [1979]).

50   Mojtaba Zadeh-Moaammadi, *Lompen-ha dar siyasat-e 'asr-e pahlavi*, 3rd edn.
     (Tehran: Nashr-e markaz, 1392 h. sh. [=2013]), 100.

51   Ibid., 112

52   Georgi Derluguian and Timothy Earle, 'Strong Chieftaincies out of Weak States, or
     Elemental Power Unbound', *Comparative Social Research*, 27, 'Troubled Regions and
     Failing States' (Bingley: Emerald Group Publishing Limited, 2010), 52.

53   David Riesman in Daniel Lerner, *Passing of Traditional Society: Modernizing the
     Middle East* (London: Macmillan, 1958), 7.

54   Leonard Binder, *Iran: Political Development in a Changing Society* (Berkeley:
     University of California Press, 1964), 158, fn 2.

55   Ibid., 158.

56   Lerner, *Passing of Traditional Society*, 399.

57   Hamid Naficy, *A Social History of Iranian Cinema*, vol. 2, *The Industrializing Years,
     1941–1978* (Durham, NC: Duke University Press, 2011), 261.

58   Ibid., 262–263.

59   Ibid., 305.

60   Ibid., 264.

61   Joanna de Groot, *Religion, Culture and Politics in Iran: From the Qajars to Khomeini*,
     Library of modern Middle East studies 25 (London: I.B. Tauris, 2007), 51.

62   Sarshar, *Sha'ban Ja'fari*, 89

63   Mohsen Mobasser, 6 October 1984 in *Iranian Oral History Collection, Harvard
     University*, ed. Habib Ladjevardi, transcript 2, 2; Zadeh-Mohammadi, *Lompan-ha dar
     siyasat-e 'asr-e pahlavi*, 109.

64   Sarshar, *Sha'ban Ja'fari*, 207.

65   Ibid., 249–274.

66   Cf. H. E. Chehabi, 'Ja'fari, Ša'bān', *Encyclopædia Iranica*. Available online: http://
     www.iranicaonline.org/articles/jafari-saban(accessed5August2016): 'While there
     is general agreement that he had originally been a *čāqukeš* (thug), from the mid-
     1950s onwards his demeanor became more respectable as he came to concentrate on
     traditional athletics. As *sarparast-e varzeš-e bāstāni* (head of ancient sport) he played
     a major part in keeping alive Iran's athletic tradition at a time when the country's
     physical education establishment was mostly committed to propagating Western
     disciplines and looked down on Ja'fari and the *zur-ḵāna* tradition (Ja'fari; Saršār,
     pp. 304–305). His tireless efforts to recruit young Iranian men for what was by now
     called "ancient" (*bāstāni*) sports played a major part in ensuring the generational
     renewal of that tradition at a time when most young people were attracted to
     Western sports. The Ja'fari club was Iran's first modern *zur-kānā* and paved the way
     for others, such as that of the Bānk-e Melli and the ones built after the revolution.
     Since the revolution, the premises of his club have housed the National Federation of
     Ancient Sports.'

67   Ibid.

68   Geruh-e farhangi-ye Shahid-e Ebrahimhadi, *Tayyeb*, 88.

69   Fakhreddin Azimi, 'Khomeini and the "White Revolution"', in *A Critical Introduction
     to Khomeini*, ed. Arshin Adib-Moghaddam (New York: Cambridge University Press,
     2014), 36.

70   Ibid.

71   Fathi, 'The Role of the "Rebels" in the Constitutional Movement in Iran', 58.

72   Groot, *Religion, Culture and Politics in Iran*, 170.
73   Theodor W. Adorno, 'Reflexionen zur Klassentheorie [1942]', in *Gesellschaftstheorie und Kulturkritik*, 1. Aufl., Edition Suhrkamp 772 (Frankfurt am Main: Suhrkamp, 1975), 7–25; Max Horkheimer, 'Die Rackets und der Geist [1943]', in *Gesammelte Schriften: Band 12: Nachgelassene Schriften 1931–1949*, ed. Gunzelin Schmid Noerr (Frankfurt am Main: Fischer, 1985), 287–291; Max Horkheimer, 'Zur Soziologie der Klassenverhältnisse [1943]', in *Gesammelte Schriften: Band 12: Nachgelassene Schriften 1931–1949*, ed. Gunzelin Schmid Noerr (Frankfurt am Main: Fischer, 1985, 75–104).
74   Horkheimer, 'Die Rackets und der Geist [1943]', 287.
75   Max Horkheimer and Theodor W. Adorno, *Dialektik der Aufklärung: Philosophische Fragmente*, 21st edn. (Frankfurt am Main: Fischer Taschenbuch Verlag, 2013).
76   Max Horkheimer, 'Herrschende Klasse, die von den Rackets beherrschte Klasse und die Rolle der Fachleute: [Späne. 1957–1967]', in *Gesammelte Schriften: Band 14: Nachgelassene Schriften 1949–1972*, ed. Alfred Schmidt and Gunzelin Schmid Noerr (Frankfurt am Main: Fischer, 1988), 334.
77   Kai Lindemann, 'Der Racketbegriff als Herrschaftskritik', in *Staat und Politik bei Horkheimer und Adorno*, eds Ulrich Ruschig and Hans-Ernst Schiller, Staatsverständnisse Band 64 (Baden-Baden: Nomos, 2014), 118.
78   'Der Unterschied von Ausbeutern und Ausgebeuteten tritt nicht so in Erscheinung, daß er den Ausgebeuteten Solidarität als ihre ultima ratio vor Augen stell: Konformität ist ihnen rationaler. Die Zugehörigkeit zur gleichen Klasse setzt längst nicht in Gleichheit des Interesses und der Aktion um.' Adorno, 'Reflexionen zur Klassentheorie [1942]', 11.
79   'Die Geschichte ist, nach dem Bilde der letzten ökonomischen Phase, die Geschichte von Monopolen. Nach dem Bilde der manifesten Usurpation, die von den einträchtigen Führern von Kapital und Arbeit heute verübt wird, ist sie die Geschichte von Bandenkämpfen, Gangs und Rackets.' Adorno, 'Reflexionen zur Klassentheorie [1942]', 15.
80   Horkheimer, 'Die Rackets und der Geist [1943]', 290.
81   Charles Tilly, 'War Making and State Making as Organized Crime', in *Bringing the State Back In*, ed. Peter B. Evans (Cambridge: Cambridge University Press, 1985), 170–171.
82   Peter M. R. Stirk, *Max Horkheimer: A New Interpretation* (Hemel Hempstead: Harvester Wheatsheaf; Barnes & Noble, 1992), 141.
83   Ibid., 143.
84   Rahnema, *Behind the 1953 Coup in Iran*, 295.
85   Ibid., 297.

Chapter 11

1   This chapter is a revised, extended and adapted version of the article published (Open Access) in *Ethnography* (Sage Publications). See Maziyar Ghiabi, 'Under the Bridge in Tehran: Addiction, Poverty and Capital', *Ethnography*, https://doi.org/10.1177/1466138118787534. Published online August 2, 2018. It shares some of the ethnographic vignettes but explores the historical and theoretical aspects of the Iranian case in more depth.

2   Maziyar Ghiabi, Masoomeh Maarefvand, Hamed Bahari and Zohreh Alavi, 'Islam
    and Cannabis: Legalisation and Religious Debate in Iran', *International Journal of
    Drug Policy* 56 (2018): 121–127; Rudolph P. Matthee, *The Pursuit of Pleasure: Drugs
    and Stimulants in Iranian History, 1500–1900* (Princeton, NJ: Princeton University
    Press, 2005).
3   Maziyar Ghiabi, 'The Opium of the State', in *The Age of Aryamehr: Local and Global
    Entanglements of Late Pahlavi Iran, 1941–1979*, ed. R. Alvandi (London: Gingko
    Library Press, 2018).
4   Merrill Singer and J. Bryan Page. *The Social Value of Drug Addicts: Uses of the Useless*
    (London: Routledge, 2016), 153.
5   Maziyar Ghiabi, 'Deconstructing the Islamic Bloc: The Middle East and North Africa
    and Pluralistic Drug Policy', in *Collapse of the Global Order on Drugs? From UNGASS
    2016 to the High Level Review 2019*, eds Blaine Stothard and Axel Klein (London:
    Emerald, 2018), 167–189.
6   By the late nineteenth century, the definition of 'dangerous class' applied to plebeian
    groups, its borders shifting based on the political persuasion of the time. Karl Marx
    discussed the political dangers of this category in the *Eighteen Brumaire of Louis
    Napoleon*, calling them the lumpenproletariat, i.e. 'what is lower than the proletariat'.
    A century later, Michel Foucault turned Marx's criticism of the reactionary nature
    of lumpen politics upside down by claiming, in *Les Anormaux*, that only those at
    the very margins of the social order disposed of true revolutionary power. Michel
    Foucault, 'Les Anormaux', *Cours au Collège de France* (Paris: Seiul, 1999).
7   Philippe I. Bourgois and Jeffrey Schonberg, *Righteous Dopefiend*, vol. 21 (Los
    Angeles: University of California Press, 2009); Tim Rhodes, Merrill Singer, Philippe
    Bourgois, Samuel R. Friedman and Steffanie A. Strathdee, 'The Social Structural
    Production of HIV Risk Among Injecting Drug Users', *Social Science & Medicine* 61,
    no. 5 (2005): 1026–1044; Philippe Bourgois, *In Search of Respect: Selling Crack in El
    Barrio*, vol. 10 (New York: Cambridge University Press, 2003).
8   See the case of black Americans, powerfully illustrated in Michelle Alexander, *The
    New Jim Crow: Mass Incarceration in the Age of Colorblindness* (New York: The New
    Press, 2012).
9   Philippe Bourgois, 'Lumpen Abuse: the Human Cost of Righteous Neoliberalism',
    City & Society 23, no. 1 (2011): 7.
10 Maziyar Ghiabi, *Drugs Politics: Managing Disorder in the Islamic Republic of Iran*
    (London: Cambridge University Press, 2019).
11 Singer and Page, *The Social Value of Drug Addicts*, 172.
12 Rakhshan Bani Etemad, dir., *Zir-e Pust-e Shahr* [Under the Skin of the City] (Tehran,
    2003).
13 Truth be told, pharmaceutical companies own a legal monopoly on all opiate
    substances, sold and distributed in the form of morphine-derivate products.
14 Michael Denning, 'Wageless life', *New Left Review* 66 (2010): 81.
15 In Karl Marx, *Grundrisse* (London: Penguin, 1993) cited also by Denning, 'Wageless
    Life'.
16 Giorgio Agamben, *Homo Sacer: Sovereign Power and Bare Life* (Stanford, CA:
    Stanford University Press, 1998).
17 See Didier Fassin, *At the Heart of the State* (London: Pluto Press, 2015), 2.
18 Cesare Lombroso, *L'uomo delinquente in rapporto all'antropologia: alla giurisprudenza
    ed alle discipline carcerarie. 1896–1897*, vol. 2 (Torino: Fratelli Bocca, 1896).

19   In Franco Basaglia and Franca Basaglia-Ongaro, *La maggioranza deviante: (L'ideologia del controllo sociale totale)* (Torino: Einaudi, 1971), 168.

20   The word can mean different things, but it has acquired a specific meaning in drug parlance.

21   *Tabnak*, 29 July 2013. Available online: http://www.tabnak.ir/fa/news/335027 (accessed 14 June 2018).

22   Maziyar Ghiabi, 'Drogues Illégales et Gestion de l'espace dans l'Iran Moderne', *Hérodote* 2 (2018): 133–151.

23   Reuters in Ankara, 'Iran Bans Magazine after 'White Marriage' Special', *The Guardian*, 27 April 2015. Available online: https://www.theguardian.com/world/2015/apr/27/iran-bans-magazine-white-marriage-unmarried-couples-cohabiting (accessed 2 June 2019).

24   In Iran, as elsewhere, methadone is legal when sold as a prescription substance in clinics, but there is an active black market for it too.

25   *ADNA*, 'Hezar mo'tad-e karton-khab dar keshvar shenasai shodand' 12 June 2016. Available online: http://adna.ir/news/1590/42- accessed on August 22, 2018

26   Michel Foucault, *Discipline & Punish: The Birth of the Prison* (London: Vintage, 2012), 278.

27   Shahram Khosravi, *Precarious Lives: Waiting and Hope in Iran* (Philadelphia: University of Pennsylvania Press, 2017), 104–105.

28   The abundance of 'social pathology' as a discipline studying urban phenomena is a distinct trait of Iranian social sciences today. Cf. Mohammad Kaveh, *Asib-shenasi-ye Bimari-ha-ye Ejtema'i*, vol. 1–2 (Tehran: Jame'eshanan, 2010).

29   Maziyar Ghiabi, 'Drugs and Revolution in Iran: Islamic Devotion, Revolutionary Zeal and Republican Means', *Iranian Studies* 48, no. 2 (2015): 139–163.

30   Yet, already in the early 1980s there was a shift in policy with the government's refusal to expropriate large land holdings and the inability to formalize the illegal settlements in Tehran's shantytowns.

31   Frantz Fanon, Jean-Paul Sartre and Constance Farrington, *The Wretched of the Earth*, vol. 36 (New York: Grove Press, 1963).

32   Didier Fassin, *Enforcing Order: An Ethnography of Urban Policing* (New York: Polity, 2013).

33   The story is an amalgam of factual elements from the life of several young plebeians, with whom I carried out fieldwork between 2012 and 2016.

34   Cf. Khosravi, *Precarious Lives.*

35   Walter Benjamin. *Selected Writings* II 1927-1934. Trans. Rodney Livingstone et al. Eds. Michael W. Jennings, Howard Eiland and Gary Smith (Cambridge, MA: Harvard Universiy Press, 1999).

36   Maziyar Ghiabi, 'Maintaining Disorder: the Micropolitics of Drug Policy in Iran', *Third World Quarterly* 38, no. 2 (2017): 277–297.

37   Unpublished data and statistics by the United Nations Office on Drugs and Crime, Tehran [Excel file].

38   Jean Comaroff, 'Beyond Bare Life: AIDS, (bio) Politics, and the Neoliberal Order', *Public Culture* 19, no. 1 (2007): 197.

39   Ruhollah Faghihi, 'Grave sleepers shock Iranians', *Al-Monitor*, 27 December 2016. Available online: www.al-monitor.com/pulse/originals/2016/12/iran-grave-sleepers-shahrvand-rouhani-asghar-farhadi.html?utm_source=Boomtrain&utm_medium=manual&utm_campaign=20161229&bt_ee=gkfARQJWWIBnqjsWENPS

fFLwkdpbFzyAuZ/R7s10NqLK0ETGDRslQQY2CICcr0Og&bt_ts=1483032217060 (accessed 29 August 2018).

40   A longer analysis of this paradox can be found in a piece I wrote in response to *Shahrvand*'s report, Maziyar Ghiabi, 'Mas'aleh-i faratar az gurkhabi', *Shahrvand*, 27 December 2016. Available online: http://shahrvand-newspaper.ir/News:NoMobile/Main/86383 (accessed 29 August 2018).

41   *Vaqaye' Ettefaqiyeh*, 4 July 2017. Available online: http://www.vaghayedaily.ir/fa/News/76102 (accessed August 30, 2018).

42   Reported in Ahmad Masjed Jamei, *Darvazeh Ghar* (Tehran: Thaleth, 2016), 15.

43   Ibid., 16. The area itself deserves detailed historical study. The history of *ashura'*, coffeehouses, *zurkhaneh*, *lutigari* and much more is inevitably omitted here.

44   *Sharq*, 16 November 2015. Available online: http://www.sharghdaily.ir/News/78788 (accessed 16 August 2018).

45   She has also worked with the award-winning Iranian film director Rakhshan Bani on the documentary titled *Khaneh-ye Khorshid*.

46   I recorded the speech. Available online: http://www.entekhab.ir/fa/news/229385 (accessed July 20, 2018).

47   Mitra Asfari, 'An integrated group of strangers called *Ghorbat*', presentation at the International Society of Iranian Studies Conference, Vienna, 2017.

48   Basaglia, *La Maggioranza Deviante*, 71.

49   Ela R. Bhatt, *We are Poor but So Many: The Story of Self-employed Women in India* (Oxford: Oxford University Press, 2005), 89, cited in Denning, 'Wageless Life'.

50   See Melissa Gira Grant, *Playing the Whore: The Work of Sex Work* (London: Verso Books, 2014). Shira M. Goldenberg, Steffanie A. Strathdee, Manuel Gallardo, Tim Rhodes, Karla D. Wagner and Thomas L. Patterson, '"Over Here, it's Just Drugs, Women and all the Madness": The HIV Risk Environment of Clients of Female Sex Workers in Tijuana, Mexico', *Social Science & Medicine* 72, no. 7 (2011): 1185–1192; Trung Nam Tran, Roger Detels, Nguyen Tran Hien, Hoang Thuy Long and Pham Thi Hoang Nga, 'Drug Use, Sexual Behaviours and Practices Among Female Sex Workers in Hanoi, Viet Nam – a Qualitative Study', *International Journal of Drug Policy* 15, no. 3 (2004): 189–195.

51   *ADNA* 'Dar payetakht gorosneh-ye motlaq nadarim', 3 January 2017. Available online: http://adna.ir/news/1973/در-پایتخت-گرسنه-مطلق-نداریم-به-م-ی-گوی-م د ر-تهران-ب-ی-خانمان-نداریم- (accessed July 20, 2018).

Bibliography

Archives

Al-Mahalla Misdemeanor Court Records, Egypt
Archives Nationales d'Outre Mer (ANOM), France
Başbakanlık Osmanlı Arşivi (The Ottoman Archives of the Prime Minister's Office, BOA)
Dar al-Mahfuzat al-'Umumiyya (National Archive), Cairo
Egyptian National Library and Archives
Foreign Broadcast Information Service (FBIS)
İçişleri Bakanlığı Arşivi (Interior Ministry Archive, Turkey, İBA)
India Office Records
Library, Museum and Document Center of the Iranian Parliament
The National Archives at College Park, Maryland (NACP)
The National Archives of the United Kingdom (TNA)
Parliamentary Papers of the British House of Commons (HCPP)
Başbakanlık Cumhuriyet Arşivi (Prime Ministry Republican Archive, Turkey, BCA)
Public Record Office (PRO), UK
Sazman-e Asnad-e Melli-ye Iran (National Archives of Iran)
Société des Missionnaires d'Afrique
Tanta Criminal Court Records

Newspapers and periodicals

Cumhuriyet
Deutsches Handelsarchiv
The Guardian
Hadiqat al-Akbar
İkdam
Iran-i naw
Konstantinopler Handelsblatt
Köroğlu
L'Echo d'Oran
La Revue algérienne illustrée
The Levant Herald
Lisan al-Hal
Orak Çekiç
Resmi Gazete
Salname suriye
Servet-i Fünun

Shahrvand
Sharq
Shefaq-e Sorkh
Son Posta
Suriye
Tabnak
Taqqadum
Thamarat al-Funun
Ülkü
Vakit
Vaqaye'-e Ettefaqiyeh
Yeni Türk

Books and articles

'Abd al-Wahid, Fatima 'Alam al-Din. *Tatawural-Naqlwaal-Muwasalatal-Dakhiliyya fi Misr fi 'ahd al-Ihtilal al-Britani 1882–1914* [The Development of Domestic Transportation in Egypt under the British Occupation, 1882–1914]. Cairo: al-Hay'a al-Misriyya al-'Amma lil-kitab, 1989.

Abrahamian, Ervand. *The Coup: 1953 the CIA and the Roots of Modern U.S.-Iranian Relations.* New York: The New Press, 2013.

Abolhassan Hadjiheidari, 'Nāyeb Ḥoseyn Kāšī, Strassenräuber oder Revolutionär?: eine Untersuchung zur neueren iranischen Geschichte (1850–1920)' (Berlin: Klaus Schwarz Verlag, 2011)

Abu-Lughod, Leila. 'The Romance of Resistance: Tracing Transformations of Power Through Bedouin Women'. *American Ethnologist* 17, no. 1 (February 1990): 41–55.

Abu-Manneh, Butrus. 'The Genesis of Midḥat Pasha's Governorship in Syria 1878–1880'. In *The Syrian Land: Processes of Integration and Fragmentation; Bilād al-Shām from the 18th to the 20th Century,* edited by Thomas Philipp and Birgit Schaebler, 251–267. Stuttgart: Franz Steiner Verlag, 1998.

Adelkhah, Fariba. *Being Modern in Iran,* translated by Jonathan Derrick. London: Hurst & Co. in association with the Centre d'Etudes et de Recherches Internationales Paris, 1999.

Adli, Younes. *Si Mohand ou Mhand.* Alger: EDIF, [2000] 2001.

Adorno, Theodor W. 'Reflexionenen zur Klassentheorie [1942]'. In *Gesellschaftstheorie und Kulturkritik,* 1. Aufl., Edition Suhrkamp 772, 7–25. Frankfurt am Main: Suhrkamp, 1975.

Afary, Janet. *The Iranian Constitutional Revolution, 1906–1911: Grassroots Democracy, Social Democracy, & the Origins of Feminism.* New York: Columbia University Press, 1996.

Afkhami, Gholam Reza. *The Life and Times of the Shah.* Berkeley: University of California Press, 2009.

Afshari, Reza. 'The Historians of the Constitutional Movement and the Making of the Iranian Populist Tradition'. *International Journal of Middle East Studies* 25, no. 3 (1993): 477–494.

Agamben, Giorgio. *Homo Sacer: Sovereign Power and Bare Life.* Stanford, CA: Stanford University Press, 1998.

Agamben, Giorgio. *State of Exception*. Chicago: University of Chicago Press, 2005.

Ageron, Charles Robert. *Les Algériens musulmans et la France (1871–1919)*, vol. 1. Saint-Denis: Bouchène, [1968] 2005.

Ağir, Seven. 'The Evolution of Grain Policy: The Ottoman Experience'. *Journal of Interdisciplinary History* 43, no. 4 (2013): 571–598.

Akçetin, Elif. 'Anatolian Peasants in the Great Depression, 1929–1933'. *New Perspectives on Turkey*, no. 23 (September 2000): 79–102.

Akdağ, Mustafa. *Türk Halkının Dirlik ve Düzenlik Kavgası*. Ankara: Bilgi Yayınları, 1975.

Aksoy, Refet, *Köylülerimizle Başbaşa*. Yozgat: Yozgat İlbaylik Basımevi, 1936.

Al-Babli, Muhammad. *Al-Ijram fi Misr: Asbabuh wa Turq ʾIlajih* [Criminality in Egypt: Its Causes and Remedies]. Cairo: Matbaʿat Dar al-Kutub, 1941.

al-Bustani, Butrus. *Kitab muhit al-muhit: Qamus mutawwal li-l-lugha al-ʿarabiyya*, vol. 2. Bayrut, 1286 aH [1869–70].

Al-Davud, Seyyedʾ Ali. *Nayeb Hossein Kashi Dar Khur Biabanak*. Tehran: Ketabkhaneh, Muzeh va Markaz-e Asnad-e Majles-e Shura-ye Eslami, 1394 [2015].

Al-Dunya al-Musawara. 'Jihad al-Bulis fi Mukafahat al-Mujrimin min al-Jins al-Latif' [The Police Struggle against Criminals of the Gentle Sex], 20 March 1930.

Al-Misri, Kamil, ed. *Qanun al-ʾUqubat al-Ahli Mudhayyal bi-Ahkam al-Mahakim al-Ahliyyah li-ghayat 1930* [The Penal Code with Verdicts of the National Courts until 1930]. Cairo: al Maktaba al-Tujariyya al-Kubra, 1931.

al-Qarrarat wa al Manshurat al-Sadirah sanat-1885. Cairo: al-Matbaʿah al-Amiriyyah bi-Bulaq, 1886.

al-Qasimi, *Jamal al-Din* and Khalil al-ʾAzm, *Qāmūs al-sinaʾat al-shamiyya*, Vol. 2, ed. Zafir al-Qasimi (Paris: Mouton & co., 1960).

Al-Tarabulsi, Muhammad Nabih. *Al-Mujrimun al-ahdath fi al-qanun al-Misri wa al-Tashriʾ al-Muqaran* [Child Criminals in the Egyptian Code and Comparative Law]. Cairo: Dar al-fikr alʾArabi, 1948.

al-ʿUyun, Mahmud Abu. *Mushkilah al-Bighaʾ al- Rasmi*. Cairo: Matbaʿat al-Hilal, 1933.

al-ʿUyun, Mahmud Abu. 'Chastity Screams'. *Al-Ahram*. 8 December 1923, n.p.

Alexander, Michelle. *The New Jim Crow: Mass Incarceration in the Age of Colorblindness*. New York: The New Press, 2012.

Ali, HusaynMuhammad. 'Al-Nashl: Asalibahu wa Mawasimahu fi Madinat al-Qahira' ['Pickpocketing: Its Methods and Seasons in Cairo'], 56–81. *Majallat al-Amn al-ʾAmm*, April 1959.

ʾAli, Muhammad Khayri Muhammad. *Al-Rif wa al-Hadar wa Zahirat al-Jarima: Dirasa Nazariyya wa Maydaniyya* [The Phenomenon of Crime in the Countryside and City: A Theoretical and Empirical Study]. Cairo: Dar al-Nahda, 1965.

Alyot, Halim. *Türkiye'de Zabıta: Tarihi Gelişim ve Bugünkü Durum*. Ankara: İçişleri Bakanlığı Yayınları, 1947.

Amanat, Abbas. 'Bāqer Khan Sālār-e melli'. *Encyclopædia Iranica (Online)* 3, no. 7 (1988): 726–728. Available online: http://www.iranicaonline.org/articles/baqer-khan-salar-melli (accessed 30 October 2017).

Amirahmadi, Hooshang. *The Political Economy of Iran under the Qajars: Society, Politics, Economics and Foreign Relations, 1796–1926*. London: I.B. Tauris, 2012.

Amrouni, Hassina. 'Les bandits d'honneur d'Algérie'. *Memoria*, 19 September 2016. Available online: https://www.memoria.dz/sep-2016/dossier/les-bandits-dhonneur-dalg-rie (accessed 4 June 2019).

Amster, Ellen J. *Medicine and the Saints. Science, Islam, and the Colonial Encounter in Morocco, 1877–1956*. Austin: University of Texas Press, 2014.

Anarfi, J. K. 'Ghanaian Women and Prostitution in Cote d'Ivoire'. In *Global Sex Workers: Rights, Resistance, and Redefinition,* edited by Kamala Kempadoo and Jo Doezema, 104–113. New York: Routledge, 1998.

Anderson, Kyle J. 'The Egyptian Labor Corps: Workers, Peasants, and the State in World War I'. *International Journal of Middle East Studies* 49 (2017): 5–24.

Anscombe, Frederick. 'Albanians and "Mountain Bandits"'. *Princeton Papers: Interdisciplinary Journal of Near Eastern Studies* 13 (2006): 87–114; reprinted in *The Ottoman Balkans, 1750–1830,* edited by Frederick F. Anscombe, 87–113. Princeton, NJ: Markus Wiener Publishers, 2006.

Antony, Robert J. 'Peasants, Heroes and Brigands: The Problems of Social Banditry in Early Nineteenth-Century South China'. *Modern China* 15, no. 2 (April 1989): 123–148.

Arasteh, Reza. 'The Character, Organization and Social Role of the Lutis (Javan-Mardan) in the Traditional Iranian Society of the Nineteenth Century'. *Journal of the Economic and Social History of the Orient* 4, no. 1 (February 1961): 47–52.

Araz, Yahya. *Osmanlı Toplumunda Çocuk Olmak* (16. Yüzyıldan 19. Yüzyıl Başlarına). İstanbul: Kitap Yayınevi, 2013.

Arnold, David. 'Dacoity and Rural Crime in Madras, 1860–1940'. *Journal of Peasant Studies* 6 (1979): 140–167.

Aryanpur, Amir Hushang. *Hamase-ye Toghiyan: Barresi-ye Jonbesh-e Nayebiyan-e Kashan Bar Asas-e Asnad.* Tehran: Ketab-e Ameh, 1388.

Asfari, Mitra. 'An integrated group of strangers called *Ghorbat*'. Presentation at the International Society of Iranian Studies Conference, Vienna, 2017.

Atabaki, Touraj, ed. *Iran and the First World War: Battleground of the Great Powers.* London: I.B. Tauris, 2006.

Atabaki, Touraj and Zürcher, Eric Jan (eds), *Men of Order : authoritarian modernization under Atatürk and Reza Shah* (London: I.B. Tauris, 2003).

Axworthy, Michael. *Revolutionary Iran: A History of the Islamic Republic.* London: Allen Lane, 2013.

Ayalon, Ami. 'From Fitna to Thawra'. *Studia Islamica* 66, no. 66 (1987): 145–174.

Aytaç, Ayfet. *Alim Efe.* Afyon: Tuna Yayınları, 2011.

Azimi, Fakhreddin. 'Khomeini and the "White Revolution"'. In *A Critical Introduction to Khomeini,* edited by Arshin Adib-Moghaddam, 19–42. New York: Cambridge University Press, 2014.

Azimi, Fakhreddin. 'The Overthrow of the Government of Mosaddeq Reconsidered'. *Iranian Studies* 45, no. 5 (2012): 693–712.

Badran, Margot. *Feminists, Islam, and Nation: Gender and the Making of Modern Egypt.* Princeton, NJ: Princeton University Press, 1995.

Baer, Gabriel. 'Popular Revolt in Ottoman Cairo'. *Der Islam* 54, no. 2 (1977): 213–242.

Bakr, ʿAbdal-Wahab. *al-Shawariʿ al-Khalfiyya: al-Jarima fi Misr fi al-Nisf al-Thani min al-Qarn al-ʿIshrin* [The Backstreets: Crimes in Egypt in the First Half of the Twentieth Century]. Cairo: Dar al-Wathaʾiq al-Qawmiyya, 2005.

Bakr, ʿAbdal-Wahab. *Mujtamaʿ al-Qahira al-Sirri, 1900–1951* [Cairo's Underground Society, 1900–1951]. Cairo: al-ʿArabi lil-Nashr wa al-Tawziʿ, 2001.

Baldwin, James E. 'Prostitution, Islamic Law and Ottoman Societies'. *Journal of the Economic and Social History of the Orient* 55 (2012): 117–152.

Balkelis, Tomas. 'Social Banditry and Nation-Making: The Myth of a Lithuanian Robber'. *Past and Present* 198, no. 1 (2008): 111–145.

Bani Etemad, Rakhshan (dir.). *Zir-e Pust-e Shahr* [Under the Skin of the City]. 1996.

Bankoff, Greg. 'Bandits, Banditry and Landscapes of Crime in the Nineteenth-Century Phillipines'. *Journal of Southeast Asian Studies* 29, no. 2 (1998): 319–339.

Barak, On. *On Time: Technology and Temporality in Modern Egypt*. Berkeley: University of California Press, 2013.

Bardakçı, Cemal. *Toprak Dâvasından Siyasî Partilere*. İstanbul: Işıl Matbaası, 1945.

Barkan, Ömer Lütfi. '"Çiftçiyi Topraklandırma Kanunu" ve Türkiye'de Zirai Bir Reformun Ana Meseleleri'. In *Türkiye'de Toprak Meselesi: Toplu Eserler 1*, 54–145. İstanbul: Gözlem Yayınları, 1980.

Barkey, Karen. *Bandits and Bureaucrats: The Ottoman Route to Centralization*. Ithaca, NY: Cornell University Press, 1994.

Baron, Beth. *Egypt as a Woman: Nationalism, Gender, and Politics*. Berkeley: University of California Press, 2005.

Basaglia, Franco and Basaglia-Ongaro. Franca, *La maggioranza deviante: (L'ideologia del controllo sociale totale)*. Milan: Einaudi, 1971.

Başaran, Betül. *Selim III, Social Control, and Policing in Istanbul at the end of the 18th Century*. Leiden: Brill, 2014.

Bast, Oliver. 'Disintegrating the "Discourse of Disintegration": Some Reflections on the Historiography of the Late Qajar Period and Iranian Cultural Memory'. In *Iran in the 20th Century: Historiography and Political Culture*, edited by Touraj Atabaki, 55–68. London: I.B. Tauris, 2009.

Bateson, M.C., J.W. Clinton, J.B.M. Kassarjian, H. Safavi and M. Soraya. 'Ṣafā-yi Bāṭin: A Study of the Interrelations of a Set of Iranian Ideal Character Types'. In *Psychological Dimensions of Near Eastern Studies*, edited by Leon C. Brown and Norman Itzkowitz, Princeton Studies on the Near East. Princeton, NJ: Darwin Press, 1977.

Bayandor, Darioush. *Iran and the CIA: The Fall of Mosaddeq Revisited*. Basingstoke: Palgrave Macmillan, 2010.

Bayat, Asef. 'Cairo's Poor: Dilemmas of Survival and Solidarity'. *Middle East Report* 202 (1997): 7–12.

Bayat, Asef. 'From "Dangerous Classes" to "Quiet Rebels": Politics of the Urban Subaltern in the Global South'. *International Sociology* 15, no. 3 (2000): 533–557.

Bayat, Asef. 'Squatters and the state: Back street politics in the Islamic Republic'. *Middle East Report* 191 (1994): 10–14.

Bayat, Kaveh. 'Riza Shah and the Tribes: An Overview'. In *The Making of Modern Iran: State and Society under Riza Shah, 1921–1941*, edited by Stephanie Cronin, 213–219. Abingdon: Routledge, 2003.

Bayat, Kaveh. 'Toghyan Bar Zed-e Tarikh'. *Nashr-e Danesh* 10, no. 3 (1369): 32–37.

Bayrak, Mehmet. *Eşkiyalık ve Eşkiya Türküleri: İnceleme, Antoloji*. Ankara: Yorum Yayınevi, 1985.

Bayrak, Mehmet. *Öyküleriyle Halk Anlatı Türküleri*. Ankara: Özge Yayınları, 1996.

Beck, Lois. *The Qashqa'i of Iran*. New Haven, CT: Yale University Press, 1986.

Becker, Howard Saul and Dudouet, François-Xavier, *Le Grand Deal De L'opium: Histoire Du Marché Légal Des Drogues*. Paris: Dauphine University, 2009.

Beinin, Joel and Lockman, Zachary, *Workers on the Nile: Nationalism, Communism, Islam, and the Egyptian Working Class, 1882–1954* (Cairo: American University in Cairo Press, 1998).

Bell, Robert Joseph. 'Luti Masculinity in Iranian Modernity, 1785–1941: Marginalization and the Anxieties of Proper Masculine Comportment'. MA Thesis, City University of New York, 2015.

Bendedouche, Nadia. *Bouzian el Kalaï*. Manuscript, 1977.

Bender, Cemşid. *Genelkurmay Belgelerinde Kürt İsyanları*. İstanbul: Kaynak Yayınları, 1992.

Benjamin, Walter. 'The Return of the Flâneur, 1929'. In *Selected Writings*, vol. 2, part 1, 1927–1943, translated by Rodney Livingstone and others, edited by Michael W. Jennings, Howard Eiland and Gary Smith, 262–267. Cambridge, MA: Belknap Press, 1999.

Berkes, Niyazi. *Bazı Ankara Köyleri Üzerine Bir Araştırma*. Ankara: Uzluk Basımevi, 1942.

Beşikçi, İsmail. *Doğu Anadolu'nun Düzeni*. İstanbul: İsmail Beşikçi Vakfı, 2014.

Biancani, Francesca. *Sex Work in Colonial Egypt: Women, Modernity and the Global Economy*. London: I.B.Tauris, 2018.

Bilbaşar, Kemal. *Memo*. İstanbul: Tekin Yayınevi, 1969–70.

Binder, Leonard. *Iran: Political Development in a Changing Society*. Berkeley: University of California Press, 1964.

Birtek, Faruk and Keyder, Çağlar, "Agriculture and the State: An Inquiry into Agricultural Differentiation and Political Alliances: The Case of Turkey," *The Journal of Peasant Studies* 2/4 (1975), pp. 447–463.

Blackwood, Alice. 'Criminal or Nationalist? The Social Purposes and Results of the Creation of a "Social Bandit" Mythos in the Balkans'. *Balkan Folklore*, 2 December 2011. Available online: https://www.academia.edu/4457176/Criminal_or_Nationalist_The_Social_Purposes_and_Results_of_the_Creation_of_a_Social_Bandit_Mythos_in_the_Balkans (accessed 3 June 2019).

Blok, Anton. *The Mafia of a Sicilian Village, 1860–1960: A Study of Violent Peasant Entrepreneurs*. Oxford: Basil Blackwell, 1974.

Blok, Anton. 'The Peasant and the Brigand: Social Banditry Reconsidered'. *Comparative Studies in Society and History* 14, no. 4 (September 1972): 494–503.

Bohstedt, John. 'Gender, Household and Community Politics: Women in English Riots 1790–1810'. *Past and Present* 120, no. 1 (1988): 88–122.

Bohstedt, John. 'The Moral Economy and the Discipline of Historical Context'. *Journal of Social History* 26, no. 2 (1992): 265–284.

Bohstedt, John. *Riots and Community Politics in England and Wales 1790–1810*. Cambridge, MA: Harvard University Press, 1983.

Bonello, Giovanni. 'Pirates in the Early British Era: The Malta Connections'. *The Malta Historical Society*, 2010. Available online: http://maltahistory.eu5.net/60/60_21.html (accessed 15 June 2019).

Booth, Marilyn. 'Disruptions of the Local, Eruptions of the Feminine: Local Reportage and National Anxieties in Egypt's 1890s'. In *The Press in the Middle East and North Africa, 1850–1950: Politics, Social History, and Culture*, edited by Anthony Gorman and Didier Monciaud. Edinburgh: Edinburgh University Press, 2019.

Boratav, Pertev Naili. 'Mudurnu'nun Abant-Dibi Köyleri Üzerine 1940 Yılında Yapılmış Bir İncelemeden Notlar'. In *Sosyoloji Konferansları*, vol. 17, *On Yedinci Kitap*, 94–122. İstanbul: İstanbul Üniversitesi İktisat Fakültesi Yayını, no. 446, 1979.

Borgzanoa, Alexander. *Asrar al-Nashshalin wa ma Yutakhaz Limukafahatihim* [The Secrets of Pickpockets and What Is Done to Fight Them]. Cairo: Matba'at Misr, 1927.

Bosworth, C. E. 'Banū Sāsān'. *Encyclopaedia Iranica* 111, no. 7 (1988): 721–722.

Bosworth, C. E. 'Begging'. *Encyclopaedia Iranica* 4, no. 1 (1989): 80–84.

Bosworth, C. E. *The Mediaeval Islamic Underworld: The Banu Sasan in Arabic Society and Literature*. Leiden: Brill, 1976.

Bourgois, Philippe. 'Lumpen Abuse: The Human Cost of Righteous Neoliberalism'. *City & Society* 23, no. 1 (2011): 2–12.

Bourgois, Philippe. *In Search of Respect: Selling Crack in El Barrio*, vol. 10. Cambridge: Cambridge University Press, 2003.

Bourgois, Philippe and Schonberg, Jeffrey, Righteous dopefiend, Vol. 21 (Univ of California Press, 2009).

Boutilly, M. *Recueil de la législation forestière algérienne*. Paris: Berger-Levrault Editeurs, 1904.

Boyar, Ebru. 'An Imagined Moral Community: Ottoman Female Public Presence, Honour and Marginality'. In *Ottoman Women in Public Space*, edited by Ebru Boyar and Kate Fleet, 187–229. Leiden: Brill, 2016.

Boyar, Ebru. 'The Press and the Palace: The Two-Way Relationship Between Abdülhamid II and the Press, 1876–1908'. *Bulletin of the School of Oriental and African Studies* 69, no. 3 (2006): 417–432.

Brace, Charles Loring. *The Dangerous Classes and Twenty Years' Work Among Them*. New York: Wynkoop & Hallenbeck, 1872.

Bracewell, Catherine Wendy. *The Uskoks of Senj: Piracy, Banditry, and Holy War in the Sixteenth-Century Adriatic*. Ithaca, NY: Cornell University Press, 1992.

Breyley, G.J. and Fatemi, Sasan, *Iranian Music and Popular Entertainment: From Motrebi to Losanjelesi and Beyond* (Abingdon: Routledge, 2016).

Brown, Nathan. 'Brigands and State Building: The Invention of Banditry in Modern Egypt'. *Comparative Studies in Society and History* 32, no. 2 (April 1990): 258–281.

Brown, Nathan, *Peasant Politics in Modern Egypt: The Struggle Against the State*. New Haven, CT: Yale University Press, 1990.

Browne, Edward G. *A Year Amongst the Persians*. London: Adam and Charles Black, 1893.

Brummett, Palmira. 'Classifying Ottoman Mutiny: The Act and Vision of Rebellion'. *Turkish Studies Association Bulletin* 22, no. 1 (1998): 91–107.

Brummett, Palmira. 'Dogs, Women, Cholera, and Other Menaces in the Streets: Cartoon Satire in the Ottoman Revolutionary Press'. *International Journal of Middle East Studies* 27, no. 4 (1995): 433–460.

Bulut, Faik. *Dersim Raporları*. İstanbul: Evrensel Basım Yayın, 1992.

Burg, David F. *A World History of Tax Rebellions: An Encyclopedia of Tax Rebels, Revolts, and Riots from Antiquity to the Present*. New York: Routledge, 2004.

Burke III, Edmund. 'Collective Action and Discursive Shifts: A Comparative Historical Perspective'. Working Paper, 26 February 2004. Available online: http://escholarship. org/uc/item/40p248x1 (accessed 2 May 2013).

Burke III, Edmund. 'Towards a History of Urban Collective Action in the Middle East: Continuities and Change 1750–1980'. In *État, Ville et Mouvements Sociaux au Maghreb et au Moyen-Orient: Actes du Colloque C.N.R.S.-E.S.R.C*, Paris, 23–27 Mai 1986, edited by Kenneth L. Brown, 42–56. Paris: l'Harmattan, 1989.

Burke III, Edmund. 'Understanding Arab Protest Movements'. *Arab Studies Quarterly* 8, no. 4 (1986): 333–345.

Burtuqalis Bey. *al-Bigha' aw Khatar 'aharah fi-l- Qutr al-Misri*, translated by Dawwud Barakat. Cairo: Matba'ah Hindiyyah, 1907.

Bussard, Robert L. 'The "Dangerous Class" of Marx and Engels: The Rise of the Idea of the Lumpenproletariat'. *History of European Ideas* 8, no. 6 (1987): 675–692.

Cahen, C.l. and Hanaway, W. L. Jr., ''Ayyār', *Encyclopaedia Iranica*, http://www. iranicaonline.org/articles/ayyar (last accessed 7 August 2018).

Cairo Police. *Annual Report 1931*. Cairo: al-Matb'a al-Amiriyya, 1932.

Calmard, Jean. 'Chodźko, Aleksander Borejko'. *Encyclopaedia Iranica* 5, no. 5 (1991): 502–504.

Cejpek, Jiři. 'Iranian Folk Literature'. In *History of Iranian Literature*, edited by Jan Rypka, 607–705. Dordrecht: D. Reidel, 1968.

Çetin, Güneş. 'Vergi Aflarının Vergi Mükelleflerinin Tutum ve Davranışları Üzerindeki Etkisi'. *Yönetim ve Ekonomi* 14, no. 2 (2007): 171–187.

Chalcraft, John. 'Engaging the State: Peasants and Petitions in Egypt on the Eve of Colonial Rule'. *International Journal of Middle East Studies* 37 (2005): 303–325.

Chalcraft, John. *Popular Politics in the Making of the Modern Middle East*. Cambridge: Cambridge University Press, 2016.

Chambre de Commerce Française de Constantinople, ed. *Poids, mesures, monnaies et cours du change dans les principales localités de l'Empire ottoman à la fin du 19e siècle*. Istanbul: Isis, [1893] 2002.

Chandler, Billy Jaynes. *The Bandit King: Lampiao of Brazil*. Austin: Texas A&M University Press, 1978.

Cheah, Boon Kheng. *The Peasant Robbers of Kedah, 1900–1919: Historical and Folk Perceptions*. London, Singapore: Oxford University Press, 1988.

Chehabi, H. E. 'Jaʿfari, Šaʿbān'. *Encyclopædia Iranica (Online)* 14, no. 4 (2008): 366–367. Available online: http://www.iranicaonline.org/articles/jafari-saban (accessed 5 August 2016).

Chehabi, H. E. 'Voices Unveiled: Women Singers in Iran'. In *Iran and Beyond: Essays in Middle Eastern History in Honor of Nikki R. Keddie*, edited by Beth Baron and Rudi Matthee, 151–166. Costa Mesa, CA: Mazda Publishers, 2000.

Chevalier, Louis. *Labouring and Dangerous Classes in Paris during the First Half of the Nineteenth Century*, translated by Frank Jellinek. London: Routledge & Kegan Paul, [1958] 1973.

Chodzko, Alexander. *Specimens of the Popular Poetry of Persia: As Found in the Adventures and Improvisations of Kurroglou, the Bandit-Minstrel of Northern Persia and in the Songs of the People Inhabiting the Shores of the Caspian Sea*. London: Printed for the Oriental Translation Fund of Great Britain and Ireland, 1842.

Clancy-Smith, Julia. *Mediterraneans: North Africa and Europe in an Age of Migrations, c. 1800–1900*. Berkeley: University of California Press, 2010.

Clément, Anne. 'Rethinking "Peasant Consciousness" in Colonial Egypt: An Exploration of the Performance of Folksongs by Upper Egyptian Agricultural Workers on the Archaeological Excavation Sites of Karnak and Dendera at the Turn of the Twentieth Century (1885–1914)'. *History and Anthropology* 21, no. 2 (June 2010): 73–100.

Cohen, Stanley. 'Bandits, Rebels or Criminals: African History and Western Criminology'. *Africa: Journal of the International African Institute* 56, no. 4 (1986): 468–483.

Çoker, Fahri. *Türk Parlamento Tarihi: TBMM IV. Dönem (1931–1935)*, vol. 1. Ankara: Türkiye Büyük Millet Meclisi Vakfı, 1996.

Colonna, Fanny. *Le Meunier, les moines et le bandit: Des vies quotidiennes dans l'Aurès (Algerie) du XXe siècle*. Paris: Sindbad, 2010.

Comaroff, Jean. 'Beyond Bare Life: AIDS, (Bio) Politics, and the Neoliberal Order'. *Public Culture* 19, no. 1 (2007): 197–2019.

Cooper, Frederick. *Colonialism in Question*. Berkeley: University of California Press, 2005.

Corbain, Alain. *Women for Hire, Prostitution and Sexuality in France after 1850*. Cambridge, MA: Harvard University Press, 1996.

Cronin, Stephanie. 'Bread and Justice in Qajar Iran: The Moral Economy, the Free Market and the Hungry Poor'. *Middle Eastern Studies* 54, no. 6 (2018): 843–877.

Cronin, Stephanie. 'Introduction: Coercion or Empowerment? Anti-veiling Campaigns: A Comparative Perspective'. In *Anti-Veiling Campaigns in the Muslim World: Gender,*

Modernism and the Politics of Dress, edited by Stephanie Cronin, 1–36. Abingdon: Routledge, 2014.

Cronin, Stephanie. *Soldiers, Shahs and Subalterns in Iran: Opposition, Protest and Revolt, 1921–1941*. Basingstoke: Palgrave Macmillan, 2010.

Cronin, Stephanie. *The Army and the Creation of the Pahlavi State in Iran, 1910–1926*. London: I.B.Tauris, 1996.

Cronin, Stephanie. *Tribal Politics in Iran: Rural Conflict and the New State, 1921–1941*. Abingdon: Routledge, 2007.

Crummey, Donald. 'African Banditry Revisited'. https://www.brunel.ac.uk/__data/assets/pdf_file/0018/110736/Donald-Crummey,-African-Banditry-Revisited--an-essay.pdf (accessed 27 June 2019).

Crummey, Donald, ed. *Banditry, Rebellion and Social Protest in Africa*. London: James Curry, 1986.

Davis, D. K. *Resurrecting the Granary of Rome: Environmental History and French Colonia Expansion in North Africa*. Athens: Ohio University Press, 2007.

de Certeau, Michel. *The Practice of Everyday Life*, translated by Steven F. Rendall. Berkeley: University of California Press, 1984.

de Groot, Joanna. *Religion, Culture and Politics in Iran: From the Qajars to Khomeini*, Library of Modern Middle East Studies 25. London: I.B. Tauris, 2007.

de Moraes Ruehsen, Moyara. 'Operation "Ajax" Revisited: Iran, 1953'. *Middle Eastern Studies* 29, no. 3 (1993): 467–486.

Dejeux, Jean. 'Un Bandit d'honneur dans l'Aures, de 1917 à 1921'. *Revue de l'Occident musulman et de la Méditerranée* 26 (1978): 35–54.

Denning, Michael. 'Wageless life'. *New Left Review* 66 (2010): 79–97.

Deringil, Selim. '"They Live in a State of Nomadism and Savagery": The Late Ottoman Empire and the Post-Colonial Debate'. *Comparative Studies in Society and History* 45, no. 2 (2003): 311–342.

Derluguian, Georgi and Earle, Timothy, "Strong Chieftaincies out of Weak States, or Elemental Power Unbound," in Kristian Berg Harpviken (ed.) Troubled Regions and Failing States: The Clustering and Contagion of Armed Conflicts, Comparative Social Research vol 27, 2010.

Devi, Phoolan with Cuny, Marie-Therese and Rambali, I, Paul, *Phoolan Devi: The Autobiography of India's Bandit Queen* (Little, Brown and Company: New York, 1996).

Dildum, Iskandar, Mustafa La'l Shakiri and Hadi Vakili. 'Naqsh-i ruspiyan-i Shahr-i naw dar Coup du-ta-yi 28 murdad-i 1332'. *Ganjina-'i Asnad* 26, no. 1 (21 May 2016): 60–81.

Diyab, Muhammad Tawfiq. 'Mushkilatal-Khadimat fi Misr' [The Problem of Maids in Egypt]. *Al-Siyasa al-Usbu'iyya*, January 1928.

Doezema, Jo. 'Ouch!: Western Feminists' "Wounded Attachment" to the "Third World Prostitute"'. *Feminist Review* 67, no. 1 (2001): 16–38.

Doğruel, Fatma and Doğruel, A. Suut, *Osmanlı'dan Günümüze Tekel* (İstanbul: Tekel & Tarih Vakfı Yurt Yayınları, 2000).

Dubber, Markus D. 'Histories of Crime and Criminal Justice'. In *The Oxford Handbook of the History of Crime and Criminal Justice*, edited by Paul Knepper and Anja Johansen, 597–614. London: Oxford University Press, 2016.

Duben, Alan and Behar, Cem, *İstanbul Haneleri: Evlilik, Aile ve Doğurganlık, 1880–1940* İstanbul: İletişim Yayınları, 1996.

Dubshan, S. Syphilis wa mukhtasat-i intishar-i an dar Iran. Tehran: Matba'a-yi majlis, 1930.

Dündar, Safiye. *Kürtler ve Azınlık Tartışmaları: Tarih, Kimlik, İsyanlar, Sosyo-Kültürel Yapı, Terör.* İstanbul: Doğan Kitap, 2009.

Dunne, Bruce W. 'French Regulation of Prostitution in Nineteenth-Cetury Colonial Algeria'. *Arab Studies Journal* 2, no. 1 (1994): 24–30.

Dunne, Bruce W. 'Sexuality and the Civilizing Process in Modern Egypt'. PhD Thesis, Georgetown University, 1996.

Dural, Halil. *Bize Derler Çakırca: 19. ve 20. Yüzyılda Ege'de Eşkıyalar.* İstanbul: Tarih Vakfı Yurt Yayınları, 1999.

Dyson-Hudson, Rada and Dyson-Hudson, Neville, 'Nomadic Pastoralism', *Annual Review of Anthropology* 9 (1980): 15–61.

Ecevid, Fahri. 'Suçluluk Bakımından Köylümüzün Ruhi Yapılışı'. *Polis Dergisi* 25, no. 3–4 (October 1938).

Effimianidis, Yorğaki. *Cihan İktisad Buhranı Önünde Türkiye.* İstanbul: Kaadçılık ve Matbaacılık Anonim Şirketi, 1935–36.

Egmond, Florike. *Underworlds: Organized Crime in the Netherlands, 1650–1800.* Cambridge: Polity Press, 1993.

Ehlers, Eckart and Floor, Willem, "Urban Change in Iran, 1920-1941," *Iranian Studies*, vol. 26, nos 3–4 (1993): 251–275.

El Shakry, Omnia. *The Great Social Laboratory: Subjects of Knowledge in Colonial and Postcolonial Egypt.* Stanford, CA: Stanford University Press, 2007.

El Shakry, Omnia. 'Peasants, Crime, and Tea in Interwar Egypt'. *ISIM Review* 21 (2008): 44–45.

El-Aswad, el-Sayed. 'Thaqafat al-Satr wa Dilalatiha al-Ramziyya fi al-hayyah al-Sha'biyya al-'Arabiyya' [Covering-Up Culture and Its Symbolic Meaning in Arab Popular Life]. *Al-Ma'thurat al-Sha'biyya*, 8–27 July 2004.

el-Azhary Sonbol, Amira. *The Creation of a Medical Profession in Egypt.* Syracuse, NY: Syracuse University Press, 1991.

el-Ghoul, Yahya. 'Bled et beldi, kbâr et a'yân: aspects linguistiques et historiques'. *IBLA: Revue de l'Institut des Belles Lettres Arabes* 60, no. 179 (1997): 37–53.

Emiroğlu, Cezmi. *Türkiye'de Vergi Sistemi: Vasıtasız Vergiler.* Ankara: Damga Matbaası, 1932.

Enayat, Hadi. *Law, State and Society in Modern Iran: Constitutionalism, Autocracy, and Legal Reform, 1906–1941.* Basingstoke: Palgrave Macmillan, 2013.

Ener, Mine. *Managing Egypt's Poor and the Politics of Benevolence, 1800–1952.* Princeton, NJ: Princeton University Press, 2003.

Ener, Mine. 'Prohibitions on Begging and Loitering in Nineteenth-Century Egypt'. *Die Welt des Islams*, n.s., 39, no. 3 (1999): 319–339.

Ener, Mine. 'Religious Prerogatives and Policing the Poor in Ottoman Contexts'. *Journal of Interdisciplinary History* 35, no. 3 (2005): 501–511.

Engels, Frederick. *The Condition of the Working-Class in England in 1844.* London: The Project Gutenberg eBook, 2005, translated by Florence Kelley Wischnewetzky. Available online: http://www.gutenberg.org/files/17306/17306-h/17306-h.htm (accessed 26 October 2017).

Ennaji, Mohammed. *Serving the Master: Slavery and Society in Nineteenth-Century Morocco*, translated by Seth Graebner. Basingstoke: Macmillan, 1999.

Erami, Narges and Keshavarzian, Arang, 'When ties don't bind: smuggling effects, bazaars and regulatory regimes in postrevolutionary Iran', *Economy and Society*, vol. 44, no. 1, (February 2015): 110–139.

Ergin, Osman Nuri. *Mecelle-i Umûr-ı Belediyye*, 9 vols, vol. 6. İstanbul: İstanbul Büyükşehir Belediyesi Kültür İşleri Daire Başkanlığı Yayınları, 1995.

Ergut, Ferdan. *Modern Devlet ve Polis: Osmanlı'dan Cumhuriyet'e Toplumsal Denetimin Diyalektiği*. İstanbul İletişim Yayınları 2004.

Ergut, Ferdan. 'Policing the Poor in the Late Ottoman Empire'. *Middle Eastern Studies* 38, no. 2 (2002): 149–164.

Erk, Hasan Basri. *Kaçakçılık İşleri*. İstanbul: Cumhuriyet Matbaası, 1946.

Esenel, Mediha. *Geç Kalmış Kitap: 1940'lı Yıllarda Anadolu Köylerinde Araştırmalar ve Yaşadığım Çevreden İzlenimler*. İstanbul: Sistem Yayıncılık, 1999.

Eshaghi, Peyman. 'Quietness beyond Political Power: Politics of Taking Sanctuary (Bast Neshini) in the Shi'ite Shrines of Iran'. *Iranian Studies* 49, no. 3 (2016): 493–514.

Eski, Mustafa. *İsmet İnönü'nün Kastamonu Gezileri*. İstanbul: Çağdaş Yayınları, 1995.

Ettehadieh, Mansoureh. 'Crime, Security, and Insecurity: Socio-Political Conditions of Iran, 1875–1924'. In *War and Peace in Qajar Persia: Implications Past and Present*, edited by Roxane Farmanfarmaian, 174–182. London: Routledge, 2008.

Evered, Emine Ö. and Evered, Kyle T., "'Protecting the National Body': Regulating the Practice and the Place of Prostitution in Early Republican Turkey," *Gender, Place & Culture* 20, no. 7, 1 November 2013: 839–857.

Ezzeldin, Mohammed Saaid. 'History and Memory of Bandits in Modern Egypt: The Controversy of Adham al-Sharqawi'. MA thesis, Georgetown University, 2013. Available online: https://repository.library.georgetown.edu/bitstream/handle/10822/709716/Ezzeldin_georgetown_0076M_12481.pdf;sequence=1 (accessed 15 June 2019).

Fahmy, Khaled. 'Modernizing Cairo: A Revisionist Narrative'. In *Making Cairo Medieval*, edited by Nezar AlSayyad, Irene A. Bierman and Nasser Rabat, 173–199. Lanham, MD: Lexington Books, 2005.

Fahmy, Khaled. 'Prostitution in Nineteenth-Century Egypt'. In *Outside In: On the Margins of the Modern Middle East*, edited by Eugene Rogan, 77–103. London: I.B. Tauris, 2002.

Falierou, Anastasia and Köksal, Duygu, eds., *A Social History of Late Ottoman Women: New Perspectives* (Leiden: Brill 2013).

Fanon, Frantz, Sartre, Jean-Paul and Farrington. Constance, *The wretched of the earth*. Vol. 36 (New York: Grove Press, 1963).

Faraj, Fakhr Mikha'il, *Taqrir 'an Intishar al-Bigha' wa al-Amrad al-Tanassuliyyah bi-l- Qutr al Masri wa ba'd al-Turuq al-Mumkin Ittiba'iha li-Muharibatihima*. Cairo: al-Matba'ah al-'Asriyyah, 1924.

Farman-farma'iyan, Sattareh. Piramun-i ruspigari dar shahr-i Tehran, 2nd ed. Tehran: Amuzishgah-i 'ali-yi khadamat-i ijtima'i, 1970.

Farman-farma'iyan, Sattareh. Dukhtari az Iran, translated by Maruam A'layi. Tehran: Nashr-i Karang, 2004.

Faroqhi, Suraiya. *Coping with the State: Political Conflict and Crime in the Ottoman Empire, 1550–1720*. Istanbul: Isis Press, 1995.

Fassin, Didier. *At the Heart of the State*. London: Pluto Press, 2015.

Fassin, Didier. *Enforcing Order: An Ethnography of Urban Policing*. New York: Polity, 2013.

Fathi, Asghar. 'The Role of "Rebels" in the Constitutional Movement in Iran'. *International Journal of Middle East Studies* 10, no. 1 (February 1979): 55–66.

Fleet, Kate and Boyar, Ebru, ed., *Ottoman Women in Public Space* (Leiden: Brill, 2016).

Floor, Willem M. 'Change and Development in the Judicial System of Qajar Iran (1800–1925)'. In *Qajar Iran: Political, Social and Cultural Change*, edited by Clifford E.

Bosworth and Carole Hillenbrand, 113–147. Edinburgh: Edinburgh University Press, 1983.

Floor, Willem M. 'Luṭi'. *Encyclopædia Iranica (Online)*, 15 March 2012. Available online: http://www.iranicaonline.org/articles/luti (accessed 30 October 2017).

Floor, Willem M. 'The lutis: A Social Phenomenon in Qajar Persia: A Reappraisal'. *Die Welt des Islams* 13, no. 1/2 (1971): 103–120

Floor, Willem M. 'The Political Role of Lutis in Iran'. In *Modern Iran: The Dialectics of Continuity and Change*, edited by Michael E. Bonine and Nikki R. Keddie, 83–95. Albany: State University of New York Press, 1981.

Floor, Willem M. *A Social History of Sexual Relations in Iran*. Washington, DC: Mage Publishers, 2008.

Foran, John. 'The Concept of Dependent Development as a Key to the Political Economy of Qajar Iran (1800–1925)'. *Iranian Studies* 22, no. 2–3 (1989): 5–56.

Foucault, Michel. *The Birth of Biopolitics: Lectures at the Collège de France, 1978–1979*. Basingstoke: Palgrave Macmillan, 2008.

Foucault, Michel. *Discipline and Punish, the Birth of the Prison*. New York: Vintage Books, 1995.

Foucault, Michel. *The History of Sexuality, Vol. 1, the Will to Knowledge*. New York: Vintage Books, 1980.

Foucault, Michel. 'Les Anormaux'. *Cours au Collège de France*. Paris: Gallimard/Seuil, 1999.

Foucault, Michel. *Society Must be Defended. Lectures at the Collège de France, 1975–76*. London: Penguin Books, 2003.

Fregier, Honore Antoine. *Des Classes Dangereuses de* la Population Dans Les Grandes Villes, Et Des Moyens De Les Rendre Meilleures…* Paris: Chez J.-B. Baillière, 1840.

Frierson, Elizabeth. *Mirrors Out, Mirrors In: Domestication and Rejection of the Foreign in the Ottoman Women's Magazines*. New York: State University of New York, 2000.

Frierson, Elizabeth B. 'Unimagined Communities: Women and Education in the Late-Ottoman Empire, 1876–1909'. *Critical Matrix, The Princeton Journal of Women, Gender, and Culture* 9, no. 2 (1995): 55–90.

Gahan, Jairan. 'Intimating Tehran: Affective Narrativization in Iranian Popular Literature on Prostitution, 1920–1960'. In *Iranian Literary Modernity and Historiography*, ed. Hamid Rezaie-Yazdi and Arshavez Muzzafari. London: Routledge, 2019.

Gallagher, Nancy E. *Egypt's Other Wars: Epidemics and the Politics of Public Health*. Syracuse, NY: Syracuse University Press, 1990.

Gallagher, Nancy E. *Medicine and Power in Tunisia, 1790–1900*. Cambridge: Cambridge University Press, 1983.

Garcia, Angela. *The Pastoral Clinic: Addiction and Dispossession Along the Rio Grande*. Oakland: University of California Press, 2010.

Garland, David. *Punishment and Welfare: A History of Penal Strategies*. Aldershot: Gower, 1985.

Gasiorowski, Mark J. 'The 1953 Coup d'État against Mosaddeq'. In *Mohammad Mosaddeq and the 1953 Coup in Iran*, edited by Mark J. Gasiorowski and Malcom Byrne, 1st edn., Modern Intellectual and Political History of the Middle East, 227–260. Syracuse, NY: Syracuse University Press, 2004.

Gasiorowski, Mark J. 'The Causes of Iran's 1953 Coup: A Critique of Darioush Bayandor's Iran and the CIA'. *Iranian Studies* 45, no. 5 (2012): 669–678.

Gazerani, Ameneh. 'Thugs, Thieves, Tricksters or Popular Heroes? A Comparative Look at the Phenomenon of 'Ayyari'. MA thesis, Ohio State University, 2003.

Geertz, Clifford. 'Religion as Cultural System'. In *The Interpretation of Cultures: Selected Essays*, 87–125. New York: Basic Books, 1993.

Gelvin, James L. 'Demonstrating Communities in Post-Ottoman Syria'. *Journal of Interdisciplinary History* 25, no. 1 (1994): 23–44.

Gelvin, James L. *Divided Loyalties: Nationalism and Mass Politics in Syria at the Close of Empire*. Berkeley: University of California Press, 1998.

George, Annie, Vindhya, U. and Ray, Sawmya, "Sex Trafficking and Sex Work: Definitions, Debates and Dynamics — A Review of Literature," *Economic and Political Weekly* 45, no. 17 (2010): 64–73.

Georgy, Sami. 'Ziyadat al-Jara'im: Asbabiha wa 'Ilajaha' [The Increase in Crimes: Its Causes and Solutions]. *al-Murshid*, 28 September 1936.

Geruh-e farhangi-ye Shahid-e Ebrahimhadi. *Tayyeb: Zendeginameh va khaterat-e Horr-e nehzat-e Imam Khomeyni Shahid-e Tayyeb-e Hajj Reza 'i*. Tehran: Nashr-e Aminan, 1392 h. sh. [=2013].

Ghiabi, Maziyar. 'Deconstructing the Islamic Bloc: The Middle East and North Africa and Pluralistic Drugs Policy'. In *Collapse of the Global Order on Drugs: From Ungass 2016 to Review 2019*, edited by Axel Klein and Blain Stothard, 167–189. Bingley: Emerald Publishing Limited, 2018.

Ghiabi, Maziyar. 'Drogues Illégales Et Gestion De L'espace Dans L'iran Moderne'. *Hérodote*, no. 2 (2018): 133–151.

Ghiabi, Maziyar. 'Drugs and Revolution in Iran: Islamic Devotion, Revolutionary Zeal and Republican Means', *Iranian Studies* 48, no. 2 (2015): 139–163.

Ghiabi, Maziyar. *Drugs Politics: Managing Disorder in the Islamic Republic of Iran*. Cambridge: Cambridge University Press, 2019.

Ghiabi, Maziyar. 'Maintaining Disorder: the micropolitics of drug policy in Iran'. *Third World Quarterly* 38, no. 2 (2017): 277–297.

Ghiabi, Maziyar. 'The Opium of the State'. In *The Age of Aryamehr: Local and Global Entanglements of Late Pahlavi Irani, 1941–1979*, edited by R. Alvandi. London: Gingko Library Press, 2018.

Ghiabi, Maziyar. 'Under the Bridge in Tehran: Addiction, Poverty and Capital'. *Ethnography* (2018).

Ghiabi, Maziyar, Masoomeh Maarefvand, Hamed Bahari, and Zohreh Alavi. 'Islam and Cannabis: Legalisation and Religious Debate in Iran'. *International Journal of Drug Policy* 56 (2018): 121–127.

Gilfoyle, Timothy J. 'Prostitutes in History: From Parables of Pornography to Metaphors of Modernity'. *American Historical Review* 104, no. 1 (February 1999): 117–141.

Gingeras, Ryan. 'Beyond Istanbul's 'Laz Underworld': Ottoman Paramilitarism and the Rise of Turkish Organised Crime'. *Contemporary European History* 19, no. 3 (2010): 215–230.

Ginio, Eyal. 'Piracy and Redemption in the Aegean Sea during the First Half of the Eighteenth Century'. *Turcica* 33 (2001): 135–147.

Goldberg, Ellis. 'Peasants in Revolt – Egypt 1919'. *International Journal of Middle East Studies* 24, no. 2 (1992), 261–280.

Goldenberg, Shira M., Strathdee, Steffanie A., Gallardo, Manuel, Rhodes, Tim, Wagner, Karla D. and Patterson. Thomas L., "'Over here, it's just drugs, women and all the madness": The HIV risk environment of clients of female sex workers in Tijuana, Mexico." Social Science & Medicine 72, no. 7, 2011: 1185–1192.

Gordon, Stewart N., 'Bhils and the Idea of A Criminal Tribe in Nineteenth-Century India', in *Crime and Criminality in British India*, ed. Anand A. Yang (Tucson: University of Arizona Press, 1985), 128–139.

Gould, Andrew G. 'Lords or Bandits? The Derebeys of Cilicia'. *International Journal of Middle East Studies* 7, no. 4 (1976): 485–506.

Gouvernement Général de l'Algérie. *Exposé de la situation de l'Algérie*. Alger: Imprimerie Juillet-Saint-Lager, 1904.

Grallert, Till. 'To Whom Belong the Streets? Property, Propriety, and Appropriation: The Production of Public Space in Late Ottoman Damascus, 1875–1914'. PhD diss., Freie Universität Berlin, April 2014.

Gramsci, Antonio. *Selections from the Prison Notebooks of Antonio Gramsci*, translated by Quintin Hoare and Geoffrey Nowell-Smith, repr. London: Lawrence and Wishart, 2007.

Grant, Melissa Gira. *Playing the Whore: The Work of Sex Work*. London: Verso Books, 2014.

Grehan, James. *Everyday Life and Consumer Culture in 18th-Century Damascus*. Seattle: University of Washington Press, 2007.

Grehan, James. 'Smoking and "early Modern" Sociability: The Great Tobacco Debate in the Ottoman Middle East (Seventeenth to Eighteenth Centuries)'. *American Historical Review* 111, no. 5 (2006): 1352–1377.

Grehan, James. 'Street Violence and Social Imagination in Late-Mamluk and Ottoman Damascus (Ca. 1500–1800)'. *International Journal of Middle East Studies* 35 (2003): 215–236.

Grew, Joseph C. *Atatürk ve Yeni Türkiye (1927–1932)*. İstanbul: Gündoğan Yayınları, 2002.

Grobba, Fritz. *Die Getreidewirtschaft Syriens und Palästinas seit Beginn des Weltkrieges*. Hannover: H. Lafaire, 1923.

Guha, Ranajit. *Elementary Aspects of Peasant Insurgency in Colonial India*. Delhi: Oxford University Press, 1983.

Guignard, Didier. 'Conservatoire ou révolutionnaire? Le sénatus-consulte de 1863 appliqué au régime foncier d'Algérie'. *Revue d'histoire du XIXe siècle* 41 (2010): 81–95.

Güler, Birgün Ayman, ed. *Açıklamalı Yönetim Zamandizini, 1929–1939*. Ankara: Ankara Üniversitesi Basımevi, 2007.

Gürbüz, A. Cenani. *Mondros'tan Milenyuma Türkiye'de İsyanlar*. İstanbul: Bilge Karınca Yayınları, 2006.

Guzarish-i sah salah-yi qismat-i bihdasht va umur-i 'umumi-yi sazman-i barnamah az Mihr 1334 ta Mihr 1337'. Tehran: Sazman-i barnamah, 1337 [1985].

Ha'erizadah, Abdul'hasan. Mashruh-i muzakirat-i majlis, darah 16, Majlis-i shawra-yi milli, jalasah 117. Bahman 26, 1329/[16 February 1951].

Hadjiheidari, Abolhassan. '"Nayeb Hoseyn-e Kasi Strasenräuber Oder Revolutionär?" Eine Untersuchung Der Iranischen Geschichte 1850–1920'. PhD Thesis, University of Tübingen, 2008.

Haeri, Shahla. *Law of Desire: Temporary Marriage in Iran*. London: I.B. Tauris, 1989.

Hafez, Melis. 'The Lazy, the Idle, and the Industrious: Discourse of Work and Productivity in Late Ottoman Society'. PhD thesis, University of California Los Angeles, 2012. Available online: https://escholarship.org/uc/item/3pj7009t (accessed 15 June 2019).

Hakamizadah, Akbar. Ranj-i bihudah: guftar-i haftum, Humayun 1, no. 10 (Tir 1314/June 1935), 26.

Hakimilahi, Hidayatullah. Ba man bi artish bi-yayid. Tehran, 1948.

Hakimilahi, Hidayatullah. Ba man bi dar al-majanin bi-yayid. Tehran 1947.

Hakimilahi, Hidayatullah. Ba man bi Tehran bi-yayid, Tehran, 1947.

Hakimilahi, Hidayatullah. Ba man bi Shahr-i naw bi-yayid, vol. 1. Tehran, 1946.

Hakimilahi, Hidayatullah. Ba man bi Shahr-i naw bi-yayid, vol. 2. Tehran, 1947.

Hakīmilāhī, Hidāyatullah. *Bā man bi Tehran bī-yayīd*. Tehran, 1947.

Hall, Stuart and Scraton, Phil, `Law, Class and Control', in *Crime and Society: Readings in History and Theory*, ed. Mike Fitzgerald, Gregor MacLennan, and Jennie Pawson (London: Routlege & K. Paul, 1981).

Hallı, Reşat. *Türkiye Cumhuriyeti'nde Ayaklanmalar (1924–1938)*. Ankara: Genelkurmay Harb Tarihi Başkanlığı, 1972.

Hamadeh, Shirine. 'Mean Streets: Space and Moral Order in Early Modern Istanbul'. *Turcica* 44 (2013): 249–277.

Hamdi, Husayn. *Mushkilat al-Batala: Bahth ʿilmi wa Dirasa Muqarna* [The Unemployment Problem: A Scientific and Comparative Study]. Cairo: Jamaʿat al-kuttab, 1944.

Hammad, Hanan. 'Between Egyptian National Purity and Local Flexibility: Prostitution in al Mahallaal-Kubra in the First Half of the Twentieth Century'. *Journal of Social History* 44, no. 3 (2011): 751–783.

Hammad, Hanan. *Industrial Sexuality: Mechanization, Sex, Gender, and Social Transformation in Modern Egypt*. Austin: University of Texas Press, 2016.

Harsin, Jill. *Policing Prostitution in Nineteenth Century Paris*. Princeton, NJ: Princeton University Press, 1985.

Hart, David M. *Banditry in Islam: Case studies from Morocco, Algeria and the Pakistan North West Frontier*. Wisbech: Menas Press, 1987.

Hashemi, Zakariyyā. *Tūti*. Tehran: Hadaf, 1969.

Hatipoğlu, Şevket Raşit. *Türkiye'de Ziraî Buhran*. Ankara: Yüksek Ziraat Enstitüsü, 1936.

Hay, Douglas, Peter Linebaugh, John G. Rule, E.P. Thompson and Cal Winslow. *Albion's Fatal Tree: Crime and Society in Eighteenth-Century England*, rev. edn. London: Verso, [1975] 2011.

Haykal, Muhammad Husayn. 'Hijrat al-rif ila al-mudun' [Rural Immigration to Cities]. *Al Siyasa al-Usbu'iyya*, 20 April 1940.

Hayvanlar Vergisi Dökümanları. Ankara: T. C. Ziraat Vekâleti Birinci Köy ve Ziraat Kalkınması Kongresi Yayını, 1939.

Hershlag, Z. Yehuda. *Turkey: The Challenge of Growth*. Leiden: E. J. Brill, 1968.

Hijazi, Amina. *al-Jarima fi Misr, 1919–1939* [Crime in Egypt, 1919–1939]. Cairo: Dar al-Wathaʾiq al-Qawmiyya, 2014.

Hilal, Imad. *Al-Baghaya fi Misr: Dirasa Tarikhiyya Ijtimaʿiyya, 1834–1949* [Prostitutes in Egypt: A Sociohistorical Study, 1834–1949]. Cairo: al-ʿArabi lil-nashr wa-al-tawziʿ, 2001.

Hobsbawm, Eric J. *Age of Extremes: A History of the World, 1914–1991*. New York: Vintage Books, 1994.

Hobsbawm, Eric J. *Bandits*. London: Weidenfeld and Nicolson, [1969] 2000.

Hobsbawm, Eric J. *Primitive Rebels: Studies in Archaic Forms of Social Movements in the 19th and 20th Centuries*. Manchester: Manchester University Press, 1959.

Hooglund, Eric J. *Land and Revolution in Iran, 1960–1980*. Austin: University of Texas Press, 1982.

Horkheimer, Max. 'Die Rackets und der Geist [1943]'. In *Gesammelte Schriften: Band 12: Nachgelassene Schriften 1931–1949*, edited by Gunzelin Schmid Noerr, 287–291. Frankfurt am Main: Fischer, 1985.

Horkheimer, Max. 'Herrschende Klasse, die von den Rackets beherrschte Klasse und die Rolle der Fachleute: [Späne. 1957–1967]'. In *Gesammelte Schriften: Band 14: Nachgelassene Schriften 1949–1972*, edited by Alfred Schmidt and Gunzelin Schmid Noerr, 334–335. Frankfurt am Main: Fischer, 1988.

Horkheimer, Max. 'Zur Soziologie der Klassenverhältnisse [1943]'. In *Gesammelte Schriften: Band 12: Nachgelassene Schriften 1931–1949*, edited by Gunzelin Schmid Noerr, 75–104. Frankfurt am Main: Fischer, 1985.

Horkheimer, Max and Adorno, Theodor W., *Dialektik der Aufklärung: Philosophische Fragmente*, 21st ed. (Frankfurt am Main: Fischer Taschenbuch Verlag, 2013).

Hostettler, John. *A History of Criminal Justice in England and Wales*. Sherfield on Loddon: Waterside, 2009.

Hourani, Albert. 'Ottoman Reform and the Politics of Notables'. In *The Modern Middle East: A Reader*, edited by. Albert Hourani, Philip S Khoury, and Mary C Wilson, 83–110. Berkeley: University of California Press, [1968] 1993.

Howell, Philip. *Geographies of Regulation, Policing Prostitution in Nineteenth Century Britain and the Empire*. Cambridge: Cambridge University Press, 2009.

Howell, Philip. 'Historical Geographies of the Regulation of Prostitution in Britain and the British Empire'. Available online: http://www.geog.cam.ac.uk/research/projects/prostitutionregulation/ (accessed 1 May 2017).

Howell, Philip. 'Race, Space and the Regulation of Prostitution in Colonial Hong Kong'. *Urban History* 31, no. 2 (2004): 229–248.

Hoyle, Mark. *Mixed Courts of Egypt*. London: Graham and Trotman, 1968.

Hüsrev (Tökin), İsmail. *Türkiye Köy İktisadiyatı*. İstanbul: Matbaacılık ve Neşriyat Türk Anonim Şirketi, 1934.

Idarat ʿUmum al-Amn al-ʿAmm. *Taqrir ʿan Halat al-Amn al-ʿAm bil-Mamlaka al-Misriyya* [Public Security Department: A Report on the State of Public Security in the Egyptian Kingdom]. Cairo: al-Matb ʿa al-amiriyya bi-Bulaq, 1938.

İleri, Nurçin. 'Between the Real and the Imaginary: Late Ottoman Istanbul as a Crime Scene'. *Journal of the Ottoman and Turkish Studies Association* 4, no. 1 (2017): 95–116.

İnalcık, Halil. 'Introduction to Ottoman Metrology'. In *Studies in Ottoman Social and Economic History*, 311–348. London: Variorum Reprints, 1985.

İnan, Afet. *Yurt Bilgisi Notlarımdan: Vergi Bilgisi*. İstanbul: Devlet Matbaası, 1930.

Isaacman, Allen. 'Social Banditry in Zimbabwe (Rhodesia) and Mozambique, 1894–1907: An Expression of Early Peasant Protest'. *Journal of Southern African Studies* 4, no. 1 (1977): 1–30.

International Bureau for the Suppression of Traffic in Women and Children. *The Case for the Abolition of the Government Regulation of Prostitution*. Cairo: Nile Mission Press, 1939.

Ismail, Salwa. *Political Life in Cairo's New Quarters: Encountering the Everyday State*. Minneapolis: University of Minnesota Press, 2006.

Issawi, Charles. *The Economic History of Iran, 1800–1914*. Chicago: University of Chicago Press, 1971.

Issawi, Charles. *Egypt at Mid-century: An Economic Survey*. Oxford: Oxford University Press, 1954.

Issawi, Charles. *The Fertile Crescent 1800–1914: A Documentary Economic History*. Oxford: Oxford University Press, 1988.

Jagailloux, Serge. *La Médicalization de l'Egypte au XIXe siècle, 1798–1918*. Paris: Editions Recherches sur les Civilizations, 1986.

Jallad, Fillib. *Qamus al-Qada' wa al-Idarah*, vol. 3. al-Iskandariyyah: Lagoudakis, 1906.

Jamei, Ahmad Masjed. *Darvazeh Ghar*. Tehran: Thaleth, 2016.

Jamieson, Alan G. *Lords of the Sea: A History of the Barbary Corsairs*. London: Reaktion Books, 2012.

Jefroudi, Maral. 'The Opening-Up of the Past and the Possibilities of Global History for Iranian Historiography'. In *Iran in the Middle East: Transnational Encounters and Social History*, edited by Houchang Chehabi, Peyman Jafari and Maral Jefroudi, 235–248. London: I.B. Tauris, 2015.

Johnson, Amy J. *Reconstructing Rural Egypt: Ahmed Hussein and the History of Egyptian Development.* Syracuse, NY: Syracuse University Press, 2004.

Joseph, Gilbert M. 'On the Trail of Latin American Bandits: A Reexamination of Peasant Resistance'. *Latin American Research Review* 25, no. 3 (1990): 7–53.

Joubin, Rebecca. 'The Politics of the Qabaday (Tough Man) and the Changing Father Figure in Syrian Televsion Drama'. *Journal of Middle East Women's Studies* 12, no. 1 (2016): 50–56.

Junaydi al-Bigha', Muhammad Farid. *Bahth 'ilmi 'amali.* Cairo: Matba'at al-Nasr, 1934.

Jwaideh, Wadie. *Kürt Milliyetçiliğinin Tarihi: Kökenleri ve Gelişimi*, 5th edn. İstanbul: İletişim Yayınları, 2008.

Kaddache, Mahfoud. *Histoire du nationalisme algérien*, vol. 1. Alger: EDIF 2000; Paris: Paris Méditerranée, 2003.

Karabuda, Barbro. *Goodbye to the Fez: A Portrait of Modern Turkey*, translated by Maurice Michael. London: Denis Dobson Books, 1959.

Karimi, Pamela. *Domesticity and Consumer Culture in Iran: Interior Revolutions of the Modern Era.* New York: Routledge, 2013.

Kashani-Sabet, Firoozeh. 'The Haves and Have Nots: A Historical Study of Disability in Modern Iran'. *Iranian Studies* 43, no. 2 (2010): 167–195.

Kaveh, Mohammad. *Asib-shenasi-ye Bimari-ha-ye Ejtema'i*, vols 1–2. Tehran: Jame'eshanan, 2010.

Kazemi, Farhad and Abrahamian, Ervand, 'The Nonrevolutionary Peasantry of Modern Iran', *Iranian Studies* 11, 1978: 259–304.

Kazemi, Ranin. 'Of Diet and Profit: On the Question of Subsistence Crises in Nineteenth-Century Iran'. *Middle Eastern Studies* 52, no. 2 (2016): 335–358.

Kazemi, Ranin. 'The Tobacco Protest in Nineteenth-Century Iran: The View from a Provincial Town'. *Journal of Persianate Studies* 7 (2014): 251–295.

Keddie, Nikki R. and Baron, Beth, *Women in Middle Eastern History: Shifting Boundaries in Sex and Gender* (New Haven: Yale University Press, 1991).

Keller, Richard C. *Colonial Madness: Psychiatry in French North Africa.* Chicago: University of Chicago Press, 2007.

Kelly, J.B., Imber, C.H. and Pellat, Ch., 'Kursān', *Encyclopaedia of Islam* (second edition, Leiden: 1960-2004). Available online: https://referenceworks.brillonline.com/browse/encyclopaedia-of-islam-2 (accessed 15 June 2019).

Kemal, Yaşar. *İnce Memed.* İstanbul: Çağlayan Yayınları, 1955.

Kempadoo, Kamala. 'Freelancers, Temporary Wives, and Beach-Boys: Researching Sex Work in the Caribbean'. *Feminist Review* 67, no. 1 (2001): 39–62.

Kempadoo, Kamala, Sanghera, Jyoti and Pattanaik, Bandana, *Trafficking and Prostitution Reconsidered: New Perspectives on Migration, Sex Work, and Human Rights* (Boulder, Colo.: Paradigm Publishers, 2005).

Kempadoo, Kamala. 'The Modern-Day White (Wo)Man's Burden: Trends in Anti-Trafficking and Anti-Slavery Campaigns'. *Journal of Human Trafficking* 1, no. 1 (2 January 2015): 8–20.

Kempadoo, Kamala. 'The War on Human Trafficking in the Caribbean'. *Race & Class* 49, no. 2 (1 October 2007): 79–85.

Keyder, Çağlar. 'Türk Demokrasisinin Ekonomi Politiği'. In *Geçiş Sürecinde Türkiye*, edited by Irvin Cemil Shick and Ertuğrul Ahmet Tonak, 38–75. İstanbul: Belge Yayınları, 1998.

Keyder, Çağlar. 'Türk Tarımında Küçük Meta Üretiminin Yerleşmesi (1946–1960)'. In *Türkiye'de Tarımsal Yapılar*, edited by Şevket Pamuk and Zafer Toprak, 163–174. Ankara: Yurt Yayınevi, 1988.

Khaldun, Ibn. *The Muqaddimah: An Introduction to History*, edited by N. J. Dawood and Franz Rosenthal. London: Routledge and Kegan Paul in association with Secker and Warburg, 1967.

Khater, Akram Fouad. '"House" to "Goddess of the House": Gender, Class, and Silk in 19th-Century Mount Lebanon'. *International Journal of Middle East Studies* 28, no. 3 (1996): 325–348.

Kholoussy, Hanan. 'Monitoring and Medicalising Male Sexuality in Semi-Colonial Egypt'. *Gender & History* 22, no. 3 (2010): 677–691.

Khosravi, Muhammad Reaa. *Toghiyan-e Nayebiyan Dar Jariyan-e Enqelab-e Mashrutiyate Iran*. Tehran: Beh Negar, 1368.

Khosravi, Shahram. *Precarious Lives: Waiting and Hope in Iran*. Philadelphia: University of Pennsylvania Press, 2017.

Khoury, Phillip S. 'Abu Ali al-Kilawi: A Damascus Qabaday'. In *Struggle and Survival in the Modern Middle East*, edited by Edmund Burke III and David N. Yaghoubian, 152–163. Berkeley: University of California Press, 2006.

Khoury, Philip S. *Urban Notables and Arab Nationalism: The Politics of Damascus, 1860–1920*. New York: Cambridge University Press, 1983.

Khoury, Philip S. 'The Urban Notable Paradigm Revisited'. *Revue Des Mondes Musulmans Et de La Méditerranée*, no. 55–56 (1990): 215–228.

Khoury, Philip S. and Kostiner, Joseph, eds., *Tribes and State Formation in the Middle East* (Berkeley: University of California Press, 1990).

Khwashir, F. M. *Tajrobe-ye bist-o-hasht-e mordad*. Tehran: Entasharat-e Hezb-e Tudeh-ye Iran, 1359 h. sh. [=1979].

King, Peter. *Crime, Justice, and Discretion in England, 1740–1820*. Oxford: Oxford University Press, 2000.

Kıvılcımlı, Hikmet. *Yol/İhtiyat Kuvvet Milliyet (Şark)*. İstanbul: Yol Yayınları, 1979.

Knepper, Paul. *Writing the History of Crime*. London: Bloomsbury Academic, 2016.

Koliopoulos, John S. *Brigands with a Cause: Brigandage and Irredentism in Modern Greece, 1821–1912*. Oxford: Clarendon Press, 1987.

Kozma, Liat. 'Girls, Labor, and Sex in Precolonial Egypt, 1850–1882'. In *Girlhood: A Global History*, edited by Jennifer Helgren and Colleen A. Vasconcellos, 344–362. New Brunswick, NJ: Rutgers University Press, 2010.

Kozma, Liat. *Global Women, Colonial Ports: Prostitution in the Interwar Middle East*. Albany: State University of New York Press, 2017.

Kozma, Liat. *Policing Egyptian Women: Sex, Law, and Medicine in Khedival Egypt*. Syracuse, NY: Syracuse University Press, 2011.

Kozma, Liat. 'Wandering About as She Pleases: Prostitutes, Adolescent Girls, and Female Slaves in Cairo's Public Space, 1850–1882'. *Journal of Women of the Middle East and the Islamic World* 10 (2012): 18–36.

Kozma, Liat. '"We, the Sexologists …": Arabic Medical Writing on Sexuality'. *Journal of the History of Sexuality* 22, no. 3 (2013): 426–445.

Kuhnke, LaVerne. *Lives at Risk: Public Health in Nineteenth Century Egypt*. Berkeley: University of California Press, 1990.

Kuruç, Bilsay. *Belgelerle Türkiye İktisat Politikası* 1. Ankara: Ankara Üniversitesi Basımevi, 1988.

Kuruç, Bilsay. *Belgelerle Türkiye İktisat Politikası* 2. Ankara: Ankara Üniversitesi Siyasal Bilgiler Fakültesi Yayınları, 1993.

Lafi, Nora. 'Introduction'. In *Municipalités méditerranéennes: les réformes urbaines ottomanes au miroir d'une histoire comparée (Moyen-Orient, Maghreb, Europe méridionale)*, edited by Nora Lafi, 11–34. Berlin: Klaus Schwarz Verlag, 2005.

Lafi, Nora. 'The Ottoman Municipal Reforms Between Old Regime and Modernity: Towards a New Interpretative Paradigm'. In *First International Symposium on Eminönü*, edited by Fatih Sadırlı, 348–355. Istanbul: Eminönü Belediyesi, 2007.

Lafi, Nora. *Une ville du maghreb entre ancien régime et réformes ottomanes: Genèse des institutions municipales à tripoli de barbarie, 1795–1911*. Paris: l'Harmattan, 2002.

Lambton, Ann K. S. *Landlord and Peasant in Persia: A Study of Land Tenure and Land Revenue Administration*. London: Oxford University Press, 1953.

Lasswell, Harold D. *Politics: Who Gets What, When, How?*. Cleveland, OH: World Pub. Co., 1958.

Lawrence, Paul. 'The Historiography of Crime and Criminal Justice'. In *The Oxford Handbook of the History of Crime and Criminal Justice*, edited by Paul Knepper and Anja Johansen, 17–37. London: Oxford University Press, 2016.

Lea, John. 'Social Crime Revisited'. *Theoretical Criminology* 3, no. 3 (1999): 307–325.

Lefebvre, Henri. *Critique of Everyday Life: The One-Volume Edition*. London: Verso, 2014.

Legg, Stephen. 'Beyond the European province: Foucault and postcolonialism'. In *Space, Knowledge and Power. Foucault and Geography*, edited by J. W. Crampton and S. Elden, 265–288. Aldershot: Routledge, 2007.

Legg, Stephen. 'Governing Prostitution in Colonial Delhi: from Cantonment Regulations to International Hygiene (1864–1939)'. *Social History* 34 (2009): 447–467.

Legg, Stephen. *Prostitution and the Ends of Empire, Scales, Governmentality, and Interwar India*. Durham, NC: Duke University Press, 2014.

Lerner, Daniel. *Passing of Traditional Society: Modernizing the Middle East*. Glencoe, IL: Macmillan, 1958.

Levine, Phillippa. 'Modernity, Medicine and Colonialism: the Contagious Diseases Ordinances in Hong Kong and the Straits Settlements'. *Positions* 6 (1998): 675–705.

Levy, Noemi and Toumarkine, Alexandre, eds., *Osmanlı'da Asayiş, Suç ve Ceza, 18.-20. Yüzyıllar* (İstanbul: Tarih Vakfı Yurt Yayınları, 2007).

Lévy-Aksu, Noémi. *Osmanlı İstanbulu'nda Asayiş 1879–1909*, translated by Serra Akyüz Gönen. Istanbul İletişim Yayınları, 2017.

Liauzu, Claude. 'Crises urbaines, crise de l'état, mouvements sociaux'. In *État, ville et mouvements sociaux au Maghreb et au Moyen-Orient: actes du colloque C.N.R.S.-E.S.R.C. Paris, 23–27 mai 1986*, edited by Kenneth L. Brown, 23–41. Paris: L'Harmattan, 1989.

Lindemann, Kai. 'Der Racketbegriff als Herrschaftskritik'. In *Staat und Politik bei Horkheimer und Adorno*, edited by Ulrich Ruschig and Hans-Ernst Schiller, Staatsverständnisse Band 64, 102–126. Baden-Baden: Nomos, 2014.

Linke, Lilo. *Allah Dethroned*. London: Constable & Co. Ltd., 1937.

Lombroso, Cesare. *L'uomo delinquente in rapporto all'antropologia: alla giurisprudenza ed alle discipline carcerarie. 1896–1897*, vol. 2. Turin: Fratelli Bocca, 1896.

Lombroso, Cesare and Ferrero, Guglielmo, *Criminal Woman, the Prostitute, and the Normal Woman*, translated by Nicole Hahn Rafter and Mary Gibson (Durham, NC: Duke University Press, 2004).

Lopez, Shaun. 'Madams, Murders, and the Media: *Akbar al-Hawadith* and the Emergence of a Mass Culture in Egypt'. In *Re-Envisioning Egypt 1919–1952*, edited by Arthur Goldschmidt and Amy J. Johnson, 371–397. Cairo: American University in Cairo Press, 2005.

Lüdtke, Alf. 'Introduction: What Is the History of Everyday Life and Who Are Its Practitioners?'. In *The History of Everyday Life: Reconstructing Historical Experiences and Ways of Life*, edited by Alf Lüdtke, translated by William Templer. Princeton, NJ: Princeton University Press, 1995.

Lutfi, Husayn. 'Asbab Kathrat Hawadith al-Sariqa' [Causes of the Increase in Theft]. *Al Muqattam*, 26 June 1939.

Madanoğlu, Cemal. *Anılar (1911–1938)*. İstanbul: Çağdaş Yayınları, 1982.

Maghraoui, Driss. 'Gendering Urban Colonial Casablanca: the Case of the Quartier Resérvé of Bousbir'. In *Gendering Urban Space in the Middle East, South Asia and Africa*, edited by M. Rieker and K. Ali, 17–44. New York: Palgrave, 2008.

Mahé, A. *Histoire de la Grande-Kabylie*. Paris: Bouchene, [2001] 2006.

Mahmood, Saba. *Politics of Piety: The Islamic Revival and the Feminist Subject*. Princeton, NJ: Princeton University Press, 2012.

Majallat Ra'msis. 'Al-Insan al-Mujrim' [The Criminal]. December/January 1920/21, 640–642.

Maksudyan, Nazan. 'Orphans, Cities, and the State: Vocational Orphanages (Islahhanes) and Reform in the Late Ottoman Urban Space'. *International Journal of Middle East Studies* 43 (2011): 493–511.

Maksudyan, Nazan. *Orphans and Destitude Children in the Late Ottoman Empire*. New York: Syracuse University Press, 2014.

Maksudyan, Nazan, ed. *Women and the City, Women in the City: A genderd Perspective on Ottoman Urban History*. New York: Berghahn, 2014.

Marc, Henri. *Notes sur les Forêts en Algérie*. Paris: Larose, 1930.

Martin, Vanessa. 'The Lutis – The Turbulent Urban Poor', in *The Qajar Pact: Bargaining, Protest and the State in Nineteenth-Century Persia*, International library of Iranian studies 4 (London: Tauris, 2005).

Martin, Vanessa. *Iran between Islamic Nationalism and Secularism: The Constitutional Revolution of 1906*. London: I.B. Tauris, 2013.

Martin, Vanessa. *The Qajar Pact: Bargaining, Protest and the State in 19th-Century Persia*. London: I.B. Tauris, 2005.

Marx, Karl. 'The Eighteenth Brumaire of Louis Napoleon'. In *Surveys from Exile*, translated and introduced by David Fernbach, 146–249. Harmondsworth: Penguin, 1973.

Marx, Karl. *Grundrisse*. London: Penguin, 1993.

Massey, Doreen. *For Space*. London: Sage, 2005.

Matthee, Rudi. 'Prostitutes, Courtesans and Dancing Girls: Women Entertainers in Safavid Iran'. In *Iran and Beyond: Essays in Middle Eastern History in Honor of Nikki R. Keddie*, edited by Beth Baron and Rudi Matthee, 121–150. Costa Mesa, CA: Mazda Publishers, 2000.

Matthee, Rudi. *The Pursuit of Pleasure: Drugs and Simulants in Iranian History, 1500–1900*. Princeton, NJ: Princeton University Press, 2005.

McDowall, David. *A Modern History of the Kurds*. London: I.B. Tauris, 2004.

Meftahi, Ida. *Gender and Dance in Modern Iran: Biopolitics on Stage*. New York: Routledge, 2016.

Meier, William. Property Crime in London, 1850–Present. New York: Palgrave Macmillan, 2011.

Metinsoy Mahir, İkbal Elif. 'Poor Ottoman Turkish Women During World War I: Women's Experiences and Politics in Everyday Life, 1914–1923'. PhD diss., Boğaziçi University, 2012.

Metinsoy, Murat. *İkinci Dünya Savaşı'nda Türkiye: Savaş ve Gündelik Yaşam*. İstanbul: Homer Kitabevi, 2007; 2nd edn. İş Bankası Kültür Yayınları, 2016.

Migdal, Joel S. *State in Society: Studying How States and Societies Transforms and Constitute One Another*. Cambridge: Cambridge University Press, 2001.

Migdal, Joel S. *Strong Societies and Weak States: State-Society Relations and State Capabilities in the Third World*. Princeton, NJ: Princeton University Press, 1988.

Milani, Abbas. *Eminent Persians: The Men and Women Who Made Modern Iran, 1941–1979*. New York: Persian World Press, 2008.

Mimaroğlu, M. Reşat. *Gördüklerim ve Geçirdiklerim'den: Memurluk Hayatımın Hatıraları*. Ankara: T.C. Ziraat Bankası Matbaası, 1946.

Minamizuka, Shingo. *A Social Bandit in Nineteenth Century Hungary: Rózsa Sándor*. Boulder, CO: East European Monographs, 2008.

Ministry of Finance, Statistical and Census Department. *The Census of Egypt Taken in 1937*. Cairo: Government Press, 1941.

Ministry of Finance, Statistical Department. *Population Censuses Conducted in Egypt 1907*. Cairo: Government Press, 1909.

Ministry of Finance, Statistical Department. *Population Censuses Conducted in Egypt 1947*. Cairo: al-Matba'a al-amiriyya, 1953.

Ministry of Interior. *Bolis Madinat al-Qahira: al-Taqrir al-Sanawi li-sanat 1939* [Cairo Police: Annual Report for 1939]. Cairo: al-Matba'a al-Amiriyya, 1940.

Ministry of Interior of Egypt. *La'ihah Maktab al-Kashf 'ala al-Niswah al-'Ahirat* (An Ordinance on the Medical Inspections of Prostitutes), article 14, 1885.

Mir'Ābedini, Hasan. 'Moshfeq-e Kazemi, Sayyed Mortaza'. *Encyclopaedia Iranica*, 21 January 2011. Available online: http://www.iranicaonline.org/articles/moshfeq-kazemi (accessed 3 June 2019).

Miroğlu, Orhan. *Hevsel Bahçesinde Bir Dut Ağacı: Canip Yıldırım'la Söyleşi*. İstanbul: İletişim, 2005.

Mirzai, Behnaz A. *A History of Slavery and Emancipation in Iran, 1800–1929*. Austin: University of Texas Press, 2017.

Mitchell, Timothy. *Colonising Egypt*. Cambridge: Cambridge University Press, 1988.

Mitchell, Timothy. 'Everyday Metaphors of Power', *Theory and Society* 19, no. 5 (October 1990): 545–577.

Mobasser, Mohsen. '6. October 1984'. In *Iranian Oral History Collection, Harvard University*, edited by Habib Ladjevardi, transcript 2.

Mokhtari, Fariborz. 'Iran's 1953 Coup Revisited: Internal Dynamics versus External Intrigue'. *Middle East Journal* 62, no. 3 (2008): 457–488.

Moore, Arthur. *The Orient Express*. London: Constable & Company, 1914.

Morizot, Jean. *L'Aurès ou le mythe de la montagne rebelle*. Paris: L'Harmattan, 1992.

Morrison, Heidi. *Childhood and Colonial Modernity in Egypt*. New York: Palgrave Macmillan, 2015.

Muir, Edward and Ruggiero, Guido, eds., *History From Crime* (Baltimore: Johns Hopkins University Press, 1994).

Naficy, Hamid. *A Social History of Iranian Cinema*, vol. 2, *The Industrializing Years, 1941–1978*. Durham, NC: Duke University Press, 2011.

Najmabadi, Afsaneh. *The Story of the Daughters of Quchan: Gender and National Memory in Iranian History*. Syracuse, NY: Syracuse University Press, 1998.

Naraqi, Hassan. *Kashan Dar Jonbesh-e Mashrute-ye Iran*. Tehran: Entesharat-e Iran, 1364.

Navaei, ʿAbdolhoseyn and Muhammad Baqaei Shireh-Jini. *Nayebiyan-e Kashan (Bar Asas-e Asnad)* (Tehran: Sazman-e Asnad-e Melli-ye Iran, 1379).

Newman, Bernard. *Turkish Crossroads*. London: Robert Hale Ltd., 1951.

Nightingale, Charles H. *Segregation: A Global History of Divided Cities*. Chicago: University of Chicago Press, 2014.

Nizarah al-Dakhiliyyah. *al-Qawanin al-Idariyyah wa al-Jinaʾiyyah, al-Juzʾ al-Rabiʿ al-Qawanin al-Khususiyyah*. Cairo: al-Matbaʿah al-Amiriyyah bi-Bulaq, n.d.

Nizarah al-Dakhiliyyah. *Idarah ʿUmum al-Sahhah, Dikritat wa Lawaʾih Sahhiyyah*. Cairo: al-Matbaʿah al-Amiriyyah bi-Bulaq, 1895.

Nouraei, Morteza and Martin, Vanessa, 'Part II: The Karguzar and Security, the Trade Routes of Iran and Foreign Subjects 1900–1921ʾ, *Journal of the Royal Asiatic Society* 16, no. 1, April 2006: 29–41.

Nouschi, André. *Enquête sur le niveau de vie des populations rurales constantinoises*. Saint-Denis: Bouchène, [1961] 2013.

Nouschi, André. 'La dépossession foncière et la paupérisation de la paysannerie algérienne'. In *Histoire de l'Algérie à la période coloniale*, edited by Abderrahmane Bouchène, Jean-Pierre Peyroulou, Ouanassa Siari Tengour and Sylvie Thénault, 189–193. Alger: Barzakh; Paris: La Découverte, 2012.

O'Hanlon, Rosalind. 'Recovering the Subject: Subaltern Studies and Histories of Resistance in Colonial South Asiaʾ. *Modern Asian Studies* 22, no. 1 (1988): 189–224.

O'Malley, Pat. 'Class Conflict, Land and Social Banditry: Bushranging in Nineteenth Century Australiaʾ. *Social Problems* 26, no. 3 (1979): 271–283.

O'Malley, Pat. 'Social Bandits, Modern Capitalism and the Traditional Peasantry. A Critique of Hobsbawmʾ. *Journal of Peasant Studies* 6, no. 9 (1979): 489–501.

Oberling, Pierre. *The Qashqaʾi Nomads of Fars*. The Hague: Mouton, 1974.

Oberling, Pierre. 'The Tribes of Qaraca Dag: A Brief Historyʾ. *Oriens* 17 (December 1964): 60–95.

Önder, İzzettin. 'Cumhuriyet Döneminde Tarım Kesimine Uygulanan Vergi Politikasıʾ. In *Türkiye'de Tarımsal Yapılar*, edited by Şevket Pamuk and Zafer Toprak, 113–133. Ankara: Yurt Yayınevi, 1988.

Osokina, Elena. *Our Daily Bread: Socialist Distribution and the Art of Survival in Stalin's Russia, 1927–1941*, edited by Kate Transchel and translated by Kate Transchel and Greta Bucher. Armonk, NY: Sharpe, 2001.

Ouatmani, Settar. 'Arezki L'Bachir Un « bandit d'honneur » en Kabylie au xixe siècleʾ. *Revue des mondes musulmans et de la Méditerranée*, 136 (2014): 187–202.

Özbek, Nadir. '"Beggars" and "Vagrants" in State Policy and Public Discourse During the Late Ottoman Empire: 1876–1914ʾ. *Middle Eastern Studies* 45, no. 5 (2009): 783–801.

Özbek, Nadir. *Osmanlı İmparatorluğu'nda Sosyal Devlet: Siyaset, İktidar ve Meşruiyet (1876–1914)*. İstanbul: İletişim Yayınları, 2002.

Ozkan, Fulya. 'Gravediggers of the Modern State: Highway Robbers on the Trabzon-Bayezid Road, 1850s–1910sʾ. *Journal of Persianate Studies* 7 (2014): 219–250.

Pamuk, Şevket. 'War, State Economic Policies, and Resistance by Agricultural Producers in Turkey, 1939–1945ʾ. In *Peasants & Politics in The Modern Middle East*, edited by

Farhad Kazemi and John Waterbury, 125–142. Miami: Florida International University Press, 1991.

Parascandola, John. *Sex, Sin, and Science: A History of Syphilis in America, Healing Society – Disease, Medicine, and History*. Westport, CT: Praeger, 2008.

Parent-Duchâtelet, J. B. *De la prostitution dans la ville de Paris: considérée sous le rapport de l'hygiéne publique, de la morale et de l'administration*, 2 vols. Paris, 1836.

Patel, Raj and McMichael, Philip, "A Political Economy of the Food Riot," *Review-Fernand Braudel Center for the Study of Economies, Historical Systems, and Civilizations* 32, no. 1, 2009.

Peirce, Leslie. 'Abduction with (Dis)honor: Sovereigns, Brigands, and Heroes in the Ottoman World'. *Journal of Early Modern History* 15 (2001): 311–329.

Perry, Elizabeth J. 'Social Banditry Revisited: The Case of Bai Lang, a Chinese Brigand'. *Modern China* 9, no. 3 (1983): 355–382.

Perry, John R. 'Ḥaydari and Neʿmati'. *Encyclopædia Iranica (Online)* 12, no. 2 (2003): 70–73. Available online: http://www.iranicaonline.org/articles/haydari-and-nemati (accessed 30 October 2017).

Peters, Rudolph. 'Prisons and Marginalization in Nineteenth-Century Egypt'. In *Outside In: Marginality in the Modern Middle East*, edited by Eugene Rogan, 31–52. London: Tauris, 2002.

Peyerimhoff, Henri. *Enquête sur les résultats de la colonisation officielle*. Alger: Imprimerie Torrent, 1906.

Philipp, Thomas. *Acre: The Rise and Fall of a Palestinian City, 1730–1831*. New York: Columbia University Press, 2001.

Pistor-Hatam, Anja. 'The Iranian Constitutional Revolution as Lieu(x) de Memoire: Sattar Khan'. In *Iran's Constitutional Revolution: Popular Politics, Cultural Transformations and Transnational Connections*, edited by H. E. Chehabi and Vanessa Martin, 33–44. London: I.B. Tauris, 2010.

Pistor-Hatam, Anja. 'Sattār Khan'. *Encyclopædia Iranica (Online)*, 20 July 2009. Available online: http://www.iranicaonline.org/articles/sattar-khan-one-of-the-most-popular-heroes-from-tabriz-who-defended-the-town-during-the-lesser-autocracy-in-1908-09 (accessed 30 October 2017).

Plarier, Antonin. 'Banditisme et dépossession foncière en Algérie'. In *Propriété et Société en Algérie contemporaine*, edited by D. Guignard, 194–205. Aix-en-Provence: IREMAM, 2017.

Plarier, Antonin. *Le banditisme en Algérie pendant la Première Guerre mondiale*. Paris: Karthala, forthcoming.

Prakash, Gyan. *Another Reason: Science and the Imagination of Modern India*. Princeton, NJ: University Press, 1999.

Prochaska, David. 'Fire on the Mountain: Resisting Colonialism in Algeria'. In *Banditry, Rebellion and Social Protest in Africa*, edited by Donald Crummey, 229–252. London: James Currey, 1986.

Quataert, Donald. 'Ottoman Reform and Agriculture in Anatolia, 1876–1908'. PhD diss., University of California, 1973.

Quataert, Donald. 'The Régie, Smugglers and the Government'. In *Social Disintegration and Popular Resistance in the Ottoman Empire, 1881–1908, Reactions to European Economic Penetration*, 13–40. New York: New York University Press, 1983.

Rahnama-yi muʾassisat-i ijtimaʿi wa khairiyyah dar Iran. Tehran: Bashgah-i bain al-milali-yi zanan-i Iran, n.d.

Rahnema, Ali. *Behind the 1953 Coup in Iran: Thugs, Turncoats, Soldiers, and Spooks.* Cambridge: Cambridge University Press, 2015.

Rebhan, Helga. *Geschichte und Funktion einiger politischer Termini im Arabischen des 19. Jahrhunderts, 1798–1882.* Wiesbaden: Harrassowitz, 1986.

Rediker, Marcus. *Outlaws of the Atlantic: Sailors, Pirates and Motley Crews in the Age of Sail.* London: Verso, 2014.

Rediker, Marcus. *Villains of All Nations: Atlantic Pirates in the Golden Age.* London: Verso, 2004.

Reilly, James A. 'Inter-Confessional Relations in Nineteenth-*Century Syria: Damascus, Homs and Hama Compared'. Islam* and Christian-Muslim Relations 7, no. 2 (1996): 213–224.

Reilly, James A. 'Origins of Peripheral Capitalism in the Damascus Region, 1830–1914'. PhD diss., Georgetown University, 1987.

Reilly, James A. 'Women in the Economic Life of Late-Ottoman Damascus'. *Arabica* 42, no. 1 (1995).

Reinarman, Craig and Levine, Harry Gene, eds., *Crack in America: Demon drugs and social justice* (University of California Press, 1997).

Reinkowski, Maurus. *Die Dinge der Ordnung: eine vergleichende Untersuchung über die osmanische Reformpolitik im 19. Jahrhundert.* Munich: Oldenbourg, 2005.

Rejali, Darius M. *Torture & Modernity: Self, Society, and State in Modern Iran.* Boulder, CO: Westview Press, 1994.

Reynolds, Nancy. *A City Consumed: Urban Commerce, the Cairo Fire, and the Politics of Decolonization in Egypt.* Stanford, CA: Stanford University Press, 2012.

Reynolds, Nancy, 'Sharikat al-Baytal-Misri: Domesticating Commerce in Egypt, 1931– 1956', *Arab Studies Journal* 7, no. 2–8, 1 (1999–2000): 75–107.

Rezaei, Ensiah and Azari, Shahla, *Guzarish-ha-yi nazmiyyah az mahallat-i Tehran: rapurt-i vaqayi'-i mukhtalifah-yi mahallat-i dar al-khilafah*, vol. 1 (Tehran: Iran National Archive Organization, 1999).

Rhodes, Tim, Singer, Merrill, Bourgois, Philippe, Friedman, Samuel R. and Strathdee, Steffanie A., "The social structural production of HIV risk among injecting drug users." Social Science & Medicine 61, no. 5, 2005: 1026–1044.

Rizq, Yunan Labib. 'Safety First'. *al-Ahram Weekly Online*, 6–12 December 2001, no. 563. Available online: http://weekly.ahram.org.eg/2001/563/chrncls.htm (accessed 1 May 2017).

Robin, Corey. *Fear: The History of a Political Idea.* Oxford: Oxford University Press, 2004.

Roded, Ruth Michal. 'The Syrian Urban Notables: Elite, Estates, Class?'. *Asian and African Studies* 20 (1986): 375–384.

Roded, Ruth Michal. 'Tradition and Change in Syria during the Last Decades of Ottoman Rule: The Urban Elite of Damaskus, Aleppo, Homs and Hama, 1876–1918'. PhD diss., University of Denver, 1984.

Rudé, George F. E. *Ideology and Popular Protest.* Chapel Hill: University of North Carolina Press, 1995.

Ruiz, Mario M. 'Criminal Statistics in the Long. In *The Long 1890s in Egypt: Colonial Quiescence, Subterranean Resistance*, edited by Marilyn Booth and Anthony Gorman, 141–166. Edinburgh: Edinburgh University Press, 2014.

Rule, John. 'Social Crime in the Rural South in the Eighteenth and Nineteenth Centuries'. In *Crime, Protest, and Popular Politics in Southern England, 1740–1850*, edited by John Rule and Roger A. E. Wells, 153–168. London: Hambledon Press, 1997.

Russell, Mona L. *Creating the New Egyptian Woman: Consumerism, Education, and National Identity, 1863–1922.* New York: Palgrave Macmillan, 2004.

Russell Pasha, Thomas. *Egyptian Service 1902–1946.* London: J. Murray, 1949.

Sabatier, Camille. *La Question de la sécurité, insurrections, criminalité: les difficultés algériennes.* Alger: A. Jourdan, 1882.

Sabra, Adam. *Poverty and Charity in Medieval Islam: Mamluk Egypt, 1250–1517.* Cambridge: Cambridge University Press, 2000.

Saddat, Seyyed Mahmoud, Nouraei, Morteza and Mir Ja'fari, Hossein, 'An Analysis of the Performance of Nayebi Exiles to Kashan (Causes and Factors of the Occurrence and Continuance of Their Rebellion)', *Interdisciplinary Journal of Contemporary Research in Business* 5, no. 1, May 2013: 113–130.

Safiri, Floreeda. 'The South Persian Rifles' PhD thesis, University of Edinburgh, 1976.

Sainte-Marie, A. *Réflexions sur l'histoire du grand-banditisme.* Oran: CRIDSSH, 1984.

Sajdi, Dana. 'Peripheral Visions: The Worlds and Worldviews of Commoner Chroniclers in the 18th Century Ottoman Levant'. PhD diss., Columbia University, 2002.

Salami, Qulam Riza and Najmabadi, Afsaneh, *Nahzat-i nisvan-i Sharq*, Chap-i 1, Majmū'ah-'i mutala'at-i zanan 2 (Tehran: Shirazah, 1384).

Salhi, M. B. 'L'insurrection de 1871'. In *Histoire de l'Algérie à la période colonial, 1830–1962*, edited by Abderrahmane Bouchene, Jean-Pierre Peyroulou, Ouanassa Siari Tengour and Sylvie Thénault. Paris: La Découverte, 2014.

Salih, Nahid. 'Al-'Awd ila al-Ijram 'Inda al-Mar'a' [Recidivism among Women]. *al-Majalla al-jina'iyya al-qawmiyya* 9, no. 2 (1966): 215–247.

Salzmann, Ariel. 'An Ancien Regime Revisited: "Privatization" and Political Economy in the Eighteenth-Century Ottoman Empire'. *Politics Society* 21, no. 4 (1993): 393–423.

Salzmann, Ariel. *Tocqueville in the Ottoman Empire: Rival Paths to the Modern State.* Boston, MA: Brill, 2004.

Sariyannis, Marinos. 'Images of the Mediterranean in an Ottoman Pirate Novel from the Late Seventeenth Century'. *Journal of Ottoman Studies* 39 (2012): 189–204.

Sariyannis, Marinos. '"Mobs", "Scamps" and Rebels in Sevententh Century Istanbul: Some Remarks on Ottoman Social Vocabulary'. *International Journal of Turkish Studies* 11, nos 1–2 (2005): 1–15.

Sariyannis, Marinos. '"Neglected Trades": Glimpses into the 17th Century Istanbul Underworld'. *Turcica* 38 (2006): 155–179.

Sarshar, Huma. Chi kasi bi yad-i kahnum mudir ast? Qulam Riza Salami and Afsaneh Najmabadi, Nihzat-i nisvan-i sharq, Chap-i 1, Majmu'ah-'i zanan 2, 313–329. Tehran: Shirazah, 1384.

Sarshar, Homa. *Sha'ban Ja'fari*, 2nd edn. Los Angeles: Nāb, 1381 h. sh. [=2002].

Sassen, Saskia. 'Women's Burden: Counter-Geographies of Globalization and the Feminization of Survival'. *Journal of International Affairs* 53, no. 2 (2000): 503–524.

Schatkowski Schilcher, Linda. *Families in Politics: Damascene Factions and Estates of the 18th and 19th Centuries.* Stuttgart: Steiner-Verlag-Wiesbaden, 1985.

Schayegh, Cyrus. 'Criminal-Women and Mother-Women: Socio-Cultural Transformations and the Critique of Criminality in Early Post-World War 11 Iran'. *Journal of Middle East Women's Studies* 2, no. 3 (2006): 1–21.

Schayegh, Cyrus. 'Serial Murder in Tehran: Crime, Science, and the Formation of Modern State and Society in Interwar Iran'. *Comparative Studies in Society and History* 47, no. 4 (October 2005): 836–862.

Schayegh, Cyrus. "'A Sound Mind Lives in a Healthy Body": Texts and Contexts in the Iranian Modernists' Scientific Discourse of Health, 1910s–1940s'. *International Journal of Middle East Studies* 37, no. 2 (2005): 167–188.

Schayegh, Cyrus. *Who is Knowledgeable is Strong: Science, Class, and the Formation of Modern Iranian Society, 1900–1950.* Berkeley: University of California Press, 2009.

Scheele, Judith. *Smugglers and Saints of the Sahara.* Cambridge: Cambridge University Press, 2015.

Schilcher, Linda. 'The Grain Economy of Late Ottoman Syria and the Issue of Large-Scale Commercialization'. In *Landholding and Commercial Agriculture in the Middle East*, edited by Keyder Çağlar and Faruk Tabak, 173–195. Albany: State University of New York Press, 1991.

Schulze Tanielian, Melanie. 'Feeding the City: The Beirut Municipality and the Politics of Food during World War I'. *International Journal of Middle East Studies* 46, no. 4 (2014): 737–758.

Scott, James C. *The Art of Not Being Governed: An Anarchist History of Upland Southeast Asia.* New Haven, CT: Yale University Press, 2009.

Scott, James C. *Domination and the art of resistance.* New Haven, CT: Yale University Press, 1990.

Scott, James C. *The Moral Economy of the Peasant: Rebellion and Subsistence in Southeast Asia.* New Haven, CT: Yale University Press, 1976.

Scott, James C. *Weapons of the Weak : Everyday Forms of Peasant Resistance.* New Haven, CT: Yale University Press, 1985.

Seal, Graham. 'The Robin Hood Principle: Folklore, History and the Social Bandit'. *Journal of Folklore Research* 46, no. 1 (2009): 67–89.

Segrave, Kerry. *Shoplifting: A Social History* (Jefferson, NC: McFarland, 2001).

Semerdijan, Elise. *Off the Straight Path: Illicit Sex, Law, and Community in Ottoman Aleppo.* Syracuse, NY: Syracuse University Press, 2008.

Sen, Amartya. *Poverty and Famines: An Essay on Entitlement and Deprivation.* Oxford: Oxford University Press, 1981.

Sertel, Yıldız. *Ardımdaki Yıllar.* İstanbul: İletişim Yayınları, 2001.

Şevki, Mehmet Ali. *Kurna Köyü. (Kocaeli Yarımadası) Monografisinden Üç Makale* [Articles published in *Siyasi İlimiler Mecmuası*, nos.77–79 and 90] (1939).

Seyf, Ahmad. 'Commercialization of Agriculture: Production and Trade of Opium in Persia, 1850–1906'. *International Journal of Middle East Studies* 16, no. 2 (May 1984): 233–250.

Shahin, Muhammad. *Kifah al-Jarima* [Fighting Crime]. Cairo: al-Matb'a al-Mutawasita, 1936.

Shahin, Muhammad. *Taqrir min-Mukafahat-al-Amrad al-Zahriyyah bi-l-Qutr al-Masri.* Cairo: n.p., 1933.

Shahrī, Ja'far. *Tehran-i qadīm*, 5 vols. Tehran: Mu'īn, 1383.

Shakya, Tsering. 'Ga rgya 'gram nag: A bandit or proto-rebel? The question of banditry as social protest in Nag chu', in *Trails of the Tibetan Tradition: Papers for Elliot Sperling.* Dharamshala: Amnye Machen Institute, 2014.

Shalabi, Hilmi Ahmad. *Fusul fi Tarikh Tahdith al-Mudun* [Chapters on Modernizing Cities]. Cairo: al-Hayy'a al-Misriyya al-'amma lil-kitab, 1988.

Shan, Patrick Fuliang. 'Insecurity, Outlawry and Social Order: Banditry in China's Heilongjiang Frontier Region, 1900–1931'. *Journal of Social History* 40, no. 1 (2006): 25–54.

Shanin, Teodor. 'Peasantry As a Class'. In *Peasants and Peasant Societies*, edited by Teodor Shanin. Oxford: Blackwell, 1987.

Shields, Sarah D. 'Regional Trade and 19th-Century Mosul: Revising the Role of Europe in the Middle East Economy'. *International Journal of Middle East Studies* 23, no. 1 (1991): 19–37.

Shore, Heather. 'A Brief History of the Underworld and Organised Crime, c. 1750–1950'. In *The Oxford Handbook of the History of Crime and Criminal Justice*, edited by Paul Knepper and Anja Johansen, 170–191. London: Oxford University Press, 2016.

Şimşir, Bilâl N. *Kürtçülük II, 1924–1999*. Ankara: Bilgi Yayınevi, 2009.

Singer, Merrill and Page, J. Bryan, The Social Value of Drug Addicts: Uses of the Useless (Routledge, 2016).

Sirjani, ʿAli Akbar Saʿidi. *Vaqayeʿ-e Ettefaqiyeh: Majmuʿeh-e Gozareshha-ye Khafiyeh Nevisan-e Inglis Dar Velayat-e Jonubi-ye Iran Az Sal-e 1291 Ta 1322*. Tehran: Entesharat-e Novin, 1383.

Sılan, Necmeddin Sahir. *Doğu Sorunu: Necmeddin Sahir Sılan Raporları (1939–1953)*. İstanbul: Tarih Vakfı Yurt Yayınları, 2010.

Sladen, Douglas. *Oriental Cairo, the City of the Arabian Nights*. London, 1911.

Slatta, Richard W., ed. *Bandidos: The Varieties of Latin American Banditry*. New York: Greenwood Press, 1987.

Smith Cooke, William. *The Ottoman Empire and its Tributary States (Excepting Egypt) With a Sketch of Greece*, repr. Amsterdam: Grüner, [1876] 1968.

Staszak, Jean-François. 'Planning Prostitution in Colonial Marocco: Bousbir, Casablanca's Quartier Réservé'. In *(Sub)urban Sexscapes: Geographies and Regulation of Sex Industry*, edited by P. J. Maginn and C. Steinmetz, 175–196. New York, 2015.

Stebbins, Lyman. 'British Imperialism, Regionalism, and Nationalism in Iran, 1890–1919'. In *Iran Facing Others: Identity Boundaries in a Historical Perspective*, edited by Abbas Amanat and Farzin Vejdani, 153–169. New York: Palgrave Macmillan, 2012.

Stirk, Peter M. R. *Max Horkheimer: A New Interpretation*. Hemel Hempstead: Harvester Wheatsheaf; Lanham, MD: Barnes & Noble, 1992.

Stirling, Paul. *Culture and Economy: Changes in Turkish Villages*. Huntingdon: Eothen, 1993.

Swedenburg, Ted. *Memories of Revolt: The 1936–1939 Rebellion and the Palestinian National Past*. Minneapolis: University of Minnesota Press, 1995.

Sweet, Louise E. 'Camel Raiding of North Arabian Bedouin: A Mechanism of Ecological Adaptation'. *American Anthropologist* 67, no. 5 (October 1965): 1132–1150.

Szyliowicz, Joseph. *Political Change in Rural Turkey: Erdemli*. The Hague: Mouton, 1966.

Tafrishi, Murtiza. Pulis-i khafiyyah-yi Iran: murmuri bar rukhdad-ha-yi siyasi wa tarikhchah-yi shahrbani (1299-1320). Tehrna: Quqnus, 1989.

Tahir, Kemal. *Rahmet Yolları Kesti*. İstanbul: Düşün Yayınevi, 1957.

Takla, Mary Nefertiti. 'Murder in Alexandria: The Gender, Sexual and Class Politics of Criminality in Egypt, 1914–1921'. PhD thesis, University of California, Los Angeles, 2016, https://escholarship.org/uc/item/4r35401h (accessed 16 June 2019).

Talatoff, Kamran. *Modernity, Sexuality, and Ideology in Iran: The Life and Legacy of a Popular Female Artist*. Syracuse, NY: Syracuse University Press, 2011.

Tapper, Richard. 'Raiding, Reaction and Rivalry: The Shāhsevan in the Constitutional Period'. *Bulletin of the School of Oriental and African Studies* 49, no. 3 (October 1986): 508–531.

Tapper, Richard. 'The Tribes in Eighteenth and Nineteenth Century Iran'. In *The Cambridge History of Iran. Vol. 7*, edited by Peter Avery, Gavin Hambly and C. P. Melville, 506–541. Cambridge: Cambridge University Press, 1991.

Taylor, Lynne. 'Food Riots Revisited'. *Journal of Social History* 30, no. 2 (1996): 483–496.

Thaurad, Christine. 'Colonialist Regulationist Prostitution in the Maghreb and the Struggle for Abolition'. In *Trafficking in Women, 1924–1926, The Paul Kinsie Report for the League of Nations*, edited by J. M. Chaumont, M. Rodriguez Garcia, and P. Servais, vol. 2. Geneva: United Nations, 2017.

Tharaud, Christelle. *La prostitution coloniale in Algérie, Tunisie, Maroc, 1830–1910*. Paris: Éditions Payot & Rivages, 2003.

Thénault, Sylvie. *Violence ordinaire dans l'Algérie coloniale*. Paris: Odile Jacob, 2012.

Thieck, Jean-Pierre. 'Décentralisation ottomane et affirmation urbaine à Alep à la fin du XVIIIème siècle'. In *Mouvements communautaires et Espaces urbains au Machreq*, edited by Mona Zakaria and Bachchar Chbarou, 117–168. Beirut: CERMOC, 1985.

Thompson, E. P. *Customs in Common: Studies in Traditional Popular Culture*. New York: New Press, 1993.

Thompson, E. P. *The Making of the English Working Class*, rev. edn. London: Penguin, [1963] 2013.

Thompson, E.P. 'The Moral Economy of the English Crowd in the Eighteenth Century'. *Past and Present* 50, no. 1 (1971): 76–136.

Thompson, E. P. *Whigs and Hunters, the Origin of the Black Act*. London: Allen Lane, 1975.

Thornton, Guy. *With the Anzacs in Cairo, the Tale of a Great Fight*. London: H.R. Allenson, 1916.

Ticktin, Miriam. 'Transnational Humanitarianism'. *Annual Review of Anthropology* 43, no. 1 (21 October 2014): 273–289.

Tilly, Charles. 'The Analysis of Popular Collective Action'. *European Journal of Operational Research* 30, no. 3 (1987): 223–229.

Tilly, Charles. 'Contentious Repertoires in Great Britain, 1758–1834'. *Social Science History* 17, no. 2 (1993): 253–280.

Tilly, Charles. 'War Making and State Making as Organized Crime'. In *Bringing the State Back In*, edited by Peter B. Evans, 169–191. Cambridge: Cambridge University Press, 1985.

Tilly, Louise A. 'The Food Riot as a Form of Political Conflict in France'. *Journal of Interdisciplinary History* 2, no. 1 (1971): 23–57.

Todorova, Maria, ed. *Balkan Identities: Nation and Memory*. New York: New York University Press, 2004.

Togsoy, Ali Enver. 'Cenub Hudutlarımızda Kaçakçılık'. *Resimli Ay*, no. 28 (June 1938): 20.

Toprak, Zafer. *Türkiye'de Kadın Özgürlüğü ve Feminizm*. Istanbul: Tarih Vakfı Yurt Yayınları, 2014.

Tran, Trung Nam, Detels, Roger, Tran Hien, Nguyen, Long, Hoang Thuy and Nga, Pham Thi Hoang, "Drug use, sexual behaviours and practices among female sex workers in Hanoi, Viet Nam—a qualitative study," International Journal of Drug Policy 15, no. 3, 2004: 189–195.

Tripp, Charles. *The Power and the People: Paths of Resistance in the Middle East*. New York: Cambridge University Press, 2013.

Tucker, Judith. *Women in Nineteenth Century Egypt*. Cambridge: Cambridge University Press, 1985.

Tuluʻi, Muhammad. Pidar wa pisar: Naguftah-ha az zindagi wa ruzgar-i Pahlavi-ha. Tehran: Intisharat-i ʻilmi, 1993.

Tumaniyans, Surin. Chira suzak wa syphilis muʻalihah nimishavad. Tehran: Baradaran-i baghirzadah, 1309 [=1930].

Tunçay, Mete. *Türkiye'de Sol Akımlar*. İstanbul: BDS Yayınları, 1991.

Turan, Kemal. *Yeni Vergi Kanunları'nın Tatbiki Mahiyeti ve Tediye Kabiliyeti Hakkında Tahliller.* İzmir: Hafız Ali Matbaası, 1931.

T. C. Başbakanlık İstatistik Genel Müdürlüğü. *Hayvanlar İstatistiği 1944.* [İstanbul]: Hüsnütabiat Basımevi, 1946.

Us, Asım, *Asım Us'un Hatıra Notları: 1930'dan 1950 Yılına Kadar Atatürk ve İsmet İnönü Devirlerine Ait Seçme Fıkralar* (İstanbul: Vakit Matbaası, 1966).

Uthman, Taha Sa'd. '*Kifah 'Ummal al-Nasij, Mudhakkarat wa-watha'iq min tarikh 'ummal Misr: Kifah 'ummal al-nasij, 1938-1947* [Memoirs and Documents from the History of Egypt's Workers: The Struggle of Textile Workers, 1938-1947]. Cairo: Maktabat Madbuli, 1983.

'Uways, Sayyid. 'Dhahirat Jara'im al-Nashl fi Muhit al-Nisa' fi Muhafazat al-Qahira' [The Pickpocketing Phenomenon among Women in the Cairo Province]. *Al-Majalla al-Jina'iyya al-Qawmiyya* 8, no. 1 (1965): 67-94.

Van Bruinessen, Martin. *Kürdistan Üzerine Yazılar.* İstanbul: İletişim Yayınları, 2002.

Vejdani, Farzin. 'Illict Acts and Sacred Space: Everyday Crime in the Shrine City of Mashhad, 1913-1914'. *Journal of Persianate Studies* 7 (2014): 22-54.

Vejdani, Farzin. 'Urban Violence and Space: Lutis, Seminarians, and Sayyids in Late Qajar Iran'. *Journal of Social History* 52, no. 4 (2019): 1185-1211.

Vincent, Bernard, ed. *Les Marginaux et les exclus dans l'histoire.* Paris: Union Générale d'Edition, 1979.

Vitkus, Daniel J., ed. *Piracy, Slavery and Redemption: Barbary Captivity Narratives from Early Modern England.* New York: Columbia University Press, 2001.

Vizarat-i bihdari. Guzarish-i 'amaliyat-i sal-i 1334.Tehran: Vizarat-i bihdari (Ministry of Health), 1954.

Wagner, Kim A. 'Thuggee and Social Banditry Reconsidered'. *Historical Journal* 50, no. 2 (2007): 353-376.

Walkowitz, Judith R. *City of Dreadful Delight: Narratives Of Sexual Danger In Late-Victorian London.* Chicago: University of Chicago Press, 1992.

Walkowitz, Judith R. *Prostitution and Victorian Society: Women, Class and the State.* Cambridge: Cambridge University Press, 1996.

Walton, John and Seddon, David, *Free Markets &; Food Riots* (Oxford: Blackwell, 1994).

Waters, Chris. 'Sexology'. In *Palgrave Advances in the Modern History of Sexuality,* edited by H. G. Cocks and M. Houlbrook, 41-63. Basingstoke: Palgrave Macmillan, 2006.

Weber, Max. *Weber's Rationalism and Modern Society.* New York: Palgrave Macmillan, 2015.

White, Richard., 'Outlaw Gangs of the Middle Border: American Social Bandits'. *Western Historical Quarterly* 12, no. 4 (October 1981): 387-408.

Wilber, Donald N. *[CIA-files] Overthrow of Premier Mossadeq of Iran: November 1952 - August 1953.* CIA, (written 1954) 1969, Clandestine Service History, 63.

Wild, Stefan. 'Jugglers and Fraudulent Sufis'. *Proceedings of the VIth Congress of Arabic and Islamic Studies,* edited by Frithiof Rundgren, Visby, 13-16 August, Stockholm, 17-19 August 1972, pp. 58-62.

Wilks, Judith M. 'The Persianization of Köroğlu: Banditry and Royalty in Three Versions of the Köruğlu "Destan"'. *Asian Folklore Studies* 60, no. 2 (2001): 305-318.

Willis, N. W. *Anti-Christ in Egypt.* London: Anglo-Eastern Publishing Company Co., 1914.

Wilson, Arnold. SW. *Persia: A Political Officer's Diary 1907-1914.* London: Oxford University Press, 1941.

Wizarat al-Dakhiliyyah-Bulis Madinat al-Qahirah. *Taqrir Sanawi-al-'am 1930.* al-Matba'ah al-Amiriyyah bi-Bulaq, 1931.

Wizarat al-Dakhiliyyah-Bulis Madinat al-Qahirah. *Taqrir Sanawi al-'am 1933*. al-Matba'ah al-Amiriyyah bi-Bulaq, 1934.

Wizarat al-Dakhiliyya-Bulis Madinat al-Qahirah. *Taqrir Sanawi al-'am 1935*. al-Matba'ah al-Amiriyyah bi-Bulaq, 1936.

Wizarat al-Dakhaliyyah-Bulis Madinat al-Qahirah. *Taqrir Sanawi al-'am 1937*. al-Matba'ah al-Amiriyyah bi-Bulaq, 1938.

Wizarat al-Dakhiliyyah-Bulis Madinat al-Qahirah. *Taqrir Sanawi 'an A'mal Taftish Sahhat al-Qahirah li-sanawat 1922, 1925, 1927*.

Wizarat al-Dakhaliyyah-Bulis Madinat al-Qahirah. *Taqrir Sanawi li-sanat- 1944*. Matba'ah al-Amiriyyah bi-Bulaq bi-l-Qahirah, 1944.

Wizarat al-Dakhiliyyah-Bulis Madinat al-Qahirah. *Taqrir Sanawi li-sanatay 1942–1943*. al-Matb'ah al-Amiriyyah bi-l-Qahirah, 1944.

Wizarat al-Sahhah al-'Umumiyyah. *al-Taqrir al-Sanawi al-'amm li-sanat 1943*. Matba'ah al-Amiriyyah bi-Bulaq bi-l-Qahirah.

Wizarat al-Sahhah al-'Umumiyyah. *Taqrir Sanawi 'an A'mal Taftish Sahhat- al-Qahirah li-'am 1936*. al-Matba'ah al-Amiriyyah bi-Bulaq, 1939.

Wizarat al-Sahhah al-'Umumiyyah. *Taqrir Sanawi 'an sanat-1937*. Dar al-Tiba'ah al-Fayyada, al- Qahirah, 1939.

Wizarat al-Sahhah al-'Umumiyyah. *Taqrīr Sanawi li-sanat 1946*. Matba'ah al-Amiriyyah bi-Bulaq bi-l-Qahirah.

Wyers, Mark David. *Wicked Istanbul: The Regulation of Prostitution in the Early Turkish Republic*. Istanbul: Libra Kitapçılık ve Yayıncılık, 2013.

Yağcı, İsmail. 'Tuz, Tahta Kaşık Kaçakçılığı ve Yol Parası'. *Türkiye Gazetesi*, 18 July 2007. Available online: http://m.turkiyegazetesi.com.tr/yazarlar/ismail-yagci/338738.aspx (accessed 16 June 2019).

Yaghmaei, A. *Hamase-ye Fathname-ye Nayebi*. Tehran: Esparak, 1368.

Yang, Anand A., ed. *Crime and Criminality in British India*. Tucson: University of Arizona Press, 1985.

Yang, Anand A. 'Dangerous Castes and Tribes: The Criminal Tribes Act and the Magahiya Doms of Northeast India'. In *Crime and Criminality in British India*, edited by Anand A. Yang, 108–127. Tucson: University of Arizona Press, 1985.

Yasa, İbrahim. *Hasanoğlan Köyü'nün İçtimaî-İktisadî Yapısı*. Ankara: Doğuş Ltd. O. Matbaası for Türkiye ve Orta Doğu Amme İdaresi Enstitüsü, 1955.

Yasa, İbrahim. *Sindel Köyü'nün Toplumsal ve Ekonomik Yapısı*. Ankara: Türkiye ve Orta Doğu Amme İdaresi Enstitüsü, 1960.

Yetkin, Sabri. *Ege'de Eşkıyalar*. İstanbul: Tarih Vakfı Yurt Yayınları, 1996.

Yıldırmaz, Sinan. *Politics and the Peasantry in Post-War Turkey: Social History, Culture and Modernization*, Library of Ottoman Studies 46. London: I.B. Tauris, 2017.

Yılmaz, İlkay. *Serseri, Anarşist ve Fesadın Peşinde: II. Abdülhami Dönemi Güvenlik Politikaları Ekseninde Mürur Tezkerleriö Pasaportlar ve Otel Kayıtları*. İstanbul: Tarih Vakfı Yurt Yayınları 2014.

Young, Frank. 'The Cheapest Thing in Egypt'. *Egyptian Gazette*, 7 October 1913.

Yurtsever, Cezmi. *Kadirli Tarihi*. Osmaniye: Kadirli Hizmet Birliği Kültür Yayınları, 1999.

Zadeh-Mohammadi, Mojtaba. *Lompan-ha dar siyasat-e 'asr-e pahlavi*, 3rd edn. Tehran: Nashr-e markaz, 1392 h. sh. [=2013].

Zakeri, Mohsen. *Sasanid Soldiers in Early Muslim Society: The Origins of 'Ayyaran and Futuwwa*. Wiesbaden: Harrassowitz Verlag, 1995.

Zand-Muqaddam, Mahmud. *Qal'ah*. Tehran: Maziar Publishing House, 1958.

Zand-Muqaddam, Mahmud, *Shahr-i naw, Qal'ah-'i Zahidi 1348: Hamrah ba du didar az mujtami'-i bihzisti* 1368, Chap-i nukhust. Gothenberg: Khanah-yi hunar wa adabiyat: Kitab-i arzan, 2012.

Zarinebaf-Sharh, Fariba. *Crime and Punishment in Istanbul, 1700–1800* Los Angles: University of California Press, 2010.

Zarinebaf-Sharh, Farıba, *Women on the Margins: Gender, Charity and Justice in the Early Modern Middle East.* Istanbul: Isıs Press, 2014.

Zeki, Salih, *Türkiye'de Tütün, Ziraat Zanaat ve Ticareti.* İstanbul: Cumhuriyet Matbaası, 1928.

Zwiedinek von Südenhorst, Julius. *Syrien und seine Bedeutung für den Welthandel.* Vienna: A.Hölder, 1873.

Index

www.ingramcontent.com/pod-product-compliance
Lightning Source LLC
Chambersburg PA
CBHW060145280326
41932CB00012B/1638